Beginning ASP.NET 2.0 E-Commerce in C# 2005

From Novice to Professional

Cristian Darie and Karli Watson

Beginning ASP.NET 2.0 E-Commerce in C# 2005: From Novice to Professional

Copyright © 2006 by Cristian Darie and Karli Watson

ISBN (pbk): 1-59059-468-1

Printed and bound in the United States of America 9 8 7 6 5 4 3 2 1

Trademarked names may appear in this book. Rather than use a trademark symbol with every occurrence of a trademarked name, we use the names only in an editorial fashion and to the benefit of the trademark owner, with no intention of infringement of the trademark.

Lead Editor: Ewan Buckingham

Technical Reviewer: Paul Sarknas

Editorial Board: Steve Anglin, Dan Appleman, Ewan Buckingham, Gary Cornell, Tony Davis, Jason Gilmore, Jonathan Hassell, Chris Mills, Dominic Shakeshaft, Jim Sumser

Project Manager: Kylie Johnston

Copy Edit Manager: Nicole LeClerc

Copy Editor: Julie McNamee

Assistant Production Director: Kari Brooks-Copony

Production Editor: Linda Marousek

Compositor: Susan Glinert Stevens

Proofreader: Nancy Sixsmith

Indexer: Broccoli Information Management

Artist: Kinetic Publishing Services, LLC

Cover Designer: Kurt Krames

Manufacturing Director: Tom Debolski

Distributed to the book trade worldwide by Springer-Verlag New York, Inc., 233 Spring Street, 6th Floor, New York, NY 10013. Phone 1-800-SPRINGER, fax 201-348-4505, e-mail orders-ny@springer-sbm.com, or visit http://www.springeronline.com.

For information on translations, please contact Apress directly at 2560 Ninth Street, Suite 219, Berkeley, CA 94710. Phone 510-549-5930, fax 510-549-5939, e-mail info@apress.com, or visit http://www.apress.com.

The source code for this book is available to readers at http://www.apress.com in the Source Code section.

Contents at a Glance

Contents

About the Authors

CRISTIAN DARIE, currently technical lead for the Better Business Bureau Romania, is an experienced programmer specializing in Microsoft and open source technologies, and relational database management systems. Having worked with computers since he was old enough to press the keyboard, he initially tasted programming success with a first prize in his first programming contest at the age of 12. From there, Cristian moved on to many other similar achievements in the following years, and now he is studying advanced distributed application architectures for his PhD degree. Cristian co-authored several programming books for Apress, Wrox Press, and Packt Publishing. He can be contacted through his personal web site at http://www.CristianDarie.ro.

KARLI WATSON is the technical director of 3form Ltd. (http://www.3form.net) and a freelance writer. He started out with the intention of becoming a world-famous nanotechnologist, so perhaps one day you might recognize his name as he receives a Nobel Prize. For now, though, Karli's computer interests include all things mobile and everything .NET. Karli is also a snow-boarding enthusiast and wishes he had a cat.

About the
Technical Reviewer

PAUL SARKNAS currently is the president of his own consulting company, Sarknasoft Solutions LLC, which provides enterprise solutions to a wide array of companies utilizing the .NET platform. He specializes in C#, ASP.NET, and SQL Server. Paul works intimately with all aspects of software, including project planning, requirements gathering, design, architecture, development, testing, and deployment. Paul's experience spans more than eight years working with Microsoft technologies, and he has used .NET since its early conception.

Along with authoring and technical reviewing for Apress, Paul has also co-authored books for Wrox Press.

Paul can be contacted via his consulting company's web site (http://www.sarknasoft.com) or his personal site (http://www.paulsarknas.com), and he welcomes questions and feedback of any kind.

Introduction

Welcome to *Beginning ASP.NET 2.0 E-Commerce in C# 2005: From Novice to Professional!* The explosive growth of retail over the Internet is encouraging more small- to medium-sized businesses to consider the benefits of setting up e-commerce web sites. Although online retailing has great and obvious advantages, there are also many hidden pitfalls that may be encountered when developing a retail web site. This book provides you with a practical, step-by-step guide to setting up an e-commerce site. Guiding you through every aspect of the design and build process, this book will have you building high-quality, extendable e-commerce web sites quickly and easily.

Over the course of this book, you will develop all the skills necessary to get your business up on the web and available to a worldwide audience, without having to use high-end, expensive solutions. Except for the operating system, the software required for this book can be downloaded free. We present this information in a book-long case study, the complexity of which develops as your knowledge increases through the book.

The case study is presented in three phases. The first phase focuses on getting the site up and running as quickly as possible, and at a low cost. That way, the financial implications if you are not publishing the site are reduced, and also, should you use the site, you can start to generate revenue quickly. At the end of this phase, you'll have a working site that you can play with or go live with if you want to. The revenue generated can be used to pay for further development.

The second phase concentrates on increasing revenue by improving the shopping experience and actively encouraging customers to buy more by implementing product recommendations. Again at the end of this phase, you'll have a fully working site that you can go live with.

By the third phase, you'll have the site up and running, and doing very well. During this phase, you'll look at increasing your profit margins by reducing costs through automating and streamlining order processing and administration, and by handling credit card transactions yourself. You'll also learn how to communicate with external systems, by integrating the Amazon E-Commerce Service (formerly known as Amazon Web Services—AWS), into your web site.

Who This Book Is For

This book is aimed at developers looking for a tutorial approach to building a full e-commerce web site from design to deployment.

Although this book explains the techniques used to build the site, you should have some previous experience programming ASP.NET 2.0 with C#. Having a reference book such as *Beginning Visual Web Developer 2005 Express: From Novice to Professional* (Apress, 2005) on hand is highly recommended.

This book may also prove valuable for ASP.NET 1.x, ASP 3, PHP, or Java developers who learn best by example and want to experience ASP.NET 2.0 development techniques firsthand.

What This Book Covers

In this book you'll learn to

- Build an online product catalog that can be browsed and searched.

- Implement the catalog administration pages that allow adding, modifying, and removing products, categories, and departments.

- Create your own shopping basket and checkout in ASP.NET.

- Increase sales by implementing product recommendations.

- Handle payments using PayPal, DataCash, and VeriSign Payflow Pro.

- Implement a customer accounts system.

- Integrate with XML Web Services, such as Amazon E-Commerce Service.

How This Book Is Structured

The following sections present a brief roadmap of where this book is going to take you. The first phase of the book, Chapters 1 through 8, takes you through the process of getting your site up and running. In the second phase of the book, Chapters 9 through 11, you'll create your own shopping cart. And in the third phase, Chapters 12 through 17, you'll start processing orders and integrating external systems.

Chapter 1: Starting an E-Commerce Site

In this chapter you'll see some of the principles of e-commerce in the real world. You'll learn the importance of focusing on short-term revenue and keeping risks down. We look at the three basic ways in which an e-commerce site can make money. We then apply those principles to a three-phase plan that continues to expand throughout the book, providing a deliverable, usable site at each stage.

Chapter 2: Laying Out the Foundations

After deciding to develop a web site, we start to look in more detail at laying down the foundations for the future web site. We'll talk about what technologies and tools you'll use and, even more important, how you'll use them.

Chapter 3: Creating the Product Catalog: Part I

After you've learned about the three-tier architecture and implemented a bit of your web site's main page, it's time to continue your work by starting to create the product catalog. You'll develop the first database table, create the first stored procedure, implement generic data access code, learn how to handle errors and email their details to the administrator, work with the web.config ASP.NET configuration file, implement the business logic, and finally use data gathered from the database through the business logic mechanism to compose dynamic content for your visitor.

Chapter 4: Creating the Product Catalog: Part II

This chapter continues the work started in Chapter 3 by adding many new product catalog features. Here you'll learn about relational data and about the types of relationships that occur between data tables, how to join data tables, how to work with stored procedures, and how to display categories, products, and product details.

Chapter 5: Searching the Catalog

"What are you looking for?" There is no place where you'll hear this question more frequently than in both brick-and-mortar and e-commerce stores. Like any other quality web store around, your site should allow visitors to search through the product catalog. In this chapter, you'll see how easy it is to add new functionality to a working site by integrating the new components into the existing architecture.

Chapter 6: Improving Performance

Why walk when you can run? No, we won't talk about sports cars in this chapter. Instead, we'll analyze a few possibilities to improve the performance of your project. Although having a serious discussion on improving ASP.NET performance is beyond the scope of this book, in this chapter, you'll learn a few basic principles that you can follow to improve your web site's performance.

Chapter 7: Receiving Payments Using PayPal

Let's collect some money! Your e-commerce web site needs a way to receive payments from customers. The preferred solution for established companies is to open a merchant account, but many small businesses choose to start with a solution that's simpler to implement, where they don't have to process credit card or payment information themselves. In this chapter, you'll learn how to receive payments through PayPal.

Chapter 8: Catalog Administration

The final detail to take care of before launching the site is to create the administrative interface. In the previous chapters, you worked with catalog information that already existed in the database. You've probably inserted some records yourself, or maybe you downloaded the database information. For a real web site, both of these methods are unacceptable, so you need to write some code to allow easy management of the web store data. In this chapter, you'll implement a catalog administration page. With this feature, you complete the first stage of your web site's development.

Chapter 9: Creating a Custom Shopping Cart

Welcome to the second phase of development, where you'll start improving and adding new features to the already existing, fully functional e-commerce site. In this chapter, you'll implement the custom shopping basket, which will store its data into the local database. This will provide you with more flexibility than the PayPal shopping basket, over which you have no control and which you can't save into your database for further processing and analysis.

Chapter 10: Dealing with Customer Orders

The good news is that your brand-new shopping cart looks good and is fully functional. The bad news is that it doesn't allow visitors to actually place orders, making it totally useless in the context of a production system. You'll deal with that problem in this chapter, in two separate stages. In the first part of the chapter, you'll implement the client-side part of the order-placing mechanism. In the second part of the chapter, you'll implement a simple orders administration page where the site administrator can view and handle pending orders.

Chapter 11: Making Product Recommendations

One of the most important advantages of an online store as compared to a brick-and-mortar store is the capability to customize the web site for each visitor based on his or her preferences, or based on data gathered from other visitors with similar preferences. If your web site knows how to suggest additional products to an individual visitor in a clever way, he or she might end up buying more than initially planned. In this chapter, you'll implement a simple but efficient product recommendations system in your web store.

Chapter 12: Adding Customer Accounts

So far in this book, you've built a basic (but functional) site and hooked it into PayPal for taking payments and confirming orders. In this last section of the book, you'll take things a little further. By cutting out PayPal from the ordering process, you can gain better control and reduce over-heads. This isn't as complicated as you might think, but you must be careful to do things right. This chapter lays the groundwork for this task by implementing a customer account system.

Chapter 13: Advanced Customer Orders

Your e-commerce application is shaping up nicely. You've added customer account function-ality, and you're keeping track of customer addresses and credit card information, which is stored in a secure way. However, you're not currently using this information—you're delegating responsibility for this to PayPal. In this chapter, you'll make the modifications required for customers to place orders that are associated with their user profile.

Chapter 14: Order Pipeline

In this and the next chapter, you'll build your own order-processing pipeline that deals with credit card authorization, stock-checking, shipping, sending email notifications, and so on. We'll leave the credit card processing specifics until Chapter 16, but we'll show you where this process fits in before then.

Chapter 15: Implementing the Pipeline

Here you complete the previous chapter's work by adding the required pipeline sections so that you can process orders from start to finish. We'll also look at the web administration of orders by modifying the order administration pages added earlier in the book to take into account the new order-processing system.

Chapter 16: Credit Card Transactions

The last thing you need to do before launching the e-commerce site is enable credit card processing. In this chapter, we'll look at how you can build this into the pipeline you created in the last chapter. You'll learn how to process payments through DataCash and using the VeriSign Payflow Pro service.

Chapter 17: Integrating Amazon Web Services

In the dynamic world of the Internet, sometimes it isn't enough to just have an important web presence; you also need to interact with functionality provided by third parties to achieve your goals. So far in this book, you've seen how to integrate external functionality to process payments from your customers. In this chapter, you'll learn new possibilities for integrating functionality from an external source, this time through a web service.

Appendix A: Installing the Software

Here you'll learn how to set up your machine for the e-commerce site you'll build throughout the book. You're shown the steps to install Visual Web Developer 2005 Express Edition, SQL Server 2005 Express Edition, SQL Server Express Manager, and IIS 5.x.

Appendix B: Project Management Considerations

Although the way you build your e-commerce web site throughout this book (by designing and building one feature at a time) is ideal for learning, in real-world projects, you need to design everything from the start, otherwise you risk ending up with a failed project. Appendix B is a very quick introduction to the most popular project-management methodologies and gives you a few guidelines about how to successfully manage building a real-world project.

Downloading the Code

The code for this book is available for download in the Source Code area of the Apress web site (http://www.apress.com). Unzip the file and open Welcome.html for installation details.

Contacting the Authors

Cristian Darie can be contacted through his personal web site at http://www.CristianDarie.ro. Karli Watson can be contacted through http://www.3form.net.

CHAPTER 1

■■■

Starting an E-Commerce Site

The word "e-commerce" has had a remarkable fall from grace in the past few years. Just the idea of having an e-commerce web site was enough to get many business people salivating with anticipation. Now it's no longer good enough to just say, "E-commerce is the future—get online or get out of business." You now need compelling, realistic, and specific reasons to take your business online.

This book focuses on programming and associated disciplines, such as creating, accessing, and manipulating databases. Before we jump into that, however, we need to cover the business decisions that lead to the creation of an e-commerce site in the first place.

If you want to build an e-commerce site today, you must answer some tough questions. The good news is these questions do have answers, and we're going to have a go at answering them in this chapter:

- So many big e-commerce sites have failed. What can e-commerce possibly offer me in today's tougher environment?

- Most e-commerce companies seemed to need massive investment. How can I produce a site on my limited budget?

- Even successful e-commerce sites expect to take years before they turn a profit. My business can't wait that long. How can I make money now?

Deciding Whether to Go Online

Although there are hundreds of possible reasons to go online, they tend to fall into the following motivations:

- Getting more customers

- Making customers spend more

- Reducing the costs of fulfilling orders

We'll look at each of these in the following sections.

Getting More Customers

Getting more customers is immediately the most attractive reason. With an e-commerce site, even small businesses can reach customers all over the world. This reason can also be the most dangerous because many people set up e-commerce sites assuming that the site will reach customers immediately. It won't. In the offline world, you need to know a shop exists before you can go into it. This is still true in the world of e-commerce—people must know your site exists before you can hope to get a single order.

■Note The need to register and optimize your site for good search engine placement (with Google, Yahoo!, and so on) has given birth to an entire services industry (and many spam emails). For example, many services offer to register your site for a fee, but actually you can do it yourself with a bit of effort—the link to register yourself with Google is `http://www.google.com/addurl.html`.

Addressing this issue is largely a question of advertising, rather than the site itself. Because this is a programming book, we won't cover this aspect of e-commerce, and we suggest you consult additional books and resources if you're serious about doing e-commerce.

Anyway, because an e-commerce site is always available, some people may stumble across it. It's certainly easier for customers to tell their friends about a particular web address than to give them a catalog, mailing address, or directions to their favorite offline store.

Making Customers Spend More

Assuming your company already has customers, you probably wish that they bought more. What stops them? If the customers don't want any more of a certain product, there's not a lot that e-commerce can do, but chances are there are other reasons, too:

- Getting to the shop/placing an order by mail is a hassle.

- Some of the things you sell can be bought from more convenient places.

- You're mostly open while your customers are at work.

- Buying some products just doesn't occur to your customers.

An e-commerce site can fix those problems. People with Internet access will find placing an order online far easier than any other method—meaning that when the temptation to buy strikes, it will be much easier for them to give in. Of course, the convenience of being online also means that people are more likely to choose your site over other local suppliers.

Because your site is online 24 hours a day, rather than the usual 9 to 5, your customers can shop at your store outside of their working hours. Having an online store brings a double blessing to you if your customers work in offices because they can indulge in retail therapy directly from their desks.

Skillful e-commerce design can encourage your customers to buy things they wouldn't usually think of. You can easily update your site to suggest items of particular seasonal interest or to announce interesting new products.

Many of the large e-commerce sites encourage shoppers to buy useful accessories along with the main product or to buy a more expensive alternative to the one they're considering. Others give special offers to regular shoppers or suggest impulse purchases during checkout. You'll learn how to use some of these methods in later chapters, and by the end of the book, you'll have a good idea of how to add more features for yourself.

Finally, it's much easier to learn about your customers via e-commerce than in face-to-face shops, or even through mail order. Even if you just gather email addresses, you can use these to send out updates and news. More sophisticated sites can automatically analyze a customer's buying habits to suggest other products the customer might like to buy.

Another related benefit of e-commerce is that you can allow people to browse without buying at no real cost to you. In fact, getting people to visit the site as often as possible can be valuable. You should consider building features into the site that are designed purely to make people visit regularly; for example, you might include community features such as forums or free content related to the products you're selling. Although we won't cover these features explicitly, by the end of the book you will have learned enough to easily add them for yourself.

Reducing the Costs of Fulfilling Orders

A well-built e-commerce site will be much cheaper to run than a comparable offline business. Under conventional business models, a staff member must feed an order into the company's order-processing system. With e-commerce, the customer can do this for you—the gateway between the site and the order processing can be seamless.

Of course, after your e-commerce site is up and running, the cost of actually taking orders gets close to zero—you don't need to pay for checkout staff, assistants, security guards, or rent in a busy shopping mall.

If you have a sound business idea, and you execute the site well, you can receive these benefits without a massive investment. It's important to always focus on the almighty dollar: Will your site, or any particular feature of it, help you get more customers, get customers to spend more, or reduce the costs and therefore increase your profit margins?

Now it's time to introduce the site we'll be using as the example in this book, and see just how all these principles relate to your own shop.

Making Money

We're going to build an online balloon shop. On all the e-commerce sites we've worked on, there's been a great deal of tension between wanting to produce an amazing site that everybody will love and needing to create a site with a limited budget that will make money. Usually, we're on the trigger-happy, really-amazing-site side, but we're always grateful that our ambitions are reined in by the actual business demands. If you're designing and building the site for yourself and you are the client, then you have a challenge: keeping your view realistic while maintaining your enthusiasm for the project.

This book shows you a logical way to build an e-commerce site that delivers what it needs to be profitable. However, when designing your own site, you need to think carefully about exactly who your customers are, what they need, how they want to place orders, and what they are most likely to buy. Most important of all, you need to think about how they will come to your site in the first place. You should consider the following points before you start to visualize or design the site, and certainly before you start programming:

- *Getting customers*: How will you get visitors to the site in the first place?

- *Offering products*: What will you offer, and how will you expect customers to buy? Will they buy in bulk? Will they make a lot of repeat orders? Will they know what they want before they visit, or will they want to be inspired? These factors will influence how you arrange your catalog and searching, as well as what order process you use. A shopping basket is great if people want to browse. If people know exactly what they want, then they may prefer something more like an order form.

- *Processing orders*: How will you turn a customer order into a parcel ready for mailing? How will you ship the products (for example, FedEx, UPS, or DHL)? Your main consideration here is finding an efficient way to process payments and deliver orders to whoever manages your stocks or warehouse. You must give your customers confidence in your ability to protect their data and deliver their purchases on time.

- *Servicing customers*: Will customers require additional help with products that they buy from you? Do you need to offer warranties, service contracts, or other support services?

- *Bringing customers back*: How will you entice customers back to the site? Are they likely to only visit the site to make a purchase, or will there be e-window shoppers? Are your products consumables, and can you predict when your customers will need something new?

After you've answered these questions, you can start designing your site, knowing that you're designing for your customers—not just doing what seems like a good idea. Determining the answers to these questions also helps ensure that your design covers all the important areas, without massive omissions that will be a nightmare to fix later.

The example presented in this book takes a deliberate generic approach to show you the most common e-commerce techniques. To really lift yourself above the competition, however, you don't need fancy features or Flash movies—you just need to understand, attract, and serve your customers better than anybody else. Think about this before you launch into designing and building the site itself.

Considering the Risks and Threats

All this might make it sound as if your e-commerce business can't possibly fail. Well, it's time to take a cold shower and realize that even the best-laid plans often go wrong. Some risks are particularly relevant to e-commerce companies, such as

- Hacking and identity theft

- Credit-card scams

- Hardware failures

- Unreliable shipping services

- Software errors

- Changing laws

You can't get rid of these risks, but you can try to understand them and defend yourself from them. The software developed in this book goes some way to meeting these issues, but many of the risks have little to do with the site itself.

An important way to defend your site from many risks is to keep backups. You already know backups are important; however, if you're anything like us, when it gets to the end of the day, saving five minutes and going home earlier seems even more important. When you have a live web site, this simply isn't an option.

Coding with security in mind is also essential. In this book, you'll learn how to protect yourself by implementing a good error-handling strategy and validating user input. Using SSL (Secure Sockets Layer) connections is vital for securing sensible pages, such as the ones that contain credit-card data, and we'll cover this as well.

We haven't talked much about the legal side of e-commerce in this book because we're programmers, not lawyers. However, if you're setting up an e-commerce site that goes much beyond an online garage sale, you'll need to look into these issues before putting your business online.

While we're on the subject of risks and threats, one issue that can really damage your e-commerce site is unreliable order fulfillment. An essential part of the processes is getting the products delivered. To do this, you need a good logistics network set up before launching your shop. If your store doesn't deliver the goods, customers won't come back or refer their friends.

■**Tip** Webmonkey provides an excellent general e-commerce tutorial that covers taxation, shipping, and many of the issues you'll face when designing your site at `http://hotwired.lycos.com/webmonkey/e-business/building/tutorials/tutorial3.html`. Check this out before you start designing your own site.

Designing for Business

Building an e-commerce site requires a significant investment. If you design the site in phases, you can reduce the initial investment, and therefore cut your losses if the idea proves unsuccessful. You can use the results from an early phase to assess whether it's worthwhile to add extra features, and even use revenue from the site to fund future development. If nothing else, planning to build the site in phases means that you can get your site online and receive orders much earlier than if you build every possible feature into the first release.

Even after you've completed your initial planned phases, things may not end there. Whenever you plan a large software project, it's important to design in a way that makes unplanned future growth easy. In Chapter 2, where we'll start dealing with the technical details of building e-commerce sites, you'll learn how to design the web site architecture to allow for long-term development flexibility and scalability.

If you're building sites for clients, they will like to think their options are open. Planning the site, or any other software, in phases will help your clients feel comfortable doing business with you. They will be able to see that you are getting the job done, and they can decide to end the project at the end of any phase if they feel—for whatever reason—that they don't want to continue to invest in development.

Phase I: Getting a Site Up

Chapters 2 through 8 concentrate on establishing the basic framework for a site and putting a product catalog online. We'll start by putting together the basic site architecture, deciding how the different parts of our application will work together. We'll then build the product catalog into this architecture. You'll learn how to

- Design a database for storing a product catalog containing categories, subcategories, and products.

- Write the SQL (Structured Query Language) code and C# code for accessing that data.

- Build an attractive and functional user interface (UI) that allows for easy catalog browsing.

- Implement an efficient error-reporting system that notifies the administrator in case the site runs into trouble and displays an *Ooops* message to the visitor when a critical error occurs.

- Integrate an external payment processor (with examples for PayPal) to allow visitors to order your products.

- Provide a free-text search engine for the database.

- Give the site's administrators a private section of the site where they can modify the catalog online.

After you've built this catalog, you'll see how to offer the products for sale by integrating it with PayPal's shopping cart and order-processing system, which will handle credit-card transactions for you and email you with details of orders. These orders will be processed manually because in the early stages of an e-commerce site, the time you lose processing orders will be less than the time it would have taken to develop an automated system.

Phase II: Creating Your Own Shopping Cart

Using PayPal's shopping cart is okay and really easy, but it does mean you lose a lot of advantages. For example, you can't control the look and feel of PayPal's shopping cart, but if you use your own, you can make it an integral part of the site.

This is a significant advantage, but it's superficial compared to some of the others. For example, with your own shopping cart, you can store complete orders in your database as part of the order process, and then use that data to learn about your customers. With additional work, you also can use the shopping basket and checkout as a platform for selling more products. How often have you been tempted by impulse purchases near the checkout of your local store? Well, this also works with e-commerce. Having your own shopping cart and checkout gives you the option of later offering low-cost special offers from there. You can even analyze and make suggestions based on the contents of the cart. These optional features are outside the scope of this book, but will be easy to plug into the infrastructure you develop here—remember, your site is designed for growth!

Chapters 9 through 11 show you how to

- Build your own ASP.NET (Active Server Pages .NET) shopping cart.

- Pass a complete order through to PayPal for credit-card processing.

- Create an orders administration page.

- Implement a product recommendations system in the form of a "customers who bought this product also bought" list.

Once again, at the end of Phase II, your site will be fully operational. If you want, you can leave it as it is or add features within the existing PayPal-based payment system. When the site gets serious, however, you'll want to start processing orders and credit cards yourself. This is the part where things get complicated, and you need to be serious and careful about your site's security.

Phase III: Processing Orders

The core of e-commerce, and the bit that really separates it from other web-development projects, is handling orders and credit cards. PayPal has helped you put this off, but there are many good reasons why—eventually—you'll want to part company with PayPal:

- *Cost*: PayPal is not expensive, but the extra services it offers must be paid for somehow. Moving to a simpler credit-card processing service will mean lower transaction costs, although developing your own system will obviously incur upfront costs.

- *Freedom*: PayPal has a fairly strict set of terms and conditions and is designed for residents of a limited number of countries. By taking on more of the credit-card processing responsibility yourself, you can better control the way your site works. As an obvious example, you can accept payment using regional methods such as the Switch debit cards common in the United Kingdom.

- *Integration*: If you deal with transactions and orders using your own system, you can integrate your store and your warehouse to whatever extent you require. You could even automatically contact a third-party supplier that ships the goods straight to the customer.

- *Information*: When you handle the whole order yourself, you can record and collate all the information involved in the transaction—and then use it for marketing and research purposes.

By integrating the order processing with the warehouse, fulfillment center, or suppliers, you can reduce costs significantly. This might mean that it reduces the need for staff in the fulfillment center, or at least that the business can grow without requiring additional staff.

Acquiring information about customers can feed back into the whole process, giving you valuable information about how to sell more. At its simplest, you could email customers with special offers, or just keep in touch with a newsletter. You also could analyze buying patterns and use that data to formulate targeted marketing campaigns.

During Phase III (in Chapters 12 through 17), you will learn how to

- Build a customer accounts module, so that customers can log in and retrieve their details every time they make an order.

- Establish secure connections using SSL so that data sent by users is encrypted on its travels across the Internet.

- Authenticate and charge credit cards using third-party companies such as DataCash and VeriSign, and their XML (Extensible Markup Language) web services.

- Store credit-card numbers securely in a database.

- Learn how to integrate the Amazon E-Commerce Service into your web site.

This third phase is the most involved of all and requires some hard and careful work. By the end of Phase III, however, you will have an e-commerce site with a searchable product catalog, shopping cart, secure checkout, and complete order-processing system.

The Balloon Shop

As we said earlier, we're going to build an online shop called BalloonShop. Figure 1-1 shows how BalloonShop will look at some point during the second stage of development.

Figure 1-1. *BalloonShop during Phase II of development*

■Tip You can preview the online version of BalloonShop at `http://web.cristiandarie.ro/` `BalloonShop`. Many thanks go to `http://www.balloon-shop.com/` for allowing us to use some of their products to populate our virtual BalloonShop store.

For the purposes of this book, we'll assume that the client already exists as a mail-order company and has a good network of customers. The company is not completely new to the business and wants the site to make it easier and more enjoyable for its existing customers to buy—with the goal that they'll end up buying more.

Knowing this, we suggest the phased development because

- The company is unlikely to get massive orders initially, so you should keep the initial cost of building the web site down as much as possible.

- The company is accustomed to manually processing mail orders, so manually processing orders emailed by PayPal will not introduce many new problems.

- The company doesn't want to invest all of its money in a massive e-commerce site, only to find that people actually prefer mail order after all! Or, after Phase I, the company might realize that the site already meets its needs and there's no reason to expand it further. Either way, you hope that offering a lower initial cost gives your bid the edge. (It might also mean you can get away with a higher total price.)

Because this company is already a mail-order business, it probably already has a merchant account and can process credit cards. Thus, moving on to Phase III as soon as possible would be best for this company so it can benefit from the preferential card-processing rates.

Summary

In this chapter, we've covered some of the principles of e-commerce in the real, hostile world where it's important to focus on short-term revenue and keep risks down. We've discussed the three basic motivations for taking your business online:

- Acquiring more customers

- Making customers spend more

- Reducing the costs of fulfilling orders

We've shown you how to apply those principles to a three-phase plan that provides a deliverable, usable site at each stage. We'll continue to expand on this plan throughout the book.

At this point, you've presented your plan to the owners of the balloon shop. In the next chapter, you'll put on your programming hat, and start to design and build your web site (assuming you get the contract, of course).

CHAPTER 2

■■■

Laying Out the Foundations

Now that you've convinced the client that you can create a cool web site to complement the client's store activity, it's time to stop celebrating and start thinking about how to put into practice all the promises made to the client. As usual, when you lay down on paper the technical requirements you must meet, everything starts to seem a bit more complicated than initially anticipated.

■Note It is strongly recommended to consistently follow an efficient project-management methodology to maximize the chances of the project's success, on budget and on time. Most project-management theories imply that an initial requirements/specifications document containing the details of the project you're about to create has been signed by you and the client. You can use this document as a guide while creating the solution, and it also allows you to charge extra in case the client brings new requirements or requests changes after development has started. See Appendix B for more details.

To ensure this project's success, you need to come up with a smart way to implement what you've signed the contract for. You want to make your life easy and develop the project smoothly and quickly, but the ultimate goal is to make sure the client is satisfied with your work. Consequently, you should aim to provide your site's increasing number of visitors with a pleasant web experience by creating a nice, functional, and responsive web site by implementing each one of the three development phases described in the first chapter.

The requirements are high, but this is normal for an e-commerce site today. To maximize the chances of success, we'll try to analyze and anticipate as many of the technical requirements as possible, and implement the solution in way that supports changes and additions with minimal effort.

In this chapter, we'll lay down the foundations for the future BalloonShop web site. We'll talk about what technologies and tools you'll use, and even more important, how you'll use them. Let's consider a quick summary of the goals for this chapter before moving on:

- Analyze the project from a technical point of view.

- Analyze and choose an architecture for your application.

- Decide which technologies, programming languages, and tools to use.

- Discuss naming and coding conventions.

- Create the basic structure of the web site and set up the database.

Designing for Growth

The word "design" in the context of a Web Application can mean many things. Its most popular usage probably refers to the visual and user interface (UI) design of a web site.

This aspect is crucial because, let's face it, the visitor is often more impressed with how a site looks and how easy it is to use than about which technologies and techniques are used behind the scenes, or what operating system the web server is running. If the site is hard to use and easy to forget, it just doesn't matter what rocket science was used to create it.

Unfortunately, this truth makes many inexperienced programmers underestimate the importance of the way the invisible part of the site is implemented—the code, the database, and so on. The visual part of a site gets visitors interested to begin with, but its functionality makes them come back. A web site can sometimes be implemented very quickly based on certain initial requirements, but if not properly architected, it can become difficult, if not impossible, to change.

For any project of any size, some preparation must be done before starting to code. Still, no matter how much planning and design work is done, the unexpected does happen and hidden catches, new requirements, and changing rules always seem to work against deadlines. Even without these unexpected factors, site designers are often asked to change or add new functionality after the project is finished and deployed. This also will be the case for BalloonShop, which you'll implement in three separate stages, as discussed in Chapter 1.

You'll learn how to create the web site so that the site (or you) will not fall apart when functionality is extended or updates are made. Because this is a programming book, it doesn't address important aspects of e-commerce, such as designing the UI, marketing techniques, or legal issues. You'll need additional material to cover that ground. Instead, in this book, we'll pay close attention to constructing the code that makes the site work.

The phrase "designing the code" can have different meanings; for example, we'll need to have a short talk about naming conventions. Still, the most important aspect that we need to look at is the architecture to use when writing the code. The architecture refers to the way you split the code for a simple piece of functionality (for example, the product search feature) into smaller, interconnected components. Although it might be easier to implement that functionality as quickly and as simply as possible, in a single component, you gain great long-term advantages by creating more components that work together to achieve the desired result.

Before considering the architecture itself, you must determine what you want from this architecture.

Meeting Long-Term Requirements with Minimal Effort

Apart from the fact that you want a fast web site, each of the phases of development we talked about in Chapter 1 brings new requirements that must be met.

Every time you proceed to a new stage, you want to **reuse** most of the already existing solution. It would be very inefficient to redesign the site (not just the visual part, but the code as well!) just because you need to add a new feature. You can make it easier to reuse the solution by planning ahead so that any new functionality that needs to be added can slot in with ease, rather than each change causing a new headache.

When building the web site, implementing a **flexible architecture** composed of pluggable components allows you to add new features—such as the shopping cart, the departments list, or the product search feature—by coding them as separate components and plugging them into the existing application. Achieving a good level of flexibility is one of the goals regarding the application's architecture, and this chapter shows how you can put this into practice. You'll see that the level of flexibility is proportional to the amount of time required to design and implement it, so we'll try to find a compromise that provides the best gains without complicating the code too much.

Another major requirement that is common to all online applications is to have a **scalable architecture**. Scalability is defined as the capability to increase resources to yield a linear increase in service capacity. In other words, in a scalable system, the ratio (proportion) between the number of client requests and the hardware resources required to handle those requests is constant, even when the number of clients increases (ideally). An unscalable system can't deal with an increasing number of clients, no matter how many hardware resources are provided. Because we're optimistic about the number of customers, we must be sure that the site will be able to deliver its functionality to a large number of clients without throwing out errors or performing sluggishly.

Reliability is also a critical aspect for an e-commerce application. With the help of a coherent error-handling strategy and a powerful relational database, you can ensure data integrity and ensure that noncritical errors are properly handled without bringing the site to its knees.

The Magic of the Three-Tier Architecture

Generally, the architecture refers to splitting each piece of the application's functionality into separate components based on what they do and grouping each kind of component into a single logical tier.

The three-tier architecture has become popular today because it answers most of the problems discussed so far by splitting an application's functionality unit into three logical tiers:

- The presentation tier

- The business tier

- The data tier

The **presentation tier** contains the UI elements of the site, and includes all the logic that manages the interaction between the visitor and the client's business. This tier makes the whole site feel alive, and the way you design it is crucially important to the site's success. Because your application is a web site, its presentation tier is composed of dynamic web pages.

The **business tier** (also called the *middle tier*) receives requests from the presentation tier and returns a result to the presentation tier depending on the business logic it contains. Almost any event that happens in the presentation tier results in the business tier being called (except events that can be handled locally by the presentation tier, such as simple input data validation). For example, if the visitor is doing a product search, the presentation tier calls the business tier and says, "Please send me back the products that match this search criterion." Almost always, the business tier needs to call the data tier for information to respond to the presentation tier's request.

The **data tier** (sometimes referred to as the *database tier*) is responsible for storing the application's data and sending it to the business tier when requested. For the BalloonShop e-commerce site, you'll need to store data about products (including their categories and their departments), users, shopping carts, and so on. Almost every client request finally results in the data tier being interrogated for information (except when previously retrieved data has been cached at the business tier or presentation tier levels), so it's important to have a fast database system. In Chapters 3 and 4, you'll learn how to design the database for optimum performance.

These tiers are purely logical—there is no constraint on the physical location of each tier. You're free to place all the application, and implicitly all its tiers, on a single server machine. Alternatively, you can place each tier on a separate machine or even split the components of a single tier over multiple machines. Your choice depends on the particular performance requirements of the application. This kind of flexibility allows you to achieve many benefits, as you'll soon see.

An important constraint in the three-layered architecture model is that information must flow in sequential order between tiers. The presentation tier is only allowed to access the business tier and never directly the data tier. The business tier is the "brain" in the middle that communicates with the other tiers and processes and coordinates all the information flow. If the presentation tier directly accessed the data tier, the rules of three-tier architecture programming would be broken. When you implement a three-tier architecture, you must be consistent and obey its rules to reap the benefits.

Figure 2-1 is a simple representation of how data is passed in an application that implements the three-tier architecture.

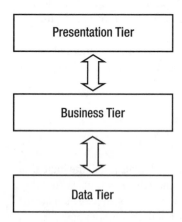

Figure 2-1. *Simple representation of the three-tier architecture*

A Simple Scenario

It's easier to understand how data is passed and transformed between tiers if you take a closer look at a simple example. To make the example even more relevant to the project, let's analyze a situation that will actually happen in BalloonShop. This scenario is typical for three-tier applications.

Like most e-commerce sites, BalloonShop will have a shopping cart, which we'll discuss later in the book. For now, it's enough to know that the visitor will add products to the shopping cart by clicking an Add to Cart button. Figure 2-2 shows how the information flows through the application when that button is clicked.

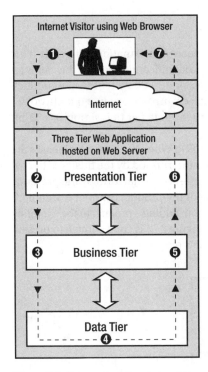

Figure 2-2. *Internet visitor interacting with a three-tier application*

When the user clicks the Add to Cart button for a specific product (Step 1), the presentation tier (which contains the button) forwards the request to the business tier—"Hey, I want this product added to the visitor's shopping cart!" (Step 2). The business tier receives the request, understands that the user wants a specific product added to the shopping cart, and handles the request by telling the data tier to update the visitor's shopping cart by adding the selected product (Step 3). The data tier needs to be called because it stores and manages the entire web site's data, including users' shopping cart information.

The data tier updates the database (Step 4) and eventually returns a success code to the business tier. The business tier (Step 5) handles the return code and any errors that might have occurred in the data tier while updating the database and then returns the output to the presentation tier.

Finally, the presentation tier generates an updated view of the shopping cart (Step 6). The results of the execution are wrapped up by generating an HTML (Hypertext Markup Language) web page that is returned to the visitor (Step 7), where the updated shopping cart can be seen in the visitor's favorite web browser.

Note that in this simple example, the business tier doesn't do a lot of processing, and its business logic isn't very complex. However, if new business rules appear for your application, you would change the business tier. If, for example, the business logic specified that a product could only be added to the shopping cart if its quantity in stock were greater than zero, an additional data tier call would have been made to determine the quantity. The data tier would only be requested to update the shopping cart if products were in stock. In any case, the presentation tier is informed about the status and provides human-readable feedback to the visitor.

What's in a Number?

It's interesting to note how each tier interprets the same piece of information differently. For the data tier, the numbers and information it stores have no significance because this tier is an engine that saves, manages, and retrieves numbers, strings, or other data types—not product quantities or product names. In the context of the previous example, a product quantity of 0 represents a simple, plain number without any meaning to the data tier (it is simply 0, a 32-bit integer).

The data gains significance when the business tier reads it. When the business tier asks the data tier for a product quantity and gets a "0" result, this is interpreted by the business tier as "Hey, no products in stock!" This data is finally wrapped in a nice, visual form by the presentation tier, for example, a label reading, "Sorry, at the moment the product cannot be ordered."

Even if it's unlikely that you want to forbid a customer from adding a product to the shopping cart if the product isn't in stock, the example (described in Figure 2-3) is good enough to present in yet another way how each of the three tiers has a different purpose.

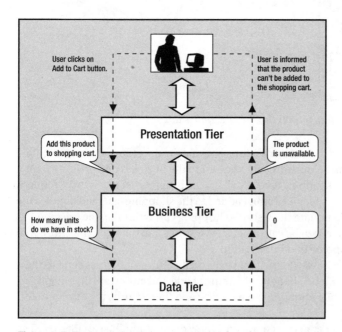

Figure 2-3. *Internet visitor interacting with a three-tier application*

The Right Logic for the Right Tier

Because each layer contains its own logic, sometimes it can be tricky to decide where exactly to draw the line between the tiers. In the previous scenario, instead of reading the product's quantity in the business tier and deciding whether the product is available based on that number (resulting in two data tier, and implicitly database, calls), you could have a single data tier method named `AddProductIfAvailable` that adds the product to the shopping cart only if it's available in stock.

In this scenario, some logic is transferred from the business tier to the data tier. In many other circumstances, you might have the option to place the same logic in one tier or another, or maybe in both. In most cases, there is no single best way to implement the three-tier architecture, and you'll need to make a compromise or a choice based on personal preference or external constraints.

Occasionally, even though you know the right way (in respect to the architecture) to implement something, you might choose to break the rules to get a performance gain. As a general rule, if performance can be improved this way, it's okay to break the strict limits between tiers *just a little bit* (for example, add some of the business rules to the data tier or vice versa), if these rules are not likely to change in time. Otherwise, keeping all the business rules in the middle tier is preferable because it generates a "cleaner" application that is easier to maintain.

Finally, don't be tempted to access the data tier directly from the presentation tier. This is a common mistake that is the shortest path to a complicated, hard-to-maintain, and inflexible system. In many data access tutorials or introductory materials, you'll be shown how to perform simple database operations using a simple UI application. In these kinds of programs, all the logic is probably written in a short, single file instead of separate tiers. Although the materials might be very good, keep in mind that most of these texts are meant to teach you how to do different individual tasks (for example, access a database) and not how to correctly create a flexible and scalable application.

A Three-Tier Architecture for BalloonShop

Implementing a three-tiered architecture for the BalloonShop web site will help you achieve the goals listed at the beginning of the chapter. The coding discipline imposed by a system that might seem rigid at first sight allows for excellent levels of flexibility and extensibility in the long run.

Splitting major parts of the application into separate, smaller components also encourages reusability. More than once when adding new features to the site you'll see that you can reuse some of the already existing bits. Adding a new feature without needing to change much of what already exists is, in itself, a good example of reusability. Also, smaller pieces of code placed in their correct places are easier to document and analyze later.

Another advantage of the three-tiered architecture is that, if properly implemented, the overall system is resistant to changes. When bits in one of the tiers change, the other tiers usually remain unaffected, sometimes even in extreme cases. For example, if for some reason the backend database system is changed (say, the manager decides to use Oracle instead of SQL Server), you only need to update the data tier. The existing business tier should work the same with the new database.

Why Not Use More Tiers?

The three-tier architecture we've been talking about so far is a particular (and the most popular) version of the *n*-Tier Architecture, which is a commonly used buzzword these days. *n*-Tier architecture refers to splitting the solution into a number (*n*) of logical tiers. In complex projects, sometimes it makes sense to split the business layer into more than one layer, thus resulting in an architecture with more than three layers. However, for this web site, it makes most sense to stick with the three-layered design, which offers most of the benefits while not requiring too many hours of design or a complex hierarchy of framework code to support the architecture.

Maybe with a more involved and complex architecture, you would achieve even higher levels of flexibility and scalability for the application, but you would need much more time for design before starting to implement anything. As with any programming project, you must find a fair balance between the time required to design the architecture and the time spent to implement it. The three-tier architecture is best suited to projects with average complexity, like the BalloonShop web site.

You also might be asking the opposite question, "Why not use fewer tiers?" A two-tier architecture, also called client-server architecture, can be appropriate for less-complex projects. In short, a two-tier architecture requires less time for planning and allows quicker development in the beginning, although it generates an application that's harder to maintain and extend in the long run. Because we're expecting to extend the application in the future, the client-server architecture isn't appropriate for this application, so it won't be discussed further in this book.

Now that you know the general architecture, let's see what technologies and tools you'll use to implement it. After a brief discussion of the technologies, you'll create the foundation of the presentation and data tiers by creating the first page of the site and the backend database. You'll start implementing some real functionality in each of the three tiers in Chapter 3 when you start creating the web site's product catalog.

Choosing Technologies and Tools

No matter which architecture is chosen, a major question that arises in every development project is which technologies, programming languages, and tools are going to be used, bearing in mind that external requirements can seriously limit your options.

■**Note** In this book, we're creating a web site using Microsoft technologies. Keep in mind, however, that when it comes to technology, problems often have more than one solution, and rarely is there only a single best way to solve the problem. Although we really like Microsoft's technologies as presented in this book, it doesn't necessarily mean they're the best choice for any kind of project, in any circumstances. Additionally, in many situations, you must use specific technologies because of client requirements or other external constraints. The *System Requirements* and *Software Requirements* stages in the software development process will determine which technologies you must use for creating the application. See Appendix B for more details.

This book is about programming e-commerce web sites with **ASP.NET 2.0** (Active Server Pages .NET 2.0) and **C#**. The tools you'll use are **Visual Web Developer 2005 Express Edition** and **SQL Server 2005 Express Edition**, which are freely available from Microsoft's web site. See Appendix A for installation instructions. Although the book assumes a little previous experience with each of these, we'll take a quick look at them and see how they fit into the project and into the three-tier architecture.

> ■**Note** This book builds on *Beginning ASP.NET 1.1 E-Commerce: From Novice to Professional* (Apress, 2004), which used ASP.NET 1.1, Visual Studio .NET 2003, and SQL Server 2000. If you're an open source fan, you might also want to check out *Beginning PHP 5 and MySQL E-Commerce: From Novice to Professional* (Apress, 2004).

Using ASP.NET 2.0

ASP.NET 2.0 is Microsoft's latest technology set for building dynamic, interactive web content. Compared to its previous versions, ASP.NET 2.0 includes many new features aimed at increasing the web developer's productivity in building web applications.

Because this book is targeted at both existing ASP.NET 1.1 and existing ASP.NET 2.0 developers, we'll highlight a number of ASP.NET 2.0-specific techniques along the way and try to provide useful tips and tricks that increase your coding efficiency by making the most of this technology. However, do keep in mind that while building your e-commerce web site with this book, we only cover a subset of the vast number of features ASP.NET 2.0 has to offer. Therefore, you still need additional ASP.NET 2.0 books (or other resources) to use as a reference and to complete your knowledge on theory issues that didn't make it into this book. In the Apress technology tree, reading this book comes naturally after *Beginning ASP.NET 2.0 in C#: From Novice to Professional* (Apress, 2005), but you can always use the beginners' books of your choice instead.

ASP.NET is not the only server-side technology around for creating professional e-commerce web sites. Among its most popular competitors are PHP (Hypertext Preprocessor), JSP (JavaServer Pages), ColdFusion, and even the outdated ASP 3.0 and CGI (Common Gateway Interface). Among these technologies are many differences, but also some fundamental similarities. For example, pages written with any of these technologies are composed of basic HTML, which draws the static part of the page (the template), and code that generates the dynamic part.

Web Clients and Web Servers

You probably already know the general principles about how dynamic web pages work. However, as a short recap, Figure 2-4 shows what happens to an ASP.NET web page from the moment the client browser (no matter if it's Internet Explorer, Mozilla Firefox, or any other web browser) requests it to the moment the browser actually receives it.

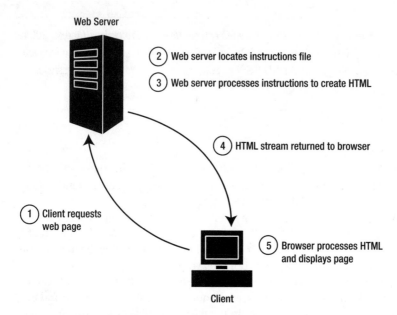

Figure 2-4. *Web server processing client requests*

After the request, the page is first processed at the server before being returned to the client (this is the reason ASP.NET and the other mentioned technologies are called server-side technologies). When an ASP.NET page is requested, its underlying code is first executed on the server. After the final page is composed, the resulting HTML is returned to the visitor's browser.

The returned HTML can optionally contain client-side script code, which is directly interpreted by the browser. The most popular client-side scripting technologies are JavaScript and VBScript. JavaScript is usually the better choice because it has wider acceptance, whereas only Internet Explorer recognizes VBScript. Other important client-side technologies are Macromedia Flash and Java applets, but these are somewhat different because the web browser does not directly parse them—Flash requires a specialized plug-in and Java applets require a JVM (Java Virtual Machine). Internet Explorer also supports ActiveX controls and .NET assemblies.

The Code Behind the Page

From its first version, ASP.NET encouraged (and helped) developers to keep the code of a web page physically separated from the HTML layout of that page. Keeping the code that gives life to a web page in a separate file from the HTML layout of the page was an important improvement over other server-side web-development technologies whose mix of code and HTML in the same file often led to long and complicated source files that were hard to document, change, and maintain. Also, a file containing both code and HTML is the subject of both programmers' and designers' work, which makes team collaboration unnecessarily complicated and increases the chances of the designer creating bugs in the code logic while working on cosmetic changes.

ASP.NET 1.0 introduced a **code-behind** model, used to separate the HTML layout of a web page from the code that gives life to that page. Although it was possible to write the code and HTML in the same file, Visual Studio .NET 2002 and Visual Studio .NET 2003 always automatically generated two separate files for a Web Form: the HTML layout resided in the .ASPX file and the code resided in the code-behind file. Because ASP.NET allowed the developer to write the code in the programming language of his choice (such as C# or VB .NET), the code-behind file's extension depended on the language it was written in (such as .ASPX.CS or .ASPX.VB).

ASP.NET 2.0 uses a refined code-behind model. Although the new model is more powerful, the general principles (to help separate the page's looks from its brain) are still the same. We'll look over the differences a bit later, especially for existing ASP.NET 1.x developers migrating to ASP.NET 2.0.

Before moving on, let's summarize the most important general features of ASP.NET:

- The server-side code can be written in the .NET language of your choice. By default, you can choose from C#, VB .NET, and J#, but the whole infrastructure is designed to support additional languages. These languages are powerful and fully object oriented.

- The server-side code of ASP.NET pages is fully compiled and executed—as opposed to being interpreted line by line—which results in optimal performance and offers the possibility to detect a number of errors at compile-time instead of runtime.

- The concept of code-behind files helps separate the visual part of the page from the (server-side) logic behind it. This is an advantage over other technologies, in which both the HTML and the server-side code reside in the same file (often resulting in the popular "spaghetti code").

- Visual Web Developer 2005 is an excellent and complete visual editor that represents a good weapon in the ASP.NET programmer's arsenal (although you don't need it to create ASP.NET Web Applications). Visual Web Developer 2005 Express Edition is free, and you can use it to develop the examples in this book.

ASP.NET Web Forms, Web User Controls, and Master Pages

ASP.NET web sites are developed around ASP.NET **Web Forms**. ASP.NET Web Forms have the .aspx extension and are the standard way to provide web functionality to clients. A request to an ASPX resource, such as http://web.cristiandarie.ro/BalloonShop/default.aspx, results in the default.aspx file being executed on the server (together with its code-behind file) and the results being composed as an HTML page that is sent back to the client. Usually, the .aspx file has an associated code-behind file, which is also considered part of the Web Form.

Web User Controls and **Master Pages** are similar to Web Forms in that they are also composed of HTML and code (they also support the code-behind model), but they can't be directly accessed by clients. Instead, they are used to compose the content of the Web Forms.

Web User Controls are files with the .ascx extension that can be included in Web Forms, with the parent Web Form becoming the container of the control. Web User Controls allow you to easily reuse pieces of functionality in a number of Web Forms.

Master Pages are a new feature of ASP.NET 2.0. A Master Page is a template that can be applied to a number of Web Forms in a site to ensure a consistent visual appearance and functionality throughout the various pages of the site. Updating the Master Page has an immediate effect on every Web Form built on top of that Master Page.

Web User Controls, Web Server Controls, and HTML Server Controls It's worth taking a second look at Web User Controls from another perspective. Web User Controls are a particular type of server-side control. Server-side controls generically refer to three kinds of controls: Web User Controls, Web Server Controls, and HTML Server Controls. All these kinds of controls can be used to reuse pieces of functionality inside Web Forms.

As stated in the previous section, Web User Controls are files with the .ascx extension that have a structure similar to the structure of Web Forms, but they can't be requested directly by a client web browser; instead, they are meant to be included in Web Forms or other Web User Controls.

Web Server Controls are compiled .NET classes that, when executed, generate HTML output (eventually including client-side script). You can use them in Web Forms or in Web User Controls. The .NET Framework ships with a large number of Web Server Controls (many of which are new to version 2.0 of the framework), including simple controls such as Label, TextBox, or Button, and more complex controls, such as validation controls, data controls, the famous GridView control (which is meant to replace the old DataGrid), and so on. Web Server Controls are powerful, but they are more complicated to code because all their functionality must be implemented manually. Among other features, you can programmatically declare and access their properties, make these properties accessible through the Visual Web Developer designer, and add the controls to the toolbox, just as in Windows Forms applications or old VB6 programs.

HTML Server Controls allow you to programmatically access HTML elements of the page from code (such as from the code-behind file). You transform an HTML control to an HTML Server Control by adding the runat="server" attribute to it. Most HTML Server Controls are doubled by Web Server Controls (such as labels, buttons, and so on). For consistency, we'll stick with Web Server Controls most of the time, but you'll need to use HTML Server Controls in some cases.

For the BalloonShop project, you'll use all kinds of controls, and you'll create a number of Web User Controls.

Because you can develop Web User Controls independently of the main web site and then just plug them in when they're ready, having a site structure based on Web User Controls provides an excellent level of flexibility and reusability.

ASP.NET and the Three-Tier Architecture

The collection of Web Forms, Web User Controls, and Master Pages form the presentation tier of the application. They are the part that creates the HTML code loaded by the visitor's browser.

The logic of the UI is stored in the code-behind files of the Web Forms, Web User Controls, and Master Pages. Note that although you don't need to use code-behind files with ASP.NET (you're free to mix code and HTML just as you did with ASP), we'll exclusively use the code-behind model for the presentation-tier logic.

In the context of a three-tier application, the logic in the presentation tier usually refers to the various event handlers, such as Page_Load and someButton_Click. As you learned earlier, these event handlers should call business-tier methods to get their jobs done (and never call the data tier directly).

Using C# and VB .NET

C# and VB .NET are languages that can be used to code the Web Forms' code-behind files. In this book, we're using C#; in a separate version of this book called *Beginning ASP.NET E-Commerce in VB .NET: From Novice to Professional*, we'll present the same functionality using VB .NET. Unlike its previous version (VB6), VB .NET is a fully object-oriented language and takes advantage of all the features provided by the .NET Framework.

ASP.NET 2.0 even allows you to write the code for various elements inside a project in different languages, but we won't use this feature in this book. Separate projects written in different .NET languages can freely interoperate, as long as you follow some basic rules. For more information about how the .NET Framework works, you should read a general-purpose .NET book.

■**Note** Just because you *can* use multiple languages in a single language, doesn't mean you *should* overuse that feature, if you have a choice. Being consistent is more important than playing with diversity if you care for long-term ease of maintenance and prefer to avoid unnecessary headaches (which is something that most programmers do).

In this book, apart from using C# for the code-behind files, you'll use the same language to code the middle tier classes. You'll create the first classes in Chapter 3 when building the product catalog, and you'll learn more details there, including a number of new features that come with .NET 2.0.

Using Visual Studio 2005 and Visual Web Developer 2005 Express Edition

Visual Studio 2005 is by far the most powerful tool you can find to develop .NET applications. Visual Studio is a complete programming environment capable of working with many types of projects and files, including Windows and Web Forms projects, setup and deployment projects, and many others. Visual Studio also can be used as an interface to the database to create tables and stored procedures, implement table relationships, and so on.

Visual Web Developer 2005 Express Edition is a free version of Visual Studio 2005, focused on developing Web Applications with ASP.NET 2.0. Because the code in this book can be built with any of these products, we'll use the terms *Visual Web Developer* and *Visual Studio* interchangeably.

A significant new feature in Visual Studio .NET 2005 and Visual Web Developer 2005 compared to previous versions of Visual Studio is the presence of an integrated web server, which permits you to execute your ASP.NET Web Applications even if you don't have IIS (Internet Information Services) installed on your machine. This is good news for Windows XP Home Edition users, who can't install IIS on their machines because it isn't supported by the operating system.

Although we'll use Visual Web Developer 2005 Express Edition for writing the BalloonShop project, it's important to know that you don't have to. ASP.NET and the C# and VB .NET compilers are available as free downloads at `http://www.microsoft.com` as part of the .NET Framework SDK (Software Developers Kit), and a simple editor such as Notepad is enough to create any kind of web page.

■**Tip** In the ASP.NET 1.x days when there were no free versions of Visual Studio, many developers preferred to use a neat program called Web Matrix—a free ASP.NET development tool whose installer (which can still be downloaded at `http://www.asp.net/webmatrix`) was only 1.3MB. Development of Web Matrix has been discontinued though, because Visual Web Developer 2005 Express Edition is both powerful and free.

Visual Studio 2005 and Visual Web Developer 2005 come with many new features compared to its earlier versions, and we'll study a part of them while creating the BalloonShop project.

Using SQL Server 2005

Along with .NET Framework 2.0 and Visual Studio 2005, Microsoft also released a new version of its player in the Relational Database Management Systems (RDBMS) field—SQL Server 2005. This complex software program's purpose is to store, manage, and retrieve data as quickly and reliably as possible. You'll use SQL Server to store all the information regarding your web site, which will be dynamically placed on the web page by the application logic. Simply said, all data regarding the products, departments, users, shopping carts, and so on will be stored and managed by SQL Server.

The good news is that a lightweight version of SQL Server 2005, named SQL Server 2005 Express Edition, is freely available. Unlike the commercial versions, SQL Server 2005 Express Edition doesn't ship by default with any visual-management utilities. However, a very nice tool called SQL Server Express Manager is also freely available. Appendix A contains details for installing both SQL Server 2005 Express Edition and SQL Server Express Manager.

■**Tip** To learn more about the differences between SQL Server 2005 Express Edition and the other versions, you can check `http://www.microsoft.com/sql/2005/productinfo/sql2005features.asp`.

The first steps in interacting with SQL Server come a bit later in this chapter when you create the BalloonShop database.

SQL Server and the Three-Tier Architecture

It should be clear by now that SQL Server is somehow related to the data tier. However, if you haven't worked with databases until now, it might be less than obvious that SQL Server is more than a simple store of data. Apart from the actual data stored inside, SQL Server is also capable of storing logic in the form of stored procedures, maintaining table relationships, ensuring that various data integrity rules are obeyed, and so on.

You can communicate with SQL Server through a language called T-SQL (Transact-SQL), which is the SQL dialect recognized by SQL Server. SQL, or Structured Query Language, is the language used to interact with the database. SQL is used to transmit to the database instructions such as "Send me the last 10 orders" or "Delete product #123."

Although it's possible to compose T-SQL statements in your C# code and then submit them for execution, this is generally a *bad practice*, because it incurs security, consistency, and performance penalties. In our solution, we'll store all data tier logic using **stored procedures**. Historically, stored procedures were programs that were stored internally in the database and were written in T-SQL. This still stands true with SQL Server 2005, which also brings the notion of *managed stored procedures* that can be written in a .NET language such as C# and VB.NET and are, as a result, compiled instead of interpreted.

■**Note** Writing stored procedures in C#, also called *managed stored procedures*, doesn't just sound interesting, it actually is. However, managed stored procedures are very powerful weapons, and as with any weapon, only particular circumstances justify using them. Typically it makes sense to use managed stored procedures when you need to perform complex mathematical operations or complex logic that can't be easily implemented with T-SQL. However, learning how to do these tasks the right way requires a good deal of research, which is outside the scope of this book. Moreover, the data logic in this book didn't justify adding any managed stored procedures, and as a result you won't see any here. Learning how to program managed stored procedures takes quite a bit of time, and you might want to check out one of the books that are dedicated to writing managed code under SQL Server.

The stored procedures are stored internally in the database and can be called from external programs. In your architecture, the stored procedures will be called from the business tier. The stored procedures in turn manipulate or access the data store, get the results, and return them to the business tier (or perform the necessary operations).

Figure 2-5 shows the technologies associated with every tier in the three-tier architecture. SQL Server contains the data tier of the application (stored procedures that contain the logic to access and manipulate data) and also the actual data store.

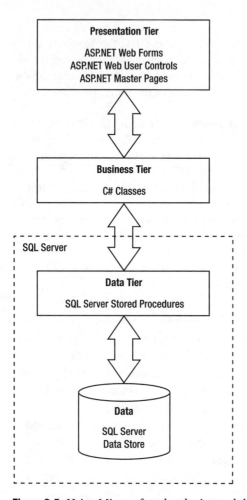

Figure 2-5. *Using Microsoft technologies and the three-tier architecture*

Following Coding Standards

Although coding and naming standards might not seem that important at first, they definitely shouldn't be overlooked. Not following a set of rules for your code almost always results in code that's hard to read, understand, and maintain. On the other hand, when you follow a consistent way of coding, you can say your code is already half documented, which is an important contribution toward the project's maintainability, especially when many people are working at the same project at the same time.

Naming conventions refer to many elements within a project, simply because almost all of a project's elements have names: the project itself, namespaces, Web Forms, Web User Controls, instances of Web User Controls and other interface elements, classes, variables, methods, method parameters, database tables, database columns, stored procedures, and so on. Without some discipline when naming all those elements, after a week of coding, you won't understand a line of what you've written.

This book tries to stick to Microsoft's recommendations regarding naming conventions. Now the philosophy is that a variable name should express what the object does and not its data type. We'll talk more about naming conventions while building the site. Right now, it's time to play.

Creating the Visual Web Developer Project

Our favorite toy is, of course, Visual Web Developer. It allows you to create all kinds of projects, including Web Site projects (formerly known as Web Application projects). The other necessary toy is SQL Server, which will hold your web site's data. We'll deal with the database a bit later in this chapter.

The first step toward building the BalloonShop site is to open Visual Web Developer and create a new ASP.NET Web Site project. If with previous versions of Visual Studio you needed to have IIS installed, due to the integrated web server of Visual Studio .NET 2005 (named Cassini), you can run the ASP.NET Web Application from any physical folder on your disk. As a result, when creating the Web Site project, you can specify for destination either a web location (such as `http://localhost/BalloonShop`) or a physical folder on your disk (such as `C:\BalloonShop`).

If you have a choice, usually the preferred solution is still to use IIS because of its better performance and because it guarantees that the pages will display the same as the deployed solution. Cassini (the integrated web server) does an excellent job of simulating IIS, but it still shouldn't be your first option. For this book, you can use either option, although our final tests and screenshots were done using IIS.

You'll create the BalloonShop project step-by-step in the exercises that follow. To ensure that you always have the code we expect you to have and to eliminate any possible frustrations or misunderstandings, we'll always include the steps you must follow to build your project in separate Exercise sections. We know it's very annoying when a book tells you something, but the computer's monitor shows you another thing, so we did our best to eliminate this kind of problems.

Let's go.

Exercise: Creating the BalloonShop Project

Follow the steps in this exercise to create the ASP.NET Web Site project.

1. Start Visual Web Developer 2005 Express Edition, choose **File ➤ New Web Site**. In the dialog box that opens, select **ASP.NET Web Site** from the Templates panel, and **Visual C#** for the Language.

2. In the first Location combo box, you can choose from File System, HTTP, and FTP, which determine how your project is executed. If you choose to install the project on the File System, you need to choose a physical location on your disk, such as C:\BalloonShop\. In this case, the Web Application is executed using Visual Web Developer's integrated web server (Cassini). If you choose an HTTP location (such as http://localhost/BalloonShop), the Web Application will be executed through IIS.

   Make a choice that fits you best. If you go the HTTP way and you're developing on your local machine, make sure that your machine has IIS installed (see Appendix A). For the purpose of this exercise, we're creating the project in the http://localhost/BalloonShop location, as shown in Figure 2-6.

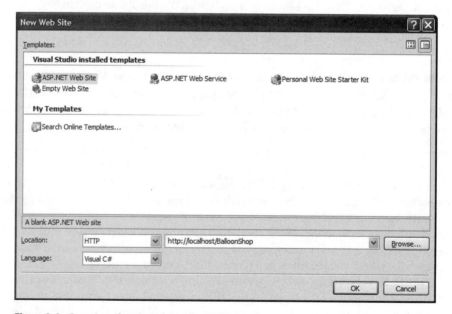

Figure 2-6. *Creating the Visual Studio .NET project*

■**Note** When creating the project on an HTTP location with the local IIS server, the project is physically created, by default, under the `\InetPub\wwwroot` folder. If you prefer to use another folder, use the Internet Information Services applet by choosing Control Panel ➤ Administrative Tools to create a virtual folder pointing to the physical folder of your choice prior to creating the Web Application with Visual Web Developer. If this note doesn't make much sense to you, ignore it for now.

3. Click **OK**. Visual Studio now creates the new project in the BalloonShop folder you specified.

In the new project, a new Web Form called Default.aspx is created by default, as shown in Figure 2-7.

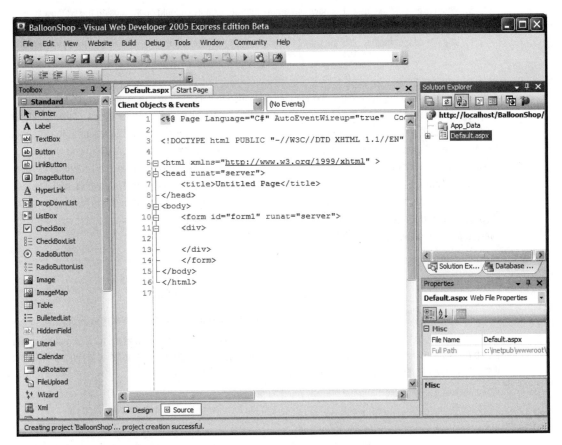

Figure 2-7. *The BalloonShop project in Visual Web Developer 2005 Express Edition*

4. Execute the project in debug mode by pressing **F5**. At this point, Visual Web Developer will complain (as shown in Figure 2-8) that it can't debug the project as long as debugging is not enabled in web.config (actually, at this point, the web.config file doesn't even exist). Click **OK** to allow Visual Studio to enable debug mode for you. Feel free to look at the newly created web.config file to see what has been done for you.

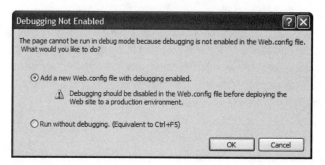

Figure 2-8. *Debugging must be enabled in* `web.config`

5. When executing the project, a new and empty Internet Explorer should open. Closing the window will also stop the project from executing (the Break and Stop Debugging symbols disappear from the Visual Web Developer toolbar, and the project becomes fully editable again).

■**Note** When executing the project, the web site is loaded in your system's default web browser. For the purposes of debugging your code, we recommend configuring Visual Web Developer to use Internet Explorer by default, even if your system's preferred browser is (for example) Mozilla Firefox. The reason is that Internet Explorer integration seems to work better. For example, Visual Web Developer knows when you close the Internet Explorer window and automatically stops the project from debug mode so you can continue development work normally; however, with other browsers, you may need to manually Stop Debugging (click the Stop square button in the toolbar, or press Shift+F5 by default). To change the default browser to be used by Visual Web Developer, right-click the root node in Solution Explorer, choose Browse With, select a browser from the Browsers tab, and click Set as Default.

How It Works: Your Visual Web Developer Project

Congratulations! You have just completed the first step in creating your e-commerce store!

Unlike with previous versions of ASP.NET, you don't need an IIS virtual directory (or IIS at all, for that matter) to run a Web Application, because you can create the ASP.NET Web Site project in a physical location on your drive. Now it's up to you where and how you want to debug and execute your Web Application!

When not using IIS and executing the project, you'll be pointed to an address like `http://localhost:5392/ BalloonShop/Default.aspx`, which corresponds to the location of the integrated web server.

At this moment your project contains three files:

- `Default.aspx` is your Web Form.

- `Default.aspx.cs` is the code-behind file of the Web Form.

- `web.config` is the project's configuration file.

We'll have a closer look at these files later.

Implementing the Site Skeleton

The visual design of the site is usually agreed upon after a discussion with the client and in collaboration with a professional web designer. Alternatively, you can buy a web site template from one of the many companies that offer this kind of service for a reasonable price.

Because this is a programming book, we won't discuss web design issues. Furthermore, we want a simple design that allows you to focus on the technical details of the site. A simplistic design will also make your life easier if you'll need to apply your layout on top of the one we're creating here.

All pages in BalloonShop, including the first page, will have the structure shown in Figure 2-9. In later chapters, you'll add more components to the scheme (such as the login box or shopping cart summary box), but for now, these are the pieces we're looking to implement in the next few chapters.

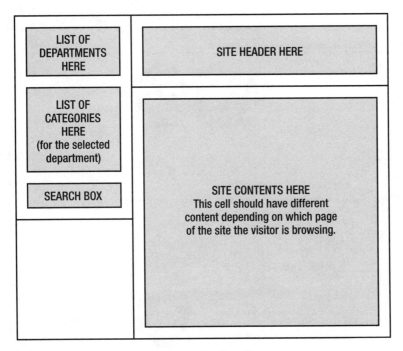

Figure 2-9. *Structure of web pages in BalloonShop*

Although the detailed structure of the product catalog is covered in the next chapter, right now you know that the main list of departments needs to be displayed on every page of the site. You also want the site header to be visible in any page the visitor browses.

You'll implement this structure by creating the following:

- A Master Page containing the general structure of all the web site's pages, as shown in Figure 2-9

- A number of Web Forms that use the Master Page to implement the various locations of the web site, such as the main page, the department pages, the search results page, and so on

- A number of Web User Controls to simplify reusing specific pieces of functionality (such as the departments list box, the categories list box, the search box, the header, and so on)

Figure 2-10 shows a few of the Web User Controls you'll create while developing BalloonShop.

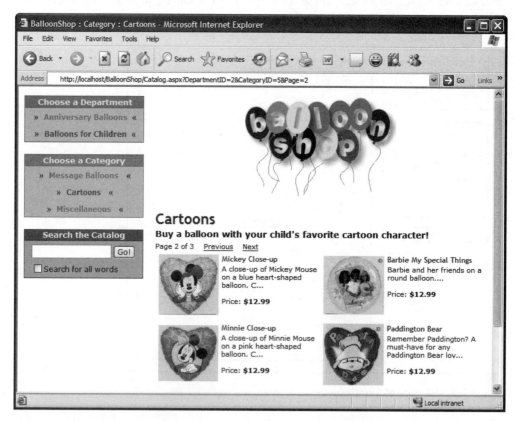

Figure 2-10. *Using Web User Controls to generate content*

Using Web User Controls to implement different pieces of functionality has many long-term advantages. Logically separating different, unrelated pieces of functionality from one another gives you the flexibility to modify them independently and even reuse them in other pages without having to write HTML code and the supporting code-behind file again. It's also extremely easy to extend the functionality or change the place of a feature implemented as a user control in the parent web page; changing the location of a Web User Control is anything but a complicated and lengthy process.

In the remainder of this chapter, we'll write the Master Page of the site, a Web Form for the first page that uses the Master Page, and the Header Web User Control. We'll deal with the other user controls in the following chapters. Finally, at the end of the chapter, you'll create the BalloonShop database, which is the last step in laying the foundations of the project.

Building the First Page

At the moment, you have a single Web Form in the site, Default.aspx, which Visual Web Developer automatically created when you created the project. By default, Visual Web Developer didn't generate a Master Page for you, so you'll do this in the following exercise.

1. Click **Website ➤ Add New Item** (or press **Ctrl+Shift+A**). In the dialog box that opens, choose **Master Page** from the Visual Studio Installed Templates list.

2. Choose **Visual C#** for the language, check the **Place code in a separate file** check box, and change the page name to **BalloonShop.master** (the default name MasterPage.master isn't particularly expressive). The Add New Item dialog box should now look like Figure 2-11.

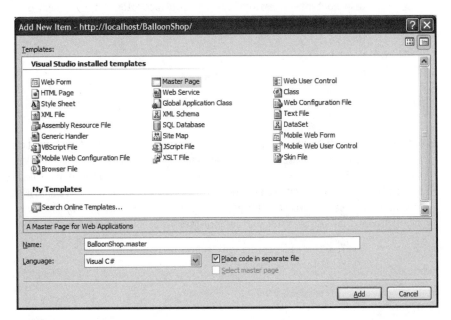

Figure 2-11. *Adding a new Master Page to the project*

3. Click **Add** to add the new Master Page to the project. The new Master Page will be opened with some default code in Source View. If you switch to Design View, you'll see the ContentPlaceHolder object that it contains. While in Source View, update its code like this:

```
<%@ Master Language="C#" AutoEventWireup="true"
CodeFile="BalloonShop.master.cs" Inherits="BalloonShop" %>
<!DOCTYPE html PUBLIC "-//W3C//DTD XHTML 1.1//EN"
"http://www.w3.org/TR/xhtml11/DTD/xhtml11.dtd">
<html xmlns="http://www.w3.org/1999/xhtml">
<head runat="server">
  <title>BalloonShop</title>
</head>
<body>
  <form id="Form1" runat="server">
    <table cellspacing="0" cellpadding="0" width="770" border="0">
      <tr>
        <td width="220" valign="top">
          List of Departments
          <br />
          List of Categories
          <br />
        </td>
        <td valign="top">
          Header
          <asp:ContentPlaceHolder ID="contentPlaceHolder" runat="server">
          </asp:ContentPlaceHolder>
        </td>
      </tr>
    </table>
  </form>
</body>
</html>
```

4. Now switch again to Design View; you should see something like Figure 2-12. If you haven't changed the default behavior of Visual Web Developer, you'll see that the ContentPlaceHolder object is marked with a little green arrow sign (which is probably hardly visible in the figure). This indicates that the control is marked to be executed at server-side (on the server). All server-side controls (including Labels, TextBoxes, and so on) on the page will be marked with the same green symbol. If you look at the HTML code of the ContentPlaceHolder, you'll see the runat="server" clause:

```
<asp:contentplaceholder id="contentPlaceHolder" runat="server">
</asp:contentplaceholder>
```

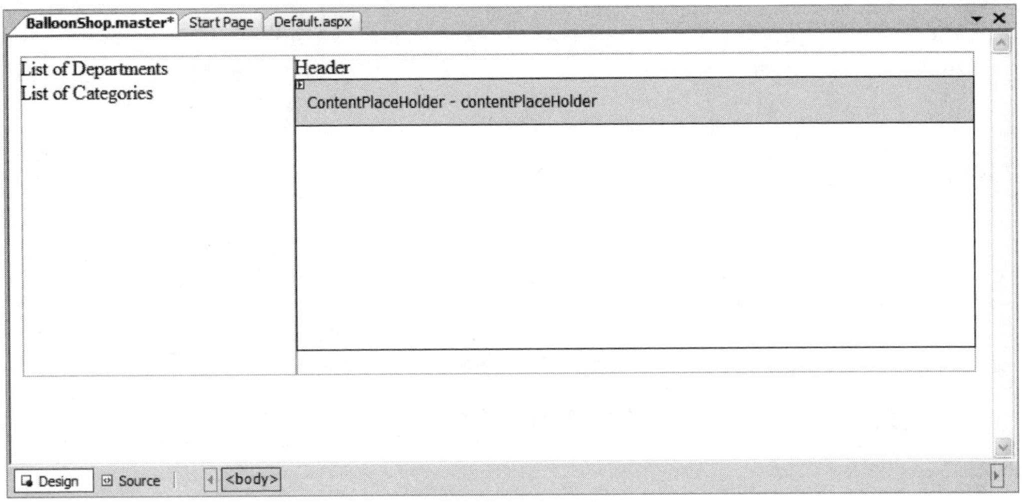

Figure 2-12. *Your New Master Page in Design View*

Master Pages are not meant to be accessed directly by clients, but to be implemented in Web Forms. You'll use the Master Page you've just created to establish the template of the Default.aspx Web Form. Because the Default.aspx page that Visual Web Developer created for you was not meant to be used with Master Pages (it contains code that should be inherited from the Master Page), it's easier to delete and re-create the file.

5. Right-click Default.aspx in Solution Explorer and choose **Delete**. Confirm the deletion.

6. Right-click the project root in Solution Explorer and select **Add New Item**. Choose the Web Form template, leave its name as Default.aspx, make sure both check boxes **Place code in separate file** and **Select Master Page** are checked, verify that the language is **Visual C#**, and click **Add**. When asked for a Master Page file, choose BalloonShop.master and click **OK**. Your new page will be created with just a few lines of code, all the rest being inherited from the Master Page:

```
<%@ Page Language="C#" MasterPageFile="~/BalloonShop.master"
AutoEventWireup="true" CodeFile="Default.aspx.cs" Inherits="_Default"
Title="Untitled Page" %>
<asp:Content ID="Content1" ContentPlaceHolderID="contentPlaceHolder"
Runat="Server">
</asp:Content>
```

When you switch to Design View, Default.aspx will look like Figure 2-13.

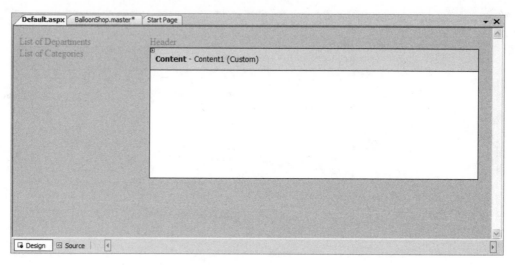

Figure 2-13. *Default.aspx in Design View*

7. Change the title of the page from "Untitled Page" to "Welcome to BalloonShop!" by either using the Properties window in Design View (see Figure 2-14) or by editing the code in Source View like this:

```
<%@ Page Language="C#" MasterPageFile="~/BalloonShop.master"
AutoEventWireup="true" CodeFile="Default.aspx.cs" Inherits="_Default"
Title="Welcome to BalloonShop!" %>
```

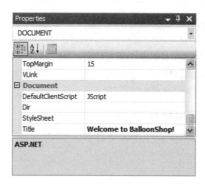

Figure 2-14. *Changing the form name using the Properties window*

8. Press **F5** to execute the project. You should get a page similar to the one in Figure 2-15.

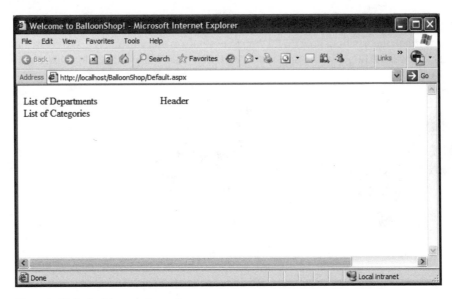

Figure 2-15. *Default.aspx in action*

■**Note** You need to close the browser window or manually stop the project from running before you can use the Designer window to edit your forms at full power again.

How It Works: The Main Web Page

Right now you have the skeleton of the first BalloonShop page in place. Perhaps it's not apparent right now, but working with Master Pages will save you a lot of headaches later on when you extend the site.

The Master Page establishes the layout of the pages that implement it, and these pages have the freedom to update the contents of the ContentPlaceHolder elements. In our case, the header, the list of departments, and the list of categories are standard elements that will appear in every page of the web site (although the list of categories will have blank output in some cases and will appear only when a department is selected—you'll see more about this in the next chapter). For this reason, we included these elements directly in the Master Page, and they are not editable when you're designing Default.aspx. The actual contents of every section of the web site (such as the search results page, the department and category pages, and so on) will be generated by separate Web Forms that will be differentiated by the code in the ContentPlaceHolder object.

■**Note** A Master Page can contain more than one ContentPlaceHolder object.

The list of departments and the list of categories will be implemented as Web User Controls that generate their output based on data read from the database. You'll implement this functionality in Chapters 3 and 4.

Adding the Header to the Main Page

After so much theory about how useful Web User Controls are, you finally get to create one. The Header control will populate the upper-right part of the main page and will look like Figure 2-16.

Figure 2-16. *The BalloonShop logo*

To keep your site's folder organized, you'll create a separate folder for all the user controls. Having them in a centralized location is helpful, especially when the project grows and contains a lot of files.

Exercise: Creating the Header Web User Control

Follow these steps to create the Web User Control and add it to the Master Page:

1. Download the code for this book from the Source Code area at http://www.apress.com, unzip it somewhere on your disk, and copy the ImageFolders\Images folder to your project's directory (which will be \Inetpub\wwwroot\BalloonShop\ if you used the default options when creating the project). The Images folder contains, among other files, a file named BalloonShopLogo.png, which is the logo of your web site. Now, if you save, close, and reload your solution, the Images folder will show up in Solution Explorer.

2. Make sure that the project isn't currently running (if it is, the editing capabilities are limited), and that the Solution Explorer window is visible (if it isn't, choose **View ➤ Solution Explorer** or use the default **Ctrl+Alt+L** shortcut). Right-click the root entry and select **Add Folder ➤ Regular Folder**.

3. Enter **UserControls** as the name of the new folder, as shown in Figure 2-17.

Figure 2-17. *Adding a new folder to the BalloonShop project*

4. Create the Header.ascx user control in the UserControls folder. Right-click **UserControls** in Solution Explorer and click **Add New Item**. In the form that appears, choose the **Web User Control** template and change the default name to **Header.ascx**. Leave the other options in place (as shown in Figure 2-18), and click **Add**.

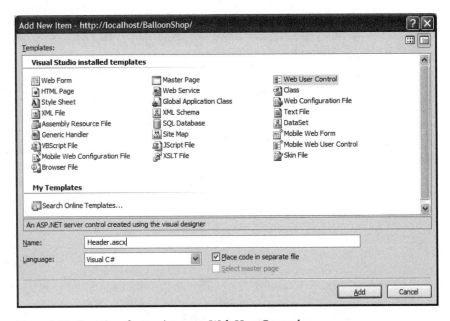

Figure 2-18. *Creating the Header.ascx Web User Control*

5. The Header Web User Control automatically opens in Source View. Modify the HTML code like this:

```
<%@ Control Language="C#" AutoEventWireup="true" CodeFile="Header.ascx.cs"
Inherits="Header" %>
<p align="center">
  <a href="Default.aspx">
    <img src="Images/BalloonShopLogo.png" border="0">
  </a>
</p>
```

■**Note** If you switch the control to Design View right now, you won't see the image because the relative path to the Images folder points to a different absolute path at designtime than at runtime. At runtime, the control is included and run from within BalloonShop.master, not from its current location (the UserControls folder).

---

6. Open BalloonShop.master in Design View, drag Header.ascx from Solution Explorer, drop it near the "Header" text, and then delete the "Header" text from the cell. The Design view of BalloonShop.master should now look like Figure 2-19.

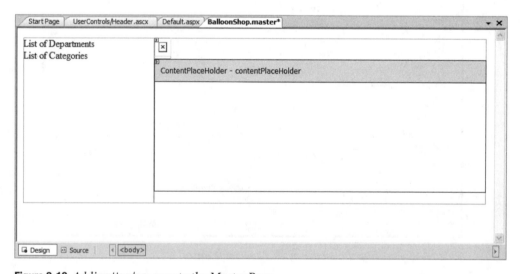

Figure 2-19. *Adding* Header.ascx *to the Master Page*

7. Click **Debug ➤ Start** (**F5** by default) to execute the project. The web page will look like Figure 2-20.

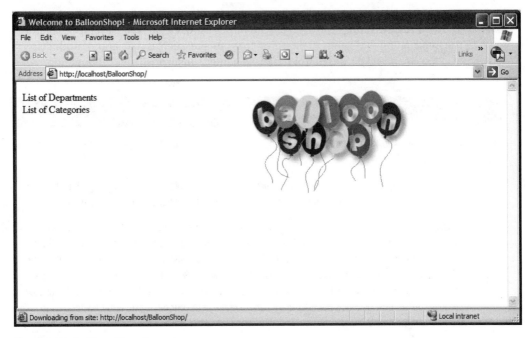

Figure 2-20. *BalloonShop in action*

How It Works: The Header Web User Control

Congratulations once again! Your web site has a perfectly working header! If you don't find it all that exciting, then get ready for the next chapter, where you'll get to write some real code and show the visitor dynamically generated pages with data extracted from the database. The final step you'll make in this chapter is to create the BalloonShop database (in the next exercise), so everything will be set for creating your product catalog!

Until that point, make sure you clearly understand what happens in the project you have at hand. The Web User Control you just created is included in the BalloonShop.master Master Page, so it applies to all pages that use this Master Page, such as Default.aspx. Having that bit of HTML written as a separate control will make your life just a little bit easier when you need to reuse the header in other parts of the site. If at any point the company decides to change the logo, changing it in one place (the Header.ascx control) will affect all pages that use it.

This time you created the control by directly editing its HTML source, but it's always possible to use the Design View and create the control visually. The HTML tab of the Toolbox window in Visual Studio contains all the basic HTML elements, including Image, which generates an img HTML element.

Let's move on.

Creating the SQL Server Database

The final step in this chapter is to create the SQL Server database, although you won't get to effectively use it until the next chapter. SQL Server 2005 Express Edition, the free version of SQL

Server, doesn't ship with the SQL Server Management Studio (formerly known as the Enterprise Manager). However, now you can also create databases using Visual Web Developer's features.

All the information that needs to be stored for your site, such as data about products, customers, and so on, will be stored in a database named, unsurprisingly, BalloonShop.

Exercise: Creating a New SQL Server Database

The following steps show how to create the BalloonShop database using Visual Studio. However, feel free to use the tool of your choice.

1. In your Visual Web Developer project, make sure the Database Explorer window is open. If it isn't, you can either select **View ➤ Database Explorer** or press the default shortcut keys **Ctrl+Alt+S**.

2. In Server Explorer, right-click the **Data Connections** entry, and select **Create New SQL Server Database**. In the window that appears (see Figure 2-21), enter the name of the SQL Server instance where you want to create the database (note that you can use (local) instead of the local computer's name), the login information, and the name of the new database. If you installed SQL Server Express using the default options as shown in Appendix A, then your server name should be (local)\SqlExpress; in the installation process you are provided with the necessary data to connect to your database. Enter **BalloonShop** for the name of the new database.

Figure 2-21. *Creating a new SQL Server database using Visual Web Developer*

■**Note** Using Windows Authentication, your local Windows account will be used to log in to SQL Server. If you installed SQL Server yourself, you'll have full privileges to SQL Server, and everything will run smoothly; otherwise, you'll need to make sure you're provided with administrative privileges on the SQL Server instance. With SQL Server Authentication, you need to provide a username and password, but note that this authentication mode is disabled by default in SQL Server.

How It Works: The SQL Server Database

That's it! You've just created a new SQL Server database! The Server Explorer window in Visual Studio allows you to control many details of the SQL Server instance. After creating the BalloonShop database, it appears under the Data Connections node in Server Explorer. Expanding that node reveals a wide area of functionality you can access directly from Visual Web Developer (see Figure 2-22). Because the database you just created is (obviously) empty, its subnodes are also empty, but you'll take care of this detail in the following chapters.

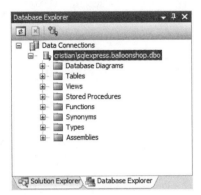

Figure 2-22. *Accessing the BalloonShop database from the Database Explorer*

Downloading the Code

The code you have just written is available in the Source Code area of the Apress web site at http://www.apress.com or at the author's web site at http://www.CristianDarie.ro. It should be easy for you to read through this book and build your solution as you go; however, if you want to check something from our working version, you can. Instructions on loading the chapters are available in the Welcome.html document in the download. You can also view the online version of BalloonShop at http://web.cristiandarie.ro/BalloonShop.

Summary

We covered a lot of ground in this chapter, didn't we? We talked about the three-tier architecture and how it helps you create powerful flexible and scalable applications. You also saw how each of the technologies used in this book fits into the three-tier architecture.

So far you have a very flexible and scalable application because it only has a main web page formed from a Web Form, a Master Page, and the Header Web User Control, but you'll feel the real advantages of using a disciplined way of coding in the next chapters. In this chapter, you have only coded the basic, static part of the presentation tier and created the BalloonShop database, which is the support for the data tier. In the next chapter, you'll start implementing the product catalog and learn a lot about how to dynamically generate visual content using data stored in the database with the help of the middle tier and with smart and fast presentation tier controls and components.

■■■

CHAPTER 3

Creating the Product Catalog: Part I

After learning about the three-tier architecture and implementing a bit of your web site's main page, it's time to continue your work by starting to create the BalloonShop product catalog.

Because the product catalog is composed of many components, you'll create it over two chapters. Be warned that this chapter is a particularly intense chapter, especially if you're a beginner, because it introduces a lot of new theory. It's important to understand this theory well, so please don't rush into doing the exercises before reading and understanding the preceding theory sections. Don't hesitate to use additional material, such as *Beginning ASP.NET 2.0 in C#: From Novice to Professional* (Apress, 2006), to learn more about the bits we didn't have space to fully cover in this book.

In this chapter, you'll create the first database table, create the first stored procedure, implement generic data access code, learn how to handle errors and email their details to the administrator, work with the `web.config` ASP.NET configuration file, implement the business logic, and finally use data gathered from the database through the business logic mechanism to compose dynamic content for your visitor.

The main topics we'll touch on in this chapter are

- Analyzing the structure of the product catalog and the functionality it should support

- Creating the database structures for the catalog and the data tier of the catalog

- Implementing the business tier objects required to make the catalog run, and putting a basic but functional error-handling strategy in place

- Implementing a functional UI for the product catalog

Showing Your Visitor What You've Got

One of the essential features required in any e-store is to allow the visitor to easily browse through the products. Just imagine what Amazon.com would be like without its excellent product catalog!

Whether your visitors are looking for something specific or just browsing, it's important to make sure their experience with your site is a pleasant one. When looking for a specific product or product type, you want the visitor to find it as easily as possible. This is why you'll want to add search functionality to the site and find a clever way of structuring products into categories so they can be quickly and intuitively accessed.

Depending on the size of the store, it might be enough to group products under a number of categories, but if there are a lot of products, you'll need to find even more ways to categorize them.

Determining the structure of the catalog is one of the first tasks to accomplish in this chapter. Keep in mind that using a professional approach, these details would have been established before starting to code when building the requirements document for the project, as explained in Appendix B. However, for the purposes of this book, we prefer to deal with things one at a time.

After the structure of the catalog is established, you'll start writing the code that makes the catalog work as planned.

What Does a Product Catalog Look Like?

Today's web surfers are more demanding than they used to be. They expect to find information quickly on whatever product or service they have in mind, and if they don't find it, they are likely to go to the competition before giving the site a second chance. Of course, you don't want this to happen to *your* visitors, so you need to structure the catalog to make it as intuitive and helpful as possible.

Because the e-store will start with around 100 products and will probably have many more in the future, it's not enough to just group them in categories. The store has a number of departments, and each department will contain a number of categories. Each category can then have any number of products attached to it.

■**Note** Later in the book, you'll also create the administrative part of the web site, often referred to as the *Control Panel*, which allows the client to update department, category, and product data. Until then, you'll manually fill in the database with data (or you can "cheat" by using the SQL scripts provided in the Source Code area on the Apress web site [http://www.apress.com], as you'll see).

Another particularly important detail that you need to think about is whether a category can exist in more than one department, and whether a product can exist in more than one category. This decision can have implications on the way you code the product catalog (most important, as you'll see, it affects the design of the database), so you need to consult your client on this matter.

For the BalloonShop product catalog, each category can exist in only one department, but a product can exist in more than one category. For example, the product "Today, Tomorrow & Forever" will appear in both the "Love & Romance" and "Birthdays" categories. (Not that the authors are very romantic by nature, but the example is good enough to illustrate the idea.)

Finally, apart from having the products grouped in categories, we also want to have featured products. For this web site, a product can be featured either on the front page or in the department pages. Let's look at a few screenshots that explain this.

Previewing the Product Catalog

Although we'll have the fully functional product catalog finished by the end of Chapter 4, look at it now to help you get a better idea about where you're heading. In Figure 3-1, you can see the BalloonShop front page and four of its featured products.

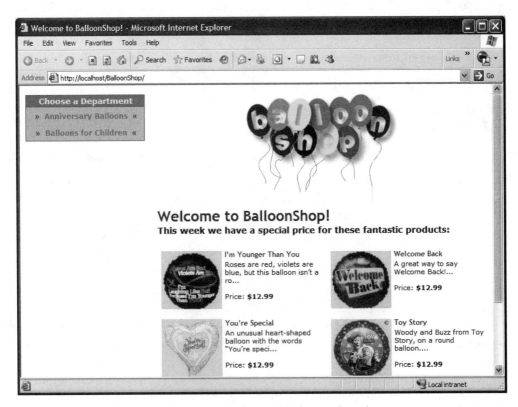

Figure 3-1. *The BalloonShop front page and some of its featured products*

Note the Choose a Department list in the upper-left corner of the page. The list of departments is dynamically generated with data gathered from the database; you'll implement the list of departments in this chapter.

When site visitors click a department in the departments list, they go to the main page of the specified department. This replaces the store's list of catalog-featured products with a page containing information specific to the selected department—including the list of featured products for that department. In Figure 3-2, you see the page that will appear when the "Anniversary Balloons" department is clicked.

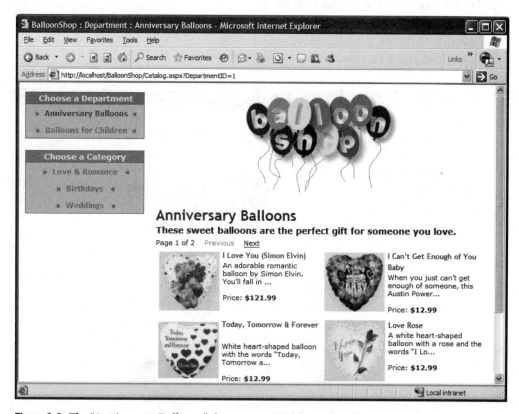

Figure 3-2. *The "Anniversary Balloons" department and four of its featured products*

Under the list of departments, you can now see the Choose a Category list of categories that belong to the selected department. In the right side of the screen, you can see the name, description, and featured products of the selected department. We decided to list only the featured products in the department page, in part because the complete list would be too long. The text above the list of featured products is the description for the selected department, which means you'll need to store in the database both a name and a description for each department.

In this page, when a particular category from the categories list is selected, all of its products are listed, along with updated title and description text. In Figure 3-3, you can see how that page appears when selecting the "Birthdays" category. Also note the paging controls, which appear in any product listings that contain more than an established number of products.

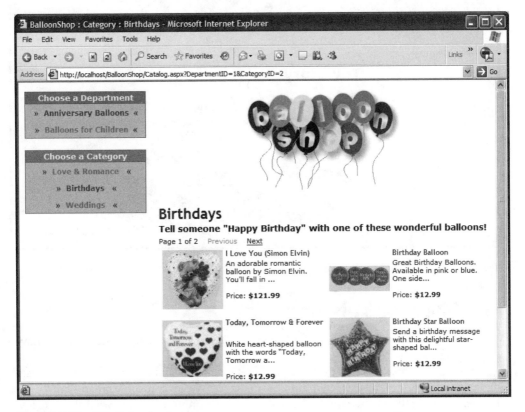

Figure 3-3. *The "Birthdays" category*

In any page that displays products, you can click the name or the picture of a product to view its product details page (see Figure 3-4). In later chapters, you'll add more functionality to this page, such as product recommendations.

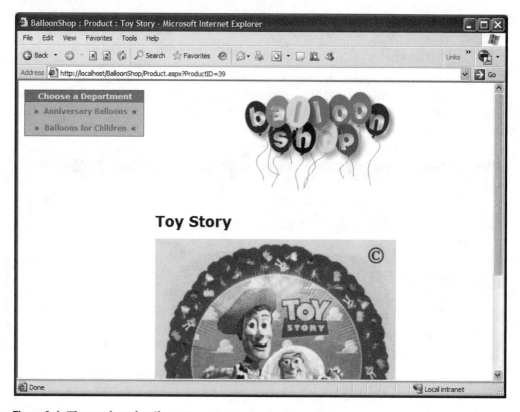

Figure 3-4. *The product details page*

Roadmap for This Chapter

We'll cover a lot of ground in this chapter. To make sure you don't get lost on the way, let's have a look at the big picture.

The departments list will be the first dynamically generated data in your site, as the names of the departments will be extracted from the database. We cover just the creation of the department list in this chapter, in the form of a Web User Control, because we'll also take a closer look at the mechanism that makes the control work. After you understand what happens behind the list of departments, you'll quickly implement the other components in Chapter 4.

In Chapter 2, we discussed the three-tiered architecture that you'll use to implement the Web Application. The product catalog part of the site makes no exception to the rule, and its components (including the departments list) will be spread over the three logical layers. Figure 3-5 previews what you'll create at each tier in this chapter to achieve a functional departments list.

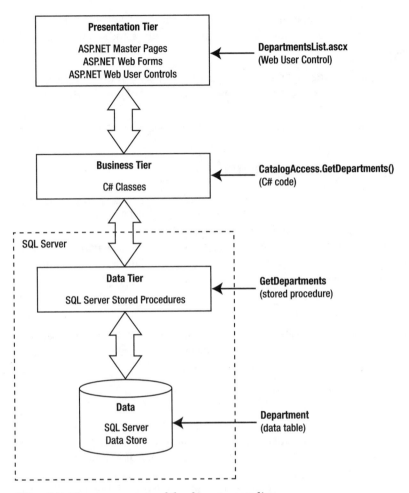

Figure 3-5. *The components of the departments list*

To implement the departments list, you'll start with the database and make your way to the presentation tier:

1. You'll create the Department table in the database. This table will store data regarding the store's departments. Before adding this table, you'll learn the basic concepts of working with relational databases.

2. You'll add the GetDepartments stored procedure to the database, which (like all the other stored procedures you'll write) is logically located in the data tier part of the application. At this step, you'll learn how to speak with relational databases using SQL.

3. You'll create the business tier components of the departments list. You'll learn how to communicate with the database by calling the stored procedure and sending the results to the presentation tier.

4. Finally, you'll implement the DepartmentsList.ascx Web User Control to display a dynamic list of departments for your visitor, which is the goal of this chapter.

You'll implement the rest of the product catalog in Chapter 4. So, let's start with the database.

Storing Catalog Information

The vast majority of Web Applications, e-commerce web sites being no exception, live around the data they manage. Analyzing and understanding the data you need to store and process is an essential step in successfully completing your project.

The typical data storage solution for this kind of application is a relational database. However, this is not a requirement—you have the freedom to create your own data access layer and have whatever kind of data structures to support your application.

■**Note** In some particular cases, it may be preferable to store your data in plain text files or XML files instead of databases, but these solutions are generally not suited for applications like BalloonShop, so we won't cover them in this book. However, it's good to know there are options.

Although this is not a book about databases or relational database design, you'll learn all you need to know to understand the product catalog and make it work. For more information about database programming using SQL Server, you should read an SQL Server book such as *Beginning SQL Server 2005 Programming* (Wiley, 2005).

Essentially, a relational database is made up of data tables and the relationships that exist between them. Because in this chapter you'll work with a single data table, we'll cover only the database theory that applies to the table as a separate, individual database item. In the next chapter, when you add the other tables to the picture, we'll take a closer look at more theory behind relational databases by analyzing how the tables relate to each other and how SQL Server helps you deal with these relationships.

■**Note** In a real world situation, you would probably design the whole database (or at least all the tables relevant to the feature you build) from the start. However, we chose to split the development over two chapters to maintain a better balance of theory and practice.

So, let's start with a little bit of theory, after which you'll create the Department data table and the rest of the required components.

Understanding Data Tables

This section is a quick database lesson that covers the essential information you need to know to design simple data tables. We'll briefly discuss the main parts that make up a database table:

- Primary keys

- Unique columns

- SQL Server data types

- Nullable columns and default values

- Identity columns

- Indexes

■**Note** If you have enough experience with SQL Server, you might want to skip this section and go directly to the "Creating the Department Table" section.

A data table is made up of columns and rows. Columns are also referred to as **fields**, and rows are sometimes called **records**. Still, in a relational database, a good deal of hidden logic exists behind a simple list of data rows.

The Department Table

The database element of the product catalog is composed of tables, table relationships, and stored procedures. Because this chapter only covers the departments list, you'll only need to create one data table: the Department table. This table will store your departments' data and is one of the simplest tables you'll work with.

With the help of tools such as the Visual Studio .NET or Visual Web Developer, it's easy to create a data table in the database if you know what kind of data it will store. When designing a table, you must consider which fields it should contain and which data types should be used for those fields. Besides a field's data type, there are a few more properties to consider; we'll learn about them in the following pages.

To determine which fields you need for the Department table, write down a few examples of records that would be stored in that table. Remember from the previous figures that there isn't much information to store about a department—just the name and description for each department. The table containing the departments' data might look like Figure 3-6.

Name	Description
Anniversary Balloons	These sweet balloons are the perfect gift for someone you love.
Balloons for Children	These colorful and funny balloons will make any child smile!

Figure 3-6. *Data from the Department table*

From a table like this, the names would be extracted to populate the list in the upper-left part of the web page, and the descriptions would be used as headers for the featured products list.

Primary Keys

The way you work with data tables in a relational database is a bit different from the way you usually work on paper. A fundamental requirement in relational databases is that each data row in a table must be **uniquely identifiable**. This makes sense because you usually save records into a database so that you can retrieve them later; however, you can't do that if each row isn't uniquely identifiable. For example, suppose you add another record to the Department table shown previously in Figure 3-6, making it look like the table shown in Figure 3-7.

Name	Description
Anniversary Balloons	These sweet balloons are the perfect gift for someone you love.
Balloons for Children	These colorful and funny balloons will make any child smile!
Balloons for Children	Totally different department... ooops!

Figure 3-7. *Two departments with the same name*

Now look at this table, and tell me the description of the "Balloons for Children" department. Yep, we have a problem! The problem arises because there are two departments with this name. If you queried the table using the Name column and wanted to add new products to the "Balloons for Children" department, to change the department's name, or to do literally anything, you would get two results!

To solve this problem, you use a **primary key**, which allows you to uniquely identify a specific row out of many rows. Technically, a PRIMARY KEY is a **constraint** applied on a table column that guarantees that the column will have unique values across the table.

■**Note** Applying a PRIMARY KEY constraint on a field also generates a unique index by default. Indexes are objects that improve the performance of many database operations, speeding up your Web Application (you'll learn more about indexes a bit later).

A table can have a single PRIMARY KEY constraint, which can be composed of one or more columns. Note that the primary key is not a column itself; instead, it's a *constraint* that applies to one or more of the existing columns. Constraints are rules that apply to data tables and make up part of the data integrity rules of the database. The database takes care of its own integrity and makes sure these rules aren't broken. If, for example, you try to add two identical values for a column that has a PRIMARY KEY constraint, the database will refuse the operation and generate an error. We'll do some experiments later in this chapter to show this.

> ■ **Note** Although a PRIMARY KEY is not a column, but a constraint that applies to that column, from now on, for the sake of simplicity, when we refer to primary key, we'll be talking about the column that has the PRIMARY KEY constraint applied to it.

Back to the example, setting the Name column as the primary key of the Department table would solve the problem because two departments would not be allowed to have the same name. If Name is the primary key of the Department table, searching for a row with a specific Name will always produce exactly one result if the name exists, or no results if no records have the specified name.

An alternative solution, and usually the preferred one, is to have an additional column in the table, called an ID column, to act as its primary key. With an ID column, the Department table would look like Figure 3-8.

DepartmentID	Name	Description
1	Anniversary Balloons	These sweet balloons are the perfect gift for someone you love.
2	Balloons for Children	These colorful and funny balloons will make any child smile!

Figure 3-8. *Adding an ID column as the primary key of* Department

The primary key column is named DepartmentID. We'll use the same naming convention for primary key columns in the other data tables we'll create.

There are two main reasons why it's better to create a separate numerical primary key column than to use Name (or another existing column) as the primary key:

- *Performance*: The database engine handles sorting and searching operations much faster with numerical values than with strings. This becomes even more relevant in the context of working with multiple related tables that need to be frequently joined (you'll learn more about this in Chapter 4).

- *Department name changes*: If you need to rely on the ID value being stable in time, creating an artificial key solves the problem because it's unlikely you'll ever need to change the ID.

In Figure 3-8, the primary key is composed of a single column, but this is not a requirement. If the primary key is composed of more than one column, the group of primary key columns (taken as a unit) is guaranteed to be unique (but the individual columns that form the primary key can have repeating values in the table). In Chapter 4, you'll see an example of a multivalued primary key. For now, it's enough to know that they exist.

Unique Columns

UNIQUE is yet another kind of constraint that can be applied to table columns. This constraint is similar to the PRIMARY KEY constraint because it doesn't allow duplicate data in a column. Still, there are differences. Although there is only one PRIMARY KEY constraint per table, you are allowed to have as many UNIQUE constraints as you like.

Columns with the UNIQUE constraint are useful when you already have a primary key, but you still have columns for which you want to have unique values. You can set Name to be unique in the Department table if you want to forbid repeating values, when the DepartmentID column is the primary key. (We won't use the UNIQUE constraint in this book, but we mention it here for completeness.) We decided to allow identical department names because only site administrators will have the privileges to modify or change department data.

The facts that you need to remember about UNIQUE constraints are

- The UNIQUE constraint forbids having identical values on the field.

- You can have more that one UNIQUE field in a data table.

- Unlike with primary keys, a UNIQUE constraint can't apply to more than one field.

- A UNIQUE field is allowed to accept NULL values, in which case it can only accept one NULL value.

- Indexes are automatically created on UNIQUE and PRIMARY KEY columns.

Columns and Data Types

Each column in a table has a particular data type. By looking at the previously shown Figure 3-8 with the Department table, it's clear that DepartmentID has a numeric data type, whereas Name and Description contain text.

It's important to consider the many data types that SQL Server supports so that you can make correct decisions concerning how to create your tables. Table 3-1 isn't an exhaustive list of SQL Server data types, but it focuses on the main types you might come across in your project. Refer to SQL Server 2005 Books Online, which can be freely accessed and downloaded from http://msdn.microsoft.com/sql/, for a more detailed list.

■Note Table 3-1 was created with SQL Server 2005 in mind, but these data types exist in SQL Server 2000 as well, and even SQL Server 7 comes close. The differences between SQL Server versions are reflected in details such as the maximum size for character data.

To keep the table short, under the Data Type heading we've listed only the most frequently used types, while similar data types are explained under the Description and Notes heading. You don't need to memorize the list, but you should get an idea of which data types are available.

Table 3-1. *SQL Server 2005 Data Types*

Data Type	Size in Bytes	Description and Notes
Int	4	Stores whole numbers from -2,147,483,648 to 2,147,483,647. You'll use them for ID columns and in other circumstances that require integer numbers. Related types are SmallInt and TinyInt. A Bit data type is able to store values of 0 and 1.
Money	8	Stores monetary data with values from -2^{63} to 2^{63} -1 with a precision of four decimal places. You'll use this data type to store product prices, shopping cart subtotals, and so on. SQL Server also supports the Float data type, which holds floating-point data, but Float is not recommended for storing monetary information because of its lack of precision. A variation of Money is SmallMoney, which has a smaller range, but the same precision.
DateTime	8	Supports date and time data from January 1, 1753 through December 31, 9999 with an accuracy of three hundredths of a second. A SmallDateTime type has a range from January 1, 1900 to June 6, 2079 with an accuracy of one minute. You'll use this data type to store information such as order shipping dates.
UniqueIdentifier	16	Stores a numerical Globally Unique Identifier (GUID). A GUID is guaranteed to be unique; this property makes it very useful in certain situations. In this book, we prefer to generate unique identifiers using other methods, but it's good to know there are options.
VarChar, NVarChar	Variable	Stores variable-length character data. NVarChar stores Unicode data with a maximum length of 4,000 characters and VarChar non-Unicode data with a maximum length of 8,000 characters. This data type is best used for storing short strings (note their length limitation) without fixed lengths.
Char, NChar	Fixed	Stores fixed-length character data. Values shorter than the declared size are padded with spaces. NChar is the Unicode version and goes to a maximum of 4,000 characters, whereas Char can store 8,000 characters. When the size of the strings to be stored is fixed, it's more efficient to use Char rather than VarChar.
Text, NText	Fixed	Stores large character data. NText is the Unicode version and has a maximum size of 1,073,741,823 characters. Text has double this maximum size. Using these data types can slow down the database, and it's generally recommended to use Char, VarChar, NChar, or NVarChar instead. When adding Text or NText fields, their length is fixed to 16, which represents the size of the pointer that references the location where the actual text is stored, and not the size of the text itself. The Text data type can be used to store large character data such as paragraphs, long product descriptions, and so on. We won't use this data type in this book.

Table 3-1. *SQL Server 2005 Data Types (Continued)*

Data Type	Size in Bytes	Description and Notes
Binary, VarBinary	Fixed/Variable	Stores binary data with a maximum length of 8,000 bytes.
Image	Variable	Stores binary data of maximum 2^{31} - 1 bytes. Despite its name, this field can store any kind of binary data, not just pictures. In most circumstances, it's easier and faster to store the files in the OS file system and store only their names in the database, but there are situations when it makes more sense to use the database for storing binary data. For BalloonShop, you'll store the product images in the file system.

■**Note** The names of the SQL Server 2005 data types are not case sensitive, and most programmers write them either in full uppercase or lowercase. We've cased them properly in the table for readability.

Now let's get back to the Department table and determine which data types to use. Don't worry that you don't have the table yet in your database, you'll create it a bit later. For now, you just need to understand how data types work with SQL Server.

If you know what these data types mean, Figure 3-9 is self-explanatory. DepartmentID is an Int, and Name and Description are VarChar data types. The little golden key at the left of DepartmentID specifies that the column is the primary key of the Department table.

	Column Name	Data Type	Allow Nulls
🔑	DepartmentID	int	☐
	Name	varchar(50)	☐
	Description	varchar(1000)	☑

Figure 3-9. *Designing the Department table*

You can also see the length of the VarChar fields. Note that "length" means different things for different data types. For numerical data types, the length is usually fixed (so it doesn't show up in some designers, such as the one in Figure 3-9) and it specifies the number of bytes it takes to store one record, whereas for string data types (excluding Text and NText), the length specifies the number of characters that can be stored in a record. This is a subtle but important difference because for Unicode text data (NChar, NVarChar, NText), the actual storage space needed is 2 bytes per character.

We choose to have 50 characters available for the department's name and 1,000 for the description. Some prefer to use NVarChar instead of VarChar—this is actually a requirement when you need to store Unicode characters (such as Chinese text). Otherwise, the non-Unicode versions are usually preferred because they occupy half the size their Unicode pairs need. With large databases, the smaller size of the non-Unicode versions can make some difference.

Nullable Columns and Default Values

Observe the **Allow Nulls** column in the design window of the Department table—some fields have this check box checked, but others don't. If the check box is checked, the column is allowed to store the NULL value.

The best and shortest definition for NULL is "undefined." In your Department table, only DepartmentID and Name are required, so Description is optional—meaning that you are allowed to add a new department without supplying a description for it. If you add a new row of data without supplying a value for columns that allow nulls, NULL is automatically supplied for them.

Especially for character data, a subtle difference exists between the NULL value and an "empty" value. If you add a product with an empty string for its description, this means that you actually set a value for its description; it's an empty string, not an undefined (NULL) value.

The primary key field never allows NULL values. For the other columns, it's up to you to decide which fields are required and which are not.

In some cases, instead of allowing NULLs, you'll prefer to specify default values. This way, if the value is unspecified when creating a new row, it will be supplied with the default value. The default value can be a literal value (such as 0 for a Salary column or "Unknown" for a Description column), or it can be a system value (such as the GETDATE function, which returns the current date). In Chapter 10, you'll have a column named DateCreated, which can be set to have the default value supplied by the GETDATE function.

Identity Columns

Identity columns are "auto-numbered" columns. This behavior is similar to AutoNumber columns in Microsoft Access. When a column is set as an identity column, SQL Server automatically provides values for it when inserting new records into the table; by default, the database doesn't permit manually specified values for identity columns.

SQL Server guarantees that the generated values are always unique, which makes them especially useful when used in conjunction with the PRIMARY KEY constraint. You already know that primary keys are used on columns that uniquely identify each row of a table. If you set a primary key column to also be an identity column, SQL Server automatically fills that column with values when adding new rows (in other words, it generates new IDs), ensuring that the values are unique.

When setting an identity column, you must specify an identity seed, which is the first value that SQL Server provides for that column, and an identity increment value, which specifies the number of units to increase between two consecutive records.

By default, identity seed and identity increment values are both set to 1, meaning that the first value will be 1 and the following ones will be generated by adding 1 to the last created value. You don't need to specify other values because you don't care what values are generated anyway.

Although it wasn't shown in the earlier Figure 3-9, DepartmentID in your Department table is an identity column. You'll learn how to set identity columns a bit later, when creating the Department table.

■**Note** The generated values for identity columns are unique over the life of your table. A value that was generated once will never be generated again, even if you delete all the rows from the table. If you want SQL Server to restart numbering from the initial value, you need to either delete and re-create the table or *truncate* the table using the TRUNCATE SQL command. Truncating a table has the same effect as deleting and creating it again.

Indexes

Indexes are related to SQL Server performance tuning, so we'll mention them only briefly. For more in-depth information about SQL Server indexes, read a specialized book on SQL Server 2005.

Indexes are database objects meant to increase the overall speed of database operations. Indexes work on the assumption that the vast majority of database operations are read operations. Indexes increase the speed of search operations, but slow down insert, delete, and update operations. Usually, the gains of using indexes considerably outweigh the drawbacks.

On a table, you can create one or more indexes, with each index working on one column or on a set of columns. When a table is indexed on a specific column, its rows are either indexed or physically arranged based on the values of that column and of the type of index. This makes search operations on that column very fast. If, for example, an index exists on DepartmentID, and then you do a search for department 934, the search is performed very quickly. Adding or updating new rows is a bit slower because the index must be actualized (or the table rows rearranged) each time these operations occur.

You should keep the following in mind about indexes:

- Indexes greatly increase search operations on the database, but they slow down operations that change the database (delete, update, and insert operations).

- Having too many indexes can slow down the general performance of the database. The general rule is to set indexes on columns frequently used in WHERE, ORDER BY, and GROUP BY clauses, used in table joins, or having foreign-key relationships with other tables.

- By default, indexes are automatically created on primary key and unique table columns.

You can use dedicated tools to test the performance of a database under stress conditions with and without particular indexes; in fact, a serious database administrator will want to make some of these tests before deciding on a wining combination for indexes. You can also use the Database Tuning Advisor that can be accessed through SQL Server Management Studio (this doesn't ship with the Express Edition, however). Consult a specialized SQL Server book for more details on these subjects.

In your application, you'll rely on the indexes that are automatically created on the primary key columns, which is a safe combination for our kind of web site.

Creating the Department Table

You created the BalloonShop database in Chapter 2. In the following exercise, you'll add the Department table to it.

We recommend that you create the Department table by following the steps in the exercise. Alternatively, you can use the SQL scripts for this book in the Source Code area of the Apress web site (http://www.apress.com/) to create and populate the Department table. The script file that creates the Department table is named CreateDepartment.sql, and you can execute it using the SQL Server Express Manager utility (see Appendix A for installation instructions).

Exercise: Creating the Department Table

1. Using the Database Explorer window in Visual Web Developer, open the BalloonShop data connection that you created in Chapter 2. Remember, if Database Explorer is not visible, activate it using **View ➤ Database Explorer** or by using the default shortcut **Ctrl+Alt+S**.

2. Expand the **BalloonShop** database connection node, right-click the **Tables** node, and select **Add New Table** from the context menu. Alternatively, after connecting to the database, you can choose **Data ➤ Add New ➤ Table.**

3. A form appears where you can add columns to the new table. Using this form, add three columns, with the properties described in Table 3-2.

Table 3-2. *Designing the Department Table*

Field Name	Data Type	Other Properties
DepartmentID	int	Primary Key and Identity column
Name	varchar(50)	Don't allow NULLs
Description	varchar(1000)	Allow NULLs

■**Note** You set a column to be the primary key by right-clicking it and clicking the **Set Primary Key** item from the context menu. You set a column to be an identity column by expanding the **Identity Specification** item from its Column Properties window, and setting the **(Is Identity)** node to **Yes**. You can also access the Identity Increment and Identity Seed values, if you should ever want to use other values than the defaults.

After adding these fields, the form should look like Figure 3-10 in Visual Studio.

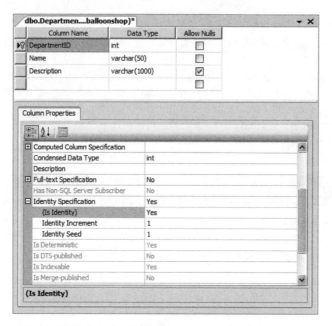

Figure 3-10. *The three fields of the Department table*

4. Now that everything is in place, you need to save the newly created table. Press **Ctrl+S** or select **File ➤ Save Table1**. When asked, type `Department` for the table name.

5. After creating the table in the database, you can open it to add some data. To open the `Department` table for editing, right-click it in **Database Explorer** and select **Show Table Data** from the context menu. (Alternatively, you can choose **Database ➤ Show Table Data** after selecting the table in Database Explorer.) Using the integrated editor, you can start adding rows. Because `DepartmentID` is an identity column, you cannot manually edit its data—SQL Server automatically fills this field, depending on the identity seed and identity increment values that you specified when creating the table.

6. Add two departments, as shown in Figure 3-11.

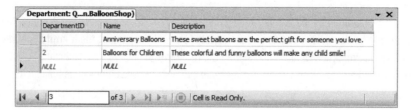

Figure 3-11. *Adding two sample rows to the Department table*

■**Note** To ensure consistency with the scripts in the Source Code area on the Apress web site (and to make your life easier), make sure the department IDs are 1 and 2, as shown in Figure 3-11. Because `DepartmentID` is an identity column, an ID value is generated only once, even if you remove records from the table in the meantime. The only way to reset the identity values generator is to delete and re-create the table, or to *truncate* the table. The easiest way to truncate the table is to start SQL Server Express Manager, log in to your local SQL Server Express Instance (by default, named `localhost\SqlExpress`), and execute the following SQL commands:

```
USE BalloonShop
TRUNCATE TABLE Department
```

How It Works: The Database Table

You have just created your first database table! You also set a primary key, set an identity column, and then filled the table with some data. As you can see, as soon as you have a clear idea about the structure of a table, Visual Web Developer and SQL Server make it very easy to implement.

Let's continue by learning how to programmatically access and manipulate this data with SQL code.

Communicating with the Database

Now that you have a table filled with data, let's do something useful with it. The ultimate goal with this table is to get the list of department names from the database using C# code.

To get data from a database, you first need to know how to communicate with the database. SQL Server understands a language called Transact-SQL (T-SQL). The usual way of communicating with SQL Server is to write a T-SQL command, send it to SQL Server, and get the results back. However, these commands can be sent either directly from the business tier to SQL Server (without having an intermediary data tier) or can be centralized and saved as stored procedures as part of the database.

Stored procedures are database objects that store programs written in T-SQL. Much like normal functions, stored procedures accept input and output parameters and have return values.

■**Note** As mentioned in Chapter 2, SQL Server 2005 introduces for the first time the notion of *managed stored procedures*, which are programs written in a .NET language that execute inside SQL Server. Writing managed stored procedures is an advanced topic outside the scope of this book, but it's good to know that they exist.

You don't need to use stored procedures if you want to perform database operations. You can directly send the SQL commands from an external application to SQL Server. When using stored procedures, instead of passing the SQL code you want executed, you just pass the name of the stored procedure, and the values for any parameters it might have. Using stored procedures for data operations has the following advantages:

- Storing SQL code as a stored procedure usually results in better performance because SQL Server generates and caches the stored procedure execution plan when it's first executed.

- Using stored procedures allows for better maintainability of the data access and manipulation code, which is stored in a central place, and permits easier implementation of the three-tier architecture (the stored procedures forming the data tier).

- Security can be better controlled because SQL Server permits setting different security permissions for each individual stored procedure.

- SQL queries created ad hoc in C# code are more vulnerable to SQL injection attacks, which is a major security threat. Many Internet resources cover this security subject, such as the article at http://www.sitepoint.com/article/sql-injection-attacks-safe.

- This might be a matter of taste, but having the SQL logic separated from the C# code keeps the C# code cleaner and easier to manage; it looks better to call the name of a stored procedure than to join strings to create an SQL query to pass to the database.

Your goal for this section is to write the GetDepartments stored procedure, but first, let's take a quick look at SQL.

Speaking the Database Language

SQL (Structured Query Language) is the language used to communicate with modern Relational Database Management Systems (RDBMS). Most database systems support a particular dialect of SQL, such as T-SQL (Transact-SQL) for SQL Server and PL/SQL (Procedural Language extensions to SQL) for Oracle. Because T-SQL is a big subject when analyzed in detail, we'll briefly introduce it and cover just enough so you'll understand the code in your stored procedures.

■**Tip** If you're interested in entering the world of SQL, we recommend another book we've authored called *The Programmer's Guide to SQL* (Apress, 2003). It covers the SQL standard and its dialects implemented in SQL Server, Oracle, DB2, MySQL, and Access.

The basic and most important SQL commands are SELECT, INSERT, UPDATE, and DELETE. Their names are self-explanatory, and they allow you to perform basic operations on the database.

You can use SQL Server Express Manager to test these commands with your newly created Department table. Start SQL Server Express Manager, log in to your local SQL Server Express Instance (by default, named localhost\SqlExpress), and then execute the following command that connects you to the BalloonShop database (to execute the command, you can use the Execute button on the toolbar, or choose Query ➤ Execute, or press the F5 shortcut key):

```
USE BalloonShop
```

After executing this command, you should get a "Command(s) completed successfully" message. After you connect to the database, you're ready to test the SQL commands you're about to learn.

Be aware that each SQL command has many optional arguments, and they can become more complex than those presented here. Still, to keep the presentation short and simple, you'll learn the most important and frequently used parameters, and we'll get into more details later in the book.

SELECT

The SELECT statement is used to query the database and retrieve selected data that match the criteria you specify. Its basic structure is

```
SELECT <column list>
FROM <table name(s)>
[WHERE <restrictive condition>]
```

■**Note** Although SQL is not case sensitive, in this book the SQL commands and queries appear in uppercase for consistency and clarity. The WHERE clause appears in brackets because it's optional.

The simplest SELECT command you can execute on your BalloonShop database is

```
SELECT * FROM Department
```

If you've created and populated the Department table as described in the exercises, you should get the results shown in Figure 3-12.

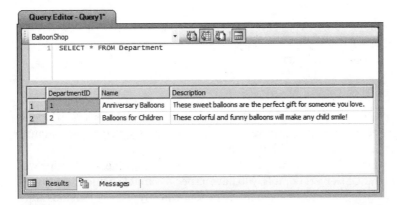

Figure 3-12. *Executing a simple SQL command using SQL Express Manager*

The "*" wildcard you used in the SQL query means "all columns." Most of the time, unless you have a serious reason to use it, it's good to avoid using this wildcard and to specify the columns you want returned manually, like this:

```
SELECT DepartmentID, Name, Description
FROM Department
```

The following command returns the name of the department that has the DepartmentID of 1. In your case, the returned value is "Anniversary Balloons", but you would receive no results if there were no departments with an ID of 1.

```
SELECT Name FROM Department WHERE DepartmentID = 1
```

INSERT

The INSERT statement is used to insert or add a row of data into the table. Its syntax is as follows:

```
INSERT [INTO] <table name> (column list) VALUES (column values)
```

The following INSERT statement adds a department named "Mysterious Department" to the Department table:

```
INSERT INTO Department (Name) VALUES ('Mysterious Department')
```

■**Tip** The INTO keyword is optional, but including it makes the statement easier to read.

We didn't specify any value for the Description field because it was marked to allow NULLs in the Department table. This is why you can omit specifying a value, if you want to. However, the Name field is required, so if you tried, for example, to specify a description without specifying a name, you would get an error:

```
INSERT INTO Department (Description) VALUES ('Some Description Here')
```

The error message specifies

```
.Net SqlClient Data Provider: Msg 515, Level 16, State 2, Line 1
Cannot insert the value NULL into column 'Name',
table 'balloonshop.dbo.Department'; column
does not allow nulls. INSERT fails.
The statement has been terminated.
```

Also note that you didn't specify a DepartmentID. Because DepartmentID was set as an identity column, you're not allowed to manually specify values for this column. SQL Server can guarantee this has unique values, but only if you don't interfere with it.

So, if you can't specify a value for DepartmentID, how can you determine which value was automatically supplied by SQL Server? For this, you have a special variable named @@IDENTITY. You can type its value by using the SELECT statement. The following two SQL commands add a new record to Department and return the DepartmentID of the row just added:

```
INSERT INTO Department (Name) Values ('Some New Department')
SELECT @@IDENTITY
```

UPDATE

The UPDATE statement is used to modify existing data and has the following syntax:

```
UPDATE <table name>
SET <column name> = <new value> [, <column name> = <new value> ...]
[WHERE <restrictive condition>]
```

The following query changes the name of the department with the ID of 43 to Cool➥ Department. If there were more departments with that ID, all of them would be modified, but because DepartmentID is the primary key, you can't have more departments with the same ID.

```
UPDATE Department SET Name='Cool Department' WHERE DepartmentID = 43
```

Be careful with the UPDATE statement, because it makes it easy to mess up an entire table. If the WHERE clause is omitted, the change is applied to every record of the table, which you usually don't want to happen. SQL Server will be happy to change all your records; even if all departments in the table would have the same name and description, they would still be perceived as different entities because they have DepartmentIDs.

DELETE

The syntax of the DELETE command is actually very simple:

```
DELETE [FROM] <table name>
[WHERE <restrictive condition>]
```

The FROM keyword is optional and can be omitted. We generally use it because it makes the query sound more like normal English.

Most times, you'll want to use the WHERE clause to delete a single row:

```
DELETE FROM Department
WHERE DepartmentID = 43
```

As with UPDATE, be careful with this command, because if you forget to specify a WHERE clause, you'll end up deleting all the rows in the specified table. The following query deletes all the records in Department. The table itself isn't deleted by the DELETE command.

```
DELETE FROM Department
```

■**Tip** As with INSERT [INTO], the FROM keyword is optional. Add it if you feel it makes the statement easier to understand.

Creating Stored Procedures

You need to create the GetDepartments stored procedure, which returns department information from the Department table. This stored procedure is part of the data tier and will be accessed from the business tier. The final goal is to have this data displayed in the user control.

The SQL code that retrieves the necessary data and that you need to save to the database as the GetDepartments stored procedure is the following:

```
SELECT DepartmentID, Name, Description FROM Department
```

This command returns all the department information.

■**Caution** Unless you have a specific reason to do so, never ask for all columns (using the * wildcard) when you only need a part of them. This generates more traffic and stress on the database server than necessary and slows down performance. Moreover, even if you do need to ask for all columns in the table, it's safer to mention them explicitly to protect your application in case the number or order of columns changes in future.

Saving the Query As a Stored Procedure

As with data tables, after you know the structure, implementing the stored procedure is a piece of cake. Now that you know the SQL code, the tools will help you save the query as a stored procedure easily.

The syntax for creating a stored procedure that has no input or output parameters is as follows:

```
CREATE PROCEDURE <procedure name>
AS
  <stored procedure code>
```

If the procedure already exists and you just want to update its code, use ALTER PROCEDURE instead of CREATE PROCEDURE.

Stored procedures can have input or output parameters. Because GetDepartments doesn't have any parameters, you don't have to bother about them right now. You'll learn how to use input and output parameters in Chapter 4.

In the following exercise, you'll add the GetDepartments stored procedure to your database.

■**Note** Alternatively, you can execute the GetDepartments.sql script file in the BalloonShop database, which creates the GetDepartments stored procedure.

Exercise: Writing the Stored Procedure

1. Make sure the data connection to the BalloonShop database is expanded and selected in **Database Explorer**. Choose **Data ➤ Add New ➤ Stored Procedure**. Alternatively, you can right-click the Stored Procedures node in Server Explorer and select Add New Stored Procedure.

2. Replace the default text with your GetDepartments stored procedure:

```
CREATE PROCEDURE GetDepartments AS
SELECT DepartmentID, Name, Description
FROM Department
```

3. Press **Ctrl+S** to save the stored procedure. Unlike with the tables, you won't be asked for a name because the database already knows that you're talking about the GetDepartments stored procedure.

■**Note** Saving the stored procedure actually executes the SQL code you entered, which creates the stored procedure in the database. After saving the procedure, the CREATE keyword becomes ALTER, which is the SQL command that changes the code of an existing procedure.

---

4. Now test your first stored procedure to see that it's actually working. Navigate to the GetDepartments stored procedure node in **Database Explorer** and select **Execute**, as shown in Figure 3-13.

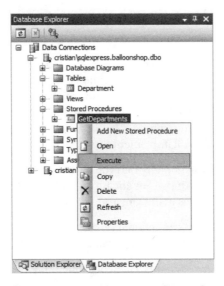

Figure 3-13. *Executing a stored procedure from Visual Web Developer*

5. After running the stored procedure, you can see the results in the Output window (see Figure 3-14). You can open the Output window by choosing **View ➤ Other Windows ➤ Output** or by pressing **Ctrl+Alt+O**.

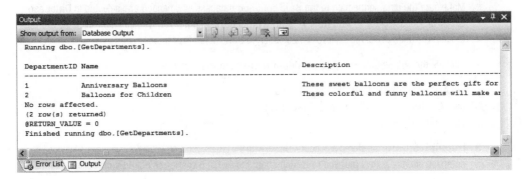

Figure 3-14. *The Output window shows the results.*

How it Works: The `GetDepartments` Stored Procedure

You've just finished coding the data tier part that reads the departments list!

The results in the Output window confirm your stored procedure works as expected. You can also test the stored procedure by using SQL Express Manager and executing the stored procedure from there:

```
USE BalloonShop
EXEC GetDepartments
```

Adding Logic to the Site

The business tier (or middle tier) is said to be the brains of the application because it manages the application's business logic. However, for simple tasks such as getting a list of departments from the data tier, the business tier doesn't have much logic to implement. It just requests the data from the database and passes it to the presentation tier.

For the business tier of the departments list, you'll implement three classes:

- `GenericDataAccess` implements common functionality that you'll then reuse whenever you need to access the database. Having this kind of generic functionality packed in a separate class saves keystrokes and avoids bugs in the long run.

- `CatalogAccess` contains product catalog specific functionality, such the `GetDepartments` method that will retrieve the list of departments from the database.

- `BalloonShopConfiguration` and `Utilities` contain miscellaneous functionality such as sending emails, which will be reused in various places in BalloonShop.

In Chapter 4, you'll keep adding methods to these classes to support the new pieces of functionality.

Connecting to SQL Server

The main challenge is to understand how the code that accesses the database works. The .NET technology that permits accessing a database from C# code is called **ADO.NET**. ADO.NET groups all .NET classes that are related to database access. This is the most modern Microsoft data-access technology, and it can be used from any .NET language.

ADO.NET is a complex subject that requires a separate book by itself, so we'll cover just enough to help you understand how your business tier works. For more information about ADO.NET, refer to *Beginning ASP.NET 2.0 Databases: From Novice to Professional* (Apress, 2005).

The data access class named GenericDataAccess that you'll write will make extensive use of many ADO.NET features, including features new to ADO.NET 2.0 (we'll highlight these features at the proper time). The GenericDataAccess class deals with accessing the database, executing stored procedures, and returning the retrieved data. This class will be part of the business tier and will provide generic functionality for the other business tier classes.

Each database operation always consists of three steps:

1. *Open* a connection to the SQL Server database.

2. *Perform* the needed operations with the database and get back the results.

3. *Close* the connection to the database.

Before you implement the GenericDataAccess class itself, which implements all these steps, we'll have a quick look at each step individually.

■**Tip** Always try to make the second step (executing the commands) as fast as possible. Keeping a data connection open for too long or having too many database connections open at the same time is expensive for your application's performance. The golden rule is to open the connection as late as possible, perform the necessary operations, and then close it immediately.

The class used to connect to SQL Server is SqlConnection. When creating a new database connection, you always need to specify at least three important pieces of data:

- The name of the SQL Server instance you're connecting to

- The authentication information that will permit you to access the server

- The database you want to work with

This connection data is grouped in a connection string, which needs to be passed to the SqlConnection object. The following code snippet demonstrates how to create and open a database connection:

```
// Create the connection object
SqlConnection connection = new SqlConnection();
// Set the connection string
connection.ConnectionString = "Server=(local)\SqlExpress; " +
                              "User ID=johnny; Password=qwerty;" +
                              "Database=BalloonShop";
// Open the connection
connection.Open();
```

The code is fairly straightforward: you first create a SqlConnection object, then set its ConnectionString property, and finally open the connection. A connection needs to be opened before using it for any operations.

Understanding the connection string is important—if your program has problems connecting to the database, these problems likely can be solved by "fixing" the connection string (assuming that SQL Server is properly configured and that you actually have access to it).

The connection string contains the three important elements. The first is the name of the SQL Server instance you're connecting to. For the SQL Server 2005 Express Edition, the default instance name is (local)\SqlExpress. You'll want to change this if your SQL Server instance has another name. You can use your computer name instead of (local). Of course, if you connect to a remote SQL Server instance, you'll need to specify the complete network path instead of (local).

After specifying the server, you need to supply security information needed to log in to the server. You log in to SQL Server by either using SQL Server Authentication (in which case you need to supply a SQL Server username and password as shown in the code snippet) or by using Windows Authentication (also named Windows Integrated Security). With Windows Integrated Security, you don't have to supply a username and password because SQL Server uses the Windows login information of the currently logged-in user.

To log in using Windows Authentication, you'll need to supply Integrated Security=True (or Integrated Security=SSPI) instead of User ID=username; Password=password. The final part of the connection string specifies the database you'll be working with.

Instead of setting the connection string after creating the SqlConnection object, you can provide the connection string right when creating the SqlConnection object:

```
// Create the connection object and set the connection string
SqlConnection connection = new SqlConnection("... connection string ...");
// Open the connection
connection.Open();
```

A final note about the connection string is that several synonyms can be used inside it; for example, instead of Server, you can use Data Source or Data Server, and instead of Database, you can use Initial Catalog. The list is much longer, and the complete version can be found in SQL Server 2005 Books Online.

CONFIGURING SQL SERVER SECURITY

Because connection problems are common, many readers have asked for additional information about fixing connection problems. Let's talk about configuring SQL Server to accept connections from within your web site, considering that you have done the installation procedures as explained in Appendix A. If you're using an external SQL Server instance, such as the one provided by your web hosting company, you'll need to request the connection string details from the system administrator or the hosting company.

Because the configuration details can be boring, you can skip these sections for now, if you want. If the BalloonShop project throws a connectivity exception when executed, you can come back and see what's wrong.

SQL Server can be configured to work in **Windows Authentication Mode** or in **Mixed Mode**. In Mixed Mode, SQL Server accepts connections through both Windows Authentication and SQL Server Authentication. You can't set SQL Server to accept connection only through SQL Server Authentication.

If you don't specify otherwise at installation, by default SQL Server works in Windows Authentication Mode, in which SQL Server recognizes you by your Windows login. This is why you don't need to specify any extra credentials when accessing SQL Server from Visual Web Developer or when connecting to your database using SQL Express Manager.

However, an ASP.NET application running through IIS will authenticate itself using a special account named **ASPNET** (in Windows 2003 Server, this account is named **Network Service**), which doesn't have by default privileges to access SQL Server, not to mention the BalloonShop database. As a result, if you're using IIS, you'll need to give rights to the ASPNET account to access the BalloonShop database, in order for your application to function properly. The integrated web server that ships with Visual Web Developer runs under the credentials of the logged-in user, making your life easier from this point of view (you don't need to set any security options, as your site will have full privileges to the BalloonShop database by default).

Alternative methods to solve the connection problem when you use IIS include enabling SQL Server Authentication and using a user ID and password in the connection string, or using a technique called **ASP.NET impersonation**, when the ASP.NET application is executed under the credentials of another Windows user than ASPNET. However, we'll not discuss the details of using these techniques here.

To enable the ASPNET account to access the BalloonShop database, you need to follow these steps:

1. Start SQL Express Manager, specify the SQL Server Instance name (localhost\SqlExpress by default), and log in using Windows Authentication.

2. Use the sp_grantlogin stored procedure to add a Windows user account to the SQL Server database. This command grants the ASPNET account the privilege to connect to SQL Server. Be sure to use the name of your local machine instead of *MachineName*.

   EXEC sp_grantlogin '*MachineName*\ASPNET'

3. After giving the ASPNET account the privilege to connect to SQL Server, you need to give it the privilege to access to the BalloonShop database:

   USE BalloonShop
   EXEC sp_grantdbaccess '*MachineName*\ASPNET'

4. Finally, you need to give the ASPNET account privileges to the objects inside the BalloonShop database, such as the privilege to execute stored procedures, read and modify tables, and so on. The simplest way is to assign the ASPNET account with the db_owner role in the BalloonShop database. Assuming that you already connected to the BalloonShop database at the previous step (with USE BalloonShop), type the following:

```
EXEC sp_addrolemember 'db_owner', 'MachineName\ASPNET'
```

That's it, now you can connect to SQL Server from your Web Application using Windows Authentication.

Issuing Commands and Executing Stored Procedures

After you have an open connection to the database, you usually need to create an SqlCommand object to perform operations. Because there are more tricks you can do with the SqlCommand object, we'll take them one at a time.

Creating an SqlCommand Object

SqlCommand will be your best friend when implementing the data access code. This class is capable of storing information about what you want to do with the database—it can store an SQL query or the name of a stored procedure that needs to be executed. The SqlCommand is also aware of stored procedure parameters—you'll learn more about these in Chapter 4, because the stored procedure you work with in this chapter (GetDepartments) doesn't have any parameters.

Following is the standard way of creating and initializing an SqlCommand object:

```
// Create the command object
SqlCommand command = new SqlCommand();
command.Connection = connection;
command.CommandText = "GetDepartments";
command.CommandType = CommandType.StoredProcedure;
```

Once again, there's no mystery about the code. You first create an SqlCommand object and then set some of its properties. The most important property that needs to be set is Connection, because each command needs to be executed on a specific connection. The other important property is CommandText, which specifies the command that needs to be executed. This can be an SQL query such as SELECT * FROM Department, but in your application this will always be the name of a stored procedure.

By default, the CommandText property receives SQL queries. Because you are supplying the name of a stored procedure instead of an SQL query, you need to inform the SqlCommand object about this by setting its CommandType property to CommandType.StoredProcedure.

The previous code snippet shows a simple and structured way to create and configure the SqlCommand object. However, it's possible to achieve the same result using less code by passing some of the information when creating the Command object:

```
// Create the command object
SqlCommand command = new SqlCommand("GetDepartments", connection);
command.CommandType = CommandType.StoredProcedure;
```

Executing the Command and Closing the Connection

This is the moment of glory—finally, after creating a connection, creating an SqlCommand object, and setting various parameters, you're ready to execute the command. It is important always to close the connection as soon as possible, immediately after the necessary database operation has been performed, because open connections consume server resources, which finally results in poor performance if not managed carefully.

You can execute the command in many ways, depending on the specifics. Does it return any information? If so, what kind of information, and in which format? You'll analyze the various scenarios later, when you actually put the theory into practice, but for now let's take a look at the three Execute methods of the SqlCommand class: ExecuteNonQuery, ExecuteScalar, and ExecuteReader.

ExecuteNonQuery is used to execute an SQL statement or stored procedure that doesn't return any records. You'll use this method when executing operations that update, insert, or delete information in the database. ExecuteNonQuery returns an integer value that specifies how many rows were affected by the query—this proves useful if you want to know, for example, how many rows were deleted by the last delete operation. Of course, in case you don't need to know that number, you can simply ignore the return value. Here's a simple piece of code that shows how to open the connection, execute the command using ExecuteNonQuery, and immediately close the connection afterward:

```
connection.Open();
command.ExecuteNonQuery();
command.Close();
```

ExecuteScalar is like ExecuteNonQuery in that it returns a single value, although it returns a value that has been read from the database instead of the number of affected rows. It is used in conjunction with SELECT statements that select a single value. If SELECT returns more rows and/or more columns, only the first column in the first row is returned.

ExecuteReader is used with SELECT statements that return multiple records (with any number of fields). ExecuteReader returns an SqlDataReader object, which contains the results of the query. An SqlDataReader object reads and returns the results one by one, in a forward-only and read-only manner. The good news about the SqlDataReader is that it represents the fastest way to read data from the database, and the bad news is that it needs an open connection to operate—no other database operations can be performed on that connection until the reader is closed. In our solution, you'll load all the data returned by the SqlDataReader into a DataTable object (which is capable of storing the data offline without needing an open connection), which will allow you to close the database connection very quickly.

The DataTable class can store a result set locally without needing an open connection to SQL Server, and it isn't data provider-specific, like the other ADO.NET objects mentioned so far (whose names begin with SQL because they're SQL Server-specific).

■**Tip** A "parent" of the DataTable object is the DataSet, which is a very smart object that represents something like an "in-memory" database. DataSet is capable of storing data tables, their data types, relationships between tables, and so on. Because of their complexity, DataSets consume a lot of memory so it's good to avoid them when possible. We won't use any DataSets when building BalloonShop.

Here's a simple example of reading some records from the database and saving them to a DataTable:

```
// Open the connection
conn.Open();
// Create the SqlDataReader object by executing the command
SqlDataReader reader = comm.ExecuteReader();
// Create a new DataTable and populate it from the SqlDataReader
DataTable table = new DataTable();
table.Load(reader);
// Close the reader and the connection
reader.Close();
conn.Close();
```

Implementing Generic Data Access Code

So far in the examples we used classes whose names start with *Sql*: SqlConnection, SqlCommand, and SqlDataReader. These objects and all the others whose names start with *Sql* are specifically created for SQL Server, and are part of the **SQL Server Managed Data Provider**. The SQL Server Managed Data Provider is the low-level interface between the database and your program. The ADO.NET objects that use this provider are grouped in the System.Data.SqlClient namespace, so you need to import this namespace when you need to access these classes directly.

The .NET Framework ships with Managed Data Providers for SQL Server (System.Data. SqlClient namespaces), Oracle (System.Data.Oracle), OLE DB (System.Data.OleDb), and ODBC (System.Data.Odbc).

To keep your application as independent as possible to the backend database, we'll use a trick to avoid using database-specific classes, such as SqlConnection, and so on. Instead, we'll let the application decide at runtime which provider to use, depending on the connection string provided. Moreover, because of a cool new ADO.NET 2.0 feature, we can implement this trick without affecting the application's performance!

■**Tip** If you're familiar with Object-Oriented Programming (OOP) theory, you'll find it interesting to hear this extra bit of information. In our code, we'll use database-agnostic classes, such as DbConnection and DbCommand, instead of SqlConnection and SqlCommand. At execution time, objects of these classes will contain instances of their database-specific variants, through polymorphism. As a result, for example, calling a method on the DbConnection class will have the similar method from SqlConnection executed. Using this trick, if you change the backend database, the compiled code keeps working with absolutely no changes, as long as the stored procedures are implemented the same under the new database. You can download some free material on OOP with C# from my personal web site at http://www.CristianDarie.ro.

Although using SQL Server-specific classes was better for the sake of keeping examples simple, in practice we'll use a method that doesn't make the C# code depend (in theory, at least) on a specific database server product.

The new ADO.NET 2.0 classes that allow for generic data access functionality (they weren't available in ADO.NET 1.0 or 1.1)—such as in DbConnection, DbCommand, and so on—are grouped under the System.Data.Common namespace.

The first step in implementing database-agnostic data access is to use the DbProviderFactory class to create a new database provider factory object:

```
// Create a new database provider factory
DbProviderFactory factory =
                DbProviderFactories.GetFactory("System.Data.SqlClient");
```

This piece of code, because of the System.Data.SqlClient parameter passed, will have the factory object contain an SQL Server database provider factory (the term *factory* generally refers to a class that builds other classes for you). In practice, the System.Data.SqlClient string parameter is kept in a configuration file, allowing you to have C# code that really doesn't know what kind of database it's dealing with.

The database provider factory class is capable of creating a database-specific connection object through its CreateConnection object. However, you'll keep the reference to the connection object stored using the generic DbConnection reference:

```
// Obtain a database specific connection object
DbConnection conn = factory.CreateConnection();
```

So, in practice, the connection object will actually contain a SqlCommand object if the backend database is SQL Server, an OracleCommand if the backend database is Oracle, and so on. However, instead of working with SqlCommand or OracleCommand objects, we simply use DbCommand and let it decide at runtime what kind of object to create in the background.

After you have a connection object, you can simply set its properties the familiar way, just as you would with a "normal" connection object:

```
// Set the connection string
conn.ConnectionString = "... connection string ...";
```

Okay, so you have the connection, but what about executing the command? Well, it just so happens that the connection object has a method named CreateCommand that returns a database command object. Just like with the connection object, CreateCommand returns a database-specific command object, but you'll keep the reference stored using a database-neutral object: DbCommand. Here's the line of code that does the job:

```
// Create a database specific command object
DbCommand comm = conn.CreateCommand();
```

Now that you have a connection object and a command object, you can play with them just like the good old days. Here's a fairly complete (and almost working) ADO.NET 2.0 code listing that loads the list of departments into a DataTable without knowing what kind of database it's working with:

```
// Create a new database provider factory
DbProviderFactory factory =
                DbProviderFactories.GetFactory("System.Data.SqlClient");
// Create the connection object
DbConnection conn = factory.CreateConnection();
// Initialize the connection string
conn.ConnectionString = "... connection string ...";
// Create the command object and set its properties
DbCommand comm = conn.CreateCommand();
comm.CommandText = "GetDepartments";
comm.CommandType = CommandType.StoredProcedure;
// Open the connection
conn.Open();
// Execute the command and save the results in a DataTable
DbDataReader reader = comm.ExecuteReader();
DataTable table = new DataTable();
table.Load(reader);
// Close the reader and the connection
reader.Close();
conn.Close();
```

Catching and Handling Exceptions

The rule is, of course, that your web site will always work fine, and no problems of any kind will ever happen. Exceptions to that rule can happen during development, however, and even more important, in a production system. It's needless to mention the many aspects out of your control, like hardware failure, software crashes, and viruses that can cause your software to work not exactly the way you designed it to work. Even better known are the errors that can happen because of bad (or unexpected) user input data combined with weaknesses in the application logic.

Common and particularly dangerous are the errors that can happen when accessing the database or executing a stored procedure. This can be caused by too many reasons to list, but the effects can show the visitor a nasty error message or keep database resources locked, which would cause problems to all the visitors accessing the site at that time.

Exceptions are the modern way of intercepting and handling runtime errors in object-oriented languages. When a runtime error occurs in your code, the execution is interrupted, and an exception is generated (or *raised*). If the exception is not handled by the local code that generated it, the exception goes up through the methods in the stack trace. If it isn't handled anywhere, it's finally caught by the .NET Framework, which displays an error message. If the error happens in an ASP.NET page during a client request, ASP.NET displays an error page, eventually including debugging information, to the visitor. (The good news in this scenario is that ASP.NET can be instructed to display a custom error page instead of the default one—you'll do that by the end of the chapter.)

On the other hand, if the exception is dealt with in the code, execution continues normally, and the visitor will never know a problem ever happened when handling the page request.

The general strategy to deal with runtime exceptions is as follows:

- If the error is not critical, deal with it in code, allowing the code to continue executing normally, and the visitor will never know an error happened.

- If the error is critical, handle it partially with code to reduce the negative effects as much as possible, and then let the error propagate to the presentation tier that will show the visitor a nice looking "Houston, there's a problem" page.

- For the errors that you can't anticipate, the last line of defense is still the presentation tier, which politely asks the visitor to come back later.

For any kind of error, it's good to let the site administrator (or the technical staff) know about the problem. Possible options include sending details about the error to a custom database table, to the Windows Event log, or by email. At the end of this chapter, you'll learn how to send an email to the site administrator with detailed information when an error happens.

In our data access code, you'll consider any error as critical. As a result, you'll minimize potential damage by closing the database connection immediately, logging the error, and then letting it propagate to the presentation tier.

■**Note** The business logic you see in the business tier code can control which exceptions pass through it. Any exception generated by the data access code can be caught and handled by the business tier. In case the business tier doesn't handle it, the exception propagates to the presentation tier, where it's logged once again (so the administrator will know it was a critical error), and the visitor is shown a nice error message asking him to come back later.

So, data access errors that are handled somewhere before getting to the visitor are logged only once (in the data access code). Critical errors that affect the visitor's browsing experience (by displaying the error message) are logged twice—the first time when they are thrown by the data access code and the second time when they display the error message for the visitor.

The theory sounds good enough, but how do we put it in practice? First, you need to learn about exceptions. Exceptions are dealt with in C# code using the `try-catch-finally` construct, whose simple version looks something like

```
try
{
  // code that might generate an exception
}
catch (Exception ex)
{
  // code that is executed only in case of an exception
  // (exception's details are accessible through the ex object)
}
finally
{
  // code that executes at the end, no matter if
  // an exception was generated or not
}
```

You place inside the try block any code that you suspect might possibly generate errors. If an exception is generated, the execution is immediately passed to the catch block. If no exceptions are generated in the try block, the catch block is bypassed completely. In the end, no matter whether an exception occurred or not, the finally block is executed.

The finally block is important because it's guaranteed to execute no matter what happens. If any database operations are performed in the try block, it's a standard practice to close the database connection in the finally block to ensure that no open connections remain active on the database server. This is useful because open connections consume resources on the database server and can even keep database resources locked, which can cause problems for other concurrently running database activities.

Both the finally and catch blocks are optional, but (obviously) the whole construct only makes sense if at least one of them is present. If no catch block exists (and you have only try and finally), the exception is not handled; the code stops executing, and the exception propagates to the higher levels in the class hierarchy, but not before executing the finally block (which, as stated previously, is guaranteed to execute no matter what happens).

Runtime exceptions propagate from the point they were raised through the call stack of your program. So, if an exception is generated in the database stored procedure, it is immediately passed to the data access code. If the data tier handles the error using a try-catch construct, then everything's fine, and the business tier and the presentation tier will never know that an error occurred. If the data tier doesn't handle the exception, the exception is then propagated to the business tier, and if the business tier doesn't handle it, the exception then propagates to the presentation tier. If the error isn't handled in the presentation tier either, the exception is finally propagated to the ASP.NET runtime that will deal with it by presenting an error page to the visitor.

There are cases when you want to catch the exception, respond to it somehow, and then allow it to propagate through the call stack anyway. This will be the case in the BalloonShop data access code, where we want to catch the exceptions to log them, but afterward we let them propagate to higher-level classes that know better how to handle the situation and decide how critical the error is. To rethrow an error after you've caught it in the catch block, you use the throw statement:

```
try
{
  // code that might generate an exception
}
catch (Exception ex)
{
  // code that is executed only in case of an exception
  throw ex;
}
```

As you can see in the code snippet, exceptions are represented in .NET code by the Exception class. The .NET Framework contains a number of specialized exception classes that are generated on certain events, and you can even create your own. However, these topics are out of the scope of this book.

See the C# language reference for complete details about using the try-catch-finally construct. In this chapter, you'll see it in action in the data access code, where it catches potential data access errors to report them to the administrator.

Sending Emails

Speaking of reporting errors, in BalloonShop you'll report errors by emailing them to the site administrator (or to the person you designate to handle them). Alternatives to this solution consist of using the Windows Event log, saving the error to the database, or even saving to a text file.

To send emails, you need the SmtpClient and MailMessage classes from the System.Web.Mail namespace.

MailMessage has four important properties that you set before sending an email: From, To, Subject, and Body. These properties can also be set through MailMessage's constructor, which accepts them as parameters. After the MailMessage object is properly set up, you send it using the SmtpMail class.

When working with SmtpClient, you can set its Host property to the address of an external SMTP (Simple Mail Transfer Protocol) server; otherwise, the mail is sent through the local SMTP service in Windows. Note that the SMTP service must be installed in Windows before you can use it. This service is a component of IIS, and you can install it by following the instructions in Appendix A.

The standard code that sends an email looks like the following code snippet (you need to replace the text in italics with your own data):

```
// Configure mail client (may need additional
// code for authenticated SMTP servers)
SmtpClient smtpClient = new SmtpClient("SMTP server address");
// Create the mail message
MailMessage mailMessage = new MailMessage("from", "to", "subject", "body");
// Send mail
smtpClient.Send(mailMessage);
```

If you're working with your local SMTP server, ensure that the server is started using the IIS Configuration console. Also, you may need to enable relaying for the local machine. For this, you need to open the IIS configuration console, expand your computer's node, right-click Default SMTP Virtual Server, select Properties, go to the Access tab, click the Relay button, add **127.0.0.1** to the list, and finally restart the SMTP server.

If you're having problems, before trying Google, first look at http://www.systemwebmail.com/default.aspx—although designed for .NET 1.1, this site may contain the solution to your problem.

Writing the Business Tier Code

It's time to upgrade your BalloonShop solution with some new bits of code. The following exercise uses much of the theory presented so far, while implementing the business tier code. You'll add the following C# classes to your application:

- GenericDataAccess contains the generic database access code, implementing basic error-handling and logging functionality.

- CatalogAccess contains the product catalog business logic.

- BalloonShopConfiguration provides easy access to various configuration settings (that are generally read from web.config), such as the database connection string, and so on.

- Utilities contains miscellaneous functionality such as sending emails, which will be used from various places in BalloonShop.

Follow the steps of the exercise to add these classes to your project.

Exercise: Implementing the Data Access Code

1. Open the web.config configuration file (double-click on its name in **Solution Explorer**) and update the connectionStrings element like this:

```
<configuration xmlns="http://schemas.microsoft.com/.NetConfiguration/v2.0">
  <appSettings/>
  <connectionStrings>
    <add name="BalloonShopConnection" connectionString="Server=
(local)\SqlExpress;
Integrated Security=True;Database=BalloonShop"
providerName="System.Data.SqlClient"/>
  </connectionStrings>
  <system.web>
    <!--
```

■**Note** You might need to adapt the connection string to match your particular SQL Server configuration. Also, you should type the <add> element on a single line, not split in multiple lines as shown in the previous code snippet.

2. Add the other necessary configuration data under the <appSettings> node in web.config, as shown here:

```
<appSettings>
  <add key="MailServer" value="localhost" />
  <add key="EnableErrorLogEmail" value="true" />
  <add key="ErrorLogEmail" value="errors@yourballoonshopxyz.com" />
</appSettings>
```

■**Note** Make sure you include a working server address instead of *localhost* and a valid email account instead of *errors@yourballoonshopxyz.com*, if you intend to use the email logging feature. Otherwise, just set EnableErrorLogEmail to false.

3. Right-click the project's name in **Solution Explorer** and choose **Add New Item** from the context menu.

4. Choose the **Class** template, and set its name to ApplicationConfiguration.cs. Click **Add**.

5. You'll be asked about adding the class into the App_Code folder. This is a special folder in ASP.NET 2.0. Choose **Yes**.

6. Modify the ApplicationConfiguration class like this:

```
using System;
using System.Configuration;

/// <summary>
/// Repository for BalloonShop configuration settings
/// </summary>
public static class BalloonShopConfiguration
{
  // Caches the connection string
  private static string dbConnectionString;
  // Caches the data provider name
  private static string dbProviderName;

  static BalloonShopConfiguration()
  {
    dbConnectionString =
ConfigurationManager.ConnectionStrings["BalloonShopConnection"].
ConnectionString;
    dbProviderName =
ConfigurationManager.ConnectionStrings["BalloonShopConnection"].
ProviderName;
  }

  // Returns the connection string for the BalloonShop database
  public static string DbConnectionString
  {
    get
    {
      return dbConnectionString;
    }
  }

  // Returns the data provider name
  public static string DbProviderName
  {
    get
    {
      return dbProviderName;
    }
  }
}
```

```csharp
    // Returns the address of the mail server
    public static string MailServer
    {
      get
      {
        return ConfigurationManager.AppSettings["MailServer"];
      }
    }

    // Send error log emails?
    public static bool EnableErrorLogEmail
    {
      get
      {
        return bool.Parse(ConfigurationManager.AppSettings
["EnableErrorLogEmail"]);
      }
    }

    // Returns the email address where to send error reports
    public static string ErrorLogEmail
    {
      get
      {
        return ConfigurationManager.AppSettings["ErrorLogEmail"];
      }
    }
  }
}
```

7. Right-click the project's name in **Solution Explorer** and choose **Add New Item** from the context menu.

8. Choose the `Class` template and set its name to `Utilities.cs`. Click **Add**. You'll be asked about adding the class into the App_Code folder. Choose **Yes**.

9. Write the following code into `Utilities.cs` (note that we've removed the unnecessary using statements):

```csharp
using System;
using System.Net.Mail;

/// <summary>
/// Class contains miscellaneous functionality
/// </summary>
public static class Utilities
{
  static Utilities()
  {
    //
    // TODO: Add constructor logic here
    //
  }
```

```csharp
  // Generic method for sending emails
  public static void SendMail(string from, string to, string subject,
string body)
  {
    // Configure mail client (may need additional
    // code for authenticated SMTP servers)
    SmtpClient mailClient = new SmtpClient
(BalloonShopConfiguration.MailServer);
    // Create the mail message
    MailMessage mailMessage = new MailMessage(from, to, subject, body);
/*
// For SMTP servers that require authentication
message.Fields.Add
("http://schemas.microsoft.com/cdo/configuration/smtpauthenticate", 1);
message.Fields.Add
("http://schemas.microsoft.com/cdo/configuration/sendusername",
"SmtpHostUserName");
message.Fields.Add
("http://schemas.microsoft.com/cdo/configuration/sendpassword",
"SmtpHostPassword");
*/
    // Send mail
    mailClient.Send(mailMessage);
  }

  // Send error log mail
  public static void LogError(Exception ex)
  {
    // get the current date and time
    string dateTime = DateTime.Now.ToLongDateString() + ", at "
                  + DateTime.Now.ToShortTimeString();
    // stores the error message
    string errorMessage = "Exception generated on " + dateTime;
    // obtain the page that generated the error
    System.Web.HttpContext context = System.Web.HttpContext.Current;
    errorMessage += "\n\n Page location: " + context.Request.RawUrl;
    // build the error message
    errorMessage += "\n\n Message: " + ex.Message;
    errorMessage += "\n\n Source: " + ex.Source;
    errorMessage += "\n\n Method: " + ex.TargetSite;
    errorMessage += "\n\n Stack Trace: \n\n" + ex.StackTrace;
    // send error email in case the option is activated in Web.Config
    if (BalloonShopConfiguration.EnableErrorLogEmail)
    {
```

```
          string from = "noreply@cristiandarie.ro";
          string to = BalloonShopConfiguration.ErrorLogEmail;
          string subject = BalloonShopConfiguration.SiteName + " error report";
          string body = errorMessage;
          SendMail(from, to, subject, body);
        }
      }
    }
```

10. Right-click the project's name in **Solution Explorer** and choose **Add New Item** from the context menu. Choose the `Class` template and set its name to **GenericDataAccess.cs**. Click **Add**. You'll be asked about adding the class into the App_Code folder. Choose **Yes**.

11. Write the following code into `GenericDataAccess.cs`:

```csharp
using System;
using System.Data;
using System.Data.Common;
using System.Configuration;


/// <summary>
/// Class contains generic data access functionality to be accessed from
/// the business tier
/// </summary>
public static class GenericDataAccess
{
  // static constructor
  static GenericDataAccess()
  {
    //
    // TODO: Add constructor logic here
    //
  }

  // executes a command and returns the results as a DataTable object
  public static DataTable ExecuteSelectCommand(DbCommand command)
  {
    // The DataTable to be returned
    DataTable table;
    // Execute the command making sure the connection gets closed in the end
    try
    {
      // Open the data connection
      command.Connection.Open();
      // Execute the command and save the results in a DataTable
      DbDataReader reader = command.ExecuteReader();
      table = new DataTable();
      table.Load(reader);
```

```
    // Close the reader
    reader.Close();
  }
  catch (Exception ex)
  {
    Utilities.LogError(ex);
    throw ex;
  }
  finally
  {
    // Close the connection
    command.Connection.Close();
  }
  return table;
}

// creates and prepares a new DbCommand object on a new connection
public static DbCommand CreateCommand()
{
  // Obtain the database provider name
  string dataProviderName = BalloonShopConfiguration.DbProviderName;
  // Obtain the database connection string
  string connectionString = BalloonShopConfiguration.DbConnectionString;
  // Create a new data provider factory
  DbProviderFactory factory = DbProviderFactories.
GetFactory(dataProviderName);
  // Obtain a database specific connection object
  DbConnection conn = factory.CreateConnection();
  // Set the connection string
  conn.ConnectionString = connectionString;
  // Create a database specific command object
  DbCommand comm = conn.CreateCommand();
  // Set the command type to stored procedure
  comm.CommandType = CommandType.StoredProcedure;
  // Return the initialized command object
  return comm;
  }
}
```

12. In **Solution Explorer**, right-click on the App_Code folder and choose **Add New Item.** Using the window that appears, create a new class named CatalogAccess (which would reside in a file named CatalogAccess.cs). Add the new code to the file:

```
using System;
using System.Data;
using System.Data.Common;

/// <summary>
/// Product catalog business tier component
/// </summary>
public static class CatalogAccess
{
  static CatalogAccess()
  {
    //
    // TODO: Add constructor logic here
    //
  }

  // Retrieve the list of departments
  public static DataTable GetDepartments()
  {
    // get a configured DbCommand object
    DbCommand comm = GenericDataAccess.CreateCommand();
    // set the stored procedure name
    comm.CommandText = "GetDepartments";
    // execute the stored procedure and return the results
    return GenericDataAccess.ExecuteSelectCommand(comm);
  }
}
```

How It Works: The Business Tier

Let's take some time to understand the code you just wrote.

First, you added some configuration settings to the web.config configuration file. web.config is an external configuration XML file managed by ASP.NET. This complex and powerful file can include many options regarding the application's security, performance, behavior, and so on.

Saving data to web.config is beneficial because you can change it independently of your C# code, which now doesn't need to be recompiled when you change the address of the mail server or the database connection string. This detail, combined with the fact that the data access code is written to be database-independent, makes the whole data access code powerful.

Then, you added the BalloonShopConfiguration class, which is simply a collection of static properties that return data from web.config. Using this class instead of needing to read web.config all the time will make your life easier in the long run. The performance is improved as well because the class can cache the values read from web.config instead of reading them on every request. The first place you use the BalloonShopConfiguration class is the Utility class, which for now only contains code that sends emails.

Next, you implemented the GenericDataAccess class, whose purpose is to store a series of common database access operations, to avoid typing it all over again in other places. The two methods it contains now are

- CreateCommand creates a DbCommand object, sets some standard properties to it, and returns the configured object. If you preferred to use a database-specific command object, such as SqlCommand, the code would have been a bit simpler, but in this case we prefer to have database-independent access code, as explained earlier in this chapter. The CreateCommand method uses the steps presented earlier in this chapter to create a command object specific to the database implementation you're working with, wrap that instance into a generic DbCommand reference, and return this reference. This way, external classes will be able to call CreateCommand to get an already configured—with a prepared connection—DbCommand object.

- ExecuteSelectCommand is essentially a wrapper for DbCommand's ExecuteReader method, except it returns the results as a DataTable instead of a DataReader. Using the DataTable ensures that the database connection is kept open as short as possible. In this method, you implement an error-handling technique that guarantees that in case of an exception, the administrator is informed by email (if the application is configured to do so), the database connection is properly closed and the error is rethrown. We decided to let the error propagate because this class is at too low a level to know how to properly handle the errors. At this point, we're only interested in keeping the database safe (by closing the connection) and reporting any eventual error. The best example of how a client class can use GenericDataAccess to work with the BalloonShop database is the GetDepartments method in the CatalogAccess class.

All the classes you've added are static classes, which are composed exclusively of static members. Note that some understanding of basic OOP terminology—such as classes, objects, constructors, methods, properties, fields, instance members and static members, public data and private data, and so on—is an important prerequisite for this book. These topics are covered in many articles on the Internet, such as the ones you can find for free download at http://www.cristiandarie.ro/downloads.html.

■**Note** Static class members (such as static properties and static methods) can be called by external classes without creating an instance of the class first; instead, they can be called directly using the class name. The perfect example for this is the Math class, which contains a number of static methods to perform various operations, such as Math.Cos, and so on. Under the hood, the static class members are called on a global instance of that class, which is not destroyed by the GC (Garbage Collector) after execution. When the first static member of a class is called, the global instance of the class is created, and its static constructor is executed. Because the static constructor is called only once per application's lifetime, and the global instance is never destroyed, we can ensure that any initializations performed by the static constructor (such as reading the database connection string) are performed only once, and the values of any static members are persisted. A static class member can call or access another static class member directly. However, if you needed to access an instance class member (nonstatic class member) from a static class member, you had to create an instance of the class, even from a method of that class, to access that member.

We've chosen to use static members mainly to improve performance. Because static classes and static members are initialized only once, they don't need to be reinstantiated each time a new visitor makes a new request; instead, their "global" instances are used. In the presentation tier, you'll display your list of departments with a call like this:

```
list.DataSource = CatalogAccess.GetDepartments();
```

If GetDepartments would have been an instance method, you would have needed to create a separate instance of the CatalogAccess class instead of using the static instance, which would have had, obviously, a bigger performance impact:

```
CatalogAccess catalogAccess = new CatalogAccess();
list.DataSource = catalogAccess.GetDepartments();
```

In BalloonShopConfiguration, you've implemented even an additional trick to improve performance by caching connection string data using static fields (dbConnectionString and dbProviderName), whose data is read in from web.config in the class's static constructor. The static class constructor is called only once per application's life cycle, so the web.config file won't be read on every database operation, but just once when the class is initialized.

Displaying the List of Departments

Now that everything is in place in the other tiers, all you have to do is create the presentation tier part—the final goal you've been working toward from the beginning. As you saw in the figures at the beginning of this chapter, the departments list needs to look something like Figure 3-15 when the site is loaded in the web browser.

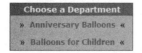

Figure 3-15. *The departments list when loaded in the web browser*

You'll implement this as a separate Web User Control named DepartmentsList, just as you did with the Header control in Chapter 2, and then you'll add the user control to the Master Page to make it available to all the site's pages.

The list of departments needs to be dynamically generated based on what you have in the database. Fortunately, the .NET Framework provides a few useful web controls that can help you solve this problem without writing too much code. For example, the DataList control can be set to simply take a DataTable object as input and generate content based on it.

Before actually writing the user control, let's prepare the BalloonShop CSS file.

Preparing the Field: Themes, Skins, and Styles

Cascading Style Sheets (CSS) files are a standard repository for font and formatting information that can be easily applied to various parts of the site. For example, instead of setting fonts, colors, and dimensions for a Label control, you can set its CssClass property to one of the existing styles. The CSS file is applied at the client side and doesn't imply any server-side processing on the ASP.NET application. A typical CSS style definition looks like this:

```
.AdminButtonText
{
  color: Black;
  font-family: Verdana, Helvetica, sans-serif;
  font-size: 12px;
}
```

ASP.NET 2.0 brings in the notions of themes and skins. **Skins** are like CSS files in that they contain various properties, but they do this on a control-type basis, they allow setting properties that aren't accessible through CSS (such as image's `src` property), and they are applied at server side. Skin definitions are saved in files with the `.skin` extension (these files can store one or more skin definitions) and look much like the definition of an ASP.NET control. A typical skin definition looks like this:

```
<asp:Image runat="server" SkinID="BalloonShopLogo" src="/Images/BalloonShop.png"/>
```

This skin entry is a named skin because it has a `SkinID`. In this case, when adding images that you want to implement this skin, you need to set their `SkinID` properties to `BalloonShopLogo`. If you don't specify a `SkinID` when creating the skin, that skin becomes the default skin for its control type.

Just as with CSS files, you use skins when you want to reuse a particular control format in more controls. However, your `DepartmentsList.ascx` and its contents will be one-of-a-kind, and using a skin for just one instance of a control wouldn't bring much of a benefit. As a result, we won't build any skins in this chapter, but you'll meet them later in the book, where it makes more sense to use them.

A **theme** is a collection of CSS files, skins, and images. You can add more themes to a web site and allow for easily changing the look of your site by switching the active theme at design-time or even at runtime.

In the exercise, you'll create a new theme called `BalloonShopDefault`, and you'll add a CSS file to it, which will be then used to display the list of departments.

Exercise: Preparing the Styles

1. Right-click the root entry in **Solution Explorer**, and then choose **Add Folder ➤ Theme Folder**. Set the name of the new folder to **BalloonShopDefault**, as shown in Figure 3-16.

Figure 3-16. *The departments list when loaded in the web browser*

2. Right-click the `BalloonShopDefault` entry in **Solution Explorer** and then choose **Add New Item**. From the **Templates** window, choose **Style Sheet** and name it `BalloonShop.css`. Click **Add**.

3. Open `BalloonShop.css` by double-clicking it in **Solution Explorer**. Delete its contents and add these styles to it:

```
.DepartmentListHead
{
  border-right: #01a647 1px solid;
  border-top: #01a647 1px solid;
  border-left: #01a647 1px solid;
  border-bottom: #01a647 1px solid;
  background-color: #30b86e;
  font-family: Verdana, Arial;
  font-weight: bold;
  font-size: 10pt;
  color: #f5f5dc;
  padding-left: 3px;
  text-align: center;
}
.DepartmentListContent
{
  border-right: #01a647 1px solid;
  border-top: #01a647 1px solid;
  border-left: #01a647 1px solid;
  border-bottom: #01a647 1px solid;
  background-color: #9fe1bb;
  text-align: center;
}
a.DepartmentUnselected
{
  font-family: Verdana, Arial;
  font-weight: bold;
  font-size: 9pt;
  color: #5f9ea0;
  line-height: 25px;
  padding-left: 5px;
  text-decoration: none;
}
a.DepartmentUnselected:hover
{
  padding-left: 5px;
  color: #2e8b57;
}
a.DepartmentSelected
{
  font-family: Verdana, Arial;
  font-weight: bold;
```

```
    font-size: 9pt;
    color: #556b2f;
    line-height: 25px;
    padding-left: 5px;
    text-decoration: none;
}
```

4. Finally, open web.config to enable the default theme:

```
<system.web>
    <pages theme="BalloonShopDefault"/>
...
```

How It Works: Using Themes

Having a central place to store style information helps you to easily change the look of the site without changing a line of code.

At this moment, BalloonShop.css contains a few styles you'll need for displaying the departments list. These styles refer to the way department names should look when they are unselected, unselected but with the mouse hovering over them, or selected. The CSS file and skin file are added to the default theme, which is enabled in web.config, so they'll be accessible from any page of the site.

While you're here, it's worth noticing the built-in features Visual Web Developer has for editing CSS files. While BalloonShop.css is open in edit mode, right-click one of its styles and click the Build Style menu option. You'll get a dialog box such as the one in Figure 3-17, which permits editing the style visually.

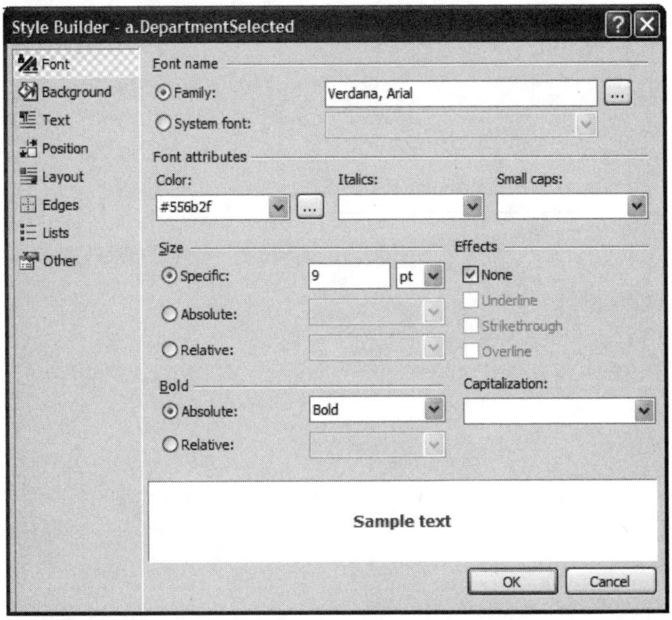

Figure 3-17. *Editing a style in Visual Web Developer*

Displaying the Departments

Now everything is in place, the only missing part being the DepartmentsList user control itself. This user control will contain a DataList control that generates the list of departments.

In this exercise, you'll implement most functionality by using the Design View of Visual Web Developer, and you'll see the HTML code that it generates. In other exercises, you'll work directly in Source View mode.

Exercise: Creating DepartmentsList.ascx

1. First create a new Web User Control in the UserControls folder. Right-click the UserControls folder and then choose **Add New Item**. Select the **Web User Control** template and name it DepartmentsList.ascx (or simply DepartmentsList). Check the **Place Code in separate file** check box, make sure the language is **Visual C#**, and click **Add**.

2. Switch DepartmentsList.ascx to Design View. Make sure the toolbox is visible (**Ctrl+Alt+X**), open the **Data** tab, and double-click the **DataList** entry. This will add a DataList control to DepartmentsList.ascx.

3. Use the **Properties** window (see Figure 3-18) to change the properties of your DataList, as shown in Table 3-3.

Table 3-3. *Setting the DataList Properties*

Property Name	Value
(ID)	list
Width	200px
CssClass	DepartmentListContent
HeaderStyle-CssClass	DepartmentListHead

Figure 3-18. *Changing the name of the DataList control*

4. Open `DepartmentsList.ascx` in Design View, right-click the `DataList`, and select **Edit Template ➤ Header and Footer Templates**.

5. Type **Choose a Department** in the Header template.

6. Right-click the `DataList` and select **Edit Template ➤ Item Templates**.

7. Add a `HyperLink` control from the **Standard** tab of the **Toolbox** to the `ItemTemplate`.

8. Set the `Text` property of the `HyperLink` to an empty string. The `list` control should then look like Figure 3-19.

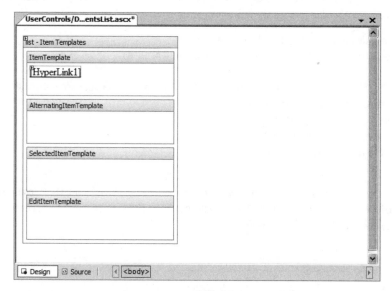

Figure 3-19. *Editing the templates of the* `DataList`

9. Switch to Source View, where you need to make few changes to the `HyperLink` control. Here's the full code of the `DataList` control:

```
<asp:DataList ID="list" runat="server" Width="200px">
  <ItemTemplate>
     &raquo;
    <asp:HyperLink
      ID="HyperLink1"
      Runat="server"
      NavigateUrl='<%# "../Catalog.aspx?DepartmentID=" +
Eval("DepartmentID")%>'
      Text='<%# Eval("Name") %>'
      ToolTip='<%# Eval("Description") %>'
      CssClass='<%# Eval("DepartmentID").ToString() ==
Request.QueryString["DepartmentID"] ? "DepartmentSelected" :
"DepartmentUnselected"
%>'>
```

```
      </asp:HyperLink>
       &laquo;
    </ItemTemplate>
     <HeaderTemplate>
       Choose a Department
     </HeaderTemplate>
     <ItemStyle CssClass="DepartmentListContent" />
     <HeaderStyle CssClass="DepartmentListHead" />
    </asp:DataList>
```

10. Now open the code-behind file of the user control (DepartmentsList.ascx.cs) and modify the Page_Load event handler function like this:

```
    // Load department details into the DataList
    protected void Page_Load(object sender, EventArgs e)
    {
        // CatalogAccess.GetDepartments returns a DataTable object containing
        // department data, which is read in the ItemTemplate of the DataList
        list.DataSource = CatalogAccess.GetDepartments();
        // Needed to bind the data bound controls to the data source
        list.DataBind();
    }
```

11. Open BalloonShop.master in Design View. Drag DepartmentsList.ascx from Solution Explorer and drop it near the "List of Departments" text. Delete the text from the cell, so that only the user control should be there, as shown in Figure 3-20.

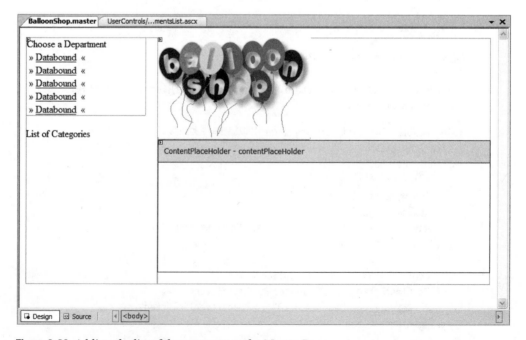

Figure 3-20. *Adding the list of departments to the Master Page*

12. Finish the exercise by creating `Catalog.aspx`, the page that is referenced by the departments list links. Right-click the name of the project in **Solution Explorer** and select **Add New Item**. Choose the **Web Form** template, set its name to `Catalog.aspx`, make sure both check boxes **Place Code in separate file** and **Select Master Page** are checked, and click **Add**. When asked for a Master Page file, choose `Balloonshop.master`.

13. Open `Catalog.aspx` in Source View and change its title to **BalloonShop – The Product Catalog**:

```
<%@ Page Language="C#" MasterPageFile="~/BalloonShop.master"
AutoEventWireup="true" CodeFile="Catalog.aspx.cs"
Inherits="Catalog" Title="BalloonShop : The Product Catalog" %>
```

14. Press **F5** to execute the project (see Figure 3-21). Then select one of the departments.

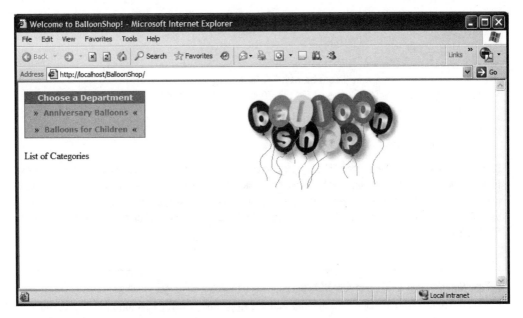

Figure 3-21. *Executing the BalloonShop project*

■**Note** If you get an error at this point, you either didn't enter the code correctly or there is a problem connecting to SQL Server. Review the "Configuring SQL Server Security" section earlier in this chapter.

How It Works: The DepartmentsList User Control

The heart of the `DepartmentsList` Web User Control is its `DataList` control, which generates the list of departments. To make a `DataList` work, you need to edit its `ItemTemplate` property at the least. You also edited its `HeaderTemplate`.

The templates can be edited either in Design View mode or in Source View mode. It's easier to work with the designer, but editing the HTML directly is more powerful and allows some tweaks that aren't always possible with the designer.

The DataList control, which generates the list of departments, is flexible and configurable. The most important step for configuring this control is to set its ItemTemplate property. When the DataList is bound to a data source, the ItemTemplate generates a new data list entry for each row of the data source. In our case, the DataList object contains a HyperLink control in its ItemTemplate, so we'll have one hyperlink for each record returned from the database. It's important to understand how the data-binding process works. Let's have another look at the code of the HyperLink:

```
<asp:HyperLink
    ID="HyperLink1"
    Runat="server"
    NavigateUrl='<%# "../Catalog.aspx?DepartmentID=" +
Eval("DepartmentID")%>'
    Text='<%# Eval("Name") %>'
    ToolTip='<%# Eval("Description") %>'
    CssClass='<%# Eval("DepartmentID").ToString() ==
Request.QueryString["DepartmentID"] ? "DepartmentSelected" :
"DepartmentUnselected"
%>'>
    </asp:HyperLink>
```

Basically, this piece of code generates a link of the form http://*webserver*/Catalog.aspx?DepartmentID=XXX for each row retrieved from the data source. In our case, the data source is a DataTable that contains this information about each department: the DepartmentID, the Name, and the Description. These details are extracted using the Eval() function. For example, Eval("Name") will return the Name field of the row being processed by the DataList.

■**Tip** With previous versions of ASP.NET, the code used to look a bit longer, such as in DataBinder. Eval(Container.DataItem, "Name") instead of Eval("Name"). The new form was introduced to make things a little bit easier for programmers' fingers.

Perhaps the most interesting detail about the piece of code that creates the hyperlinks is the way you set CssClass. The code should make sense if you're familiar with the ternary operator. The expression assigned to the CssClass property returns "DepartmentSelected" in case the DepartmentID from the query string is the same as the DepartmentID of the row being read from the data source or returns "DepartmentUnselected" otherwise. This ensures that after the visitor clicks a department and the page gets reloaded with a new query string, the selected department is painted using a different style than the other departments in the list.

■**Tip** The ternary operator has the form `condition ? value1 : value2`. If the condition is true, `value1` is returned, otherwise, `value2` is returned. The expression could be rewritten as

```
if (condition) return value1 else return value2;
```

Back to the `DataList`, it's important to know that it accepts more templates that can be used to customize its appearance, using a schema like the following:

```
<asp:DataList id="list" runat="server">
  <HeaderTemplate>
    <!- contents -->
  </HeaderTemplate>
  <SelectedItemTemplate>
    <!- contents -->
  </SelectedItemTemplate>
  <ItemTemplate>
    <!- contents -->
  </ItemTemplate>
  <AlternatingItemTemplate>
    <!- contents -->
  </AlternatingItemTemplate>
  <FooterTemplate>
    <!- contents -->
  </FooterTemplate>
</asp:DataList>
```

The last piece of the puzzle that makes the list of departments work is the C# code you wrote in `DepartmentsList.ascx.cs`. The `Page_Load` event is fired when loading the data list, with which you ask for the list of departments from the business tier, and bind that list to the `DataList`:

```
// Load department details into the DataList
protected void Page_Load(object sender, EventArgs e)
{
  // CatalogAccess.GetDepartments returns a DataTable object containing
  // department data, which is read in the ItemTemplate of the DataList
  list.DataSource = CatalogAccess.GetDepartments();
  // Needed to bind the data bound controls to the data source
  list.DataBind();
}
```

It's exciting how the full power of the business tier code you implemented earlier can now be used to populate a `DataList` control with just a couple of lines of code, isn't it? Keep in mind that you're working on the presentation tier right now. It doesn't matter how the `CatalogAccess` class or the `GetDepartments` method is implemented. You just need to know that `GetDepartments` returns a list of (DepartmentID, Name) pairs. While you are on the presentation tier, you don't really care how `Catalog.GetDepartments` does what it's supposed to do.

Adding a Custom Error Page

Now, at the final bit of this chapter, you complete the last piece of error-handling functionality for BalloonShop.

At this point, the single piece of error handling that you've implemented is in the data access code. The data access code can't know if an error is serious or if it can simply be ignored, so the only purpose is to make sure the database connection is closed properly and to report the error to the administrator. The exception is rethrown, and it's up to the upper layers of the architecture to decide what to do next with the exception.

The problem is, if the error isn't properly handled anywhere, it generates an ugly error message that your visitors will see—you don't want this to happen.

In the next exercise you will

- Add a custom error page to your site that your visitor will see in case an unhandled error happens. That page will politely ask the visitor to come back later.

- Report the error once again, so the administrator knows that this serious error gets to the visitor and needs to be taken care of as soon as possible.

Adding the custom error page is a very simple task, consisting of building a simple Web Form and configuring it as the default error page in web.config. Reporting unhandled errors is equally simple, by using a class named the Global Application Class. Follow the steps in the exercise to apply all this in practice.

Exercise: Adding a Custom Error Page and Reporting Unhandled Errors

1. Right-click the project entry in **Solution Explorer** and then select **Add New Item.**

2. Choose the **Global Application Class** template and click **Add**.

3. Modify Application_Error like this:

```
void Application_Error(Object sender, EventArgs e)
{
  // Log all unhandled errors
  Utilities.LogError(Server.GetLastError());
}
```

4. In Solution Explorer, double-click web.config and add the following element as a child of the <system.web> element:

```
<customErrors mode="RemoteOnly" defaultRedirect="Oooops.aspx" />
```

■**Note** After this change, remote clients will be forwarded to Oooops.aspx when unhandled exceptions are thrown; however, on the local machine, you'll still receive detailed error information. If you want to see the same error message as your visitors, set mode to On instead of RemoteOnly.

---

5. Add a new Web Form to your application's root, named Oooops.aspx, based on BalloonShop.master.

6. While in Source View, modify the page by changing its title and adding content to its content placeholder:

```
<%@ Page Language="C#" MasterPageFile="~/BalloonShop.master"
AutoEventWireup="true" CodeFile="Oooops.aspx.cs" Inherits="Oooops"
Title="BalloonShop - Oooops!" %>
<asp:Content ID="Content1" ContentPlaceHolderID="contentPlaceHolder"
runat="Server">
  <p align="center">
    <span class="CatalogTitle">Your request generated an internal error!
</span>
    <br />
    <br />
    <span class="CatalogDescription">We apologize for the inconvenience!
The error has been reported. </span>
  </p>
</asp:Content>
```

How It Works: Error Reporting

Right now your web site, no matter what happens, will look good. In case of an error, instead of displaying the default error message (which is, of course, not colorful enough for our customers' tastes), it will display a nice-looking error message page. For a short test, configure your application to show the error page to you as well, not only to your visitors (there's a note about how to do this in the exercise). Remember to unset this option, however, because you need exception details when building and debugging the application.

Then, execute the project, click on a department, and add a few letters to the department ID, like this:

```
http://localhost/BalloonShop/Catalog.aspx?DepartmentID=1ABC
```

Trying to load this page generates an exception because the department ID is supposed to be numerical, and the business tier code tries to convert this to an integer before sending it to the database (this is a good technique to prevent sending bogus values to the database).

Have a look at the custom error page in Figure 3-22.

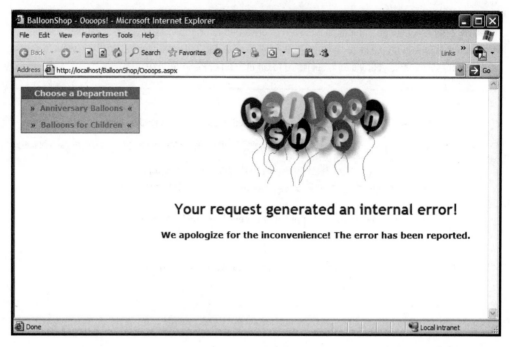

Figure 3-22. *Oooops!*

First, this exception is caught in the data tier, which simply reports it and then rethrows it. The report from the data tier generates an email with contents like this:

```
Exception generated on Sunday, September 25, 2005, at 1:15 AM

Page location: /BalloonShop/Catalog.aspx?DepartmentID=1ABC

Message: Failed to convert parameter value from a String to a Int32.

Source: System.Data

Method: System.Object CoerceValue(System.Object, System.Data.SqlClient
.MetaType)

Stack Trace:

   at System.Data.SqlClient.SqlParameter.CoerceValue(Object value, MetaType
destinationType)
   at System.Data.SqlClient.SqlParameter.GetCoercedValue()
   at System.Data.SqlClient.SqlParameter.Validate(Int32 index)
   at System.Data.SqlClient.SqlCommand.SetUpRPCParameters(_SqlRPC rpc, Int32
startCount, Boolean inSchema, SqlParameterCollection parameters)
```

```
    at System.Data.SqlClient.SqlCommand.BuildRPC(Boolean inSchema,
SqlParameterCollection parameters, _SqlRPC& rpc)
    at System.Data.SqlClient.SqlCommand.RunExecuteReaderTds(CommandBehavior
cmdBehavior, RunBehavior runBehavior, Boolean returnStream, Boolean async)
    at System.Data.SqlClient.SqlCommand.RunExecuteReader(CommandBehavior
cmdBehavior, RunBehavior runBehavior, Boolean returnStream, String method,
DbAsyncResult result)
    at System.Data.SqlClient.SqlCommand.RunExecuteReader(CommandBehavior
cmdBehavior, RunBehavior runBehavior, Boolean returnStream, String method)
    at System.Data.SqlClient.SqlCommandExecuteReader(CommandBehavior behavior,
String method)
    at System.Data.SqlClient.SqlCommand.ExecuteDbDataReader(CommandBehavior
behavior)
    at System.Data.Common.DbCommand.ExecuteReader()
    at GenericDataAccess.ExecuteSelectCommand(DbCommand command) in
c:\Inetpub\wwwroot\BalloonShop\App_Code\GenericDataAccess.cs:line 31
```

This email contains all the significant details about the error. However, the error is rethrown, and because it isn't handled anywhere else, it's finally caught by the presentation tier, which displays the nice error page. A second email is generated, which should be taken seriously because the error caused the visitor to see an error message:

```
Exception generated on Sunday, September 25, 2005, at 1:15 AM

 Page location: /BalloonShop/Catalog.aspx?DepartmentID=1ABC

 Message: Exception of type 'System.Web.HttpUnhandledException' was thrown.

 Source: System.Web

 Method: Boolean HandleError(System.Exception)

 Stack Trace:

    at System.Web.UI.Page.HandleError(Exception e)
    at System.Web.UI.Page.ProcessRequestMain(Boolean
includeStagesBeforeAsyncPoint, Boolean includeStagesAfterAsyncPoint)
    at System.Web.UI.Page.ProcessRequest(Boolean includeStagesBeforeAsyncPoint,
 Boolean includeStagesAfterAsyncPoint)
    at System.Web.UI.Page.ProcessRequest()
    at System.Web.UI.Page.ProcessRequest(HttpContext context)
    at
System.Web.HttpApplication.CallHandlerExecutionStep.System.
Web.HttpApplication.IexecutionStep.Execute()
    at System.Web.HttpApplication.ExecuteStep
(IExecutionStep step, Boolean& completedSynchronously)
```

Summary

This long chapter was well worth the effort, when you consider how much theory you've learned and applied to the BalloonShop project! In this chapter, you accomplished the following:

- Created the Department table and populated it with data

- Added a stored procedure to the database and added code to access this stored procedure from the middle tier using a special data access class

- Added a number of configuration options to web.config, such as the database connection string, to make things easier if you need to change these options

- Wrote error-handling and reporting code to keep the administrator notified of any errors that happen to the web site

- Added the DepartmentList Web User Control to the site

In the next chapter, you'll continue building the site to include even more exciting functionality!

CHAPTER 4

■■■

Creating the Product Catalog: Part II

The fun isn't over yet! In the previous chapter, you created a selectable list of departments for BalloonShop. However, there's much more to a product catalog than a list of departments. In this chapter, you'll add many new product catalog features. This chapter has a similar structure to the last chapter, but there's a lot of new functionality to add, which involves quite a bit of code.

Review Figures 3-1, 3-2, 3-3, and 3-4 from Chapter 3 to get a visual feeling of the new functionality you'll implement in this chapter.

In this chapter, you will

- Learn about relational data and the types of relationships that occur between data tables, and then create the new data structures in your database.

- Understand how to join related data tables, how to use subqueries, how to implement paging at the data tier level, and even more theory about T-SQL functions and techniques.

- Complete business tier functionality to work with the new stored procedures, including stored procedures with input and output parameters, and use simple data structures to pass requested data to the presentation tier.

- Create new Web Forms and Web User Controls to show your visitor details about your categories, your products, and more.

Yep, that's a lot of material to get through! Take a deep breath, and let's get started!

Storing the New Data

Given the new functionality you are adding in this chapter, it's not surprising that you need to add more data tables to the database. However, this isn't just about adding new data tables. You also need to learn about relational data and the relationships that you can implement between the data tables, so that you can obtain more significant information from your database.

What Makes a Relational Database

It's no mystery that a database is something that stores data. However, today's modern Relational Database Management Systems (RDBMS), such as MySQL, PostgreSQL, SQL Server, Oracle, DB2, and others, have extended this basic role by adding the capability to store and manage relational data.

So what does *relational data* mean? It's easy to see that every piece of data ever written in a real-world database is somehow related to some already existing information. Products are related to categories and departments, orders are related to products and customers, and so on. A relational database keeps its information stored in data tables but is also aware of the relations between them.

These related tables form the *relational database*, which becomes an object with a significance of its own, rather than simply being a group of unrelated data tables. It is said that *data* becomes *information* only when we give significance to it, and establishing relations with other pieces of data is a good means of doing that.

Look at the product catalog to see what pieces of data it needs and how you can transform this data into information. For the product catalog, you'll need at least three data tables: one for departments, one for categories, and one for products. It's important to note that physically each data table is an independent database object, even if logically it's part of a larger entity— in other words, even though we say that a category *contains* products, the table that contains the products is not inside the table that contains categories. This is not in contradiction with the relational character of the database. Figure 4-1 shows a simple representation of three data tables, including some selected sample data.

When two tables are related, this more specifically means that the *records* of those tables are related. So, if the products table is related to the categories table, this translates into each product record being somehow related to one of the records in the categories table.

Figure 4-1 doesn't show the physical representation of the database, so we didn't list the table names there. Diagrams like this are used to decide *what* needs to be stored in the database. After you know *what* to store, the next step is to decide *how* the listed data is related, which leads to the physical structure for the database. Although Figure 4-1 shows three kinds of data that you want to store, you'll learn later that to implement this structure in the database, you'll actually use four tables.

So, now that you know the data you want to store, let's think about how the three parts relate to each other. Apart from knowing that the records of two tables are related *somehow*, you also need to know *the kind of relationship* between them. Let's now take a closer look at the different ways in which two tables can be related.

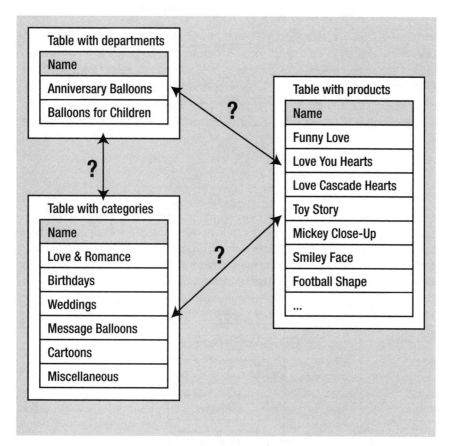

Figure 4-1. *Unrelated departments, categories, and products*

Relational Data and Table Relationships

To continue exploring the world of relational databases, let's further analyze the three logical tables we've been looking at so far. To make life easier, let's give them names now: the table containing products is Product, the table containing categories is Category, and the last one is our old friend, Department. No surprises here! These tables implement the most common kinds of relationships that exist between tables, the **One-to-Many** and **Many-to-Many** relationships, so you have the chance to learn about them.

■**Note** Some variations of these two relationship types exist, as well as the less popular One-to-One relationship. In the One-to-One relationship, each row in one table matches exactly one row in the other. For
example, in a database that allowed patients to be assigned to beds, you would hope that there would be a
one-to-one relationship between patients and beds! Database systems don't support enforcing this kind of
relationship, because you would have to add matching records in both tables at the same time. Moreover, two
tables with a One-to-One relationship can be joined to form a single table. No One-to-One relationships are
used in this book.

One-to-Many Relationships

The One-to-Many relationship happens when one record in a table can be associated with
multiple records in the related table, but not vice versa. In our catalog, this happens for the
Department–Category relation. A specific department can contain any number of categories,
but each category belongs to exactly one department. Figure 4-2 better represents the One-to-
Many relationship between departments and categories.

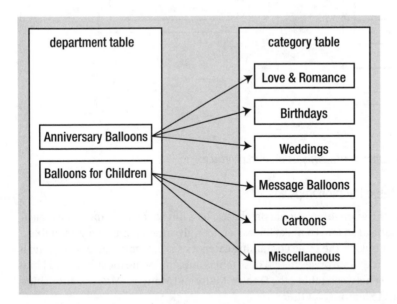

Figure 4-2. *A One-to-Many relationship between departments and categories*

Another common scenario in which you see the One-to-Many relationship is with the
Order–Order Details tables, where Order contains general details about the order (such as date,
total amount, and so on) and Order Details contains the products related to the order.

Many-to-Many Relationships

The other common type of relationship is the Many-to-Many relationship. This kind of relationship is implemented when records in both tables of the relationship can have multiple matching records in the other. In our scenario, this happens between the Product and Category tables, because a product can exist in more than one category (*one* product—*many* categories), and also a category can have more than one product (*one* category—*many* products).

This happens because we decided earlier that a product could be in more than one category. If a product belonged to a single category, you would have another One-to-Many relationship, just like that between departments and categories (where a category can't belong to more than one department).

If you represent this relationship with a picture as shown previously in Figure 4-2, but with generic names this time, you get something like what is shown in Figure 4-3.

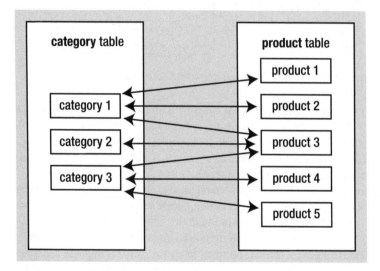

Figure 4-3. *The Many-to-Many relationship between categories and products*

Although logically the Many-to-Many relationship happens between two tables, databases don't have the means to physically implement this kind of relationship by using just two tables, so we cheat by adding a third table to the mix. This third table, called a junction table (also known as a *linking table* or *associate table*) and two One-to-Many relationships will help achieve the Many-to-Many relationship.

The junction table is used to associate products and categories, with no restriction on how many products can exist for a category or how many categories a product can be added to. Figure 4-4 shows the role of the junction table.

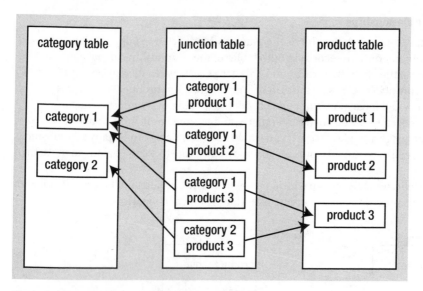

Figure 4-4. *The Many-to-Many relationship between categories and products*

Note that each record in the junction table links one category with one product. You can have as many records as you like in the junction table, linking any category to any product. The linking table contains two fields, each one referencing the primary key of one of the two linked tables. In our case, the junction table will contain two fields: a CategoryID field and a ProductID field.

Each record in the junction table will consist of a (ProductID, CategoryID) pair, which is used to associate a particular product with a particular category. By adding more records to the junction table, you can associate a product with more categories or a category with more products, effectively implementing the Many-to-Many relationship.

Because the Many-to-Many relationship is implemented using a third table that makes the connection between the linked tables, there is no need to add additional fields to the related tables in the way that you added DepartmentID to the category table for implementing the One-to-Many relationship.

There's no definitive naming convention to use for the junction table. Most of the time it's okay to just join the names of the two linked tables—in this case, our junction table will be named ProductCategory.

Enforcing Table Relationships with the FOREIGN KEY Constraint

Relationships between tables are physically enforced in the database using FOREIGN KEY constraints, or simply *foreign keys*.

You learned in the previous chapter about the PRIMARY KEY and UNIQUE constraints. We covered them there because they apply to the table as an individual entity. Foreign keys, on the other hand, always occur between two tables: the table in which the foreign key is defined (the referencing table) and the table the foreign key references (the referenced table).

> **Tip** Actually, the referencing table and the referenced table can be one and the same. You won't see this too often in practice, but it's not unusual, either. For example, you can have a table with employees, where each employee references the employee that is her or his boss (in this case, the big boss would probably reference itself).

SQL Server Books Online defines a foreign key as a column or combination of columns used to establish or enforce a link between data in two tables (usually representing a One-to-Many relationship). Foreign keys are used both to ensure data integrity and to establish a relationship between tables.

To enforce database integrity, the foreign keys, like the other types of constraints, apply certain restrictions. Unlike PRIMARY KEY and UNIQUE constraints that apply restrictions to a single table, the FOREIGN KEY constraint applies restrictions on both the referencing and referenced tables. For example, when enforcing a One-to-Many relationship between the Department table and the Category table by using a FOREIGN KEY constraint, the database includes this relationship as part of its integrity. The foreign key won't allow you to add a category to a nonexistent department, and it won't allow you to delete a department if categories belong to it.

You now know the general theory of foreign keys. You'll implement them in the following exercise, where you'll have the chance to learn more about how foreign keys work. A bit later, in the "Creating a Database Diagram" exercise, you'll learn how to visualize and implement foreign keys using the integrated diagramming feature in Visual Web Developer.

In the following exercises, you'll put into practice the new theory you learned on table relationships by creating and populating these tables:

- Category

- Product

- ProductCategory

Adding Categories

> **Tip** Remember that you can use the code in the Source Code area of the Apress web site (http://www.apress.com) to create and populate the data tables.

Exercise: Creating the Product Table and Relating It to Department

Essentially, creating the Category table is pretty much the same as the Department table you've already created, so we'll move pretty quickly. What makes this exercise special is that you'll learn how to implement and enforce the One-to-Many relationship between the Category and Department tables.

1. Using the **Database Explorer** (**Ctrl+Alt+S**), open the data connection to the BalloonShop database. When the database is selected, choose **Data ➤ Add New ➤ Table**. Alternatively, you can right-click the **Tables** node under **BalloonShop** and select **Add New Table**.

2. Add the columns shown in Table 4-1 using the form that appears.

Table 4-1. *Designing the Category Table*

Field Name	Data Type	Other Properties
CategoryID	int	Primary Key and Identity column
DepartmentID	int	Don't allow NULLs
Name	varchar(50)	Don't allow NULLs
Description	varchar(1000)	Allow NULLs

■**Tip** A quick reminder from the previous chapter: you set a column to be the primary key by right-clicking on it and clicking the **Set Primary Key** item from the context menu. You set it to be an identity column by expanding the **Identity Specification** item from its Column Properties window, and setting the **(Is Identity)** node to **Yes**. At this moment the form should look like Figure 4-5.

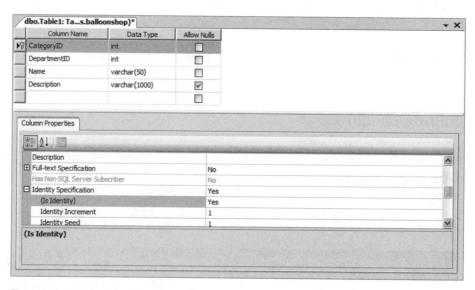

Figure 4-5. *Creating the Category table*

3. Press **Ctrl+S** to save the table. When asked, type **Category** for the table's name.

4. While the Category table is still selected, click **Table Designer ➤ Relationships**. Here is where you specify the details for the foreign key. This works by relating a column of the referencing table (Category) to a column of the referenced table (Department). You need to relate the DepartmentID column in Category with the DepartmentID column of the Department table.

5. In the dialog box that appears, click **Add**.

6. Select the **Tables and Columns Specifications** entry and click the "..." button that appears. In the dialog box that opens (see Figure 4-6), choose **Department** for the **Primary key table** and **DepartmentID** for the column on both tables.

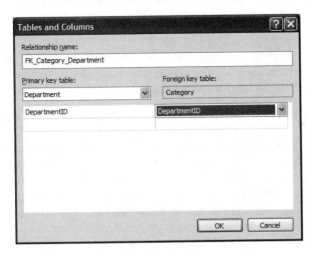

Figure 4-6. *Creating a new foreign key*

7. Click **OK** and then **Close** to save the relationship.

■**Tip** If anything goes wrong, delete the relationship, and then create it again.

---

8. Press **Ctrl+S** to save the table again. You'll be warned about the Category and Department tables being updated and asked for confirmation. This confirms again that a foreign-key relationship affects both tables that take part in the relationship. Click **Yes**.

How It Works: The One-to-Many Relationship

Okay, so you created and then enforced a relationship between the Category and Department tables. But how does it work, and how does it affect your work and life? Let's study how you implemented this relationship.

In the Category table, apart from the primary key and the usual CategoryID, Name and Description columns, you added a DepartmentID column. This column stores the ID of the department the category belongs to. Because the DepartmentID field in Category doesn't allow NULLs, you must supply a department for each category. Furthermore, because of the foreign-key relationship, the database won't allow you to specify a nonexistent department.

Actually, you can ask the database not to enforce the relationship. In the Foreign Key Relationships dialog box where you created the relationship, you can set a number of options for your foreign key. We left them with the default value, but let's see what they do:

- *Check existing data on creation:* If you set this to Yes, it doesn't allow the creation of the relationship if the existing database records don't comply with it. In other words, the relationship can't be created if orphaned categories are in the database (you have categories with a DepartmentID that references a nonexistent department).

- *Enforce For Replication:* This option applies to database replication, which is beyond the scope of this book. Replication is a technology that allows the synchronization of data between multiple SQL Servers situated at different locations.

- *Enforce Foreign Key Constraint:* This is probably the most important of the options. It tells SQL Server to make sure that database operations on the tables involved in the relationship don't break the relationship. When this option is selected, by default SQL Server won't allow you to add categories to nonexistent departments or delete departments that have related categories.

- *INSERT and UPDATE specification:* These options allow you to fine-tune the way SQL Server behaves when you delete or update data that would break data integrity. For example, if you set the Update Rule to Cascade, changing the ID of an existing department would cause the change to propagate to the Category table to keep the category-department associations intact. This way, even after you change the ID of the department, its categories would still belong to it (you can leave this option set to No Action because you won't need to change departments IDs.) Setting the Delete Rule to Cascade is a radical solution for keeping data integrity. If this is selected and you delete a department from the database, SQL Server automatically deletes all the department's related categories. This is a sensitive option and you should be very careful with it. You won't use it in the BalloonShop project.

In the One-to-Many relationship (and implicitly the FOREIGN KEY constraint), you link two columns from two different tables. One of these columns is a primary key, and it defines the One part of the relationship. In our case, DepartmentID is the primary key of Department, so Department is the one that connects to many categories. A primary key must be on the One part to ensure that it's unique—a category can't be linked to a department if you can't be sure that the department ID is unique. You must ensure that no two departments have the same ID; otherwise, the relationship wouldn't make much sense.

Now that you've created the Category table, you can populate it with some data. We'll also try to add data that would break the relationship that you established between the Department and Category tables.

Exercise: Adding Categories

1. Open the Category table for editing (right-click the table in **Database Explorer** and select **Show Table Data**).

2. Using the editor integrated with Visual Web Developer, you can start adding rows. Because `CategoryID` has been set as an identity column, you cannot manually edit its data—SQL Server automatically fills this field for you. However, you'll need to manually fill the `DepartmentID` field with ID values of existing departments. Alternatively, you can populate the `Category` table using the scripts from the Source Code area on the Apress web site (`http://www.apress.com`). Add categories as shown in Figure 4-7.

	CategoryID	DepartmentID	Name	Description
▶	1	1	Love & Romance	Here's our collection of balloons with romantic messages.
	2	1	Birthdays	Tell someone "Happy Birthday" with one of these wonderful balloons!
	3	1	Weddings	Going to a wedding? Here's a collection of balloons for that special event!
	4	2	Message Balloons	Why write on paper, when you can deliver your message on a balloon?
	5	2	Cartoons	Buy a balloon with your child's favorite cartoon character!
	6	2	Miscellaneous	Various baloons that your kid will most certainly love!
✳	NULL	NULL	NULL	NULL

Category: Quer...s.balloonshop)*

I◀ ◀ [1]   of 6 ▶ ▶I ▶▣ ⬤

Figure 4-7. *Populating the* Category *table*

■**Tip** Keep the `CategoryID` numbers in sequential order to make your life easier when associating them with product IDs later in this chapter. Remember that you can use the `TRUNCATE TABLE` command to empty the table's contents and reset the identity value.

---

3. Now, try to break the database integrity by adding a category to a nonexistent department (for example, set the `DepartmentID` to 500). After filling the new category data, try to move to the next row. At this point, Visual Web Developer submits the newly written data to SQL Server. If you've created the relationship properly, an error should occur (see Figure 4-8). For more detailed information about the error, click the **Help** button.

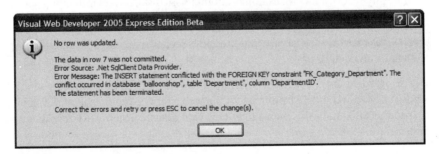

Visual Web Developer 2005 Express Edition Beta   [?][X]

ⓘ No row was updated.

The data in row 7 was not committed.
Error Source: .Net SqlClient Data Provider.
Error Message: The INSERT statement conflicted with the FOREIGN KEY constraint "FK_Category_Department". The conflict occurred in database "balloonshop", table "Department", column 'DepartmentID'.
The statement has been terminated.

Correct the errors and retry or press ESC to cancel the change(s).

[OK   ]

Figure 4-8. *The foreign key in action*

How It Works: Populating the Categories Table

Visual Web Developer makes it very easy to add new records to a data table. The only trick is to keep the generated CategoryID numbers in sequential order, as shown earlier in Figure 4-7. Otherwise, you won't be able to use the SQL scripts from the Source Code area on the Apress web site to populate the tables that relate to Category.

This can be tricky if you delete and add records in the table, because the autogenerated number keeps increasing, and you can't specify the ID manually. Erasing all the records of the table doesn't reset the autoincrement number. Instead, you need to truncate the table, or delete and re-create it. Another solution is to temporarily disable the (Is Identity) option, change the IDs manually, and then activate the option again.

Adding Products

Now that you've added categories and departments to the database, the next logical step is to add products. This is different from what you did when adding categories, because between Product and Category, you must implement a Many-to-Many relationship.

Here you'll create the Product and ProductCategory tables. The Product table contains a few more fields than the usual ProductID, Name, and Description. Most of them are pretty self-explanatory, but for completeness, let's look at each of them:

- ProductID uniquely identifies a product. It's the primary key of the table.

- Name stores the product's name.

- Description stores the product's description.

- Price stores the product's price.

- Image1FileName stores the name of the product's primary picture file (to be displayed on product lists). SQL Server can store binary data, including pictures, directly in the database, but we chose to store only the file names in the database and store the actual picture files in the Windows file system. This method also allows you to save the images in a separate physical location (for example, another hard disk), further improving performance for high-traffic web sites.

- Image2FileName stores the name of the product's secondary picture file, which is displayed on the product details page.

- OnCatalogPromotion is a bit field (can be set to either 0 or 1) that specifies whether the product is featured on the front page of the web site. The main page of the site will list the products that have this bit set to 1. This field doesn't accept NULLs and has a default value of 0.

- OnDepartmentPromotion is a bit field that specifies whether the product is featured on the department pages. When visiting a department, the visitor is shown only the featured products of that department. If a product belongs to more than one department (remember, it can belong to more than one category), it will be listed as featured on all those departments. This field doesn't accept NULLs and has a default value of 0.

Using those bit fields allows you to let the site administrators highlight a set of products that are particularly important at a specific time (for example, before Valentine's Day they will draw attention to the pink balloons, and so on).

Okay, enough talk; let's add the Product table to the database.

Exercise: Creating the Product Table and Relating It to Category

1. Using the steps that you already know, create a new Product table with the fields shown in Table 4-2.

Table 4-2. *Designing the Product Table*

Field Name	Data Type	Other Properties
ProductID	int	Primary Key and Identity column
Name	varchar(50)	Doesn't allow NULLs
Description	varchar(5000)	Doesn't allow NULLs
Price	money	Doesn't allow NULLs
Image1FileName	varchar(50)	Default value is GenericImage1.png
Image2FileName	varchar(50)	Default value is GenericImage2.png
OnCatalogPromotion	bit	Doesn't allow NULLs and has a default value of 0
OnDepartmentPromotion	bit	Doesn't allow NULLs and has a default value of 0

Tip You set a column's default value from the Default Value or Binding property in its Column Properties window.

After adding the fields, your table window will look like Figure 4-9.

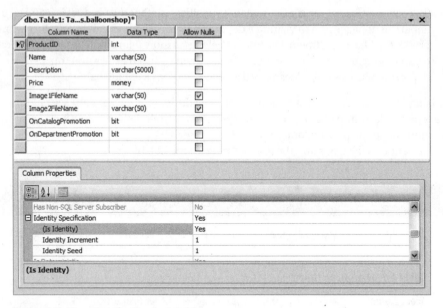

Figure 4-9. *Creating the Product table*

2. Press **Ctrl+S** to save the table and type **Product** for its name. Now you have a brand new Product table!

3. Because there are many products, populate this table by executing the PopulateProduct.sql script provided in the Source Code area on the Apress web site.

4. Now let's create the junction table to associate products to categories (implementing the Many-to-Many relationship between Product and Category). Create a new table with two fields, as shown in Figure 4-10.

Column Name	Data Type	Allow Nulls
ProductID	int	☑
CategoryID	int	☑
		☐

Figure 4-10. *Creating the Product table*

5. Now select both fields, ProductID and CategoryID, and click **Table Designer ➤ Set Primary Key**. Two golden keys appear on the left side, and the **Allow Nulls** check boxes are automatically unchecked (see Figure 4-11).

Column Name	Data Type	Allow Nulls
ProductID	int	☐
CategoryID	int	☐
		☐

Figure 4-11. *Creating the Product table*

6. Press **Ctrl+S** to save the newly created table. Its name is ProductCategory.

7. Expand your database node in Database Explorer, right-click the **Database Diagrams** node, and select **Add New Diagram** from the context menu (alternatively, you can choose **Data ➤ Add New ➤ Diagram**). If a dialog box that asks about creating database objects required for diagramming shows up, click **Yes**.

8. You'll see a dialog box as shown in Figure 4-12. Click **Add** four times to add all your tables to the diagram, and then click **Close**.

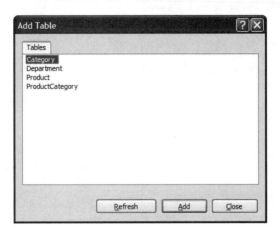

Figure 4-12. *Adding tables to the diagram*

9. Feel free to zoom the window and rearrange the tables on the diagram to fit nicely on the screen. With the default options, your diagram will look like Figure 4-13.

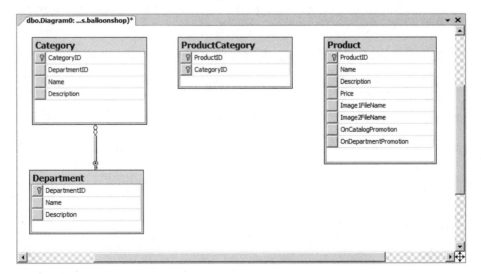

Figure 4-13. *Adding tables to the diagram*

To enforce the Many-to-Many relationship between Category and Product, you need to add two FOREIGN KEY constraints. In this exercise, you'll create these constraints visually.

10. Click the ProductID key in the ProductCategory table and drag it over the ProductID column of the Product table. The dialog box that adds a new foreign-key relationship shows up, already filled with the necessary data (see Figure 4-14).

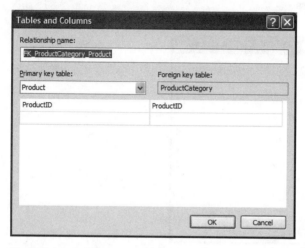

Figure 4-14. *Creating a new foreign key*

11. Click **OK** to confirm adding the foreign key, and then click **OK** again to close the Foreign Key Relationship dialog box.

12. Create a new relationship between the Category and ProductCategory tables on their CategoryID columns in the same way you did in steps 11 and 12. The diagram now reflects the new relationships (see Figure 4-15).

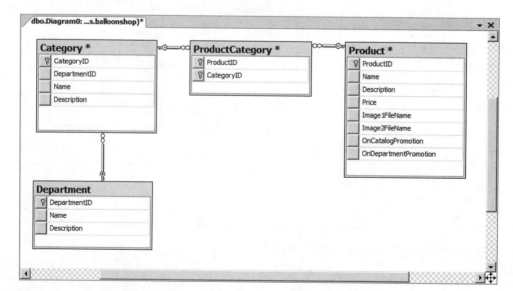

Figure 4-15. *Viewing tables and relationships using the database diagram*

13. Press **Ctrl+S** to save your diagram and the changes you made to your tables. When asked for a diagram name, type **CatalogDiagram**. You'll be warned that Product, Category, and ProductCategory will be saved to the database. Click **Yes** to confirm.

14. Populate the ProductCategory table by running the PopulateProductCategory.sql script provided in the Source Code area on the Apress web site.

How It Works: Many-to-Many Relationships and Database Diagrams

In this exercise, you created the Product table and implemented (and enforced) a Many-to-Many relationship with Category.

Many-to-Many relationships are created by adding a third table, called a junction table, which is named ProductCategory in this case. This table contains (ProductID, CategoryID) pairs, and each record in the table associates a particular product with a particular category. So, if you see a record such as (1,4) in ProductCategory, you know that the product with ProductID 1 belongs to the category with CategoryID 4.

The Many-to-Many relationship is physically enforced through two FOREIGN KEY constraints—one that links Product to ProductCategory, and the other that links ProductCategory to Category. In English, this means, "one product can be associated with many product-category entries, each of those being associated with one category." The foreign keys ensure that the products and categories that appear in the ProductCategory table actually exist in the database and won't allow you to delete a product if you have a category associated with it and vice versa.

This is also the first time that you set a primary key consisting of more than one column. The primary key of ProductCategory is formed by both its fields: ProductID and CategoryID. This means that you won't be allowed to have two identical (ProductID, CategoryID) pairs in the table. However, it's perfectly legal to have a ProductID or CategoryID appear more than once, as long as it's part of a unique (ProductID, CategoryID) pair. This makes sense, because you don't want to have two identical records in the ProductCategory table. A product can be associated with a particular category, or not; it cannot be associated with a category multiple times.

At first, all the theory about table relationships can be a bit confusing, until you get used to them. To understand the relationship more clearly, you can get a picture by using database diagrams like the ones you worked with in this exercise. Database diagrams are very useful. If, until now, you could only imagine the relationships between the different tables, the diagram allows you to see what actually happens. The diagram you created shows your three One-to-Many relationships.

The diagram also shows the type and direction of the relationships. Note that a key symbol appears at the One part of each relationship and an infinity symbol appears at the Many side of the relationship. The table whose whole primary key is involved in the relationship is at the One side of the relationship and is marked with the little golden key.

One of the most useful things about diagrams is that you can edit database objects directly from the diagram. If you right-click a table or a relationship, you'll see a lot of features there. Feel free to experiment a bit to get a feeling for the features available. Not only can you create foreign keys through the diagram, you can also create new tables, or design existing ones, directly within the diagram. To design one of the existing tables, you must switch the table to normal mode by right-clicking the table, and then choosing Table View ➤ Standard. When the table is in Standard View mode, you can edit it directly in the diagram, as shown in Figure 4-16.

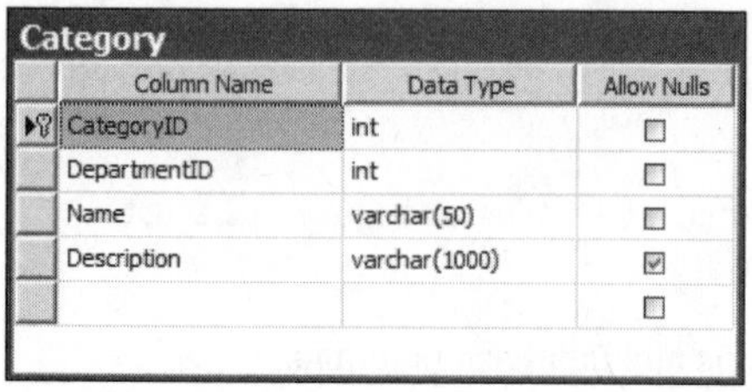

Figure 4-16. *Editing the table directly in the diagram*

Querying the New Data

Now you have a database with a wealth of information just waiting to be read by somebody. However, the new elements bring with them a set of new things you need to learn.

For this chapter, the data-tier logic is a little bit more complicated than in the previous chapter, because it must answer to queries like "give me the second page of products from the 'Cartoons' category" or "give me the products on promotion for department X." Before moving on to writing the stored procedures that implement this logic, let's first cover the theory about

- Retrieving short product descriptions

- Joining data tables

- Implementing paging

Let's deal with these monsters one by one.

Retrieving Short Product Descriptions

In our web site, product lists don't display complete product descriptions, but only a portion of them (the full descriptions are shown only in the product details pages). In T-SQL, you get the first characters of a string using the LEFT function. After extracting a part of the full description, you append "..." to the end using the + operator.

The following SELECT query returns all product's descriptions trimmed at 60 characters, with "..." appended:

```
SELECT LEFT(Description, 60) + '...' AS 'Short Description'
FROM Product
```

The new column generated by the (LEFT(Description, 60) + '...') expression doesn't have a name, so we created an alias for it using the AS keyword. With your current data, this query would return something like this:

```
Short Description
-----------------------------------------------------------------
An adorable romantic balloon by Simon Elvin. You'll fall in ...
A heart-shaped balloon with the great Elvis on it and the wo...
A red heart-shaped balloon with "I love you" written on a wh...
White heart-shaped balloon with the words "Today, Tomorrow a...
Red heart-shaped balloon with a smiley face. Perfect for say...
A red heart-shaped balloon with "I Love You" in script writi...
Red heart-shaped balloon with a smiley face and three kisses...
...
```

Joining Data Tables

Because the data is stored in several tables, you'll frequently run into situations in which not all the information you want is in one table. Take a look at the following list, which contains data from both the Department and Category tables:

```
Department Name                          Category Name
----------------------------------       -----------------------------------------
Anniversary Balloons                     Love & Romance
Anniversary Balloons                     Birthdays
Anniversary Balloons                     Weddings
Balloons for Children                    Message Balloons
Balloons for Children                    Cartoons
Balloons for Children                    Miscellaneous
```

In other cases, all the information you need is in just one table, but you need to place conditions on it based on the information in another table. You cannot get this kind of result set with simple queries such as the ones you've used so far. Needing a result set based on data from multiple tables is a good indication that you might need to use **table joins**.

When extracting the products that belong to a category, the SQL query isn't the same as when extracting the categories that belong to a department. This is because products and categories are linked through the ProductCategory junction table.

To get the list of products in a category, you first need to look in the ProductCategory table and get all the (ProductID, CategoryID) pairs where CategoryID is the ID of the category you're looking for. That list contains the IDs of the products in that category. Using these IDs, you can generate the required product list. Although this sounds complicated, it can be done using a single SQL query. The real power of SQL lies in its capability to perform complex operations on large amounts of data using simple queries.

You'll learn how to make table joins by analyzing the Product and ProductCategory tables and by analyzing how to get a list of products that belong to a certain category. Tables are joined in SQL using the JOIN clause. Joining one table with another table results in the columns (not the rows) of those tables being joined. When joining two tables, there always must be a common column on which the join will be made.

Suppose you want to get all the products in the category where CategoryID = 5. The query that joins the Product and ProductCategory tables is as follows:

```
SELECT ProductCategory.ProductID, ProductCategory.CategoryID, Product.Name
FROM ProductCategory INNER JOIN Product
ON Product.ProductID = ProductCategory.ProductID
```

The result will look something like this (to save space, the listing doesn't include all returned rows:

```
ProductID    CategoryID    Name
-----------  -----------   -------------------------------------------------
1            1             I Love You (Simon Elvin)
1            2             I Love You (Simon Elvin)
2            1             Elvis Hunka Burning Love
2            4             Elvis Hunka Burning Love
2            6             Elvis Hunka Burning Love
3            1             Funny Love
3            3             Funny Love
3            4             Funny Love
...
```

The resultant table is composed of the requested fields from the joined tables synchronized on the `ProductID` column, which was specified as the column to make the join on. You can see that the products that exist in more categories are listed more than once, once for each category they belong in, but this problem will go away after we filter the results to get only the products for a certain category.

Note that in the `SELECT` clause, the column names are prefixed by the table name. This is a requirement if columns exist in more than one table participating in the table join, such as `ProductID` in our case. For the other column, prefixing its name with the table name is optional, although it's a good practice to avoid confusion.

The query that returns only the products that belong to category 5 is

```
SELECT Product.ProductID, Product.Name
FROM ProductCategory INNER JOIN Product
ON Product.ProductID = ProductCategory.ProductID
WHERE ProductCategory.CategoryID = 5
```

The results are

```
ProductID    Name
-----------  ----------------------------------------------------
21           Baby Hi Little Angel
25           Tweety Stars
39           Toy Story
40           Rugrats Tommy & Chucky
41           Rugrats & Reptar Character
42           Tweety & Sylvester
43           Mickey Close-up
44           Minnie Close-up
45           Teletubbies Time
```

46	Barbie My Special Things
47	Paddington Bear
48	I Love You Snoopy
49	Pooh Adult
50	Pokemon Character
51	Pokemon Ash & Pikachu
53	Smiley Face
54	Soccer Shape
55	Goal Ball

A final thing worth discussing here is the use of **aliases**. Aliases aren't necessarily related to table joins, but they become especially useful (and sometimes necessary) when joining tables, and they assign different (usually) shorter names for the tables involved. Aliases are necessary when joining a table with itself, in which case you need to assign different aliases for its different instances to differentiate them. The following query returns the same products as the query before, but it uses aliases:

```
SELECT p.ProductID, p.Name
FROM ProductCategory pc INNER JOIN Product p
ON p.ProductID = pc.ProductID
WHERE pc.CategoryID = 5
```

Showing Products Page by Page

In case certain web sections need to list large numbers of products, it's useful to let the visitor browse them page by page, with a predefined (or configurable by the visitor) number of products per page.

Depending on the tier on your architecture where paging is performed, there are two main ways to implement paging:

- *Paging at the data tier level*: In this case, the database returns only the page of products the visitor wants to see.

- *Paging at the presentation tier level*: In this scenario, the data tier always returns the complete list of products for a certain section of the site, and the presentation tier objects (such as the GridView control) extract the requested page of products from the complete list. This method has potential performance problems especially when dealing with large result sets, because it transfers unnecessarily large quantities of data from the database to the presentation tier. Additional data also needs to be stored on the server's memory, unnecessarily consuming server resources.

In our web site, we'll implement paging at the data tier level, not only because of its better performance, but also because it allows you to learn some very useful tricks about database programming that you'll find useful when developing your web sites. Paging at the data tier level can be done in two main ways:

- You can use ASP.NET 2.0's new feature of the DbDataReader object, which has an overload of the ExecuteReader method that takes as parameter the page of records you're interested in.

- You can write stored procedures that return only the requested page of products.

The second alternative is more powerful because of flexibility and performance reasons. The automatic paging feature offered by ADO.NET usually doesn't yield optimal performance because under the hood it uses cursors. In case you aren't a database professional, you don't need to know what cursors are, besides the fact they usually offer the slowest method of SQL Server data access.

In the following pages, you'll learn how to write smart stored procedures that return a specific page of records. Say, the first time the visitor searches for something, only the first n matching products are retrieved from the database. Then, when the visitor clicks *Next page*, the next n rows are retrieved from the database, and so on. Because for your own project you may need to use various versions of SQL Server, we'll cover this theory for both SQL Server 2005 and SQL Sever 2000. The optimal method to implement paging using T-SQL code is different for each case because SQL Server 2005 has improvements to the T-SQL language that make your life easier.

Implementing Paging Using SQL Server 2005

Unlike SQL Server 2000, SQL Server 2005 has a new feature that allows for a very easy implementation of the paging functionality.

With SQL Server 2000 (and other relational database systems), the main problem is that result sets are always perceived as a group, and individual rows of the set aren't numbered (ranked) in any way. As a consequence, there was no straightforward way to say "I want the sixth to the tenth records of this list of products," because the database actually didn't know which those records were.

Note The problem was sometimes even more serious because unless some sorting criteria was implemented, the database didn't (and doesn't) guarantee that if the same SELECT statement is run twice, you get the resulted rows in the same order. Therefore, you couldn't know for sure that after the visitor sees the first five products and clicks "Next", products "six to ten" returned by the database are the ones you would expect.

To demonstrate the paging feature, we'll use the SELECT query that returns all the products of the catalog:

```
SELECT Name
FROM Product
```

Now, how do you take just one portion from this list of results, given that you know the page number and the number of products per page? (To retrieve the first n products, the simple answer is to use the TOP keyword in conjunction with SELECT, but that wouldn't work to get the *next* page of products.)

SQL Server 2005 has a ROW_NUMBER function that assigns consecutive row numbers, starting with 1, for each row returned by a SELECT statement. Because numbering can only be guaranteed to be consistent if a sorting criteria applies to the query, when using ROW_NUMBER, you also need to specify a column on which the rows are ordered prior to being numbered:

```
SELECT ROW_NUMBER() OVER (ORDER BY ProductID) AS Row, Name
FROM Product
```

This query will have a list of results such as the following:

```
Row                      Name
-------------------- ---------------------------------------------------
1                        I Love You (Simon Elvin)
2                        Elvis Hunka Burning Love
3                        Funny Love
4                        Today, Tomorrow & Forever
5                        Smiley Heart Red Balloon
6                        Love 24 Karat
7                        Smiley Kiss Red Balloon
8                        Love You Hearts
9                        Love Me Tender
10                       I Can't Get Enough of You Baby
...
```

To retrieve five products, namely the sixth to the tenth products of the list, you transform the previous query into a subquery and filter the results on the WHERE clause of the main query. The results of a subquery can be interpreted as a separate table, on which the main query applies (the AS keyword that follows the subquery assigns a name to this virtual "table"). The following T-SQL code returns the specified list of products:

```
SELECT Row, Name
FROM(
     SELECT ROW_NUMBER() OVER (ORDER BY ProductID) AS Row, Name
     FROM Product
     ) AS ProductsWithRowNumbers
WHERE Row >= 6 AND Row <= 10
```

Using Table Variables

If you get a set of data that you need to make further operations on, you're likely to need to save it either as a temporary table or in a TABLE variable. Both temporary tables and TABLE variables can be used just like normal tables, and are very useful for storing temporary data within the scope of a stored procedure.

In the stored procedures that return pages of products, you'll save the complete list of products in a TABLE variable, allowing you to count the total number of products (so you can tell the visitor the number of pages of products) before returning the specified page.

The code listing that follows shows you how to create a TABLE variable named @Products:

```
-- declare a new TABLE variable
DECLARE @Products TABLE
(RowNumber INT,
 ProductID INT,
 Name VARCHAR(50),
 Description VARCHAR(5000))
```

After creating this variable, you'll populate it with data using `INSERT INTO`:

```
-- populate the table variable with the complete list of products
INSERT INTO @Products
SELECT ROW_NUMBER() OVER (ORDER BY Product.ProductID) AS Row,
       ProductID, Name, Description
FROM Product
```

You can then retrieve data from this table object like this:

```
-- extract the requested page of products
SELECT Name, Description FROM @Products
WHERE RowNumber >= 6 AND RowNumber <= 10
```

IMPLEMENTING PAGING USING SQL SERVER 2000

The presented solution doesn't work with SQL Server 2000, because SQL Server 2000 doesn't support the `ROW_NUMBER` function used to generate the rank column. Instead, you need to use an `IDENTITY` column, which generates the rank you need. `IDENTITY` columns work with both `TABLE` variables and with temporary tables.

Of course, this technique works with SQL Server 2005 as well (actually, it works even better with SQL Server 2005). The technique is somewhat flawed because SQL Server 2000 (unlike SQL Server 2005) doesn't guarantee the temporary table will always get populated in the same order and that each product will get the same row number on two consecutive executions. In the worst scenario (which is likely to happen very rarely), the visitor can be presented, for example, the same product in two different pages of products. We'll consider this to be a minor disadvantage compared to the dramatic performance gains you'll get by using the paging technique that uses a temporary table, compared with other kinds of paging queries (that we don't cover in this book).

For variety, this time instead of using a `TABLE` variable, we'll use a temporary table. Temporary tables are just like normal data tables, except their names begin with # or ##. Using # specifies a **local temporary table** and ## marks a **global temporary table**. Local temporary tables are unique to the connection that created them, whereas global temporary tables are visible to all connections.

The following piece of code creates a local temporary table named `#Products` with three fields (`Row`, `ProductID`, and `Name`). Note the first field is an `IDENTITY` (auto-numbered) field. `IDENTITY` fields were discussed in Chapter 3.

```
/* Create the temporary table that will contain the search results */
CREATE TABLE #Products
(Row SMALLINT NOT NULL IDENTITY(1,1),
 ProductID INT,
 Name VARCHAR(50),
 Description VARCHAR(5000))
```

The next step is to populate this temporary table with the complete list of products using the `INSERT`➥ `INTO` statement. This process automatically assigns a row number to each product on the `IDENTITY` column:

```
/* Populate the temporary table, automatically assigning row numbers */
INSERT INTO #Products (ProductID, Name, Description)
SELECT ProductID, Name, Description
FROM Product
```

Finally, you extract the needed page of products from this temporary table:

```
/* Get page of products */
SELECT Name, Description
FROM #Products
WHERE Row >= 6 AND Row <= 10
```

Note Because you work with a local temporary table, if multiple users are performing searches at the same time, each user will create a separate version of the #Products table, because different users will access the database on different database connections. It's easy to imagine that things won't work exactly well if all connections worked with a single ##Products table.

Writing the New Stored Procedures

It's time to add the new stored procedures to the BalloonShop database, and then you'll have the chance to see them in action. For each stored procedure, you'll need its functionality somewhere in the presentation tier. You may want to refresh your memory by having a look at the first four figures in Chapter 3.

In this chapter, the data you need from the database depends on external parameters (such as the department selected by a visitor, the number of products per pages, and so on). You'll send this data to your stored procedures in the form of stored procedure parameters.

The syntax used to create a stored procedure with parameters is

```
CREATE PROCEDURE <procedure name>
[(
    <parameter name> <parameter type> [=<default value>] [INPUT|OUTPUT],
    <parameter name> <parameter type> [=<default value>] [INPUT|OUTPUT],
    ...
    ...
)]
AS
    <stored procedure body>
```

The portions between the square brackets are optional. Specifying parameters is optional, but if you specify them, they must be within parentheses. For each parameter, you must supply at least its name and data type.

You can optionally supply a default value for the parameter. In this case, if the calling function doesn't supply a value for this parameter, the default value will be used instead. Also you can specify whether the parameter is an input parameter or output parameter. By default, all parameters are input parameters. The value of output parameters can be set in the stored procedure and then read by the calling function after the stored procedure executes.

Stored procedure parameters are treated just like any other SQL variables, and their names start with @, as in @DepartmentID, @CategoryID, @ProductName, and so on. The simplest syntax for setting the value of an output parameter, inside the stored procedure, is as follows:

```
SELECT @DepartmentID = 5
```

Because you already know how to add stored procedures, we won't be using Exercises this time. Add the stored procedures discussed in the following sections to the BalloonShop database.

GetDepartmentDetails

The GetDepartmentDetails stored procedure is needed when the user selects a department in the product catalog. When this happens, the database must be queried again to find out the name and the description of the particular department.

The stored procedure receives the ID of the selected department as a parameter and returns its name and description. A bit later, when you create the business tier, you'll learn how to extract these values into individual variables after executing the stored procedure.

The code for GetDepartmentDetails is as follows:

```
CREATE PROCEDURE GetDepartmentDetails
(@DepartmentID int)
AS
SELECT Name, Description
FROM Department
WHERE DepartmentID = @DepartmentID
```

GetCategoryDetails

The GetCategoryDetails stored procedure is called when the visitor selects a category, and wants to find out more information about it, such as its name and description. Here's the code:

```
CREATE PROCEDURE GetCategoryDetails
(@CategoryID int)
AS
SELECT DepartmentID, Name, Description
FROM Category
WHERE CategoryID = @CategoryID
```

GetProductDetails

The GetCategoryDetails stored procedure is called to display a product details page. The information it needs to display is the name, description, price, and the second product image.

```
CREATE PROCEDURE GetProductDetails
(@ProductID int)
AS
SELECT Name, Description, Price, Image1FileName, Image2FileName,
       OnDepartmentPromotion, OnCatalogPromotion
FROM Product
WHERE ProductID = @ProductID
```

GetCategoriesInDepartment

When the visitor selects a particular department, apart from showing the department's details, you also want to display the categories that belong to that department. This is done using the GetCategoriesInDepartment procedure, which returns the list of categories in a department.

GetCategoriesInDepartment returns the IDs, names, and descriptions for the categories that belong to the department mentioned by the @DepartmentID input parameter:

```
CREATE PROCEDURE GetCategoriesInDepartment
(@DepartmentID int)
AS
SELECT CategoryID, Name, Description
FROM Category
WHERE DepartmentID = @DepartmentID
```

GetProductsOnCatalogPromotion

GetProductsOnCatalogPromotion returns a page of products that are on catalog promotion (have the OnCatalogPromotion bit field set to 1). This stored procedure employs much of the theory presented earlier in this chapter:

- The stored procedure saves the total number of products into the @HowManyProducts variable.

- A TABLE variable holds the complete list of products.

- The ROW_NUMBER function implements paging.

```
CREATE PROCEDURE GetProductsOnCatalogPromotion
(@DescriptionLength INT,
@PageNumber INT,
@ProductsPerPage INT,
@HowManyProducts INT OUTPUT)
AS

-- declare a new TABLE variable
DECLARE @Products TABLE
(RowNumber INT,
 ProductID INT,
 Name VARCHAR(50),
 Description VARCHAR(5000),
 Price MONEY,
 Image1FileName VARCHAR(50),
 Image2FileName VARCHAR(50),
 OnDepartmentPromotion bit,
 OnCatalogPromotion bit)
```

```
-- populate the table variable with the complete list of products
INSERT INTO @Products
SELECT ROW_NUMBER() OVER (ORDER BY Product.ProductID),
       ProductID, Name,
       SUBSTRING(Description, 1, @DescriptionLength) + '...' AS Description, Price,
       Image1FileName, Image2FileName, OnDepartmentPromotion, OnCatalogPromotion
FROM Product
WHERE OnCatalogPromotion = 1

-- return the total number of products using an OUTPUT variable
SELECT @HowManyProducts = COUNT(ProductID) FROM @Products

-- extract the requested page of products
SELECT ProductID, Name, Description, Price, Image1FileName,
       Image2FileName, OnDepartmentPromotion, OnCatalogPromotion
FROM @Products
WHERE RowNumber > (@PageNumber - 1) * @ProductsPerPage
  AND RowNumber <= @PageNumber * @ProductsPerPage
```

GetProductsInCategory

When a visitor selects a particular category from a department, you'll want to list all the products that belong to that category. For this, you'll use the GetProductsInCategory stored procedure. This stored procedure is much the same as GetProductsOnCatalogPromotion, except the actual query is a bit more complex (it involves a table join to retrieve the list of products in the specified category):

```
CREATE PROCEDURE GetProductsInCategory
(@CategoryID INT,
@DescriptionLength INT,
@PageNumber INT,
@ProductsPerPage INT,
@HowManyProducts INT OUTPUT)
AS

-- declare a new TABLE variable
DECLARE @Products TABLE
(RowNumber INT,
 ProductID INT,
 Name VARCHAR(50),
 Description VARCHAR(5000),
 Price MONEY,
 Image1FileName VARCHAR(50),
 Image2FileName VARCHAR(50),
 OnDepartmentPromotion bit,
 OnCatalogPromotion bit)
```

```
-- populate the table variable with the complete list of products
INSERT INTO @Products
SELECT ROW_NUMBER() OVER (ORDER BY Product.ProductID),
       Product.ProductID, Name,
       SUBSTRING(Description, 1, @DescriptionLength) + '...' AS Description, Price,
       Image1FileName, Image2FileName, OnDepartmentPromotion, OnCatalogPromotion
FROM Product INNER JOIN ProductCategory
  ON Product.ProductID = ProductCategory.ProductID
WHERE ProductCategory.CategoryID = @CategoryID

-- return the total number of products using an OUTPUT variable
SELECT @HowManyProducts = COUNT(ProductID) FROM @Products

-- extract the requested page of products
SELECT ProductID, Name, Description, Price, Image1FileName,
       Image2FileName, OnDepartmentPromotion, OnCatalogPromotion
FROM @Products
WHERE RowNumber > (@PageNumber - 1) * @ProductsPerPage
  AND RowNumber <= @PageNumber * @ProductsPerPage
```

GetProductsOnDepartmentPromotion

When the visitor selects a particular department, apart from needing to list its name, description, and list of categories (you wrote the necessary stored procedures for these tasks earlier), you also want to display the list of featured products for that department.

GetProductsOnDepartmentPromotion needs to return all the products that belong to a department and have the OnDepartmentPromotion bit set to 1. In GetProductsInCategory, you needed to make a table join to find out the products that belong to a specific category. Now that you need to do this for departments, the task is a bit more complicated because you can't directly know which products belong to which departments.

You know how to find categories that belong to a specific department (you did this in GetCategoriesInDepartment), and you know how to get the products that belong to a specific category (you did that in GetProductsInCategory). By combining this information, you can determine the list of products in a department. For this, you need two table joins. You'll also filter the final result to get only the products that have the OnDepartmentPromotion bit set to 1.

You'll also use the DISTINCT clause to filter the results to make sure you don't get the same record multiple times. This can happen when a product belongs to more than one category, and these categories are in the same department. In this situation, you would get the same product returned for each of the matching categories, unless you filter the results using DISTINCT. (Using DISTINCT also implies using a SELECT subquery that doesn't return row numbers when populating the @Products variable, because the rows would become different and using DISTINCT would make no more difference.)

```
CREATE PROCEDURE GetProductsOnDepartmentPromotion
(@DepartmentID INT,
@DescriptionLength INT,
@PageNumber INT,
@ProductsPerPage INT,
@HowManyProducts INT OUTPUT)
AS

-- declare a new TABLE variable
DECLARE @Products TABLE
(RowNumber INT,
 ProductID INT,
 Name VARCHAR(50),
 Description VARCHAR(5000),
 Price MONEY,
 Image1FileName VARCHAR(50),
 Image2FileName VARCHAR(50),
 OnDepartmentPromotion bit,
 OnCatalogPromotion bit)

-- populate the table variable with the complete list of products
INSERT INTO @Products
SELECT ROW_NUMBER() OVER (ORDER BY ProductID) AS Row,
       ProductID, Name, SUBSTRING(Description, 1, @DescriptionLength)
+ '...' AS Description,
       Price, Image1FileName, Image2FileName, OnDepartmentPromotion,
OnCatalogPromotion
FROM
(SELECT DISTINCT Product.ProductID, Product.Name,
  SUBSTRING(Product.Description, 1, @DescriptionLength) + '...' AS Description,
  Price, Image1FileName, Image2FileName, OnDepartmentPromotion, OnCatalogPromotion
  FROM Product INNER JOIN ProductCategory
                    ON Product.ProductID = ProductCategory.ProductID
             INNER JOIN Category
                    ON ProductCategory.CategoryID = Category.CategoryID
  WHERE Product.OnDepartmentPromotion = 1
    AND Category.DepartmentID = @DepartmentID
) AS ProductOnDepPr

-- return the total number of products using an OUTPUT variable
SELECT @HowManyProducts = COUNT(ProductID) FROM @Products

-- extract the requested page of products
SELECT ProductID, Name, Description, Price, Image1FileName,
       Image2FileName, OnDepartmentPromotion, OnCatalogPromotion
FROM @Products
WHERE RowNumber > (@PageNumber - 1) * @ProductsPerPage
  AND RowNumber <= @PageNumber * @ProductsPerPage
```

Using ADO.NET with Parameterized Stored Procedures

In this section, you'll learn a few more tricks for ADO.NET, mainly regarding dealing with stored procedure parameters. Let's start with the usual theory part, after which you'll write the code.

The ADO.NET class that deals with input and output stored procedure parameters is DbCommand. This shouldn't come as a big surprise—DbCommand is responsible for executing commands on the database, so it makes sense that it should also deal with their parameters. (Remember that DbCommand is just a generic class that will always contain a reference to a "real" command object, such as SqlCommand.)

Using Input Parameters

When adding an input parameter to a command object, you need to specify the parameter's name, data type, and value. The DbCommand object stores its parameters in a collection named Parameters, which contains DbParameter objects. Each DbParameter instance represents a parameter.

Given that you have a DbCommand object named comm, the following code snippet creates a DbParameter object for the command using the CreateParameter method, sets its properties, and adds the parameter to the command's Parameters collection.

```
// create a new parameter
DbParameter param = comm.CreateParameter();
param.ParameterName = "@DepartmentID";
param.Value = value;
param.DbType = DbType.Int32;
comm.Parameters.Add(param);
```

The command's CreateParameter method always returns a parameter object type specific to the data provider you're using, so the DbParameter object will actually reference a SqlParameter instance if you're using SQL Server, and so on.

Another important property of DbParameter is size, which is good to set for data types that don't have fixed values, such as VarChar. For numerical columns, specify the parameter size in bytes. For columns that store strings (such as Char, VarChar, or even Text), specify the size in number of characters. Longer strings are automatically truncated to the size specified for the parameter.

Using Output Parameters

Output stored procedure parameters behave like Out parameters in C#. They are much like return values, in that you set their value in the stored procedure and read it from the calling function after executing the procedure. Output parameters are especially useful when you have more return values, when you want to return noninteger data, or when you prefer to keep using the return value for indicating executing success (or for some other purpose).

The code that creates an output parameter is as follows:

```
// create a new parameter
param = comm.CreateParameter();
param.ParameterName = "@HowManyProducts";
param.Direction = ParameterDirection.Output;
param.DbType = DbType.Int32;
comm.Parameters.Add(param);
```

This is almost the same as the code for the input parameter, except instead of supplying a value for the parameter, you set its `Direction` property to `ParameterDirection.Output`. This tells the command that `@HowManyProducts` is an output parameter.

Stored Procedure Parameters Are Not Strongly Typed

When adding stored procedure parameters, you should use exactly the same name, type, and size as in the stored procedure. You don't always have to do it, however, because SQL Server is very flexible and automatically makes type conversions. For example, you could add `@DepartmentID` as a `VarChar` or even `NVarChar`, as long as the value you set it to is a string containing a number.

We recommend always specifying the correct data type for parameters, however, especially in the business tier. The `DbParameter` object will always check the value you assign to see if it corresponds to the specified data type, and if it doesn't, an exception is generated. This way, you can have the data tier check that no bogus values are sent to the database to corrupt your data.

The C# methods in the business tier (the `CatalogAccess` class) always take their parameters from the presentation tier as strings. We chose this approach for the architecture to keep the presentation tier from being bothered with the data types; for example, it simply doesn't care what kind of product IDs it works with (123 is just as welcome as ABC). It's the role of the business tier to interpret the data and test for its correctness.

Getting the Results Back from Output Parameters

After executing a stored procedure that has output parameters, you'll probably want to read the values returned in those parameters. You can do this by reading the parameters' values from the `DbParameter` object after executing it and closing the connection.

In your business tier code, you'll have a line like this, which will retrieve the value of the `@HowManyProducts` output parameter:

```
int howManyProducts = Int32.Parse(comm.Parameters["@HowManyProducts"].ToString());
```

In this example, `ToString()` is called to convert the returned value to a string, which is then parsed and transformed into an integer.

Completing the Business Tier Code

Most of your business tier code will consist of the new code you'll add to the `CatalogAccess` class. That code will use a few new configuration settings that you'll add to `web.config`:

- `ProductsPerPage` stores the maximum number of products to list on a page of products. If the entire list contains more items, the paging controls (next page/previous page) appear.

- ProductDescriptionLength stores the length of the product descriptions to be used in product lists. The entire description is shown only in the product details page.

- SiteName stores the name of your store, which will be used to compose catalog page names.

Let's add these settings in a short exercise.

Exercise: Adding New Configuration Settings

1. Open web.config and add the following entries to the <appSettings> node:

```
<appSettings>
  <add key="MailServer" value="localhost" />
  <add key="EnableErrorLogEmail" value="true" />
  <add key="ErrorLogEmail" value="errors@yourballoonshopxyz.com" />
  <add key="ProductsPerPage" value="6"/>
  <add key="ProductDescriptionLength" value="60"/>
  <add key="SiteName" value="BalloonShop"/>
</appSettings>
```

2. Open the BalloonShopConfiguration class and add two fields, whose values are loaded once by the static constructor of the class:

```
public static class BalloonShopConfiguration
{
  // Caches the connection string
  private readonly static string dbConnectionString;
  // Caches the data provider name
  private readonly static string dbProviderName;
  // Store the number of products per page
  private readonly static int productsPerPage;
  // Store the product description length for product lists
  private readonly static int productDescriptionLength;
  // Store the name of your shop
  private readonly static string siteName;

  // Initialize various properties in the constructor
  static BalloonShopConfiguration()
  {
    dbConnectionString =
ConfigurationManager.ConnectionStrings
["BalloonShopConnection"].ConnectionString;
    dbProviderName =
ConfigurationManager.ConnectionStrings["BalloonShopConnection"].ProviderName;
    productsPerPage =
Int32.Parse(ConfigurationManager.AppSettings["ProductsPerPage"]);
    productDescriptionLength =
```

```
    Int32.Parse(ConfigurationManager.AppSettings["ProductDescriptionLength"]);
      siteName = ConfigurationManager.AppSettings["SiteName"];
  }
```

3. Also in the `BalloonShopConfiguration` class, add the corresponding properties to return the values of the fields you've added in the previous step:

```
// Returns the maximum number of products to be displayed on a page
public static int ProductsPerPage
{
  get
  {
    return productsPerPage;
  }
}

// Returns the length of product descriptions in products lists
public static int ProductDescriptionLength
{
  get
  {
    return productDescriptionLength;
  }
}
// Returns the length of product descriptions in products lists
public static string SiteName
{
  get
  {
    return siteName;
  }
}
```

How It Works: Read-Only Fields and Constants

The `productsPerPage` and `productDescriptionLength` fields are marked as `readonly`. This mainly means that after setting their values in the class constructor, you can't change their values any more in any method. If you're curious to find more details about `readonly` and how `readonly` is different from `const`, read on.

The major similarity between the `readonly` and `const` fields is that you aren't allowed to change their values inside class methods or properties. The main difference is that whereas for constants you need to set their value at the time you write the code (their values must be known at compile-time), with `readonly` fields you are allowed to dynamically set their values in the class constructor.

Constant values are always replaced with their literal values by the compiler. If you look at the compiled code, you'll never know constants were used. You can use the `const` keyword only with value types (the primitive data types: `Int`, `Char`, `Float`, `Bool`, and so on), but not with reference types (such as the classes you're creating).

Readonly fields are handled differently. They don't have to be value types, and they can be initialized in the class constructor. Static `readonly` fields can be initialized only in the static class constructor, and instance `readonly` fields can be initialized only in the instance class constructor.

Note that in case of `readonly` fields of reference types, only the reference is kept read only. The inner data of the object can still be modified.

Let's now implement the business-tier methods. Each method calls exactly one stored procedure, and the methods are named exactly like the stored procedures they are calling. In Visual Studio, open the `CatalogAccess.cs` file you created in the previous chapter, and prepare to fill it with business logic.

GetDepartmentDetails

`GetDepartmentDetails` is called from the presentation tier when a department is clicked to display its name and description. The presentation tier passes the ID of the selected department, and you need to send back the name and the description of the selected department.

The `GetDepartmentDetails` method of the business tier uses the `GenericDataAccess.CreateCommand` method to get a `DbCommand` object and execute the `GetDepartmentDetails` stored procedure. The business tier wraps the returned data into a separate object and sends this object back to the presentation tier.

What object, you say? The technique is to create a separate class (or **struct**, in our case) for the particular purpose of storing data that you want to pass around. This struct is named `DepartmentDetails` and looks like this:

```
public struct DepartmentDetails
{
    public string Name;
    public string Description;
}
```

STRUCTS

A struct is a user-defined data type that is very similar to a class; it can contain constructors, fields, methods, and properties. Structs are declared using the `struct` keyword instead of `class`. Please consult separate documentation for more details, but as a quick reference here are some differences you should keep in mind:

- A struct is a value type, whereas classes are reference types. Internally, structs are implicitly derived from `System.ValueType`.

- Inheritance doesn't work with structs. A struct cannot derive from a class or from another struct; a class cannot derive from a struct.

- Structs always contain by default a parameterless, default constructor, which does nothing. You're allowed to add more overloads, but you can't add a parameterless constructor.

- Although structs are very powerful, they are mainly designed to act as containers for data rather than as fully featured objects. Because they are value types (and are stored on the stack), passing them around can be very fast. MSDN says that data structures smaller than 16 bytes may be handled more efficiently as structs rather than as classes.

You wrap the department's name and description into one DepartmentDetails object and send it back to the presentation tier. The DepartmentDetails class can be added in a separate file in the BusinessObjects folder or added to one of the existing files. Most of the time, you'll want to create a separate file for each class, but because in this case DepartmentDetails is more like a tool for the CatalogAccess class, we chose to add it to CatalogAccess.cs.

Add the DepartmentDetails class at the beginning of CatalogAccess.cs (but not inside the CatalogAccess class) like this:

```
using System;
using System.Data;
using System.Data.Common;

/// <summary>
/// Wraps department details data
/// </summary>
public struct DepartmentDetails
{
  public string Name;
  public string Description;
}


/// <summary>
/// Product catalog business tier component
/// </summary>
public class CatalogAccess
```

Now add the GetDepartmentDetails method to the CatalogAccess class. The exact location doesn't matter, but to keep the code organized, add it just after the GetDepartments method:

```
// get department details
public static DepartmentDetails GetDepartmentDetails(string departmentId)
{
  // get a configured DbCommand object
  DbCommand comm = GenericDataAccess.CreateCommand();
  // set the stored procedure name
  comm.CommandText = "GetDepartmentDetails";
  // create a new parameter
  DbParameter param = comm.CreateParameter();
  param.ParameterName = "@DepartmentID";
  param.Value = departmentId;
  param.DbType = DbType.Int32;
  comm.Parameters.Add(param);
  // execute the stored procedure
  DataTable table = GenericDataAccess.ExecuteSelectCommand(comm);
  // wrap retrieved data into a DepartmentDetails object
  DepartmentDetails details = new DepartmentDetails();
  if (table.Rows.Count > 0)
  {
```

```
      details.Name = table.Rows[0]["Name"].ToString();
      details.Description = table.Rows[0]["Description"].ToString();
    }
  // return department details
  return details;
}
```

You know what happens in this function fairly well because we analyzed portions of it in the first part of the chapter. Its main purpose is to send back the name and description of the relevant department. To do this, it calls the GetDepartmentDetails stored procedure, supplying it with a department ID. After execution, the function reads the @DepartmentName and @DepartmentDescription output parameters, saves them into a DepartmentDetails object, and sends this object back to the calling function.

GetCategoryDetails

History repeats itself in this section. Just as you needed to return a name and description for the selected department, now you need to do the same thing for the categories. You'll use the same technique here and wrap the data into a separate class.

Add the CategoryDetails struct at the beginning of CatalogAccess.cs. Don't place it inside the CatalogAccess class!

```
/// <summary>
/// Wraps category details data
/// </summary>
public struct CategoryDetails
{
  public int DepartmentId;
  public string Name;
  public string Description;
}
```

Next, add the GetCategoryDetails method to the CatalogAccess class. Except for the fact that it calls another stored procedure and uses another class to wrap the return information, it is identical to GetDepartmentDetails:

```
// Get category details
public static CategoryDetails GetCategoryDetails(string categoryId)
{
  // get a configured DbCommand object
  DbCommand comm = GenericDataAccess.CreateCommand();
  // set the stored procedure name
  comm.CommandText = "GetCategoryDetails";
  // create a new parameter
  DbParameter param = comm.CreateParameter();
  param.ParameterName = "@CategoryID";
  param.Value = categoryId;
  param.DbType = DbType.Int32;
  comm.Parameters.Add(param);
```

```
    // execute the stored procedure
    DataTable table = GenericDataAccess.ExecuteSelectCommand(comm);
    // wrap retrieved data into a CategoryDetails object
    CategoryDetails details = new CategoryDetails();
    if (table.Rows.Count > 0)
    {
      details.DepartmentId = Int32.Parse(table.Rows[0]["DepartmentID"].ToString());
      details.Name = table.Rows[0]["Name"].ToString();
      details.Description = table.Rows[0]["Description"].ToString();
    }
    // return department details
    return details;
}
```

GetProductDetails

Let's do the same with the product details now. Add the ProductDetails struct at the beginning of Catalog.cs. Don't place it inside the CatalogAccess class!

```
/// <summary>
/// Wraps product details data
/// </summary>
public struct ProductDetails
{
  public string Name;
  public string Description;
  public decimal Price;
  public string Image1FileName;
  public string Image2FileName;
  public bool OnDepartmentPromotion;
  public bool OnCatalogPromotion;
}
```

Add the GetProductDetails method to the CatalogAccess class:

```
// Get product details
public static ProductDetails GetProductDetails(string productId)
{
  // get a configured DbCommand object
  DbCommand comm = GenericDataAccess.CreateCommand();
  // set the stored procedure name
  comm.CommandText = "GetProductDetails";
  // create a new parameter
  DbParameter param = comm.CreateParameter();
  param.ParameterName = "@ProductID";
  param.Value = productId;
  param.DbType = DbType.Int32;
  comm.Parameters.Add(param);
```

```
  // execute the stored procedure
  DataTable table = GenericDataAccess.ExecuteSelectCommand(comm);
  // wrap retrieved data into a ProductDetails object
  ProductDetails details = new ProductDetails();
  if (table.Rows.Count > 0)
  {
    // get the first table row
    DataRow dr = table.Rows[0];
    // get product details
    details.Name = dr["Name"].ToString();
    details.Description = dr["Description"].ToString();
    details.Price = Decimal.Parse(dr["Price"].ToString());
    details.Image1FileName = dr["Image1FileName"].ToString();
    details.Image2FileName = dr["Image2FileName"].ToString();
    details.OnDepartmentPromotion =
bool.Parse(dr["OnDepartmentPromotion"].ToString());
    details.OnCatalogPromotion = bool.Parse(dr["OnCatalogPromotion"].ToString());
  }
  // return department details
  return details;
}
```

GetCategoriesInDepartment

The GetCategoriesInDepartment method is called to retrieve the list of categories that belong to a department. Add this function to the CatalogAccess class:

```
// retrieve the list of categories in a department
public static DataTable GetCategoriesInDepartment(string departmentId)
{
  // get a configured DbCommand object
  DbCommand comm = GenericDataAccess.CreateCommand();
  // set the stored procedure name
  comm.CommandText = "GetCategoriesInDepartment";
  // create a new parameter
  DbParameter param = comm.CreateParameter();
  param.ParameterName = "@DepartmentID";
  param.Value = departmentId;
  param.DbType = DbType.Int32;
  comm.Parameters.Add(param);
  // execute the stored procedure
  return GenericDataAccess.ExecuteSelectCommand(comm);
}
```

GetProductsOnCatalogPromotion

The methods that return products (GetProductsOnCatalogPromotion, GetProductsOn➡ DepartmentPromotion, GetProductsInCategory) are a bit more complex because they need to manage paging. This implies adding three parameters to the command objects: @PageNumber,

@ProductsPerPage, and @HowManyProducts. The latter is an output parameter, which will be set by the stored procedure to the total number of products for the section (so you can calculate and tell the visitor the number of pages of products). Another new parameter is @DescriptionLength, which specifies how many characters the product's description should be trimmed down to (remember that we don't show full product descriptions in product lists).

The GetProductsOnCatalogPromotion method gets the list of products featured on the main page of the site. It has two parameters: pageNumber and howManyPages. The latter parameter, howManyPages, is an out parameter. The values for the other two parameters needed for the GetProductsOnCatalogPromotion stored procedure (@DescriptionLength and @ProductsPerPage) are taken from the productsPerPage and productDescriptionLength class fields that you added earlier to the class.

When the presentation tier calls GetProductsOnCatalogPromotion, you send back the requested list of products in the form of a DataTable and the number of product subpages using the howManyPages out parameter.

Add this method to the CatalogAccess class:

```
// Retrieve the list of products on catalog promotion
public static DataTable GetProductsOnCatalogPromotion(string pageNumber,
                                                      out int howManyPages)
{
  // get a configured DbCommand object
  DbCommand comm = GenericDataAccess.CreateCommand();
  // set the stored procedure name
  comm.CommandText = "GetProductsOnCatalogPromotion";
  // create a new parameter
  DbParameter param = comm.CreateParameter();
  param.ParameterName = "@DescriptionLength";
  param.Value = BalloonShopConfiguration.ProductDescriptionLength;
  param.DbType = DbType.Int32;
  comm.Parameters.Add(param);
  // create a new parameter
  param = comm.CreateParameter();
  param.ParameterName = "@PageNumber";
  param.Value = pageNumber;
  param.DbType = DbType.Int32;
  comm.Parameters.Add(param);
  // create a new parameter
  param = comm.CreateParameter();
  param.ParameterName = "@ProductsPerPage";
  param.Value = BalloonShopConfiguration.ProductsPerPage;
  param.DbType = DbType.Int32;
  comm.Parameters.Add(param);
  // create a new parameter
  param = comm.CreateParameter();
  param.ParameterName = "@HowManyProducts";
  param.Direction = ParameterDirection.Output;
  param.DbType = DbType.Int32;
  comm.Parameters.Add(param);
```

```
  // execute the stored procedure and save the results in a DataTable
  DataTable table = GenericDataAccess.ExecuteSelectCommand(comm);
  // calculate how many pages of products and set the out parameter
  int howManyProducts = Int32.Parse(comm.Parameters
["@HowManyProducts"].Value.ToString());
  howManyPages = (int)Math.Ceiling((double)howManyProducts /
                  (double)BalloonShopConfiguration.ProductsPerPage);
  // return the page of products
  return table;
}
```

GetProductsOnDepartmentPromotion

The GetProductsOnDepartmentPromotion function returns the list of products featured for a
particular department. The department's featured products must be displayed when the
customer visits the home page of a department.

```
// retrieve the list of products featured for a department
public static DataTable GetProductsOnDepartmentPromotion
(string departmentId, string pageNumber, out int howManyPages)
{
  // get a configured DbCommand object
  DbCommand comm = GenericDataAccess.CreateCommand();
  // set the stored procedure name
  comm.CommandText = "GetProductsOnDepartmentPromotion";
  // create a new parameter
  DbParameter param = comm.CreateParameter();
  param.ParameterName = "@DepartmentID";
  param.Value = departmentId;
  param.DbType = DbType.Int32;
  comm.Parameters.Add(param);
  // create a new parameter
  param = comm.CreateParameter();
  param.ParameterName = "@DescriptionLength";
  param.Value = BalloonShopConfiguration.ProductDescriptionLength;
  param.DbType = DbType.Int32;
  comm.Parameters.Add(param);
  // create a new parameter
  param = comm.CreateParameter();
  param.ParameterName = "@PageNumber";
  param.Value = pageNumber;
  param.DbType = DbType.Int32;
  comm.Parameters.Add(param);
  // create a new parameter
  param = comm.CreateParameter();
  param.ParameterName = "@ProductsPerPage";
  param.Value = BalloonShopConfiguration.ProductsPerPage;
  param.DbType = DbType.Int32;
```

```
  comm.Parameters.Add(param);
  // create a new parameter
  param = comm.CreateParameter();
  param.ParameterName = "@HowManyProducts";
  param.Direction = ParameterDirection.Output;
  param.DbType = DbType.Int32;
  comm.Parameters.Add(param);
  // execute the stored procedure and save the results in a DataTable
  DataTable table = GenericDataAccess.ExecuteSelectCommand(comm);
  // calculate how many pages of products and set the out parameter
  int howManyProducts = Int32.Parse
(comm.Parameters["@HowManyProducts"].Value.ToString());
  howManyPages = (int)Math.Ceiling((double)howManyProducts /
                  (double)BalloonShopConfiguration.ProductsPerPage);
  // return the page of products
  return table;
}
```

GetProductsInCategory

GetProductsInCategory returns the list of products that belong to a particular category. Add the
following method to the CatalogAccess class:

```
// retrieve the list of products in a category
public static DataTable GetProductsInCategory
(string categoryId, string pageNumber, out int howManyPages)
{
  // get a configured DbCommand object
  DbCommand comm = GenericDataAccess.CreateCommand();
  // set the stored procedure name
  comm.CommandText = "GetProductsInCategory";
  // create a new parameter
  DbParameter param = comm.CreateParameter();
  param.ParameterName = "@CategoryID";
  param.Value = categoryId;
  param.DbType = DbType.Int32;
  comm.Parameters.Add(param);
  // create a new parameter
  param = comm.CreateParameter();
  param.ParameterName = "@DescriptionLength";
  param.Value = BalloonShopConfiguration.ProductDescriptionLength;
  param.DbType = DbType.Int32;
  comm.Parameters.Add(param);
  // create a new parameter
  param = comm.CreateParameter();
  param.ParameterName = "@PageNumber";
```

```
    param.Value = pageNumber;
    param.DbType = DbType.Int32;
    comm.Parameters.Add(param);
    // create a new parameter
    param = comm.CreateParameter();
    param.ParameterName = "@ProductsPerPage";
    param.Value = BalloonShopConfiguration.ProductsPerPage;
    param.DbType = DbType.Int32;
    comm.Parameters.Add(param);
    // create a new parameter
    param = comm.CreateParameter();
    param.ParameterName = "@HowManyProducts";
    param.Direction = ParameterDirection.Output;
    param.DbType = DbType.Int32;
    comm.Parameters.Add(param);
    // execute the stored procedure and save the results in a DataTable
    DataTable table = GenericDataAccess.ExecuteSelectCommand(comm);
    // calculate how many pages of products and set the out parameter
    int howManyProducts = Int32.Parse
(comm.Parameters["@HowManyProducts"].Value.ToString());
    howManyPages = (int)Math.Ceiling((double)howManyProducts /
                   (double)BalloonShopConfiguration.ProductsPerPage);
    // return the page of products
    return table;
}
```

Implementing the Presentation Tier

Once again, it's time to see some colors! Believe it or not, right now the data and business tiers of the product catalog are complete for this chapter (finally!). All you have to do is use their functionality in the presentation tier. In this final section, you'll create a few Web Forms and Web User Controls and integrate them into the existing project.

If you now execute the BalloonShop project and click one of the departments, you are redirected to Catalog.aspx (which at this moment doesn't exist), with a DepartmentID parameter in the query string that specifies the ID of the selected department:

http://localhost/BalloonShop/Catalog.aspx?DepartmentID=1

In the following sections, you'll write code that makes the catalog more friendly by actually responding when the visitor clicks on those links. In the following sections, you will

- Write the CategoriesList.ascx control, which will display the list of categories for the selected department. This new control is similar to DepartmentsList.ascx that you wrote in the previous chapter.

- Complete the functionality in Catalog.aspx, making it display the name and description of the selected department or category.

- Implement ProductsList.ascx, which will display the products for the currently visited page (the main page, a department page, or a category page).

- Implement Product.aspx, which will be the product details page. When the visitors click on a product in the products list, they will be redirected to an address like http://localhost:13319/BalloonShop/Product.aspx?ProductID=1.

Displaying the List of Categories

CategoriesList is similar to the DepartmentsList Web User Control. It consists of a DataList control that is populated with data retrieved from the business tier. The DataList control will contain links to Catalog.aspx, but this time the query string will also contain a CategoryID parameter, showing that a category has been clicked, like this:

http://localhost/BalloonShop/Catalog.aspx?DepartmentID=1&CategoryID=2

The steps in the following exercise are similar to the steps you followed to create the DepartmentsList user control, so we'll move a bit more quickly this time.

Exercise: Creating the CategoriesList Web User Control

1. Create a new Web User Control in the UserControls folder. In Solution Explorer, right-click the UserControls folder, and then choose **Add New Item**. Select the **Web User Control** template, and set CategoriesList.ascx (or simply CategoriesList) as its name. Make sure **Place code in separate file** is checked and click **Add**.

2. Set the properties on the DataList object as shown in Table 4-3.

Table 4-3. *Setting the DataList Properties*

Property Name	Value
(ID)	list
Width	200px
CssClass	CategoryListContent
HeaderStyle-CssClass	CategoryListHead

3. Switch to Design View, right-click the DataList, and select **Edit Template ➤ Header and Footer Templates**. Type **Choose a Category** in the **Header** template.

4. Right-click the DataList and select **Edit Template ➤ Item Templates**. Add a HyperLink control from the Standard tab of the toolbox to the **ItemTemplate**. Set the **Text** property of the HyperLink to an empty string.

5. Switch to Source View. The code auto-generated by Visual Studio for the hyperlink should look like this:

```
<asp:DataList ID="list" runat="server" CssClass="CategoryListContent"
Width="200px">
  <ItemTemplate>
    <asp:HyperLink ID="HyperLink1" runat="server"></asp:HyperLink>
  </ItemTemplate>
  <HeaderTemplate>
    Choose a Category
  </HeaderTemplate>
  <HeaderStyle CssClass="CategoryListHead" />
</asp:DataList>
```

6. Modify the code of the <ItemTemplate> element like this:

```
<ItemTemplate>
   &raquo;
  <asp:HyperLink
    ID="HyperLink1"
    Runat="server"
    NavigateUrl='<%# "../Catalog.aspx?DepartmentID=" +
Request.QueryString["DepartmentID"] +
"&CategoryID=" + Eval("CategoryID")  %>'
    Text='<%# Eval("Name") %>'
    ToolTip='<%# Eval("Description") %>'
    CssClass='<%# Eval("CategoryID").ToString() ==
Request.QueryString["CategoryID"] ?
"CategorySelected" : "CategoryUnselected" %>'>>
  </asp:HyperLink>
   &laquo;
</ItemTemplate>
```

7. Add a Label control after the DataList with no text. When the categories list is populated with data, you'll set the text of this label to <br/> for cosmetic reasons.

```
<asp:Label ID="brLabel" runat="server" Text="" />
```

Switching to Design View should reveal a window such as the one in Figure 4-17.

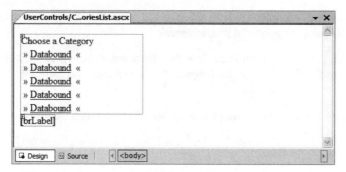

Figure 4-17. *CategoriesList.ascx* in Design View

8. Add the following styles to BalloonShop.css:

```css
.CategoryListHead
{
  border-right: #ea6d00 1px solid;
  border-top: #ea6d00 1px solid;
  border-left: #ea6d00 1px solid;
  border-bottom: #ea6d00 1px solid;
  background-color: #ef8d0e;
  font-family: Verdana, Arial;
  font-weight: bold;
  font-size: 10pt;
  color: #f5f5dc;
  text-align: center;
}
.CategoryListContent
{
  border-right: #ea6d00 1px solid;
  border-top: #ea6d00 1px solid;
  border-left: #ea6d00 1px solid;
  border-bottom: #ea6d00 1px solid;
  background-color: #f8c78c;
  text-align: center;
}
a.CategoryUnselected
{
  font-family: Verdana, Arial;
  font-weight: bold;
  font-size: 9pt;
  color: #cd853f;
  line-height: 25px;
  padding-right: 5px;
  padding-left: 5px;
  text-decoration: none;
}
```

```
a.CategoryUnselected:hover
{
  color: #d2691e;
  padding-right: 5px;
  padding-left: 5px
}
a.CategorySelected
{
  font-family: Verdana, Arial;
  font-weight: bold;
  font-size: 9pt;
  color: #a0522d;
  line-height: 25px;
  padding-right: 5px;
  padding-left: 5px;
  text-decoration: none
}
```

9. Now open the code-behind file of the user control (CategoriesList.ascx.cs) and modify the Page_Load event handler like this:

```
protected void Page_Load(object sender, EventArgs e)
{
  // Obtain the ID of the selected department
  string departmentId = Request.QueryString["DepartmentID"];
  // Continue only if DepartmentID exists in the query string
  if (departmentId != null)
  {
    // Catalog.GetCategoriesInDepartment returns a DataTable
    // object containing category data, which is displayed by the DataList
    list.DataSource =
CatalogAccess.GetCategoriesInDepartment(departmentId);
    // Needed to bind the data bound controls to the data source
    list.DataBind();
    // Make space for the next control
    brLabel.Text = "<br />";
  }
}
```

10. Open BalloonShop.master in Design View. Drag CategoriesList.ascx from **Solution Explorer** and drop it near the text that reads "List of Categories." Delete the text so that only the user control is there.

11. Execute the project, select a department, and then select a category. You should see something like Figure 4-18.

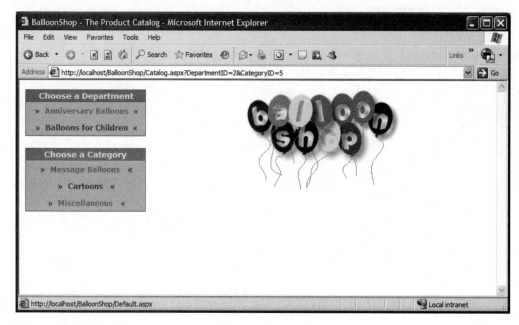

Figure 4-18. *BalloonShop with a brand new list of categories*

How It Works: The CategoriesList User Control

The important detail to know about CategoriesList is what happens when you click a category link: Catalog.aspx is reloaded, but this time, CategoryID is appended to the query string. In some of the other controls you'll create, you'll check for CategoryID in the query string—when it's present, this indicates that the visitor is browsing a category.

CategoriesList works like DepartmentsList, they are both used in the Master Page, and they both get loaded at the same time. However, when CategoriesList gets loaded and its Page_Load function executes, the code checks to determine whether a department was selected:

```
void Page_Load(object sender, EventArgs e)
{
    // Obtain the ID of the selected department
    string departmentId = Request.QueryString["DepartmentID"];
    // Continue only if DepartmentID exists in the query string
    if (departmentId != null)
    {
    ...
    ...
...
```

If the DataList isn't populated with data, it doesn't show at all. This is important, because if the visitor is on the main page and a department was not selected, no categories should show up.

On the other hand, if a department was selected, the business tier GetCategoriesInDeparment method of the CatalogAccess class is called to obtain the list of categories in that department:

```
// Continue only if DepartmentID exists in the query string
if (departmentId != null)
{
  // Catalog.GetCategoriesInDepartment returns a DataTable object
  // containing category data, which is displayed by the DataList
  list.DataSource =
CatalogAccess.GetCategoriesInDepartment(departmentId);
  // Needed to bind the data bound controls to the data source
  list.DataBind();
  // Make space for the next control
  brLabel.Text = "<br />";
}
```

> **Note** A final note about CategoriesList.ascx is that you're free to use it in other pages or even for other user controls. For example, you might want to add CategoriesList inside the SelectedItemTemplate element of the DataList in the DepartmentsList instead of placing in directly on the Master Page. Feel free to experiment and see how easy it is to change the look of the web site with just a few clicks!

Displaying Department and Category Details

Now the visitor can visit the main web page and select a department or a category. In each of these cases, your page contents cell must update itself with data about the selected department or category.

The good thing is that category and department pages have similar structure: they display the name of the selected category or department on the top, then the description, and finally a list of products. You'll use a single Web Form named Catalog.aspx, which handles generating both category and department pages. The list of products in those pages is generated by a separate Web User Control that you'll implement later.

In the following exercise, you implement Catalog.aspx, which hosts the details of the selected department of category.

Exercise: Displaying Department and Category Data

1. Open Catalog.aspx in **Source View**. You need to add two labels, named catalogTitleLabel and catalogDescriptionLabel, to the content part of the page. Feel free to use Design View to add them the way you like. Alternatively, use Source View to add the following HTML code, which also contains the mentioned labels:

```
<%@ Page Language="C#" MasterPageFile="~/BalloonShop.master"
AutoEventWireup="true" CodeFile="Catalog.aspx.cs" Inherits="Catalog"
Title="BalloonShop - The Product Catalog" %>
<asp:Content ID="content" ContentPlaceHolderID="contentPlaceHolder"
Runat="Server">
  <asp:Label ID="catalogTitleLabel" CssClass="CatalogTitle"
Runat="server" />
  <br />
  <asp:Label ID="catalogDescriptionLabel" CssClass="CatalogDescription"
 Runat="server" />
  <br />
  [Place List of Products Here]
</asp:Content>
```

2. Open `Default.aspx` in **Source View** and edit the content placeholder like this:

```
<asp:Content ID="content" ContentPlaceHolderID="contentPlaceHolder"
 Runat="server">
  <span class="CatalogTitle">Welcome to BalloonShop! </span>
  <br />
  <span class="CatalogDescription">This week we have a special price
 for these fantastic products: </span>
  <br />
  [Place List of Products Here]
</asp:Content>
```

3. Add the following styles to `BalloonShop.css`:

```
.CatalogTitle
{
  color: red;
  font-family: 'Trebuchet MS', Comic Sans MS, Arial;
  font-size: 24px;
  font-weight: bold;
}
.CatalogDescription
{
  color: Black;
  font-family: Verdana, Helvetica, sans-serif;
  font-weight: bold;
  font-size: 14px;
}
```

4. It's time to write the code that populates the two labels with data from the database. Add the following code to the `Catalog` class, in `Catalog.aspx.cs`:

```csharp
public partial class Catalog : System.Web.UI.Page
{
  protected void Page_Load(object sender, EventArgs e)
  {
    PopulateControls();
  }
  // Fill the page with data
  private void PopulateControls()
  {
    // Retrieve DepartmentID from the query string
    string departmentId = Request.QueryString["DepartmentID"];
    // Retrieve CategoryID from the query string
    string categoryId = Request.QueryString["CategoryID"];
    // If browsing a category...
    if (categoryId != null)
    {
      // Retrieve category details and display them
      CategoryDetails cd = CatalogAccess.GetCategoryDetails(categoryId);
      catalogTitleLabel.Text = cd.Name;
      catalogDescriptionLabel.Text = cd.Description;
      // Set the title of the page
      this.Title = BalloonShopConfiguration.SiteName +
                " : Category : " + cd.Name;
    }
    // If browsing a department...
    else if (departmentId != null)
    {
      // Retrieve department details and display them
      DepartmentDetails dd =
  CatalogAccess.GetDepartmentDetails(departmentId);
      catalogTitleLabel.Text = dd.Name;
      catalogDescriptionLabel.Text = dd.Description;
      // Set the title of the page
      this.Title = BalloonShopConfiguration.SiteName +
                " : Department : " + dd.Name;
    }
  }
}
```

5. Execute the project and click one of the departments. You should get something like Figure 4-19. Then do the same test for categories.

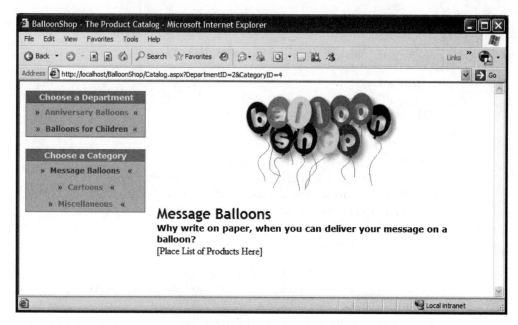

Figure 4-19. *Displaying category and department details*

How It Works: Displaying Department and Category Data

BalloonShop started looking almost like a real web site, didn't it? In this exercise you started by adding some controls to Catalog.aspx that display the name and description of the selected department or category. You also added some text to Default.aspx that gets displayed on the main page of your catalog. Both Catalog.aspx and Default.aspx contain the [Place list of products here] text; you'll replace this text with the actual list of products in the next section.

The work of displaying department and category data is done in the PopulateControls method in Catalog.aspx.cs. To determine whether the visitor is browsing a department or a category, the method needs to check out the values of CategoryID and DepartmentID in the query string, so it saves the values of these parameters as local variables:

```
// Retrieve DepartmentID from the query string
string departmentId = Request.QueryString["DepartmentID"];
// Retrieve CategoryID from the query string
string categoryId = Request.QueryString["CategoryID"];
```

Next it determines whether a value has been supplied for CategoryID; if it hasn't, CategoryID will be NULL. Otherwise, if CategoryId has a value, its details are obtained using the CatalogAccess.GetCategoryDetails method of the business tier. These details come packed as a CategoryDetails object:

```
// If browsing a category...
if (categoryId != null)
{
  // Retrieve category details and display them
  CategoryDetails cd = CatalogAccess.GetCategoryDetails(categoryId);
  catalogTitleLabel.Text = cd.Name;
  catalogDescriptionLabel.Text = cd.Description;
}
```

If `CategoryId` is NULL, you could assume the visitor is browsing a department and display the department's data (Catalog.aspx is loaded only if the visitor has clicked on a department or a category). However, for safety, you do an extra check on `DepartmentId`'s value, and if it's not NULL, loads its data from the business tier:

```
// If browsing a department...
else if (departmentId != null)
{
  // Retrieve department details and display them
  DepartmentDetails dd = CatalogAccess.GetDepartmentDetails(departmentId);
  catalogTitleLabel.Text = dd.Name;
  catalogDescriptionLabel.Text = dd.Description;
}
```

Displaying Product Lists

So where's the meat? Your web site will display product lists using a Web User Control named `ProductsList.ascx`. In theory, this control is very much alike `CategoriesList.ascx` and `DepartmentsList.ascx`, in that it uses a `DataList` control to generate a list of items. In practice, implementing this control is a little bit more complicated because there's more code to write.

This control also needs to support the paging feature offered by the business tier. It needs to display controls to allow the visitor to move forward and backward between pages of products. The product's name and picture are links to the product details page, which is dealt with by a Web Form named `Product.aspx` (you'll write this one later).

Let's go.

Exercise: Creating the `ProductsList` Web User Control

1. Copy the **ProductImages** folder from the Source Code area on the Apress web site to your BalloonShop solution.

2. Add a new Web User Control named **ProductsList** to the UserControls folder.

3. While in Source View, add the following code that will generate the "Page x of y … Previous … Next" text in sections of products that have more pages.

```
<asp:Label ID="pagingLabel" Runat="server"
         CssClass="PagingText" Visible="false" />
  
<asp:HyperLink ID="previousLink" Runat="server"
           CssClass="PagingText" Visible="false">Previous</asp:HyperLink>
  
<asp:HyperLink ID="nextLink" Runat="server"
             CssClass="PagingText" Visible="false">Next</asp:HyperLink>
```

4. Open the control in Design View, and drag a DataList control from the toolbox to the bottom of the control.

5. Rename the ID of the DataList to **list**, and set its **RepeatColumns** property to **2** (specifies the number of products to be displayed per row), and **RepeatDirection** to **Horizontal**.

6. Edit the DataList's code directly in Source View:

```
<asp:DataList ID="list" Runat="server" RepeatColumns="2">
  <ItemTemplate>
    <table cellPadding="0" align="left">
      <tr height="105">
        <td align="center" width="110">
          <a href='Product.aspx?ProductID=<%# Eval("ProductID")%>'>
            <img width="100" src='ProductImages/
<%# Eval("Image1FileName") %>' border="0"/>
          </a>
        </td>
        <td vAlign="top" width="250">
          <a class="ProductName" href='Product.aspx?ProductID=
<%# Eval("ProductID")%>'>
            <%# Eval("Name") %>
          </a>
          <br/>
          <span class="ProductDescription">
            <%# Eval("Description") %>
            <br/><br/>
            Price:
          </span>
          <span class="ProductPrice">
            <%# Eval("Price", "{0:c}") %>
          </span>
        </td>
      </tr>
    </table>
  </ItemTemplate>
</asp:DataList>
```

7. Add these styles to `BalloonShop.css`:

```
a.ProductName
{
  color: Red;
  font-family: 'Trebuchet MS';
  text-decoration: none;
  font-weight: bold;
  font-size: 12px;
}
a.ProductName:hover
{
  text-decoration: underline;
}
.ProductDescription
{
  color: Black;
  font-family: Verdana, Helvetica, sans-serif;
  font-size: 11px;
}
.ProductPrice
{
  color: Black;
  font-family: Verdana, Helvetica, sans-serif;
  font-weight: bold;
  font-size: 11px;
}
.PagingText
{
  font-family: Verdana, Helvetica, sans-serif;
  font-size: 11px;
  color: Black;
}
```

8. The way ASP.NET outputs product prices to the visitor depends on the culture settings of the computer running the site. You told ASP.NET which numbers represent prices by using the {0:C} formatting parameter in the `Eval` expression. For example, if the default culture is set to `fr-FR`, instead of $1.23 you would see 1,23EUR. (For more information on internationalization issues, consult an advanced ASP.NET book.) For now, to make sure the prices are expressed in the same currency (U.S. dollars for this example), double-click `web.config` in Solution Explorer and add the `<globalization>` element under `<system.web>`, like this:

```
...
    <globalization requestEncoding="utf-8" responseEncoding="utf-8"
                   culture="en-US"/>
  </system.web>
</configuration>
```

This ensures that no matter how the development (or production) machine is set up, your prices will always be expressed in the same currency.

9. Modify `ProductsList` class in `ProductsList.ascx.cs` like this:

```
using System.Collections.Specialized;

public partial class ProductsList : System.Web.UI.UserControl
{
  protected void Page_Load(object sender, EventArgs e)
  {
    PopulateControls();
  }

  private void PopulateControls()
  {
    // Retrieve DepartmentID from the query string
    string departmentId = Request.QueryString["DepartmentID"];
    // Retrieve CategoryID from the query string
    string categoryId = Request.QueryString["CategoryID"];
    // Retrieve Page from the query string
    string page = Request.QueryString["Page"];
    if (page == null) page = "1";
    // How many pages of products?
    int howManyPages = 1;
    // If browsing a category...
    if (categoryId != null)
    {
      // Retrieve list of products in a category
      list.DataSource =
CatalogAccess.GetProductsInCategory(categoryId, page, out howManyPages);
      list.DataBind();
    }
    else if (departmentId != null)
    {
      // Retrieve list of products on department promotion
      list.DataSource = CatalogAccess.GetProductsOnDepartmentPromotion
(departmentId, page, out howManyPages);
      list.DataBind();
    }
    else
    {
      // Retrieve list of products on catalog promotion
      list.DataSource =
CatalogAccess.GetProductsOnCatalogPromotion(page, out howManyPages);
      list.DataBind();
    }
```

```
    // display paging controls
    if (howManyPages > 1)
    {
      // have the current page as integer
      int currentPage = Int32.Parse(page);
      // make controls visible
      pagingLabel.Visible = true;
      previousLink.Visible = true;
      nextLink.Visible = true;
      // set the paging text
      pagingLabel.Text = "Page " + page + " of " + howManyPages.ToString();
      // create the Previous link
      if (currentPage == 1)
        previousLink.Enabled = false;
      else
      {
        NameValueCollection query = Request.QueryString;
        string paramName, newQueryString = "?";
        for (int i = 0; i < query.Count; i++)
          if (query.AllKeys[i] != null)
            if ((paramName = query.AllKeys[i].ToString()).ToUpper() != "PAGE")
              newQueryString += paramName + "=" + query[i] + "&";
        previousLink.NavigateUrl = Request.Url.AbsolutePath + newQueryString
+ "Page=" + (currentPage - 1).ToString();
      }
      // create the Next link
      if (currentPage == howManyPages)
        nextLink.Enabled = false;
      else
      {
        NameValueCollection query = Request.QueryString;
        string paramName, newQueryString = "?";
        for (int i = 0; i < query.Count; i++)
          if (query.AllKeys[i] != null)
            if ((paramName = query.AllKeys[i].ToString()).ToUpper() != "PAGE")
              newQueryString += paramName + "=" + query[i] + "&";
        nextLink.NavigateUrl = Request.Url.AbsolutePath + newQueryString +
"Page=" + (currentPage + 1).ToString();
      }
    }
  }
}
```

10. Open **Catalog.aspx** in Design View. Drag **ProductsList.ascx** from Solution Explorer, drop it near
    the **[Place List of Products Here]** text, and then delete the text, as shown in Figure 4-20.

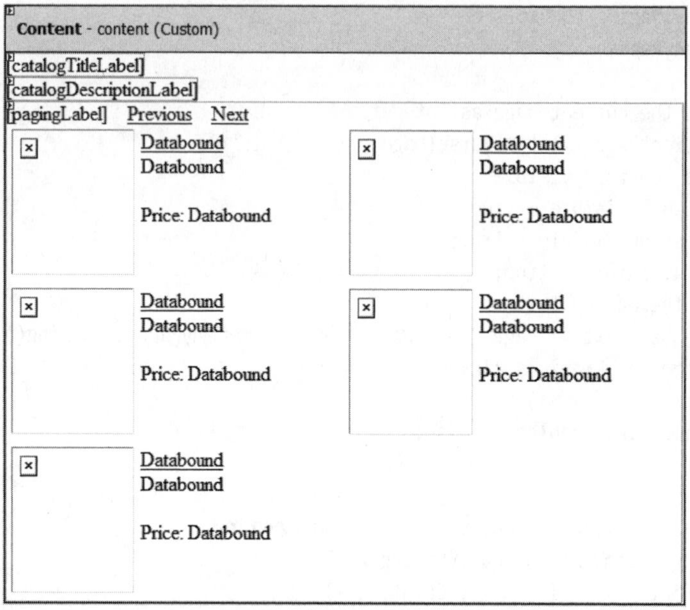

Figure 4-20. *Adding ProductsList.ascx to Catalog.aspx*

11. Now do the same in Default.aspx.

12. Press **F5** to execute the project. The main page should now be populated with its featured products (see Figure 4-21).

■Note To see the product images, make sure you have the ProductImages folder available (located in your project's folder) from the Source Code area on the Apress web site (http://www.apress.com).

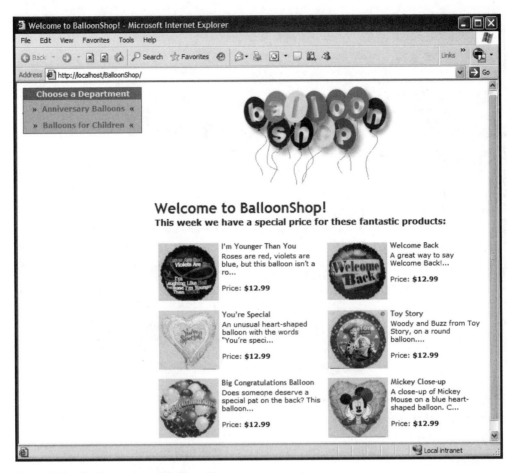

Figure 4-21. *The front page of BalloonShop*

13. Now click a department to see the department's featured products, and then click a category to see all the products in that category. Figure 4-22 shows the paging feature in action.

Figure 4-22. *Paging in action*

How It Works: The `ProductsList` Web User Control

`ProductsList.ascx`, just like `CategoriesList.ascx` and `DepartmentsList.ascx`, uses a `DataList` to paint a list of items. Because `ProductsList.ascx` will be reused in both `Default.aspx` and `Catalog.aspx`, you can't know beforehand exactly what it needs to display. Is it the list of products on catalog promotion, or is it the list of products in a particular category? In the usual style, `ProductsList` decides what it needs to display by analyzing the query string parameters. The logic is simple, so we won't go through it again here.

The first two new issues you played with in this exercise are the globalization setting and the paging controls. Setting the application to use the `en-US` culture ensures that monetary data (product prices) will always be displayed using the dollar symbol, no matter the settings of the computer that hosts the application.

Paging works through a query string parameter named `Page`. When a list of products is to be displayed and `Page` doesn't show up in the query string, the code automatically assumes the visitor is on the first page. For example, both these links would forward the visitor to the first page of products for the main page of the catalog:

```
http://localhost/BalloonShop/Catalog.aspx?DepartmentID=1
http://localhost/BalloonShop/Catalog.aspx?DepartmentID=1&Page=1
```

The Previous and Next links have the simple role of incrementing or decrementing the value of the Page query string parameter. Note that the paging controls only appear if there's more than one subpage of products. You find out this detail from the business tier GetProducts... functions, which return the total number of subpages through the howManyPages out parameter:

```
    // If browsing a category...
    if (categoryId != null)
    {
        // Retrieve list of products in a category
        list.DataSource =
  CatalogAccess.GetProductsInCategory(categoryId, page, out howManyPages);
        list.DataBind();
    }
```

You make the paging controls visible only if the number of subpages is greater than 1:

```
        // display paging controls
        if (howManyPages > 1)
```

When making the paging controls visible, the main challenge is to build the links for Previous and Next. For example, the Next link should be the same as the currently loaded page, except the Page value in the query string should incremented by one, but it shouldn't be enabled if the visitor is on the last page. You do this by browsing through the collection of query string parameters and reconstructing the complete query string:

```
        // create the Next link
        if (currentPage == howManyPages)
          nextLink.Enabled = false;
        else
        {
          NameValueCollection query = Request.QueryString;
          string paramName, newQueryString = "?";
          for (int i = 0; i < query.Count; i++)
            if (query.AllKeys[i] != null)
              if ((paramName = query.AllKeys[i].ToString()).ToUpper() != "PAGE")
                newQueryString += paramName + "=" + query[i] + "&";
          nextLink.NavigateUrl = Request.Url.AbsolutePath +
      newQueryString + "Page=" + (currentPage + 1).ToString();
        }
```

The logic that builds the Previous link is similar to the code for the Next link.

Displaying Product Details

This is the last bit of the UI for this chapter. Product lists contain links to the product details pages, which is dealt with by a Web Form named Product.aspx that you'll write in the following exercise.

Exercise: Displaying Product Details

1. Add a new Web Form named **Product.aspx** to your project, based on the **BalloonShop.master** Master Page.

2. The Web Form opens by default in Source View. The product details page needs to display the product's name in a Label control named titleLabel, the product's description in a Label named descriptionLabel, the price in a Label named priceLabel, and the image in an Image control named productImage. Feel free to arrange these items in any way you like. Here's how we placed them in Product.aspx (note their CssLabel property as well):

```
<%@ Page Language="C#" MasterPageFile="~/BalloonShop.master"
AutoEventWireup="true" CodeFile="Product.aspx.cs" Inherits="Product"
Title="BalloonShop - Product Details Page" %>
<asp:Content ID="content" ContentPlaceHolderID="contentPlaceHolder"
Runat="Server">
<br/>
<asp:Label CssClass="ProductTitle" ID="titleLabel"
Runat="server" Text="Label"></asp:Label>
<br/><br/>
<asp:Image ID="productImage" Runat="server" />
<br/>
<asp:Label CssClass="ProductDescription" ID="descriptionLabel"
Runat="server" Text="Label"></asp:Label>
<br/><br/>
<span class="ProductDescription">Price:</span> 
<asp:Label CssClass="ProductPrice" ID="priceLabel"
Runat="server" Text="Label"></asp:Label>
<br/><br/>
</asp:Content>
```

3. Add the following style to BalloonShop.css:

```
.ProductTitle
{
  color: Blue;
  font-family: Verdana, Helvetica, sans-serif;
  text-decoration: none;
  font-size: 24px;
  font-weight: bold;
  line-height: 15px;
}
```

4. Let's now read the necessary data from the database to set up the labels and the image. Add the following code to the page's Page_Load event handler method in Product.aspx.cs:

```
public partial class Product : System.Web.UI.Page
{
  protected void Page_Load(object sender, EventArgs e)
  {
    PopulateControls();
  }

  // Fill the control with data
  private void PopulateControls()
  {
    // Retrieve ProductID from the query string
    string productId = Request.QueryString["ProductID"];
    // stores product details
    ProductDetails pd;
    // Retrieve product details
    pd = CatalogAccess.GetProductDetails(productId);
    // Display product details
    titleLabel.Text = pd.Name;
    descriptionLabel.Text = pd.Description;
    priceLabel.Text = String.Format("{0:c}", pd.Price);
    productImage.ImageUrl = "ProductImages/" + pd.Image2FileName;
    // Set the title of the page
    this.Title = BalloonShopConfiguration.SiteName +
                 " : Product : " + pd.Name;
  }
}
```

5. Congratulations, you've finished! Execute the project to ensure everything works as expected.

Summary

You've done a lot of work in this chapter. You finished building the product catalog by implementing the necessary logic in the data, business, and presentation tiers. On the way, you learned about many new theory issues, including

- Relational data and the types of relationships that can occur between tables

- How to obtain data from multiple tables in a single result set using JOIN and how to implement paging at the data tier level

- How to work with stored procedure input and output parameters

Chapter 5 will be at least as exciting as this one, because you'll learn how to add a dynamic site map to your web site!

CHAPTER 5

■ ■ ■

Searching the Catalog

"What are you looking for?" There is no place where you'll hear this question more frequently than in both brick-and-mortar and e-commerce stores. Like any other quality web store around, your BalloonShop will allow visitors to search through the product catalog. You'll see how easy it is to add new functionality to a working site by integrating the new components into the existing architecture.

In this chapter, you will

- Analyze the various ways in which the product catalog can be searched

- Implement a custom search engine that works with SQL Server Express

- Write the data tier and business tier code that interacts with the search stored procedure

- Create the user interface of the catalog search feature

Choosing How to Search the Catalog

As always, you need to think about a few things before starting to code. Always keep in mind that when designing a new feature, you must analyze that feature from the final user's perspective.

For the visual part, you'll use a text box in which the visitor can enter one or more words to search for. In BalloonShop, the words entered by the visitor will be searched for in the products' names and descriptions. The text entered by the visitor can be searched for in several ways:

- *Exact-match search*: If the visitor enters an entire phrase, this phrase is searched in the database as it is, without splitting the words and searching for them separately.

- *All-words search*: The phrase entered by the visitor is split into words, causing a search for products that contain every word entered by the visitor. This is like the exact-match search in that it still searches for all the entered words, but this time the order of the words is no longer important.

- *Any-words search*: Products must contain at least one of the entered words.

This simple classification isn't by any means complete. The search engine can be as complex as the one offered by modern search engines, which provides many options and features and shows a ranked list of results, or as simple as searching the database for the exact string provided by the visitor.

BalloonShop will support the any-words and all-words search modes. This decision leads to the visual design of the search feature (see Figure 5-1).

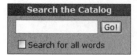

Figure 5-1. *The search box*

The text box is there, as expected, along with a check box that allows the visitor to choose between an all-words search and an any-words search.

Another decision you need to make here concerns how the matching products are displayed. The simplest solution to display the search results is to reuse the `ProductsList.ascx` web control you built in the previous chapter. A sample search page will look like Figure 5-2.

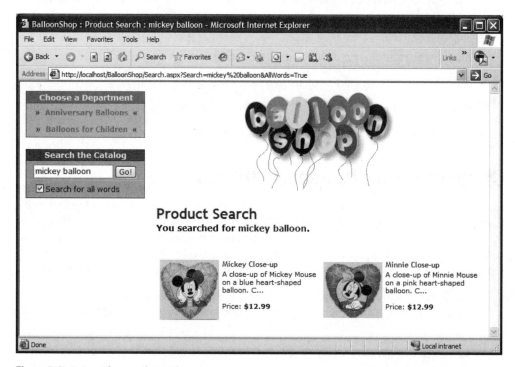

Figure 5-2. *A sample search results page*

The search results page employs paging, just as the other pages that contain product lists. If there are a lot of search results, you'll only present a fixed (but configurable) number of products per page and allow the visitor to browse through the pages using `Previous` and `Next` links.

Let's begin implementing the functionality by starting, as usual, with the data tier.

Teaching the Database to Search Itself

Within the database, there are two main ways to implement searching. You can implement database searching by using

- *SQL Server's Full-Text Search feature*: This feature—available with SQL Server Workgroup, Standard, and Enterprise editions—allows for advanced keyword searches (see `http://www.microsoft.com/sql/2005/productinfo/sql2005features.asp` for a comparison of the features in these SQL Server editions). These include searching using the Boolean operators (AND, AND NOT, OR) and searching for inflected forms of words, such as plurals and various verb tenses, or words located in close proximity. Additionally, the Full-Text Search feature can also sort the results based on rank, placing the most likely matches at the top.

- *A custom search solution for which you need stored procedures, user-defined functions, and courage*: This solution is very useful for your clients that are not ready to purchase an expensive version of SQL Server that contains the Full-Text Search engine.

The technical difference between the two approaches affects only the data tier, so if your customer starts with the custom solution, it will be easy to upgrade the web site to use Full-Text Search.

In this chapter, we'll analyze the custom search engine because it works with all editions of SQL Server 2005 (including the Express Edition), whereas you need a commercial version of SQL Server to use the Full-Text Search feature.

■**Note** You can visit `http://www.cristiandarie.ro` for updated information on how to integrate the Full-Text Search instead of the custom search engine into BalloonShop.

Implementing a Custom Search Engine

We'll start by presenting the custom search feature. Before moving on, it's good to know the disadvantages of this method as compared with using Full-Text Search:

- Manual searches of the catalog are much slower than SQL Server's Full-Text Search feature, which uses internal search indexes and features advanced search algorithms. However, this won't be a problem for your site until you have a large number of visitors and a large products database.

- You can't easily implement all the features that you could use with SQL Server's Full-Text Search, such as allowing the visitor to search using Boolean operators (AND, OR). Also, manually implementing advanced features such as searching for similar words adds even more performance penalties.

The good part about implementing the custom search engine is that you get to play a little more with some lesser-known features of SQL Server, so get ready. When it comes to manually searching the catalog, you have some options to choose from, as detailed in the following sections.

Searching Using WHERE and LIKE

The straightforward solution, most widely used in such situations, consists of using LIKE in the WHERE clause of the SELECT statement. The following query returns all the products that have the word "mask" somewhere in their description:

```
SELECT Name FROM Product WHERE Description LIKE '%mask%'
```

The percent (%) wildcard is used to specify any string of zero or more characters. Placing it before and after the word to be searched for guarantees that you'll get all the products whose description contains the word "mask."

This technique—using WHERE and LIKE—was used when building the SearchCatalog stored procedure for the ASP.NET 1.0 (but not in the ASP.NET 1.1) edition of this book, and is also presented in the Product Catalog case study in *The Programmer's Guide to SQL* (Apress, 2003). This is the fastest method for manually searching the catalog. In this edition of the book, we chose to present two other methods, which are not as fast as this one, but provide better search results.

Searching for Product Data in the Search String

This is yet another search strategy that doesn't provide the best search results, but it's worth taking a look at. This is the search method used in the Community Starter Kit (CSK).

■**Note** The CSK is a complex, free, and customizable application (provided with full source code) from Microsoft that allows you to build powerful community web sites quickly and easily. By default, the CSK comes with out-of-the box functionality that supports nine types of content, including articles, books, events, photo galleries, downloads, user polls, and more. It also supports features such as moderation, upload quotas, comments, ratings, newsletters, advertisements, web services, and security. However, by the time of this writing, the CSK hasn't been updated for ASP.NET 2.0. (You can download the CSK at http://www.asp.net.)

Like with BalloonShop, the CSK also implements a custom search feature instead of relying on SQL Server's Full-Text Search, making it possible to use MSDE as the database server.

The typical search method when Full-Text Search is not available is to split the search string into words and then look into the database for these words. However, the search algorithm in the CSK goes the other way round: It takes every word from the searchable database content and verifies whether it exists in the search string. The method doesn't offer much search flexibility, but it works.

In BalloonShop, the searchable content is the products' names and descriptions. These are split into separate words called *search keys*. The search keys are saved into a special data table in the database whenever new content is added or updated in the database.

■**Tip** To learn more about the CSK, check out another book I co-authored, *Building Websites with the ASP.NET Community Starter Kit* (Packt Publishing, 2004). Find more details about it at http://www.CristianDarie.ro/books.html.

These two methods are okay, but in BalloonShop, you'll implement something even better.

Searching by Counting the Number of Appearances

The disadvantage when searching with LIKE is that the search results are returned in random order. Today's smart search engines provide a ranking system that places the results with higher rankings at the top of the search results page.

An intuitive solution for implementing a simple ranking system is to count how many times the words you're searching for appear in the product's name or description. Moreover, you can give higher ranking to products that have matching words in their names, rather than in their descriptions.

This solution can't be implemented with LIKE and WHERE. LIKE returns True or False, specifying whether you have a match or not, but can't tell you how many times a word appears in a phrase.

Because SQL Server doesn't provide an easy way to count how many times a substring appears in a string, you'll manually implement this functionality as an SQL Server User-Defined Function.

■**Note** SQL Server User-Defined Functions (UDFs) implement common functionality that can be called from stored procedures. Unlike stored procedures, which can be accessed from client applications, UDFs are created for database internal usage and can be called from stored procedures or from other UDFs. UDFs must return data to the caller function or stored procedure before exiting (their last command must be RETURN) and are not allowed to modify data—their role is to return information.

For the catalog, you'll create a UDF named WordCount. It will take as parameters two strings and will return a SMALLINT value specifying how many times the first string appears in the second. The definition of WordCount is

```
CREATE FUNCTION dbo.WordCount
(@Word VARCHAR(20),
@Phrase VARCHAR(1000))
RETURNS SMALLINT
```

This looks similar to how you create stored procedures, except that you use FUNCTION instead of PROCEDURE, you need to explicitly specify the user who owns the function (which, in the example, is dbo), and you need to specify the return data type.

■**Note** dbo is a special database user who has full privileges on the database. If you're not permitted to use dbo, use the username under which you have privileges on the database.

Inside WordCount, the challenge is to find an effective way to count how many times @Word appears in @Phrase, because SQL Server doesn't provide a function for this (otherwise, you would have used that function instead of creating your own, right?).

The straightforward solution, which implies splitting the phrase where it has spaces (or other delimiter characters) and comparing word by word, is very slow. We've found a trick that performs the same functionality about five times faster.

SQL Server provides the REPLACE function, which replaces all occurrences of a substring in a string with another substring. REPLACE doesn't tell you how many replacements it did, but it returns the modified initial string. REPLACE works much faster than a custom created UDF or stored procedure because it's an internal SQL Server function.

You'll use REPLACE to replace the word to search for with a word that is one character longer. Say you want to count how many times the word "red" appears in "This is a red, red mask." Replacing "red" with "redx" generates "This is a redx, redx mask." The length difference between the initial phrase and the modified phrase tells you how many times the word "red" appears in the initial phrase (nice trick, eh?).

The code that does this appears as follows:

```
/* @BiggerWord is a string one character longer than @Word */
DECLARE @BiggerWord VARCHAR(21)
SELECT @BiggerWord = @Word + 'x'

/* Replace @Word with @BiggerWord in @Phrase */
DECLARE @BiggerPhrase VARCHAR(2000)
SELECT @BiggerPhrase = REPLACE (@Phrase, @Word, @BiggerWord)

/* The length difference between @BiggerPhrase and @phrase
   is the number we're looking for */
RETURN LEN(@BiggerPhrase) - LEN(@Phrase)
```

Searching for Similar Words

The implementation shown earlier is fast, but has one drawback: It can't be used to search for words that are similar to (sound like) the words entered by the visitor. For example, in the current database, searching for "balloon" generates many results, whereas searching for "balloons" generates a single result. This may or may not be what you want—you must decide what works best for your site.

You can change this behavior by changing the WordCount function. However, the version that recognizes similar versions of words is very slow because you can't use the REPLACE function anymore—you need to manually split the phrase word-by-word in SQL code, which is a time-consuming process. We'll present this modified version of WordCount at the end of the chapter for your reference.

■**Tip** You can implement the WordCount stored procedure in many ways, so we encourage you to play with it until you get the best results for your solution.

Introducing the SearchCatalog Stored Procedure

SearchCatalog is the stored procedure that will perform the actual database search. When building it, you need to address three main issues:

- The form in which you'll pass the search string to the stored procedure

- The way to use the WordCount UDF to calculate ranking within search results

- The need to support the paging functionality for the presentation tier

Let's analyze these requirements one at a time.

Passing the Search String to the Stored Procedure

The SearchCatalog stored procedure will receive the words to search for as separate INPUT parameters. But wait, how do you know how many keywords the search string will contain? Well, you don't, and the workaround is to assume a maximum number of keywords.

In this case, you'll have five input parameters named @Word1 through @Word5. These parameters will have a default value of NULL, so the business tier won't have to supply values for all of them if the visitor is searching for fewer than five words.

The obvious disadvantage is that you'll always have a maximum number of keywords that can be accepted (five words, in this example). If a visitor ever introduces more than the maximum number of words, the additional words are simply ignored—the business tier doesn't send them to the stored procedure at all. This suggests the second drawback: The business tier needs to know about the data-tier logic (regarding the maximum number of allowed words); this is a data-tier limitation that has to be handled by the business tier.

■**Note** You might not like the limitation about the number of words you can search for in the database. However, if you set the limit high enough, the visitors are not likely to feel this limitation. Even Google has (at the moment of writing) a maximum number of allowed search words (ten), and we haven't heard anyone complaining about this, so far.

The alternative to sending separate words to SearchCatalog is to send the entire search string from the business tier and then split it into separate words in the stored procedure. Then, after extracting the words, you have to build the SQL query that does the search by joining strings, and save it in a VarChar variable. When you have a query saved in a VarChar variable, named @SearchQuery for instance, you can execute it using sp_executesql as follows:

```
/* Execute the query using the SQL Server's sp_executesql stored procedure*/
EXEC sp_executesql @SearchQuery
```

This solution isn't preferred because it results in messy SQL code (don't we all like simple and clear solutions?), and dynamically creating SQL queries isn't a very elegant solution (it's almost like building the query in the business tier by joining strings). Also, the query will probably perform more slowly because SQL Server can't precompile and save the execution plan of a dynamically created query, as it does with stored procedures.

Calculating Product Ranking Using WordCount

You've decided SearchCatalog will receive the search string as separate words, named @Word1 to @Word5. The second challenge with this stored procedure is how to calculate a ranking for each matching product, so you can place the higher-ranking records first.

To assign a rank to each product in the database when doing an any-words search, you need a query like this one:

```
SELECT Product.Name,
       3 * WordCount(@Word1, Name) + WordCount(@Word1, Description) +
       3 * WordCount(@Word2, Name) + WordCount(@Word2, Description) +
       ...
       AS TotalRank
FROM Product
```

■**Tip** TotalRank, in this example, is a calculated column. It doesn't exist in the database, but it's generated using a formula you define.

This query gives three ranking points for each time one of the search string words is found in the product's name, and one ranking point for each time the words are found in the description. The query uses the WordCount function, which returns a number specifying how many times a word appears in a phrase.

If none of the search words is found in a product's name or description, its ranking is 0. If any of the words are found, the ranking is a positive number. The search results will consist of the products that have a positive ranking number.

In case the business tier sends fewer than five words to the procedure, the remaining @Word parameters are NULL, for which WordCount returns 0. This is okay for any-words searches, because you don't want any ranking points added for nonmatching words, and you also don't want a product eliminated because of a nonmatching word.

Things are a bit more complicated for all-words searches. With all-words searches, when a single word isn't found in the product's name or description, the product must not be included in the search results.

One solution to implement the all-words search is to multiply the individual rankings of each word (using 1 for NULL @Word parameters), instead of adding them; this way, if a word has a ranking of 0, the total rank will be 0, and the product is excluded from the list. The query that returns the names and rankings for each product in the Product table for an all-words search looks like the following:

```
SELECT Product.Name,
       (3 * WordCount(@Word1, Name) + WordCount(@Word1, Description)) *
       CASE
          WHEN @Word2 IS NULL THEN 1
             ELSE 3 * WordCount(@Word2, Name) + WordCount(@Word2, Description)
       END *
       ...
```

```
        AS TotalRank
FROM Product
```

If for any reason you want to avoid multiplying the partial rank numbers, the workaround is to continue adding the partial ranks, while granting negative ranks for the words that don't match. So, if the WordCount function returns a positive number, that number is used as the word's partial rank; if WordCount returns 0, that number is substituted with a negative number (-1000 in the following code) that ensures the total sum is negative. Here's how to do that:

```
SELECT Product.Name,
       CASE
          WHEN @Word1 IS NULL THEN 0
          ELSE ISNULL(NULLIF(dbo.WordCount(@Word1, Name + ' ' + Description),
0), -1000)
       END +
       CASE
          WHEN @Word2 IS NULL THEN 0
          ELSE ISNULL(NULLIF(dbo.WordCount(@Word2, Name + ' ' + Description), 0),
 -1000)
       END +
       ...
       AS TotalRank
FROM Product
```

Note Using the ISNULL and NULLIF functions avoids calling WordCount twice for each word (this trick significantly improves performance). Visit SQL Server 2005 Books Online for more information about how these functions work.

Implementing Paging

You'll implement paging in a bit different way than you did in Chapter 4. Back then, you populated the @Products table variable while assigning a row number to each row using the ROW_NUMBER() function, like this:

```
INSERT INTO @Products
SELECT ROW_NUMBER() OVER (ORDER BY Product.ProductID) AS Row,
...
```

As you can see, the list of products is sorted on their product IDs before being numbered. This criterion doesn't apply to the list of search results, which need to be sorted in descending order on their search ranking (so more relevant search results are always listed first). We can solve this problem by performing the search in a subquery and then applying the ROW_NUMBER() function on the results (so, using the same technique as in Chapter 4) or by using a new trick. We chose the latter method, of course, to play with yet a new T-SQL thing.

This time, when creating the @Products table variable (see the following code snippet), you'll make RowNumber an IDENTITY column. This means that it will be automatically assigned incrementing numbers, without you needing to explicitly calculate them using a function such as ROW_NUMBER().

```
/* Create the table variable that will contain the search results */
DECLARE @Products TABLE
(RowNumber SMALLINT IDENTITY (1,1) NOT NULL,
 ProductID INT,
 Name VARCHAR(50),
 Description VARCHAR(1000),
 Price MONEY,
 Image1FileName VARCHAR(50),
 Image2FileName VARCHAR(50),
 Rank INT)
```

Okay, enough with the theory. Let's go back to the keyboard.

Writing the Code

You're probably eager to write some code! Let's implement the WordCount function and the SearchCatalog stored procedure in the following exercise.

Exercise: Adding Search Functionality to the Data Tier

1. Let's first add the WordCount function. Navigate to the BalloonShop connection in **Database Explorer**, right-click **Functions**, and choose **Add New ➤ Scalar-valued Function**. Change the function skeleton Visual Web Developer created for you with the following code:

```
CREATE FUNCTION dbo.WordCount
(@Word VARCHAR(15),
@Phrase VARCHAR(1000))
RETURNS SMALLINT
AS
BEGIN

/* If @Word or @Phrase is NULL the function returns 0 */
IF @Word IS NULL OR @Phrase IS NULL RETURN 0

/* @BiggerWord is a string one character longer than @Word */
DECLARE @BiggerWord VARCHAR(21)
SELECT @BiggerWord = @Word + 'x'

/* Replace @Word with @BiggerWord in @Phrase */
DECLARE @BiggerPhrase VARCHAR(2000)
SELECT @BiggerPhrase = REPLACE (@Phrase, @Word, @BiggerWord)

/* The length difference between @BiggerPhrase and @phrase
   is the number we're looking for */
```

```
RETURN LEN(@BiggerPhrase) - LEN(@Phrase)
END
```

2. Now add the `SearchCatalog` stored procedure. This stored procedure uses `WordCount` to calculate the search results. Using the steps you already know, add this stored procedure to your BalloonShop database:

```
CREATE PROCEDURE SearchCatalog
(@DescriptionLength INT,
 @PageNumber TINYINT,
 @ProductsPerPage TINYINT,
 @HowManyResults SMALLINT OUTPUT,
 @AllWords BIT,
 @Word1 VARCHAR(15) = NULL,
 @Word2 VARCHAR(15) = NULL,
 @Word3 VARCHAR(15) = NULL,
 @Word4 VARCHAR(15) = NULL,
 @Word5 VARCHAR(15) = NULL)
AS

/* Create the table variable that will contain the search results */
DECLARE @Products TABLE
(RowNumber SMALLINT IDENTITY (1,1) NOT NULL,
 ProductID INT,
 Name VARCHAR(50),
 Description VARCHAR(1000),
 Price MONEY,
 Image1FileName VARCHAR(50),
 Image2FileName VARCHAR(50),
 Rank INT)

/* Populate @Products for an any-words search */
IF @AllWords = 0
   INSERT INTO @Products
   SELECT ProductID, Name,
       SUBSTRING(Description, 1, @DescriptionLength) + '...' AS Description,
       Price, Image1FileName, Image2FileName,
       3 * dbo.WordCount(@Word1, Name) + dbo.WordCount(@Word1, Description) +
       3 * dbo.WordCount(@Word2, Name) + dbo.WordCount(@Word2, Description) +
       3 * dbo.WordCount(@Word3, Name) + dbo.WordCount(@Word3, Description) +
       3 * dbo.WordCount(@Word4, Name) + dbo.WordCount(@Word4, Description) +
       3 * dbo.WordCount(@Word5, Name) + dbo.WordCount(@Word5, Description)
           AS Rank
   FROM Product
   ORDER BY Rank DESC

/* Populate @Products for an all-words search */
IF @AllWords = 1
```

```
      INSERT INTO @Products
      SELECT ProductID, Name,
             SUBSTRING(Description, 1, @DescriptionLength) +
'...' AS Description,
             Price, Image1FileName, Image2FileName,
             (3 * dbo.WordCount(@Word1, Name) + dbo.WordCount
(@Word1, Description)) *
             CASE
              WHEN @Word2 IS NULL THEN 1
              ELSE 3 * dbo.WordCount(@Word2, Name) + dbo.WordCount(@Word2,
Description)
             END *
             CASE
              WHEN @Word3 IS NULL THEN 1
              ELSE 3 * dbo.WordCount(@Word3, Name) + dbo.WordCount(@Word3,
Description)
             END *
             CASE
              WHEN @Word4 IS NULL THEN 1
              ELSE 3 * dbo.WordCount(@Word4, Name) + dbo.WordCount(@Word4,
Description)
             END *
             CASE
              WHEN @Word5 IS NULL THEN 1
              ELSE 3 * dbo.WordCount(@Word5, Name) + dbo.WordCount(@Word5,
Description)
             END
             AS Rank
      FROM Product
      ORDER BY Rank DESC

   /* Save the number of searched products in an output variable */
   SELECT @HowManyResults = COUNT(*)
   FROM @Products
   WHERE Rank > 0

   /* Send back the requested products */
   SELECT ProductID, Name, Description, Price, Image1FileName,
    Image2FileName, Rank
   FROM @Products
   WHERE Rank > 0
     AND RowNumber BETWEEN (@PageNumber-1) * @ProductsPerPage + 1
                     AND @PageNumber * @ProductsPerPage
   ORDER BY Rank DESC
```

How It Works: WordCount and SearchCatalog

In the first step of the exercises, you wrote the WordCount function. This function returns the number of times the @Word string appears in @Phrase (@Word and @Phrase are its input parameters). We discussed how this function works earlier in this chapter.

■**Note** The function is completely unaware of the fact that you're searching for words; it simply searches for substrings. The effect is that if you search for "love," it finds a match on "lovely," for example. If you don't like this behavior, there are a number of ways to change it. One of them is to append a space before and after the word to search for, do some preparation on the phrase (such as add leading and trailing spaces), and then perform the search with these.

SearchCatalog is a bit more complex. First of all, let's analyze its parameters:

- @DescriptionLength is the maximum length of the product description.

- @PageNumber specifies the page of results the visitor has requested.

- @ProductsPerPage specifies how many records to return. If @PageNumber is 3 and @ProductPerPage is 5, the procedure will return the 11th to 15th records from the search results.

- @HowManyResults is an output parameter, which you'll set to the total number of search results. This will be read from the C# code to calculate the number of search results pages.

- @AllWords is a bit input parameter that specifies whether you should do an all-words or any-words search.

- @Word1 to @Word5 are the words to be searched for. They all have a default value of NULL.

The stored procedure starts by creating the @Products table variable:

```
/* Create the table variable that will contain the search results */
DECLARE @Products TABLE
(RowNumber SMALLINT IDENTITY (1,1) NOT NULL,
 ProductID INT,
 Name VARCHAR(50),
 Description VARCHAR(1000),
 Price MONEY,
 Image1FileName VARCHAR(50),
 Image2FileName VARCHAR(50),
 Rank INT)
```

The RowNumber field is used for paging, as you learned in Chapter 4. This time it's also an IDENTITY column, to make its calculation a bit easier later on.

We also have a field called Rank that contains the search result ranking (products with higher values are listed first).

After creating the table variable, you populate it by searching the product catalog. For this, the stored procedure reads the @AllWords bit parameter and decides what kind of search to do depending on its value (an all-words search versus an any-words search). The logic of searching the catalog was explained earlier in this chapter.

After searching the catalog and populating @Products, you set the value of the @HowManyResults output parameter (which will be read from the business tier), by counting the number of rows in @Products:

```
/* Save the number of searched products in an output variable */
SELECT @HowManyResults = COUNT(*)
FROM @Products
WHERE Rank > 0
```

Finally, you get back the portion of records from @Products based on the @PageNumber and @ProductsPerPage input parameters:

```
/* Send back the requested products */
SELECT ProductID, Name, Description, Price, Image1FileName,
  Image2FileName, Rank
FROM @Products
WHERE Rank > 0
  AND RowNumber BETWEEN (@PageNumber-1) * @ProductsPerPage + 1
                 AND @PageNumber * @ProductsPerPage
ORDER BY Rank DESC
```

Implementing the Business Tier

The business tier consists of the SearchCatalog method, which calls the SearchCatalog stored procedure. This data feeds our older friend, the ProductsList.ascx Web User Control, which displays the search results.

Apart from a little bit of logic to handle splitting the search phrase into separate words (the presentation tier sends the whole phrase, but the data tier needs individual words) and to ensure we send a valid True/False value for the @AllWords parameter to the SearchCatalog stored procedure, there's nothing fantastic about this new method.

Like always, you set up the stored procedure parameters, execute the command, and return the results. Add the Search method to your CatalogAccess class:

```
// Search the product catalog
public static DataTable Search(string searchString, string allWords,
string pageNumber, out int howManyPages)
{
  // get a configured DbCommand object
  DbCommand comm = GenericDataAccess.CreateCommand();
  // set the stored procedure name
  comm.CommandText = "SearchCatalog";
  // create a new parameter
  DbParameter param = comm.CreateParameter();
  param.ParameterName = "@DescriptionLength";
  param.Value = BalloonShopConfiguration.ProductDescriptionLength;
  param.DbType = DbType.Int32;
  comm.Parameters.Add(param);
```

```
// create a new parameter
param = comm.CreateParameter();
param.ParameterName = "@AllWords";
param.Value = allWords.ToUpper() == "TRUE" ? "True" : "False";
param.DbType = DbType.Boolean;
comm.Parameters.Add(param);
// create a new parameter
param = comm.CreateParameter();
param.ParameterName = "@PageNumber";
param.Value = pageNumber;
param.DbType = DbType.Int32;
comm.Parameters.Add(param);
// create a new parameter
param = comm.CreateParameter();
param.ParameterName = "@ProductsPerPage";
param.Value = BalloonShopConfiguration.ProductsPerPage;
param.DbType = DbType.Int32;
comm.Parameters.Add(param);
// create a new parameter
param = comm.CreateParameter();
param.ParameterName = "@HowManyResults";
param.Direction = ParameterDirection.Output;
param.DbType = DbType.Int32;
comm.Parameters.Add(param);

// define the maximum number of words
int howManyWords = 5;
// transform search string into array of words
char[] wordSeparators = new char[] { ',', ';', '.', '!', '?', '-', ' ' };
string[] words = searchString.Split(wordSeparators,
StringSplitOptions.RemoveEmptyEntries);
int index = 1;

// add the words as stored procedure parameters
for (int i = 0; i <= words.GetUpperBound(0) && index <= howManyWords; i++)
  // ignore short words
  if (words[i].Length > 2)
  {
    // create the @Word parameters
    param = comm.CreateParameter();
    param.ParameterName = "@Word" + index.ToString();
    param.Value = words[i];
    param.DbType = DbType.String;
    comm.Parameters.Add(param);
    index++;
  }
```

```
    // execute the stored procedure and save the results in a DataTable
    DataTable table = GenericDataAccess.ExecuteSelectCommand(comm);
    // calculate how many pages of products and set the out parameter
    int howManyProducts =
Int32.Parse(comm.Parameters["@HowManyResults"].Value.ToString());
    howManyPages = (int)Math.Ceiling((double)howManyProducts /
                    (double)BalloonShopConfiguration.ProductsPerPage);
    // return the page of products
    return table;
}
```

Because the code is pretty clear, it's not worth analyzing it again in detail. However, note the following aspects:

- To guard against bogus values, we make sure to set the @AllWords parameter strictly to True or False, using the allWords.ToUpper() == "TRUE" ? "True" : "False" construct.

- The words in the search phrase are split on the list of characters contained in the wordSeparators array.

- There's a for loop to add the @Word parameters. Short words (fewer than three letters long) are considered noise words and are not used for the search. Feel free to change this rule to suit your particular solution.

- The words searched for are returned though an out parameter, so the presentation tier is able to tell the visitor which words were actually used for searching.

- The number of pages is given by dividing the number of products by the number of products per page.

■**Note** The maximum number of allowed words and the list of characters used to split the search string are hard-coded. In case you think any of these could ever change, it's strongly recommended to save their values in web.config. Also note that increasing the maximum number of allowed words implies updating the SearchCatalog stored procedure as well.

Let's now create the presentation tier, where you'll use all the logic implemented so far.

Implementing the Presentation Tier

Let's see some colors now! The Search Catalog feature has two separate interface elements that you need to implement. The first one is the place where the visitor enters the search string, shown earlier in Figure 5-1.

This part of the UI will be implemented as a separate user control named SearchBox.ascx, which provides a text box and a check box for the visitor. The other part of the UI consists of the search results page (Search.aspx), which displays the products matching the search criteria (refer to Figure 5-2).

The Search Box consists of a text box, a button, and a check box. Many times, ASP.NET programmers have complained about TextBox and Button controls working well together, especially when you want the same functionality to happen both when the Enter key is pressed while editing the TextBox and when the Button is clicked. For example, the standard way to respond to the Enter key in the text box is handling its TextChanged event, but this event is also raised when the button is clicked (in which case, it's called twice). Other problems involve circumstances when you have more buttons on the form, and you need to associate their actions with the visitor hitting Enter in different text boxes.

The solution presented in this book is a bit more involved than other possible solutions, but it's very powerful because after it's in place, you can easily reuse it in other parts of the site, as you'll see when adding new functionality in later chapters. You'll add a method called TieButton to the Utilities class that can be called from any presentation tier component (Web User Controls, Web Forms, and so on) and that associates a TextBox control with an existing Button control. TieButton ensures than when the visitor presses Enter while editing the text box, the Click event of the Button is raised. This way you won't need to deal with the TextChanged event of the TextBox any more.

This way of doing things is not exactly the "ASP.NET way," which by design encourages you to handle everything with server-side code, but in this case breaking the rules a little bit brings some long-term benefits, and you'll probably come to use the TieButton method in your other web projects as well. However, because the code is beyond the scope of this book, we won't analyze the inner workings of TieButton here.

Creating the Search Box

Because there are more steps to follow to create the SearchBox.ascx control, let's do them in the following exercise.

Exercise: Creating the SearchBox Web User Control

1. First let's handle adding the required new functionality to Utilities.cs. Open **Utilities.cs** and add the following references at the beginning of the file:

```
using System;
using System.Net.Mail;
using System.Web.UI;
using System.Web.UI.WebControls;
using System.Web.UI.HtmlControls;
```

2. Add the following method to your Utilities class:

```
// Configures what button to be clicked when the uses presses Enter in a
// text box. The text box doesn't have to be a TextBox control, but it must
// be derived from either HtmlControl or WebControl, and the HTML control it
// generates should accept an 'onkeydown' attribute. The HTML generated by
// the button must support the 'Click' event
public static void TieButton(Page page, Control TextBoxToTie,
Control ButtonToTie)
```

```
{
  // Init jscript
  string jsString = "";

  // Check button type and get required jscript
  if (ButtonToTie is LinkButton)
  {
    jsString = "if ((event.which && event.which == 13) ||
(event.keyCode && event.keyCode == 13)) {"
        + page.ClientScript.GetPostBackEventReference
(ButtonToTie, "").Replace(":", "$") + ";return false;} else return true;";
  }
  else if (ButtonToTie is ImageButton)
  {
    jsString = "if ((event.which && event.which == 13) ||
(event.keyCode && event.keyCode == 13)) {"
        + page.ClientScript.GetPostBackEventReference
(ButtonToTie, "").Replace(":", "$") + ";return false;} else return true;";
  }
  else
  {
    jsString = "if ((event.which && event.which == 13) ||
(event.keyCode && event.keyCode == 13)) {document."
        + "forms[0].elements['" + ButtonToTie.UniqueID.Replace
(":", "_") + "'].click();return false;} else return true; ";
  }

  // Attach jscript to the onkeydown attribute—we have to
cater for HtmlControl or WebControl
  if (TextBoxToTie is HtmlControl)
  {
    ((HtmlControl)TextBoxToTie).Attributes.Add("onkeydown", jsString);
  }
  else if (TextBoxToTie is WebControl)
  {
    ((WebControl)TextBoxToTie).Attributes.Add("onkeydown", jsString);
  }
}
```

3. First, create a Web User Control named SearchBox.ascx in the UserControls folder.

4. You can create the control either by using the Design View window or by directly modifying the HTML. In this case, add the following HTML code to the file:

```
<table border="0" cellpadding="0" cellspacing="0" width="200px">
  <tr>
    <td class="SearchBoxHead">
      Search the Catalog
```

```
      </td>
    </tr>
    <tr>
      <td class="SearchBoxContent">
        <asp:TextBox ID="searchTextBox" Runat="server" Width="128px"
CssClass="SearchBox" BorderStyle="Dotted" MaxLength="100" Height="16px" />
        <asp:Button ID="goButton" Runat="server" CssClass="SearchBox"
Text="Go!" Width="36px" Height="21px" /><br />
        <asp:CheckBox ID="allWordsCheckBox" CssClass="SearchBox" Runat="server"
Text="Search for all words" />
      </td>
    </tr>
</table>
```

5. Switch to Design View. The control should look like Figure 5-3.

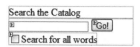

Figure 5-3. *SearchBox.ascx in Design View*

Note the CssClass used for both controls will be applied at runtime and also note the maximum size of 100 characters was set for the text box.

6. Add the following styles to BalloonShop.css:

```
.SearchBoxHead
{
  border-right: #0468a4 1px solid;
  border-top: #0468a4 1px solid;
  border-bottom: #0468a4 1px solid;
  border-left: #0468a4 1px solid;
  background-color: #0583b5;
  font-family: Verdana, Arial;
  font-weight: bold;
  font-size: 10pt;
  color: #f5f5dc;
  text-align: center;
}
.SearchBoxContent
{
  border-right: #0468a4 1px solid;
  border-top: #0468a4 1px solid;
  border-left: #0468a4 1px solid;
  border-bottom: #0468a4 1px solid;
  background-color: #8bc8dd;
  font-family: Arial, Verdana;
  font-size: 9pt;
```

```
      color: darkblue;
      padding-top: 5px;
      padding-left: 12px;
      padding-bottom: 5px;
    }
    .SearchBox
    {
      font-family: Verdana, Helvetica, sans-serif;
      font-size: 9pt;
      margin-bottom: 5px;
    }
```

7. Open the code-behind file, **SearchBox.ascx.cs**, and complete the Page_Load method like this:

```csharp
protected void Page_Load(object sender, EventArgs e)
{
  // don't repopulate control on postbacks
  if (!IsPostBack)
  {
    // tie the search text box to the Go button
    Utilities.TieButton(this.Page, searchTextBox, goButton);
    // load search box controls' values
    string allWords = Request.QueryString["AllWords"];
    string searchString = Request.QueryString["Search"];
    if (allWords != null)
      allWordsCheckBox.Checked = (allWords.ToUpper() == "TRUE");
    if (searchString != null)
      searchTextBox.Text = searchString;
  }
}
```

8. Switch to SearchBox.ascx.cs in Design View, double-click the **Go** button to generate its Click event handler, and complete it like this:

```csharp
// Perform the product search
protected void goButton_Click(object sender, EventArgs e)
{
  ExecuteSearch();
}

// Redirect to the search results page
private void ExecuteSearch()
{
  if (searchTextBox.Text.Trim() != "")
    Response.Redirect(Request.ApplicationPath +
                "/Search.aspx?Search=" + searchTextBox.Text +
                "&AllWords=" + allWordsCheckBox.Checked.ToString());
}
```

9. Add the newly created user control to `BalloonShop.master` by dragging it from the **Solution Explorer** and dropping it just below the `CategoriesList` user control (see Figure 5-4).

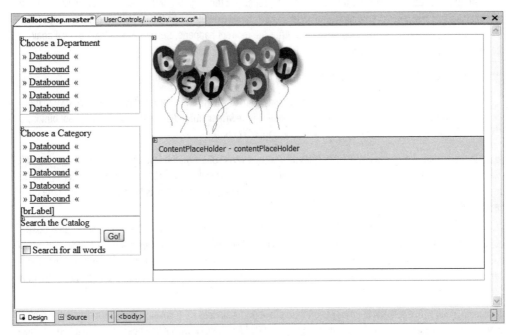

Figure 5-4. *Adding the search box to* `BalloonShop.master`

10. Press **F5** to execute the project. The search box should rest nicely in its place. Trying to search for anything would generate an error, however, because the `Search.aspx` page doesn't exist yet.

How It Works: The `SearchBox` Web User Control

The `SearchBox` user control isn't very complicated. When the visitor enters a new search string and presses Enter or clicks the Go button, the response is redirected to `Search.aspx`, which handles the search. `Search` recognizes the following query string parameters:

- `Search` specifies the search string entered by the visitor.

- `AllWords` specifies whether to do an all-words or an any-words search. You find its value by checking `allWordsCheckBox.Checked`, which returns `True` or `False`. A mighty hacker can, of course, play with the query string and change the value to something else, but our business tier contains code to guard against this kind of potential problem.

- `PageNumber` appears only in case the number of products is larger than the number of products per page (which you saved in `web.config`).

The `Page_Load` method first uses the `Utilities.TieButton` method, which configures the text box to "click" the Go! button when the Enter key is pressed. Details about `TieButton` have been presented prior to this exercise.

`Page_Load` then checks the query string parameters and fills the search box contents accordingly. When the visitor performs a search, the page is reloaded (with a `Response.Redirect` to the `Search.aspx` page), so implicitly the search box contents are cleared. If you want to keep the values there (the string of the text box and the status of the check box), you must do this manually.

While we're here, note the check for the `IsPostBack` property of the page. After the visitor clicks the Go! button to perform a search, the `SearchBox` control is loaded (`Page_Load` executes) and the `Click` event handler executes, which causes a page redirect (to `Search.aspx`). After the redirect happens, `SearchBox` is loaded once again in the new page (so `Page_Load` executes again). This suggests two problems:

- A performance problem because the `Page_Load` method is called twice.

- Functionality problem because you actually only want to set the check box and text box values when the control is reloaded in a new page. If their values are rewritten immediately after clicking the Go! button, the user's input would be ignored (which is bad, of course).

To avoid these kind of problems, ASP.NET offers the `Page.IsPostBack` method, which tells you if `Page_Load` is executed as a result of a postback, which is true when the method is executed in response to a user clicking the Go! button or pressing Enter and false when the method is executed when the control is loaded for the first time on a new page.

The first time `Page_Load` executes (after the button click), `IsPostBack` returns `true`. The second time `Page_Load` executes (the control is loaded in a fresh page), `IsPostBack` returns `false`. You don't want to fill the contents of the search box from the query string when the page is loaded from a postback event, because it will be filled with data from the previous search. To test this, remove the `if` statement from `Page_Load` and try to do some consecutive different searches.

Because playing with postback is mostly used to improve performance, we'll cover it more seriously in the next chapter, where you'll use this technique in more pages of BalloonShop. However, you needed to use it here to make the search functionality, well, functional.

With this new theory in mind, the implementation of `Page_Load` in `SearchBox.ascx.cs` starts to make sense:

```
protected void Page_Load(object sender, EventArgs e)
{
  // don't repopulate control on postbacks
  if (!IsPostBack)
  {
    // tie the search text box to the Go button
    Utilities.TieButton(this.Page, searchTextBox, goButton);
    // load search box controls' values
    string allWords = Request.QueryString["AllWords"];
    string searchString = Request.QueryString["Search"];
    if (allWords != null)
      allWordsCheckBox.Checked = (allWords.ToUpper() == "TRUE");
    if (searchString != null)
      searchTextBox.Text = searchString;
  }
}
```

Displaying the Search Results

Now you'll create the Web Form that displays the search results. To simplify the work, you'll reuse the ProductsList user control to display the actual list of products. This control is currently listing products for the main page, for departments, and for categories. Of course, if you want to have the searched products displayed in another format, you need to create another user control.

In the following exercise, you'll create the Search.aspx Web Form and update ProductsList.

Exercise: Displaying Search Results

1. Let's create a new Web Form in the root of the BalloonShop folder. Right-click the **BalloonShop** root entry in **Solution Explorer** and select **Add New Item**. In the **Add New Item** dialog box, write **Search.aspx** for the name, make sure the two check boxes are selected and that the language is **Visual C#**, and click **Add**.

2. In the dialog box that opens, select the **BalloonShop.master** Master Page and click **OK**.

3. Switch Search.aspx to Design View, add two Label controls, and then drag **ProductsList.ascx** from **Solution Explorer** to the **Content** area, as shown in Figure 5-5.

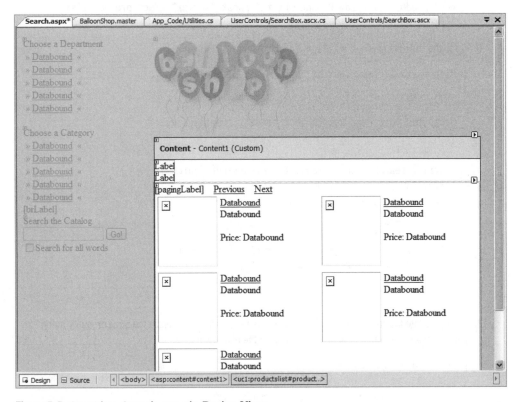

Figure 5-5. *Creating Search.aspx in Design View*

4. Clear the Text property of the Label controls. Set the name of the first label to titleLabel. The second label should be named descriptionLabel.

5. Set the CssClass property of the first Label control to CatalogTitle. Set the CssClass property of the second label to CatalogDescription.

The HTML code of the control should be like this, at this moment:

```
<%@ Page Language="C#" MasterPageFile="~/BalloonShop.master"
AutoEventWireup="true" CodeFile="Search.aspx.cs" Inherits="Search"
Title="Untitled Page" %>

<%@ Register Src="UserControls/ProductsList.ascx" TagName=
"ProductsList" TagPrefix="uc1" %>
<asp:Content ID="Content1" ContentPlaceHolderID=
"contentPlaceHolder" Runat="Server">
  <asp:Label ID="titleLabel" runat="server" CssClass="CatalogTitle">
  </asp:Label><br />
  <asp:Label ID="descriptionLabel" runat="server" CssClass=
"CatalogDescription">
  </asp:Label><br /><br />
  <uc1:productslist id="ProductsList1" runat="server"></uc1:productslist>
</asp:Content>
```

6. Go to the code file now and edit **Page_Load** like this:

```
public partial class Search : System.Web.UI.Page
{
  // Fill the form with data
  protected void Page_Load(object sender, EventArgs e)
  {
    // fill the table contents
    string searchString = Request.QueryString["Search"];
    titleLabel.Text = "Product Search";
    descriptionLabel.Text = "You searched for <font color=\"red\">"
 + searchString + "</font>.";
    // set the title of the page
    this.Title = BalloonShopConfiguration.SiteName +
                 " : Product Search : " + searchString;
  }
}
```

7. Finally, update the code-behind file of ProductsList.ascx to recognize the Search query string parameter and perform a product search in case the parameter is found:

```
private void PopulateControls()
{
  // Retrieve DepartmentID from the query string
  string departmentId = Request.QueryString["DepartmentID"];
  // Retrieve CategoryID from the query string
```

```csharp
    string categoryId = Request.QueryString["CategoryID"];
    // Retrieve Page from the query string
    string page = Request.QueryString["Page"];
    if (page == null) page = "1";
    // Retrieve Search string from query string
    string searchString = Request.QueryString["Search"];
    // How many pages of products?
    int howManyPages = 1;
    // If performing a product search
    if (searchString != null)
    {
      // Retrieve AllWords from query string
      string allWords = Request.QueryString["AllWords"];
      // Perform search
      list.DataSource = CatalogAccess.Search(searchString, allWords,
  page, out howManyPages);
      list.DataBind();
    }
    // If browsing a category...
    else if (categoryId != null)
    {
    ...
```

8. Press **F5** to execute the project. Type **love** in the search text box to get an output similar to Figure 5-6.

Figure 5-6. *Searching for love*

How It Works: Displaying Search Results

You've now finished implementing the search functionality of the catalog. Although you had quite a bit to write, the code wasn't that complicated, was it?

The single important detail of this exercise was calling the business tier `CatalogAccess.Search` method to get the search results and display them:

```
// If performing a product search
if (searchString != null)
{
  // Retrieve AllWords from query string
  string allWords = Request.QueryString["AllWords"];
  // Perform search
  list.DataSource = CatalogAccess.Search(searchString, allWords,
page, out howManyPages);
  list.DataBind();
}
```

Make sure to have a closer look at all the code that makes the product searching work. If you understand it correctly, you can easily update the code to make it work best for your particular solutions.

Searching Smarter

Okay, the search feature is working fine. Do some tests with both all-words and any-words modes to ensure that the search feature really does work. You'll notice that it's fast, too.

The major problem with the search feature is that it doesn't recognize similar word forms. If you search for "balloon," you'll be shown ten pages of results, but if you search for "balloons," you'll get only one matching product.

Depending on your client's requests, this might not be acceptable. The two solutions to this problem are to either search using SOUNDEX or search using SQL Server's Full Text Search.

SOUNDEX is an SQL Server function that allows you to check if two English words sound the same (phonetical searching). SOUNDEX was initially created to find similar person names—SOUNDEX returns the same value for, say, Charlie and Charly. Checking the SOUNDEX results for two strings reveals whether they sound the same or not. As a quick test, run these queries using SQL Server Express Manager:

```
SELECT SOUNDEX('Charly')
SELECT SOUNDEX('Charlie')
```

In both cases, the result should be C640.

> **Note** Using SOUNDEX isn't exactly the ideal search solution (which is still Full Text Search), because it doesn't offer features such as matching different verb tenses, plurals, words located in close proximity, and other advanced options. The SOUNDEX value of a string is calculated based on the first portion of that string, and the remaining characters are ignored. For more details about how SOUNDEX works, please do a Google search on "soundex algorithm."
>
> SQL Server has another related function called DIFFERENCE, which returns the phonetical difference between two words. The return value ranges from 0 to 4: 0 indicates little or no similarity, and 4 indicates strong similarity or identical values. See more details about DIFFERENCE and SOUNDEX in SQL Server 2005 Books Online.

However, searching smarter equals searching slower. To improve the search functionality using SOUNDEX, you'll need to change the WordCount function. The SearchCatalog stored procedure doesn't need to change! (nice one, right?)

Unfortunately, in WordCount, when using SOUNDEX you must manually split the phrase into separate words and compare their SOUNDEX value to the SOUNDEX value of the word you're searching for. This isn't very fast.

In tests, we discovered that the new version of WordCount is about five times slower than the previously presented one. However, if the business has grown large enough and the SQL

Server can't successfully deal any more with client requests, this is an indication that a commercial version of SQL Server should probably be purchased (which also comes with the advanced Full-Text Search functionality).

Note The main performance penalty in this version of WordCount isn't because of the SOUNDEX (or DIFFERENCE) calls, as you might think. Manually splitting the phrase into separate words is what takes a lot of time. The WordCount algorithm solution you applied earlier using the REPLACE function was cool and fast, but it can't be used any more.

After all that, here's the code for the "smarter" version of WordCount. Check the comments to understand the functionality:

```
CREATE FUNCTION dbo.WordCount
(@Word VARCHAR(20),
@Phrase VARCHAR(1000))
RETURNS SMALLINT
AS
BEGIN

/* If @Word or @Phrase is NULL, the function returns 0 */
IF @Word IS NULL OR @Phrase IS NULL RETURN 0

/* Calculate and store the SOUNDEX value of the word */
DECLARE @SoundexWord CHAR(4)
SELECT @SoundexWord = SOUNDEX(@Word)

/* Eliminate bogus characters from phrase */
SELECT @Phrase = REPLACE(@Phrase, ',', ' ')
SELECT @Phrase = REPLACE(@Phrase, '.', ' ')
SELECT @Phrase = REPLACE(@Phrase, '!', ' ')
SELECT @Phrase = REPLACE(@Phrase, '?', ' ')
SELECT @Phrase = REPLACE(@Phrase, ';', ' ')
SELECT @Phrase = REPLACE(@Phrase, '-', ' ')

/* Remove trailing spaces. Necessary because LEN doesn't
calculate trailing spaces */
SELECT @Phrase = RTRIM(@Phrase)

/* Check every word in the phrase */
DECLARE @NextSpacePos SMALLINT
DECLARE @ExtractedWord VARCHAR(20)
DECLARE @Matches SMALLINT

/* This variable keeps the number of matches */
```

```
SELECT @Matches = 0

/* Analyze the phrase word by word */
WHILE LEN(@Phrase)>0
  BEGIN
    SELECT @NextSpacePos = CHARINDEX(' ', @Phrase)
    IF @NextSpacePos = 0
      BEGIN
        SELECT @ExtractedWord = @Phrase
        SELECT @Phrase=''
      END
    ELSE
      BEGIN
        SELECT @ExtractedWord = LEFT(@Phrase, @NextSpacePos-1)
        SELECT @Phrase = RIGHT(@Phrase, LEN(@Phrase)-@NextSpacePos)
      END

    /* If there's a match... */
    IF @SoundexWord = SOUNDEX(@ExtractedWord)
      SELECT @Matches = @Matches + 1

    /* To allow for more matches, use DIFFERENCE instead of SOUNDEX:
    IF DIFFERENCE(@ExtractedWord, @Word) >= 3
      SELECT @Matches = @Matches + 1 */
  END

/* Return the number of occurences of @Word in @Phrase */
RETURN @Matches
END
```

Summary

In this chapter, you implemented the search functionality of BalloonShop. You learned many useful tricks about SQL Server and C# programming.

While implementing the data tier, you learned two ways of counting how many times a substring appears in a longer string while building the WordCount function. You learned how to use that function to implement search results ranking in the SearchCatalog procedure. You also learned how to select only a portion of the entire search results by using a table variable in SQL Server.

In the business tier, you added the logic to process the string entered by the visitor and send the words to search for to the presentation tier. The presentation tier nicely displays the search results by reusing the ProductsList controls you wrote in Chapter 4.

CHAPTER 6

■ ■ ■

Improving Performance

Why walk, when you can run? No, we won't talk about sports cars in this chapter. Instead, we'll analyze a few possibilities to improve the performance of the BalloonShop project.

For now, rest assured that you've already implemented good programming practices when building BalloonShop, such as

- Carefully designing the database; for example, having indexes on the columns used in table joins significantly improves query performance

- Writing efficient SQL code (starting from little tricks such as avoiding using the * wildcard, to implementing efficient query logic) and storing that code within stored procedures (which are easier to maintain and run faster than ad-hoc queries)

- Using smart data access techniques in the business tier

- Using fast ASP.NET objects and efficient techniques when building the presentation tier.

However, you can gain even more performance by using a few new tricks. In this chapter, you'll briefly learn about some of the most important performance tricks.

In this chapter, you'll learn how to

- Avoid populating controls with data during postback events

- Disable ViewState to pass less data in client-server roundtrips

- Enable output page caching

■**Caution** This chapter is a very short introduction to just a few topics regarding ASP.NET performance. For a serious coverage of these subjects, you should read an advanced ASP.NET 2.0 book. Also look over Alex Homer's excellent article on ASP.NET 2.0 data-caching techniques at http://www.devx.com/dotnet/Article/27327?trk=DXRSS_WEBDEV.

Handling Postback

Postback is the mechanism by which the client (the web browser) informs the server about the events that happen to its server-side controls. When an event happens at the client side (such as a button click), the data about this event is posted back to the server, where it's handled using server-side code (the C# code from the code-behind files).

For example, if a visitor clicks your Button control, the data about this event is posted back on the server. At the server side, the button's Click event method executes, and the results are sent back to the client as HTML code.

Every time such an event happens, the ASP.NET page and all its controls (including user controls) get reloaded, and their Page_Load event executes. In any data-driven application, it's likely that these Page_Load methods access the database to populate the page with information.

When each ASP.NET control has a "cache" mechanism called ViewState (which retains the control's data during postbacks), it isn't efficient to have these controls reload their data from the database (or do other initialization things) on each postback event (unless that postback event affects the database and the controls of the page actually need to get the updated information).

Thanks to this ViewState mechanism, unlike with other web-development technologies, the state of the controls in the page is not lost during postback events, even if you don't repopulate the controls in their Page_Load methods.

Note As a result, most times it makes sense to load the page or control contents only when loading the page for the first time, and reload the page or control contents during postbacks only if those postback events affect the data that needs to be displayed by the page or control.

In the BalloonShop site, you've already seen an example of postback event handling in the SearchBox control, which avoided filling its controls in Page_Load during postbacks.

Also in SearchBox.ascx, it's easy to see a possible performance problem when looking at the ExecuteSearch method:

```
// Redirect to the search results page
private void ExecuteSearch()
{
  if (searchTextBox.Text.Trim() != "")
    Response.Redirect(Request.ApplicationPath +
              "/Search.aspx?Search=" + searchTextBox.Text +
              "&AllWords=" + allWordsCheckBox.Checked.ToString());
}
```

The code in this method redirects the visitor to the search results page. However, in the postback process, the original page that initiated the event (Default.aspx, Catalog.aspx, Product.aspx, or even Search.aspx) is reloaded once before being redirected (its Page_Load method is executed). That means all the composing controls—including DepartmentsList.ascx, CategoriesList.ascx, ProductsList.ascx—and any other controls on the page are loaded twice: once in the original page, and then once again after the new page is loaded.

You can significantly improve performance by preventing Web User Controls or Web Forms from performing certain tasks (such as refreshing the DataList controls with information from the database) when they are being loaded as a result of a postback event.

The IsPostBack is a property of the Page class. Let's see how it works by updating some BalloonShop classes in the following exercise.

Exercise: Speeding Up BalloonShop

1. Open the code-behind file of **DepartmentsList** and update its **Page_Load** method as shown here:

```
// Load department details into the DataList
protected void Page_Load(object sender, EventArgs e)
{
  // don't reload data during postbacks
  if (!IsPostBack)
  {
    // CatalogAccess.GetDepartments returns a DataTable object containing
    // department data, which is read in the ItemTemplate of the DataList
    list.DataSource = CatalogAccess.GetDepartments();
    // Needed to bind the data bound controls to the data source
    list.DataBind();
  }
}
```

2. Now, do the same in **CategoriesList.ascx.cs**:

```
protected void Page_Load(object sender, EventArgs e)
{
  // don't reload data during postbacks
  if (!IsPostBack)
  {
    // Obtain the ID of the selected department
    string departmentId = Request.QueryString["DepartmentID"];
    // Continue only if DepartmentID exists in the query string
    if (departmentId != null)
    {
      // Catalog.GetCategoriesInDepartment returns a DataTable object
      // containing category data, which is displayed by the DataList
      list.DataSource = CatalogAccess.GetCategoriesInDepartment(departmentId);
      // Needed to bind the data bound controls to the data source
      list.DataBind();
      // Make space for the next control
      brLabel.Text = "<br />";
    }
  }
}
```

3. Now update the code in `Product.aspx.cs`:

```
protected void Page_Load(object sender, EventArgs e)
{
  // don't reload data during postbacks
  if (!IsPostBack)
  {
    PopulateControls();
  }
}
```

4. Apply the same change to `Catalog.aspx.cs`:

```
protected void Page_Load(object sender, EventArgs e)
{
  // don't reload data during postbacks
  if (!IsPostBack)
  {
    PopulateControls();
  }
}
```

5. Finally, open `Search.aspx.cs` and apply the following change:

```
protected void Page_Load(object sender, EventArgs e)
{
  // don't reload data during postbacks
  if (!IsPostBack)
  {
    // fill the table contents
    string searchString = Request.QueryString["Search"];
    titleLabel.Text = "Product Search";
    descriptionLabel.Text = "You searched for <font color=\"red\">"
  + searchString + "</font>.";
    // set the title of the page
    this.Title = BalloonShopConfiguration.SiteName +
              " : Product Search : " + searchString;
  }
}
```

How It Works: The `IsPostBack` Property

After completing the exercise, test your solution to see that everything works just like before. Apart from an increase in performance, nothing really changed.

In DepartmentsList.ascx.cs, the list of departments is populated in Page_Load. However, during postback events, its state is maintained by ASP.NET using the ViewState mechanism (which we'll discuss next), and the response is redirected to another page anyway. Also, there are no postback events that should affect the way the departments list looks. For these reasons, it's more efficient to query the database for the list of departments only the first time a page is loaded, and never reload the list of departments during postback events.

The Page.IsPostBack function is your best friend in this instance. IsPostBack indicates whether the page is being loaded in response to a client postback or whether it's being loaded and accessed for the first time.

■**Tip** Performance tuning can be fun to play with, but **never** do experiments on a production system. Sometimes the results are unexpected, until you learn very well how the ASP.NET internals work.

Managing ViewState

HTTP (Hypertext Transfer Protocol) is a stateless protocol—the server doesn't retain any information about the previous client request. Without an additional mechanism over this protocol, the server can't retain the state of a simple HTML page between client requests (for example, which check boxes or radio buttons are selected, and so on).

ASP.NET has a built-in technique for dealing with this problem. When sending the HTML response to the client, by default ASP.NET encodes the current state of every control in a string called ViewState, in the form of a hidden form field called __VEWSTATE.

ViewState is used to maintain the state of the web page during client postbacks. In other words, when the visitor performs any action that triggers a postback event, the page maintains its state after the event handler method executes at the server.

For this reason, in the previous exercise, you modified DepartmentsList.ascx.cs and the other controls and pages to first verify whether the control is being loaded as a result of a client postback. If it is, you don't need to query the database again, because its state is maintained by the ViewState mechanism.

The problem with ViewState is that it's transferred between the client and the server on every request. With pages that contain a large number of controls, the ViewState information can grow significantly, causing a lot of network traffic. The ViewState information can be disabled for an entire page, or for just specific controls on a page. However, when disabling ViewState for a control, you need to fill it with data even during postback events; otherwise, its contents would disappear.

■**Note** So, if you want to speed up a user control, you mainly have to choose between disabling its ViewState (causing less network traffic to happen) or letting ViewState be enabled but preventing further reprocessing of Page_Load during page postbacks (causing less database load when there are controls that work with the database). You can't apply both techniques, or you'll get empty controls when postback events occur. Which technique is best for a particular control depends on the specifics of the control.

To see the encoded ViewState information for a page, you can do a simple test. Load BalloonShop in your web browser, right-click the page, and select View Source. Inside the page

HTML code, you can see the ViewState information encoded as a hidden form element named __VIEWSTATE:

```
<input type="hidden" name="__VIEWSTATE"
value="dDwyMTAxNDE4MzM3O3Q8O2w8aTwxPjs+O2w8dDw7bDxpPDE+O2k8Mz47aTwxMT47PjtsPHQ8O2w8dGwwPjs+O2w8dDxAMDxwPHA8bDxTZWxlY3RlZEluZGV4O0RhdGFLZXlzO0 ............" />
```

■**Note** The value of the ViewState is not in human-readable form, but it isn't encrypted either. The information is stored as name-value pairs using the System.Web.UI.StateBag object. The simplest way to decipher the value stored in your ViewState is by going to a web site such as http://www.wilsondotnet.com/Demos/ViewState.aspx, which reveals what the ViewState string actually contains.

In the BalloonShop web site, you're mainly concerned about the ViewState for ProductsList.ascx, which can get quite large for a lot of products. The total page ViewState has close to 2KB if the page has six products, and less than 1KB if no products are displayed on the page.

The professional way to view how much space the ViewState occupies for every element on the page is to enable page tracing by opening a Web Form and modifying its Page directive. Update Default.aspx like this:

```
<%@ Page Trace="true" Language="C#" MasterPageFile="~/BalloonShop.master"
CompileWith="Default.aspx.cs" ClassName="Default_aspx" Title="Untitled Page" %>
```

After making this change, load Default.aspx and look at the tracing information appended at the bottom of the page. You can see a lot of info about your page, including the ViewState size for every control.

■**Note** This is obvious, but it has to be said: Always remember to turn off tracing and debug mode before releasing your pages to the web.

By default, ViewState is enabled for all server controls. However, it can be disabled for a specific control or even for an entire page. For the pages and controls where we prevented reloading during postback events, we'll leave ViewState enabled.

You should disable ViewState for ProductsList.ascx because you need to populate it every time from the database anyway—all postback events that happen in your web site affect its contents, so using the cached version from the ViewState isn't an option. Moreover, the list of products causes a lot of ViewState data, so disabling its ViewState causes a significant network traffic improvement.

To disable ViewState for a control, change its EnableViewState property to False (by default it's True). Let's disable ViewState for the DataList control in ProductsList.ascx and for the entire SearchBox.ascx control in the following exercise.

Exercise: Disabling `ViewState` for Server-Side Controls

1. Open `ProductsList.ascx` in **Design View**, select the `DataList`, and open its **Properties** window by pressing **F4**.

2. Set the `EnableViewState` property to **False**, as shown in Figure 6-1.

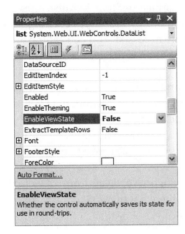

Figure 6-1. *Disabling* ViewState *for the* DataList *control*

How It Works: Disabling `ViewState` to Improve Performance

Now you have disabled `ViewState` for some of your controls. For your particular solutions, you'll decide for which controls it's best to disable `ViewState`.

So far, you've learned about letting ASP.NET manage the state of your controls, in which case you don't reload the controls with data from the database (by verifying the `IsPostBack` value), like you did with `DepartmentsList.ascx`. You also learned how to disable the `ViewState` information, in which case you rely on the control reading the database on every request.

Most of the time, you must not apply both techniques because you risk ending up with "empty" controls when client postbacks occur, because the data isn't gathered from the database or from the `ViewState`.

So far, your client's web site is an exception to that rule, however, because the only occasion (until now) in which a client postback occurs is in the `SearchBox` control, at which time the page is redirected (and so reloaded) anyway. Still, for a quick test, you can now disable `ViewState` for `DepartmentsList.ascx`, add a button somewhere in `Default.aspx`, and double-click it (in Design View) to create its `Click` event handler. Execute the page, and click the button. The list of departments should disappear because its `ViewState` is not maintained, and it's not populated from the database, either.

Using Output Cache

Output page caching is an ASP.NET feature that increases the performance of your Web Application by caching the HTML content generated from dynamic pages or controls. In other words, a page or user control that has output caching enabled is only executed the first time it is requested. On subsequent requests, the page or control is served directly from the cache, instead of being executed again.

This can have an important effect on performance for BalloonShop, because most controls access the database to populate themselves with information. With output caching enabled, the controls only read the database the first time they are accessed. You can set the interval of time at which the cache expires, so the controls have the chance to execute again, and refresh them with current information.

The drawback with output caching is that if the information in the database changes in the meantime, your page will display outdated information. For controls whose data is susceptible to frequent updates, the duration of the cache should be shorter.

Also, enabling output caching, although it saves server-processing power, consumes server memory, and should be used with caution. This is especially true when storing multiple versions of the page or user control being cached.

You can enable output page caching for a Web Form or Web User Control using the OutputCache page directive, which has a number of optional parameters:

```
<%@ OutputCache
    Duration="#ofseconds"
    Location="Any | Client | Downstream | Server | None"
    Shared="True | False"
    VaryByControl="controlname"
    VaryByCustom="browser | customstring"
    VaryByHeader="headers"
    VaryByParam="parametername" %>
```

- *Duration*: Specifies the number of seconds the page is stored in cache. A page is stored in cache the first time it's generated, which happens the first time a visitor asks for it. All the subsequent requests for that page, during the period mentioned by Duration, are served directly from cache instead of being processed again. After the cache duration expires, the page is removed from the cache.

- *Location*: Specifies the place the actual data for the cache is stored. The default value (Any) caches the page on the client browser, on the web server, or on any proxy servers supporting HTTP 1.1 caching located between the client and the server.

- *Shared*: Applies only to user controls, and specifies whether the output of the user control should be cached once for all the pages that include the control, or if multiple versions of the control should be cached for each page that contains it.

- *VaryByControl*: Used to vary the output cache depending on the values of server-side controls contained in the control or page being cached.

- *VaryByCustom*: Used to identity custom caching requirements. Its most popular value is "browser", which results in having different versions of the page cached at the server for each type of client-side browser. This feature is very useful if your dynamic web pages generate different HTML outputs depending on the client browser (this isn't the case for BalloonShop, however). If varying the output by browser type, the server retains different versions of the page that were generated for each kind and version of client browser.

- *VaryByHeader*: Used to vary the output cache by the value of different HTTP headers. When you set the value of VaryByHeader to a list of HTTP headers (separated by semicolons), multiple versions of the page are cached depending on the values of the mentioned headers. A typical value for VaryByHeader is "Accept-Language", which instructs ASP.NET to cache multiple versions of the page for different languages.

- *VaryByParam*: Varies the output cache based on the values of the parameters passed to the server, which include the query string parameters. You'll see in the exercise how to vary the output page cache based on the query string parameters.

You can enable output caching for DepartmentsList.ascx by editing the file in HTML View and by adding the following line at the beginning of the file:

```
<%@ OutputCache Duration="1000" VaryByParam="DepartmentIndex" %>
```

After adding this directive, ASP.NET retains the different output versions of DepartmentsList.ascx, depending on the value of the DepartmentIndex query string parameter.

■Caution Implementing output caching can easily affect the behavior of your web site in unexpected ways. Also, the way output caching should be implemented depends on the exact stage of your web site. For now, you shouldn't use output caching, but only keep its possibilities in mind. You can start improving performance and tweaking your Web Forms or Web User Controls after you have a working Web Application.

For controls whose output also depends on the CategoryIndex, such as CategoriesList.ascx and Catalog.ascx, you can implement caching like this:

```
<%@ OutputCache Duration="1000" VaryByParam="DepartmentIndex;CategoryIndex" %>
```

Because ProductsList.ascx has many output versions (especially if you take searching into account), it's not recommended to implement caching for it. However, if you still want to do this, you need to make it vary on every possible query string parameter that could influence its output, with an OutputCache directive like this:

```
<%@ OutputCache Duration="1000"
VaryByParam="DepartmentIndex;CategoryIndex;Search;AllWords;PageNumber;
ProductsOnPage" %>
```

Alternatively, the "*" wildcard can be used to vary the output cache on any possible query string parameter:

```
<%@ OutputCache Duration="1000" VaryByParam="*" %>
```

■**Note** You can test caching to make sure it actually works by either placing breakpoints in code (the code shouldn't execute at all when caching is enabled) or even by temporarily stopping SQL Server and then browsing through pages that were stored in cache (although for this to work, you'll need to implement caching on all the controls that perform data access).

Although implementing output page caching saves the database, it occupies web server memory. For this reason, it isn't feasible to implement output caching for controls such as ProductsList, which have a very large number of display possibilities. ProductsList has a different output for every department and category, not to mention the endless search possibilities.

■**Note** For your own solutions, you'll need to carefully decide on which user controls to implement output page caching. You can start experimenting by playing with the different controls that you implemented for BalloonShop so far. One thing you should be aware of is that output page caching doesn't always behave as expected during client postbacks generated by other user controls in the page. For this reason, it's advisable to test your solution seriously every time you change output cache options.

Summary

This chapter was very short, indeed, especially since it covered a topic that's very complex by its nature. Although ASP.NET performance tuning is out of the scope of this book, you took a quick look at the most useful features that allow you to improve a web site's performance.

In the next chapter, you'll learn how to accept payments for BalloonShop using PayPal.

CHAPTER 7

■■■

Receiving Payments Using PayPal

Let's collect some money! Your e-commerce web site needs a way to receive payments from customers. The preferred solution for established companies is to open a merchant account, but many small businesses choose to start with a solution that's simpler to implement, where they don't have to process credit card or payment information themselves.

A number of companies and web sites can help individuals or small businesses that don't have the resources to process credit card and wire transactions. These companies can be used to intermediate the payment between online businesses and their customers. Many of these payment-processing companies are relatively new, and the handling of any individual's financial details is very sensitive. Additionally, a quick search on the Internet will produce reports from both satisfied and unsatisfied customers for almost all of these companies. For these reasons, we are not recommending any specific third-party company.

Instead, this chapter lists some of the companies currently providing these services, and then demonstrates some of the functionality they provide with PayPal. You'll learn how to integrate PayPal with BalloonShop in the first two stages of development. In this chapter, you will

- Learn how to create a new PayPal account

- Learn how to integrate PayPal in stage 1 of development, where you'll need a shopping cart and custom checkout mechanism

- Learn how to integrate PayPal in stage 2 of development, where you'll have your own shopping cart, so you'll need to guide the visitor directly to a payment page

- Learn how to configure PayPal to automatically calculate shipping costs

---

Note This chapter is not a PayPal manual, but a quick guide to using PayPal. For any complex queries about the services provided, visit PayPal (`http://www.paypal.com`) or the Internet Payment Service Provider you decide to use. Also, you can buy components that make it easier to interact with these systems, such as the free ComponentOne PayPal eCommerce for ASP.NET by ComponentOne (`http://www.componentone.com`).

Considering Internet Payment Service Providers

Take a look at this list of Internet Payment Service Provider web sites. This is a diverse group, each having its advantages. Some of the providers transfer money person to person, and payments need to be verified manually; others offer sophisticated integration with your web site. Some providers work anywhere on the globe, whereas others work only for a single country.

The following list is not complete. You can find many other such companies by doing a Google search on "Internet Payment Service Providers." An online resource with a list of such companies that I've found helpful is http://www.online-payment-processing.com.

- *2Checkout*: http://www.2checkout.com

- *AnyPay*: http://www.anypay.com

- *CCNow*: http://www.ccnow.com

- *Electronic Transfer*: http://www.electronictransfer.com

- *Moneybookers*: http://www.moneybookers.com

- *MultiCards*: http://www.multicards.com

- *Pay By Web*: http://www.paybyweb.com

- *Paymate*: http://www.paymate.com.au

- *PayPal*: http://www.paypal.com

- *PaySystems*: http://www.paysystems.com

- *ProPay*: http://www.propay.com

- *QuickPayPro*: http://www.quickpaypro.com

- *WorldPay*: http://worldpay.com

For the demonstration in this chapter, we chose to use PayPal. Apart from being quite popular, PayPal offers the services that fit very well into our web site for the first two stages of development. PayPal is available in a number of countries—the most up-to-date list can be found at http://www.paypal.com.

For the first stage of development—where you only have a searchable product catalog—and with only a few lines of HTML code, PayPal enables you to add a shopping cart with checkout functionality. For the second stage of development, in which you need to manually record orders in the database, PayPal has a feature called Single Item Purchases that can be used to send the visitor directly to a payment page without the intermediate shopping cart. You'll use this feature of PayPal in Chapter 10.

For a summary of the features provided by PayPal, point your browser to http://www.paypal.com and click the Merchant Tools link. That page contains a few other useful links that will show you the main features available from PayPal.

Getting Started with PayPal

Probably the best description of this service is the one found on its web site: "PayPal is an account-based system that lets anyone with an email address securely send and receive online payments using their credit card or bank account."

PayPal is one of the companies that allow a small business like your BalloonShop to receive payments from its customers. The visitor, instead of paying the client directly, pays PayPal using a credit card or bank account. The client then uses its PayPal account to get the money received from the customers. At the time of writing, creating a new PayPal account is free, and the service for the buyer is free. The fees involved when receiving money are shown at `http://www.paypal.com/cgi-bin/webscr?cmd=_display-fees-outside`.

Visit the PayPal web site to get updated and complete information, and, of course, visit its competitors before making a decision for your own e-commerce site. You'll also want to check which of the services are available in your country, what kind of credit cards and payment methods each company accepts, information about currency conversions, and so on.

PAYPAL LINKS AND RESOURCES

Check out these resources when you need more information than this short chapter provides:

- *Website Payments Standard Integration Guide*: Contains information previously contained in separate manuals, such as the Shopping Cart manual and the Instant Payments Notification manual. Get it at `https://www.paypal.com/en_US/pdf/PP_WebsitePaymentsStandard_IntegrationGuide.pdf`.

- *The PayPal Developer Network*: The official resource for PayPal developers. Access it at `https://www.paypal.com/pdn`.

- *PayPalDev*: According to the site, this is an independent forum for PayPal developers. Access it at `http://www.paypaldev.org/`. You can also find numerous links to various other PayPal resources as well.

In the following exercise, you'll create a new PayPal account and then integrate it with BalloonShop. (These steps are also described in more detail in the PayPal manuals mentioned earlier.)

Exercise: Creating the PayPal Account

1. Browse to `http://www.paypal.com` using your favorite web browser.

2. Click the `Sign Up` link.

3. PayPal supports three account types: Personal, Premier, and Business. To receive credit card payments, you need to open a **Premier** or **Business** account. Choose your country from the combo box, and click **Continue**.

4. Complete all the requested information and you'll receive an email asking you to revisit the PayPal site to confirm the details you have entered.

■**Note** The email address you provide during the registration process will be your PayPal ID, and it will be shown to your customers when they pay for your products.

How It Works: The PayPal Account

After the PayPal account is set up, the email address you provided will be your PayPal ID.

The PayPal service provides a lot of functionality, and because the site is easy to use and many of the functions are self-explanatory, we won't describe everything here. Remember that these sites are there for your business, so they're more than happy to assist with any of your queries.

Now let's see how you can actually use the new account for the web site.

Integrating the PayPal Shopping Cart and Checkout

In the first stage of development (the current stage), you need to integrate the shopping cart and checkout functionality from PayPal. In the second stage of development, after you create your own shopping cart, you'll only need to rely on PayPal's checkout mechanism.

To accept payments, you need to add two important elements to the user interface part of the site: Add to Cart buttons for each product and a View Cart button somewhere on the page. PayPal makes adding these buttons a piece of cake.

The functionality of those buttons is performed by secure links to the PayPal web site. For example, the following form represents the Add to Cart button for a product named "Welcome Back" that costs $12.99:

```
<form target="paypal" action="https://www.paypal.com/cgi-bin/webscr" method="post">
  <input type="hidden" name="cmd" value="_cart">
  <input type="hidden" name="business" value="your_email_address">
  <input type="hidden" name="item_name" value="Welcome Back">
  <input type="hidden" name="amount" value="12.99">
  <input type="hidden" name="currency" value="USD">
  <input type="image" src="Images/AddToCart.gif" name="submit">
  <input type="hidden" name="add" value="1">
</form>
```

The fields are predefined and their names are self-explanatory. The most important is business, which must be the email address you used when you registered the PayPal account (the email address that will receive the money). Consult PayPal's Website Payments Standard Integration Guide for more details.

The View Cart button can be generated using a similar structure. In your web site, because ASP.NET works by default using a main form (and forms cannot be nested), you'll generate the buttons using links such as

```
https://www.paypal.com/cgi-bin/webscr?
cmd=_cart&business=your_email_address&item_name=Welcome Back&
amount=12.99&currency=USD&add=1
```

■**Caution** Yes, it's just that simple to manufacture an `Add to Cart` link! The drawback of this simplicity is that it can be potentially used against you. After PayPal confirms the payment, you can ship the products to your customer. On each payment, you need to carefully check that the product prices correspond to the correct amounts, because it's very easy for anyone to add a fake product to the shopping cart, or an existing product with a modified price. This can be done so simply by fabricating one of those PayPal `Add to Cart` links and navigating to it. You can read a detailed article about this problem at `http://www.alphabetware.com/pptamper.asp`.

You need to make sure this HTML code gets added to each product, so you'll have Add to Cart buttons for each product. To do this, you must modify the `ItemTemplate` of the `DataList` control in the `ProductsList` user control. Then, you'll add the View Cart button somewhere on `default.aspx`, so it's accessible at any time for the visitor.

In BalloonShop, you need to add links such as the one shown previously (`Add to Cart` links) in the product details pages (`Product.aspx`), and you need to add the `View Cart` link on the main web page (so you'll update `BalloonShop.master` as well).

■**Tip** Although we won't use them for our site, it's good to know that PayPal provides button generators based on certain data you provide (product name, product price), giving you an HTML code block similar to the one shown previously. Click the `Developers` link at the bottom of the first page and then click `PayPal Solutions` in the menu on the left to find the button generators.

You'll implement the PayPal integration in the next exercise.

Exercise: Integrating the PayPal Shopping Cart and Custom Checkout

1. Open `BalloonShop.master` in Source View and add the following JavaScript function inside the `<HEAD>` element:

```
<head runat="server">
  <title>BalloonShop</title>
  <script language="JavaScript">
```

```
<!--
var PayPalWindow = null;

// Opens a PayPal window
function OpenPayPalWindow(url)
{
  if ((!PayPalWindow) || PayPalWindow.closed)
    // If the PayPal window doesn't exist, we open it
    PayPalWindow = window.open(url, "cart", "height=300, width=500");
  else
  {
    // If the PayPal window exists, we make it show
    PayPalWindow.location.href=url;
    PayPalWindow.focus();
  }
}
// -->
</script>
</head>
```

Note JavaScript is case sensitive, so you need to be very careful to reproduce the code exactly; otherwise, it won't work as expected.

---

2. While `BalloonShop.master` is in Source View, add the View Cart button on the main page, just below the `SearchBox` control.

```
<uc4:SearchBox id="SearchBox1" runat="server">
</uc4:SearchBox>
<p align="center">
  <a href="JavaScript: OpenPayPalWindow('https://www.paypal.com/cgi-bin/webscr
            ?cmd=_cart
            &business=youremail@yourserver.com
            &display=1
            &return=www.yourwebsite.com
            &cancel_return=www.yourwebsite.com')">
    <IMG src="Images/ViewCart.gif" border="0">
  </a>
</p>
```

Note You must write the `OpenPayPalWindow` call on a single line in the HTML source. We split it on multiple lines in the code snippet to make it easier to read.

---

3. Next, to add the PayPal **Add to Cart** button in `Product.aspx`, open **Product.aspx** and add an HTML Server Control just below the product price:

```
<asp:Label CssClass="ProductPrice" ID="priceLabel" Runat="server"
 Text="Label"/>
<br /><br />
<a runat="server" id="addToCartLink">
  <IMG src="Images/AddToCart.gif" border="0">
</a>
```

Your form should look like Figure 7-1 in Design View.

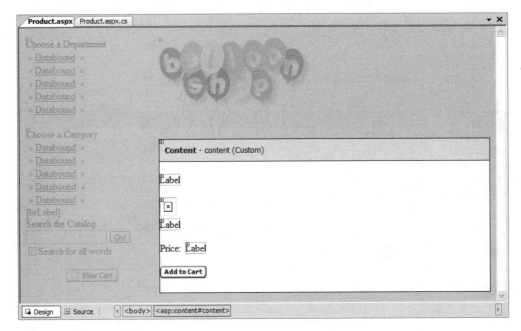

Figure 7-1. *The Add to Cart button in* `Product.aspx`

4. Append the following code to the `PopulateControls` method in `Product.aspx.cs`:

```
// Create the "Add to Cart" PayPal link
string link =
    "JavaScript: OpenPayPalWindow(\"https://www.paypal.com/cgi-bin/webscr"
    + "?cmd=_cart" + // open shopping cart command
    "&business=youremail@yourserver.com" + // your PayPal account
    "&item_name=" + pd.Name + // product name
    "&amount=" + String.Format("{0:0.00}", pd.Price) + // product price
    "&currency=USD" + // currency
    "&add=1" + // quantity to add to the shopping cart
    "&return=www.yourwebsite.com" + // return address
    "&cancel_return=www.yourwebsite.com\")"); // cancel return address)
```

```
// Encode link characters to be included in HTML file
string encodedLink = Server.HtmlEncode(link);
// The the link of the HTML Server Control
addToCartLink.HRef = encodedLink;
```

5. Make sure you replace **youremail@yourserver.com** in every link with the email address you submitted when you created your PayPal account for all Add to Cart and View Cart buttons. Also, replace **www.yourwebsite.com** with the address of your e-commerce store. Alternatively, you can remove the return and cancel_return variables if you don't want PayPal to redirect back to your web site after the customer completes or cancels a payment.

Caution You need to use the correct email address for the money to get into your account.

---

6. Press **F5** to execute the project. Your first page should look like Figure 7-2 now.

Figure 7-2. *Integrating the PayPal shopping cart*

7. Experiment with the PayPal shopping cart to make sure that it works as advertised. Figure 7-3 shows the PayPal shopping cart in action.

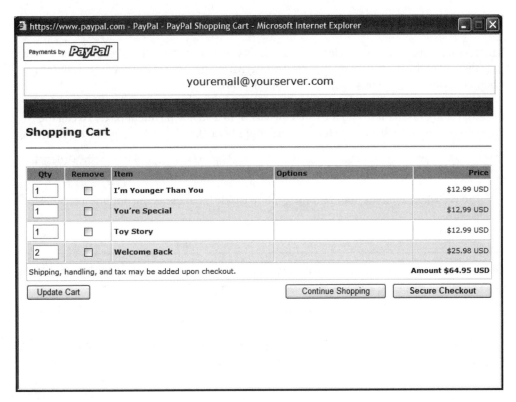

Figure 7-3. *The PayPal shopping cart*

How It Works: PayPal Integration

Yes, it was just that simple. Right now, all visitors became potential customers! They can click the Checkout button of the PayPal shopping cart, which allows them to buy the products!

After a customer makes a payment on the web site, an email notification is sent to the email address registered on PayPal and also to the customer. Your PayPal account reflects the payment, and you can view the transaction information in your account history or as a part of the history transaction log.

We touched on a few of the details of the PayPal shopping cart, but for a complete description of its functionality, you should read PayPal's Website Payments Standard Integration Guide. If you decide to use PayPal for your own web site, make sure you learn about all its features. For example, you can teach PayPal to automatically calculate shipping costs and tax for each order.

This was also the first time you created an HTML Server Control, when you added the Add to Cart link in Product.aspx. The HTML Server Control is just a simple HTML tag that has the runat="server" attribute. After you add that attribute, you can access its properties from the code-behind file, just as you did when setting the link's HRef property.

Among the alternative solutions is the use of an ImageButton control, whose OnClientClick property could contain the JavaScript function call that opens the PayPal shopping cart.

Using the PayPal Single Item Purchases Feature

Single Item Purchases is a PayPal feature that allows you to send the visitor directly to a payment page instead of the PayPal shopping cart. The PayPal shopping cart will become useless in Chapter 9, where you'll create your own shopping cart.

In Chapter 10, you'll implement the Place Order button in the shopping cart, which saves the order into the database and forwards the visitor to a PayPal payment page. To call the PayPal payment page (bypassing the PayPal shopping cart), redirect to a link like the following:

```
https://www.paypal.com/xclick/business=youremail@yourserver.com&item_name=Order#1
23&item_number=123&amount=123.00&currency=USD
```

The Website Payments Standard Integration Guide includes all the options available for this feature.

Note You'll create your own complete order-processing system in the third phase of development (starting with Chapter 12), where you'll process credit card transactions.

When you implement the PayPal Single Item Purchases in Chapter 10 (just after creating the Place Order button), you'll need to add the following code to checkoutButton_Click in the code-behind file of ShoppingCart.ascx:

```
// create a new order and redirect to a payment page
protected void checkoutButton_Click(object sender, EventArgs e)
{
  // Store the total amount because the cart
  // is emptied when creating the order
  decimal amount = ShoppingCartAccess.GetTotalAmount();
  // Create the order and store the order ID
  string orderId = ShoppingCartAccess.CreateOrder();
  // Create the PayPal redirect location
  string redirect = "";
  redirect += "https://www.paypal.com/xclick/business=youremail@server.com";
  redirect += "&item_name=" + BalloonShopConfiguration.SiteName + " Order "
                            + orderId;
  redirect += "&item_number=" + orderId;
  redirect += "&amount=" + String.Format("{0:0.00} ", amount);
  redirect += "&currency=USD";
  redirect += "&return=http://www.YourWebSite.com";
  redirect += "&cancel_return=http://www.YourWebSite.com";
  // Redirect to the payment page
  Response.Redirect(redirect);
}
```

Of course, don't forget to replace youremail@server.com with your registered PayPal email address and replace http://www.YourWebSite.com with the address of your e-commerce store.

The `return` and `cancel_return` parameters specify the web pages to return to after the payment is made or canceled. Figure 7-4 shows the PayPal Single Item Purchase screen.

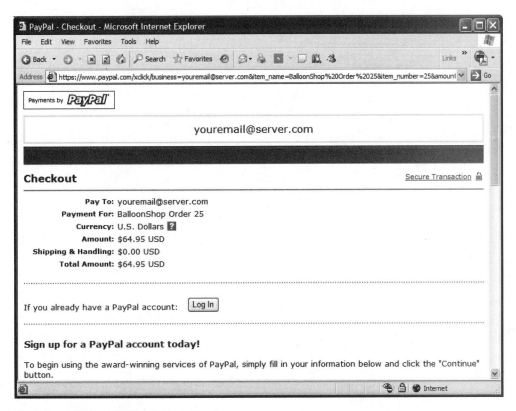

Figure 7-4. *The PayPal Single Item Purchase screen*

Summary

In this chapter, you saw how to integrate PayPal into an e-commerce site—a simple payment solution that many small businesses choose so they don't have to process credit card or payment information themselves.

First we listed some of the alternatives to PayPal, before guiding you through the creation of a new PayPal account. We then covered how to integrate PayPal in stages 1 and 2 of development, first discussing a shopping cart, a custom checkout mechanism, and then how to direct the visitor straight to the payment page.

In the next chapter, we'll move on to look at a catalog administration page for BalloonShop.

CHAPTER 8

■■■

Catalog Administration

The final detail to take care of before launching BalloonShop is to create the administrative interface.

In the previous chapters, you worked with catalog information that already existed in the database. You've probably inserted some records yourself, or maybe you downloaded the department, category, and product information from the Source Code area of the Apress web site. Obviously, for a real web site, both ways are unacceptable, so you need to write some code to allow easy management of the web store data.

In this chapter, you'll implement a catalog administration page. With this feature, you complete the first stage of your web site's development!

Because this page can be done in many ways, a serious discussion with the client is required to get the specific list of required features. In our case, the catalog administration page should allow the client to

- Add or remove departments, and update the details of existing departments

- View and manage the categories that belong to a department

- Manage the list of products in a specific category, and edit product details

- Assign an existing product to an additional category (a product can belong to multiple categories), or move it to another category

- Remove a product from a category or delete the product from the catalog

The administration page also needs to ask for a username and password, so that only the site administrator is allowed to perform administrative tasks.

Preparing to Create the Catalog Administration Page

Although the list of objectives might look intimidating at first, it will be easy to implement. We have already covered most of the theory in the previous chapters, but you'll still learn a few new bits of information in this chapter.

The first step toward creating the catalog administration page is to create a simple login mechanism for administrators. This mechanism will be extended in Chapter 12, where you'll add customer accounts. The user interface bit of the login functionality consists of a control named UserInfo that allows the administrator to authenticate himself or herself (see Figure 8-1).

Figure 8-1. *BalloonShop with a login box*

After logging in as an administrator, the UserInfo box displays links to the administrative parts of the site. The first page of the catalog administration section that you'll build in this chapter will look like Figure 8-2 (note that it reuses the UserInfo control).

■**Tip** Although the list of departments looks like a DataList control, it's actually a GridView. You'll learn more about this control later, when you create the DepartmentsAdmin Web User Control. For now, it's important to know that it allows for easy integration of edit, select, and delete functionalities. When the Edit, Edit Categories (Select), or Delete buttons are clicked, events are generated that can be handled in code.

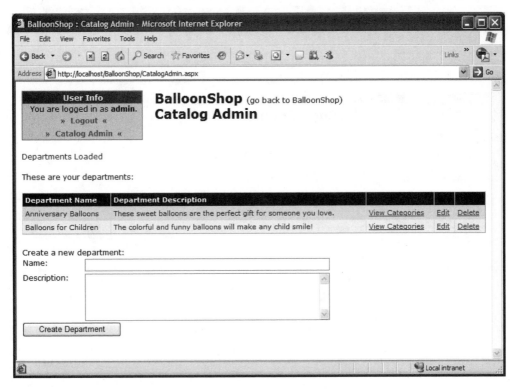

Figure 8-2. *Administering departments*

The functionality you'll implement for departments is much the same as you'll see for categories and products. More specifically, the administrator can

- Edit the department's name or description by clicking the Edit button.

- Edit the categories for a specific department by clicking the Edit Categories button.

- Completely remove a department from the database by clicking the Delete button (this works only if the department has no related categories; otherwise, the administrator is notified that the operation couldn't be completed).

When clicking the Edit button, the grid enters edit mode, and its fields become editable TextBox controls, as shown in Figure 8-3. Also, as you can see, instead of the Edit button, you get Update and Cancel buttons. Clicking Update updates the database with the changes, whereas clicking Cancel simply quits edit mode.

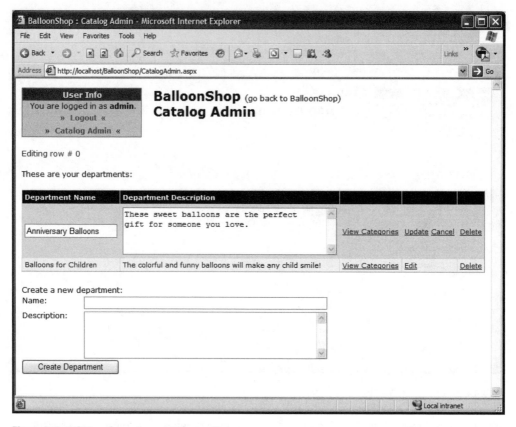

Figure 8-3. *Editing department information*

The administrator can add new departments by writing the new department's name and description in the TextBox controls below the grid, and clicking the Add button.

When the administrator clicks the Edit Categories button, the page is reloaded, but with an additional parameter in the query string: DepartmentID. The user is presented with a similar page where he or she can edit the categories that belong to the selected department (see Figure 8-4).

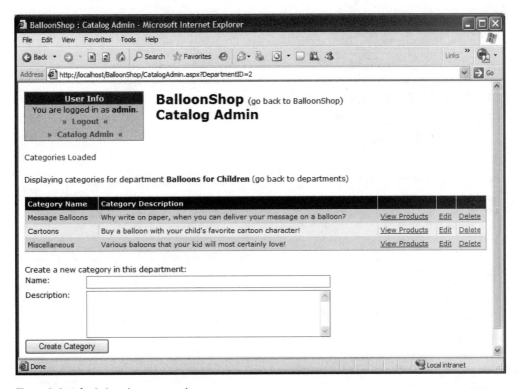

Figure 8-4. *Administering categories*

This page works similar to the one for editing departments, but there is an additional link that takes you back to the departments' page. When selecting a category, the page loads the list of products for that category (see Figure 8-5).

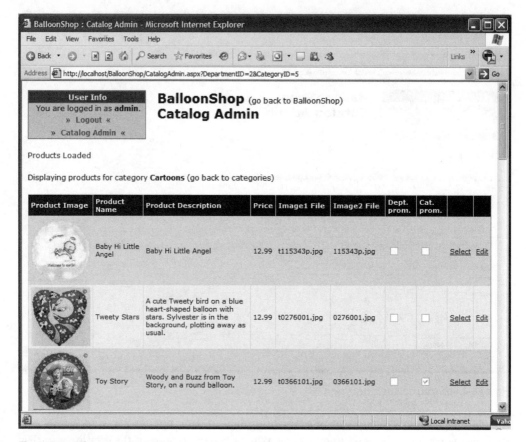

Figure 8-5. *Administering products*

Finally, the last page allows you to do additional product details management, such as changing the product's category, removing a product from a category or from the catalog, and so on (see Figure 8-6).

The navigation logic between the department, category, and product administration pages is done using query string parameters.

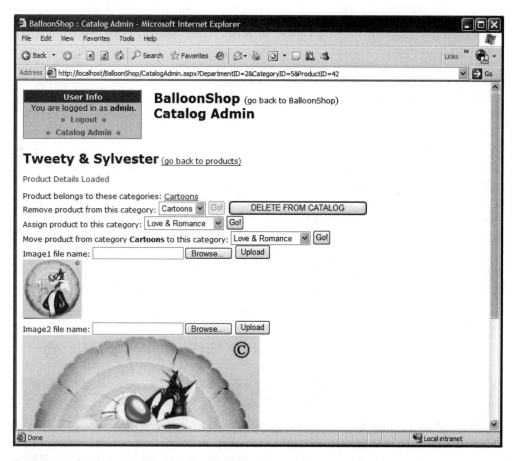

Figure 8-6. *Administering product details*

Authenticating Administrators

Because you want only certain persons to access the catalog administration page, you need to implement some sort of security mechanism that controls access to the sensitive pages in the site.

Implementing security implies dealing with two important concepts: **authentication** and **authorization**. Authentication is the process in which users are uniquely identified (most often by supplying a username and password); authorization refers to which resources the authenticated user can access.

Users who want to access the catalog administration page should first authenticate themselves. After you know who they are, you decide whether they are authorized to access the administration page.

In BalloonShop, you'll use an authentication method called `Forms authentication`, which allows you to control the login process through a Web Form. After the client is authenticated, ASP.NET automatically generates a cookie on the client, which is used to authenticate all subsequent requests. If the cookie is not found, the client is redirected to the login Web Form.

■**Tip** You should know that ASP.NET supports more authentication methods, which are presented in the MSDN article on ASP.NET authentication at `http://msdn.microsoft.com/library/default.asp?url=/library/en-us/vsent7/html/vxconASPNETAuthentication.asp`. Two other interesting and detailed articles on ASP.NET security are "Building Secure ASP.NET Applications: Authentication, Authorization, and Secure Communication" (`http://msdn.microsoft.com/library/default.asp?url=/library/en-us/dnnetsec/html/secnetlpMSDN.asp`) and "Improving Web Application Security: Threats and Countermeasures" (`http://msdn.microsoft.com/library/default.asp?url=/library/en-us/dnnetsec/html/ThreatCounter.asp`).

Authorization to access various resources can be applied to individual users or to **roles**.

ROLES

A role is a named set of permissions. In other words, a role contains permissions. Roles can be granted to or revoked from users; granting a role to a user has the same effect as granting the user all the permissions in that role. Roles are important because they allow the administrator to manage user privileges in a much more convenient way.

In this chapter, you'll create a new role named Administrators, which will have the privilege to access the web site administration pages. You'll add new roles in the following chapters.

The username and password combinations can be saved in various formats and can be physically stored in different places. ASP.NET stores the passwords in **hashed form** by default.

HASHING

Hashing is a common method for storing passwords. The hash value of a password is calculated by applying a mathematical function (hash algorithm) to it. The essential property about the hash algorithm is that you can't obtain the original password from its hash value (the algorithm is one-way).

Hashing is different from encryption in that it can't be undone, whereas encrypted data can be decrypted given the correct decrypt key is known. With hashing, even if some unauthorized person gets access to the database, he or she won't be able to find out the stored passwords (in practice, scientists have found vulnerabilities with the popular MD5, SHA-0, and SHA-1 hashing algorithms—see `http://www.broadbandreports.com/shownews/52284`).

User passwords are stored in hashed form, so when the user tries to authenticate, the entered password is hashed, and the resulted hash value is compared to the hash value of the original (correct) password. If the two values are identical, then the entered password is the correct one.

You can store the hashed versions of user passwords directly in `web.config` (although in this chapter you'll use a new ASP.NET 2.0 technique that uses the database for storage). To calculate the hash value of a password for storing in `web.config`, you can use the very intuitively named function `FormsAuthentication.HashPasswordForStoringInConfigFile`. You can find examples about how to use this function in MSDN and in a number of other articles, such as the ones at `http://www.stardeveloper.com/articles/display.html?article=2003062001&page=1` or `http://www.c-sharpcorner.com/Code/2003/Feb/HashPassword.asp`.

Alternatively, you can even hash your password online on a site such as `http://aspnetresources.com/tools/pwdhash.aspx`. For example, the hash value of the password "admin" using the SHA-1 algorithm is `D033E22AE348AEB5660FC2140AEC35850C4DA997`. In the following example, you'll simply store this hash value in `web.config`.

ASP.NET 2.0 works by default with an SQL Server Express database named ASPNETDB, located in the application's `App_Data` folder, whose data can be managed by the ASP.NET Web Site Administration Tool.

ASP.NET 2.0 and Using Declarative Security

To build the skeleton of your site's security mechanism, you'll use many of the new login controls offered by ASP.NET 2.0. At this stage, the functionality you implement is limited, because you only need to authenticate administrators, but you'll add more features in Chapter 12, when adding customer accounts. Here, you'll implement complete, working login/logout functionality and apply security restrictions to the admin pages without writing a single line of code! Everything is as simple as combining some login controls and applying templates to define the way they look and behave.

You can see the list of login controls packaged with ASP.NET 2.0 under the Login tab of the toolbox. The controls you'll use in this chapter are

- `Login` is perhaps the most useful control of all. It displays a login box asking for the username and password and a check box for the "remember me next time" feature. It has a number of color templates that you can apply, and if you don't like any of these templates, you can convert the whole control into a template (you'll see how to do this later in this chapter). This gives you access to all the individual controls that make up the `Login` control, so you can customize them separately. You'll use the template not only for changing colors and styles, but also to tie the text boxes and check boxes to the Log In button using the `TieButton` method you added in Chapter 5.

- `LoginView` is capable of displaying various templates depending on which user is logged in at the moment. The `AnonymousTemplate` is displayed if no user is logged in, and you'll generally want it to display the "You are not logged in" text and a link to the login page. If an administrator is logged in, your `LoginView` control displays links to the various administrative pages. In Chapter 12, when you'll allow your customers to create accounts on your site, your `LoginView` control will be updated to recognize the customers and display links to their personal pages.

- `LoginName` is a simple control that displays the name of the logged-in user. You'll use this control inside some templates of the `LoginView` control, to display the "You're logged in as *username*" text.

- `LoginStatus` simply generates a `Login` link in case no user is logged in and a `Logout` link in case a user is logged in.

Implementing Security

Let's add the security mechanism in the following exercise, where you'll

- Create a role named Administrators for your application, and then a user named admin that is associated with the role.

- Add the `UserInfo` control to your application that displays data about the currently logged-in user (refer to Figure 8-1).

- Create a login page named `Login.aspx`.

- Create the skeleton of the catalog administration page (`CatalogAdmin.aspx`).

- Make the `CatalogAdmin.aspx` page accessible only by users of the Administrators role.

Exercise: Implementing the Login Mechanism

1. The first step is to create an admin user to be recognized by your ASP.NET application. This user will have the privilege to access the catalog administration page. Start the ASP.NET Web Site Administration Tool by clicking **WebSite ➤ ASP.NET Configuration**.

2. Click the **Security** tab. You should get a screen like the one shown in Figure 8-7.

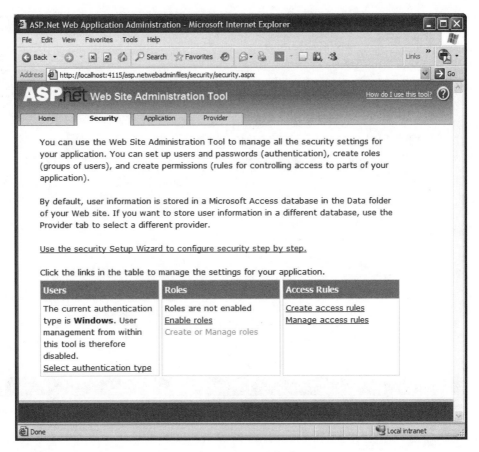

Figure 8-7. *The ASP.NET Web Site Administration Tool*

3. Click **Enable roles**.

4. Click **Create or Manage roles** and create a new role named **Administrators**. Click **Back**.

5. The default authentication type is Windows. Click **Select authentication type** and select the **From the Internet** option. Click **Done**.

6. Click **Create user** and add a new user that will be allowed to perform catalog administration tasks. We'll assume you add a new user named **admin** with the password **BalloonShop!**. Add some text of your choice for E-mail, Security Question, and Security Answer. Assign the user to the **Administrators** role by checking the check box, and click **Create User** (see Figure 8-8).

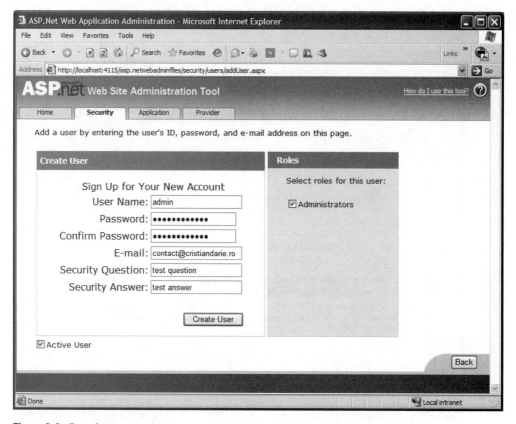

Figure 8-8. *Creating a new user*

■**Note** The default security settings require users to have strong passwords, so your password may be rejected if you try simpler passwords. This is because the ASP.NET membership system applies several rules to passwords, which are defined in `machine.config`. By default, passwords require a minimum length of seven characters, including at least one nonalphanumeric character (that is, a symbol character such as [, *, !, and so on). These settings can be changed by editing the `machine.config` file, which is located in `<Windows Install Directory>\Microsoft.NET\Framework\<Version>\CONFIG\`. Look for the definition of the `AspNetSqlMembershipProvider` provider, which can include the `minRequiredPasswordLength` and `minRequiredNonalphanumericCharacters` attributes to define the length and complexity of the password (or you can do this in one go using the `passwordStrengthRegularExpression` parameter). However, be aware that changes you make in `machine.config` apply to *all* the web sites on your computer. An alternative is to override the definition of this provider in `web.config`—you'll learn more details about this in Chapter 12.

---

7. Click **Back** to get to the main Security page. Make sure that you have one role and one user and then close the window.

8. Switch back to **Visual Studio**. You'll probably be asked to reload web.config, which was modified by an external program. Select **Yes**.

9. Next you'll create the UserInfo Web User Control, the Login Web Form, and the skeleton of the CatalogAdmin Web Form. First add the following styles to BalloonShop.css, which will be used in these pages:

```css
.UserInfoHead
{
  border-right: #cc6666 1px solid;
  border-top: #cc6666 1px solid;
  border-left: #cc6666 1px solid;
  border-bottom: #cc6666 1px solid;
  background-color: #dc143c;
  font-family: Verdana, Arial;
  font-weight: bold;
  font-size: 10pt;
  color: #f5f5dc;
  padding-left: 3px;
  text-align: center;
}
.UserInfoContent
{
  border-right: #cc6666 1px solid;
  border-top: #cc6666 1px solid;
  border-left: #cc6666 1px solid;
  border-bottom: #cc6666 1px solid;
  background-color: #ffcccc;
  text-align: center;
}
.UserInfoText
{
  font-family: Verdana, Arial;
  font-size: 9pt;
  padding-left: 5px;
  text-decoration: none;
}
a.UserInfoLink
{
  font-family: Verdana, Arial;
  font-weight: bold;
  font-size: 9pt;
  color: #ed486d;
  line-height: 15px;
  padding-left: 5px;
  text-decoration: none;
}
```

```
a.UserInfoLink:hover
{
  padding-left: 5px;
  color: #dc143c;
}
.Button
{
  color: Black;
  font-family: Verdana, Helvetica, sans-serif;
  font-size: 12px;
}
.AdminTitle
{
  color: Black;
  font-family: Verdana, Helvetica, sans-serif;
  text-decoration: none;
  font-size: 21px;
  font-weight: bold;
  line-height: 25px;
}
.AdminPageText
{
  color: Navy;
  font-family: Verdana, Helvetica, sans-serif;
  text-decoration: none;
  font-size: 12px;
}
a.AdminPageText
{
  color: Navy;
  font-family: Verdana, Helvetica, sans-serif;
  text-decoration: none;
  font-size: 12px;
}
a.AdminPageText:hover
{
  color:Red;
}
```

10. Now, create a Web User Control named **UserInfo.ascx** in your **UserControls** folder.

11. In UserInfo, you'll use a new ASP.NET 2.0 control named LoginView, which can display different data (through templates) depending on the currently logged-in user. For users of the Administrators role, you'll display links to the administration pages, and if no users are logged in, you simply display a login link (using the LoginStatus control). You can edit the templates of the LoginView control by either using Design View or Source View. Either way, make sure your UserInfo Web User Control contains the following code:

```
<%@ Control Language="C#" AutoEventWireup="true" CodeFile="UserInfo.ascx.cs"
Inherits="UserInfo" %>
<table cellspacing="0" border="0" width="200px" class="UserInfoContent">
  <tr>
    <td class="UserInfoHead">
      User Info</td>
  </tr>
  <asp:LoginView ID="LoginView1" runat="server">
    <AnonymousTemplate>
      <tr>
        <td>
          <span class="UserInfoText">You are not logged in.</span>
        </td>
      </tr>
      <tr>
        <td>
           &raquo;
            <asp:LoginStatus ID="LoginStatus1" runat="server"
CssClass="UserInfoLink" />
           &laquo;
        </td>
      </tr>
    </AnonymousTemplate>
    <RoleGroups>
      <asp:RoleGroup Roles="Administrators">
        <ContentTemplate>
          <tr>
            <td>
              <asp:LoginName ID="LoginName2" runat="server" FormatString=
"You are logged in as <b>{0}</b>. "
                CssClass="UserInfoText" />
            </td>
          </tr>
          <tr>
            <td>
               &raquo;
                <asp:LoginStatus ID="LoginStatus2" runat="server" CssClass=
"UserInfoLink" />
               &laquo;
            </td>
          </tr>
          <tr>
            <td>
               &raquo;
                <a class="UserInfoLink" href="CatalogAdmin.aspx">
```

```
Catalog Admin</a>
                 &laquo;
            </td>
          </tr>
        </ContentTemplate>
      </asp:RoleGroup>
    </RoleGroups>
  </asp:LoginView>
</table>
```

12. Open `BalloonShop.master` and drag the `UserInfo` control from **Solution Explorer** just before the list of departments, as shown in Figure 8-9.

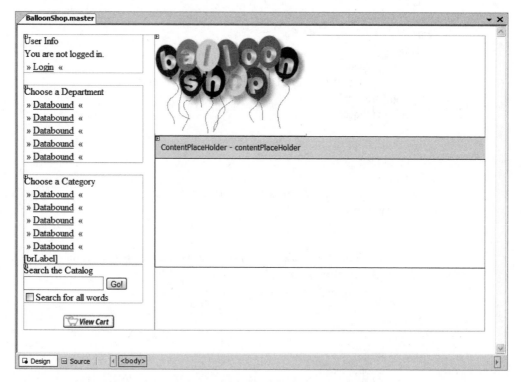

Figure 8-9. *Adding the* `UserInfo` *control to the Master Page*

13. Start your project and ensure that your `UserInfo` control looks good. The next step is to create the login page. Right-click the root entry in **Solution Explorer**, select **Add New Item**, choose the **Web Form** template, and name it `Login.aspx`. Make sure the two check boxes are checked and click **Add**.

14. In the dialog box that opens, select the **BalloonShop.master** entry and click **OK**.

15. Switch `Login.aspx` to **Design View**, add a **Login** control from the **Login** tab of the toolbox to the content placeholder, and then rename the control from **Login1** to **login**, as shown in Figure 8-10.

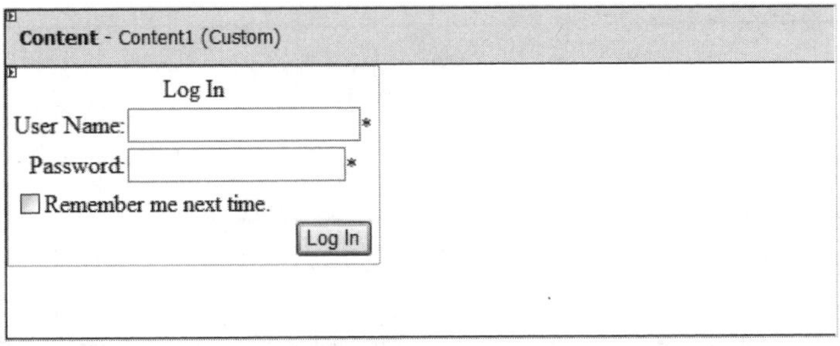

Figure 8-10. *The content area of Login.aspx in Design View*

16. Open `web.config` and change the `<authentication>` element under the `<system.web>` node, as shown next. This registers `Login.aspx` as the default login page, which visitors will be forwarded to if they click the `Login` link or when they try to access an unauthorized page.

```
<authentication mode="Forms">
  <forms name="BalloonShopLogin"
      loginUrl="Login.aspx" path="/" protection="All" timeout="60">
  </forms>
</authentication>
```

At this point, you have a working login and logout mechanism! Start your project to ensure the login and logout features are fully working (try to log in with the username admin, which should have as the password BalloonShop!, if you followed the instructions).

■**Note** After you type your username and password, it's not enough to just press the Enter key while the focus is on the Password text box or on the check box. You need to press the Tab key to give the Log In button the focus or click the Log In button with the mouse. You'll fix this problem in the next steps by using the `TieButton` method that you implemented in Chapter 5 (I told you that method would be useful!).

---

17. Continue by doing a few cosmetic changes to your page. To make the `Login` control fully customizable by having access to its individual constituent controls, you need to convert it to a template. Click its **Smart Link** and choose **Convert to Template**, as shown in Figure 8-11.

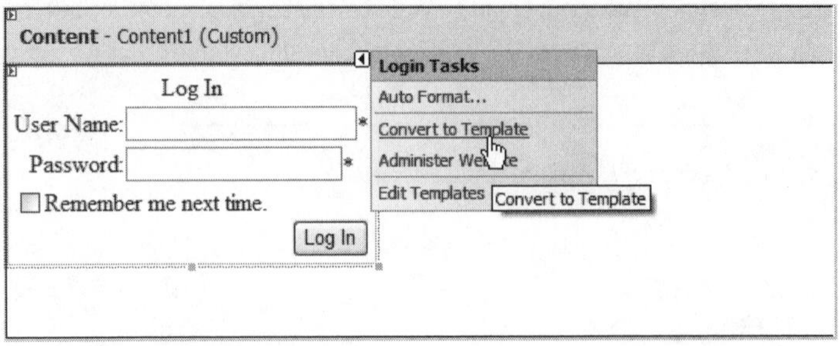

Figure 8-11. *Converting the* Login *control to a template*

18. Switch to **Source View**. After converting the control to a template, you'll see all of its constituent controls generated inside its <LayoutTemplate>. Modify the template as shown in the following code snippet:

```
<LayoutTemplate>
  <table border="0" cellpadding="1">
    <tr class="UserInfoText">
      <td>
        <table border="0" cellpadding="0">
          <tr>
            <td class="CatalogTitle" align="left" colspan="2">
              Who Are You?<br /><br />
            </td>
          </tr>
          <tr>
.....
```

19. Remember the TieButton method you wrote in Chapter 5? You'll use it here again to link the username and password text boxes to the Log In button. After converting the Login control to use templates, not only is it easy to change how the control looks, but you can also see the names of the constituent controls (more specifically, you want to find the names of the two TextBox controls and the name of the Button control). Open the code-behind file **Login.aspx.cs** and modify **Page_Load** like this:

```
protected void Page_Load(object sender, EventArgs e)
{
  // get references to the button, checkbox and textboxes
  TextBox usernameTextBox = (TextBox)login.FindControl("UserName");
  TextBox passwordTextBox = (TextBox)login.FindControl("Password");
  CheckBox persistCheckBox = (CheckBox)login.FindControl("RememberMe");
  Button loginButton = (Button)login.FindControl("LoginButton");
  // tie the two textboxes and the checkbox to the button
  Utilities.TieButton(this.Page, usernameTextBox, loginButton);
  Utilities.TieButton(this.Page, passwordTextBox, loginButton);
  Utilities.TieButton(this.Page, persistCheckBox, loginButton);
```

```
    // set the page title
    this.Title = BalloonShopConfiguration.SiteName + " : Login";
    // set focus on the username textbox when the page loads
    usernameTextBox.Focus();
}
```

20. Now your login page not only that works well, but it also looks good and is very user-friendly. The next and final task for this exercise is to create the skeleton of your administrative part of the site. Start by creating a new Master Page to be used by all the admin pages you'll build for BalloonShop. Right-click the project name in **Solution Explorer**, choose **Add New Item**, select **Master Page**, and type **Admin.master** for the name. Choose **Visual C#** for the language, make sure **Place code in separate file** is checked, and click **Add**.

21. While editing the page in **Source View**, modify the body like this:

```
<body>
  <form id="form1" runat="server">
    <table cellspacing="0" cellpadding="0" border="0" width="100%">
      <tr = valign="top">
        <td width="220">
          <uc1:UserInfo ID="UserInfo1" runat="server" />
        </td>
        <td valign="top">
          <span class="AdminTitle">
            <% Response.Write(BalloonShopConfiguration.SiteName); %>
          </span>
          (<a href="Default.aspx" class="AdminPageText">go back
          to BalloonShop</a>)
          <br />
          <asp:ContentPlaceHolder ID="ContentPlaceHolder1" runat="server">
          </asp:ContentPlaceHolder>
        </td>
      </tr>
    </table>
    <br />
    <asp:ContentPlaceHolder ID="ContentPlaceHolder2" runat="server">
    </asp:ContentPlaceHolder>
  </form>
</body>
```

22. Switch to **Design View** and drag the UserInfo.ascx control you wrote earlier from the **Solution Explorer**, near the "Login here" text in your page. Delete the "Login here" text, and your page should look like Figure 8-12.

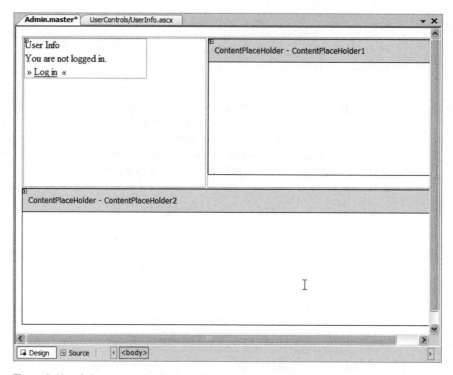

Figure 8-12. *Admin.master in Design View*

23. Add a new Web Form called **CatalogAdmin.aspx** to the project. Make sure its language is **Visual C#** and that both check boxes (**Place code in separate file** and **Select master page**) are checked. Click **Add**, choose the **Admin.master** Master Page, and then click **OK**.

24. In `CatalogAdmin.aspx`, write the following code in the first content area:

```
<asp:Content ID="Content1" ContentPlaceHolderID="ContentPlaceHolder1"
Runat="server">
  <span class="AdminTitle">Catalog Admin</span>
</asp:Content>
```

25. Add a **PlaceHolder** object from the toolbox to the second content area and change its **ID** to **adminPlaceHolder**.

26. Double-click `web.config` in **Solution Explorer** and add the following sections to it. Be aware that the default authentication mode is `Windows`, and you'll need to change it to `Forms`:

```
<?xml version="1.0" encoding="utf-8" ?>
<configuration xmlns="http://schemas.microsoft.com/.NetConfiguration/v2.0">
  <appSettings>
    ...
  </appSettings>

  <connectionStrings>
    ...
```

```
</connectionStrings>

<!-- Only administrators are allowed to access CatalogAdmin.aspx -->
<location path="CatalogAdmin.aspx">
  <system.web>
    <authorization>
      <allow roles="Administrators" />
      <deny users="*" />
    </authorization>
  </system.web>
</location>

<system.web>
  ...
```

How It Works: The Security Mechanism

Congratulations for finishing this long exercise! First, test that your new features work as expected. Try also to access the CatalogAdmin.aspx page without being logged in as Administrator or try to log out when you're in the admin page. You should be forwarded to the login page.

In this exercise, you first added the Administrators role and the admin user to your site. You performed these tasks using the ASP.NET Web Application Administration page. Feel free to check out other options of that page as well. For instance, you can access and manage the options you saved to web.config (such as SiteName, and so on) by going to the Application tab, and then clicking Create/Manage application settings.

The security data is saved in the App_Data folder of your application, in either an Access database or in an SQL Server Express database named ASPNETDB. After this database is created, you can access it from the Database Explorer window. You can change the engine used for this database from the ASP.NET Configuration page, on the Provider tab.

After adding the admin user, you created the UserInfo Web User Control. There you used a number of the new .NET 2.0 login controls that were explained previously. You could have used the designer to build these controls and their templates—and you can still use the designer to edit them, which I encourage you to test—but in this exercise, it was easier to simply type the code. Let's see how these controls were used:

- LoginView is capable of displaying various templates depending on what user is logged in at the moment. The AnonymousTemplate is displayed if no user is logged in, and it generates the "You are not logged in" text and a link to the login page.

```
<AnonymousTemplate>
  <tr>
    <td>
      <span class="UserInfoText">You are not logged in.</span>
    </td>
  </tr>
  <tr>
    <td>
       &raquo;
        <asp:LoginStatus ID="LoginStatus1" runat="server"
```

```
                CssClass="UserInfoLink" />
                     </asp:HyperLink>
                      &laquo;
                   </td>
                 </tr>
               </AnonymousTemplate>
```

- Then, under the `RoleGroups` template, you can find the HTML code that is displayed when an administrator is logged in.

- `LoginName` simply displays the "You are logged in as *username*" text. This text is defined in its `FormatString` property, where `{0}` is the username.

```
<asp:LoginName ID="LoginName2" runat="server"
FormatString="You are logged in as <b>{0}</b>. " CssClass="UserInfoText" />
```

- `LoginStatus` displays a `Login` link that forwards you to the login page you configured in `web.config`, or a Logout button that logs out the currently logged-in user and clears the current session information.

```
<asp:LoginStatus ID="LoginStatus1" runat="server" CssClass="UserInfoLink" />
```

After writing the `UserInfo` control, you created `Login.aspx`. Creating this page was extremely simple, because its only role is to contain a `Login` control. That control does the login work by itself, without requiring you to write any line of code or configure any settings. The extra steps you took for creating `Login.aspx` were for customizing the look of the `Login` control and converting it into a template to have access to its inner controls. Knowing the names of the inner controls helped you use the `Utilities.TieButton` method to tie the two text boxes and the one check box to the Log In button. This way, if the visitor presses Enter while any of the text boxes or the check box has focus, the Log In button is automatically clicked (otherwise, the page would have been refreshed without performing any login functionality).

Finally, `CatalogAdmin.aspx` was created to serve as a skeleton for the future catalog admin page. You configured it through `web.config` to be only accessible by users of the Administrators role:

```
<!-- Only administrators are allowed to access CatalogAdmin.aspx -->
<location path="CatalogAdmin.aspx">
  <system.web>
    <authorization>
      <allow roles="Administrators" />
      <deny users="*" />
    </authorization>
  </system.web>
</location>
```

Note that the authorization list is interpreted in sequential order. The following combination would reject all login attempts:

```
        <deny users="*" />
        <allow roles="Administrators" />
```

The * wildcard is used for "all identities." The other wildcard character, *?*, means "anonymous users." If you wanted all anonymous users to be denied, you could have used the following:

```
<location path="CatalogAdmin.aspx">
  <system.web>
    <authorization>
      <deny users="?" />
    </authorization>
  </system.web>
</location>
```

With this setting, any logged-in users (not only administrators) would be allowed access to the admin page.

Tip By default, all visitors are allowed access to all pages, so you need to explicitly deny access to the sensitive pages.

Administering Departments

The department administration section will allow your client to add, remove, or change department information. To implement this functionality, you'll need to write the code for the presentation, business, and data layers.

One fundamental truth regarding *n*-Tiered applications (which also applies to this particular case) is that the business and database tiers are ultimately created to support the presentation tier. Drawing it on paper and establishing exactly how you want the site to look (in other words, what functionality needs to be supported by the user interface) will provide you with a good indication of what the database and business tier will contain.

With the proper design work, you would know exactly what to place in each tier, so the order of writing the code wouldn't matter. When the design is clearly established, a team of programmers can work at the same time and implement the three tiers concurrently, which is one of the benefits of having a tiered architecture.

However, this rarely happens in practice, except for the largest projects that really need very careful design and planning. In our case, usually the best way is to start with the lower levels (the database) to get the basics established before creating the user interface. For this to happen, you need to analyze first what functionality is required for the user interface; otherwise, you won't know what to write in the data and business tiers.

Because you already have a working architecture, it will be simple to write components as needed for each tier. Of course, if you had to implement something new or more complicated, we would have spent some time analyzing the full implications, but here you won't do anything more complicated than the code in the previous chapters.

This being said, you'll implement all features for this chapter in the classical order, starting with the data tier.

Stored Procedures for Departments Administration

Four stored procedures perform the four basic tasks for departments: retrieve departments, update departments, delete departments, and insert departments. The procedure for retrieving departments already exists in the database, so you just need to add the other three.

AddDepartment

AddDepartment inserts a new department into the database. Add this stored procedure to the BalloonShop database:

```
CREATE PROCEDURE AddDepartment
(@DepartmentName varchar(50),
@DepartmentDescription varchar(1000))
AS
INSERT INTO Department (Name, Description)
VALUES (@DepartmentName, @DepartmentDescription)
```

UpdateDepartment

The UpdateDepartment stored procedure updates the name and description of an existing department using the UPDATE SQL statement. Add it to the BalloonShop database:

```
CREATE PROCEDURE UpdateDepartment
(@DepartmentID int,
@DepartmentName varchar(50),
@DepartmentDescription varchar(1000))
AS
UPDATE Department
SET Name = @DepartmentName, Description = @DepartmentDescription
WHERE DepartmentID = @DepartmentID
```

DeleteDepartment

DeleteDepartment deletes an existing department from the database. Add this stored procedure to the BalloonShop database:

```
CREATE PROCEDURE DeleteDepartment
(@DepartmentID int)
AS
DELETE FROM Department
WHERE DepartmentID = @DepartmentID
```

Middle-Tier Methods for Departments Administration

In this section, you'll add two new methods to the GenericDataAccess class, called ExecuteNonQuery and ExecuteScalar, which will wrap DbCommand's ExecuteNonQuery and ExecuteScalar methods in the same way ExecuteSelectCommand works with ExecuteReader.

You'll then add three methods to the CatalogAccess class that you'll need to call from the DepartmentsAdmin control (you'll also use the GetDepartments method that already exists):

- UpdateDepartment

- DeleteDepartment

- AddDepartment

Start by adding these methods to the GenericDataAccess class:

```
// execute an update, delete, or insert command
// and return the number of affected rows
public static int ExecuteNonQuery(DbCommand command)
{
  // The number of affected rows
  int affectedRows = -1;
  // Execute the command making sure the connection gets closed in the end
  try
  {
    // Open the connection of the command
    command.Connection.Open();
    // Execute the command and get the number of affected rows
    affectedRows = command.ExecuteNonQuery();
  }
  catch (Exception ex)
  {
    // Log eventual errors and rethrow them
    Utilities.LogError(ex);
    throw ex;
  }
  finally
  {
    // Close the connection
    command.Connection.Close();
  }
  // return the number of affected rows
  return affectedRows;
}

// execute a select command and return a single result as a string
public static string ExecuteScalar(DbCommand command)
{
  // The value to be returned
  string value = "";
  // Execute the command making sure the connection gets closed in the end
  try
  {
```

```
    // Open the connection of the command
    command.Connection.Open();
    // Execute the command and get the number of affected rows
    value = command.ExecuteScalar().ToString();
  }
  catch (Exception ex)
  {
    // Log eventual errors and rethrow them
    Utilities.LogError(ex);
    throw ex;
  }
  finally
  {
    // Close the connection
    command.Connection.Close();
  }
  // return the result
  return value;
}
```

The functionality in these two methods is similar to the one you wrote for ExecuteSelectCommand in Chapter 4, so we won't analyze them again here.

The next step is to update CatalogAccess. Add these methods to your CatalogAccess class, inside CatalogAccess.cs:

```
// Update department details
public static bool UpdateDepartment(string id, string name, string description)
{
  // get a configured DbCommand object
  DbCommand comm = GenericDataAccess.CreateCommand();
  // set the stored procedure name
  comm.CommandText = "UpdateDepartment";
  // create a new parameter
  DbParameter param = comm.CreateParameter();
  param.ParameterName = "@DepartmentId";
  param.Value = id;
  param.DbType = DbType.Int32;
  comm.Parameters.Add(param);
  // create a new parameter
  param = comm.CreateParameter();
  param.ParameterName = "@DepartmentName";
  param.Value = name;
  param.DbType = DbType.String;
  param.Size = 50;
  comm.Parameters.Add(param);
```

```csharp
  // create a new parameter
  param = comm.CreateParameter();
  param.ParameterName = "@DepartmentDescription";
  param.Value = description;
  param.DbType = DbType.String;
  param.Size = 1000;
  comm.Parameters.Add(param);
  // result will represent the number of changed rows
  int result = -1;
  try
  {
    // execute the stored procedure
    result = GenericDataAccess.ExecuteNonQuery(comm);
  }
  catch
  {
    // any errors are logged in GenericDataAccess, we ignore them here
  }
  // result will be 1 in case of success
  return (result != -1);
}

// Delete department
public static bool DeleteDepartment(string id)
{
  // get a configured DbCommand object
  DbCommand comm = GenericDataAccess.CreateCommand();
  // set the stored procedure name
  comm.CommandText = "DeleteDepartment";
  // create a new parameter
  DbParameter param = comm.CreateParameter();
  param.ParameterName = "@DepartmentId";
  param.Value = id;
  param.DbType = DbType.Int32;
  comm.Parameters.Add(param);
  // execute the stored procedure; an error will be thrown by the
  // database if the department has related categories, in which case
  // it is not deleted
  int result = -1;
  try
  {
    result = GenericDataAccess.ExecuteNonQuery(comm);
  }
  catch
  {
```

```
      // any errors are logged in GenericDataAccess, we ignore them here
    }
    // result will be 1 in case of success
    return (result != -1);
}


// Add a new department
public static bool AddDepartment(string name, string description)
{
    // get a configured DbCommand object
    DbCommand comm = GenericDataAccess.CreateCommand();
    // set the stored procedure name
    comm.CommandText = "AddDepartment";
    // create a new parameter
    DbParameter param = comm.CreateParameter();
    param.ParameterName = "@DepartmentName";
    param.Value = name;
    param.DbType = DbType.String;
    param.Size = 50;
    comm.Parameters.Add(param);
    // create a new parameter
    param = comm.CreateParameter();
    param.ParameterName = "@DepartmentDescription";
    param.Value = description;
    param.DbType = DbType.String;
    param.Size = 1000;
    comm.Parameters.Add(param);
    // result will represent the number of changed rows
    int result = -1;
    try
    {
        // execute the stored procedure
        result = GenericDataAccess.ExecuteNonQuery(comm);
    }
    catch
    {
        // any errors are logged in GenericDataAccess, we ignore them here
    }
    // result will be 1 in case of success
    return (result != -1);
}
```

The DepartmentsAdmin User Control

Figure 8-13 shows how the DepartmentsAdmin Web User Control will look.

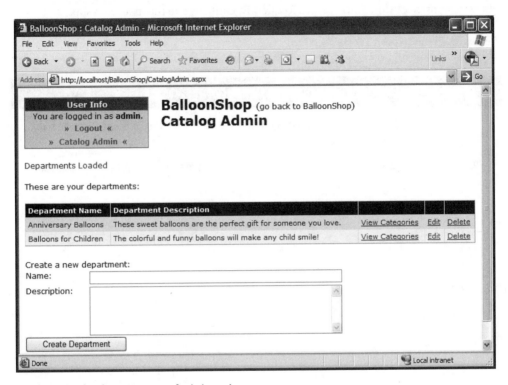

Figure 8-13. *The departments administration page*

The control is formed from a list populated with the departments' information, and it also has four additional controls (a label, two text boxes, and a button) used to add new departments to the list.

The list control you see in Figure 8-13 is not a DataList, but a GridView control.

■Tip The GridView object is more powerful than the DataList, but its power comes at the expense of speed. For this reason, when the GridView's extra features are not used, you should stick with the DataList. ASP.NET also provides an even simpler and faster object, named Repeater. We don't use the Repeater object in this book, but you should take a look at its documentation for more information.

The GridView is more powerful than DataList and has many more features; in this chapter, you'll only use a part of GridView's possibilities, particularly the ones that allow for easy integration of Edit, Select, and Delete buttons, and database-bound column editing in Design View. You can see the mentioned controls in Figure 8-13, where the Select button is called Edit Categories.

Everything you do here with `GridView` is also possible to do with `DataList`, but using `GridView` eases your work considerably because of its rich set of built-in features. You don't have to worry about the performance penalty for using a more complex control, because the administration page won't be accessed frequently, compared to the main web site.

You'll implement `DepartmentsAdmin.ascx` in the following exercise, and then we'll discuss the details in the "How it Works" section.

Exercise: Implementing `DepartmentsAdmin.ascx`

1. Create a new Web User Control named **DepartmentsAdmin** in the **UserControls** folder (be sure to check the **Place code in separate file** option).

2. Switch to **Design View**. From the toolbox, add two `Label` controls and a `GridView` control, as shown in Figure 8-14.

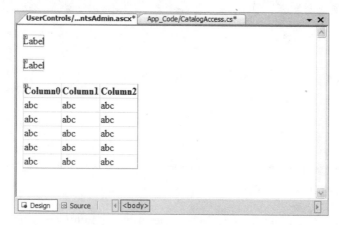

Figure 8-14. *Adding controls to* `DepartmentsAdmin.ascx`

3. Set the properties for the controls as shown in Table 8-1.

Table 8-1. *Setting the Properties for the Controls in* `CategoriesAdmin.ascx`

Control Type	ID **Property**	Text **Property**	CssClass **Property**
Label	statusLabel	Departments Loaded	AdminPageText
Label	locationLabel	These are your departments:	AdminPageText
GridView	grid		

4. Set the `DataKeyNames` property of the grid to **DepartmentID** and set its `Width` property to **100%**.

■Note Setting the DataKeyNames allows you to find the DepartmentID of the selected departments.

5. Switch to **Source View** and add the controls that will allow new departments to be added:

```
<br />
<span class="AdminPageText">Create a new department:</span>
<table class="AdminPageText" cellspacing="0">
  <tr>
    <td valign="top" width="100">Name:
    </td>
    <td>
      <asp:TextBox cssClass="AdminPageText" ID="newName" Runat="server"
Width="400px" />
    </td>
  </tr>
  <tr>
    <td valign="top" width="100">Description:
    </td>
    <td>
      <asp:TextBox cssClass="AdminPageText" ID="newDescription"
Runat="server" Width="400px" Height="70px" TextMode="MultiLine"/>
    </td>
  </tr>
</table>
<asp:Button ID="createDepartment" Text="Create Department" Runat="server"
CssClass="AdminButtonText" />
```

6. Click GridView's **Smart Link** and choose **Add New Column**. Use this command to add two columns with the properties shown in Table 8-2.

Table 8-2. *Adding Bound Fields to Your Grid*

Field Type	Header Text	Data Field	Other Properties
BoundField	Department Name	Name	
BoundField	Department Description	Description	

Your Add Field window should look like Figure 8-15 when adding the Department Name bound field.

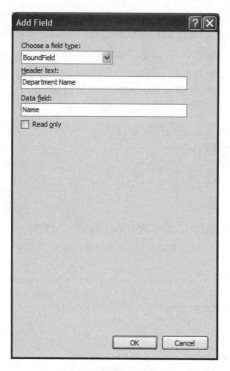

Figure 8-15. *Adding a bound column*

7. Add the **View Categories** column by adding a HyperLinkField with a text of **View Categories**. Set the data field to **DepartmentID** and the **URL format string** to **../CatalogAdmin.aspx?DepartmentID={0}**, as shown in Figure 8-16.

8. Now add the functionality that allows the administrator to edit department details. Use the **Add New Column** command again to add a CommandField. Leave the header text empty, leave button type set to **Link**, check the **Edit/Update** check box, and leave the **Show cancel button** check box checked. Click **OK**.

9. Finally, add the Delete button by clicking the **Smart Link** and choosing **Add New Column**. Choose the **ButtonField** field type, choose **Delete** for the command name, modify the text to **Delete**, and click **OK**.

10. Click GridView's **Smart Link** and choose **Edit Columns**. In the dialog box that opens, deselect **Auto-Generate Fields** (because you manually specified which columns to display). If you leave this check box checked, the GridView appends all columns retrieved from the data source to the manually created ones. At the end of this exercise, you might want to experiment with checking this check box, but for now, leave it unchecked. Click **OK**.

Okay, you finished working on the columns, so your control should now look like Figure 8-17.

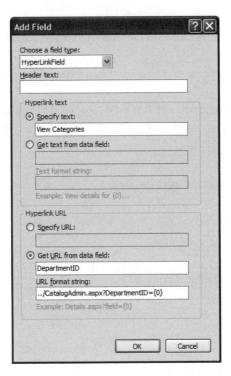

Figure 8-16. *Adding a HyperLinkField column*

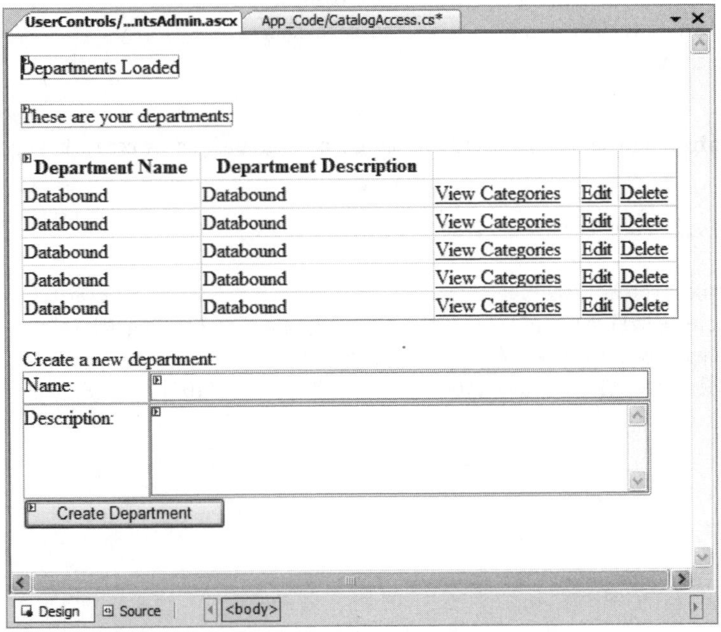

Figure 8-17. *Designing DepartmentsAdmin.ascx*

■Note Right now the CSS styles don't have any effect because BalloonShop.css is part of a skin, which is loaded at runtime.

---

11. To make the data grid functional, you need to populate it with data in the **Page_Load** method of **DepartmentsAdmin.ascx.cs**:

```
protected void Page_Load(object sender, EventArgs e)
{
  // Load the grid only the first time the page is loaded
  if (!Page.IsPostBack)
  {
    // Load the departments grid
    BindGrid();
    // Set control properties
    statusLabel.ForeColor = System.Drawing.Color.Red;
  }
}

// Populate the GridView with data
private void BindGrid()
{
  // Get a DataTable object containing the catalog departments
  grid.DataSource = CatalogAccess.GetDepartments();
  // Bind the data bound controls to the data source
  grid.DataBind();
}
```

12. Update **CatalogAdmin.aspx.cs** to load the admin user controls by adding this code to its **Page_Load** method:

```
protected void Page_Load(object sender, EventArgs e)
{
  // Set the title of the page
  this.Title = BalloonShopConfiguration.SiteName + " : Catalog Admin";
  // Get DepartmentID from the query string
  string departmentId = Request.QueryString["DepartmentID"];
```

```
    // Get CategoryID from the query string
    string categoryId = Request.QueryString["CategoryID"];
    // Get ProductID from the query string
    string productId = Request.QueryString["ProductID"];
    // Load the appropriate control into the place holder
    if (departmentId == null)
    {
      Control c = Page.LoadControl(Request.ApplicationPath +
                         "/UserControls/DepartmentsAdmin.ascx");
      adminPlaceHolder.Controls.Add(c);
    }
    else if (categoryId == null)
    {
      Control c = Page.LoadControl(Request.ApplicationPath +
                          "/UserControls/CategoriesAdmin.ascx");
      adminPlaceHolder.Controls.Add(c);
    }
    else if (productId == null)
    {
      Control c = Page.LoadControl(Request.ApplicationPath +
                          "/UserControls/ProductsAdmin.ascx");
      adminPlaceHolder.Controls.Add(c);
    }
    else
    {
      Control c = Page.LoadControl(Request.ApplicationPath +
                          "/UserControls/ProductDetailsAdmin.ascx");
      adminPlaceHolder.Controls.Add(c);
    }
  }
}
```

13. Pause here to test whether what you've been working on so far works. Execute the project, log in as administrator, and go to the catalog admin page. The GridView control doesn't look like much at the moment, but you'll take care of its looks a bit later. If everything works as expected, you should be presented with a page that looks like Figure 8-18.

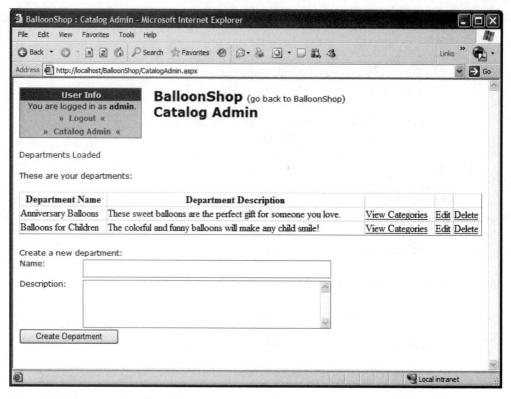

Figure 8-18. *Executing* CatalogAdmin.aspx

14. To change the looks of the DataGrid, you'll use a skin, which will define the appearance of every GridView in the site. Open the **App_Themes** folder in **Solution Explorer**.

15. Right-click the **BalloonShopDefault** folder and choose **Add New Item.**

16. Select the **Skin File** template and change the name to **BalloonShop.skin**.

17. Add the following code, which represents the default skin for GridView controls, to BalloonShop.skin:

```
<asp:GridView runat="server" CssClass="Grid" CellPadding="4"
AutoGenerateColumns="False">
  <SelectedRowStyle BackColor="#738A9C" Font-Bold="True"
ForeColor="#F7F7F7" />
  <HeaderStyle CssClass="GridHeader" />
  <RowStyle CssClass="GridRow" />
  <AlternatingRowStyle CssClass="GridAlternateRow" />
</asp:GridView>
```

18. Add the following styles to BalloonShop.css:

```
.Grid
{
  border-color: #E7E7FF;
  width: 100%;
}
.GridHeader
{
  color: White;
  background-color: Navy;
  font-family: Verdana, Helvetica, sans-serif;
  text-decoration: none;
  font-size: 11px;
  text-align: left;
}
.GridRow
{
  color: Navy;
  background-color: #E7E7FF;
  font-family: Verdana, Helvetica, sans-serif;
  text-decoration: none;
  font-size: 11px;
  text-align: left;
}
.GridEditingRow
{
  color: Navy;
  font-family: Verdana, Helvetica, sans-serif;
  text-decoration: none;
  font-size: 11px;
  text-align: left;
}
.GridAlternateRow
{
  color: Navy;
  background-color: #F7F7F7;
  font-family: Verdana, Helvetica, sans-serif;
  text-decoration: none;
  font-size: 11px;
  text-align: left;
}
```

19. Execute your project again to make sure your new skin and styles are in effect, as shown in Figure 8-19. Feel free to change your skin and styles files until the grid looks like you want it to.

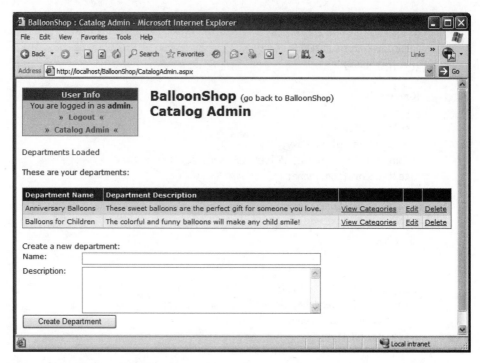

Figure 8-19. *Executing CatalogAdmin.aspx with skins and styles*

20. Now that everything looks good, you can implement the functionality by writing the event handlers for the Edit, View Categories, and Delete buttons. You'll start with the row editing functionality. Open DepartmentsAdmin.ascx in **Design View** and select the GridView control.

Figure 8-20. *Using Visual Web Developer to generate new event handlers*

21. In the **Properties window**, double-click the **RowEditing** entry (as shown in Figure 8-20). Visual Web Developer generates the grid_RowEditing event handler for you in the code-behind file, This method is executed when the visitor clicks the Edit button in the grid, and it must enable edit mode for that row. Modify the code in grid_RowEditing like this:

```
// Enter row into edit mode
protected void grid_RowEditing(object sender, GridViewEditEventArgs e)
{
    // Set the row for which to enable edit mode
    grid.EditIndex = e.NewEditIndex;
    // Set status message
    statusLabel.Text = "Editing row # " + e.NewEditIndex.ToString();
    // Reload the grid
    BindGrid();
}
```

22. While in edit mode, instead of the Edit button, the `GridView` places two buttons: Update and Cancel. To make editing functional, you need to supply code that reacts when these buttons are clicked. Let's start with the code that deals with the Cancel button. Follow the same procedure to generate `grid_RowCancelingEdit` and complete its code like this:

```
// Cancel edit mode
protected void grid_RowCancelingEdit(object sender,
GridViewCancelEditEventArgs e)
{
    // Cancel edit mode
    grid.EditIndex = -1;
    // Set status message
    statusLabel.Text = "Editing canceled";
    // Reload the grid
    BindGrid();
}
```

Now you have functional Edit and Cancel buttons. When the Edit button is clicked, the grid enters into edit mode, as shown in Figure 8-21.

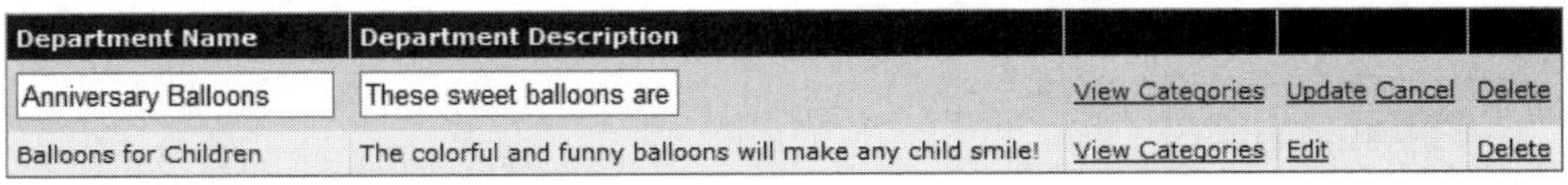

Department Name	Department Description				
Anniversary Balloons	These sweet balloons are		View Categories	Update Cancel	Delete
Balloons for Children	The colorful and funny balloons will make any child smile!	View Categories	Edit		Delete

Figure 8-21. *Editing department information*

■**Note** The problem with automatically generated editing controls is that they aren't configurable, unless transformed to **template columns**. You'll do this later in a separate exercise for the department description column, where the edit text box needs to be larger than the default size.

---

23. When the Update button is clicked, a `RowUpdating` event is raised. Generate its event handler like you did for the other two. Now add the following code for these two events:

```
// Update row
protected void grid_RowUpdating(object sender, GridViewUpdateEventArgs e)
{
  // Retrieve updated data
  string id = grid.DataKeys[e.RowIndex].Value.ToString();
  string name = ((TextBox)grid.Rows[e.RowIndex].Cells[0].Controls[0]).Text;
  string description = ((TextBox)grid.Rows[e.RowIndex].
Cells[1].Controls[0]).Text;
  // Execute the update command
  bool success = CatalogAccess.UpdateDepartment(id, name, description);
  // Cancel edit mode
  grid.EditIndex = -1;
  // Display status message
  statusLabel.Text = success ? "Update successful" : "Update failed";
  // Reload the grid
  BindGrid();
}
```

24. Finally, here's the code for the `DeleteCommand` event handler. Let Visual Web Developer generate its signature for you, and then add the following code:

```
// Delete a record
protected void grid_RowDeleting(object sender, GridViewDeleteEventArgs e)
{
  // Get the ID of the record to be deleted
  string id = grid.DataKeys[e.RowIndex].Value.ToString();
  // Execute the delete command
  bool success = CatalogAccess.DeleteDepartment(id);
  // Cancel edit mode
  grid.EditIndex = -1;
  // Display status message
  statusLabel.Text = success ? "Delete successful" : "Delete failed";
  // Reload the grid
  BindGrid();
}
```

25. The last bit of code to write in this exercise consists of adding the `addDepartmentButton_Click` event handler method. Generate its signature by double-clicking the **Add** button in the **Design View** window and complete the code like this:

```
// Create a new department
protected void createDepartment_Click(object sender, EventArgs e)
{
  // Execute the insert command
  bool success = CatalogAccess.AddDepartment(newName.Text,
```

```
        newDescription.Text);
          // Display status message
          statusLabel.Text = success ? "Insert successful" : "Insert failed";
          // Reload the grid
          BindGrid();
        }
```

■**Tip** The presentation tier should do input validation when possible—for example, you can check whether the department name and description are valid before trying to add them to the database. Later in this chapter, you'll learn how to implement validation using the .NET validator controls.

How It Works: DepartmentsAdmin.ascx

Be sure to test that the new features are functional. Try to add a new department, rename it, and then delete it.

This is the first exercise in which you worked with a `GridView` control, and it's important to understand how this complex control works. The `GridView` control is smart enough to be aware of the columns it reads from the data source and display them to the user. Moreover, as you saw when writing the code, you just tell the grid what row you want to enter edit mode, and it automatically transforms the labels into text boxes.

The `GridView` control supports a number of built-in column types: `BoundField`, `CheckBoxField`, `HyperLinkField`, `ButtonField`, `CommandField`, `ImageField`, and `TemplateField`. The last one, `TemplateField`, really lets you write your own HTML code for that column, whereas the others have predefined behavior. In this example, you met some of these column types, but you'll get to work with all of them by the end of this chapter!

`BoundField` is the most usual field type, simply reading the value from the database and displaying it in the grid. Each column type has a number of options you can set that affect its behavior. The most common options are shown in the Add New Column dialog box that you used to add your fields, but you can access more of their properties by clicking `GridView`'s Smart Link and choosing the Edit Columns entry.

To change the default look of the `GridView`, you have three main options: You can use the Auto Format feature of the grid (accessible by clicking the Smart Link), you can transform the columns into template columns and edit their format manually, or you can use skins. For this case, we chose to create a default skin for the `GridView`, because it offers the maximum efficiency with the least effort. Default skins apply to all controls of that kind in a web site, so your work will also be much easier when creating other grids later in this book. If you want to have more skins for a certain type of control, you need to create named skins by adding a `SkinID` property to their definition. However, here we preferred to build a default skin to format all the grids in BalloonShop in an identical way.

The simplest way to create a skin is to create a control instance using the designer, rip the unnecessary details, and copy what remains to the `.skin` file. For BalloonShop, we used styles from the CSS file in the skin, in an effort to keep all the site's colors in one place.

Your new C# code deals with the `GridView` control. For example, to enter a row into edit mode, you just need to set the `GridView`'s `EditItemIndex` property to the index of the column you want to change in the `EditCommand` event handler method:

```
// Enter row into edit mode
protected void grid_RowEditing(object sender, GridViewEditEventArgs e)
{
  // Set the row for which to enable edit mode
  grid.EditIndex = e.NewEditIndex;
  // Set status message
  statusLabel.Text = "Editing row # " + e.NewEditIndex.ToString();
  // Reload the grid
  BindGrid();
}
```

The RowEditing event handler receives a GridViewEditEventArgs object named e, which contains, among other details, the index of the row on which the Edit button was clicked (e.NewItemIndex). You use this value to inform the GridView to enter in edit mode for that row. You take similar action in the CancelCommand event handler, where you cancel edit mode by setting GridView's EditIndex to -1. The way these two event handlers work is fairly standard.

The methods that modify data (the event handlers for the Update and Delete buttons) need to read information from the data grid and the ID of the item on which the action happens. Because delete and update operations are based on departments' IDs, you need to obtain somehow the ID of the department to be updated or deleted. The problem is that you can't extract DepartmentID from the visible part of the GridView, because we chose not to display it for the user (it's a low-level detail, useless for the user).

So, how do you know the ID associated with a GridView row? Fortunately, the designers of the GridView control anticipated this problem and added a DataKeyNames property to the GridView, which can hold one or more keys for each row in the grid. When creating the grid, you set its DataKeyNames property to DepartmentID, causing the grid to retain the ID of each loaded department.

The code in grid_RowUpdating demonstrates how to get the ID of the row that is about to updated:

```
// Update row
protected void grid_RowUpdating(object sender, GridViewUpdateEventArgs e)
{
  // Retrieve updated data
  string id = grid.DataKeys[e.RowIndex].Value.ToString();
```

The rest of the code shows how to retrieve data from the rows of the GridView. Each row in the grid is a collection of cells, and each cell is a collection of controls. Given that you know which control you are looking for, it becomes a fairly easy job to get the name or description of a department. You read the first cell of the row to obtain the name and the second cell to obtain the description. In both cases, you read the first control, which you convert to a TextBox to be able to read the Text property.

```
  // Retrieve updated data
  string id = grid.DataKeys[e.RowIndex].Value.ToString();
  string name = ((TextBox)grid.Rows[e.RowIndex].Cells[0].Controls[0]).Text;
  string description = ((TextBox)grid.Rows[e.RowIndex].Cells[1].
Controls[0]).Text;
```

To make this functionality even clearer, take a look at the following code block, which reads the department's name from the grid, but in a step-by-step fashion:

```
protected void grid_RowUpdating(object sender, GridViewUpdateEventArgs e)
{
    // Get the index of the row to be modified
    int rowIndex = e.RowIndex;
    // Get a reference to the row being updated
    GridViewRow gridViewRow = grid.Rows[rowIndex];
    // Get the first cell (one which contains the name)
    TableCell tableCell = gridViewRow.Cells[0];
    // Get the first control in the cell
    Control control = tableCell.Controls[0];
    // Access the control through a TextBox reference
    TextBox textBox = (TextBox)control;
    // Get the text from the TextBox
    string name = textBox.Text;
```

After the ID, new name, and new description of the department are known, the business tier is called to apply the changes. The CatalogAccess.UpdateDepartment method returns a Boolean value specifying whether the update was performed successfully, and then the status label is populated based on this value:

```
    // Execute the update command
    bool success = CatalogAccess.UpdateDepartment(id, name, description);
    // Cancel edit mode
    grid.EditIndex = -1;
    // Display status message
    statusLabel.Text = success ? "Update successful" : "Update failed";
    // Reload the grid
    BindGrid();
}
```

Customizing the GridView with Template Columns

In spite of the length of the exercise that you've just completed, you must admit that it was so easy to implement the editable GridView! You added columns to the GridView using Visual Web Developer's interface and set its layout and colors using a skin. Right now, the code of your grid in DepartmentsAdmin.ascx looks like this:

```
<asp:GridView ID="grid" runat="server" DataKeyNames="DepartmentID" Width="100%"
OnRowCancelingEdit="grid_RowCancelingEdit" OnRowDeleting="grid_RowDeleting"
OnRowEditing="grid_RowEditing" OnRowUpdating="grid_RowUpdating"
AutoGenerateColumns="False">
  <Columns>
    <asp:BoundField DataField="Name" HeaderText="Department Name"
SortExpression="Name" />
    <asp:BoundField DataField="Description" HeaderText="Department Description"
SortExpression="Description" />
    <asp:HyperLinkField DataNavigateUrlFields="DepartmentID"
```

```
DataNavigateUrlFormatString="../CatalogAdmin.aspx?DepartmentID={0}"
    Text="View Categories" />
  <asp:CommandField ShowEditButton="True" />
  <asp:ButtonField CommandName="Delete" Text="Delete" />
  </Columns>
</asp:GridView>
```

The interesting aspect is that you can't see any Label or TextBox controls, even though GridView generates them when showing its data and when entering edit mode. The BoundField, HyperLinkField, CommandField, and ButtonField columns take care of rendering themselves without your intervention.

The problem with these automated controls is that you don't have much flexibility with how they show their data. Although you can use a number of techniques to format your GridView's styles, colors, or fonts (such as by using a skin), the only way to have complete access to the HTML code your grid generates for a certain column is to transform that column to a **template column**, instead of using predefined column types such as BoundField, HyperLinkField, and so on.

When using template columns, you need to manually supply the code for its templates. You'll do that in the following exercise, where you'll enlarge the description editing TextBox control.

▪Note When transforming an existing field to a template field, its different display templates (such as the editing template—EditItemTemplate or the normal display template—ItemTemplate) are automatically generated for you so you won't lose any functionality.

Exercise: Implementing a Template Column

1. Open DepartmentsAdmin.ascx in **Design View**, click GridView's **Smart Link** and choose **Edit Columns**. Select the **Department Description** field and click **Convert this field into a TemplateField**.

2. You'll notice the panel on the right becomes empty, because now the GridView no longer takes care of your column's properties. Click **OK**.

3. Switch to **Source View** to see the generated code. The changes aren't so drastic, but now instead of a single line defining a BoundField entry, you can find a TemplateField entry containing the complete code for the EditItemTeamplate and ItemTemplate templates. (Note that Visual Web Developer smartly generated bound TextBox and Label controls in the two templates, so if you now execute your project, you won't lose any functionality.)

```
<asp:TemplateField HeaderText="Department Description"
SortExpression="Description">
  <ItemTemplate>
    <asp:Label ID="Label1" runat="server" Text='<%# Bind("Description") %>'>
    </asp:Label>
  </ItemTemplate>
```

```
  <EditItemTemplate>
    <asp:TextBox ID="TextBox1" runat="server"
Text='<%# Bind("Description") %>'>
    </asp:TextBox>
  </EditItemTemplate>
</asp:TemplateField>
```

4. While in **Source View**, change the name of the editing **TextBox**. Because you'll need its name to access its value from the code (when updating the departments' details), it's important to have a good name for it. Change the control's name from TextBox1 to **descriptionTextBox**:

```
<asp:TextBox ID="descriptionTextBox" runat="server"
            Text='<%# Bind("Description") %>'></asp:TextBox>
```

5. After converting the description column to a TemplateField, you can edit its templates both in Source View and in Design View. Switch to **Design View**, click GridView's **Smart Link**, and choose **Edit Templates**. Now, again using the **Smart Link**, you can choose which template to edit (see Figure 8-22).

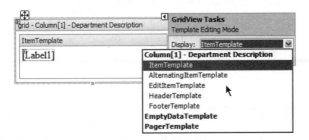

Figure 8-22. *Choosing a template to edit*

6. To modify the text box that appears when editing a department, choose **EditItemTemplate** from the list. Then, select the **TextBox** control and modify it to suit your preferences by using the **Properties window** (see Figure 8-23). For this exercise, set its TextMode property to **MultiLine**, Width to **350px**, and Height to **70px**:

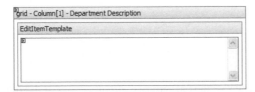

Figure 8-23. *Modifying the description editing text box*

7. The last step is to change the code-behind file for updating department data. Locate this line in the grid_RowUpdating method in DepartmentsAdmin.ascx.cs:

```
string description = ((TextBox)grid.Rows[e.RowIndex].
Cells[1].Controls[0]).Text;
```

8. Change this line to

```
string description = ((TextBox)grid.Rows[e.RowIndex].
FindControl("descriptionTextBox")).Text;
```

How It Works: Using Template Columns in the GridView Control

Execute the project and test the updated functionality to make sure that it still works. Template columns are useful because they give you full control over how the column looks and behaves. In this exercise, you modified the TextBox control used for editing the department description, but now you can use the same technique to change any field in the table.

Because you can also change the names of the controls inside your template, you can now access them by name, instead of by location:

```
string description = ((TextBox)grid.Rows[e.RowIndex].
FindControl("descriptionTextBox")).Text;
```

This piece of code demonstrates how to obtain a reference of the TextBox control named descriptionTextBox, convert its Control reference to a TextBox reference, and extract its contents from there.

You'll see some other examples of template columns later in this chapter when you'll use CheckBox controls instead of Labels and TextBoxes for displaying the value of True/False fields.

Administering Categories

The category administration bits are similar to what you did for departments, so we won't need to explain much this time. The main player in the whole categories administration part is the CategoriesAdmin.ascx Web User Control, but first you need to write the data tier and business tier code that will support its functionality.

Stored Procedures for Categories Administration

The three stored procedures that you need to add to your BalloonShop database are

- CreateCategory

- UpdateCategory

- DeleteCategory

The fourth stored procedure that you'll use, GetCategories, already exists in the database. Add these stored procedures covered in the following sections to the BalloonShop database.

CreateCategory

CreateCategory adds a new category to the database. Apart from the name and description of the new category, you also need a DepartmentID, which specifies the department the category belongs to. Note that you don't need to (in fact, you can't) specify a CategoryID because

CategoryID is an IDENTITY column in the Category table, and its value is automatically generated by the database when inserting a new record.

```
CREATE PROCEDURE CreateCategory
(@DepartmentID int,
@CategoryName varchar(50),
@CategoryDescription varchar(50))
AS
INSERT INTO Category (DepartmentID, Name, Description)
VALUES (@DepartmentID, @CategoryName, @CategoryDescription)
```

UpdateCategory

The UpdateCategory stored procedure updates the name and description of a category.

```
CREATE PROCEDURE UpdateCategory
(@CategoryID int,
@CategoryName varchar(50),
@CategoryDescription varchar(1000))
AS
UPDATE Category
SET Name = @CategoryName, Description = @CategoryDescription
WHERE CategoryID = @CategoryID
```

DeleteCategory

DeleteCategory deletes a certain category from the database. If the category has products that
belong to it, the database raises an error because the deletion affects the database integrity—
remember that you have implemented the One-to-Many relationship between Category and
Product tables using a foreign-key relationship back in Chapter 4. In this case, the error is
trapped in the business tier, which returns an error code to the presentation tier, which informs the
user that an error has occurred.

```
CREATE PROCEDURE DeleteCategory
(@CategoryID int)
AS
DELETE FROM Category
WHERE CategoryID = @CategoryID
```

Middle-Tier Methods for Categories Administration

Now you'll write the methods of the CatalogAccess class that support the functionality required
by the CategoriesAdmin user control. These methods use the stored procedures mentioned
earlier to perform their functionality: GetCategories, CreateCategory, UpdateCategory, and
DeleteCategory.

Add these methods to your CatalogAccess class in CatalogAccess.cs:

```csharp
// Create a new Category
public static bool CreateCategory(string departmentId,
 string name, string description)
{
  // get a configured DbCommand object
  DbCommand comm = GenericDataAccess.CreateCommand();
  // set the stored procedure name
  comm.CommandText = "CreateCategory";
  // create a new parameter
  DbParameter param = comm.CreateParameter();
  param.ParameterName = "@DepartmentID";
  param.Value = departmentId;
  param.DbType = DbType.Int32;
  comm.Parameters.Add(param);
  // create a new parameter
  param = comm.CreateParameter();
  param.ParameterName = "@CategoryName";
  param.Value = name;
  param.DbType = DbType.String;
  param.Size = 50;
  comm.Parameters.Add(param);
  // create a new parameter
  param = comm.CreateParameter();
  param.ParameterName = "@CategoryDescription";
  param.Value = description;
  param.DbType = DbType.String;
  param.Size = 1000;
  comm.Parameters.Add(param);
  // result will represent the number of changed rows
  int result = -1;
  try
  {
    // execute the stored procedure
    result = GenericDataAccess.ExecuteNonQuery(comm);
  }
  catch
  {
    // any errors are logged in GenericDataAccess, we ignore them here
  }
  // result will be 1 in case of success
  return (result != -1);
}
```

```csharp
// Update category details
public static bool UpdateCategory(string id, string name, string description)
{
  // get a configured DbCommand object
  DbCommand comm = GenericDataAccess.CreateCommand();
  // set the stored procedure name
  comm.CommandText = "UpdateCategory";
  // create a new parameter
  DbParameter param = comm.CreateParameter();
  param.ParameterName = "@CategoryId";
  param.Value = id;
  param.DbType = DbType.Int32;
  comm.Parameters.Add(param);
  // create a new parameter
  param = comm.CreateParameter();
  param.ParameterName = "@CategoryName";
  param.Value = name;
  param.DbType = DbType.String;
  param.Size = 50;
  comm.Parameters.Add(param);
  // create a new parameter
  param = comm.CreateParameter();
  param.ParameterName = "@CategoryDescription";
  param.Value = description;
  param.DbType = DbType.String;
  param.Size = 1000;
  comm.Parameters.Add(param);
  // result will represent the number of changed rows
  int result = -1;
  try
  {
    // execute the stored procedure
    result = GenericDataAccess.ExecuteNonQuery(comm);
  }
  catch
  {
    // any errors are logged in GenericDataAccess, we ignore them here
  }
  // result will be 1 in case of success
  return (result != -1);
}
```

```
// Delete Category
public static bool DeleteCategory(string id)
{
  // get a configured DbCommand object
  DbCommand comm = GenericDataAccess.CreateCommand();
  // set the stored procedure name
  comm.CommandText = "DeleteCategory";
  // create a new parameter
  DbParameter param = comm.CreateParameter();
  param.ParameterName = "@CategoryId";
  param.Value = id;
  param.DbType = DbType.Int32;
  comm.Parameters.Add(param);
  // execute the stored procedure; an error will be thrown by the
  // database if the Category has related categories, in which case
  // it is not deleted
  int result = -1;
  try
  {
    result = GenericDataAccess.ExecuteNonQuery(comm);
  }
  catch
  {
    // any errors are logged in GenericDataAccess, we ignore them here
  }
  // result will be 1 in case of success
  return (result != -1);
}
```

The CategoriesAdmin Web User Control

This exercise is very similar to the one in which you created the DepartmentsAdmin Web User Control. The exercise mainly consists of preparing the GridView and the other constituent controls and then implementing the code-behind functionality. Because you already have a GridView skin, you won't need to bother with that detail again here.

Exercise: Implementing CategoriesAdmin.ascx

1. Create a new Web User Control named CategoriesAdmin.ascx in the UserControls folder (make sure the **Place code in separate file** option is checked).

2. Switch to **Design View**. From the toolbox, add two Label controls, a LinkButton and a GridView control, as shown in Figure 8-24.

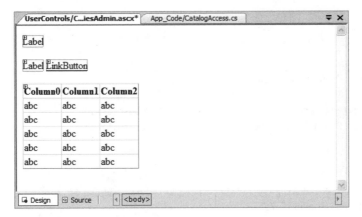

Figure 8-24. *Creating CategoriesAdmin.ascx.*

3. Set the properties for the controls as shown in Table 8-3.

Table 8-3. *Setting the Properties for the Controls in CategoriesAdmin.ascx*

Control Type	ID Property	Text Property	CssClass Property
Label	statusLabel	Categories Loaded	AdminPageText
Label	locationLabel	Displaying categories for department...	AdminPageText
LinkButton	goBackLink	(go back to departments)	AdminPageText
GridView	grid		

4. Set the DataKeyNames property of the grid to **CategoryID**, the Width property to **100%**, and the AutoGenerateColumns property to **False**.

5. Add the controls for adding a new category manually. Switch to **Source View** and add the following code:

```
<br />
<span class="AdminPageText">Create a new category in this department:</span>
<table class="AdminPageText" cellspacing="0">.
  <tr>
    <td valign="top" width="100">Name:</td>
    <td>
      <asp:TextBox cssClass="AdminPageText" ID="newName"
```

```
Runat="server" Width="400px" />
    </td>
  </tr>
  <tr>
    <td valign="top" width="100">Description:</td>
    <td>
      <asp:TextBox cssClass="AdminPageText" ID="newDescription"
Runat="server" Width="400px" Height="70px" TextMode="MultiLine"/>
    </td>
  </tr>
</table>
<asp:Button ID="createCategory" Text="Create Category" Runat="server"
CssClass="AdminButtonText" />.
```

At this point, your control should look like Figure 8-25.

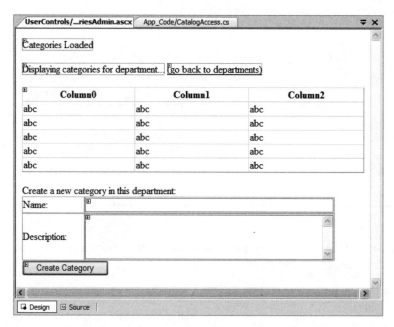

Figure 8-25. *CategoriesAdmin.ascx in Design View*

6. Click the GridView's **Smart Link** and use its **Add New Column** command to add fields with the properties shown in Table 8-4 (leave the other properties to their defaults). .

Table 8-4. *Setting GridView's Field Properties*

Column Type	Header Text	Data Field	Other Properties
BoundField	Category Name	Name	
BoundField	Category Description	Description	
TemplateField			
CommandField			Select Edit/Update and Show Cancel Button check boxes
ButtonField			Set Command Name to Delete and set Text to Delete

7. The template field from the list is the View Products link, which you're creating as a TemplateField because the HyperLinkField isn't flexible enough to generate the kind of link you need to create. Switch to **Source View** and modify the code of the template field like this:

```
<asp:TemplateField>
  <ItemTemplate>
    <asp:HyperLink
      Runat="server" ID="link"
      NavigateUrl='<%# "../CatalogAdmin.aspx?DepartmentID=" + Request
.QueryString["DepartmentID"] + "&amp;CategoryID=" + Eval("CategoryID")%>'
      Text="View Products">
    </asp:HyperLink>
  </ItemTemplate>
</asp:TemplateField>.
```

8. Transform the **Category Description** field into a template column, just like you did for the description column in DepartmentsAdmin. Then, edit the column's **EditItemTemplate** like this:

```
<asp:TemplateField HeaderText="Category Description"
SortExpression="Description">
  <ItemTemplate>
    <asp:Label ID="Label1" runat="server" Text='<%# Bind("Description") %>'>
    </asp:Label>
  </ItemTemplate>.
  <EditItemTemplate>
    <asp:TextBox ID="descriptionTextBox" runat="server" TextMode="MultiLine"
Text='<%# Bind("Description") %>' Height="70px" Width="350px" />
  </EditItemTemplate>
</asp:TemplateField>
```

Switch to **Design View** and verify that your control looks like Figure 8-26.

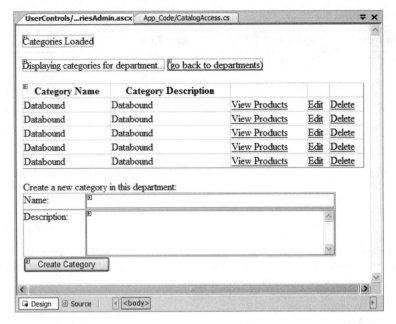

Figure 8-26. *CategoriesAdmin.ascx in Design View*

9. Now you need to deal with the code-behind file. Use the techniques you already know to have Visual Web Developer generate the method signatures for you, and write the following code to `CategoriesAdmin.ascx.cs`:

```
protected void Page_Load(object sender, EventArgs e)
{
  // Load the grid only the first time the page is loaded
  if (!Page.IsPostBack)
  {
    // Load the categories grid
    BindGrid();
    // Get DepartmentID from the query string
    string departmentId = Request.QueryString["DepartmentID"];
    // Obtain the department's name
    DepartmentDetails dd = CatalogAccess.GetDepartmentDetails(departmentId); .
    string departmentName = dd.Name;
    // Set the controls' properties
    statusLabel.ForeColor = System.Drawing.Color.Red;
    locationLabel.Text = "Displaying categories for department <b> "
      + departmentName + "</b>";
  }
}
```

```csharp
// Populate the GridView with data
private void BindGrid()
{
  // Get DepartmentID from the query string
  string departmentId = Request.QueryString["DepartmentID"];
  // Get a DataTable object containing the categories
  grid.DataSource = CatalogAccess.GetCategoriesInDepartment(departmentId);
  // Bind the data grid to the data source
  grid.DataBind();
}

// Enter row into edit mode
protected void grid_RowEditing(object sender, GridViewEditEventArgs e)
{
  // Set the row for which to enable edit mode
  grid.EditIndex = e.NewEditIndex;
  // Set status message
  statusLabel.Text = "Editing row # " + e.NewEditIndex.ToString();.
  // Reload the grid
  BindGrid();
}

// Cancel edit mode
protected void grid_RowCancelingEdit(object sender,
GridViewCancelEditEventArgs e)
{
  // Cancel edit mode
  grid.EditIndex = -1;
  // Set status message
  statusLabel.Text = "Editing canceled";
  // Reload the grid
  BindGrid();
}

// Update row
protected void grid_RowUpdating(object sender, GridViewUpdateEventArgs e)
{
  // Retrieve updated data
  string id = grid.DataKeys[e.RowIndex].Value.ToString();
  string name = ((TextBox)grid.Rows[e.RowIndex].Cells[0].Controls[0]).Text;
  string description = ((TextBox)grid.Rows[e.RowIndex].FindControl
("descriptionTextBox")).Text;
  // Execute the update command
  bool success = CatalogAccess.UpdateCategory(id, name, description); .
  // Cancel edit mode
  grid.EditIndex = -1;
```

```csharp
  // Display status message
  statusLabel.Text = success ? "Update successful" : "Update failed";
  // Reload the grid
  BindGrid();
}


// Delete a record
protected void grid_RowDeleting(object sender, GridViewDeleteEventArgs e)
{
  // Get the ID of the record to be deleted
  string id = grid.DataKeys[e.RowIndex].Value.ToString();
  // Execute the delete command
  bool success = CatalogAccess.DeleteCategory(id);
  // Cancel edit mode
  grid.EditIndex = -1;
  // Display status message
  statusLabel.Text = success ? "Delete successful" : "Delete failed";.
  // Reload the grid
  BindGrid();
}


// Create a new category
protected void createCategory_Click(object sender, EventArgs e)
{
  // Get DepartmentID from the query string
  string departmentId = Request.QueryString["DepartmentID"];
  // Execute the insert command
  bool success = CatalogAccess.CreateCategory(departmentId,
newName.Text, newDescription.Text);
  // Display results
  statusLabel.Text = success ? "Insert successful" : "Insert failed";
  // Reload the grid
  BindGrid();
}


// Redirect to the department's page
protected void goBackLink_Click(object sender, EventArgs e)
{
  Response.Redirect(Request.ApplicationPath + "/CatalogAdmin.aspx");
}
```

How It Works: CategoriesAdmin.ascx

Because this exercise was so similar to the exercise for administering departments, we won't go into many details here.

When creating the grid, the main difference was creating the View Products column as a TemplateField rather than as a HyperLinkField. This is because a more complex link had to be created, which needed to include both the CategoryID (from the data source) and the DepartmentID (from the query string).

```
    <asp:HyperLink
      Runat="server" ID="link"
      NavigateUrl='<%# "../CatalogAdmin.aspx?DepartmentID=" + Request
.QueryString["DepartmentID"] + "&amp;CategoryID=" + Eval("CategoryID")%>'
      Text="View Products">
    </asp:HyperLink>
```

Note that we used the `Eval` function here, although the code automatically generated by Visual Web Developer uses `Bind`. As far as your code is concerned, these functions have similar functionality, but in other circumstances, `Bind` can be used to implement two-way data binding (we don't use this feature in this book).

As far as the code in the code-behind file is concerned, compared to the code for administering departments, sometimes you need to read the `DepartmentID` parameter from the query string, which represents the ID of the department for which you're editing the categories.

You also have a `LinkButton` control that generates the link for going back to the main page. To implement its functionality, you composed the link to the main catalog admin page by reading the value of `Request.ApplicationPath`.

Administering Products

You're now ready for the next major part of the catalog administration page: the place where you edit the products that belong to the selected category. This one has a few more controls than the others, as shown in Figure 8-27.

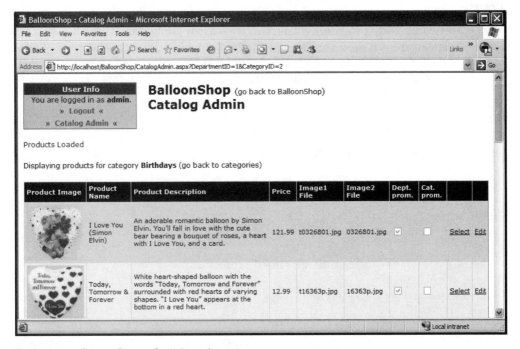

Figure 8-27. *The products administration page*

The interface is a bit more complex, but the theory isn't much more complicated. You just need to display the products that belong to a selected category and allow the user to add new products to that category. The product-deleting feature is offered via a separate page, so you won't see a Delete link here.

Stored Procedures for Products Administration

Three stored procedures support the user interface functionality: GetAllProductsIncategory, CreateProduct, and UpdateProduct. The procedures are described in the following sections.

GetAllProductsInCategory

GetAllProductsInCategory is your admin stored procedure that returns the list of products in a category and is a simplified version of GetProductsInCategory, which you created in Chapter 4. Add the stored procedure to your BalloonShop database:

```
CREATE PROCEDURE GetAllProductsInCategory
(@CategoryID INT)
AS
SELECT Product.ProductID, Name, Description, Price, Image1FileName,
       Image2FileName, OnDepartmentPromotion, OnCatalogPromotion
FROM Product INNER JOIN ProductCategory
  ON Product.ProductID = ProductCategory.ProductID
WHERE ProductCategory.CategoryID = @CategoryID
```

CreateProduct

The CreateProduct stored procedure is called to create a new product and assign it to a category. After adding the new product's record to the Product table, you read the @@Identity value to find out the generated ID, and then you assign this ID to the mentioned category. Add this stored procedure to your BalloonShop database:

```
CREATE PROCEDURE CreateProduct
(@CategoryID INT,
 @ProductName VARCHAR(50),
 @ProductDescription VARCHAR(1000),
 @ProductPrice MONEY,
 @Image1FileName VARCHAR(50),
 @Image2FileName VARCHAR(50),
 @OnDepartmentPromotion BIT,
 @OnCatalogPromotion BIT)
AS
-- Declare a variable to hold the generated product ID
DECLARE @ProductID int
-- Create the new product entry
```

```
INSERT INTO Product
    (Name,
     Description,
     Price,
     Image1FileName,
     Image2FileName,
     OnDepartmentPromotion,
     OnCatalogPromotion )
VALUES
    (@ProductName,
     @ProductDescription,
     @ProductPrice,
     @Image1FileName,
     @Image2FileName,
     @OnDepartmentPromotion,
     @OnCatalogPromotion)
-- Save the generated product ID to a variable
SELECT @ProductID = @@Identity
-- Associate the product with a category
INSERT INTO ProductCategory (ProductID, CategoryID)
VALUES (@ProductID, @CategoryID)
```

This line of code is of particular importance:

```
SELECT @ProductID = @@Identity
```

Identity columns are automatically generated by the database. If you've ever wondered how to determine which value has been generated for an identity column, here's the answer: the @@Identity system value. This needs to be saved into a variable immediately after the INSERT command because its value is reset after other SQL statements execute. After you determine which ID was generated for the new product, you can assign it to the category you received as a parameter:

```
INSERT INTO ProductCategory (ProductID, CategoryID)
VALUES (@ProductID, @CategoryID)
```

UpdateProduct

The UpdateProduct stored procedure updates the information of a product:

```
CREATE PROCEDURE UpdateProduct
(@ProductID INT,
 @ProductName VARCHAR(50),
 @ProductDescription VARCHAR(5000),
 @ProductPrice MONEY,
 @Image1FileName VARCHAR(50),
 @Image2FileName VARCHAR(50),
 @OnDepartmentPromotion BIT,
 @OnCatalogPromotion BIT)
```

```
AS
UPDATE Product
SET Name = @ProductName,
    Description = @ProductDescription,
    Price = @ProductPrice,
    Image1FileName = @Image1FileName,
    Image2FileName = @Image2FileName,
    OnDepartmentPromotion = @OnDepartmentPromotion,
    OnCatalogPromotion = @OnCatalogPromotion
WHERE ProductID = @ProductID
```

Middle-Tier Methods for Products Administration

The methods you write here, GetAllProductsInCategory, CreateProduct, and UpdateProduct, although long, are similar to what you have done so far.

What is important to note is the different error-handling strategies implemented in these methods. In GetAllProductsInCategory (and in all the other Get... methods), we consider any errors are important enough to be signaled to the user with an "oops" message, so we don't catch them in the business tier.

Errors with update- and create- type of methods are more likely due to bad input data, so we prefer to signal with a "friendlier" error message instead of allowing the error to cause the Oooops.aspx page to display. In these cases, we catch any potential exceptions to prevent them from propagating, and we return the success value as a bool value. The presentation tier decides what to tell the visitor depending on this value.

Add the following code to your CatalogAccess class:

```
// retrieve the list of products in a category
public static DataTable GetAllProductsInCategory(string categoryId)
{
  // get a configured DbCommand object
  DbCommand comm = GenericDataAccess.CreateCommand();
  // set the stored procedure name
  comm.CommandText = "GetAllProductsInCategory";
  // create a new parameter
  DbParameter param = comm.CreateParameter();
  param.ParameterName = "@CategoryID";
  param.Value = categoryId;
  param.DbType = DbType.Int32;
  comm.Parameters.Add(param);
  // execute the stored procedure and save the results in a DataTable
  DataTable table = GenericDataAccess.ExecuteSelectCommand(comm);
  return table;
}
```

```
// Create a new product
public static bool CreateProduct(string categoryId, string name, string description,
 string price, string image1FileName, string image2FileName,
string onDepartmentPromotion, string onCatalogPromotion)
{
  // get a configured DbCommand object
  DbCommand comm = GenericDataAccess.CreateCommand();
  // set the stored procedure name
  comm.CommandText = "CreateProduct";
  // create a new parameter
  DbParameter param = comm.CreateParameter();
  param.ParameterName = "@CategoryID";
  param.Value = categoryId;
  param.DbType = DbType.Int32;
  comm.Parameters.Add(param);
  // create a new parameter
  param = comm.CreateParameter();
  param.ParameterName = "@ProductName";
  param.Value = name;
  param.DbType = DbType.String;
  param.Size = 50;
  comm.Parameters.Add(param);
  // create a new parameter
  param = comm.CreateParameter();
  param.ParameterName = "@ProductDescription";
  param.Value = description;
  param.DbType = DbType.AnsiString;
  param.Size = 5000;
  comm.Parameters.Add(param);
  // create a new parameter
  param = comm.CreateParameter();
  param.ParameterName = "@ProductPrice";
  param.Value = price;
  param.DbType = DbType.Decimal;
  comm.Parameters.Add(param);
  // create a new parameter
  param = comm.CreateParameter();
  param.ParameterName = "@Image1FileName";
  param.Value = image1FileName;
  param.DbType = DbType.String;
  comm.Parameters.Add(param);
```

```csharp
    // create a new parameter
    param = comm.CreateParameter();
    param.ParameterName = "@Image2FileName";
    param.Value = image2FileName;
    param.DbType = DbType.String;
    comm.Parameters.Add(param);
    // create a new parameter
    param = comm.CreateParameter();
    param.ParameterName = "@OnDepartmentPromotion";
    param.Value = onDepartmentPromotion;
    param.DbType = DbType.Boolean;
    comm.Parameters.Add(param);
    // create a new parameter
    param = comm.CreateParameter();
    param.ParameterName = "@OnCatalogPromotion";
    param.Value = onCatalogPromotion;
    param.DbType = DbType.Boolean;
    comm.Parameters.Add(param);
    // result will represent the number of changed rows
    int result = -1;
    try
    {
      // execute the stored procedure
      result = GenericDataAccess.ExecuteNonQuery(comm);
    }
    catch
    {
      // any errors are logged in GenericDataAccess, we ignore them here
    }
    // result will be 1 in case of success
    return (result >= 1);
  }

  // Update an existing product
  public static bool UpdateProduct(string productId, string name, string description,
  string price, string image1FileName, string image2FileName, string
  onDepartmentPromotion, string onCatalogPromotion)
  {
    // get a configured DbCommand object
    DbCommand comm = GenericDataAccess.CreateCommand();
    // set the stored procedure name
    comm.CommandText = "UpdateProduct";
```

```csharp
// create a new parameter
DbParameter param = comm.CreateParameter();
param.ParameterName = "@ProductID";
param.Value = productId;
param.DbType = DbType.Int32;
comm.Parameters.Add(param);
// create a new parameter
param = comm.CreateParameter();
param.ParameterName = "@ProductName";
param.Value = name;
param.DbType = DbType.String;
param.Size = 50;
comm.Parameters.Add(param);
// create a new parameter
param = comm.CreateParameter();
param.ParameterName = "@ProductDescription";
param.Value = description;
param.DbType = DbType.AnsiString;
param.Size = 5000;
comm.Parameters.Add(param);
// create a new parameter
param = comm.CreateParameter();
param.ParameterName = "@ProductPrice";
param.Value = price;
param.DbType = DbType.Decimal;
comm.Parameters.Add(param);
// create a new parameter
param = comm.CreateParameter();
param.ParameterName = "@Image1FileName";
param.Value = image1FileName;
param.DbType = DbType.String;
param.Size = 50;
comm.Parameters.Add(param);
// create a new parameter
param = comm.CreateParameter();
param.ParameterName = "@Image2FileName";
param.Value = image2FileName;
param.DbType = DbType.String;
param.Size = 50;
comm.Parameters.Add(param);
```

```
    // create a new parameter
    param = comm.CreateParameter();
    param.ParameterName = "@OnDepartmentPromotion";
    param.Value = onDepartmentPromotion;
    param.DbType = DbType.Boolean;
    comm.Parameters.Add(param);
    // create a new parameter
    param = comm.CreateParameter();
    param.ParameterName = "@OnCatalogPromotion";
    param.Value = onCatalogPromotion;
    param.DbType = DbType.Boolean;
    comm.Parameters.Add(param);
    // result will represent the number of changed rows
    int result = -1;
    try
    {
      // execute the stored procedure
      result = GenericDataAccess.ExecuteNonQuery(comm);
    }
    catch
    {
      // any errors are logged in GenericDataAccess, we ignore them here
    }
    // result will be 1 in case of success
    return (result != -1);
}
```

■Note The product description is sent as a DbType.AnsiString parameter because DbType.String stores Unicode characters and only supports strings up to 4,000 characters.

The ProductsAdmin Web User Control

More data to display means more columns to add to your grid and more controls to add for creating a new product. In this exercise you'll also work with new types of grid columns: CheckBoxField and ImageField.

Exercise: Implementing ProductsAdmin.ascx

1. Create a new Web User Control named **ProductsAdmin.ascx** in the UserControls folder. Make sure the **Create code in a separate file** option is checked and that the language is **Visual C#**.

2. Switch to **Design View** and add two Label controls, a LinkButton and a GridView, as shown in Figure 8-28.

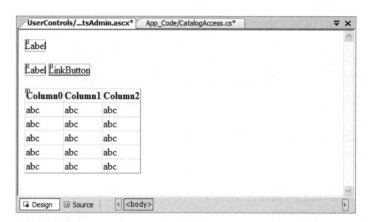

Figure 8-28. *ProductsAdmin.ascx in Design View*

3. Change the properties of the controls to the values in Table 8-5.

Table 8-5. *Setting the Properties of the Controls in ProductsAdmin.ascx*

Control Type	ID **Property**	Text **Property**	CssClass **Property**
Label	statusLabel	Products Loaded	AdminPageText
Label	locationLabel	Displaying products for category...	AdminPageText
LinkButton	goBackLink	(go back to categories)	AdminPageText
GridView	grid		

4. Change the DataKeyNames property of the GridView to **ProductID**, the Width property to **100%**, and the AutoGenerateColumns property to **False**. Right now, the control should look like Figure 8-29 when viewed in Design View. Remember that the CSS styles don't apply when designing the form, only when it is executed.

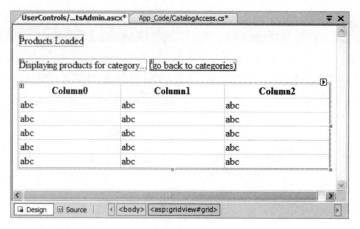

Figure 8-29. *ProductsAdmin.ascx in Design View*

5. Create the columns described in Table 8-6 by clicking the GridView's **Smart Link** and then clicking
   Add New Column.

Table 8-6. *GridView Field Properties*

Column Type	Header Text	Data Field	Other Properties
ImageField	Product Image	Image1FileName	Read Only; URL format string: ../ ProductImages/{0}
BoundField	Product Name	Name	
BoundField	Product Description	Description	
BoundField	Price	Price	
BoundField	Image1 File	Image1FileName	
BoundField	Image2 File	Image2FileName	
CheckBoxField	Dept. prom.	OnDepartmentPromotion	
CheckBoxField	Cat. prom.	OnCatalogPromotion	
TemplateField			
CommandField			Select Edit/Update and Show Cancel Button check boxes

■**Note** You didn't add a Delete button to the GridView because you'll implement this functionality later, in
the product details page.

6. In the next few steps, you'll transform all editable columns into template columns, to change the way they look when being edited (otherwise, they won't fit nicely on the screen). Moreover, you'll want to make other usability improvements such as enlarging the description text box to be multiline, or changing the format of product prices. Start with updating the **product name** by transforming the product name column into a template column and modifying its `EditItemTemplate` as shown:

```
<EditItemTemplate>
    <asp:TextBox ID="nameTextBox" runat="server" Width="97%"
                CssClass="GridEditingRow" Text='<%# Bind("Name") %>'>
    </asp:TextBox>
</EditItemTemplate>
```

7. Transform the **product description** field into a template field and then edit its `EditItemTemplate` in **Source View**:

```
<EditItemTemplate>
    <asp:TextBox ID="descriptionTextBox" runat="server"
                Text='<%# Bind("Description") %>' Height="100px" Width="97%"
                CssClass="GridEditingRow" TextMode="MultiLine" />
</EditItemTemplate>
```

8. Transform the **product price** field into a template field and edit its templates to format the price to be displayed with two decimal digits (as 19.99), instead of the default of four decimal digits (19.9900). In this case, you can also make its editing text box shorter to make better use of the space on the screen when entering edit mode:

```
<asp:TemplateField HeaderText="Price" SortExpression="Price">
    <ItemTemplate>
        <asp:Label ID="Label2" runat="server"
                Text='<%# String.Format("{0:0.00}", Eval("Price")) %>'>
        </asp:Label>
    </ItemTemplate>
    <EditItemTemplate>
        <asp:TextBox ID="priceTextBox" runat="server" Width="45px"
                Text='<%# String.Format("{0:0.00}", Eval("Price")) %>'>
        </asp:TextBox>
    </EditItemTemplate>
</asp:TemplateField>
```

9. Transform the first image field into a template field to shrink its edit text box a little bit, as highlighted in the following code:

```
<EditItemTemplate>
    <asp:TextBox ID="image1TextBox" Width="80px" runat="server"
                Text='<%# Bind("Image1FileName") %>'></asp:TextBox>
</EditItemTemplate>
```

10. Transform the second image field into a template field and set its editing `TextBox`'s width to **80px** and its name to **image2TextBox**, similar to what you did in the previous step.

11. Edit the template of the last `TemplateField` column to contain a link to the product details page (it must add a `ProductID` parameter to the query string):

```
<asp:TemplateField>
  <ItemTemplate>
    <asp:HyperLink
      Runat="server" Text="Select"
      NavigateUrl='<%# "../CatalogAdmin.aspx?DepartmentID=" +
Request.QueryString["DepartmentID"] + "&amp;CategoryID=" +
Request.QueryString["CategoryID"] + "&amp;ProductID=" +
Eval("ProductID") %>'
      ID="HyperLink1">
    </asp:HyperLink>
  </ItemTemplate>
</asp:TemplateField>
```

12. Now the `GridView` is ready. The final step for the user interface part is to create the controls for adding a new product. Feel free to add them at the bottom of the page using Design View or simply write the HTML code in Source View:

```
<span class="AdminPageText">
Create a new product and assign it to this category:</span>
<table class="AdminPageText" cellspacing="0">
  <tr>
    <td width="100" valign="top">Name:</td>
    <td>
      <asp:TextBox cssClass="AdminPageText" ID="newName" Runat="server"
Width="400px" />
    </td>
  </tr>
  <tr>
    <td width="100" valign="top">Description:</td>
    <td>
      <asp:TextBox cssClass="AdminPageText" ID="newDescription"
Runat="server" Width="400px" Height="70px" TextMode="MultiLine"/>
    </td>
  </tr>
  <tr>
    <td width="100" valign="top">Price:</td>
    <td>
      <asp:TextBox cssClass="AdminPageText" ID="newPrice" Runat="server"
```

```
Width="400px">0.00</asp:TextBox>
    </td>
  </tr>
  <tr>
    <td width="100" valign="top">Image1 File:</td>
    <td>
      <asp:TextBox cssClass="AdminPageText" ID="newImage1FileName"
Runat="server" Width="400px">Generic1.png</asp:TextBox>
    </td>
  </tr>
  <tr>
    <td width="150" valign="top">Image2 File:</td>
    <td>
      <asp:TextBox cssClass="AdminPageText" ID="newImage2FileName"
 Runat="server" Width="400px">Generic2.png</asp:TextBox>
    </td>
  </tr>
  <tr>
    <td width="150" valign="top">Dept. Promotion:</td>
    <td>
      <asp:CheckBox ID="newOnDepartmentPromotion" Runat="server" />
    </td>
  </tr>
  <tr>
    <td width="150" valign="top">Catalog Promotion:</td>
    <td>
      <asp:CheckBox ID="newOnCatalogPromotion" Runat="server" />
    </td>
  </tr>
</table>
<asp:Button ID="createProduct" CssClass="AdminButtonText"
  Runat="server" Text="Create Product" />
```

After all the changes, the user control should look Figure 8-30 when viewed in Design View:

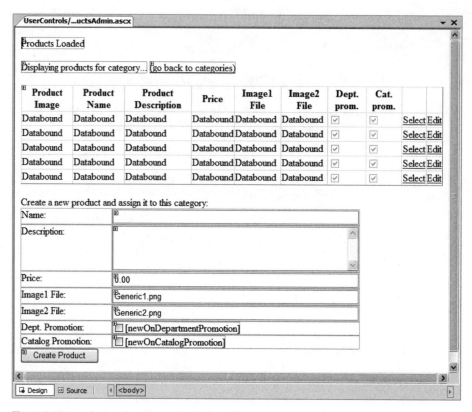

Figure 8-30. *ProductsAdmin.ascx in Design View*

13. Now it's time to write the code. Remember to use Visual Web Developer to generate the event handler signatures for you and modify their code, as shown in the following code listing:

```
protected void Page_Load(object sender, EventArgs e)
{
  // Load the grid only the first time the page is loaded
  if (!Page.IsPostBack)
  {
    // Get CategoryID from the query string
    string categoryId = Request.QueryString["CategoryID"];
    // Obtain the category's name
    CategoryDetails cd = CatalogAccess.GetCategoryDetails(categoryId);
    string categoryName = cd.Name;
    // Set controls' properties
    statusLabel.ForeColor = System.Drawing.Color.Red;
    locationLabel.Text = "Displaying products for category <b> "
                        + categoryName + "</b>";
```

```
    // Load the products grid
    BindGrid();
  }
}


// Populate the GridView with data
private void BindGrid()
{
  // Get CategoryID from the query string
  string categoryId = Request.QueryString["CategoryID"];
  // Get a DataTable object containing the products
  grid.DataSource = CatalogAccess.GetAllProductsInCategory(categoryId);
  // Needed to bind the data bound controls to the data source
  grid.DataBind();
}


// Enter row into edit mode
protected void grid_RowEditing(object sender, GridViewEditEventArgs e)
{
  // Set the row for which to enable edit mode
  grid.EditIndex = e.NewEditIndex;
  // Set status message
  statusLabel.Text = "Editing row # " + e.NewEditIndex.ToString();
  // Reload the grid
  BindGrid();
}


// Cancel edit mode
protected void grid_RowCancelingEdit(object sender,
GridViewCancelEditEventArgs e)
{
  // Cancel edit mode
  grid.EditIndex = -1;
  // Set status message
  statusLabel.Text = "Editing canceled";
  // Reload the grid
  BindGrid();
}


// Update a product
protected void grid_RowUpdating(object sender, GridViewUpdateEventArgs e)
{
```

```
  // Retrieve updated data
  string id = grid.DataKeys[e.RowIndex].Value.ToString();
  string name = ((TextBox)grid.Rows[e.RowIndex].FindControl
("nameTextBox")).Text;
  string description = ((TextBox)grid.Rows[e.RowIndex].FindControl
("descriptionTextBox")).Text;
  string price = ((TextBox)grid.Rows[e.RowIndex].FindControl
("priceTextBox")).Text;
  string image1FileName = ((TextBox)grid.Rows[e.RowIndex].FindControl
("image1TextBox")).Text;
  string image2FileName = ((TextBox)grid.Rows[e.RowIndex].FindControl
("image2TextBox")).Text;
  string onDepartmentPromotion = ((CheckBox)grid.Rows[e.RowIndex].Cells[6].
Controls[0]).Checked.ToString();
  string onCatalogPromotion = ((CheckBox)grid.Rows[e.RowIndex].Cells[7]
.Controls[0]).Checked.ToString();
  // Execute the update command
  bool success = CatalogAccess.UpdateProduct(id, name, description, price,
image1FileName, image2FileName, onDepartmentPromotion, onCatalogPromotion);
  // Cancel edit mode
  grid.EditIndex = -1;
  // Display status message
  statusLabel.Text = success ? "Product update successful" :
"Product update failed";
  // Reload grid
  BindGrid();
}

// Create a new product
protected void createProduct_Click(object sender, EventArgs e)
{
  // Get CategoryID from the query string
  string categoryId = Request.QueryString["CategoryID"];
  // Execute the insert command
  bool success = CatalogAccess.CreateProduct(categoryId, newName.Text,
newDescription.Text, newPrice.Text, newImage1FileName.Text,
newImage2FileName.Text, newOnDepartmentPromotion.Checked.ToString(),
newOnCatalogPromotion.Checked.ToString());
  // Display status message
  statusLabel.Text = success ? "Insert successful" : "Insert failed";
  // Reload the grid
  BindGrid();
}
```

```
// Go back to the list of categories
protected void goBackLink_Click(object sender, EventArgs e)
{
  // Get DepartmentID from the query string
  string departmentId = Request.QueryString["DepartmentID"];
  // Redirect
  Response.Redirect(Request.ApplicationPath + "
/CatalogAdmin.aspx?DepartmentID=" + departmentId);
}
```

How It Works: `ProductsAdmin.ascx`

Most methods are similar to those you wrote for the previous controls, except this time you did more work to customize their appearance, especially while in edit mode. Products can be updated or selected. The administrator can change the product's image using the product details admin page, which shows up when a product is selected in the list. You'll create the product details page next.

As usual, when selecting a product, you reload the form by adding its ID to the query string. `ProductDetailsAdmin` allows you to assign the selected product to an additional category, to move the product to another category, to upload a picture for the product, to remove the product from its category, or to remove the product from the database.

Administering Product Details

The products list you built earlier is wonderful, but it lacks a few important features. The final control you're implementing will take care of these missing features. `ProductDetailsAdmin. ascx` will allow you to

- View the product's pictures

- View which categories the product belongs to

- Remove the product from its category

- Remove the product from the database completely

- Assign the current product to an additional category

- Move the current product to another category

- Upload product pictures

Figure 8-31 shows how the control will look for the World's Greatest Mom product.

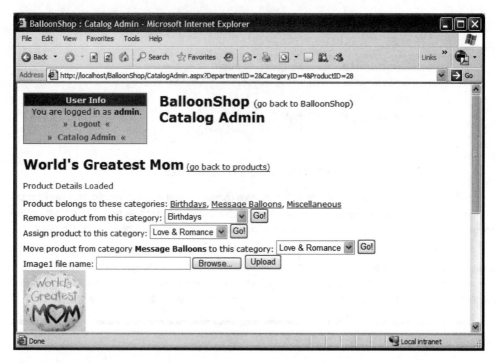

Figure 8-31. *The product details admin page in action*

When it comes to product removal, things aren't straightforward: You can either unassign the product from a category by removing the record from the ProductCategory table, or you can effectively remove the product from the Product table. Because products are accessed in the catalog by selecting a category, you must make sure there are no orphaned products (products that don't belong to any category), because they couldn't be accessed using the current administration interface.

So, if you added a Delete button to the data grid, what kind of deletion would that button have to do? Delete the product from the database? This would work, but it's a bit awkward if you have a product assigned to multiple categories, and you only want to remove it from a single category. On the other hand, if the Delete button removes the product from the current category, you can create orphaned products because they exist in the Product table. You could fix that by allowing the site administrator to see the complete list of products without locating them by department and category.

The simple solution implemented in this chapter is like that. If the product belongs to more than one category, the Delete button unassigns the product from the current category. If the product belongs to only one category, the product is first unassigned from the current category and then also removed from the Product table.

Stored Procedures for Product Details Admin

Now you'll add the following stored procedures to the BalloonShop database:

- GetCategoriesWithProduct

- GetCategoriesWithoutProduct

- AssignProductToCategory

- MoveProductToCategory

- RemoveProductFromCategory

- DeleteProduct

GetCategoriesWithProduct

The GetCategoriesWithProduct stored procedure returns a list of the categories that belong to the specified product. Only their IDs and names are returned because this is the only information we're interested in.

```
CREATE PROCEDURE GetCategoriesWithProduct
(@ProductID int)
AS
SELECT Category.CategoryID, Name
FROM Category INNER JOIN ProductCategory
ON Category.CategoryID = ProductCategory.CategoryID
WHERE ProductCategory.ProductID = @ProductID
```

GetCategoriesWithoutProduct

The GetCategoriesWithoutProduct stored procedure returns a list of the categories that don't contain a specified product. This is the list of categories that the product can be moved or assigned to.

```
CREATE PROCEDURE GetCategoriesWithoutProduct
(@ProductID int)
AS
SELECT CategoryID, Name
FROM Category
WHERE CategoryID NOT IN
   (SELECT Category.CategoryID
    FROM Category INNER JOIN ProductCategory
    ON Category.CategoryID = ProductCategory.CategoryID
    WHERE ProductCategory.ProductID = @ProductID)
```

AssignProductToCategory

The AssignProductToCategory stored procedure associates a product with a category by adding a (ProductID, CategoryID) value pair to the ProductCategory table:

```
CREATE PROCEDURE AssignProductToCategory
(@ProductID int, @CategoryID int)
AS
INSERT INTO ProductCategory (ProductID, CategoryID)
VALUES (@ProductID, @CategoryID)
```

Note that you don't do any verification here. If an error occurs (because the entered ProductID is not associated with any product or the ProductID, CategoryID pair already exists in the ProductCategory table), it is trapped at the upper levels, and the administrator is notified.

Still, since we talked about the error-handling techniques, it's worth noting that you can make the stored procedure smart enough to do some validation before attempting to add the (ProductID, CategorID) pair to ProductCategory table.

Following is a bulletproof version of the stored procedure that inserts the new record into ProductCategory only if the received ProductID and CategoryID values are valid and the pair doesn't already exist in the database:

```
CREATE PROCEDURE AssignProductToCategory
(@ProductID int, @CategoryID int)
AS
IF EXISTS
  (SELECT Name
   FROM Product
   WHERE ProductID = @ProductID)
  AND EXISTS
  (SELECT Name
   FROM Category
   WHERE CategoryID = @CategoryID)
  AND NOT EXISTS
  (SELECT *
   FROM ProductCategory
   WHERE CategoryID = @CategoryID AND ProductID = @ProductID)
INSERT INTO ProductCategory (ProductID, CategoryID)
VALUES (@ProductID, @CategoryID)
```

We won't use this version in practice because we prefer to be notified in case an illegal association is attempted.

MoveProductToCategory

MoveProductToCategory is the stored procedure that moves a product from one category to another:

```
CREATE PROCEDURE MoveProductToCategory
(@ProductID int, @OldCategoryID int, @NewCategoryID int)
AS
UPDATE ProductCategory
SET CategoryID = @NewCategoryID
WHERE CategoryID = @OldCategoryID
  AND ProductID = @ProductID
```

RemoveProductFromCategory

The RemoveProductFromCategory stored procedure verifies how many categories the product exists in. If the product exists in more than one category, the stored procedure just removes the product from the current category (ID received as a parameter). If the product is associated with a single category, it is first removed from the category and then effectively deleted from the database.

```
CREATE PROCEDURE RemoveProductFromCategory
(@ProductID int, @CategoryID int)
AS
DELETE FROM ProductCategory
WHERE CategoryID = @CategoryID AND ProductID = @ProductID
```

DeleteProduct

The DeleteProduct stored procedure verifies how many categories the product exists in. If the product exists in more than one category, the stored procedure just removes the product from the current category (ID received as a parameter). If the product is associated with a single category, it is first removed from the category and then effectively deleted from the database.

```
CREATE PROCEDURE DeleteProduct
(@ProductID INT)
AS
DELETE FROM ProductCategory WHERE ProductID=@ProductID
DELETE FROM Product where ProductID=@ProductID
```

---

2 IN 1

Don't add this new procedure to your database, but for your curiosity, here is a version of the previous two stored procedures that completely deletes a product from the catalog if it belongs to a single category, or simply removes it from the mentioned category if it belongs to more categories:

```
CREATE PROCEDURE DeleteProductFromCategoryOrFromCatalog
(@ProductID int, @CategoryID int)
AS
IF (SELECT COUNT(*) FROM ProductCategory WHERE ProductID=@ProductID)>1
  DELETE FROM ProductCategory
  WHERE CategoryID=@CategoryID AND ProductID=@ProductID
ELSE
  BEGIN
    DELETE FROM ProductCategory WHERE ProductID=@ProductID
    DELETE FROM Product where ProductID=@ProductID
  END
```

Middle-Tier Methods for Product Details Admin

Add the following methods to the CatalogAccess class:

- GetCategoriesWithProduct gets the list of categories that are related to a specified product.

- GetCategoriesWithoutProduct returns the categories that do not contain the specified product.

- AssignProductToCategory, MoveProductToCategory, and RemoveProductFromCategory do what their names imply.

- DeleteProduct completely removes a product from the product catalog.

Add the following code to the CatalogAccess class:

```
// get categories that contain a specified product
public static DataTable GetCategoriesWithProduct(string productId)
{
  // get a configured DbCommand object
  DbCommand comm = GenericDataAccess.CreateCommand();
  // set the stored procedure name
  comm.CommandText = "GetCategoriesWithProduct";
  // create a new parameter
  DbParameter param = comm.CreateParameter();
  param.ParameterName = "@ProductID";
  param.Value = productId;
  param.DbType = DbType.Int32;
  comm.Parameters.Add(param);
  // execute the stored procedure
  return GenericDataAccess.ExecuteSelectCommand(comm);
}

// get categories that do not contain a specified product
public static DataTable GetCategoriesWithoutProduct(string productId)
{
  // get a configured DbCommand object
  DbCommand comm = GenericDataAccess.CreateCommand();
  // set the stored procedure name
  comm.CommandText = "GetCategoriesWithoutProduct";
  // create a new parameter
  DbParameter param = comm.CreateParameter();
  param.ParameterName = "@ProductID";
  param.Value = productId;
  param.DbType = DbType.Int32;
  comm.Parameters.Add(param);
  // execute the stored procedure
  return GenericDataAccess.ExecuteSelectCommand(comm);
}
```

```csharp
// assign a product to a new category
public static bool AssignProductToCategory(string productId, string categoryId)
{
  // get a configured DbCommand object
  DbCommand comm = GenericDataAccess.CreateCommand();
  // set the stored procedure name
  comm.CommandText = "AssignProductToCategory";
  // create a new parameter
  DbParameter param = comm.CreateParameter();
  param.ParameterName = "@ProductID";
  param.Value = productId;
  param.DbType = DbType.Int32;
  comm.Parameters.Add(param);
  // create a new parameter
  param = comm.CreateParameter();
  param.ParameterName = "@CategoryID";
  param.Value = categoryId;
  param.DbType = DbType.Int32;
  comm.Parameters.Add(param);
  // result will represent the number of changed rows
  int result = -1;
  try
  {
    // execute the stored procedure
    result = GenericDataAccess.ExecuteNonQuery(comm);
  }
  catch
  {
    // any errors are logged in GenericDataAccess, we ignore them here
  }
  // result will be 1 in case of success
  return (result != -1);
}

// move product to a new category
public static bool MoveProductToCategory(string productId, string oldCategoryId,
  string newCategoryId)
{
  // get a configured DbCommand object
  DbCommand comm = GenericDataAccess.CreateCommand();
  // set the stored procedure name
  comm.CommandText = "MoveProductToCategory";
  // create a new parameter
  DbParameter param = comm.CreateParameter();
  param.ParameterName = "@ProductID";
```

```
    param.Value = productId;
    param.DbType = DbType.Int32;
    comm.Parameters.Add(param);
    // create a new parameter
    param = comm.CreateParameter();
    param.ParameterName = "@OldCategoryID";
    param.Value = oldCategoryId;
    param.DbType = DbType.Int32;
    comm.Parameters.Add(param);
    // create a new parameter
    param = comm.CreateParameter();
    param.ParameterName = "@NewCategoryID";
    param.Value = newCategoryId;
    param.DbType = DbType.Int32;
    comm.Parameters.Add(param);
    // result will represent the number of changed rows
    int result = -1;
    try
    {
      // execute the stored procedure
      result = GenericDataAccess.ExecuteNonQuery(comm);
    }
    catch
    {
      // any errors are logged in GenericDataAccess, we ignore them here
    }
    // result will be 1 in case of success
    return (result != -1);
  }

  // removes a product from a category
  public static bool RemoveProductFromCategory(string productId, string categoryId)
  {
    // get a configured DbCommand object
    DbCommand comm = GenericDataAccess.CreateCommand();
    // set the stored procedure name
    comm.CommandText = "RemoveProductFromCategory";
    // create a new parameter
    DbParameter param = comm.CreateParameter();
    param.ParameterName = "@ProductID";
    param.Value = productId;
    param.DbType = DbType.Int32;
    comm.Parameters.Add(param);
    // create a new parameter
    param = comm.CreateParameter();
    param.ParameterName = "@CategoryID";
```

```
    param.Value = categoryId;
    param.DbType = DbType.Int32;
    comm.Parameters.Add(param);
    // result will represent the number of changed rows
    int result = -1;
    try
    {
      // execute the stored procedure
      result = GenericDataAccess.ExecuteNonQuery(comm);
    }
    catch
    {
      // any errors are logged in GenericDataAccess, we ignore them here
    }
    // result will be 1 in case of success
    return (result != -1);
}

// deletes a product from the product catalog
public static bool DeleteProduct(string productId)
{
    // get a configured DbCommand object
    DbCommand comm = GenericDataAccess.CreateCommand();
    // set the stored procedure name
    comm.CommandText = "DeleteProduct";
    // create a new parameter
    DbParameter param = comm.CreateParameter();
    param.ParameterName = "@ProductID";
    param.Value = productId;
    param.DbType = DbType.Int32;
    comm.Parameters.Add(param);
    // result will represent the number of changed rows
    int result = -1;
    try
    {
      // execute the stored procedure
      result = GenericDataAccess.ExecuteNonQuery(comm);
    }
    catch
    {
      // any errors are logged in GenericDataAccess, we ignore them here
    }
    // result will be 1 in case of success
    return (result != -1);
}
```

The ProductDetailsAdmin Web User Control

You'll implement the control in the following exercise.

Exercise: Implementing ProductDetailsAdmin.ascx

1. Create a new user control named **ProductDetailsAdmin** in the **UserControls** folder.

2. You need to add controls to the form, as shown in Figure 8-32. Here you meet for the first time the **FileUpload** control.

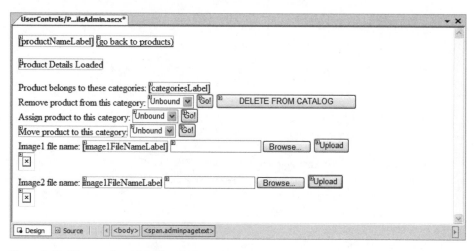

Figure 8-32. *The product details admin page*

The following is the associated source code:

```
<span class="AdminPageText">
  <asp:Label ID="productNameLabel" runat="server" CssClass="AdminTitle" />
  <asp:HyperLink ID="goBackLink" runat="server">(go back to products)
</asp:HyperLink>
  <br /><br />
  <asp:Label ID="statusLabel" runat="server" CssClass="AdminPageText"
Text="Product Details Loaded" ForeColor="Red"></asp:Label><br />
  <br />
Product belongs to these categories:
  <asp:Label ID="categoriesLabel" runat="server"></asp:Label>
  <br />
Remove product from this category:
  <asp:DropDownList ID="categoriesListRemove" runat="server">
  </asp:DropDownList>
  <asp:Button ID="removeButton" runat="server" Text="Go!"
```

```
OnClick="removeButton_Click" />
  <asp:Button ID="deleteButton" runat="server" Text="DELETE FROM CATALOG"
OnClick="deleteButton_Click" /><br />
Assign product to this category:
  <asp:DropDownList ID="categoriesListAssign" runat="server">
  </asp:DropDownList>
  <asp:Button ID="assignButton" runat="server" Text="Go!"
OnClick="assignButton_Click" />
  <br />
  <asp:Label ID="moveLabel" runat="server" Text="Move product to this
 category:"/>
  <asp:DropDownList ID="categoriesListMove" runat="server" />
  <asp:Button ID="moveButton" runat="server" Text="Go!"
OnClick="moveButton_Click" />
  <br />
Image1 file name:
  <asp:Label ID="image1FileNameLabel" runat="server" />
  <asp:FileUpload ID="image1FileUpload" runat="server" />
  <asp:Button ID="upload1Button" runat="server" Text="Upload" /><br />
  <asp:Image ID="image1" runat="server" />
  <br />
Image2 file name:
  <asp:Label ID="image2FileNameLabel " runat="server" />
  <asp:FileUpload ID="image2FileUpload" runat="server" />
  <asp:Button ID="upload2Button" runat="server" Text="Upload" /><br />
  <asp:Image ID="image2" runat="server" />
</span>
```

3. Open the code-behind file and complete the `ProductDetailsAdmin` class, as shown in the code
snippet:

```
public partial class ProductDetailsAdmin : System.Web.UI.UserControl
{
  // store product, category and department IDs as class members
  private string currentProductId, currentCategoryId, currentDepartmentId;

  protected void Page_Load(object sender, EventArgs e)
  {
    // Get DepartmentID, CategoryID, ProductID from the query string
    // and save their values
    currentDepartmentId = Request.QueryString["DepartmentID"];
    currentCategoryId = Request.QueryString["CategoryID"];
    currentProductId = Request.QueryString["ProductID"];
    // Assign buttons to the combo boxes
    Utilities.TieButton(this.Page, categoriesListRemove, removeButton);
    Utilities.TieButton(this.Page, categoriesListAssign, assignButton);
    Utilities.TieButton(this.Page, categoriesListMove, moveButton);
```

```
    // Fill the controls with data only on the initial page load
    if (!IsPostBack)
    {
      // Fill controls with data
      PopulateControls();
    }
  }

  // Populate the controls
  private void PopulateControls()
  {
    // Set the "go back to products" link
    goBackLink.NavigateUrl = Request.ApplicationPath +
        String.Format("/CatalogAdmin.aspx?DepartmentID={0}&CategoryID={1}",
                      currentDepartmentId, currentCategoryId);
    // Retrieve product details and category details from database
    ProductDetails productDetails =
CatalogAccess.GetProductDetails(currentProductId);
    CategoryDetails categoryDetails =
CatalogAccess.GetCategoryDetails(currentCategoryId);
    // Set up labels and images
    productNameLabel.Text = productDetails.Name;
    moveLabel.Text = "Move product from category <b>" +
categoryDetails.Name + "</b> to this category: ";
    image1.ImageUrl = Request.ApplicationPath + "/ProductImages/" +
productDetails.Image1FileName;
    image2.ImageUrl = Request.ApplicationPath + "/ProductImages/" +
productDetails.Image2FileName;
    // Clear form
    categoriesLabel.Text = "";
    categoriesListAssign.Items.Clear();
    categoriesListMove.Items.Clear();
    categoriesListRemove.Items.Clear();
    // Fill categoriesLabel and categoriesListRemove with data
    string categoryId, categoryName;
    DataTable productCategories =
CatalogAccess.GetCategoriesWithProduct(currentProductId);
    for (int i = 0; i < productCategories.Rows.Count; i++)
    {
      // obtain category id and name
      categoryId = productCategories.Rows[i]["CategoryId"].ToString();
      categoryName = productCategories.Rows[i]["Name"].ToString();
      // add a link to the category admin page
      categoriesLabel.Text += (categoriesLabel.Text == "" ? "" : ", ") +
          "<a href=\"" + Request.ApplicationPath + "/CatalogAdmin.aspx" +
          "?DepartmentID=" +
```

```
CatalogAccess.GetCategoryDetails(currentCategoryId).DepartmentId +
        "&CategoryID=" + categoryId + "\">" +
        categoryName + "</a>";
   // populate the categoriesListRemove combo box
   categoriesListRemove.Items.Add(new ListItem(categoryName, categoryId));
 }
 // Delete from catalog or remove from category?
 if (productCategories.Rows.Count > 1)
 {
   deleteButton.Visible = false;
   removeButton.Enabled = true;
 }
 else
 {
   deleteButton.Visible = true;
   removeButton.Enabled = false;
 }
 // Fill categoriesListMove and categoriesListAssign with data
 productCategories = CatalogAccess.GetCategoriesWithoutProduct
(currentProductId);
 for (int i = 0; i < productCategories.Rows.Count; i++)
 {
   // obtain category id and name
   categoryId = productCategories.Rows[i]["CategoryId"].ToString();
   categoryName = productCategories.Rows[i]["Name"].ToString();
   // populate the list boxes
   categoriesListAssign.Items.Add(new ListItem(categoryName, categoryId));
   categoriesListMove.Items.Add(new ListItem(categoryName, categoryId));
 }
 }
}
```

4. Open `ProductDetailsAdmin.ascx` in **Design View**, double-click the first button (`removeButton`), and then complete its `Click` event handler method like this:

```
// Remove the product from a category
protected void removeButton_Click(object sender, EventArgs e)
{
  // Check if a category was selected
  if (categoriesListRemove.SelectedIndex != -1)
  {
    // Get the category ID that was selected in the DropDownList
    string categoryId = categoriesListRemove.SelectedItem.Value;
    // Remove the product from the category
    bool success = CatalogAccess.RemoveProductFromCategory
```

```
(currentProductId, categoryId);
      // Display status message
      statusLabel.Text = success ? "Product removed successfully" :
"Product removal failed";
      // Refresh the page
      PopulateControls();
    }
    else
      statusLabel.Text = "You need to select a category";
  }
```

5. While in **Design View**, double-click the second button (`deleteButton`), and then complete its `Click`
   event handler method like this:

```
// delete a product from the catalog
protected void deleteButton_Click(object sender, EventArgs e)
{
  // Delete the product from the catalog
  CatalogAccess.DeleteProduct(currentProductId);
  // Need to go back to the categories page now
  Response.Redirect(Request.ApplicationPath + "/CatalogAdmin.aspx" +
          "?DepartmentID=" + currentDepartmentId +
          "&CategoryID=" + currentCategoryId);
}
```

6. While in **Design View**, double-click the third button (`assignButton`), and then complete its `Click`
   event handler method like this:

```
// assign the product to a new category
protected void assignButton_Click(object sender, EventArgs e)
{
  // Check if a category was selected
  if (categoriesListAssign.SelectedIndex != -1)
  {
    // Get the category ID that was selected in the DropDownList
    string categoryId = categoriesListAssign.SelectedItem.Value;
    // Assign the product to the category
    bool success = CatalogAccess.AssignProductToCategory(currentProductId,
categoryId);
    // Display status message
    statusLabel.Text = success ? "Product assigned successfully" :
"Product assignation failed";
    // Refresh the page
    PopulateControls();
  }
  else
    statusLabel.Text = "You need to select a category";
}
```

7. While in **Design View**, double-click the fourth button (moveButton), and then complete its Click event handler method like this:

```
// move the product to another category
protected void moveButton_Click(object sender, EventArgs e)
{
  // Check if a category was selected
  if (categoriesListMove.SelectedIndex != -1)
  {
    // Get the category ID that was selected in the DropDownList
    string newCategoryId = categoriesListMove.SelectedItem.Value;
    // Move the product to the category
    bool success = CatalogAccess.MoveProductToCategory(currentProductId,
currentCategoryId, newCategoryId);
    // If the operation was successful, reload the page,
    // so the new category will reflect in the query string
    if (!success)
      statusLabel.Text = "Couldn't move the product to the
specified category";
    else
      Response.Redirect(Request.ApplicationPath + "/CatalogAdmin.aspx" +
          "?DepartmentID=" + currentDepartmentId +
          "&CategoryID=" + newCategoryId +
          "&ProductID=" + currentProductId);
  }
  else
    statusLabel.Text = "You need to select a category";
}
```

8. While in **Design View**, double-click the two **Upload** buttons and complete their Click event handler code like this:

```
// upload product's first image
protected void upload1Button_Click(object sender, EventArgs e)
{
  // proceed with uploading only if the user selected a file
  if (image1FileUpload.HasFile)
  {
    try
    {
      string fileName = image1FileUpload.FileName;
      string location = Server.MapPath("./ProductImages/") + fileName;
      // save image to server
      image1FileUpload.SaveAs(location);
```

```
            // update database with new product details
            ProductDetails pd = CatalogAccess.GetProductDetails(currentProductId);
            CatalogAccess.UpdateProduct(currentProductId, pd.Name,
    pd.Description, pd.Price.ToString(), fileName, pd.Image2FileName,
    pd.OnDepartmentPromotion.ToString(), pd.OnCatalogPromotion.ToString());
            // reload the page
            Response.Redirect(Request.ApplicationPath + "/CatalogAdmin.aspx" +
                    "?DepartmentID=" + currentDepartmentId +
                    "&CategoryID=" + currentCategoryId +
                    "&ProductID=" + currentProductId);
        }
        catch
        {
          statusLabel.Text = "Uploading image 1 failed";
        }
      }
    }
  }

  // upload product's second image
  protected void upload2Button_Click(object sender, EventArgs e)
  {
    // proceed with uploading only if the user selected a file
    if (image2FileUpload.HasFile)
    {
      try
      {
        string fileName = image2FileUpload.FileName;
        string location = Server.MapPath("./ProductImages/") + fileName;
        // save image to server
        image2FileUpload.SaveAs(location);
        // update database with new product details
        ProductDetails pd = CatalogAccess.GetProductDetails(currentProductId);
        CatalogAccess.UpdateProduct(currentProductId, pd.Name,
    pd.Description, pd.Price.ToString(), pd.Image1FileName, fileName,
    pd.OnDepartmentPromotion.ToString(), pd.OnCatalogPromotion.ToString());
        // reload the page
        Response.Redirect(Request.ApplicationPath + "/CatalogAdmin.aspx" +
                "?DepartmentID=" + currentDepartmentId +
                "&CategoryID=" + currentCategoryId +
                "&ProductID=" + currentProductId);
      }
      catch
      {
        statusLabel.Text = "Uploading image 2 failed";
      }
    }
  }
```

9. Test your new catalog admin page to see that everything works as expected.

How It Works: `ProductDetailsAdmin.ascx`

It's worth taking a second look at the bits that are different from the previous exercises:

- The `TieButton` method tied the drop-down lists to their associated **Go!** buttons.

- The `FileUpload` control uploaded product pictures to the server. The code is pretty clear, so take a closer look at the `Click` event handlers of the two Upload buttons to see how the `FileUpload` control is used in practice.

- Various tests are made in the buttons' `Click` event handlers to display accurate status messages to the visitor. A novelty in this control is checking whether a value of the drop-down lists has been selected before trying to read its value (this is useful especially in the situation when the list is empty).

- The `DropDownList` controls are populated in the `PopulateControls` method, and they are capable of storing a key for each of their entries, similar to what the `DataKeyNames` property does for the `GridView`. In our case, this key retains the IDs of the listed categories. You read this ID from the `DropDownList` controls when the user tries to move, assign, or remove the product from a selected category, by reading the `SelectedItem.Value` property of the list.

Summary

You've done a lot of coding in this chapter. You implemented five user controls, along with their middle-tier methods and stored procedures for the data tier. You learned how to implement a simple authentication scheme so only administrators are allowed to access the catalog administration page.

You made contact with the `GridView`, which is probably the most powerful web control that comes packaged with the .NET Framework. You learned how to use `GridView`'s built-in features for editing, selecting, updating, and deleting records. You also learned how to use template columns to improve its functionality.

At the end of the chapter, you learned how to upload files from the client to the server using ASP.NET.

CHAPTER 9

■ ■ ■

Creating a Custom Shopping Cart

Welcome to the second stage of development! At this stage, you start improving and adding new features to the already existing, fully functional e-commerce site.

So, what can you improve about it? Well, the answer to this question isn't that hard to find if you take a quick look at the popular e-commerce sites on the web. They have user personalization and product recommendations, they remember customers' preferences, and they boast many other features that make the site easy to remember and hard to leave without first buying something.

Because in the first stage of development we extensively relied on a third-party payment processor (PayPal), which supplied an integrated shopping cart, we didn't record any shopping cart or order info into the database. Right now, your site isn't capable of displaying a list of "most wanted" products or any other information about the products that have been sold through the web site, because at this stage, you aren't tracking the products sold. This makes it impossible to implement any of the improvements listed earlier.

Obviously, saving order information into the database is your first priority and most of the features you'll want to implement next rely on having a record of the products sold. To achieve this functionality, you'll implement a custom shopping basket and a custom checkout.

In this chapter, you'll implement the custom shopping basket, which stores its data in the local BalloonShop database. This shopping basket provides you with more flexibility, compared to the PayPal shopping basket over which you have no control and which cannot be saved into your database for further processing and analysis.

In this chapter, you'll build the shopping cart page (see Figure 9-1) and a shopping cart summary control that shows up in every catalog page except the shopping cart page (see Figure 9-2). You'll also create a shopping cart administration page (see Figure 9-3), which allows the administrator to delete old shopping cart records from the database to prevent the database from growing indefinitely.

You'll also appreciate the error-handling features in both the shopping cart and the shopping cart administration page. In the shopping cart, for example, serious errors cause the site to display the Oooops! message, whereas less-serious messages are simply logged (if the site is configured to log them in web.config), and the visitor is notified with a simple message. This happens, for example, if the user tries to update the shopping cart with bogus values, such as inserting a letter for the product quantity, and so on.

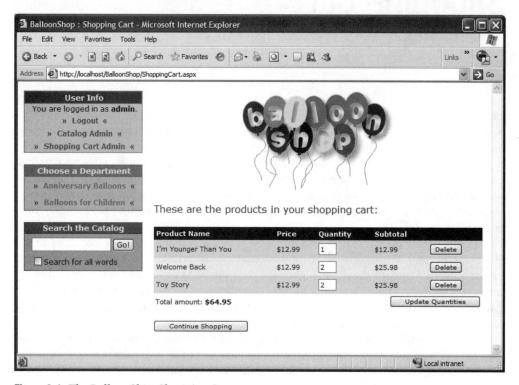

Figure 9-1. *The BalloonShop Shopping Cart*

Figure 9-2. *BalloonShop displays a Shopping Cart Summary box*

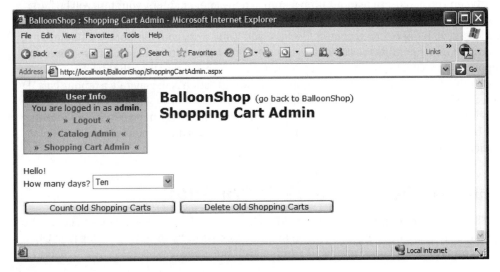

Figure 9-3. *The Shopping Cart Administration Page*

At the end of this chapter, you'll have a functional shopping basket, but the visitor won't be able to order the products contained in it yet. You'll take care of that in the next chapter, where you'll implement a custom checkout, which includes adding the Proceed to Checkout button and the functionality to administer current orders. When the visitor clicks this button, the products in the shopping basket are saved as a separate order in the database, and the visitor is redirected to a page where payments are taken. If you integrated the PayPal shopping cart for the first development stage, starting with the next chapter, PayPal will only be used to handle payments, and you won't rely on its shopping cart any more.

Before moving to the details, let's review what you'll do in this chapter:

- Design a shopping cart

- Add new data structures to store shopping cart records

- Implement the business tier methods to work with the shopping cart

- Implement the cart summary control and the shopping cart page and integrate them into the existing solution

- Create the shopping cart administration page

Designing the Shopping Cart

At this stage of the site, you won't have any user-personalization features. You won't store any user data, and BalloonShop won't know who buys the products. We're just interested in having temporary shopping carts that can be transformed into orders and paid for through a service like PayPal when the visitors decide to buy the products. The payment service provider asks for the customers' data (such as credit card information) when they decide to buy your products.

When you add user-customization features in the later chapters, your task will be fairly simple: When the visitor places an order, the visitor's temporary (anonymous) shopping cart is associated with the visitor's account. Because you'll still work with temporary shopping carts, even after implementing the customer account system, the visitor still won't be required to supply additional information (log in or create an account) earlier than the checkout stage.

Probably the best way to store shopping cart information is to generate a unique cart ID for each shopping cart and save it on the visitor's computer as a **cookie** and as **session** data. This way, even if the visitor has cookies disabled, the application can be configured to work fine by just relying on the visitor's session data. We'll discuss more about cookies and the session when we get to the business tier part.

Storing Shopping Cart Information

You'll store all shopping cart items in a single table, named ShoppingCart. You can create the new table by either following the steps in the next exercise or by simply executing the SQL script from the Source Code area on the Apress web site.

Remember that you can also create your table and implement the relationship using database diagrams, as shown in Chapter 4.

Follow the steps in the next exercise if you prefer to create your new table manually.

Exercise: Creating the ShoppingCart Table

1. In **Database Explorer**, expand your **BalloonShop** database, right-click on **Tables**, and choose **Add New Table**.

2. Add this table to your **BalloonShop** database as shown in Figure 9-4.

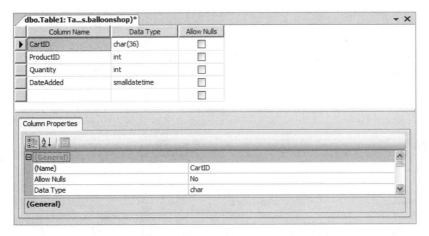

Figure 9-4. *Designing the ShoppingCart table*

■**Note** You can use either smalldatetime or datetime for the DateAdded column. smalldatetime stores the date with less precision than datetime, down to minutes, but occupies 4 bytes instead of 8.

---

3. Select both the CartID and ProductID fields and click the golden key symbol (or right-click and select **Set Primary Key**) to create a composite primary key formed of these two fields.

4. Press **Ctrl+S** to save the table. Choose **ShoppingCart** for the name and click **OK**.

5. Add a foreign key by right-clicking the table and selecting **Relationships**.

6. Click **Add** to create a new relationship entry.

7. Select the **Tables and Columns Specification** (see Figure 9-5) and then click the "**...**" button.

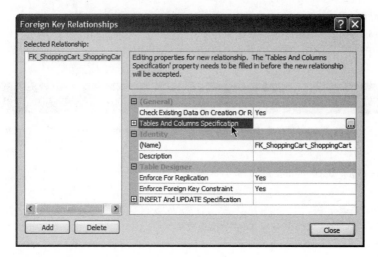

Figure 9-5. *Adding a new relationship*

8. Complete the form that appears as shown in Figure 9-6.

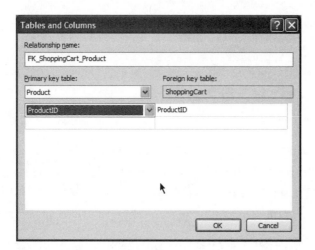

Figure 9-6. *Setting foreign key properties*

9. Click **OK** and then click **Close**.

10. Save your table. Confirm the action when asked about applying changes to the Product and ShoppingCart tables.

How It Works: The ShoppingCart Table

CartID is the unique ID you'll generate for each shopping cart. Unlike the other unique identifiers you've seen so far, this is not an integer field; instead, it's a Char(36) field, which will be filled with a GUID string. A GUID (Globally Unique Identifier) is a value guaranteed to be unique across time and space. Two generated GUIDs will never be the same. The string representation of a GUID has 36 characters: The GUID itself is 32 bytes long, and its string representation also contains 4 separating dashes. An example of a GUID is ff8029a7-91e2-4ca2-b4e7-99a7588be751.

■Tip When you know the exact length of the strings you're storing in a table field, it's better to use the Char data type instead of VarChar.

The second field is ProductID, which, as expected, holds the ID of an existing product. To ensure that the cart doesn't hold any nonexistent products, you need to enforce the One-to-Many relationship between the ShoppingCart and Product tables through a FOREIGN KEY constraint. The relationship is tied between the ProductID columns in the ShoppingCart and Product tables.

■Note The primary key is formed from both the CartID and ProductID fields (a **composite primary key**). This makes sense because a particular product can exist only once in a particular shopping cart, so a (CartID, ProductID) pair shouldn't appear more than once in the table. If the visitor adds a product more than once, you just increase the Quantity value.

Each record in ShoppingCart also has a DateAdded field, which is automatically populated with the current date when a new product is added to the cart and is useful when deleting old records.

■Tip Your implementation of the ShoppingCartAddItem procedure manually fills the DateAdded field using the GETDATE function. Alternatively, you can specify GETDATE as the default value for the DateAdded field.

Implementing the Data Tier

Because you have already created stored procedures in the previous chapters, we'll move a bit quicker this time. You need to add the following stored procedures to the BalloonShop database:

- ShoppingCartAddItem adds a product to a shopping cart.
- ShoppingCartRemoveItem deletes a record from the ShoppingCart table.
- ShoppingCartUpdateItem modifies a shopping cart record.
- ShoppingCartGetItems gets the list of products in the specified shopping cart.
- ShoppingCartGetTotalAmount returns the total cost of the products in the specified product cart.

ShoppingCartAddItem

ShoppingCartAddItem is called when the visitor clicks the Add to Cart button for one of the products. If the selected product already exists in the shopping cart, its quantity is increased by one; if the product doesn't exist, a new record is added to the shopping cart.

Not surprisingly, the parameters ShoppingCartAddItem receives are CartID and ProductID. The stored procedure first searches to determine whether the product mentioned (ProductID, CartID) pair exists in the ShoppingCart table. If it does, the stored procedure updates the current product quantity in the shopping cart by adding one unit. Otherwise, the procedure creates a new record for the product in ShoppingCart with a default quantity of 1, but not before checking whether the mentioned @ProductID is valid.

Add the following stored procedure to your BalloonShop database:

```
CREATE Procedure ShoppingCartAddItem
(@CartID char(36),
 @ProductID int)
AS
IF EXISTS
        (SELECT CartID
         FROM ShoppingCart
         WHERE ProductID = @ProductID AND CartID = @CartID)
    UPDATE ShoppingCart
    SET Quantity = Quantity + 1
    WHERE ProductID = @ProductID AND CartID = @CartID
ELSE
    IF EXISTS (SELECT Name FROM Product WHERE ProductID=@ProductID)
        INSERT INTO ShoppingCart (CartID, ProductID, Quantity, DateAdded)
        VALUES (@CartID, @ProductID, 1, GETDATE())
```

You use the GETDATE system function to retrieve the current date and manually populate the DateAdded field, but you could set the GETDATE function as the default value of that field instead.

ShoppingCartRemoveItem

Following is the stored procedure that removes a product from the shopping cart. This happens when the visitor clicks the Remove button for one of the products in the shopping cart. Add the ShoppingCartRemoveItem stored procedure to your BalloonShop database:

```
CREATE PROCEDURE ShoppingCartRemoveItem
(@CartID char(36),
 @ProductID int)
AS
DELETE FROM ShoppingCart
WHERE CartID = @CartID and ProductID = @ProductID
```

ShoppingCartUpdateItem

ShoppingCartUpdateItem is used when you want to update the quantity of an existing shopping cart item. This stored procedure receives three values as parameters: @CartID, @ProductID, and @Quantity.

If @Quantity is 0 or less, ShoppingCartUpdateItem calls ShoppingCartRemoveItem to remove the mentioned product from the shopping cart. Otherwise, it updates the quantity of the product in the shopping cart and updates DateAdded to accurately reflect the time the record was last modified.

■**Tip** Updating the DateAdded field is important because the administrator can remove old shopping carts from the database, and you don't want to remove carts that were recently updated!

Add the ShoppingCartUpdateItem stored procedure to your BalloonShop database:

```
CREATE Procedure ShoppingCartUpdateItem
(@CartID char(36),
 @ProductID int,
 @Quantity int)
AS
IF @Quantity <= 0
  EXEC ShoppingCartRemoveItem @CartID, @ProductID
ELSE
  UPDATE ShoppingCart
  SET Quantity = @Quantity, DateAdded = GETDATE()
  WHERE ProductID = @ProductID AND CartID = @CartID
```

ShoppingCartGetItems

This stored procedure returns the ID, Name, Price, Quantity, and Subtotal for each product in the shopping cart. Because the ShoppingCart table only stores the ProductID for each product it stores, you need to join the ShoppingCart and Product tables to get the information you need. Add the ShoppingCartGetItems stored procedure to your BalloonShop database:

```
CREATE PROCEDURE ShoppingCartGetItems
(@CartID char(36))
AS
SELECT Product.ProductID, Product.Name, Product.Price, ShoppingCart.Quantity,
       Product.Price * ShoppingCart.Quantity AS Subtotal
FROM ShoppingCart INNER JOIN Product
ON ShoppingCart.ProductID = Product.ProductID
WHERE ShoppingCart.CartID = @CartID
```

■**Note** Subtotal is a calculated column. It doesn't exist in any of the tables you joined, but it's generated using a formula, which in this case is the price of the product multiplied by its quantity. When sending back the results, Subtotal is regarded as a separate column.

ShoppingCartGetTotalAmount

ShoppingCartGetTotalAmount returns the total value of the products in the shopping cart. This is called when displaying the total amount for the shopping cart.

```
CREATE PROCEDURE ShoppingCartGetTotalAmount
(@CartID char(36))
AS
SELECT ISNULL(SUM(Product.Price * ShoppingCart.Quantity), 0)
FROM ShoppingCart INNER JOIN Product
ON ShoppingCart.ProductID = Product.ProductID
WHERE ShoppingCart.CartID = @CartID
```

■**Note** The ISNULL method is used to return 0 instead of a NULL total amount (this happens if the shopping cart is empty). You must do this because the business tier expects to receive a numerical value as the amount.

This stored procedure is different from the others in that it returns a single value instead of a result set. In the business tier, you'll retrieve this value using the ExecuteScalar method of the DbCommand object.

Implementing the Business Tier

You'll write the business layer methods for the shopping cart in a separate class named ShoppingCartAccess.

The ShoppingCartAccess class supports the functionality required for the presentation layer of the shopping cart and calls the stored procedures you wrote earlier. For example, when the visitor clicks the Add to Cart button, a method of the ShoppingCartAccess class named AddProduct is called.

None of the methods receives a CartID parameter, which might appear strange because all the stored procedures you've written so far require a CartID parameter. So, how does the AddItem method know which CartID to send to the ShoppingCartAddItem stored procedure?

Generating Shopping Cart IDs

Your site needs to know the Cart ID of your visitor's shopping cart to perform its shopping cart functionality. You'll create a property named shoppingCartId in the ShoppingCartAccess class, which returns the cart ID of the current visitor. It's important to understand how this latter property works.

HTTP is, by its nature, a **stateless protocol**. Each individual client request is not associated with any previous requests from the same user. ASP.NET has a number of built-in features that overcome this problem, one of them being the session state that you've already met earlier in this book.

When it comes to identifying the visitor that browses your site and keeping track of the visitor's unique shopping cart, the first thing that comes to mind is **cookies**.

COOKIES

Cookies are client-side pieces of information that are managed by the visitor's browser; they are stored as name-value pairs. Cookies have the advantages of not consuming server resources (because they are managed at the client) and having configurable expiration. By saving data unique to your visitor in a cookie (such as the visitor's shopping cart ID), you can later find its ID by requesting the cookie from the client. Cookies are also useful because you can set them to expire when the browser session ends (so a new shopping cart is created every time the visitor comes back to the site), or they can be set to exist indefinitely on the client computer, effectively allowing you to control how long the shopping cart is remembered by your application.

If you store the Cart ID in the visitor's cookie, you'll have access to it when the visitor returns after a period of time. If the shopping cart cookie doesn't exist, it can mean that the visitor used your shopping cart for the first time, so you generate a new GUID and save it to the cookie. If the cookie exists, you take the GUID from there and use the shopping cart associated with it.

What about customers that have disabled (or whose browsers don't support) cookies? Well, the backup strategy is to also use the visitor's **session**. ASP.NET's session relies, by default, on using cookies, but by changing a simple setting, you can enable cookieless session support. An alternative option to support cookieless browsers is to append the session ID to the query string, as many popular e-commerce web sites do. Both solutions have the same effect and allow the customers to use your shopping cart even if their browsers don't support cookies (however, in this case, their shopping carts are lost if they close their browser session and return after a while, unlike when using cookies).

SESSION

Session handling is a great ASP.NET feature that allows you to keep track of variables specific to a certain visitor accessing the web site. While your visitor browses various pages of the web site, its session variables are persisted by the web server, and the Web Application can keep track of certain visitor data by uniquely identifying the visitor (you can track, for example, data such as the visitor ID or the visitor's favorite background color, name, email address, and so on). The visitor's session object stores pairs of values (variable name, variable value) that are accessible for the entire visitor's visit on your web site.

In ASP.NET, you can access the session data through the `Session` object. You can use this object to preserve data between client requests. This data is stored on the server side and is not passed back and forth during requests—only a session identifier is passed. This means that storing large quantities of data in the visitor's session occupies the server's memory, but doesn't increase network traffic. In this chapter, you'll only use the session to store the ID of your visitor's shopping cart.

So, shoppingCartId is a read-only property that returns the CartID of the visitor for whom the call has been made. In this property, you'll use a cookie named BalloonShop_CartID and a session variable with the same name to keep track of your visitor's shopping cart records.

Let's create the ShoppingCartAccess class and add its shoppingCartId property in the following exercise.

Exercise: Preparing the ShoppingCartAccess Class

1. We prefer to store the number of days for the cookie expiration in the config file rather than in code, so open web.config and add this configuration setting:

   ```
   <appSettings>
     <add key="CartPersistDays" value="10" />
     ...
   ```

■**Note** Setting the expiration time to 0 generates nonpersistent cookies (they are automatically deleted when the visitor's session ends).

---

2. You now need to operate changes in the **BalloonShopConfiguration** class to make your new property easily accessible from the rest of the site. Start by adding a private field called **cartPersistDays** to the **BalloonShopConfiguration** class, located in BalloonShopConfiguration.cs:

   ```
   public static class BalloonShopConfiguration
   {
     // Store the number of days for shopping cart expiration
     private readonly static int cartPersistDays;
     ...
   ```

3. Add a new line in the static constructor to initialize your new field:

   ```
   static BalloonShopConfiguration()
   {
     cartPersistDays =
           Int32.Parse(ConfigurationManager.AppSettings["CartPersistDays"]);
     ...
   ```

4. Add the following public property to return the configuration value:

   ```
   // Returns the number of days for shopping cart expiration
   public static int CartPersistDays
   {
     get
     {
       return cartPersistDays;
     }
   }
   ```

5. Now for the real code that deals with the visitor's shopping cart. Right-click the **App_Code** folder in the **Solution Explorer** and select **Add New Item**.

6. Select **Class** from the **Templates window** and name it **ShoppingCartAccess.cs**.

7. After the file is in place, add a reference to the `System.Data.Common` assembly and write the `shoppingCartId` property as shown here:

```
using System.Data.Common;

/// <summary>
/// Supports Shopping Cart functionality
/// </summary>
public class ShoppingCartAccess
{
  public ShoppingCartAccess()
  {
    //
    // TODO: Add constructor logic here
    //
  }

  // returns the shopping cart ID for the current user
  private static string shoppingCartId
  {
    get
    {
      // get the current HttpContext
      HttpContext context = HttpContext.Current;
      // try to retrieve the cart ID from the user session object
      string cartId = "";
      object cartIdSession = context.Session["BalloonShop_CartID"];
      if (cartIdSession != null)
        cartId = cartIdSession.ToString();
      // if the ID exists in the current session...
      if (cartId != "")
        // return its value
        return cartId;
      else
      // if the cart ID isn't in the session...
      {
        // check if the cart ID exists as a cookie
        if (context.Request.Cookies["BalloonShop_CartID"] != null)
        {
          // if the cart exists as a cookie, use the cookie to get its value
          cartId = context.Request.Cookies["BalloonShop_CartID"].Value;
          // save the id to the session, to avoid reading the cookie next time
          context.Session["BalloonShop_CartID"] = cartId;
```

```
                    // return the id
                    return cartId;
                }
                else
                // if the cart ID doesn't exist in the cookie as well,
        generate a new ID
                {
                    // generate a new GUID
                    cartId = Guid.NewGuid().ToString();
                    // create the cookie object and set its value
                    HttpCookie cookie = new HttpCookie("BalloonShop_CartID",
        cartId.ToString());
                    // set the cookie's expiration date
                    int howManyDays = BalloonShopConfiguration.CartPersistDays;
                    DateTime currentDate = DateTime.Now;
                    TimeSpan timeSpan = new TimeSpan(howManyDays, 0, 0, 0);
                    DateTime expirationDate = currentDate.Add(timeSpan);
                    cookie.Expires = expirationDate;
                    // set the cookie on the client's browser
                    context.Response.Cookies.Add(cookie);
                    // save the ID to the Session as well
                    context.Session["BalloonShop_CartID"] = cartId;
                    // return the CartID
                    return cartId.ToString();
                }
            }
        }
    }
}
```

How It Works: ShoppingCartAccess and Cart IDs

The strategy of the shoppingCartID property is something like this:

1. Check whether the CartID is stored in the session. If yes, use the found value.

2. If the CartID doesn't exist in the session, try to load it from a cookie. This happens with customers that return after a while and have cookies enabled. If the cookie is found, use its value and also save the value to the session so next time it will be found from the first attempt, without needing to read the cookie from the client again.

3. If the CartID doesn't exist in the session or a cookie, generate a new GUID and save it to both the session and the cookie, effectively creating a new shopping cart.

When you set an expiration time for the cookie, it becomes a persistent cookie and is saved as a file by the computer's browser. We set our cookie to expire in ten days, so the visitor's shopping cart exists for ten days from the time it is created. If an expiration date is not specified, the cookie is stored only for the current browser session.

What If the Visitor Doesn't Like Cookies?

Using the session as a backup strategy "against" cookies isn't enough to support cookieless browsers because, by default, ASP.NET uses cookies to track session information.

To configure your web site to work with browsers that have cookies disabled, you need to configure ASP.NET's session to work without cookies. To do that, you need to open web.config and make this change:

```
<sessionState
     mode="InProc"
     stateConnectionString="tcpip=127.0.0.1:42424"
     sqlConnectionString="data source=127.0.0.1;Trusted_Connection=yes"
     cookieless="true"
     timeout="20" />
```

In cookieless mode, an ID for the session state is automatically saved by ASP.NET in the query string:

```
http://localhost/BalloonShop/(vcmq0tz22y2okxzdq1bo2w45)/default.aspx
```

Unfortunately, this looks a bit ugly, but works without using cookies. Now it's just a matter of taste and knowledge of your customers to enable or disable this feature. We won't use this feature in BalloonShop.

Implementing the Shopping Cart Access Functionality

You have five methods in the business tier that correspond to the five stored procedures you wrote earlier. Add the methods presented in the following sections to the ShoppingCartAccess class.

AddItem

AddItem calls the ShoppingCartAddItem stored procedure. If the product already exists in the shopping cart, its quantity is increased by one. Otherwise, the product is added with a default quantity of one:

```
// Add a new shopping cart item
public static bool AddItem(string productId)
{
  // get a configured DbCommand object
  DbCommand comm = GenericDataAccess.CreateCommand();
  // set the stored procedure name
  comm.CommandText = "ShoppingCartAddItem";
  // create a new parameter
  DbParameter param = comm.CreateParameter();
  param.ParameterName = "@CartID";
  param.Value = shoppingCartId;
  param.DbType = DbType.String;
  param.Size = 36;
  comm.Parameters.Add(param);
  // create a new parameter
  param = comm.CreateParameter();
```

```
      param.ParameterName = "@ProductID";
      param.Value = productId;
      param.DbType = DbType.Int32;
      comm.Parameters.Add(param);
      // returns true in case of success or false in case of an error
      try
      {
        // execute the stored procedure and return true if it executes
        // successfully, or false otherwise
        return (GenericDataAccess.ExecuteNonQuery(comm) != -1);
      }
      catch
      {
        // prevent the exception from propagating, but return false to
        // signal the error
        return false;
      }
    }
```

UpdateItem

UpdateItem calls the ShoppingCartUpdateItem stored procedure to change the quantity of a product that already exists in the shopping cart:

```
// Update the quantity of a shopping cart item
public static bool UpdateItem(string productId, int quantity)
{
  // get a configured DbCommand object
  DbCommand comm = GenericDataAccess.CreateCommand();
  // set the stored procedure name
  comm.CommandText = "ShoppingCartUpdateItem";
  // create a new parameter
  DbParameter param = comm.CreateParameter();
  param.ParameterName = "@CartID";
  param.Value = shoppingCartId;
  param.DbType = DbType.String;
  param.Size = 36;
  comm.Parameters.Add(param);
  // create a new parameter
  param = comm.CreateParameter();
  param.ParameterName = "@ProductID";
  param.Value = productId;
  param.DbType = DbType.Int32;
  comm.Parameters.Add(param);
  // create a new parameter
  param = comm.CreateParameter();
  param.ParameterName = "@Quantity";
  param.Value = quantity;
```

```
    param.DbType = DbType.Int32;
    comm.Parameters.Add(param);
    // returns true in case of success or false in case of an error
    try
    {
      // execute the stored procedure and return true if it executes
      // successfully, or false otherwise
      return (GenericDataAccess.ExecuteNonQuery(comm) != -1);
    }
    catch
    {
      // prevent the exception from propagating, but return false to
      // signal the error
      return false;
    }
}
```

RemoveItem

Now add the RemoveItem method, which causes the removal of one product from the customer's shopping cart:

```
// Remove a shopping cart item
public static bool RemoveItem(string productId)
{
  // get a configured DbCommand object
  DbCommand comm = GenericDataAccess.CreateCommand();
  // set the stored procedure name
  comm.CommandText = "ShoppingCartRemoveItem";
  // create a new parameter
  DbParameter param = comm.CreateParameter();
  param.ParameterName = "@CartID";
  param.Value = shoppingCartId;
  param.DbType = DbType.String;
  param.Size = 36;
  comm.Parameters.Add(param);
  // create a new parameter
  param = comm.CreateParameter();
  param.ParameterName = "@ProductID";
  param.Value = productId;
  param.DbType = DbType.Int32;
  comm.Parameters.Add(param);
  // returns true in case of success or false in case of an error
  try
  {
```

```
      // execute the stored procedure and return true if it executes
      // successfully, or false otherwise
      return (GenericDataAccess.ExecuteNonQuery(comm) != -1);
    }
    catch
    {
      // prevent the exception from propagating, but return false to
      // signal the error
      return false;
    }
  }
}
```

GetItems

GetItems retrieves all the products in the customer's shopping cart. This is called from the
presentation tier when the visitor wants to view the cart:

```
// Retrieve shopping cart items
public static DataTable GetItems()
{
  // get a configured DbCommand object
  DbCommand comm = GenericDataAccess.CreateCommand();
  // set the stored procedure name
  comm.CommandText = "ShoppingCartGetItems";
  // create a new parameter
  DbParameter param = comm.CreateParameter();
  param.ParameterName = "@CartID";
  param.Value = shoppingCartId;
  param.DbType = DbType.String;
  param.Size = 36;
  comm.Parameters.Add(param);
  // return the result table
  DataTable table = GenericDataAccess.ExecuteSelectCommand(comm);
  return table;
}
```

GetTotalAmount

GetTotalAmount does exactly what its name suggests, and it's a bit more interesting than the
others because it uses SqlCommand's ExecuteScalar method, which we haven't used so far. Add
it to the ShoppingCart class, and we'll discuss the details:

```
// Retrieve shopping cart items
public static decimal GetTotalAmount()
{
  // get a configured DbCommand object
  DbCommand comm = GenericDataAccess.CreateCommand();
  // set the stored procedure name
  comm.CommandText = "ShoppingCartGetTotalAmount";
```

```
// create a new parameter
DbParameter param = comm.CreateParameter();
param.ParameterName = "@CartID";
param.Value = shoppingCartId;
param.DbType = DbType.String;
param.Size = 36;
comm.Parameters.Add(param);
// return the result table
return Decimal.Parse(GenericDataAccess.ExecuteScalar(comm));
}
```

Implementing the Presentation Tier

Okay, now that the foundation functionality is in place, you can add the presentation tier bits. Building the user interface for the shopping cart functionality involves the following major steps:

- Creating Add to Cart buttons (refer to Figure 9-2)

- Showing shopping cart summary information in catalog pages (refer to Figure 9-2)

- Creating the actual shopping cart page (refer to Figure 9-1)

- Allowing the visitor to update product quantities in the shopping cart

- Implementing "Continue Shopping" functionality

Let's deal with these tasks one by one.

Creating the Add to Cart Buttons

You can choose to have Add to Cart buttons only in the products details pages (`Product.aspx`), in the product listings (`ProductsList.ascx`), or in both. Follow the steps in the following exercise to add your buttons.

Exercise: Creating the Add to Cart Buttons

1. If you implemented the PayPal shopping cart in Chapter 7, you now need to remove the PayPal Add to Cart buttons from `Product.aspx`. Open the file in **HTML View** and remove the following code:

   ```
   <a runat="server" id="addToCartLink">
     <IMG src="Images/AddToCart.gif" border="0">
   </a>
   ```

   Then remove the associated code from the `PopulateControls` method in `Product.aspx.cs`:

   ```
   // Create the "Add to Cart" PayPal link
   string link =
       "JavaScript: OpenPayPalWindow(\"https://www.paypal.com/
   ```

```
cgi-bin/webscr" +
       "?cmd=_cart" + // open shopping cart command
       "&business=youremail@yourserver.com" + // your PayPal account
       "&item_name=" + pd.Name + // product name
       "&amount=" + String.Format("{0:0.00}", pd.Price) + // product price
       "&currency=USD" + // currency
       "&add=1" + // quantity to add to the shopping cart
       "&return=www.yourwebsite.com" + // return address
       "&cancel_return=www.yourwebsite.com\")"; // cancel return address)
   // Encode the link characters to be included in HTML file
   string encodedLink = Server.HtmlEncode(link);
   // Set the link of the HTML Server Control
   addToCartLink.HRef = encodedLink;
```

2. Add the following style to **BalloonShop.css**. You'll use it for your Add to Cart buttons.

```
.SmallButtonText
{
  color: Black;
  font-family: Verdana, Helvetica, sans-serif;
  font-size: 10px;
}
```

3. Add a button to the `ItemTemplate` of the `DataList` in **ProductsList.ascx**, just below the product price. You can see the HTML code in the following snippet, but keep in mind that you can use the Edit Template feature in Design View to generate at least part of the code. In any case, make sure you have this button in the `ItemTemplate`:

```
<span class="ProductDescription">
  <%# Eval("Description") %>
  <br/><br/>
  Price:
</span>
<span class="ProductPrice">
  <%# Eval("Price", "{0:c}") %>
</span>
<br />
<asp:Button ID="addToCartButton" runat="server" Text="Add to Cart"
CommandArgument='<%# Eval("ProductID") %>' CssClass="SmallButtonText"/>
</td>
```

■**Note** Clicking a button in a `DataList` fires the `DataList`'s `ItemCommand` event. In the event handler, you read the `CommandArgument` of the button, which contains the `ID` of the product that needs to be added to the shopping cart.

---

4. Switch `ProductsList.ascx` to **Design View**, select the `DataList` control, and use the **Properties window** to add the list's `ItemCommand` event handler. Complete the generated code with the following code:

```
// fires when an Add to Cart button is clicked
protected void list_ItemCommand(object source, DataListCommandEventArgs e)
{
    // The CommandArgument of the clicked Button contains the ProductID
    string productId = e.CommandArgument.ToString();
    // Add the product to the shopping cart
    ShoppingCartAccess.AddItem(productId);
}
```

5. Now add the same functionality to `Product.aspx`. Open **Product.aspx** and add the following button at the bottom of the page (note that this new button doesn't have the `CommandArgument` property set—this button isn't part of a `DataList`, so you don't need that kind of functionality this time).

```
<br />
<asp:Button ID="addToCartButton" runat="server" Text="Add to Cart"
CssClass="SmallButtonText" />
</asp:Content>
```

6. Switch to **Design View** and double-click the button to have its `Click` event handler generated by Visual Web Developer. Complete the method signature with the following code:

```
// Add the product to cart
protected void addToCartButton_Click(object sender, EventArgs e)
{
    // Retrieve ProductID from the query string
    string productId = Request.QueryString["ProductID"];
    // Add the product to the shopping cart
    ShoppingCartAccess.AddItem(productId);
}
```

How It Works: The Add to Cart Buttons

After making the changes, build the project (Ctrl+Shift+B) and then load the site to make sure the buttons appear okay. Now click the Add to Cart button on one of the products on the site. If you don't get any errors, the product was probably successfully added to the shopping cart; right now, you can't see this in the web site, because you still need to implement functionality for viewing the shopping cart.

The `ItemCommand` event is raised by the `DataList` when one of its buttons is clicked. The `CommandArgument` parameter of the Add to Cart buttons is populated with the product ID from the database. This `ID` is read from the `ItemCommand` event handler, which passes it to `ShoppingCart.AddProduct` to have it added to the database.

Showing the Shopping Cart Summary

The shopping cart summary is implemented as a Web User Control named `CartSummary.ascx`. You'll use this control in the `BalloonShop.master` Master Page, so it shows up in every page that implements it. However, you'll write a bit of code in your control to make sure it doesn't also appear in the shopping cart page, because you don't want to show both the cart and its summary on the same page.

Exercise: Showing the Shopping Cart Summary

1. Let's start with the simple details. Add the following styles to `BalloonShop.css`:

   ```
   .CartSummary
   {
     border-right: #0468a4 2px solid;
     border-top: #0468a4 2px solid;
     border-left: #0468a4 2px solid;
     border-bottom: #0468a4 2px solid;
     background-color: snow;
     font-family: Arial;
     font-size: 9pt;
     color: Navy;
     padding-top: 3px;
     padding-left: 2px;
     padding-bottom: 5px;
   }
   a.CartLink
   {
     color: Black;
     font-family: Arial;
     text-decoration: none;
     font-size: 12px;
   }
   a.CartLink:hover
   {
     color: Red;
   }
   ```

2. Add a new **Web User Control** to your `UserControls` folder, named `CartSummary.ascx`. Make sure the language is **Visual C#** and that the **Place code in separate file** check box is checked.

3. Add the following code to `CartSummary.ascx`:

   ```
   <table border="0" cellpadding="0" cellspacing="1" width="200">
     <tr>
       <td class="CartSummary">
         <b><asp:Label ID="cartSummaryLabel" runat="server" /></b>
         <asp:HyperLink ID="viewCartLink" runat="server"
   NavigateUrl="../ShoppingCart.aspx"
           CssClass="CartLink" Text="(view details)" />
         <asp:DataList ID="list" runat="server">
           <ItemTemplate>
             <%# Eval("Quantity") %> x <%# Eval("Name") %>
   ```

```
        </ItemTemplate>
      </asp:DataList>
      <img src="Images/line.gif" border="0" width="99%" height="1" />
      Total:
      <span class="ProductPrice">
        <asp:Label ID="totalAmountLabel" runat="server" />
      </span>
    </td>
  </tr>
</table>
```

4. Go to the control's code-behind file (ShoppingCart.ascx.cs) and add the **Page_Prerender** function, along with its **PopulateControls** helper function, like this:

```
// fill cart summary contents in the PreRender stage
protected void Page_PreRender(object sender, EventArgs e)
{
  PopulateControls();
}


// fill the controls with data
private void PopulateControls()
{
  // get the items in the shopping cart
  DataTable dt = ShoppingCartAccess.GetItems();
  // if the shopping cart is empty...
  if (dt.Rows.Count == 0)
  {
    cartSummaryLabel.Text = "Your shopping cart is empty.";
    totalAmountLabel.Text = String.Format("{0:c}", 0);
    viewCartLink.Visible = false;
    list.Visible = false;
  }
  else
  // if the shopping cart is not empty...
  {
    // populate the list with the shopping cart contents
    list.Visible = true;
    list.DataSource = dt;
    list.DataBind();
    // set up controls
    cartSummaryLabel.Text = "Cart summary ";
    viewCartLink.Visible = true;
    // display the total amount
    decimal amount = ShoppingCartAccess.GetTotalAmount();
    totalAmountLabel.Text = String.Format("{0:c}", amount);
  }
}
```

5. Because you'll include the shopping cart summary control in the Master Page, normally it will show up in every page of your web site. If you don't want your shopping cart summary to show up when the visitor is viewing the shopping cart page, add the following code to the `CartSummary` class in `CartSummary.ascx.cs`:

```
// we don't want to display the cart summary in the shopping cart page
protected void Page_Init(object sender, EventArgs e)
{
  // get the current page
  string page = Request.AppRelativeCurrentExecutionFilePath;
  // if we're in the shopping cart, don't display the cart summary
  if (String.Compare(page, "~/ShoppingCart.aspx", true) == 0)
    this.Visible = false;
  else
    this.Visible = true;
}
```

6. The tough part's over now. Build the project to ensure everything compiles okay.

7. Open `BalloonShop.master` in **Source View** and remove the code of the `OpenPayPalWindow` JavaScript function, which is no longer necessary:

```
<script language="JavaScript">
<!--
...
...
...
</script>
```

8. Also in `BalloonShop.master`, remove the code that generates the PayPal View Cart button:

```
<p align="center">
  <a href="JavaScript: OpenPayPalWindow('...')">
    <IMG src="Images/ViewCart.gif" border="0">
  </a>
</p>
```

9. Switch BallonShop.master to **Design View** and then drag `CartSummary.ascx` from the **Solution Explorer** to BalloonShop.master as shown in Figure 9-7.

10. Execute the project to ensure the shopping cart summary shows up as expected. Just don't expect the view details link to work, because you haven't implemented the `ShoppingCart.aspx` file yet.

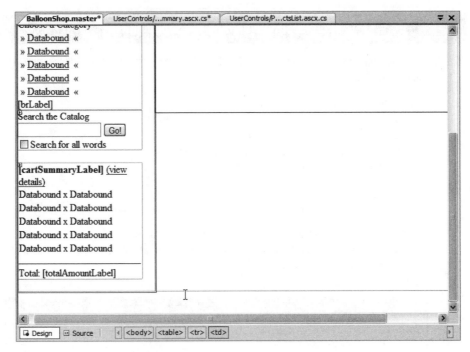

Figure 9-7. *Adding the shopping cart summary control to the Master Page*

How It Works: The Shopping Cart Summary

The important bit to understand here is the way we used the Page_PreRender method to populate the control with data.

We used Page_PreRender instead of the Load event, because Load fires *before* the Click event of the Add to Cart buttons, so the summary is updated before—not after—the cart is updated. PreRender, on the other hand, fires later in the control life cycle, so we used it to ensure that the cart summary is properly updated.

To learn more about the life cycle of ASP.NET controls, see an advanced ASP.NET book.

Displaying the Shopping Cart

Finally, you've arrived at the shopping cart, your primary goal for this chapter. The shopping cart is a Web Form named ShoppingCart.aspx, based on the BalloonShop.master Master Page.

Follow the steps in the next exercise to build your shopping cart page.

Exercise: Implementing the Shopping Cart

1. Before starting to work on the shopping cart, let's deal with a simple detail first. Add this style to your **BalloonShop.css** file.

```
.ShoppingCartTitle
{
  color: Red;
  font-family: Verdana, Helvetica, sans-serif;
  font-size: 16px;
}
```

2. Right-click the project name in **Solution Explorer** and click **Add New Item**.

3. Select the **Web Form** template, write **ShoppingCart.aspx** for its name, make sure the language is **Visual C#**, and select the two check boxes (**Place code in separate file** and **Select master page**), as shown in Figure 9-8. Click **Add**.

Figure 9-8. *Creating the ShoppingCart.aspx Web Form*

4. Choose the **BalloonShop.master** file in the dialog box that opens and click **OK**.

5. If you prefer to work in Design View, create a form as shown in Figure 9-9, and set the controls' properties as shown in Table 9-1.

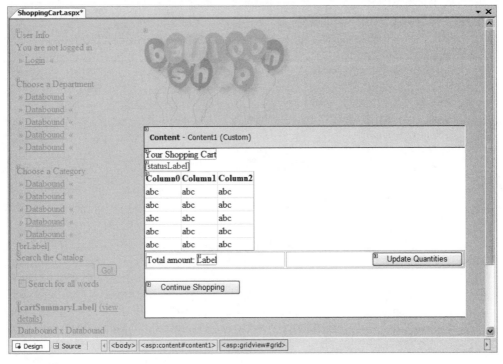

Figure 9-9. *ShoppingCart.aspx in Design View*

Table 9-1. *Control Properties in ShoppingCart.ascx*

Control Type	ID **Property**	**Text Property**	CssClass **Property**
Label	titleLabel	Your Shopping Cart	ShoppingCartTitle
Label	statusLabel	(empty)	AdminPageText
GridView	grid		
Label	totalAmountLabel		ProductPrice
Button	updateButton	Update Quantities	ButtonText
Button	continueShoppingButton	Continue Shopping	ButtonText

6. Feel free to play with the control's look to customize it according to your preferences. The source code of your page should look something like this:

```
<%@ Page Language="C#" MasterPageFile="~/BalloonShop.master"
AutoEventWireup="true" CodeFile="ShoppingCart.aspx.cs" Inherits="ShoppingCart"
 Title="Untitled Page" %>
<asp:Content ID="Content1" ContentPlaceHolderID="contentPlaceHolder"
```

```
      Runat="Server">
        <asp:Label ID="titleLabel" runat="server"
                Text="Your Shopping Cart" CssClass="ShoppingCartTitle" />
        <br />
        <asp:Label ID="statusLabel" CssClass="AdminPageText"
                ForeColor="Red" runat="server" />
        <br />
        <asp:GridView ID="grid" runat="server">
        </asp:GridView>
        <table width="100%">
          <tr>
            <td>
              <span class="ProductDescription">
                Total amount:
              </span>
              <asp:Label ID="totalAmountLabel" runat="server"
                    Text="Label" CssClass="ProductPrice" />
            </td>
            <td align="right">
              <asp:Button ID="updateButton" runat="server"
                      Text="Update Quantities" CssClass="SmallButtonText" />
            </td>
          </tr>
        </table>
        <br />
        <asp:Button ID="continueShoppingButton" runat="server"
                Text="Continue Shopping" CssClass="SmallButtonText" />
        <br /><br />
      </asp:Content>
```

7. Now it's time to deal with the GridView control. Set its AutoGenerateColumns property to **false**, DataKeyNames to **ProductID**, Width to **100%**, and BorderWidth to **0px**.

8. In **Design View**, select the **GridView**, click the **Smart Link**, and choose **Add New Column** to add the grid columns listed in Table 9-2.

Table 9-2. *Setting the Properties of the GridView Control*

Column Type	Header Text	Data Field	Other Properties
BoundField	Product Name	Name	Read Only
BoundField	Price	Price	Read Only
TemplateField	Quantity		
BoundField	Subtotal	Subtotal	Read Only
ButtonField			Command name: Delete Text: Delete Button type: Button

---

■**Note** The Product Name, Price, and Subtotal columns are marked as read-only. If you transform them to template fields, Visual Web Developer won't generate their `EditItemTemplate` but only their `ItemTemplate`. Also, they won't be editable if the `GridView` enters edit mode (we don't use this feature here, however, but you know the functionality from Chapter 8, the administration chapter).

---

9. Click `GridView`'s **Smart Link** and choose **Edit Columns**. From the **Selected Fields** list, select **Price** and set its `DataFormatString` property to **{0:c}**.

10. Do the same (set the `DataFormatString` to **{0:c}**) for the **Subtotal** field.

11. The Quantity field is a template field, so you need to fill its contents manually. Switch to **Source View** and add the following `TextBox` to the `ItemTemplate`:

```
<asp:TemplateField HeaderText="Quantity">
  <ItemTemplate>
    <asp:TextBox ID="editQuantity" runat="server" CssClass="GridEditingRow"
                 Width="24px" MaxLength="2" Text='<%#Eval("Quantity")%>' />
  </ItemTemplate>
</asp:TemplateField>
```

12. We want to use the `SmallButtonText` class for the **Delete** button. Switch to **Design View**, click the grid's **Smart Link**, and select **Edit Columns**. In the dialog box that opens, select the **Delete** field, expand its **ControlStyle** property, and set the **CssClass** to **SmallButtonText**, as shown in Figure 9-10.

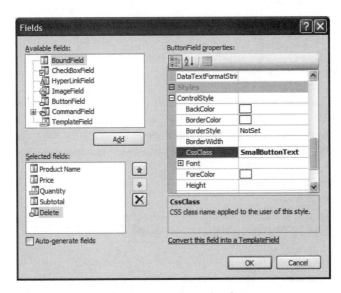

Figure 9-10. *Choosing a style for the Delete button*

13. Click **OK** to close the dialog box. Verify that the content area of your Web Form looks like Figure 9-11.

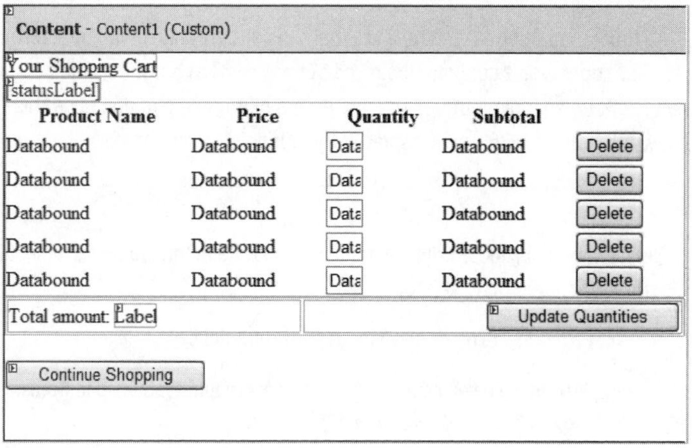

Figure 9-11. *The content area of ShoppingCart.aspx in Design View*

14. The visual part is ready. Open the code-behind file now (**ShoppingCart.aspx.cs**) and complete its Page_Load method to populate the controls, as shown in the following code listing:

```
public partial class ShoppingCart : System.Web.UI.Page
{
  protected void Page_Load(object sender, EventArgs e)
  {
    // populate the control only on the initial page load
    if (!IsPostBack)
      PopulateControls();
  }

  // fill shopping cart controls with data
  private void PopulateControls()
  {
    // set the title of the page
    this.Title = BalloonShopConfiguration.SiteName + " : Shopping Cart";
    // get the items in the shopping cart
    DataTable dt = ShoppingCartAccess.GetItems();
    // if the shopping cart is empty...
    if (dt.Rows.Count == 0)
    {
      titleLabel.Text = "Your shopping cart is empty!";
      grid.Visible = false;
      updateButton.Enabled = false;
      totalAmountLabel.Text = String.Format("{0:c}", 0);
    }
    else
    // if the shopping cart is not empty...
    {
```

```
            // populate the list with the shopping cart contents
            grid.DataSource = dt;
            grid.DataBind();
            // setup controls
            titleLabel.Text = "These are the products in your shopping cart:";
            grid.Visible = true;
            updateButton.Enabled = true;
            // display the total amount
            decimal amount = ShoppingCartAccess.GetTotalAmount();
            totalAmountLabel.Text = String.Format("{0:c}", amount);
        }
    }
}
```

How It Works: The ShoppingCart **User Control**

The steps in this exercise are probably familiar to you by now. You created a new Web Form and then added a number of controls to it, including a GridView control, to which you added and formatted columns afterwards.

Feel free to execute the project, add a few products to the cart, and then click the (view details) link in the cart summary. Your shopping cart should display your products nicely. It takes a couple of more exercises to make the Update Quantities and Continue Shopping buttons functional.

Editing Product Quantities

You learned how to work with editable GridView controls in Chapter 9. However, this time you won't use GridView's editing functionality, because you want to allow the visitor to update several product quantities at once, not only record by record. Of course, if you prefer, you can always implement the editing functionality just like you learned in Chapter 8, but in this chapter, you'll learn a new way of doing things.

Exercise: Editing Product Quantities

1. Open ShoppingCart.aspx in **Design View**, select the GridView, and use Visual Web Developer to generate the **RowDeleting** event handler.

2. Complete the code as shown in the following code listing:

```
// remove a product from the cart
protected void grid_RowDeleting(object sender, GridViewDeleteEventArgs e)
{
    // Index of the row being deleted
    int rowIndex = e.RowIndex;
    // The ID of the product being deleted
    string productId = grid.DataKeys[rowIndex].Value.ToString();
    // Remove the product from the shopping cart
    bool success = ShoppingCartAccess.RemoveItem(productId);
```

```
    // Display status
    statusLabel.Text = success ? "<br />Product successfully removed!<br />" :
                    "<br />There was an error removing the product!<br />";
    // Repopulate the control
    PopulateControls();
}
```

3. In `ShoppingCart.aspx`, double-click the **Update Quantities** button and complete the automatically generated code like this:

```
// update shopping cart product quantities
protected void updateButton_Click(object sender, EventArgs e)
{
    // Number of rows in the GridView
    int rowsCount = grid.Rows.Count;
    // Will store a row of the GridView
    GridViewRow gridRow;
    // Will reference a quantity TextBox in the GridView
    TextBox quantityTextBox;
    // Variables to store product ID and quantity
    string productId;
    int quantity;
    // Was the update successful?
    bool success = true;
    // Go through the rows of the GridView
    for (int i = 0; i < rowsCount; i++)
    {
        // Get a row
        gridRow = grid.Rows[i];
        // The ID of the product being deleted
        productId = grid.DataKeys[i].Value.ToString();
        // Get the quantity TextBox in the Row
        quantityTextBox = (TextBox)gridRow.FindControl("editQuantity");
        // Get the quantity, guarding against bogus values
        if (Int32.TryParse(quantityTextBox.Text, out quantity))
        {
            // Update product quantity
            success = success && ShoppingCartAccess.UpdateItem(productId, quantity);
        }
        else
        {
            // if TryParse didn't succeed
            success = false;
        }
```

```
      // Display status message
      statusLabel.Text = success ?
        "<br />Your shopping cart was successfully updated!<br />" :
        "<br />Some quantity updates failed! Please verify your cart!<br />";
    }
    // Repopulate the control
    PopulateControls();
  }
```

How It Works: Editing Product Quantities

Yep, this was interesting all right. Allowing the visitor to edit multiple GridView entries at once is certainly very useful. Take a close look at the code and make sure you understand how the GridView is parsed, how the proper TextBox controls is found, and how its value is read. Then, the ShoppingCartAccess class is simply used to update the product quantities.

When reading the values from the TextBox controls and converting them to integers, you use a new .NET 2.0 feature called **TryParse**. This static method of the Int32 class (you can find it in other similar classes, too) is similar to Parse, but doesn't throw an exception if the conversion cannot be done—which can easily happen if the visitor enters a letter instead of a number in the quantity box, for example.

TryParse returns a bool value representing the success of the operation and returns the converted value as an out parameter:

```
    // Get the quantity, guarding against bogus values
    if (Int32.TryParse(quantityTextBox.Text, out quantity))
```

The ShoppingCartAccess.UpdateItem method also returns a bool value specifying whether the update completed successfully or not. Should either this method or TryParse return false, you set the value of the success variable to false. If after processing all rows, the value of success is false, you inform the visitor that at least one of the rows couldn't be updated.

If ShoppingCartAccess.UpdateItem generates a database error for some reason, the error is logged using the log mechanism that you implemented in Chapter 4 —if you enabled the error-handling routine, that is—because it can be disabled by changing an option in web.config.

Adding "Continue Shopping" Functionality

Although you have the Continue Shopping button, at this point, it doesn't do much. The steps to make it work are presented in the next exercise.

Exercise: Implementing the Continue Shopping Button

1. Start editing ShoppingCart.ascx in **Design View** and double-click the **Continue Shopping** button. This automatically creates the continueShoppingButton_Click method. Modify it like this:

```
// Redirects to the previously visited catalog page
// (an alternate to the functionality implemented here is to
// Request.UrlReferrer, although that way you have no control over
// what pages you forward your visitor back to)
protected void continueShoppingButton_Click(object sender, EventArgs e)
{
  // redirect to the last visited catalog page, or to the
  // main page of the catalog
  object page;
  if ((page = Session["LastVisitedCatalogPage"]) != null)
    Response.Redirect(page.ToString());
  else
    Response.Redirect(Request.ApplicationPath);
}
```

2. Open **BalloonShop.master.cs** and modify it to save the current page location to the visitor's session:

```
public partial class BalloonShop : System.Web.UI.MasterPage
{
  // Website pages considered to be "catalog pages" that the visitor
  // can "Continue Shopping" to
  private static string[] catalogPages = { "~/Default.aspx", "~/Catalog.aspx",
"~/Search.aspx" };

  // Executes when any page based on this master page loads
  protected void Page_Load(object sender, EventArgs e)
  {
    // Don't perform any actions on postback events
    if (!IsPostBack)
    {
      /* Save the latest visited catalog page into the session
         to support "Continue Shopping" functionality */
      // Get the currently loaded page
      string currentLocation = Request.AppRelativeCurrentExecutionFilePath;
      // If the page is one we want the visitor to "continue shopping"
      // to, then save it to visitor's Session
      for (int i = 0; i < catalogPages.GetLength(0); i++)
        if (String.Compare(catalogPages[i], currentLocation, true) == 0)
        {
          // save the current location
          Session["LastVisitedCatalogPage"] = Request.Url.ToString();
          // stop the for loop from continuing
          break;
        }
    }
  }
}
```

3. Open `Product.aspx` and add a **Continue Shopping** button next to the existing **Add to Cart** button, with the following properties:

Property Name	Property Value
ID	continueShoppingButton
CssClass	SmallButtonText
Text	Continue Shopping

4. In **Design View**, double-click the button to have its `Click` event handler generated for you, and complete its code just as you did for the other Continue Shopping button:

```
// Redirects to the previously visited catalog page
protected void continueShoppingButton_Click(object sender, EventArgs e)
{
  // redirect to the last visited catalog page
  object page;
  if ((page = Session["LastVisitedCatalogPage"]) != null)
    Response.Redirect(page.ToString());
  else
    Response.Redirect(Request.ApplicationPath);
}
```

5. Execute the project and test your new Continue Shopping buttons!

How It Works: The Continue Shopping Button

Let's take a good look at the functionality you've added to the Master Page. Because the `BalloonShop.master` Master Page is used in all catalog pages, you can rely on it being called every time the visitor accesses a new catalog page. When this happens, if the accessed page is from a list of predefined page names, this location is saved to a session variable.

The list of predefined pages must contain the pages that the Continue Shopping button redirects the visitor to, and they *must not* be pages that contain Continue Shopping buttons. Otherwise, the Continue Shopping button would redirect the visitor to the page he or she is already visiting.

Note that instead of implementing this functionality, you can choose to use the value from `Request.UrlReferrer`, which contains the page the visitor was previously browsing. This technique is simpler to implement because it doesn't require you to add any code to the Master Page, but it doesn't offer much control over what page you are redirecting the visitor to. For example, if the visitor comes to BalloonShop from an external page, with the implemented solution, the Continue Shopping button will redirect her to the main BalloonShop page.

Administering the Shopping Cart

Now that you've finished writing the shopping cart, you need to take two more things into account, and both are related to administration issues:

- How to delete from the product catalog a product that exists in shopping carts.

- How to remove old shopping cart elements by building a simple shopping cart administration page. This is important, because without this feature, the ShoppingCart table keeps growing.

Deleting Products that Exist in Shopping Carts

The catalog administration pages offer the possibility to completely delete products from the catalog. Before removing a product from the Product table, however, you need to remove related records from the related tables first (otherwise, the foreign-key constraints in the database won't allow the action).

For example, look at the DeleteProduct stored procedure that first deletes all related records from ProductCategory before deleting the Product record:

```
DELETE FROM ProductCategory WHERE ProductID=@ProductID
DELETE FROM Product where ProductID=@ProductID
```

Now the problem reappears with the ShoppingCart table: The Product and ShoppingCart tables are tied through a FOREIGN KEY constraint on their ProductID fields. The database doesn't allow deleting products from Product that have related ShoppingCart records.

The solution is to update the DeleteProduct stored procedure to also remove all the references to the product from the ShoppingCart table before attempting to delete it from the database.

Update the DeleteProduct stored procedure by executing this command (you can use the same screen as the one where you create new procedures, or you can use SQL Express Manager):

```
ALTER PROCEDURE DeleteProduct
(@ProductID int, @CategoryID int)
AS
DELETE FROM ShoppingCart WHERE ProductID=@ProductID
DELETE FROM ProductCategory WHERE ProductID=@ProductID
DELETE FROM Product where ProductID=@ProductID
```

This way, the site administrators can (once again) remove products from the database.

Removing Old Shopping Carts

The second problem with the shopping cart is that at this moment no mechanism exists to delete the old records from the ShoppingCart table. On a high activity web site with many users and many shopping carts, the ShoppingCart table can grow very large.

With the default setting in web.config, shopping cart IDs are stored at the client browser for ten days. As a result, you can assume that any shopping carts that haven't been updated in the last ten days are invalid and can be safely removed.

In the following exercise, you'll quickly implement a simple shopping cart administration page, where the administrator can see how many old shopping cart entries exist and can delete them if necessary.

The most interesting aspect you need to understand is the logic behind the database stored procedure that calculates the records that need to be deleted. The goal is to delete all shopping carts that haven't been updated in a certain amount of time.

This isn't as simple as it sounds—at first sight, you might think all you have to do is delete all the records in ShoppingCart whose DateAdded value is older than a specified date. However, this strategy doesn't work with shopping carts that are modified over time (say, the visitor has been adding items to the cart each week in the past three months). If the last change to the shopping cart is recent, none of its elements should be deleted, even if some are very old. In other words, you should either remove all elements in a shopping cart or none of them. The age of a shopping cart is given by the age of its most recently modified or added product.

■**Tip** If you look at the ShoppingCartUpdateItem stored procedure, you'll notice it also updates the DateAdded field of a product each time the quantity changes.

For the shopping cart admin page, you'll build two stored procedures (ShoppingCart➥ RemoveOldCarts and ShoppingCartCountOldCarts), but they both work using the same logic to calculate the shopping cart elements that are old and should be removed. First, you should learn a little bit about the SQL logic that retrieves the old shopping cart elements.

Take a look at the following query, which returns how many days have passed since the day the last cart item was added or modified for each cart ID:

```
SELECT CartID,
       MIN(DATEDIFF(dd,DateAdded,GETDATE())) as DaysFromMostRecentRecord
FROM ShoppingCart
GROUP BY CartID
```

The DATEDIFF function returns the difference, in days (because of the dd parameter), between the date specified by DateAdded and the current date (specified by GETDATE). GROUP BY groups the results by CartID, and for each CartID, the MIN aggregate function calculates the most recent record.

To select all the elements from the carts that haven't been modified in the past ten days, you need a query like this:

```
SELECT CartID
FROM ShoppingCart
GROUP BY CartID
HAVING MIN(DATEDIFF(dd,DateAdded,GETDATE())) >= 10
```

You'll implement the shopping cart administration page in the next exercise. You'll implement everything, starting from the stored procedures and finishing with the presentation tier, in a single exercise.

Exercise: Implementing the Cart Admin Page

1. Add the **ShoppingCartRemoveOldCarts** stored procedure to the database. It receives as a parameter the maximum number of days for a shopping cart age. All shopping carts older than that are deleted.

```
CREATE PROCEDURE ShoppingCartDeleteOldCarts
(@Days smallint)
AS
DELETE FROM ShoppingCart
WHERE CartID IN
  (SELECT CartID
   FROM ShoppingCart
   GROUP BY CartID
   HAVING MIN(DATEDIFF(dd,DateAdded,GETDATE())) >= @Days)
```

2. Add **ShoppingCartCountOldCarts**, which returns the number of shopping cart elements that would be deleted by a ShoppingCartCountOldCarts call:

```
CREATE PROCEDURE ShoppingCartCountOldCarts
(@Days smallint)
AS
SELECT COUNT(CartID)
FROM ShoppingCart
WHERE CartID IN
  (SELECT CartID
   FROM ShoppingCart
   GROUP BY CartID
   HAVING MIN(DATEDIFF(dd,DateAdded,GETDATE())) >= @Days)
```

3. Add these methods to the **ShoppingCartAccess** class (located in ShoppingCartAccess.cs). They are used to interact with the two stored procedures you wrote earlier.

```
// Counts old shopping carts
public static int CountOldCarts(byte days)
{
  // get a configured DbCommand object
  DbCommand comm = GenericDataAccess.CreateCommand();
  // set the stored procedure name
  comm.CommandText = "ShoppingCartCountOldCarts";
  // create a new parameter
  DbParameter param = comm.CreateParameter();
  param.ParameterName = "@Days";
  param.Value = days;
  param.DbType = DbType.Byte;
  comm.Parameters.Add(param);
```

```
  // execute the procedure and return number of old shopping carts
  try
  {
    return Byte.Parse(GenericDataAccess.ExecuteScalar(comm));
  }
  catch
  {
    return -1;
  }
}

// Deletes old shopping carts
public static bool DeleteOldCarts(byte days)
{
  // get a configured DbCommand object
  DbCommand comm = GenericDataAccess.CreateCommand();
  // set the stored procedure name
  comm.CommandText = "ShoppingCartDeleteOldCarts";
  // create a new parameter
  DbParameter param = comm.CreateParameter();
  param.ParameterName = "@Days";
  param.Value = days;
  param.DbType = DbType.Byte;
  comm.Parameters.Add(param);
  // execute the procedure and return true if no problem occurs
  try
  {
    GenericDataAccess.ExecuteNonQuery(comm);
    return true;
  }
  catch
  {
    return false;
  }
}
```

4. Create a new Web Form at the root of the **BalloonShop** project, named **ShoppingCartAdmin.aspx**, based on the **Admin.master** Master Page.

5. While in **Source View**, add this code to the first place holder:

```
<asp:Content ID="Content1" ContentPlaceHolderID="ContentPlaceHolder1"
Runat="Server">
  <span class="AdminTitle">Shopping Cart Admin</span>
</asp:Content>
```

6. Add the following content to the second place holder:

```
<asp:Content ID="Content2" ContentPlaceHolderID="ContentPlaceHolder2"
runat="Server">
  <asp:Label ID="countLabel" runat="server" CssClass="AdminPageText">
      Hello!
  </asp:Label><br />
  <span class="AdminPageText">How many days?</span>
  <asp:DropDownList ID="daysList" runat="server">
    <asp:ListItem Value="0">All shopping carts</asp:ListItem>
    <asp:ListItem Value="1">One</asp:ListItem>
    <asp:ListItem Value="10" Selected="True">Ten</asp:ListItem>
    <asp:ListItem Value="20">Twenty</asp:ListItem>
    <asp:ListItem Value="30">Thirty</asp:ListItem>
    <asp:ListItem Value="90">Ninety</asp:ListItem>
  </asp:DropDownList><br />
  <br />
  <asp:Button ID="countButton" runat="server" Text="Count Old Shopping Carts"
CssClass="Button" />
  <asp:Button ID="deleteButton" runat="server" Text="Delete Old Shopping
Carts" CssClass="Button" />
</asp:Content>
```

Now if you switch to Design View, you should see a form like the one shown in Figure 9-12.

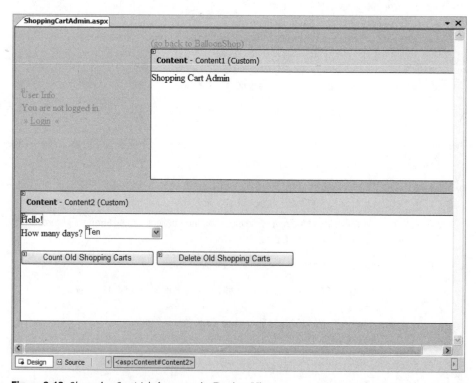

Figure 9-12. *ShoppingCartAdmin.aspx in Design View*

7. Double-click the **Delete Old Shopping Carts** button, and complete its `Click` event handler with the following code:

```
// deletes old shopping carts
protected void deleteButton_Click(object sender, EventArgs e)
{
  byte days = byte.Parse(daysList.SelectedItem.Value);
  ShoppingCartAccess.DeleteOldCarts(days);
  countLabel.Text = "The old shopping carts were removed from the database";
}
```

8. Double-click the **Count Old Shopping Carts** button and complete its `Click` event handler with the following code:

```
// counts old shopping carts
protected void countButton_Click(object sender, EventArgs e)
{
  byte days = byte.Parse(daysList.SelectedItem.Value);
  int oldItems = ShoppingCartAccess.CountOldCarts(days);
  if (oldItems == -1)
      countLabel.Text = "Could not count the old shopping carts!";
  else if (oldItems == 0)
      countLabel.Text = "There are no old shopping carts.";
  else
      countLabel.Text = "There are " + oldItems.ToString() +
                        " old shopping carts.";
}
```

9. Add this code to **Page_Load**:

```
protected void Page_Load(object sender, EventArgs e)
{
  // Set the title of the page
  this.Title = BalloonShopConfiguration.SiteName +
               " : Shopping Cart Admin";
}
```

10. To restrict this page to administrator-only access, open **web.config** and add the following block, after the one that deals with `CatalogAdmin.aspx`:

```
<!-- Only administrators are allowed to access ShoppingCartAdmin.aspx -->
<location path="ShoppingCartAdmin.aspx">
  <system.web>
    <authorization>
      <allow roles="Administrators" />
      <deny users="*" />
    </authorization>
  </system.web>
</location>
```

11. Finally, add a link to this new page. Open `UserInfo.ascx` in **Source View** and add a link to the shopping cart admin page for the **Administrators** role group, just after the link to the catalog admin page:

```
<tr>
  <td>
     &raquo;
      <a class="UserInfoLink" href="CatalogAdmin.aspx">Catalog Admin</a>
     &laquo;
  </td>
</tr>
<tr>
  <td>
     &raquo;
      <a class="UserInfoLink" href="ShoppingCartAdmin.aspx">Shopping Cart
Admin</a>
     &laquo;
  </td>
</tr>
</ContentTemplate>
```

How It Works: The Shopping Cart Admin Page

Congratulations, you're done! Your new shopping cart admin page should work as expected.

Summary

In this chapter, you learned how to store the shopping cart information in the database, and you learned a few things in the process as well. Probably the most interesting was the way you can store the shopping cart ID as a cookie on the client, because you haven't done anything similar so far in this book.

When writing the code for the user interface, you learned how to allow the visitor to update multiple GridView records with a single click, and you also implemented a clever strategy for the Continue Shopping functionality.

At the end, you updated the administrative part of the web site to deal with the new challenges implied by your custom-created shopping cart.

You'll complete the functionality offered by the custom shopping cart in the next chapter with a custom checkout system. You'll add a Place Order button to the shopping cart, which allows you to save the shopping cart information as a separate order in the database.

See you in the next chapter!

CHAPTER 10

Dealing with Customer Orders

The good news is that your brand-new shopping cart looks good and is fully functional. The bad news is that it doesn't allow the visitor to actually place an order, making it totally useless in the context of a production system.

You'll deal with that problem in this chapter, in two separate stages. In the first part of the chapter, you'll implement the client-side part of the order-placing mechanism. More precisely, you'll add a Proceed to Checkout button onto the shopping cart control, which will allow the visitor to order the products in the shopping cart.

In the second part of the chapter, you'll implement a simple orders administration page where the site administrator can view and handle pending orders.

The code for each part of the site is presented in the usual way, starting with the database tier, continuing with the business tier, and finishing with the user interface.

Implementing an Order-Placing System

The entire order-placing system is related to the Proceed to Checkout button mentioned earlier. Figure 10-1 shows how this button will look after you update the `ShoppingCart.aspx` control in this chapter.

Looking at the figure, the button looks boring for something that is the center of this chapter's universe. Still, a lot of logic is hidden behind it, so let's consider what you want to happen when the customer clicks that button. Remember that at this stage, it doesn't matter who places the order, but it's important to store information in the database about the products that were ordered.

Basically, two things need to happen when the customer clicks the Proceed to Checkout button:

- First, the order must be stored somewhere in the database. You'll save the shopping cart's products to an order named BalloonShop Order *nnn* and then clear the shopping cart.

- Secondly, the customer must be redirected to a PayPal payment page where the customer pays the necessary amount for the order.

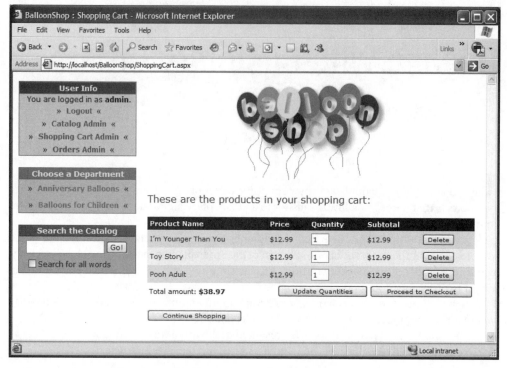

Figure 10-1. *The shopping cart with a Proceed to Checkout button*

■Note In this development stage, you still don't do the credit card transactions yourself, but use a third-party payment processor instead. You no longer need the PayPal shopping cart because you implemented your own in the previous chapter. Instead, as you'll see, you'll use the Single Item Purchases option of PayPal, which redirects the visitor directly to a payment page.

A problem that arises when using a third-party payment processor is that the customer can change her mind and cancel the order while at the checkout page. This can result in orders that are saved to the database (the order is saved *before* the page is redirected to the payment page), but for which payment wasn't completed. This makes it obvious that a payment-confirmation system is necessary, along with a database structure able to store status information about each order.

The confirmation system that you'll implement is simple. Every payment processor, including PayPal, can be instructed to send a confirmation message after a payment has been processed. The site administrator can manually check, in the administration page, which orders have been paid for. The orders for which the payment has been confirmed are known as *verified orders.* You'll see later in this chapter how to manage them in the orders management part of the site.

■**Note** PayPal and its competitors offer automated systems that notify your web site when a payment has been completed or canceled. However, in this book, we don't aim at visiting the intimate details of any of these payment systems—you'll need to do your homework and study the documentation of the company you choose. The PayPal Instant Payment Notification manual can be downloaded at `https://www.paypal.com/en_US/pdf/PP_WebsitePaymentsStandard_IntegrationGuide.pdf`.

Now that you have an idea of what the Proceed to Checkout button will do, the next major concerns are *what* product order information to store in the database and *how* to store it. As you saw in the previous chapters, deciding how to store information gives you have a better idea of how the whole system works.

Storing Orders in the Database

Two kinds of order information need to be stored in the database when a customer places an order:

- The general information about the order, including the date the order was created, the status of the order, and a few other details.

- The products that belong to that order and their quantities.

You'll need to add two tables in the database to store this information.

Creating the New Data Tables

Due to the nature of the information you need to store, two data tables are necessary: `Orders` and `OrderDetail`. The `Orders` table stores information regarding the order as a whole, while `OrderDetail` contains the products that belong to each order.

■**Tip** So far, we've consistently named our tables in singular form (`ShoppingCart`, `Department`, and so on). However, here we make an exception for the `Orders` table. Because `ORDER` is an SQL keyword, we can't use it as a name unless written with square brackets, like this: `[Order]`. For the purposes of this book, we prefer to break the naming convention to avoid any confusion while writing the SQL code.

These tables have a One-to-Many relationship, enforced through a `FOREIGN KEY` constraint on their `OrderID` fields. One-to-Many is the usual relationship implemented between an `Orders` table and an `OrderDetail` table. The `OrderDetail` table contains *many* records that belong to *one* order. You might want to revisit Chapter 4, where the table relationships are explained in more detail.

You'll create these tables in the following exercise. This time we don't explain each step in great detail, as you've been through these processes before in this book. Feel free to refer to previous chapters if anything is unclear.

Exercise: Adding the `Orders` and the `OrderDetail` Tables to the Database

1. First add the `Orders` table to the database with the columns described in Table 10-1.

Table 10-1. *The Orders Table*

Column Name	Data Type	Allow Nulls	Other Properties
OrderID	int	No	Primary Key, Identity
DateCreated	smalldatetime	No	Default: GETDATE()
DateShipped	smalldatetime	Yes	
Verified	bit	No	Default Value or Binding: 0
Completed	bit	No	Default Value or Binding: 0
Canceled	bit	No	Default Value or Binding: 0
Comments	varchar(1000)	Yes	
CustomerName	varchar(50)	Yes	
CustomerEmail	varchar(50)	Yes	
ShippingAddress	varchar(500)	Yes	

■**Caution** Don't forget to set the default of GETDATE() to the DateCreated column. Don't forget to set OrderID as a primary key and an identity column. Leave Identity Seed and Identity Increment at their default values of 1. Remember that making a column an identity column tells the database to automatically generate values for it when new records are added to the table—you can't supply your own values for that field when adding new records. The generated ID value can be found by reading the @@Identity system variable. You'll use this when creating the CreateOrder stored procedure a bit later.

2. Add the `OrderDetail` table (see Table 10-2):

Table 10-2. *The OrderDetail Table*

Column Name	Data Type	Allow Nulls	Other Properties
OrderID	int	No	Primary Key
ProductID	int	No	Primary Key
ProductName	varchar(50)	No	
Quantity	int	No	

Table 10-2. *The* `OrderDetail` *Table (Continued)*

Column Name	Data Type	Allow Nulls	Other Properties
UnitCost	money	No	
Subtotal		No	Computed Column Specification Formula: Quantity * UnitCost Is Persisted: No

■**Caution** Don't forget to set the composite primary key formed of `OrderID` and `ProductID`.

3. Enforce the One-to-Many relationship between `Orders` and `OrderDetail` by adding a `FOREIGN KEY` constraint on the `OrderID` column in `OrderDetail` to reference the `OrderID` column in `Orders`. Do this by either using database diagrams or by opening the table in **Database Explorer** and clicking **Table Designer ➤ Relationships** (as you learned in Chapter 4).

■**Note** Although `ProductID` is part of the primary key in `OrderDetail`, you don't place a `FOREIGN KEY` constraint on it (referencing the `Product` table), because products can change in time or can even be removed, while the existing orders should remain unchanged. `ProductID` is simply used to form the primary key of `OrderDetail` because at any given time, each product has a unique `ProductID`. However, the `ProductID` in `OrderDetail` is not required to point to an existing, real product.

How It Works: The Data Tables

Now that you have created the tables, take a closer look at the way they are designed.

The Orders Table

The `Orders` table basically contains two categories of information: data about the order (the first seven fields), and data about the customer that made the order (last three fields).

The professional way to store customer data is to use a separate table, named `Customer`, and reference that table from the `Orders` table. We chose not to take the professional approach in this chapter because at this stage of development, storing customer data is optional and is not one of our goals. Right now, we don't need to know who bought our products, because the third-party payment processor deals with these details. You'll create the `Customer` table in Chapter 12, where you add customer accounts functionality to BalloonShop.

Third-party payment processors, such as PayPal, store and manage the complete customer information, so it doesn't need to be stored in your database as well. The `CustomerName`, `ShippingAddress`, and `CustomerEmail` fields have been added as optional fields that can be filled by the administrator if it's easier to have this information at hand for certain (or all) orders. These are convenience fields that will be removed in Chapter 13 when you implement a serious scheme for storing customer details.

Now take a look at the other fields. OrderID is the primary key of the table, and is an identity column so you won't need to bother to find new IDs when adding new orders. DateCreated also has a pretty obvious role—you need to know the date when each order was created. This column has a default value of GETDATE(), which means that it will be automatically filled with the current date when adding new records if a specific value is not specified. DateShipped is populated with the date an order has been shipped.

Three bit fields show the status of the order: Verified, Completed, and Canceled. These fields store 0 for No and 1 for Yes. If your business grows, you'll need to extend this system to a professional order pipeline, which you'll learn how to do in Chapter 13. For now, these three bit fields will do the job.

The Verified field is set to 1 after the payment has been confirmed by the payment processor. The site administrator marks the order as verified upon receipt of the payment confirmation mail. After the payment is confirmed, the products are shipped, so the DateShipped field is populated and the Completed bit is also set to 1.

The administrator might want to mark an order as canceled (by setting the Canceled bit to 1) if it hasn't been verified in a certain amount of time or for other various reasons. The Comments field is used to record whatever special information might show up about the order.

The OrderDetail Table

Let's see now what information the OrderDetail table contains. Figure 10-2 shows what some typical OrderDetail records look like.

OrderID	Produc...	ProductName	Quantity	UnitCost	Subtotal
2	39	Toy Story	1	12.9900	12.9900
2	43	Mickey Close-up	1	12.9900	12.9900
3	21	Baby Hi Little Angel	1	12.9900	12.9900
3	25	Tweety Stars	1	12.9900	12.9900
3	39	Toy Story	1	12.9900	12.9900
3	40	Rugrats Tommy & Chucky	1	12.9900	12.9900
3	41	Rugrats & Reptar Character	1	12.9900	12.9900
3	42	Tweety & Sylvester	1	12.9900	12.9900
NULL	NULL	NULL	NULL	NULL	NULL

Figure 10-2. *Sample data in* OrderDetail

Each record in OrderDetail represents an ordered product that belongs to the order specified by OrderID. The primary key is formed by both OrderID and ProductID because a particular product can be ordered only once in one order. A Quantity field contains the number of ordered items, so it wouldn't make any sense to have one ProductID recorded more than once for one order.

You might be wondering why apart from the product ID, you also store the price and product name in the OrderDetail table. The question is valid because if you have the product ID, you can get all the product's details from the Product table without having any duplicated information.

The reason is this: The actual order detail data is stored in the ProductName, Quantity, and UnitCost fields. You can't rely on ProductID to store order data, because product IDs, names, and prices can change in time. ProductID is simply used to form the primary key (in this role, it saves you from needing to create another primary key field) and is also useful because it's the only programmatic way to link back to the original product (if the product still exists).

The last and most interesting column in OrderDetail is Subtotal, which represents the quantity multiplied by the unit price. Because it isn't persisted, this column doesn't occupy any disk space, and most importantly, it is always in sync with the other fields.

Creating Orders in the Database

Here you'll write the CreateOrder stored procedure, which takes the products from a shopping cart and creates an order with them. This procedure gets called when the customer decides that he wants to buy the products in the shopping cart and clicks the Proceed to Checkout button.

Creating a new order implies adding a new record to the Orders table and a number of records (one record for each product) to the OrderDetail table.

Add the CreateOrder stored procedure to the BalloonShop database, and then we'll talk a bit more about it:

```
CREATE PROCEDURE CreateOrder
(@CartID char(36))
AS
/* Insert a new record into Orders */
DECLARE @OrderID int
INSERT INTO Orders DEFAULT VALUES
/* Save the new Order ID */
SET @OrderID = @@IDENTITY
/* Add the order details to OrderDetail */
INSERT INTO OrderDetail
     (OrderID, ProductID, ProductName, Quantity, UnitCost)
SELECT
     @OrderID, Product.ProductID, Product.Name,
     ShoppingCart.Quantity, Product.Price
FROM Product JOIN ShoppingCart
ON Product.ProductID = ShoppingCart.ProductID
WHERE ShoppingCart.CartID = @CartID
/* Clear the shopping cart */
DELETE FROM ShoppingCart
WHERE CartID = @CartID
/* Return the Order ID */
SELECT @OrderID
```

The procedure starts by creating the new record in the Orders table. As you can see, when adding a new record, you don't specify any column values, as some of them allow NULLs, while the others have default values specified.

After adding the new record, you need to read the @@Identity system variable (which represents the order ID that was just generated) to a local variable named @OrderID:

```
/* Insert a new record into Orders*/
DECLARE @OrderID int
INSERT INTO Orders DEFAULT VALUES
/* Obtain the new Order ID */
SET @OrderID = @@IDENTITY
```

This is the standard mechanism of extracting the newly generated ID. You must save the value of @@IDENTITY immediately after the INSERT statement, because its value is lost afterward.

Using the @OrderID variable, you add the OrderDetail records by gathering information from the Product and ShoppingCart tables. From ShoppingCart, you need the list of the products and their quantities, and from Product, you get their names and prices.

After creating the order, the visitor's shopping cart is emptied. The last step for the CreateOrder stored procedure is to return the OrderID to the calling function. This is required when providing the order number to the customer.

Updating the Business Layer

Luckily, at this stage, you only need a single method named CreateOrder. Add this method to your ShoppingCartAccess class:

```
// Create a new order from the shopping cart
public static string CreateOrder()
{
  // get a configured DbCommand object
  DbCommand comm = GenericDataAccess.CreateCommand();
  // set the stored procedure name
  comm.CommandText = "CreateOrder";
  // create a new parameter
  DbParameter param = comm.CreateParameter();
  param.ParameterName = "@CartID";
  param.Value = shoppingCartId;
  param.DbType = DbType.String;
  param.Size = 36;
  comm.Parameters.Add(param);
  // return the result table
  return GenericDataAccess.ExecuteScalar(comm);
}
```

The method calls the CreateOrder stored procedure in the usual way. It returns the OrderID of the newly created order. ExecuteScalar is the DbCommand method used to execute stored procedures that return a single value.

Note that we don't catch the error here. If an exception occurs while trying to create the order, we prefer to let it propagate and have the *Oooops* message displayed to the visitor (and logged as such), because we consider this to be a critical error.

Adding the Checkout Button

This button is the only addition on the visitor side for the custom checkout. You'll place the button in the ShoppingCart Web Form and then implement the functionality by handling its Click event.

Let's do all this in the following exercise.

Exercise: Adding Proceed to Checkout Functionality

1. Open **ShoppingCart.aspx** and add the following button next to the Update Quantities button:

   ```
   <asp:Button ID="checkoutButton" runat="server" CssClass="SmallButtonText"
   Text="Proceed to Checkout" />
   ```

   In Design View, the content area of the form should look like Figure 10-3 now.

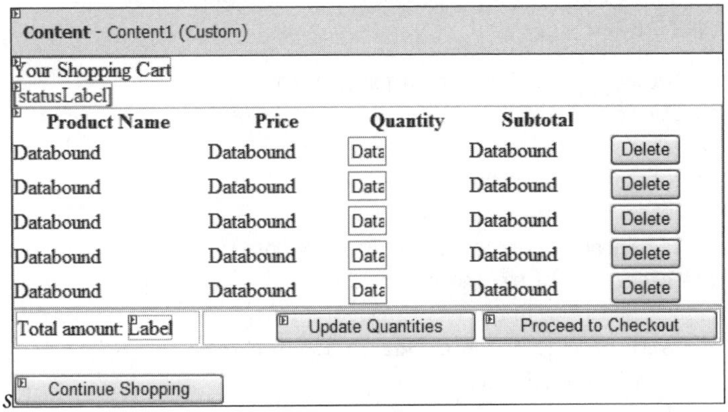

Figure 10-3. *ShoppingCart.ascx in Design View*

2. Cool, now you have a checkout button in the shopping cart. This button should be enabled only when the shopping cart is not empty. Take care of this issue by modifying **PopulateControls()** in **ShoppingCart.aspx.cs**:

   ```
   ...
     // if the shopping cart is empty...
     if (dt.Rows.Count == 0)
     {
       titleLabel.Text = "Your shopping cart is empty!";
       grid.Visible = false;
       updateButton.Enabled = false;
       checkoutButton.Enabled = false;
       totalAmountLabel.Text = String.Format("{0:c}", 0);
     }
   ```

```
    else
    // if the shopping cart is not empty...
    {
      // populate the list with the shopping cart contents
      grid.DataSource = dt;
      grid.DataBind();
      // setup controls
      titleLabel.Text = "These are the products in your shopping cart:";
      grid.Visible = true;
      updateButton.Enabled = true;
      checkoutButton.Enabled = true;
      // display the total amount
...
```

3. Now it's time to implement the checkout button's functionality. Because this functionality depends on the company that processes your payments, you might need to suit it for the payment-processing company you're working with. If you use PayPal, double-click the **checkout button** and complete its `Click` event handler like this:

```
// create a new order and redirect to a payment page
protected void checkoutButton_Click(object sender, EventArgs e)
{
  // Store the total amount because the cart
  // is emptied when creating the order
  decimal amount = ShoppingCartAccess.GetTotalAmount();
  // Create the order and store the order ID
  string orderId = ShoppingCartAccess.CreateOrder();
  // Obtain the site name from the configuration settings
  string siteName = BalloonShopConfiguration.SiteName;
  // Create the PayPal redirect location
  string redirect = "";
  redirect += "https://www.paypal.com/xclick/business=youremail@server.com";
  redirect += "&item_name=" + siteName + " Order " + orderId;
  redirect += "&item_number=" + orderId;
  redirect += "&amount=" + String.Format("{0:0.00} ", amount);
  redirect += "&currency=USD";
  redirect += "&return=http://www." + siteName + ".com";
  redirect += "&cancel_return=http://www." + siteName + ".com";
  // Redirect to the payment page
  Response.Redirect(redirect);
}
```

How It Works: Placing a New Order

First of all, if you use a company other than PayPal to process your payments, you'll need to modify the code in `checkoutButton_Click` accordingly.

When the visitor clicks the Proceed to Checkout button, three important actions happen. First, the shopping cart's total amount is saved to a temporary variable. Second, the order is created in the database by calling

ShoppingCart.CreateOrder. At this point the shopping cart is emptied, which is the reason you needed to save the total amount first.

Third, the link to the PayPal payment page is created. Note that you may want to replace the business, return, and cancel addresses with your site's specific details, the most important being the email address of your PayPal account. Optionally, you could also call the Utilities.SendMail method to email the administrator when an order is made, or you can rely on the messages that PayPal sends when a payment is processed.

For more details about the PayPal shopping cart and its options, please review its official manual at https:// www.paypal.com/en_US/pdf/PP_WebsitePaymentsStandard_IntegrationGuide.pdf.

Administering Orders

So your visitor just made an order. Now what? Well, after giving visitors the option to pay for your products, you need to make sure they actually get what they paid for.

The BalloonShop orders administration page that you'll write in what's left of this chapter allows the site administrator to review and manage pending orders. This chapter doesn't intend to create a perfect order-administration system, but rather something that is simple and functional enough to get you on the right track. You'll update the orders administration page in Chapter 13, after you implement the professional order pipeline and process credit card transactions on your own.

The orders administration part of the site will consist of a Web Form named OrdersAdmin.aspx and one Web User Control named OrderDetailsAdmin.ascx. When first loaded, the admin page will offer you various ways to select orders, as shown in Figure 10-4.

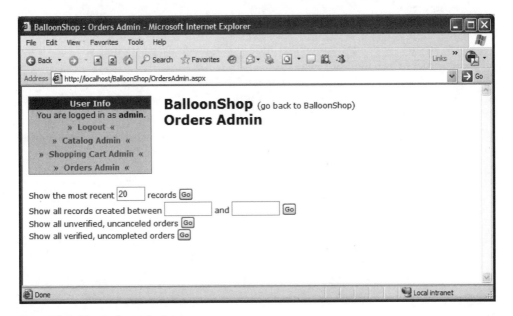

Figure 10-4. *The Orders Admin page*

After clicking one of the Go buttons, the matching orders show up in a data grid, as shown in Figure 10-5.

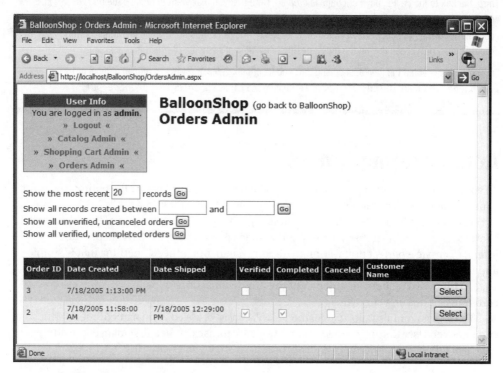

Figure 10-5. *The Orders Admin page showing a list of orders*

When you click the Select button for an order, you're sent to a page where you can view and update order information (see Figure 10-6).

A Web Form named `OrdersAdmin.aspx` handles the functionality shown in Figure 10-4 and Figure 10-5. When selecting an order, its details are displayed by a separate control you'll write later in this chapter, named `OrderDetailsAdmin.ascx`.

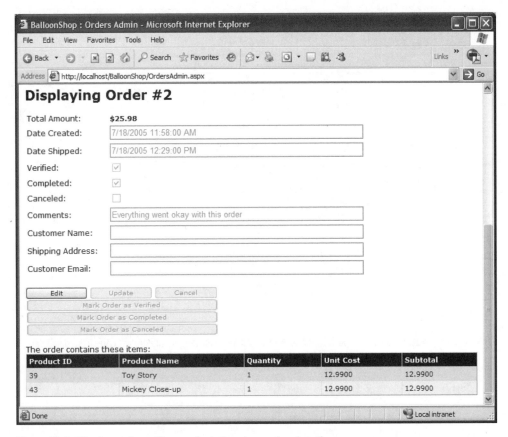

Figure 10-6. *The form that allows administering order details*

Creating the OrdersAdmin Web Form

OrdersAdmin.aspx allows the administrator to view pending and past orders according to various criteria, such as date or status. Follow the steps in the exercise to create this form.

Exercise: Creating OrdersAdmin.aspx and Integrating It into BalloonShop

1. Create a new Web Form at the root of the BalloonShop project, named OrdersAdmin.aspx, based on the Admin.master master page.

2. While in **Source View**, change the code of the first place holder like this:

```
<asp:Content ID="Content1" ContentPlaceHolderID="ContentPlaceHolder1"
Runat="Server">
  <span class="AdminTitle">Orders Admin</span>
</asp:Content>
```

3. Open the code-behind file and add this code in the **Page_Load** method;

```
protected void Page_Load(object sender, EventArgs e)
{
  // Set the title of the page
  this.Title = BalloonShopConfiguration.SiteName +
               " : Orders Admin";
}
```

4. Extend the security mechanism for the page you created. Modify **web.config** by adding the following lines just after the ones for CatalogAdmin.aspx and ShoppingCartAdmin.aspx:

```
<!-- Only administrators are allowed to access OrdersAdmin.aspx -->
<location path="OrdersAdmin.aspx">
  <system.web>
    <authorization>
      <allow roles="Administrators" />
      <deny users="*" />
    </authorization>
  </system.web>
</location>
```

5. Open UserInfo.ascx in **Source View** and add a link to the orders administration page to be displayed when an administrator logs in:

```
...
  <tr>
    <td>
       &raquo;
        <a class="UserInfoLink" href="ShoppingCartAdmin.aspx">
Shopping Cart Admin</a>
       &laquo;
    </td>
  </tr>
  <tr>
    <td>
       &raquo;
        <a class="UserInfoLink" href="OrdersAdmin.aspx">Orders Admin</a>
       &laquo;
    </td>
  </tr>
</ContentTemplate>
...
```

6. Build the web site, execute the project, login as **admin**, and go to your orders administration page that should look like Figure 10-7.

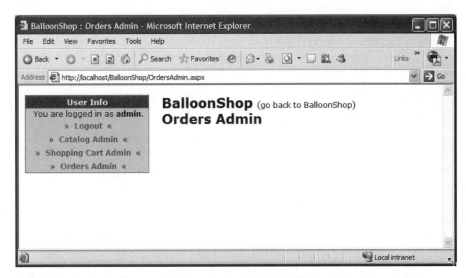

Figure 10-7. *The form that will allow administering orders*

Displaying Existing Orders

The orders administration page has two main functions:

- Allows administrators to view and filter pending and past orders

- Allows administrators to select one of the orders and to get the order details administration page, where they can see more details about the selected order

We'll deal with these requirements one at a time. For the first part, the administrator is allowed to select the orders by the following criteria:

- Show the most recent orders.

- Show orders that took place in a certain period of time.

- Show pending orders that have not been canceled. This shows the recent orders that have been placed and for which payment confirmation from PayPal is still pending. The administrator needs to mark these orders as Verified when the financial transaction is confirmed. Otherwise, if the payment is not confirmed in a reasonable amount of time, the administrator probably will want to cancel the order (marking it as Canceled), in which case the order will not appear in this list on future requests.

- Show orders that need to be shipped (they are Verified but not yet Completed). These are the orders that have been paid for, but for which the products haven't yet shipped. After the products are shipped, the administrator will mark the order as Completed.

Okay, now that you know what you need, you can start writing some code in the data tier.

The Database Stored Procedures

The stored procedures that you need to write to support the new functionality are

- OrdersGetByRecent

- OrdersGetByDate

- OrdersGetUnverifiedUncanceled

- OrdersGetVerifiedUncompleted

Add these stored procedures to the BalloonShop database, as shown in the following sections.

OrdersGetByRecent

In the OrdersGetByRecent stored procedure, the SET ROWCOUNT statement is used to limit the number of rows returned by the SELECT statement. The parameter, @Count, specifies the number of records. The SELECT command simply returns the necessary rows, in descending order of the date they were created.

```
CREATE PROCEDURE OrdersGetByRecent
(@Count smallint)
AS
-- Set the number of rows to be returned
SET ROWCOUNT @Count
-- Get list of orders
SELECT OrderID, DateCreated, DateShipped,
       Verified, Completed, Canceled, CustomerName
FROM Orders
ORDER BY DateCreated DESC
-- Reset rowcount value
SET ROWCOUNT 0
```

At the end, you set ROWCOUNT to 0, which tells SQL Server to stop limiting the number of returned rows.

ORDER BY is used to sort the returned results from the SELECT statement. The default sorting mode is ascending, but adding DESC sets the descending sorting mode (so the most recent orders will be listed first).

OrdersGetByDate

OrdersGetByDate simply returns all the records in which the current date is between the start and end dates that are supplied as parameters. The results are sorted descending by date.

```
CREATE PROCEDURE OrdersGetByDate
(@StartDate smalldatetime,
 @EndDate smalldatetime)
AS
SELECT OrderID, DateCreated, DateShipped,
       Verified, Completed, Canceled, CustomerName
```

```
FROM Orders
WHERE DateCreated BETWEEN @StartDate AND @EndDate
ORDER BY DateCreated DESC
```

OrdersGetUnverifiedUncanceled

OrdersGetUnverifiedUncanceled returns the orders that have not been verified yet but have not been canceled, either. In other words, you'll see the orders that need to be either verified (and then completed when the shipment is done) or canceled (if the payment isn't confirmed in a reasonable amount of time). The code is fairly straightforward:

```
CREATE PROCEDURE OrdersGetUnverifiedUncanceled
AS
SELECT OrderID, DateCreated, DateShipped,
       Verified, Completed, Canceled, CustomerName
FROM Orders
WHERE Verified=0 AND Canceled=0
ORDER BY DateCreated DESC
```

OrdersGetVerifiedUncompleted

OrdersGetVerifiedUncompleted returns all the orders that have been verified but not yet completed. The administrator will want to see these orders when a shipment has been done and the order needs to be marked as Completed. (When an order is marked as completed, the DateShipped field is populated.)

```
CREATE PROCEDURE OrdersGetVerifiedUncompleted
AS
SELECT OrderID, DateCreated, DateShipped,
       Verified, Completed, Canceled, CustomerName
FROM Orders
WHERE Verified=1 AND Completed=0
ORDER BY DateCreated DESC
```

The Business Tier Methods

In the business tier, you'll call the stored procedures you just wrote. First, add a new class named OrdersAccess to your application's App_Code folder. Then, add a reference to the System.Data.Common namespace, like this:

```
using System;
using System.Data;
using System.Configuration;
using System.Web;
using System.Web.Security;
using System.Web.UI;
using System.Web.UI.WebControls;
using System.Web.UI.WebControls.WebParts;
using System.Web.UI.HtmlControls;
using System.Data.Common;
```

```
/// <summary>
/// Summary description for OrdersAccess
/// </summary>
public class OrdersAccess
{
  public OrdersAccess()
  {
    //
    // TODO: Add constructor logic here
    //
  }
}
```

Now you can start adding your business tier methods to the OrdersAccess class.

GetByRecent

The GetByRecent method calls the OrdersGetByRecent stored procedure and returns a list of most recent orders to the calling function.

```
// Retrieve the recent orders
public static DataTable GetByRecent(int count)
{
  // get a configured DbCommand object
  DbCommand comm = GenericDataAccess.CreateCommand();
  // set the stored procedure name
  comm.CommandText = "OrdersGetByRecent";
  // create a new parameter
  DbParameter param = comm.CreateParameter();
  param.ParameterName = "@Count";
  param.Value = count;
  param.DbType = DbType.Int32;
  comm.Parameters.Add(param);
  // return the result table
  DataTable table = GenericDataAccess.ExecuteSelectCommand(comm);
  return table;
}
```

GetByDate

The GetByDate method returns all the orders that have been placed in a certain period of time, specified by a start date and an end date.

```
// Retrieve orders that have been placed in a specified period of time
public static DataTable GetByDate(string startDate, string endDate)
{
  // get a configured DbCommand object
  DbCommand comm = GenericDataAccess.CreateCommand();
```

```
  // set the stored procedure name
  comm.CommandText = "OrdersGetByDate";
  // create a new parameter
  DbParameter param = comm.CreateParameter();
  param.ParameterName = "@StartDate";
  param.Value = startDate;
  param.DbType = DbType.Date;
  comm.Parameters.Add(param);
  // create a new parameter
  param = comm.CreateParameter();
  param.ParameterName = "@EndDate";
  param.Value = endDate;
  param.DbType = DbType.Date;
  comm.Parameters.Add(param);
  // return the result table
  DataTable table = GenericDataAccess.ExecuteSelectCommand(comm);
  return table;
}
```

GetUnverifiedUncanceled

The GetUnverifiedUncanceled method returns a list of orders that have not been verified yet, but were not canceled, either. These are the records that need to be either verified (and then set to completed when the shipment is done) or canceled (most probable, if the payment isn't confirmed in a reasonable amount of time).

```
// Retrieve orders that need to be verified or canceled
public static DataTable GetUnverifiedUncanceled()
{
  // get a configured DbCommand object
  DbCommand comm = GenericDataAccess.CreateCommand();
  // set the stored procedure name
  comm.CommandText = "OrdersGetUnverifiedUncanceled";
  // return the result table
  DataTable table = GenericDataAccess.ExecuteSelectCommand(comm);
  return table;
}
```

GetVerifiedUncompleted

The GetVerifiedUncompleted method returns all the orders that have been verified but not yet completed. The administrator will want to see these orders when a shipment has been done to mark the order as Completed.

```
// Retrieve orders that need to be shipped/completed
public static DataTable GetVerifiedUncompleted()
{
  // get a configured DbCommand object
  DbCommand comm = GenericDataAccess.CreateCommand();
```

```
  // set the stored procedure name
  comm.CommandText = "OrdersGetVerifiedUncompleted";
  // return the result table
  DataTable table = GenericDataAccess.ExecuteSelectCommand(comm);
  return table;
}
```

Client-Side Validation and Using the ASP.NET Validator Controls

It's time to write the user interface. This time you'll learn how to use the new ASP.NET **validator controls**, which represent the standard way for ASP.NET applications to implement **client-side validation**.

Whereas server-side validation occurs on the server and you program it with C# code, client-side validation occurs in your user's browser and is implemented with JavaScript. Server-side validation is more powerful because on the server you have access to the databases and to more powerful languages and libraries; however, client-side validation is still very important and widely used because it's *fast* from the user's point of view. Although for server code to execute you need a round trip to the server, client-side code executes right away inside the browser.

As a result, using client-side validation for simple tasks such as reminding the user that he forgot to enter his phone number or credit card expiry date is beneficial and improves the overall user experience with your web site.

Then comes ASP.NET, which is a web technology that theoretically lets you do anything without writing client-side code. Although ASP.NET generates a lot of JavaScript code for you, it doesn't require you to understand it, unless you need to manually implement some fancy features—such as our `TieButton` method.

To let you have client-side validation without knowing JavaScript and to make things easier for you even if you do know JavaScript, ASP.NET contains a number of controls called validator controls. They place various conditions on the input controls of your form (such as text boxes) and don't allow the page to be submitted if the rules aren't obeyed.

■**Note** In some circumstances, if the client has JavaScript disabled, these controls don't work as expected (they won't prevent the page from being submitted), but you still can (and should) check at server side if the page is valid. In other words, in the vast majority of cases, the simple presence of the validator controls will prevent the page from being submitted with invalid values, but this is not guaranteed, so you need to do a server-side check as well as a backup strategy.

In our case, our validator controls won't allow submitting the page (such as when clicking the Go buttons), if the dates entered by the user aren't valid (see Figure 10-8).

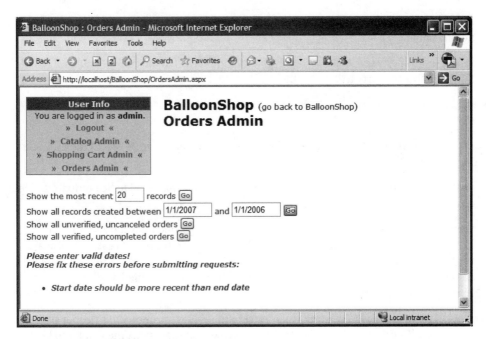

Figure 10-8. *Validator controls at work*

The .NET Framework provides more validator controls, each specialized in a certain type of validation: RequiredFieldValidator, RangeValidator, RegularExpressionValidator, CompareValidator, and CustomValidator. Also, the ValidationSummary control can display a list of all errors retrieved by all validator controls in the page.

We'll only briefly analyze the way CompareValidator and RangeValidator work, because they are used for BalloonShop. Still, the way all the validation controls work is similar, with the exception of CustomValidator, which is more powerful, and its validation logic can be programmed manually. You'll also work with the ValidationSummary control, which gathers all the error messages from the validation controls in the page and presents them in a separate list (the error message in Figure 10-8 is generated by this control).

You'll use two RangeValidator controls to test whether the data typed in the two date text boxes is correct and whether their values are in a specified range. When adding a new RangeValidator control, you usually set these properties:

- *ControlToValidate*: Set this property to the control that you want to validate (in this case, one of the text boxes).

- *Display*: If you don't use a ValidationSummary control, you can leave this set to Dynamic or Static, which results in the error message being displayed right in the place where the validator is placed. But because you'll use the ValidationSummary control to do the displaying work, set the Display to None, so that the error messages aren't displayed twice.

- *ErrorMessage*: This property contains the message to be displayed if the control is not validated.

- *Type*: This property specifies the data type that should exist in the control being validated. You'll set this property to Date for the two text boxes.

- *MinimumValue, MaximumValue*: These specify the maximum and minimum value that should exist in the control being validated.

You'll also use a CompareValidator to ensure that the end date is more recent than the start date. You'll specify these properties:

- *ControlToCompare, ControlToValidate*: The two controls that need to be compared. The one specified by ControlToValidate is the reference control.

- *Operator*: Specifies what kind of comparison should be done between the values of the two controls. Possible values are Equal, NotEqual, GreaterThan, GreaterThanEqual, LessThan, LessThanEqual, and DataTypeCheck. When DataTypeCheck is selected, only the data type of ControlToValidate is verified, and the control specified by ControlToCompare is ignored.

For the ValidationSummary control, you only set the CssClass property to a proper style for displaying errors. You also set the HeaderText property, which represents the header to be displayed before the list of errors. Other than that, there are no special properties that you'll set. Note that you can change the layout of the generated error message by setting the DisplayMode property. You also can set it up to raise a dialog box by setting the ShowMessageBox property to True.

Validation is, by default, enabled through the controls' EnableValidation property, whose default value is True. You'll set this property to False for some of the buttons, for which you don't want validation enabled.

The controls that need valid values to operate, such as the Go button associated with the dates, need to check the value of Page.IsValid to ensure the values are valid. This is important because in some cases (for example, if JavaScript is not enabled on the client), the page may submit even if the page doesn't contain valid values.

Implementing the User Interface

Okay, enough theory, let's add some code to OrdersAdmin.aspx. First, you'll add the constituent controls to the form, and then you'll write the code-behind file.

While building the user interface in the following exercise, you'll also add the validator controls. This is the first (and only) place in this book they are used, so pay special attention to them.

Exercise: Displaying Orders in OrdersAdmin.aspx

1. The first step is to add the necessary Label controls, Button controls, a GridView, and a PlaceHolder control to the second place holder in **OrdersAdmin.aspx**, as shown in Figure 10-9.

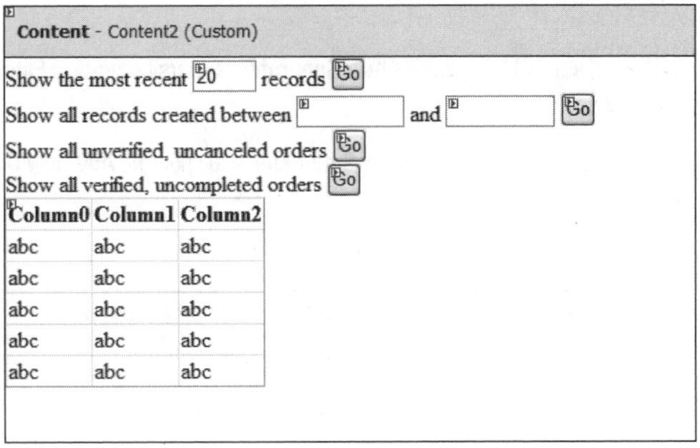

Figure 10-9. *Adding controls to OrdersAdmin.ascx*

The code that generates these controls is

```
<asp:Content ID="Content2" ContentPlaceHolderID="ContentPlaceHolder2" runat=
"Server">
  <span class="AdminPageText">
    Show the most recent
    <asp:TextBox ID="recentCountTextBox" runat="server" MaxLength="4" Width=
"40px" Text="20" />
    records
    <asp:Button ID="byRecentGo" runat="server" CssClass="SmallButtonText"
Text="Go" /><br />
    Show all records created between
    <asp:TextBox ID="startDateTextBox" runat="server" Width="72px" />
    and
    <asp:TextBox ID="endDateTextBox" runat="server" Width="72px" />
    <asp:Button ID="byDateGo" runat="server" CssClass="SmallButtonText"
Text="Go" />
    <br />
    Show all unverified, uncanceled orders
    <asp:Button ID="unverfiedGo" runat="server" CssClass="SmallButtonText"
Text="Go" />
    <br />
    Show all verified, uncompleted orders
    <asp:Button ID="uncompletedGo" runat="server" CssClass="SmallButtonText"
```

```
      Text="Go" />
        <br />
        <asp:GridView ID="grid" runat="server">
        </asp:GridView>
        <br />
      </span>
    </asp:Content>
```

2. Now edit the GridView control. First, set its ID to **grid**, its **AutoGenerateColumns** property to **False**, and its **DataKeyNames** property to **OrderID.**

3. Add columns (see Table 10-3) to the GridView by clicking its **Smart Link** and choosing **Add New Column**.

Table 10-3. *Setting the Fields of the GridView Control*

Column Type	Header Text	Data Field	Other Properties
BoundField	Order ID	OrderID	Read Only
BoundField	Date Created	DateCreated	Read Only
BoundField	Date Shipped	DateShipped	Read Only
CheckBoxField	Verified	Verified	Read Only
CheckBoxField	Completed	Completed	Read Only
CheckBoxField	Canceled	Canceled	Read Only
BoundField	Customer Name	CustomerName	Read Only
ButtonField			Set Command Name to Select, Text to Select, and Button Type to Button

■**Note** This is the first time in BalloonShop when you change the button type to Button. If you think it looks better this way, feel free to make this change in the other grid as well. Just select the grids you want to change, click their Smart Link, select Edit Columns, select the ButtonField column you want to change, and change its ButtonType property to Button.

4. Okay, your grid is ready. Now add the validator controls. You can find the range validators in the **Validation** tab of the toolbox. The validator controls provide a quick and easy way to validate the input values at the presentation-tier level. In this form, you'll test whether the values entered into the date text boxes are valid before querying the business tier with them. Just above the data grid, add a Label control (which is *not* related to the validation controls but is used for notifying the administrator about the status), two RangeValidator controls, a CompareValidator control, and a ValidationSummary control, as shown in Figure 10-10.

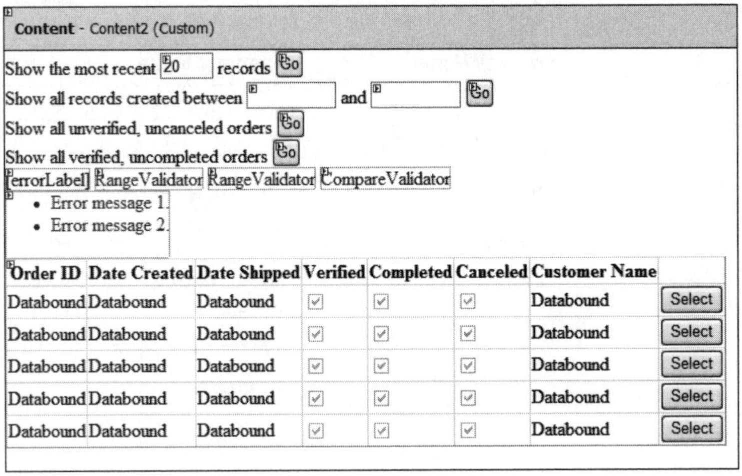

Figure 10-10. *Adding the validation controls*

5. Now set the properties for each of the newly added controls as noted in Table 10-4.

Table 10-4. *Setting the New Control's Properties in* OrdersAdmin.ascx

Control	Property Name	Property Value
Label	(ID)	errorLabel
	Text	(should be empty)
	CssClass	AdminErrorText
	EnableViewState	False
RangeValidator	(ID)	startDateValidator
	ControlToValidate	startDateTextBox
	Display	None
	ErrorMessage	Invalid start date
	MaximumValue	1/1/2009
	MinimumValue	1/1/1999
	Type	Date
RangeValidator	(ID)	endDateValidator
	ControlToValidate	endDateTextBox
	Display	None
	ErrorMessage	Invalid end date
	MaximumValue	1/1/2009
	MinimumValue	1/1/1999
	Type	Date

Table 10-4. *Setting the New Control's Properties in* OrdersAdmin.ascx *(Continued)*

Control	Property Name	Property Value
CompareValidator	(ID)	compareDatesValidator
	ControlToCompare	endDateTextBox
	ControlToValidate	startDateTextBox
	Display	None
	ErrorMessage	Start date should be more recent than end date
	Operator	LessThan
	Type	Date
ValidationSummary	(ID)	validationSummary
	CssClass	AdminErrorText
	HeaderText	Please fix these errors before submitting requests:

6. Add the following style to **BalloonShop.css**:

```
.AdminErrorText
{
  font-weight: bold;
  font-size: 12px;
  color: red;
  font-style: italic;
  font-family: Verdana, Helvetica, sans-serif;
}
```

7. Execute the project and browse to the orders admin page (you may need to login as **admin** first). Enter invalid dates and try clicking any of the admin buttons. You'll get a page like the one shown earlier in Figure 10-8.

8. A problem occurs if wrong dates are written, because *none* of the Go buttons can be used. We actually want the restrictions to apply only to the Go button associated with the dates. Change the CausesValidation property of the first, third, and fourth **Go** buttons to False (the default is True).

9. It's time to write the code. While in **Design View**, double-click the **Go** buttons to have their Click event handlers generated for you and complete their code as shown:

```
// list the most recent orders
protected void byRecentGo_Click(object sender, EventArgs e)
{
  // how many orders to list?
  int recordCount;
```

```
  // load the new data into the grid
  if (int.TryParse(recentCountTextBox.Text, out recordCount))
    grid.DataSource = OrdersAccess.GetByRecent(recordCount);
  else
    errorLabel.Text = "<br />Please enter a valid number!";
  // refresh the data grid
  grid.DataBind();
  // no order is selected
  Session["AdminOrderID"] = null;
}

// list the orders that happened between specified dates
protected void byDateGo_Click(object sender, EventArgs e)
{
  // check if the page is valid (we have date validator controls)
  if ((Page.IsValid) && (startDateTextBox.Text + endDateTextBox.Text != ""))
  {
    // get the dates
    string startDate = startDateTextBox.Text;
    string endDate = endDateTextBox.Text;
    // load the grid with the requested data
    grid.DataSource = OrdersAccess.GetByDate(startDate, endDate);
  }
  else
    errorLabel.Text = "<br />Please enter valid dates!";
  // refresh the data grid
  grid.DataBind();
  // no order is selected
  Session["AdminOrderID"] = null;
}

// get unverified, uncanceled orders
protected void unverfiedGo_Click(object sender, EventArgs e)
{
  // load the grid with the requested data
  grid.DataSource = OrdersAccess.GetUnverifiedUncanceled();
  // refresh the data grid
  grid.DataBind();
  // no order is selected
  Session["AdminOrderID"] = null;
}

// get verified, but uncompleted orders
protected void uncompletedGo_Click(object sender, EventArgs e)
{
  // load the grid with the requested data
  grid.DataSource = OrdersAccess.GetVerifiedUncompleted();
```

```
      // refresh the data grid
      grid.DataBind();
      // no order is selected
      Session["AdminOrderID"] = null;
    }
```

10. Add the following bits to **Page_Load** to associate the text boxes with their buttons:

```
    protected void Page_Load(object sender, EventArgs e)
    {
      // Set the title of the page
      this.Title = BalloonShopConfiguration.SiteName +
                   " : Orders Admin";
      // associate the check boxes with their buttons
      Utilities.TieButton(this.Page, recentCountTextBox, byRecentGo);
      Utilities.TieButton(this.Page, startDateTextBox, byDateGo);
      Utilities.TieButton(this.Page, endDateTextBox, byDateGo);
    }
```

11. Switch again to **Design View**, use Visual Web Developer to generate the **SelectedIndexChanged** event handler for the first GridView control (the one in OrdersAdmin, not the one in OrderDetailsAdmin), and then complete its code like this:

```
    // Load the details of the selected order
    protected void grid_SelectedIndexChanged(object sender, EventArgs e)
    {
      // Save the ID of the selected order in the session
      Session["AdminOrderID"] = grid.DataKeys[grid.SelectedIndex].Value.
    ToString();
    }
```

12. Feel free to play with your new administration page. Try even to break it by writing bad data to the record count or to the date text boxes. Except the Select buttons of the GridView, whose functionality hasn't been implemented yet, everything should work as expected.

How It Works: Using the Validator Controls

The two details to be aware of for this form are the way the session is used and how the validator controls work.

When selecting an order, the AdminOrderID session variable is populated with the ID of the selected order. The order details admin control reads this value and decides what to display depending on this value. The Click event handler of each of the Go buttons clears the AdminOrderID session variable, marking that no order is selected.

This form uses both server-side and client-side validation. The value for the most recent records count is verified at server side to be a valid integer. If it isn't, an error message is displayed to the visitor:

```
    // load the new data into the grid
    if (int.TryParse(recentCountTextBox.Text, out recordCount))
      grid.DataSource = OrdersAccess.GetByRecent(recordCount);
    else
      errorLabel.Text = "<br />Please enter a valid number!";
    // refresh the data grid
```

The date text boxes are validated using validation controls, which try to operate at client side, while also having a server-side mechanism in case the client doesn't support JavaScript.

```
// check if the page is valid (we have date validator controls)
if (Page.IsValid)
{
   ...
```

The validator controls you wrote apply the following requirements for the entered dates:

- The values in startDateTextBox and endDateTextBox must be correctly formatted dates between 1/1/1999 and 1/1/2009.

- The start date needs to be more recent than the end date.

The first requirement is implemented using RangeValidator controls, and the second using a CompareValidator. The ValidationSummary control gets the errors from the validator controls and displays them in a single, easy-to-read list.

When creating the control, you also added a Label control named errorLabel, which you used to display other errors than those generated by the validator controls. You set its EnableViewState property to False, so its value will be cleared after a successful Go command executes.

Administering Order Details

The OrderDetailsAdmin user control allows the administrator to edit the details of a particular order. The most common tasks are marking an unverified order as either Verified or Canceled (it can't be directly marked as Completed if it isn't verified yet) and marking a verified order as Completed when the shipment is dispatched. Refer to Figure 10-6 as a reminder of how this form will look.

Here you're providing the administrator with three very useful buttons: Mark this Order as Verified, Mark this Order as Completed, and Mark this Order as Canceled. These buttons are enabled or disabled, depending on the status of the order.

The Edit, Update, and Cancel buttons allow the administrator to manually edit any of the details of an order. When the Edit button is clicked, all the check boxes and text boxes (except for the one holding the order ID) become editable.

Now you have an idea about what you'll be doing with this control. You'll implement it in the usual style starting with the data tier.

The Database Stored Procedures

Now you'll implement the data tier logic that will support the functionality required by the user interface. You'll enable the administrator to do six operations, which you'll implement with the following stored procedures:

- OrderGetInfo returns the data needed to populate the text boxes of the form with general order information, such as the total amount, date created, date shipped, and so on. You can see the complete list in the previous figure.

- OrderGetDetails returns all the products that belong to the selected order, and its return data fills the grid at the bottom of the form.

- OrderUpdate is called when the form is in edit mode, and you submit new data to update the selected order.

- OrderMarkVerified is called to set the Verified bit of the selected order to 1.

- OrderMarkCompleted sets the Completed bit of the order to 1.

- OrderMarkCanceled sets the Canceled bit of the order to 1.

You'll now implement each of these stored procedures.

OrderGetInfo

The OrderGetInfo stored procedure returns the information necessary to fill the long list of text boxes in the OrderDetailsAdmin control.

```
CREATE PROCEDURE OrderGetInfo
(@OrderID int)
AS
SELECT OrderID,
       (SELECT SUM(Subtotal) FROM OrderDetail WHERE OrderID = @OrderID)
       AS TotalAmount,
       DateCreated,
       DateShipped,
       Verified,
       Completed,
       Canceled,
       Comments,
       CustomerName,
       ShippingAddress,
       CustomerEmail
FROM Orders
WHERE OrderID = @OrderID
```

Note that a subquery is used to generate the TotalAmount field. All the other data you need is read from the Orders table, but to get the total amount of an order, you need to look at the OrderDetail table as well.

The subquery that returns the total amount of a particular order uses the SUM function to add up the subtotal of each product in the order (remember Subtotal is a calculated column), as follows:

```
SELECT SUM(Subtotal) FROM OrderDetail WHERE OrderID = @OrderID
```

This subquery gets executed for each row of the outer query, and its result is saved as a calculated column named TotalAmount.

OrderGetDetails

OrderGetDetails returns the list of products that belongs to a specific order. This will be used to populate the data grid containing the order details, situated at the bottom of the control.

```
CREATE PROCEDURE OrderGetDetails
(@OrderID int)
AS
SELECT Orders.OrderID,
       ProductID,
       ProductName,
       Quantity,
       UnitCost,
       Subtotal
FROM OrderDetail JOIN Orders
ON Orders.OrderID = OrderDetail.OrderID
WHERE Orders.OrderID = @OrderID
```

OrderUpdate

The OrderUpdate procedure is called when the user is updating the order in the GridView.

```
CREATE PROCEDURE OrderUpdate
(@OrderID int,
 @DateCreated smalldatetime,
 @DateShipped smalldatetime = NULL,
 @Verified bit,
 @Completed bit,
 @Canceled bit,
 @Comments varchar(200),
 @CustomerName varchar(50),
 @ShippingAddress varchar(200),
 @CustomerEmail varchar(50))
AS
UPDATE Orders
SET DateCreated=@DateCreated,
    DateShipped=@DateShipped,
    Verified=@Verified,
    Completed=@Completed,
    Canceled=@Canceled,
    Comments=@Comments,
    CustomerName=@CustomerName,
    ShippingAddress=@ShippingAddress,
    CustomerEmail=@CustomerEmail
WHERE OrderID = @OrderID
```

OrderMarkVerified

OrderMarkVerified is called when the administrator clicks the Mark this Order as Verified button.

```
CREATE PROCEDURE OrderMarkVerified
(@OrderID int)
AS
UPDATE Orders
SET Verified = 1
WHERE OrderID = @OrderID
```

OrderMarkCompleted

OrderMarkCompleted is called when the administrator clicks the Mark this Order as Completed button. It not only sets the Completed bit to 1 but also updates the DateShipped field because an order is completed just after the shipment has been done.

```
CREATE PROCEDURE OrderMarkCompleted
(@OrderID int)
AS
UPDATE Orders
SET Completed = 1,
    DateShipped = GETDATE()
WHERE OrderID = @OrderID
```

OrderMarkCanceled

OrderMarkCanceled is called when the administrator clicks the Mark this Order as Canceled button.

```
CREATE PROCEDURE OrderMarkCanceled
(@OrderID int)
AS
UPDATE Orders
SET Canceled = 1
WHERE OrderID = @OrderID
```

The Business Tier Methods

Apart from the usual methods that pass data back and forth between the user interface and the database stored procedures, you'll create a struct named OrderInfo. Instances of this struct store information about one order and are used to pass order information from the business-tier methods to the presentation tier.

You learned from the previous chapters, when you built similar structures, that the code looks cleaner when using such a structure instead of passing a DataTable or a DataRow object to the presentation tier.

The OrderInfo Struct

Although you can add this struct to any of the existing files in the App_Code folder (or you can even create a new file for it if you prefer), for consistency and clarity you should add the OrderInfo struct at the beginning of the OrdersAccess.cs file, after the using statements and before the OrdersAccess class.

```
/// <summary>
/// Wraps order data
/// </summary>
public struct OrderInfo
{
  public int OrderID;
  public decimal TotalAmount;
  public string DateCreated;
  public string DateShipped;
  public bool Verified;
  public bool Completed;
  public bool Canceled;
  public string Comments;
  public string CustomerName;
  public string ShippingAddress;
  public string CustomerEmail;
}
```

After this class is in place, add the following methods to the OrdersAccess class:

- GetInfo

- GetDetails

- Update

- MarkVerified

- MarkCompleted

- MarkCanceled

GetInfo

This method gets information related to a particular order from the database and saves the data into an OrderInfo object, which is then returned.

```
// Retrieve order information
public static OrderInfo GetInfo(string orderID)
{
  // get a configured DbCommand object
  DbCommand comm = GenericDataAccess.CreateCommand();
  // set the stored procedure name
  comm.CommandText = "OrderGetInfo";
  // create a new parameter
  DbParameter param = comm.CreateParameter();
  param.ParameterName = "@OrderID";
  param.Value = orderID;
  param.DbType = DbType.Int32;
  comm.Parameters.Add(param);
```

```
  // obtain the results
  DataTable table = GenericDataAccess.ExecuteSelectCommand(comm);
  DataRow orderRow = table.Rows[0];
  // save the results into an OrderInfo object
  OrderInfo orderInfo;
  orderInfo.OrderID = Int32.Parse(orderRow["OrderID"].ToString());
  orderInfo.TotalAmount = Decimal.Parse(orderRow["TotalAmount"].ToString());
  orderInfo.DateCreated = orderRow["DateCreated"].ToString();
  orderInfo.DateShipped = orderRow["DateShipped"].ToString();
  orderInfo.Verified = bool.Parse(orderRow["Verified"].ToString());
  orderInfo.Completed = bool.Parse(orderRow["Completed"].ToString());
  orderInfo.Canceled = bool.Parse(orderRow["Canceled"].ToString());
  orderInfo.Comments = orderRow["Comments"].ToString();
  orderInfo.CustomerName = orderRow["CustomerName"].ToString();
  orderInfo.ShippingAddress = orderRow["ShippingAddress"].ToString();
  orderInfo.CustomerEmail = orderRow["CustomerEmail"].ToString();
  // return the OrderInfo object
  return orderInfo;
}
```

GetDetails

GetDetails returns the order details of the specified order.

```
// Retrieve the order details (the products that are part of that order)
public static DataTable GetDetails(string orderID)
{
  // get a configured DbCommand object
  DbCommand comm = GenericDataAccess.CreateCommand();
  // set the stored procedure name
  comm.CommandText = "OrderGetDetails";
  // create a new parameter
  DbParameter param = comm.CreateParameter();
  param.ParameterName = "@OrderID";
  param.Value = orderID;
  param.DbType = DbType.Int32;
  comm.Parameters.Add(param);
  // return the results
  DataTable table = GenericDataAccess.ExecuteSelectCommand(comm);
  return table;
}
```

Update

This stored procedure updates an order and is called when the Update button in OrderDetailsAdmin is clicked. It receives the order details as an OrderInfo parameter and saves them to the database.

```csharp
// Update an order
public static void Update(OrderInfo orderInfo)
{
  // get a configured DbCommand object
  DbCommand comm = GenericDataAccess.CreateCommand();
  // set the stored procedure name
  comm.CommandText = "OrderUpdate";
  // create a new parameter
  DbParameter param = comm.CreateParameter();
  param.ParameterName = "@OrderID";
  param.Value = orderInfo.OrderID;
  param.DbType = DbType.Int32;
  comm.Parameters.Add(param);
  // create a new parameter
  param = comm.CreateParameter();
  param.ParameterName = "@DateCreated";
  param.Value = orderInfo.DateCreated;
  param.DbType = DbType.DateTime;
  comm.Parameters.Add(param);
  // The DateShipped parameter is sent only if data is available
  if (orderInfo.DateShipped.Trim() != "")
  {
    param = comm.CreateParameter();
    param.ParameterName = "@DateShipped";
    param.Value = orderInfo.DateShipped;
    param.DbType = DbType.DateTime;
    comm.Parameters.Add(param);
  }
  // create a new parameter
  param = comm.CreateParameter();
  param.ParameterName = "@Verified";
  param.Value = orderInfo.Verified;
  param.DbType = DbType.Byte;
  comm.Parameters.Add(param);
  // create a new parameter
  param = comm.CreateParameter();
  param.ParameterName = "@Completed";
  param.Value = orderInfo.Completed;
  param.DbType = DbType.Byte;
  comm.Parameters.Add(param);
  // create a new parameter
  param = comm.CreateParameter();
  param.ParameterName = "@Canceled";
  param.Value = orderInfo.Canceled;
  param.DbType = DbType.Byte;
  comm.Parameters.Add(param);
```

```
  // create a new parameter
  param = comm.CreateParameter();
  param.ParameterName = "@Comments";
  param.Value = orderInfo.Comments;
  param.DbType = DbType.String;
  comm.Parameters.Add(param);
  // create a new parameter
  param = comm.CreateParameter();
  param.ParameterName = "@CustomerName";
  param.Value = orderInfo.CustomerName;
  param.DbType = DbType.String;
  comm.Parameters.Add(param);
  // create a new parameter
  param = comm.CreateParameter();
  param.ParameterName = "@ShippingAddress";
  param.Value = orderInfo.ShippingAddress;
  param.DbType = DbType.String;
  comm.Parameters.Add(param);
  // create a new parameter
  param = comm.CreateParameter();
  param.ParameterName = "@CustomerEmail";
  param.Value = orderInfo.CustomerEmail;
  param.DbType = DbType.String;
  comm.Parameters.Add(param);
  // return the results
  GenericDataAccess.ExecuteNonQuery(comm);
}
```

MarkVerified

The MarkVerified method is called when the Mark this Order as Verified button is clicked and sets the Verified bit of the specified order in the database to 1.

```
// Mark an order as verified
public static void MarkVerified(string orderId)
{
  // get a configured DbCommand object
  DbCommand comm = GenericDataAccess.CreateCommand();
  // set the stored procedure name
  comm.CommandText = "OrderMarkVerified";
  // create a new parameter
  DbParameter param = comm.CreateParameter();
  param.ParameterName = "@OrderID";
  param.Value = orderId;
  param.DbType = DbType.Int32;
  comm.Parameters.Add(param);
  // return the results
  GenericDataAccess.ExecuteNonQuery(comm);
}
```

MarkCompleted

The MarkCompleted method is called when the Mark this Order as Completed button is clicked and sets the Completed bit of the specified order to 1.

```
// Mark an order as completed
public static void MarkCompleted(string orderId)
{
  // get a configured DbCommand object
  DbCommand comm = GenericDataAccess.CreateCommand();
  // set the stored procedure name
  comm.CommandText = "OrderMarkCompleted";
  // create a new parameter
  DbParameter param = comm.CreateParameter();
  param.ParameterName = "@OrderID";
  param.Value = orderId;
  param.DbType = DbType.Int32;
  comm.Parameters.Add(param);
  // return the results
  GenericDataAccess.ExecuteNonQuery(comm);
}
```

MarkCanceled

The MarkCanceled method is called when the Mark this Order as Canceled button is clicked and sets the Canceled bit of the specified order to 1.

```
// Mark an order as canceled
public static void MarkCanceled(string orderId)
{
  // get a configured DbCommand object
  DbCommand comm = GenericDataAccess.CreateCommand();
  // set the stored procedure name
  comm.CommandText = "OrderMarkCanceled";
  // create a new parameter
  DbParameter param = comm.CreateParameter();
  param.ParameterName = "@OrderID";
  param.Value = orderId;
  param.DbType = DbType.Int32;
  comm.Parameters.Add(param);
  // return the results
  GenericDataAccess.ExecuteNonQuery(comm);
}
```

Creating the User Interface

Once again, you've reached the place where you wrap up all the data-tier and business-tier functionality and package it into a nice-looking user interface. You'll create the OrderDetailsAdmin user control in the following exercise.

Exercise: Creating the OrderDetailsAdmin Web User Control

1. Right-click the UserControls folder in **Solution Explorer** and select **Add New Item ➤ Web User Control**. Choose OrderDetailsAdmin.ascx for the name of the new user control.

2. Open the control in **Design View** and populate it as shown in Figure 10-11. The properties for each constituent control are shown in Table 10-5, and the GridView columns are listed in Table 10-6. For the GridView control, you also need to set its **AutoGenerateColumns** property to **False**.

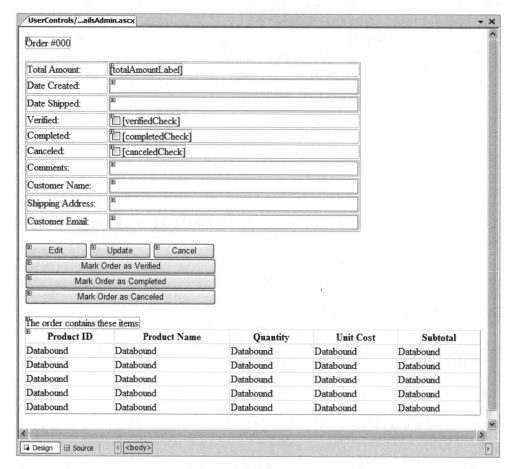

Figure 10-11. *OrderDetailsAdmin.ascx in Design View*

■Tip When setting controls' properties, remember that Visual Studio .NET allows you to set properties on more than one control at a time—you can select, for example, the TextBox controls on the right and set their Width to 400px, and so on.

Table 10-5. *Setting Controls' Properties in* OrderDetailsAdmin.ascx

Control Type	ID	Text	CssClass	Width
Label	orderIdLabel	Order #000	AdminTitle	
Label	totalAmountLabel	(empty)	ProductPrice	
TextBox	dateCreatedTextBox		AdminPageText	400px
TextBox	dateShippedTextBox		AdminPageText	400px
CheckBox	verifiedCheck		AdminPageText	400px
CheckBox	completedCheck		AdminPageText	400px
CheckBox	canceledCheck		AdminPageText	400px
TextBox	commentsTextBox		AdminPageText	400px
TextBox	customerNameTextBox		AdminPageText	400px
TextBox	shippingAddressTextBox		AdminPageText	400px
TextBox	customerEmailTextBox		AdminPageText	400px
Button	editButton	Edit	SmallButtonText	100px
Button	updateButton	Update	SmallButtonText	100px
Button	cancelButton	Cancel	SmallButtonText	100px
Button	markVerifiedButton	Mark Order as Verified	SmallButtonText	305px
Button	markCompletedButton	Mark Order as Completed	SmallButtonText	305px
Button	markCanceledButton	Mark Order as Canceled	SmallButtonText	305px
Label	(doesn't matter)	The order contains these items:	AdminPageText	
GridView	grid			100%

Table 10-6. *Setting the Fields of the* GridView *Control*

Column Type	Header Text	Data Field	Other Properties
BoundField	Product ID	ProductID	Read Only
BoundField	Product Name	ProductName	Read Only
BoundField	Quantity	Quantity	Read Only
BoundField	Unit Cost	Unit Cost	Read Only
ButtonField	Subtotal	Subtotal	Read Only

To make sure we're on the same page, here's the source code of the control:

```
<%@ Control Language="C#" AutoEventWireup="true"
CodeFile="OrderDetailsAdmin.ascx.cs" Inherits="OrderDetailsAdmin" %>
<asp:Label ID="orderIdLabel" runat="server"
            CssClass="AdminTitle" Text="Order #000" />
<br /><br />
<table class="AdminPageText">
  <tr>
    <td width="130">Total Amount:</td>
    <td>
      <asp:Label ID="totalAmountLabel" runat="server"
CssClass="ProductPrice" />
    </td>
  </tr>
  <tr>
    <td width="130">Date Created:</td>
    <td>
      <asp:TextBox ID="dateCreatedTextBox" runat="server" Width="400px" />
    </td>
  </tr>
  <tr>
    <td width="130">Date Shipped:</td>
    <td>
      <asp:TextBox ID="dateShippedTextBox" runat="server" Width="400px" />
    </td>
  </tr>
  <tr>
    <td width="130">Verified:</td>
    <td>
      <asp:CheckBox ID="verifiedCheck" runat="server" />
    </td>
  </tr>
  <tr>
    <td width="130">Completed:</td>
    <td>
      <asp:CheckBox ID="completedCheck" runat="server" />
    </td>
  </tr>
  <tr>
    <td width="130">Canceled:</td>
    <td>
      <asp:CheckBox ID="canceledCheck" runat="server" />
    </td>
  </tr>
```

```
      <tr>
        <td width="130">Comments:</td>
        <td>
          <asp:TextBox ID="commentsTextBox" runat="server" Width="400px" />
        </td>
      </tr>
      <tr>
        <td width="130">Customer Name:</td>
        <td>
          <asp:TextBox ID="customerNameTextBox" runat="server" Width="400px" />
        </td>
      </tr>
      <tr>
        <td width="130">Shipping Address:</td>
        <td>
          <asp:TextBox ID="shippingAddressTextBox" runat="server" Width="400px" />
        </td>
      </tr>
      <tr>
        <td width="130">Customer Email:</td>
        <td>
          <asp:TextBox ID="customerEmailTextBox" runat="server" Width="400px" />
        </td>
      </tr>
    </table>
    <br />
    <asp:Button ID="editButton" runat="server" CssClass="SmallButtonText"
                Text="Edit" Width="100px" />
    <asp:Button ID="updateButton" runat="server" CssClass="SmallButtonText"
                Text="Update" Width="100px" />
    <asp:Button ID="cancelButton" runat="server" CssClass="SmallButtonText"
                Text="Cancel" Width="100px" /><br />
    <asp:Button ID="markVerifiedButton" runat="server" CssClass="SmallButtonText"
                Text="Mark Order as Verified" Width="310px" /><br />
    <asp:Button ID="markCompletedButton" runat="server" CssClass="SmallButtonText"
                Text="Mark Order as Completed" Width="310px" /><br />
    <asp:Button ID="markCanceledButton" runat="server" CssClass="SmallButtonText"
                Text="Mark Order as Canceled" Width="310px" /><br />
    <br />
    <asp:Label ID="Label13" runat="server" CssClass="AdminPageText"
    Text="The order contains these items:" />
    <br />
    <asp:GridView ID="grid" runat="server" AutoGenerateColumns="False"
    BackColor="White" Width="100%">
      <Columns>
        <asp:BoundField DataField="ProductID" HeaderText="Product ID"
                        ReadOnly="True" SortExpression="ProductID" />
```

```
        <asp:BoundField DataField="ProductName" HeaderText="Product Name"
                        ReadOnly="True" SortExpression="ProductName" />
        <asp:BoundField DataField="Quantity" HeaderText="Quantity"
                        ReadOnly="True" SortExpression="Quantity" />
        <asp:BoundField DataField="UnitCost" HeaderText="Unit Cost"
                        ReadOnly="True" SortExpression="UnitCost" />
        <asp:BoundField DataField="Subtotal" HeaderText="Subtotal"
                        ReadOnly="True" SortExpression="Subtotal" />
    </Columns>
</asp:GridView>
```

3. Start writing the code-behind logic of **OrderDetailsAdmin.ascx** by adding a new field named **editMode**, "transforming" the **Page_Load** method to **Page_PreRender**, and adding some code to it:

```
public partial class OrderDetailsAdmin : System.Web.UI.UserControl
{
  // edit mode by default is false
  private bool editMode = false;

  // set up the form
  protected void Page_PreRender(object sender, EventArgs e)
  {
    // check if we must display order details
    if (Session["AdminOrderID"] != null)
    {
      // fill constituent controls with data
      PopulateControls();
      // set edit mode
      SetEditMode(editMode);
    }
    else
      // Hide
      this.Visible = false;
  }
}
```

Note the use of Session["AdminOrderID"]—this is set in OrdersAdmin.aspx, when the administrator selects an order from the list. The OrderDetailsAdmin.ascx reads this value to find out the ID of the order it needs to display details for. In the Page_PreRender function, you use two additional methods: PopulateControls, which populates all the controls on the form with data, and SetEditMode, which disables or enables the text boxes and check boxes for editing.

4. Add **PopulateControls** just after Page_PreRender. This method gets the order information into an OrderInfo object, which was especially created for this purpose, by calling the GetInfo method of the OrdersAccess class. Using the information from that object, the method fills the constituent controls with data. At the end, you call OrdersAccess.GetDetails, which returns the products in the specified order.

```csharp
// populate the form with data
private void PopulateControls()
{
  // obtain order ID from the session
  string orderId = Session["AdminOrderID"].ToString();
  // obtain order info
  OrderInfo orderInfo = OrdersAccess.GetInfo(orderId);
  // populate labels and text boxes with order info
  orderIdLabel.Text = "Displaying Order #" + orderId;
  totalAmountLabel.Text = String.Format("{0:c}", orderInfo.TotalAmount);
  dateCreatedTextBox.Text = orderInfo.DateCreated;
  dateShippedTextBox.Text = orderInfo.DateShipped;
  verifiedCheck.Checked = orderInfo.Verified;
  completedCheck.Checked = orderInfo.Completed;
  canceledCheck.Checked = orderInfo.Canceled;
  commentsTextBox.Text = orderInfo.Comments;
  customerNameTextBox.Text = orderInfo.CustomerName;
  shippingAddressTextBox.Text = orderInfo.ShippingAddress;
  customerEmailTextBox.Text = orderInfo.CustomerEmail;
  // by default the Edit button is enabled, and the
  // Update and Cancel buttons are disabled
  editButton.Enabled = true;
  updateButton.Enabled = false;
  cancelButton.Enabled = false;
  // Decide which one of the other three buttons
  // should be enabled and which should be disabled
  if (canceledCheck.Checked || completedCheck.Checked)
  {
    // if the order was canceled or completed ...
    markVerifiedButton.Enabled = false;
    markCompletedButton.Enabled = false;
    markCanceledButton.Enabled = false;
  }
  else if (verifiedCheck.Checked)
  {
    // if the order was not canceled but is verified ...
    markVerifiedButton.Enabled = false;
    markCompletedButton.Enabled = true;
    markCanceledButton.Enabled = true;
  }
  else
  {
    // if the order was not canceled and is not verified ...
    markVerifiedButton.Enabled = true;
    markCompletedButton.Enabled = false;
    markCanceledButton.Enabled = true;
  }
```

```
// fill the data grid with order details
grid.DataSource = OrdersAccess.GetDetails(orderId);
grid.DataBind();
}
```

5. Write the `SetEditMode` method now, which enables or disables edit mode for the information text boxes.

```
// enable or disable edit mode
private void SetEditMode(bool enable)
{
  dateCreatedTextBox.Enabled = enable;
  dateShippedTextBox.Enabled = enable;
  verifiedCheck.Enabled = enable;
  completedCheck.Enabled = enable;
  canceledCheck.Enabled = enable;
  commentsTextBox.Enabled = enable;
  customerNameTextBox.Enabled = enable;
  shippingAddressTextBox.Enabled = enable;
  customerEmailTextBox.Enabled = enable;
  editButton.Enabled = !enable;
  updateButton.Enabled = enable;
  cancelButton.Enabled = enable;
}
```

This method receives a `bool` parameter that specifies whether you enter or exit edit mode. When entering edit mode, all text boxes and the Update and Cancel buttons become enabled, while the Edit button is disabled. The reverse happens when exiting edit mode (this happens when one of the Cancel and Update buttons is clicked).

6. Now, start implementing the code that allows the administrator to edit order information. To make your life easier, first double-click each of the buttons (**Edit**, **Cancel**, **Update**) in **Design View** to let Visual Studio generate the signatures of the event handlers. Here's the code:

```
// enter edit mode
protected void editButton_Click(object sender, EventArgs e)
{
  editMode = true;
}

// cancel edit mode
protected void cancelButton_Click(object sender, EventArgs e)
{
  // don't need to do anything, editMode will be set to false by default
}

// update order information
protected void updateButton_Click(object sender, EventArgs e)
{
```

```
// Store the new order details in an OrderInfo object
OrderInfo orderInfo = new OrderInfo();
string orderId = Session["AdminOrderID"].ToString();
orderInfo.OrderID = Int32.Parse(orderId);
orderInfo.DateCreated = dateCreatedTextBox.Text;
orderInfo.DateShipped = dateShippedTextBox.Text;
orderInfo.Verified = verifiedCheck.Checked;
orderInfo.Completed = completedCheck.Checked;
orderInfo.Canceled = canceledCheck.Checked;
orderInfo.Comments = commentsTextBox.Text;
orderInfo.CustomerName = customerNameTextBox.Text;
orderInfo.ShippingAddress = shippingAddressTextBox.Text;
orderInfo.CustomerEmail = customerEmailTextBox.Text;
// try to update the order
try
{
  // Update the order
  OrdersAccess.Update(orderInfo);
}
catch (Exception ex)
{
    // In case of an error, we simply ignore it
}
// Exit edit mode
SetEditMode(false);
// Update the form
PopulateControls();
}
```

Note Here we didn't implement a mechanism to let the administrator know whether the update was successful or failed—if something happens, we just ignore the error. You've learned various error-handling techniques in this and previous chapters, and you can choose to implement whichever technique you think is best for your application.

7. Do the same for the last three buttons:

```
// mark order as verified
protected void markVerifiedButton_Click(object sender, EventArgs e)
{
  // obtain the order ID from the session
  string orderId = Session["AdminOrderID"].ToString();
  // mark order as verified
  OrdersAccess.MarkVerified(orderId);
  // update the form
  PopulateControls();
}
```

```
// mark order as completed
protected void markCompletedButton_Click(object sender, EventArgs e)
{
  // obtain the order ID from the session
  string orderId = Session["AdminOrderID"].ToString();
  // mark the order as completed
  OrdersAccess.MarkCompleted(orderId);
  // update the form
  PopulateControls();
}

// mark order as canceled
protected void markCanceledButton_Click(object sender, EventArgs e)
{
  // obtain the order ID from the session
  string orderId = Session["AdminOrderID"].ToString();
  // mark the order as canceled
  OrdersAccess.MarkCanceled(orderId);
  // update the form
  PopulateControls();
}
```

8. Open OrdersAdmin.aspx in **Design View** and drag OrderDetailsAdmin.ascx from the **Solution Explorer** to the bottom of the second place holder, as shown in Figure 10-12.

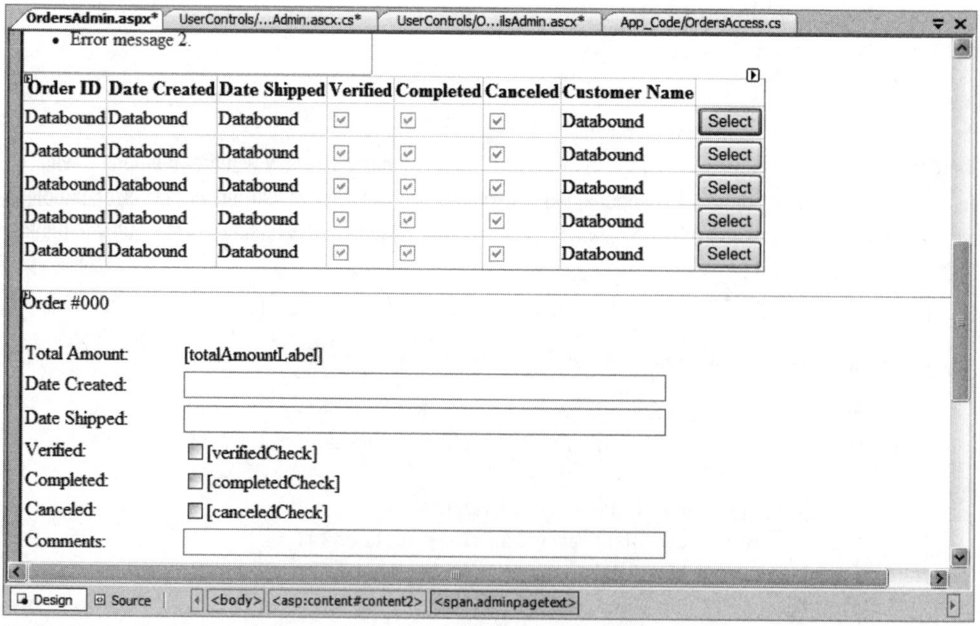

Figure 10-12. *Adding OrderDetailsAdmin.ascx to OrdersAdmin.aspx*

9. Switch `OrdersAdmin.aspx` to **Source View** and disable the view state for the `OrderDetailsAdmin.ascx` instance. Change its name from `OrderDetailsAdmin1` to `orderDetailsAdmin`:

```
        </asp:GridView>
        <br />
        <uc1:OrderDetailsAdmin EnableViewState="false"
                               id="orderDetailsAdmin" runat="server">
        </uc1:OrderDetailsAdmin>
      </span>
    </asp:Content>
```

How It Works: `OrderDetailsAdmin.ascx`

Whew, you've written a lot of code for this control. The code itself isn't complicated, but you had to deal with a lot of user interface elements. The two important details to understand are as follows:

- You used the session to persist data about the selected order. This is read in the `OrderDetailsAdmin` control to obtain the `ID` of the selected order.

- You used `Page_PreRender` instead of `Page_Load`, because it executed after the session gets the chance to be updated in the parent form.

Because we talked about each method while writing the code, it should be pretty clear how the page works. Run it now and play with the buttons to make sure everything works as it should.

Summary

We covered a lot of ground in this chapter. You implemented a system by which you can both take orders and manually administer them.

You accomplished this in two separate stages. You added a Proceed to Checkout button onto the shopping cart control to allow the visitor to order the products in the shopping cart. You implemented a simple orders administration page, where the site administrator could view and handle pending orders.

In addition, we looked at the use of validation controls and also, importantly, set the scene for entirely automating the order system.

Because order data is now stored in the database, you can create various statistics and run calculations based on the items sold. In the next chapter, you'll learn how to implement a "Visitors who bought this also bought..." feature, which wouldn't have been possible without the order data stored in the database.

CHAPTER 11

■ ■ ■

Making Product Recommendations

One of the most important advantages of an Internet store compared to a brick-and-mortar location is the capability to customize the web site for each visitor based on his or her preferences or based on data gathered from other visitors with similar preferences. If your web site knows how to suggest additional products to your visitor in a clever way, he or she might end up buying more than initially planned.

In this chapter, you'll implement a simple but efficient product recommendations system in your BalloonShop web store. You can implement a product recommendations system in several ways, depending on your kind of store. Here are a few popular ones:

- *Up-Selling*: The strategy of offering consumers the opportunity to purchase an "upgrade" or a little extra based on their requested purchases. Perhaps the most famous example of up-selling—"Would you like to super-size that?"—is mentioned to customers when they order a value meal at McDonald's. This seemingly innocent request greatly increases the profit margin.

- *Cross-Selling*: The practice of offering customers complementary products. Continuing with the McDonald's analogy, when customers order hamburgers, they'll always hear the phrase "Would you like fries with that?" because everyone knows that fries go with burgers. Because the consumers are ordering burgers, it's likely that they also like french fries—the mere mention of fries is likely to generate a new sale.

- *Featured products on the home page*: BalloonShop permits the site administrator to choose the products featured on the main page and on the department pages.

In this chapter, you'll implement a dynamic recommendations system with both up-selling and cross-selling strategies. This system has the advantage of not needing manual maintenance. Because at this point BalloonShop retains what products were sold, you can now implement a "customers who bought this product also bought . . ." feature.

Increasing Sales with Dynamic Recommendations

In BalloonShop, you'll implement the dynamic recommendations system in the visitor's shopping cart and in the product details page. After adding the new bits to your shop, the product details page will contain the product recommendations list at the bottom of the page, as shown in Figure 11-1.

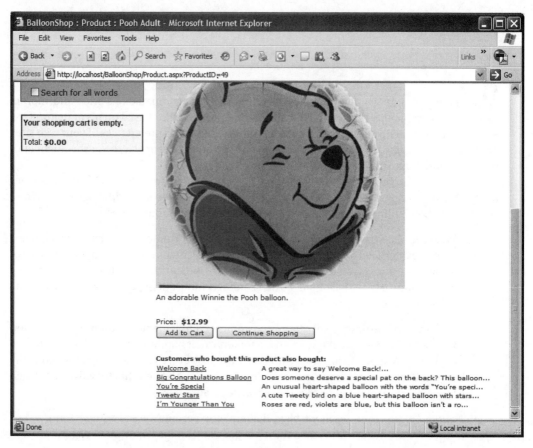

Figure 11-1. *The product details page with the dynamic recommendations system implemented*

The shopping cart page gets a similar addition, as shown in Figure 11-2.

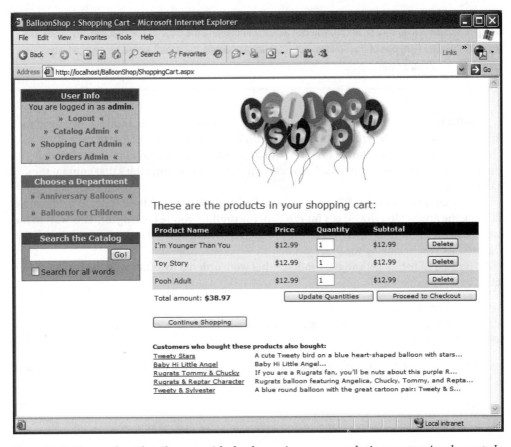

Figure 11-2. *The product details page with the dynamic recommendations system implemented*

Implementing the Data Tier

Before writing any code, you first need to understand the logic you'll implement for making product recommendations. We'll focus here on the logic of recommending products that were ordered together with another specific product. Afterward, the recommendations for the shopping cart page will function in a similar way, but will take more products into consideration.

So you need to find out what other products were bought by customers who also bought the product for which you're calculating the recommendations (in other words, determine "customers who bought this product also bought . . ." information). Let's develop the SQL logic to achieve the list of product recommendations step by step.

■**Tip** Because SQL is very powerful, you can actually implement the exact same functionality in several ways. We'll cover here one of the options, but when implementing the actual stored procedures, you'll be shown other options as well.

To find what other products were ordered together with a specific product, you need to join two instances of the OrderDetail table on their OrderID fields. Feel free to review the "Joining Data Tables" section in Chapter 4 for a quick refresher about table joins. Joining multiple instances of a single table is just like joining different data tables that contain the same data.

You join two instances of OrderDetail—called od1 and od2—on their OrderID fields, while filtering the ProductID value in od1 for the ID of the product you're looking for. This way, in the od2 side of the relationship you'll get all the products that were ordered in the orders that contain the product you're looking for.

The SQL code that gets all the products that were ordered together with the product identified by a ProductID of 4 is

```
SELECT od2.ProductID
FROM OrderDetail od1 JOIN OrderDetail od2 ON od1.OrderID = od2.OrderID
WHERE od1.ProductID = 4
```

This code returns a long list of products, which includes the product with the ProductID of 4, such as this one:

```
ProductID
-----------
1
4
7
10
14
18
22
26
30
1
4
7
10
14
18
4
14
18
22
26
30
```

Starting from this list of results, you need to get the products that are most frequently bought along with this product. The first problem with this list of products is that it includes the product with the ProductID of 4. To eliminate it from the list (because, of course, you can't put it in the recommendations list), you simply add one more rule to the WHERE clause:

```
SELECT od2.ProductID
FROM OrderDetail od1
JOIN OrderDetail od2 ON od1.OrderID = od2.OrderID
WHERE od1.ProductID = 4 and od2.ProductID != 4
```

Not surprisingly, you get a list of products that is similar to the previous one, except it doesn't contain the product with a ProductID of 4 anymore:

```
ProductID
-----------
1
7
10
14
18
22
26
30
1
7
10
14
18
14
18
22
26
30
```

Now the list of returned products is shorter, but it contains multiple entries for the products that were ordered more than once in the orders that contain the product identifier 4. To get the most relevant recommendations, you need to see which products appear more frequently in this list. You do this by grouping the results of the previous query by ProductID and sorting in descending order by how many times each product appears in the list (this number is given by the Rank calculated column in the following code snippet):

```
SELECT od2.ProductID, COUNT(od2.ProductID) AS Rank
FROM OrderDetail od1
JOIN OrderDetail od2 ON od1.OrderID = od2.OrderID
WHERE od1.ProductID = 4 AND od2.ProductID != 4
GROUP BY od2.ProductID
ORDER BY Rank DESC
```

This query now returns a list such as the following:

```
ProductID    rank
-----------  -----------
14           3
18           3
22           2
26           2
30           2
1            2
7            2
10           2
```

If you don't need the rank to be returned, you can rewrite this query by using the COUNT aggregate function directly in the ORDER BY clause. You can also use the TOP keyword to specify how many records you're interested in. If you want the top five products of the list, this query does the trick:

```
SELECT TOP 5 od2.ProductID
FROM OrderDetail od1
JOIN OrderDetail od2 ON od1.OrderID = od2.OrderID
WHERE od1.ProductID = 4 AND od2.ProductID != 4
GROUP BY od2.ProductID
ORDER BY COUNT(od2.ProductID) DESC
```

The results of this query are

```
ProductID
-----------
18
14
22
10
7
```

Because this list of numbers doesn't make much sense to a human eye, you'll also want to know the name and the description of the recommended products. The following query does exactly this by querying the Product table for the IDs returned by the previous query (the description isn't requested because of space reasons):

```
SELECT ProductID, Name
FROM Product
WHERE ProductID IN
    (
    SELECT TOP 5 od2.ProductID
    FROM OrderDetail od1
    JOIN OrderDetail od2 ON od1.OrderID = od2.OrderID
    WHERE od1.ProductID = 4 AND od2.ProductID != 4
    GROUP BY od2.ProductID
    ORDER BY COUNT(od2.ProductID) DESC
    )
```

Based on the data from the previous fictional results, this query returns something like this:

```
ProductID   Name
-----------  -------------------------------------------------
18          Love Cascade Hearts
14          Love Rose
22          I'm Younger Than You
10          I Can't Get Enough of You
7           Smiley Kiss Red Balloon
```

Alternatively, you might want to calculate the product recommendations only using data from the orders that happened in the last *n* days. For this, you need an additional join with the `orders` table, which contains the `date_created` field. The following query calculates product recommendations based on orders placed in the past 30 days:

```
SELECT ProductID, Name
FROM Product
WHERE ProductID IN
    (
    SELECT TOP 5 od2.ProductID
    FROM OrderDetail od1
    JOIN OrderDetail od2 ON od1.OrderID = od2.OrderID
    JOIN Orders ON od1.OrderID = Orders.OrderID
    WHERE od1.ProductID = 4 AND od2.ProductID != 4
      AND DATEDIFF(dd, Orders.DateCreated,GETDATE()) < 30
    GROUP BY od2.ProductID
    ORDER BY COUNT(od2.ProductID) DESC
    )
```

We won't use this trick in BalloonShop, but it's worth keeping in mind as a possibility.

Adding Product Recommendations

Make sure you understand the data tier logic explained earlier, as you'll implement it in the `GetProductRecommendations` stored procedure. The only significant difference from the queries shown earlier is that you'll also ask for the product description, which will be truncated at a specified number of characters.

The `GetProductRecommendations` stored procedure is called when displaying `Product.aspx` to show what products were ordered together with the selected product. Add this stored procedure to the `BalloonShop` database:

```
CREATE PROCEDURE GetProductRecommendations
(@ProductID INT,
 @DescriptionLength INT)
AS
SELECT ProductID,
       Name,
       SUBSTRING(Description, 1, @DescriptionLength) + '...' AS Description
FROM Product
```

```
WHERE ProductID IN
    (
    SELECT TOP 5 od2.ProductID
    FROM OrderDetail od1
    JOIN OrderDetail od2 ON od1.OrderID = od2.OrderID
    WHERE od1.ProductID = @ProductID AND od2.ProductID != @ProductID
    GROUP BY od2.ProductID
    ORDER BY COUNT(od2.ProductID) DESC
    )
```

An Alternate Solution Using SubQueries

Because SQL is so versatile, GetProductRecommendations can be written in a variety of ways. In our case, one popular alternative to using table joins is using subqueries. Here's a version of GetProductRecommendations that uses subqueries instead of joins. The commented code is self-explanatory:

```
CREATE PROCEDURE GetProductRecommendations2
(@ProductID INT,
 @DescriptionLength INT)
AS
--- Returns the product recommendations
SELECT ProductID,
       Name,
       SUBSTRING(Description, 1, @DescriptionLength) + '...' AS Description
FROM Product
WHERE ProductID IN
    (
    -- Returns the products that were ordered together with @ProductID
    SELECT TOP 5 ProductID
    FROM OrderDetail
    WHERE OrderID IN
        (
        -- Returns the orders that contain @ProductID
        SELECT DISTINCT OrderID
        FROM OrderDetail
        WHERE ProductID = @ProductID
        )
    -- Must not include products that already exist in the visitor's cart
    AND ProductID <> @ProductID
    -- Group the ProductID so we can calculate the rank
    GROUP BY ProductID
    -- Order descending by rank
    ORDER BY COUNT(ProductID) DESC
    )
```

Adding Shopping Cart Recommendations

The logic for showing shopping cart recommendations is very similar to what you did earlier, except now you need to take into account all products that exist in the shopping cart, instead of a single product. Add the following procedure to your BalloonShop database:

```
CREATE PROCEDURE GetShoppingCartRecommendations
(@CartID CHAR(36),
 @DescriptionLength INT)
AS
--- Returns the product recommendations
SELECT ProductID,
       Name,
       SUBSTRING(Description, 1, @DescriptionLength) + '...' AS Description
FROM Product
WHERE ProductID IN
    (
    -- Returns the products that exist in a list of orders
    SELECT TOP 5 od1.ProductID AS Rank
    FROM OrderDetail od1
      JOIN OrderDetail od2
        ON od1.OrderID=od2.OrderID
      JOIN ShoppingCart sp
        ON od2.ProductID = sp.ProductID
    WHERE sp.CartID = @CartID
        -- Must not include products that already exist in the visitor's cart
        AND od1.ProductID NOT IN
        (
        -- Returns the products in the specified shopping cart
        SELECT ProductID
        FROM ShoppingCart
        WHERE CartID = @CartID
        )
    -- Group the ProductID so we can calculate the rank
    GROUP BY od1.ProductID
    -- Order descending by rank
    ORDER BY COUNT(od1.ProductID) DESC
    )
```

The alternate version of this procedure, which uses subqueries instead of table joins, looks like this:

```
CREATE PROCEDURE GetShoppingCartRecommendations2
(@CartID CHAR(36),
 @DescriptionLength INT)
AS
```

```
--- Returns the product recommendations
SELECT ProductID,
       Name,
       SUBSTRING(Description, 1, @DescriptionLength) + '...' AS Description
FROM Product
WHERE ProductID IN
   (
   -- Returns the products that exist in a list of orders
   SELECT TOP 5 ProductID
   FROM OrderDetail
   WHERE OrderID IN
      (
      -- Returns the orders that contain certain products
      SELECT DISTINCT OrderID
      FROM OrderDetail
      WHERE ProductID IN
         (
         -- Returns the products in the specified shopping cart
         SELECT ProductID
         FROM ShoppingCart
         WHERE CartID = @CartID
         )
      )
   -- Must not include products that already exist in the visitor's cart
   AND ProductID NOT IN
      (
      -- Returns the products in the specified shopping cart
      SELECT ProductID
      FROM ShoppingCart
      WHERE CartID = @CartID
      )
   -- Group the ProductID so we can calculate the rank
   GROUP BY ProductID
   -- Order descending by rank
   ORDER BY COUNT(ProductID) DESC
   )
```

Implementing the Business Tier

The business tier of the product recommendations system consists of two methods named GetRecommendations. One of them is located in the CatalogAccess class and retrieves recommendations for a product details page, and the other one is located in the ShoppingCartAccess class and retrieves recommendations to be displayed in the visitor's shopping cart.

Add this GetRecommendations method to your CatalogAccess class:

```
// gets product recommendations
public static DataTable GetRecommendations(string productId)
{
  // get a configured DbCommand object
  DbCommand comm = GenericDataAccess.CreateCommand();
  // set the stored procedure name
  comm.CommandText = "GetProductRecommendations";
  // create a new parameter
  DbParameter param = comm.CreateParameter();
  param.ParameterName = "@ProductID";
  param.Value = productId;
  param.DbType = DbType.Int32;
  comm.Parameters.Add(param);
  // create a new parameter
  param = comm.CreateParameter();
  param.ParameterName = "@DescriptionLength";
  param.Value = BalloonShopConfiguration.ProductDescriptionLength;
  param.DbType = DbType.Int32;
  comm.Parameters.Add(param);
  // execute the stored procedure
  return GenericDataAccess.ExecuteSelectCommand(comm);
}
```

Add this version of the GetRecommendations method to your ShoppingCartAccess class:

```
// gets product recommendations for the shopping cart
public static DataTable GetRecommendations()
{
  // get a configured DbCommand object
  DbCommand comm = GenericDataAccess.CreateCommand();
  // set the stored procedure name
  comm.CommandText = "GetShoppingCartRecommendations";
  // create a new parameter
  DbParameter param = comm.CreateParameter();
  param.ParameterName = "@CartID";
  param.Value = shoppingCartId;
  param.DbType = DbType.String;
  param.Size = 36;
  comm.Parameters.Add(param);
  // create a new parameter
  param = comm.CreateParameter();
  param.ParameterName = "@DescriptionLength";
  param.Value = BalloonShopConfiguration.ProductDescriptionLength;
  param.DbType = DbType.Int32;
  comm.Parameters.Add(param);
  // execute the stored procedure
  return GenericDataAccess.ExecuteSelectCommand(comm);
}
```

Implementing the Presentation Tier

Creating the user interface for product recommendations implies three major steps:

- Creating a new Web User Control that displays the product recommendations. This new control will be named ProductRecommendations.ascx.

- Adding ProductRecommendations.ascx to Product.aspx, where it must display the "customers who bought this product also bought:" list.

- Adding ProductRecommendations.ascx to ShoppingCart.aspx, where it displays the "customers who bought these products also bought:" list.

Let's do these steps in the following exercise.

Exercise: Creating the User Interface

1. Add the following styles to **BalloonShop.css**:

```
.RecommendationHead
{
  color: Black;
  font-family: Verdana, Helvetica, sans-serif;
  font-weight: bold;
  font-size: 10px;
}
.RecommendationText
{
  color: Black;
  font-family: Verdana, Helvetica, sans-serif;
  font-size: 10px;
}
.RecommendationLink
{
  color: Black;
  font-family: Verdana, Helvetica, sans-serif;
  text-decoration: underline;
  font-size: 10px;
}
a.RecommendationLink:hover
{
  color: Red;
}
```

2. Add a new Web User Control named **ProductRecommendations.ascx** to your **UserControls** folder.

3. Write this code in the **Source View** window of the control, representing a DataList showing the product recommendations list:

```
<asp:Label ID="recommendationsHeader" runat="server"
CssClass="RecommendationHead" />
<asp:DataList ID="list" runat="server">
  <ItemTemplate>
    <table cellpadding="0" cellspacing="0">
      <tr>
        <td width="170px">
          <a class="RecommendationLink"
            href='Product.aspx?ProductID=<%# Eval("ProductID") %>'>
            <%# Eval("Name") %>
          </a>
        </td>
        <td class="RecommendationText" valign="top">
          <%# Eval("Description") %>
        </td>
      </tr>
    </table>
  </ItemTemplate>
</asp:DataList>
```

4. Switch to the code-behind file, change **Page_Load** to **Page_PreRender**, and complete its code like this:

```
protected void Page_PreRender(object sender, EventArgs e)
{
  // Get the currently loaded page
  string currentLocation = Request.AppRelativeCurrentExecutionFilePath;
  // If we're in Product.aspx...
  if (currentLocation == "~/Product.aspx")
  {
    // get the product ID
    string productId = Request.QueryString["ProductID"];
    // get product recommendations
    DataTable table;
    // display recommendations
    table = CatalogAccess.GetRecommendations(productId);
    list.DataSource = table;
    list.DataBind();
    // display header
    if (table.Rows.Count > 0)
      recommendationsHeader.Text =
        "Customers who bought this product also bought:";
    else
      recommendationsHeader.Text = "";
  }
```

```
    // If we're in ShoppingCart.aspx...
    else if (currentLocation == "~/ShoppingCart.aspx")
    {
      // get product recommendations
      DataTable table;
      // display recommendations
      table = ShoppingCartAccess.GetRecommendations();
      list.DataSource = table;
      list.DataBind();
      // display header
      if (table.Rows.Count > 0)
        recommendationsHeader.Text =
          "Customers who bought these products also bought:";
      else
        recommendationsHeader.Text = "";
    }
}
```

5. Open Product.aspx in **Design View** and drag ProductRecommendations.ascx from the **Solution Explorer** to the bottom of the form. Your new form will look like Figure 11-3.

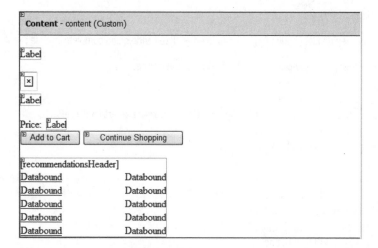

Figure 11-3. *Product.aspx in Design View*

6. Now do the same for ShoppingCart.aspx. Open ShoppingCart.aspx in **Design View** and drag ProductRecommendations.ascx from the **Solution Explorer** to the bottom of the form, as shown in Figure 11-4.

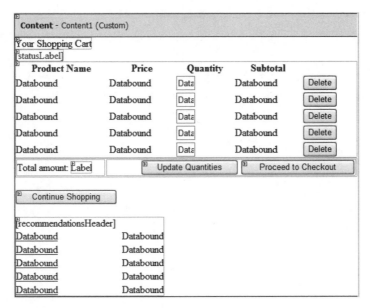

Figure 11-4. *Product.aspx in Design View*

7. Test your web site now to ensure that the new functionality works as expected. The results should resemble the screenshots presented at the beginning of this chapter.

How It Works: Showing Product Recommendations

The most complex part of this new functionality is creating the database stored procedures. In this exercise, you just needed to display the calculated products inside the Product.aspx and ShoppingCart.aspx Web Forms. The Page_PreRender event handler is used instead of Page_Load to ensure that the recommendations list is properly updated *after* the shopping cart changes, in case the visitor deletes products from the cart.

Summary

In this short chapter, you added a new and interesting functionality to the BalloonShop web site. With product recommendations, you have more chances to convince visitors to buy products from the BalloonShop web site.

In the next chapter, you'll enter the third stage of development by adding customer accounts functionality.

CHAPTER 12

■ ■ ■

Adding Customer Accounts

So far in this book, you've built a basic (but functional) site and hooked it into PayPal for taking payments and confirming orders. In this last section of the book, you'll take things a little further. By cutting out PayPal from the ordering process, you can gain better control and reduce overheads. This isn't as complicated as you might think, but you must be careful to do things right.

This chapter lays the groundwork for this task by implementing a customer account system.

To make e-commerce sites more user-friendly, details such as credit card numbers are stored in a database so that visitors don't have to retype this information each time they place an order. The customer account system you'll implement will do this and will include all the web pages required for entering such details.

As well as implementing these web pages, you'll need to take several other factors into account. First, simply placing credit card numbers, expiry dates, and so on into a database in plain text isn't ideal. This method might expose this data to unscrupulous people with access to the database. This could occur remotely or be perpetrated by individuals within your client's organization. Rather than enforcing a prohibitively restrictive access policy to such data, it's much easier to encrypt sensitive information and retrieve it programmatically when required. You'll create a security library to make this easier.

Secondly, secure communications are important because you'll be capturing sensitive information such as credit card details via the Web. You can't just put a form up for people to access via HTTP and allow them to send it to you because the data could be intercepted. You'll learn how to use SSL over HTTPS connections to solve this problem.

You'll be taking the BalloonShop application to the point where you can move on and implement your own backend order pipeline in the next chapters.

Handling Customer Accounts

You can handle customer account functionality in web sites in many ways. In general, however, they share the following features:

- Customers log in via a login page or dialog box to get access to secured areas of the web site.

- Once logged in, the Web Application remembers the customer until the customer logs out (either manually via a Log Out button or automatically if the session times out or a server error occurs).

- All secure pages in a Web Application need to check whether a customer is logged in before allowing access.

First, let's look at the general implementation details for the BalloonShop e-commerce site.

Creating a BalloonShop Customer Account Scheme

Actually, you've already done a lot of the work here—back in Chapter 9, you implemented a system whereby site administrators can log in and, among other things, edit products in the catalog. You did this using **forms authentication**, and you created a login page, Login.aspx, to allow users in an Administrators role to log in. The current login status, that is, whether a user is logged in, is shown using a user control you created, Login.ascx.

In this chapter, you'll take things a little further by extending the system for use with customers. You must make several changes to enable this, but the starting point is to include a new role, in addition to Administrators, which we'll call (surprisingly enough) Customers. Customers will then log in using the same login page as administrators, but because they are in a different role, the similarity ends there. They will not, for example, have access to the administration tools that administrators can use. They will, however, have access to a **customer details page**, where they can view and edit address, contact, and credit card details prior to placing an order. Another major addition is that of a **registration page**, where new customers can sign up on the site.

As you can see, the amount of user data you need to store has increased now that you're catering to customers, with address data and so on needing somewhere to live. Luckily, ASP.NET introduces the concept of **user profiles**, a flexible storage system that fits this need perfectly, with minimal effort. Later in the chapter, you'll see how user profiles can be quickly configured using the web.config file and how you can hook into this information from your code.

Of course, there are alternatives to using the forms authentication system. You could use Microsoft Passport authentication—although many people prefer not to because it ties accounts into a proprietary system and can be time consuming and tricky to set up correctly. You could also use Windows Authentication, where user accounts are associated with Windows accounts stored on the hosting server or in the domain of the hosting server. This solution is great for intranet sites, where users already have domain accounts, but is difficult to set up and maintain for Internet sites, and is usually avoided in such cases. Alternatively, you could implement your own custom system, which gives you the most flexibility at the cost of increased development time.

One important thing you'd have to do in a custom system, as mentioned in Chapter 9, is to secure user passwords. It isn't a good idea to store user passwords in your database in plain text, because this information is a potential target for attack. Instead, you should store what is known as the **hash** of the password. A hash is a unique string that represents the password, but cannot be converted back into the password itself. To validate the password entered by the user, you simply need to generate a hash for the password entered and compare it with the hash stored in your database. If the hashes match, the passwords entered match as well, so you can be sure that the customer is not an imposter. The ASP.NET forms authentication system you'll use in this chapter handles this side of things for you, and ensures that user passwords are stored securely (and in a case-sensitive way, providing enhanced security). However, it's still worth looking at as a general technique, and so the security library you'll create shortly includes hashing capabilities.

Hashing is a one-way system, but to store credit card details securely, you'll need to use a more advanced, bidirectional form of encryption. This enables you to store credit card details securely, but get access to them when you need to; that is, when the customer pays for an order.

The specifics of implementing this scheme in your application include the following tasks:

- Adding a user profile schema to the application

- Modifying the site to allow customer accounts, including registration and detail editing pages

- Modifying ShoppingCart.ascx, which will now redirect the user to a checkout page called Checkout.aspx

The SecurityLib Classes

The two areas you've seen so far where security functionality is required are

- Password hashing

- Credit card encryption

Both tasks can be carried out by classes in the SecurityLib directory, which you'll add as a subdirectory of App_Code. The reason for separating this functionality from the main code of the web site in this case is purely logical. Of course, at some point, you may want to access this code in another application. Having all the relevant files in one place makes it easy to copy elsewhere or even to extract it and put it into a shared class library. To facilitate all this, the classes in the SecurityLib directory are all placed in a separate namespace—also called SecurityLib. Note that to share the code in a class library requires Visual C# Express or the full version of Visual Studio, because Visual Web Developer Express doesn't allow you to create class libraries. The SecurityLib directory contains the following files:

- *PasswordHasher.cs*: Contains the PasswordHasher class, which contains the shared method Hash that returns a hash for the password supplied.

- *SecureCard.cs*: Contains the SecureCard class, which represents a credit card. This class can be initialized with credit card information, which is then accessible in encrypted format. Alternatively, it can be initialized with encrypted credit card data and provide access to the decrypted information contained within.

- *SecureCardException.cs*: Should there be any problems during encryption or decryption, the exception contained in this file, SecureCardException, is thrown by SecureCard.

- *StringEncryptor.cs*: The class contained in this file, StringEncryptor, is used by SecureCard to encrypt and decrypt data. This means that if you want to change the encryption method, you only need to modify the code here, leaving the SecureCard class untouched.

- *StringEncryptorException.cs*: Contains the StringEncryptorException exception, thrown by StringEncryptor if an error occurs.

We'll look at the code for hashing first, followed by encryption.

Hashing

Hashing, as has already been noted, is a means by which a unique value can be obtained that represents an object. In practice, this means doing the following:

1. Serialize the object being hashed into a byte array.

2. Hash the byte array, obtaining a new hashed byte array.

3. Convert the hashed byte array into the format required for storage.

For passwords this is simple because converting a string (which is an array of characters) into a byte array is no problem. Converting the resultant hashed byte array into a string for database storage and quick comparison is also simple.

The actual method used to convert the source byte array into a hashed byte array can vary. The System.Security.Cryptography namespace in .NET contains several algorithms for hashing and allows you to provide your own if necessary, although we won't go into details of this here. The two main hashing algorithms found in the .NET Framework are SHA1 (Secure Hash Algorithm) and MD5 (Message Digest, another name for the hash code generated). SHA1 generates a 160-bit hash (regardless of the size of the input data), whereas MD5 generates a 128-bit hash; therefore, SHA1 is generally considered more secure (although slower) than MD5. The Framework also contains other versions of the SHA1 hash algorithm that generate longer hashes, up to 512 bits, as well as hash algorithms that work using a key (shared secret) and the data to be hashed.

In the SecurityLib implementation, you'll use SHA1, although it's easy to change this if you require stronger security. You'll see the code that achieves this in the PasswordHasher class in the following exercise.

Exercise: Implementing the PasswordHasher Class

1. Create a new subdirectory in the App_Code directory of BalloonShop called SecurityLib.

2. Add a new class file called PasswordHasher.cs with code as follows:

```
using System;
using System.Collections.Generic;
using System.Text;
using System.Security.Cryptography;

namespace SecurityLib
{
  public static class PasswordHasher
  {
    private static SHA1Managed hasher = new SHA1Managed();

    public static string Hash(string password)
    {
```

```
    // convert password to byte array
    byte[] passwordBytes =
      System.Text.ASCIIEncoding.ASCII.GetBytes(password);

    // generate hash from byte array of password
    byte[] passwordHash = hasher.ComputeHash(passwordBytes);

    // convert hash to string
    return Convert.ToBase64String(passwordHash , 0,
      passwordHash.Length);
   }
  }
}
```

3. Add a new web page to the root of the BalloonShop web site called `SecurityLibTester.aspx`, using the usual options for having code in an external file and selecting the default BalloonShop Master Page.

4. Add the following code to `SecurityLibTester.aspx`:

```
<%@ Page Language="C#" MasterPageFile="~/BalloonShop.master"
  AutoEventWireup="true" CodeFile="SecurityLibTester.aspx.cs"
  Inherits="SecurityLibTester" Title="SecurityLib Test Page" %>

<asp:Content ID="Content1"
  ContentPlaceHolderID="contentPlaceHolder" runat="Server">
  Enter your password:<br />
  <asp:TextBox ID="pwdBox1" runat="server" />
  <br />
  Enter your password again:<br />
  <asp:TextBox ID="pwdBox2" runat="server" />
  <br />
  <asp:Button ID="processButton" runat="server" Text="Process"
    OnClick="processButton_Click" />
  <br />
  <asp:Label ID="result" runat="server" />
</asp:Content>
```

5. Modify `SecurityLibTester.aspx.cs` as follows:

```
using System;
...
using System.Text;
using SecurityLib;

public partial class SecurityLibTester : System.Web.UI.Page
{
  ...
```

```
protected void processButton_Click(object sender, EventArgs e)
{
  string hash1 = PasswordHasher.Hash(pwdBox1.Text);
  string hash2 = PasswordHasher.Hash(pwdBox2.Text);
  StringBuilder sb = new StringBuilder();
  sb.Append("The hash of the first password is: ");
  sb.Append(hash1);
  sb.Append("<br />The hash of the second password is: ");
  sb.Append(hash2);
  if (hash1 == hash2)
  {
    sb.Append("<br />The passwords match! Welcome!");
  }
  else
  {
    sb.Append("<br />Password invalid. "
      + "Armed guards are on their way.");
  }
  result.Text = sb.ToString();
 }
}
```

6. Browse to BalloonShop/SecurityLibTester.aspx, enter two passwords, and click **Process**. The
result is shown in Figure 12-1.

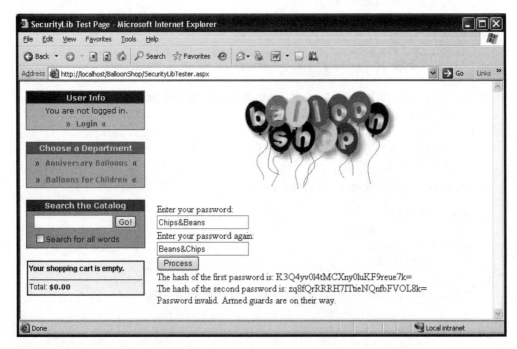

Figure 12-1. *Password hasher result*

How It Works: Implementing the `PasswordHasher` Class

The code in the `PasswordHasher` class follows the steps that were discussed earlier. First, you use the utility function `System.Text.ASCIIEncoding.ASCII.GetBytes` to convert the password string into a byte array:

```
// convert password to byte array
byte[]passwordBytes =
  System.Text.ASCIIEncoding.ASCII.GetBytes(password);
```

Next, you use the private shared member hasher, an instance of SHA1Managed, to generate a hash byte array:

```
// generate hash from byte array of password
byte[] passwordHash = hasher.ComputeHash(passwordBytes);
```

Finally, you convert the hash back into a string by using the utility function `Convert.ToBase64String` and return the result:

```
// convert hash to string
return Convert.ToBase64String(passwordHash , 0,
  passwordHash.Length);
```

All the hash algorithm classes in the .NET Framework use this ComputeHash method to get a hash from an input array of bytes. To increase the size of the hash, you can replace the hasher with another one of these, for example:

```
public static class PasswordHasher
{
  private static SHA512Managed hasher = new SHA512Managed();
  ...
}
```

This change would result in a 512-bit hash, which is probably a bit excessive in this sort of application!

The client page, SecurityLibTest.aspx, hashes two passwords and compares the result. The code is basic enough to ignore for now, but it's important to note that the generated hashes vary a great deal for even simple changes to the input data, even just changes of case—one of the defining features of good hash generation.

Encryption

Encryption comes in many shapes and sizes and continues to be a hot topic. No definitive solution to encrypting data exists, although plenty of advice can be given. In general, there are two forms of encryption:

- *Symmetric encryption*: A single key is used both to encrypt and decrypt data.

- *Asymmetric encryption*: Separate keys are used to encrypt and decrypt data. The encryption key is commonly known as the public key, and anyone can use it to encrypt information. The decryption key is known as the private key, because it can only be used to decrypt data that has been encrypted using the public key.

> ■**Note** In some situations, such as digital signing, the private key is used for encryption, and the public key is used for decryption. However, this doesn't apply to the techniques in this chapter.

Symmetric encryption is faster, but can be less secure because both the encryptor and decryptor know a single key. With Internet communications, there is often no way of ensuring that this key remains a secret from third parties when it is sent to the encryptor.

Asymmetric encryption gets around this by its key-pair method of operation, because the private key need never be divulged, making it much more difficult for a third party to break the encryption. Because the key-pair method requires a lot more processing power, the normal method of operation is to use asymmetric encryption to exchange a symmetric key over the Internet. This key is then used for symmetric encryption, safe in the knowledge that it hasn't been exposed to third parties.

In the BalloonShop application, things are much simpler than with Internet communications—you just need to encrypt data for storage in the database and decrypt it again when required—so you can use a symmetric algorithm.

> ■**Note** Behind the scenes, asymmetric encryption is going on, however, because that is the method used to encrypt the credit card details that are sent over the Internet. You don't need to do much to enable this, as you'll see in the "Secure Connections" section later in this chapter.

As with hashing, several algorithms can be used for both symmetric and asymmetric encryption. The .NET Framework contains implementations of several of these in the System.Security.Cryptography namespace.

The two available asymmetric algorithms are DSA (Digital Signature Algorithm) and RSA (Rivest-Shamir-Adleman, from the names of its inventors: Ronald Rivest, Adi Shamir, and Leonard Adleman). Of these, DSA can only be used to "sign" data so that its authenticity can be verified, whereas RSA is more versatile (although slower than DSA when used to generate digital signatures). DSA is the current standard for digital authentication used by the U.S. government.

The symmetric algorithms found in the .NET Framework are DES (Data Encryption Standard), Triple DES (3DES), RC2 ("Ron's Code," or "Rivest's Cipher" depending on who you ask, also from Ronald Rivest), and Rijndael (from the names of its inventors, John Daemen and Vincent Rijman). DES has been the standard for some time now, although this is gradually changing. It uses a 64-bit key, although, in practice, only 56 of these bits are used because 8 are "parity" bits; because of this, DES is often thought too weak to avoid being broken using today's computers (there are reports that a setup costing $400,000 managed to break DES encryption in three days). Both Triple DES and RC2 are variations of DES. Triple DES effectively encrypts data using three separate DES encryptions with three keys totaling 168 bits when parity bits are subtracted. RC2 is a variant in which key lengths up to 128 bits are possible (longer keys are also possible using RC3, RC4, and so on), so it can be made weaker or stronger than DES depending on the key size. Rijndael is a completely separate encryption method, and has now been accepted as the new AES (Advanced Encryption Standard). This standard is intended to replace DES, and several competing algorithms were considered before Rijndael was chosen. This is the standard that is gradually replacing DES as the most-used symmetric encryption algorithm.

The tasks that must be carried out when encrypting and decrypting data are a little more involved than hashing. The classes in the .NET Framework are optimized to work with data streams so you have a bit more work to do with data conversion. You also have to define both a key and an initialization vector (IV) to perform encryption and decryption. The IV is required due to the nature of encryption: Calculating the encrypted values for one sequence of bits involves using the encrypted values of the immediately preceding sequence of bits. Because no such values exist at the start of encryption, an IV is used instead. In practice, both the IV and the key can be represented as a byte array, which in the case of DES encryption is 64 bits (8 bytes) long.

The steps required for encrypting a string into an encrypted string are as follows:

1. Convert the source string into a byte array.

2. Initialize an encryption algorithm class.

3. Use the encryption algorithm class to generate an encryptor object, supporting the ICryptoTransform interface. This requires key and IV values.

4. Use the encryptor object to initialize a cryptographic stream (CryptoStream object). This stream also needs to know that you are encrypting data and needs a target stream to write encrypted data to.

5. Use the cryptographic stream to write encrypted data to a target memory stream using the source byte array created previously.

6. Extract the byte data stored in the stream.

7. Convert the byte data into a string.

Decryption follows a similar scheme:

1. Convert the source string into a byte array.

2. Fill a memory stream with the contents of the byte array.

3. Initialize an encryption algorithm class.

4. Use the encryption algorithm class to generate a decryptor object, supporting the ICryptoTransform interface. This requires key and IV values.

5. Use the decryptor object to initialize a cryptographic stream (CryptoStream object). This stream also needs to know that you are decrypting data and needs a source stream to read encrypted data from.

6. Use the cryptographic stream to read decrypted data (can use the StreamReader.ReadToEnd method to get the result as a string).

In the BalloonShop code, you'll use DES, but the code in the StringEncryptor class could be replaced with code to use any of the algorithms specified previously.

Exercise: Implementing the StringEncryptor Class

1. Add a new class to the SecurityLib directory called StringEncryptorException with code as follows:

```
using System;
using System.Collections.Generic;
using System.Text;

namespace SecurityLib
{
  public class StringEncryptorException : Exception
  {
    public StringEncryptorException(string message) : base(message)
    {
    }
  }
}
```

2. Add another new class to the SecurityLib directory called StringEncryptor with code as follows:

```
using System;
using System.Collections.Generic;
using System.Text;
using System.Security.Cryptography;
using System.IO;

namespace SecurityLib
{
  public static class StringEncryptor
  {
    public static string Encrypt(string sourceData)
    {
      // set key and initialization vector values
      byte[] key = new byte[] { 1, 2, 3, 4, 5, 6, 7, 8 };
      byte[] iv = new byte[] { 1, 2, 3, 4, 5, 6, 7, 8 };
      try
      {
        // convert data to byte array
        byte[] sourceDataBytes =
          System.Text.ASCIIEncoding.ASCII.GetBytes(sourceData);

        // get target memory stream
        MemoryStream tempStream = new MemoryStream();
```

```
      // get encryptor and encryption stream
      DESCryptoServiceProvider encryptor =
        new DESCryptoServiceProvider();
      CryptoStream encryptionStream =
        new CryptoStream(tempStream,
          encryptor.CreateEncryptor(key, iv),
          CryptoStreamMode.Write);

      // encrypt data
      encryptionStream.Write(sourceDataBytes, 0,
        sourceDataBytes.Length);
      encryptionStream.FlushFinalBlock();

      // put data into byte array
      byte[] encryptedDataBytes = tempStream.GetBuffer();

      // convert encrypted data into string
      return Convert.ToBase64String(encryptedDataBytes, 0,
        (int)tempStream.Length);
    }
    catch
    {
      throw new StringEncryptorException(
        "Unable to encrypt data.");
    }
  }

  public static string Decrypt(string sourceData)
  {
    // set key and initialization vector values
    byte[] key = new byte[] { 1, 2, 3, 4, 5, 6, 7, 8 };
    byte[] iv = new byte[] { 1, 2, 3, 4, 5, 6, 7, 8 };
    try
    {
      // convert data to byte array
      byte[] encryptedDataBytes =
        Convert.FromBase64String(sourceData);

      // get source memory stream and fill it
      MemoryStream tempStream =
        new MemoryStream(encryptedDataBytes, 0,
          encryptedDataBytes.Length);
```

```
        // get decryptor and decryption stream
        DESCryptoServiceProvider decryptor =
          new DESCryptoServiceProvider();
        CryptoStream decryptionStream =
          new CryptoStream(tempStream,
            decryptor.CreateDecryptor(key, iv),
            CryptoStreamMode.Read);

        // decrypt data
        StreamReader allDataReader =
          new StreamReader(decryptionStream);
        return allDataReader.ReadToEnd();
      }
      catch
      {
        throw new StringEncryptorException(
          "Unable to decrypt data.");
      }
    }
   }
  }
}
```

3. Add a new web page to the root of BalloonShop called **SecurityLibTester2.aspx** with the usual options and code as follows:

```
<%@ Page Language="C#" MasterPageFile="~/BalloonShop.master"
  AutoEventWireup="true" CodeFile="SecurityLibTester2.aspx.cs"
  Inherits="SecurityLibTester2" Title="SecurityLib Test Page 2" %>

<asp:Content ID="Content1"
  ContentPlaceHolderID="contentPlaceHolder" runat="Server">
  Enter data to encrypt:<br />
  <asp:TextBox ID="encryptBox" runat="server" />
  <br />
  Enter data to decrypt:<br />
  <asp:TextBox ID="decryptBox" runat="server" />
  <br />
  <asp:Button ID="processButton" runat="server" Text="Process"
    OnClick="processButton_Click" />
  <br />
  <asp:Label ID="result" runat="server" />
</asp:Content>
```

4. Modify the code in `SecurityLibTester2.aspx.cs` in `SecurityLibTester` as follows:

```
using System;
...
using System.Text;
using SecurityLib;

public partial class SecurityLibTester2 : System.Web.UI.Page
{
  ...

  protected void processButton_Click(object sender, EventArgs e)
  {
    string stringToEncrypt = encryptBox.Text;
    string stringToDecrypt = decryptBox.Text;
    string encryptedString =
      StringEncryptor.Encrypt(stringToEncrypt);
    if (stringToDecrypt == "")
    {
      stringToDecrypt = encryptedString;
    }
    string decryptedString =
      StringEncryptor.Decrypt(stringToDecrypt);

    StringBuilder sb = new StringBuilder();
    sb.Append("Encrypted data: ");
    sb.Append(encryptedString);
    sb.Append("<br />Decrypted data: ");
    sb.Append(decryptedString);
    result.Text = sb.ToString();
  }
}
```

5. Browse to `BalloonShop/SecurityLibTester2.aspx`, enter a string to encrypt in the first text box (leave the second text box blank unless you have a ready-encoded string to decrypt), and click **Process**. The result is shown in Figure 12-2.

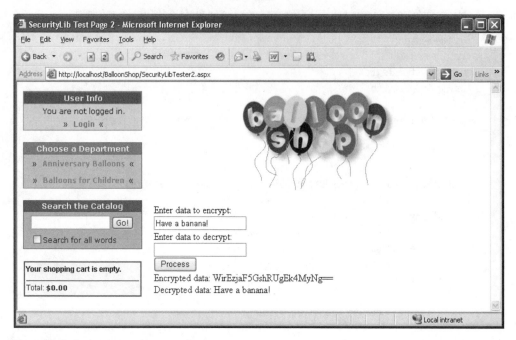

Figure 12-2. *String encryption result*

How It Works: Implementing the `StringEncryptor` Class

The `StringEncryptor` class has two shared methods, `Encrypt` and `Decrypt`, which encrypt and decrypt data. We'll look at each of these in turn.

`Encrypt` starts by defining two hard-coded byte arrays for the key and IV used in encryption:

```
public static string Encrypt(string sourceData)
{
  // set key and initialization vector values
  byte[] key = new byte[] { 1, 2, 3, 4, 5, 6, 7, 8 };
  byte[] iv = new byte[] { 1, 2, 3, 4, 5, 6, 7, 8 };
```

Both these arrays are set to temporary values here. They could just as easily take any other values, depending on the key you want to use. Alternatively, they could be loaded from disk, although having the values compiled into your code in this way could stop people from discovering the values used quite effectively. This method isn't foolproof—the data could be extracted if anyone gets access to your DLLs (Dynamic Link Libraries), but it's secure enough for our purposes. Note that you initialize these values each time the method is called rather than using constant values. One reason for this is that the `iv` array is modified as part of the encryption process, so the values would be different if you didn't re-initialize it. In effect, this would mean that the first few bytes of the decrypted data would be garbled. Therefore, you should use your own values, not the temporary ones used in the previous code snippet. You can use the classes and methods in the `System.Security.Cryptography` namespace to generate such values automatically, or you can just insert random numbers.

■**Tip** You could restrict access to this assembly to code that has been compiled using a particular key. This is possible if you strongly name your assemblies and configure code access security yourself, and you want to prevent people from using the SecurityLib assembly to decrypt credit card details from outside the BalloonShop application, unless they had access to the signature key. However, this is an advanced topic and won't be covered here.

The encryption code is contained in a try...catch block in case an error occurs. The code follows the steps laid out earlier, starting with the conversion of the source string into a byte array:

```
try
{
  // convert data to byte array
  byte[] sourceDataBytes =
    System.Text.ASCIIEncoding.ASCII.GetBytes(sourceData);
```

Next, a MemoryStream object is initialized, which is used to store encrypted data:

```
// get target memory stream
MemoryStream tempStream = new MemoryStream();
```

Now you get the encryptor object, in this case, an instance of the DESCryptoServiceProvider class, and use it with the key and IV created earlier to generate a CryptoStream object (specifying an encryption operation via the CreateEncryptor method and CryptoStreamMode.Write mode):

```
// get target memory stream
MemoryStream tempStream = new MemoryStream();

// get encryptor and encryption stream
DESCryptoServiceProvider encryptor =
  new DESCryptoServiceProvider();
CryptoStream encryptionStream =
  new CryptoStream(tempStream,
    encryptor.CreateEncryptor(key, iv),
    CryptoStreamMode.Write);
```

If you wanted to substitute a different encryption algorithm, this is where you would change the code (although you might also have to change the amount of data contained in the key and IV arrays).

■**Note** Note that the suffix of this class is CryptoServiceProvider. This indicates an unmanaged implementation of the DES encryption algorithm. There is no managed implementation of this algorithm in the .NET Framework, although there is a managed implementation of the Rijndael algorithm. In practice, however, this makes little (if any) difference to application performance.

The next section of code performs the actual encryption, writing the resultant byte array to the `MemoryStream` created earlier:

```
// encrypt data
encryptionStream.Write(sourceDataBytes, 0,
  sourceDataBytes.Length);
encryptionStream.FlushFinalBlock();
```

The `FlushFinalBlock` call here is essential. Without this call, unwritten data might be left in the buffer of the `CryptoStream`. This call forces the stream writing to complete so that all the data you require is contained in the `MemoryStream` object.

Next, you grab the data from the `MemoryStream` and place it into a byte array:

```
// put data into byte array
byte[] encryptedDataBytes = tempStream.GetBuffer();
```

Finally, you convert the resultant byte array into a string and return it:

```
// convert encrypted data into string
return Convert.ToBase64String(encryptedDataBytes, 0,
  (int)tempStream.Length);
```

If anything goes wrong during this process, a `StringEncryptorException` exception is thrown:

```
catch
{
  throw new StringEncryptorException(
    "Unable to encrypt data.");
}
}
```

Note that this exception class doesn't do very much, and you might think that just throwing a standard `Exception` would be good enough. However, by creating your own type, it's possible for Structured Exception Handling (SEH) code that uses this class to test for the specific type of this new exception, filtering out `StringEncryptorException` exceptions from others that might occur.

TheDecrypt method is very similar to `Encrypt`. You start in the same way by initializing the key and IV before moving into a `try...catch` block and converting the source string into a byte array:

```
public static string Decrypt(string sourceData)
{
  // set key and initialization vector values
  byte[] key = new byte[] { 1, 2, 3, 4, 5, 6, 7, 8 };
  byte[] iv = new byte[] { 1, 2, 3, 4, 5, 6, 7, 8 };
  try
  {
    // convert data to byte array
    byte[] encryptedDataBytes =
      Convert.FromBase64String(sourceData);
```

This time, however, you need a stream that is filled with this source byte array because the `CryptoStream` will be reading from a stream rather than writing to one:

```
// get source memory stream and fill it
MemoryStream tempStream =
  new MemoryStream(encryptedDataBytes, 0,
    encryptedDataBytes.Length);
```

The next code snippet is similar, although you use the `CreateDecryptor` method and `CryptoStreamMode.Read` mode to specify decryption:

```
// get decryptor and decryption stream
DESCryptoServiceProvider decryptor =
  new DESCryptoServiceProvider();
CryptoStream decryptionStream =
  new CryptoStream(tempStream,
    decryptor.CreateDecryptor(key, iv),
    CryptoStreamMode.Read);
```

Finally, you get the decrypted data out of the `CryptoStream` using a `StreamReader` object, which handily allows you to grab the data straight into a string for returning. As with `Encrypt`, the last step is to add the code that throws a `StringEncryptorException` exception if anything goes wrong:

```
// decrypt data
StreamReader allDataReader =
  new StreamReader(decryptionStream);
return allDataReader.ReadToEnd();
}
catch
{
  throw new StringEncryptorException(
    "Unable to decrypt data.");
}
}
```

The client code for this class simply encrypts and decrypts data, demonstrating that things are working properly. The code for this is very simple, so it's not detailed here.

Now that you have the `StringEncryptor` class code, the last step in creating the `SecureLib` library is to add the `SecureCard` class.

Exercise: Implementing the SecureCard Class

1. Add a new class to the SecurityLib directory called SecureCardException.cs with code as follows:

```
using System;

namespace SecurityLib
{
  public class SecureCardException : Exception
  {
    public SecureCardException(string message)
      : base(message)
    {
    }
  }
}
```

2. Add another new file to the SecurityLib directory called SecureCard.cs with code as follows:

```
using System;
using System.Collections.Generic;
using System.Text;
using System.Xml;

namespace SecurityLib
{
  public class SecureCard
  {
    private bool isDecrypted = false;
    private bool isEncrypted = false;
    private string cardHolder;
    private string cardNumber;
    private string issueDate;
    private string expiryDate;
    private string issueNumber;
    private string cardType;
    private string encryptedData;
    private XmlDocument xmlCardData;

    private SecureCard()
    {
      // private default constructor
    }
```

```
public SecureCard(string newEncryptedData)
{
  // constructor for use with encrypted data
  encryptedData = newEncryptedData;
  DecryptData();
}

public SecureCard(string newCardHolder,
  string newCardNumber, string newIssueDate,
  string newExpiryDate, string newIssueNumber,
  string newCardType)
{
  // constructor for use with decrypted data
  cardHolder = newCardHolder;
  cardNumber = newCardNumber;
  issueDate = newIssueDate;
  expiryDate = newExpiryDate;
  issueNumber = newIssueNumber;
  cardType = newCardType;
  EncryptData();
}

private void CreateXml()
{
  // encode card details as XML document
  xmlCardData = new XmlDocument();
  XmlElement documentRoot =
    xmlCardData.CreateElement("CardDetails");
  XmlElement child;

  child = xmlCardData.CreateElement("CardHolder");
  child.InnerXml = cardHolder;
  documentRoot.AppendChild(child);

  child = xmlCardData.CreateElement("CardNumber");
  child.InnerXml = cardNumber;
  documentRoot.AppendChild(child);

  child = xmlCardData.CreateElement("IssueDate");
  child.InnerXml = issueDate;
  documentRoot.AppendChild(child);

  child = xmlCardData.CreateElement("ExpiryDate");
  child.InnerXml = expiryDate;
  documentRoot.AppendChild(child);
```

```
      child = xmlCardData.CreateElement("IssueNumber");
      child.InnerXml = issueNumber;
      documentRoot.AppendChild(child);

      child = xmlCardData.CreateElement("CardType");
      child.InnerXml = cardType;
      documentRoot.AppendChild(child);
      xmlCardData.AppendChild(documentRoot);
    }

    private void ExtractXml()
    {
      // get card details out of XML document
      cardHolder =
        xmlCardData.GetElementsByTagName(
          "CardHolder").Item(0).InnerXml;
      cardNumber =
        xmlCardData.GetElementsByTagName(
          "CardNumber").Item(0).InnerXml;
      issueDate =
        xmlCardData.GetElementsByTagName(
          "IssueDate").Item(0).InnerXml;
      expiryDate =
        xmlCardData.GetElementsByTagName(
          "ExpiryDate").Item(0).InnerXml;
      issueNumber =
        xmlCardData.GetElementsByTagName(
          "IssueNumber").Item(0).InnerXml;
      cardType =
        xmlCardData.GetElementsByTagName(
          "CardType").Item(0).InnerXml;
    }

    private void EncryptData()
    {
      try
      {
        // put data into XML doc
        CreateXml();

        // encrypt data
        encryptedData =
          StringEncryptor.Encrypt(xmlCardData.OuterXml);
```

```
      // set encrypted flag
      isEncrypted = true;
    }
    catch
    {
      throw new SecureCardException("Unable to encrypt data.");
    }
  }

  private void DecryptData()
  {
    try
    {
      // decrypt data
      xmlCardData = new XmlDocument();
      xmlCardData.InnerXml =
        StringEncryptor.Decrypt(encryptedData);

      // extract data from XML
      ExtractXml();

      // set decrypted flag
      isDecrypted = true;
    }
    catch
    {
      throw new SecureCardException("Unable to decrypt data.");
    }
  }

  public string CardHolder
  {
    get
    {
      if (isDecrypted)
      {
        return cardHolder;
      }
      else
      {
        throw new SecureCardException("Data not decrypted.");
      }
    }
  }
```

```csharp
public string CardNumber
{
  get
  {
    if (isDecrypted)
    {
      return cardNumber;
    }
    else
    {
      throw new SecureCardException("Data not decrypted.");
    }
  }
}

public string CardNumberX
{
  get
  {
    if (isDecrypted)
    {
      return "XXXX-XXXX-XXXX-"
          + cardNumber.Substring(cardNumber.Length - 4, 4);
    }
    else
    {
      throw new SecureCardException("Data not decrypted.");
    }
  }
}

public string IssueDate
{
  get
  {
    if (isDecrypted)
    {
      return issueDate;
    }
    else
    {
      throw new SecureCardException("Data not decrypted.");
    }
  }
}
```

```csharp
public string ExpiryDate
{
  get
  {
    if (isDecrypted)
    {
      return expiryDate;
    }
    else
    {
      throw new SecureCardException("Data not decrypted.");
    }
  }
}

public string IssueNumber
{
  get
  {
    if (isDecrypted)
    {
      return issueNumber;
    }
    else
    {
      throw new SecureCardException("Data not decrypted.");
    }
  }
}

public string CardType
{
  get
  {
    if (isDecrypted)
    {
      return cardType;
    }
    else
    {
      throw new SecureCardException("Data not decrypted.");
    }
  }
}
```

```
        public string EncryptedData
        {
          get
          {
            if (isEncrypted)
            {
              return encryptedData;
            }
            else
            {
              throw new SecureCardException("Data not decrypted.");
            }
          }
        }
      }
    }
}
```

3. Add a new web page to the root of BalloonShop called **SecurityLibTester3.aspx**, with the usual options and code as follows:

```
<%@ Page Language="C#" MasterPageFile="~/BalloonShop.master"
   AutoEventWireup="true" CodeFile="SecurityLibTester3.aspx.cs"
   Inherits="SecurityLibTester3" Title="SecurityLib Test Page 3" %>

<asp:Content ID="Content1"
   ContentPlaceHolderID="contentPlaceHolder" runat="Server">
   Card holder:<br />
   <asp:TextBox ID="cardHolderBox" runat="server" />
   <br />
   Card number:<br />
   <asp:TextBox ID="cardNumberBox" runat="server" />
   <br />
   Issue date:<br />
   <asp:TextBox ID="issueDateBox" runat="server" />
   <br />
   Expiry date:<br />
   <asp:TextBox ID="expiryDateBox" runat="server" />
   <br />
   Issue number:<br />
   <asp:TextBox ID="issueNumberBox" runat="server" />
   <br />
   Card type:<br />
   <asp:TextBox ID="cardTypeBox" runat="server" />
   <br />
```

```
    <asp:Button ID="processButton" runat="server" Text="Process"
      OnClick="processButton_Click" />
    <br />
    <asp:Label ID="result" runat="server" />
  </asp:Content>
```

4. Modify the code in `SecurityLibTester3.aspx.cs` as follows:

```
using System;
...
using System.Text;
using SecurityLib;

public partial class SecurityLibTester3 : System.Web.UI.Page
{
  ...

  protected void processButton_Click(object sender, EventArgs e)
  {
    SecureCard encryptedCard =
      new SecureCard(cardHolderBox.Text, cardNumberBox.Text,
        issueDateBox.Text, expiryDateBox.Text, issueNumberBox.Text,
        cardTypeBox.Text);
    string encryptedData = encryptedCard.EncryptedData;
    SecureCard decryptedCard = new SecureCard(encryptedData);
    string decryptedData = string.Format(
      "{0}, {1}, {2}, {3}, {4}, {5}",
      decryptedCard.CardHolder, decryptedCard.CardNumber,
      decryptedCard.IssueDate, decryptedCard.ExpiryDate,
      decryptedCard.IssueNumber, decryptedCard.CardType);

    StringBuilder sb = new StringBuilder();
    sb.Append("Encrypted data:<br />");
    sb.Append("<textarea style=\"width: 400px; height: 150px;\">");
    sb.Append(encryptedData);
    sb.Append("</textarea><br />Decrypted data: ");
    sb.Append(decryptedData);
    result.Text = sb.ToString();
  }
}
```

5. Browse to `BalloonShop/SecurityLibTester3.aspx`, enter card details to encrypt, and click **Process**. The result is shown in Figure 12-3.

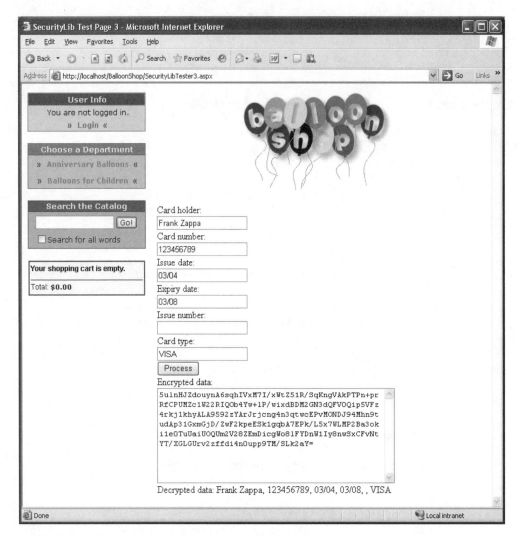

Figure 12-3. *Credit card encryption result*

How It Works: Implementing the SecureCard Class

There is a bit more code here than in previous examples, but it's all quite simple. First, you have the private member variables to hold the card details as individual strings, as an encrypted string, and in an intermediate XML document. You also have Boolean flags indicating whether the data has been successfully encrypted or decrypted:

```
using System;
using System.Collections.Generic;
using System.Text;
using System.Xml;
```

```
namespace SecurityLib
{
  public class SecureCard
  {
    private bool isDecrypted = false;
    private bool isEncrypted = false;
    private string cardHolder;
    private string cardNumber;
    private string issueDate;
    private string expiryDate;
    private string issueNumber;
    private string cardType;
    private string encryptedData;
    private XmlDocument xmlCardData;
```

Next, there are three constructors, a private default one (because you don't want the class to be instantiated with no data), and two for encrypting or decrypting credit card data:

```
    private SecureCard()
    {
      // private default constructor
    }

    public SecureCard(string newEncryptedData)
    {
      // constructor for use with encrypted data
      encryptedData = newEncryptedData;
      DecryptData();
    }

    public SecureCard(string newCardHolder,
      string newCardNumber, string newIssueDate,
      string newExpiryDate, string newIssueNumber,
      string newCardType)
    {
      // constructor for use with decrypted data
      cardHolder = newCardHolder;
      cardNumber = newCardNumber;
      issueDate = newIssueDate;
      expiryDate = newExpiryDate;
      issueNumber = newIssueNumber;
      cardType = newCardType;
      EncryptData();
    }
```

The main work is carried out in the private EncryptData and DecryptData methods, which we'll come to shortly. First, you have two utility methods for packaging and unpackaging data in XML format (which makes it easier to get at the bits you want when exchanging data with the encrypted format):

```csharp
private void CreateXml()
{
  // encode card details as XML document
  xmlCardData = new XmlDocument();
  XmlElement documentRoot =
    xmlCardData.CreateElement("CardDetails");
  XmlElement child;

  child = xmlCardData.CreateElement("CardHolder");
  child.InnerXml = cardHolder;
  documentRoot.AppendChild(child);

  child = xmlCardData.CreateElement("CardNumber");
  child.InnerXml = cardNumber;
  documentRoot.AppendChild(child);

  child = xmlCardData.CreateElement("IssueDate");
  child.InnerXml = issueDate;
  documentRoot.AppendChild(child);

  child = xmlCardData.CreateElement("ExpiryDate");
  child.InnerXml = expiryDate;
  documentRoot.AppendChild(child);

  child = xmlCardData.CreateElement("IssueNumber");
  child.InnerXml = issueNumber;
  documentRoot.AppendChild(child);

  child = xmlCardData.CreateElement("CardType");
  child.InnerXml = cardType;
  documentRoot.AppendChild(child);
  xmlCardData.AppendChild(documentRoot);
}

private void ExtractXml()
{
  // get card details out of XML document
  cardHolder =
    xmlCardData.GetElementsByTagName(
      "CardHolder").Item(0).InnerXml;
  cardNumber =
    xmlCardData.GetElementsByTagName(
      "CardNumber").Item(0).InnerXml;
  issueDate =
    xmlCardData.GetElementsByTagName(
      "IssueDate").Item(0).InnerXml;
```

```
      expiryDate =
        xmlCardData.GetElementsByTagName(
          "ExpiryDate").Item(0).InnerXml;
      issueNumber =
        xmlCardData.GetElementsByTagName(
          "IssueNumber").Item(0).InnerXml;
      cardType =
        xmlCardData.GetElementsByTagName(
          "CardType").Item(0).InnerXml;
    }
```

These methods use simple XML syntax to address data elements.

The EncryptData method starts by using the previous CreateXml method to package the details supplied in the SecureCard constructor into XML format:

```
    private void EncryptData()
    {
      try
      {
        // put data into XML doc
        CreateXml();
```

Next, the XML string contained in the resultant XML document is encrypted into a single string and stored in the _encryptedData member:

```
        // encrypt data
        encryptedData =
          StringEncryptor.Encrypt(xmlCardData.OuterXml);
```

Finally, the isEncrypted flag is set to true to indicate success—or it throws a SecureCardException exception if anything goes wrong:

```
        // set encrypted flag
        isEncrypted = true;
      }
      catch
      {
        throw new SecureCardException("Unable to encrypt data.");
      }
    }
```

The DecryptData method gets the XML from its encrypted form and uses it to populate a new XML document:

```
    private void DecryptData()
    {
      try
      {
        // decrypt data
        xmlCardData = new XmlDocument();
        xmlCardData.InnerXml =
          StringEncryptor.Decrypt(encryptedData);
```

The method then gets the data in the XML document into the private member variables for card details using
ExtractXml and either sets the isDecrypted flag to True or throws an exception, depending on whether the
code succeeds:

```
      // extract data from XML
      ExtractXml();

      // set decrypted flag
      isDecrypted = true;
    }
    catch
    {
      throw new SecureCardException("Unable to decrypt data.");
    }
  }
```

Next, you come to the publicly accessible properties of the class. There are quite a few of these, so we won't show
them all. Several are for reading card detail data, such as CardHolder:

```
  public string CardHolder
  {
    get
    {
      if (isDecrypted)
      {
        return cardHolder;
      }
      else
      {
        throw new SecureCardException("Data not decrypted.");
      }
    }
  }
```

Note that the data is only accessible when isDecrypted is true, so if an exception has been thrown during
decryption, then no data is available here (an exception is thrown instead). Also, note that the data isn't accessible
after encryption—the data used to initialize a SecureCard object is only accessible in encrypted form. This is more
a use-case decision than anything else, because this class is only really intended for encryption and decryption, not
for persistently representing credit card details. After a SecureCard instance has been used to encrypt card details,
you shouldn't subsequently need access to the unencrypted data, only the encrypted string.

One interesting property here is CardNumberX, which displays only a portion of the number on a credit card. This
is handy when showing a user existing details and is becoming standard practice because it lets the customer know
what card they have stored without exposing the details to prying eyes:

```
  public string CardNumberX
  {
    get
    {
      if (isDecrypted)
```

```
    {
      return "XXXX-XXXX-XXXX-"
        + cardNumber.Substring(cardNumber.Length - 4, 4);
    }
    else
    {
      throw new SecureCardException("Data not decrypted.");
    }
  }
}
```

The last property worth looking at is `EncryptedData`, which is used when extracting the encrypted credit card details for database storage:

```
public string EncryptedData
{
  get
  {
    if (isEncrypted)
    {
      return encryptedData;
    }
    else
    {
      throw new SecureCardException("Data not decrypted.");
    }
  }
}
```

The structure here is much like the other properties, although this time the `isEncrypted` flag restricts access rather than the `isDecrypted` flag.

Before moving on to the client code, it's important to explain and justify one design consideration that you have probably already noticed. At no point are any of the card details validated. In fact, this class will work perfectly well with empty strings for any properties. This is so the class can remain as versatile as possible. It's more likely that credit card details will be validated as part of the user interface used to enter them or even not at all. This isn't at all dangerous—if invalid details are used, then the credit card transaction simply fails, and you handle that using very similar logic to that required to deal with lack of funds (that is, you notify the customer of failure and request another card). Of course, there are also simple data-formatting issues (dates are usually MM/YY, for example), but as noted, these can be dealt with externally to the `SecureCard` class.

The client code for this class allows you to see how an encrypted card looks. As you can see, a lot of data is generated, hence the rather large column size in the Customer database. You can also see that both encryption and decryption are working perfectly, so you can now move on to the customer account section of this chapter.

Customer Logins

As mentioned earlier in this chapter, allowing customers to log in to the site simply means using the same login system that administrators use, but defining a Customers role to use rather than an Administrators role. You can do this now using the ASP.NET Web Site Administration Tool as before. This is shown in Figure 12-4.

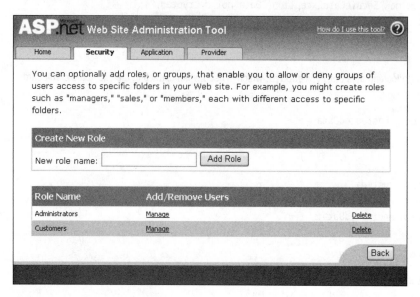

Figure 12-4. *Adding the* Customers *role*

Next, you need to make it possible for customers to create their own accounts. ASP.NET is very helpful here by providing the extremely useful CreateUserWizard control, which (as is becoming a common theme) does most of the hard work for us.

Simply adding a CreateUserWizard control to a page results in the interface shown in Figure 12-5.

Sign Up for Your New Account
User Name:
Password:
Confirm Password:
E-mail:
Security Question:
Security Answer:
Create User

Figure 12-5. *Default* CreateUserWizard *interface*

Just having this control on a site is enough to enable users to add themselves to the membership database. For BalloonShop, however, you'll need to tweak the control a little. Specifically, you'll do the following:

- Format the display of the control.

- Place the control in a `LoginView` control so that only users who aren't logged in can see it.

- Provide a link to the page containing the control so that users who aren't logged in can register.

- Add code behind so that new users are automatically added to the `Customers` role.

- Add a redirect to the customer details page for after the user has registered.

- Make the control send a "welcome" email to the new user.

To keep things simple for now, we'll have the contact details and credit card information for the user editable on a separate page, which we'll look at later in the chapter.

So, let's go ahead and add the new page. At this point, you'll create a fully functioning user registration page and update `UserInfo.ascx` accordingly, but you'll leave the emailing and customer details page unfinished for now.

Exercise: Enabling Customer Registration

1. If you haven't already done so, add the `Customers` role using the **Security** tab of the ASP.NET **Web Site Administration Tool**.

2. Add a new Web Form to the BalloonShop web site called `Register.aspx` by using the usual `BalloonShop.master` Master Page and the code-behind model.

3. In Design View, drag a `LoginView` control into the page content region.

4. Select the `LoggedInTemplate` of the `LoginView` control and add the text `"You are already registered."`, as shown in Figure 12-6.

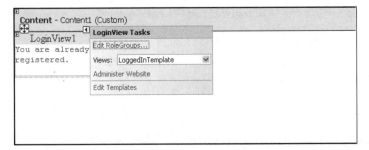

Figure 12-6. *Default CreateUserWizard interface*

5. Select the `AnonymousTemplate` in the `LoginView` control and drag a `CreateUserWizard` control to the template.

6. Autoformat the `CreateUserWizard` control with the `Professional` style.

7. Change the `CreateUserButtonText` property of the `CreateUserWizard` control to `"Sign Up"`.

8. Set the `CancelDestinationPageUrl` and `ContinueDestinationPageUrl` properties of the `CreateUserWizard` control to `~/Default.aspx`.

9. Add an event handler for the `CreatedUser` event of the `CreateUserWizard` control as follows (and, while you're looking at the code behind, add the `Title` attribute configuration code as shown):

```
protected void Page_Load(object sender, EventArgs e)
{
    // Set the title of the page
    this.Title = BalloonShopConfiguration.SiteName +
                " : Register";
}


protected void CreateUserWizard1_CreatedUser(object sender,
    EventArgs e)
{
    Roles.AddUserToRole((sender as CreateUserWizard).UserName,
        "Customers");
}
```

10. In `UserInfo.ascx`, modify the `AnonymousTemplate` to include a link to the registration page as follows:

```
<AnonymousTemplate>
  <tr>
    <td>
      <span class="UserInfoText">You are not logged in.</span>
    </td>
  </tr>
  <tr>
    <td>
       &raquo;
      <asp:LoginStatus ID="LoginStatus1" runat="server"
        CssClass="UserInfoLink" />
       &laquo;
    </td>
  </tr>
  <tr>
    <td>
       &raquo;
      <asp:HyperLink runat="server" ID="registerLink"
        NavigateUrl="~/Register.aspx" Text="Register"
        ToolTip="Go to the registration page"
        CssClass="UserInfoLink" />
       &laquo;
```

```
        </td>
      </tr>
    </AnonymousTemplate>
```

11. Also in `UserInfo.ascx`, add a new `RoleGroup` **Template** to the `RoleGroups` section for users in the
Customers role:

```
<RoleGroups>
  <asp:RoleGroup Roles="Customers">
    <ContentTemplate>
      <tr>
        <td>
          <asp:LoginName ID="LoginName1" runat="server"
            FormatString="You are logged in as <b>{0}</b>. "
            CssClass="UserInfoText" />
        </td>
      </tr>
      <tr>
        <td>
           &raquo;
          <asp:LoginStatus ID="LoginStatus1" runat="server"
            CssClass="UserInfoLink" />
           &laquo;
        </td>
      </tr>
      <tr>
        <td>
           &raquo;
          <asp:HyperLink runat="server" ID="detailsLink"
            NavigateUrl="~/CustomerDetails.aspx"
            Text="Edit Details"
            ToolTip="Edit your personal details"
            CssClass="UserInfoLink" />
           &laquo;
        </td>
      </tr>
    </ContentTemplate>
  </asp:RoleGroup>
  ...
</RoleGroups>
```

■Note This code includes a link to `CustomerDetails.aspx`, the page you'll add shortly to edit address
and credit card details for users. Rather than add this later, it's included here to save some typing later on.

12. Open the BalloonShop application in a browser, click on the `Register` link in the top left, and enter details for a new customer, as shown in Figure 12-7.

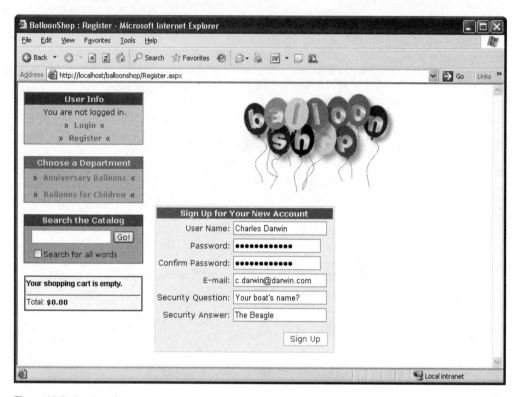

Figure 12-7. *Registering a new user*

13. Click **Sign Up**.

Note You may have your password rejected when you click Sign Up because the ASP.NET membership system applies several rules to passwords, as defined in `machine.config`. By default, passwords require a minimum length of seven characters, including at least one nonalphanumeric character (that is, a symbol character such as [, *, !, and so on). We'll look at how you can change this setting (and provide a more helpful error message) shortly.

---

14. Click Continue and verify that the UserInfo.ascx display is updated as shown in Figure 12-8.

Figure 12-8. *User info display*

How It Works: Enabling Customer Registration

The ASP.NET controls for adding membership functionality to a web site are truly a joy to use. This is the sort of thing that has often taken quite some time to implement and even longer to implement well. Now you can add this functionality in minutes.

Further customization is also possible. You can add any number of wizard pages to the CreateUserWizard control and make things work exactly as you want. For most purposes, however, the default functionality is all you need.

One thing you'll probably want to change, as noted in the exercise, is the set of rules that are applied to password complexity. This is defined by the AspNetSqlMembershipProvider provider contained in machine.config (which you can find in <Windows Install Directory>\Microsoft.NET\Framework\<Version>\ CONFIG\). The code for this provider definition is as follows:

```
<membership>
  <providers>
    <add name="AspNetSqlMembershipProvider"
      type="System.Web.Security.SqlMembershipProvider, System.Web,
        Version=2.0.0.0, Culture=neutral,
        PublicKeyToken=b03f5f7f11d50a3a"
      connectionStringName="LocalSqlServer"
      enablePasswordRetrieval="false" enablePasswordReset="true"
      requiresQuestionAndAnswer="true" applicationName="/"
      requiresUniqueEmail="false" passwordFormat="Hashed"
      maxInvalidPasswordAttempts="5" passwordAttemptWindow="10"
      passwordStrengthRegularExpression="" />
  </providers>
</membership>
```

This definition can include two additional attributes, minRequiredPasswordLength and minRequiredNonalphanumericCharacters, to define the length and complexity of the password, or you can do this in one go using the passwordStrengthRegularExpression parameter. The first two of these attributes aren't included in the default definition, but you can add them yourself. However, be aware that changes you make in machine.config will apply to *all* the web sites on your computer. An alternative is to override the definition of this provider in web.config as follows:

```
<system.web>
  ...
  <membership>
    <providers>
      <remove name="AspNetSqlMembershipProvider" />
      <add name="AspNetSqlMembershipProvider"
        type="System.Web.Security.SqlMembershipProvider,
          System.Web,
          Version=2.0.0.0, Culture=neutral,
          PublicKeyToken=b03f5f7f11d50a3a"
        connectionStringName="LocalSqlServer"
        enablePasswordRetrieval="false" enablePasswordReset="true"
        requiresQuestionAndAnswer="true" applicationName="/"
        requiresUniqueEmail="false" passwordFormat="Hashed"
        maxInvalidPasswordAttempts="5" passwordAttemptWindow="10"
        minRequiredPasswordLength="6"
        minRequiredNonalphanumericCharacters="0"
        passwordStrengthRegularExpression="" />
    </providers>
  </membership>
  ...
</system.web>
```

The passwords used on the BalloonShop site have been restricted to a minimum of six characters, but with no requirement for nonalphanumeric characters. To do this, you have to remove the definition taken from machine.config using a <remove> entry and then add it again using <add>.

■**Note** In the preceding code, the text string for the type attribute is split over multiple lines. If you use this code, remember to place the whole string on a single line to avoid errors.

Whatever complexity you use, it is worthwhile to replace the default password error message for CreateUserWizard, which displays simply "Please enter a different password.". You can do this using the PasswordRegularExpressionErrorMessage property of the CreateUserWizard control. For the preceding complexity, you can use "Your password must be at least 6 characters long.", for example.

The CreateUserWizard control also has a PasswordRegularExpression parameter that you can use to restrict the password. However, any expression you use here applies only to this control—and the restrictions from the membership provider will still be applied (assuming you use the membership provider included with ASP.NET, which we are using here).

One final point to note in the preceding exercise before we move on is the code behind:

```
protected void CreateUserWizard1_CreatedUser(object sender,
  EventArgs e)
{
  Roles.AddUserToRole((sender as CreateUserWizard).UserName,
    "Customers");
}
```

This uses one of the utility classes provided as part of the ASP.NET membership system, Roles, to perform what might otherwise be a much more complicated task—adding a user to a role. The Roles class includes several other useful methods that you might be interested in. The membership system also includes other utility classes for you to use, including Membership and MemberhipUser, as well as Profile, which you'll see in action in the next section.

Customer Details

The next thing to look at is how you store customer details, as well as enable users to edit those details. This is a feature that is common to a huge number of web sites, including a huge proportion of e-commerce sites. In fact, web developers want to implement this feature so often that ASP.NET 2.0 includes a system—**user profiles**—for doing so with very little effort. We'll look at the user profiles feature in some depth shortly.

After you've implemented a customer details scheme you'll also have to implement a Web Form where users can edit their details. This involves some of the code from earlier in the chapter, because credit card details must be encrypted. When you implement this form, you'll also be exposing customer profile details via the ObjectDataSource control. This isn't difficult and is well worth it because you can bind to customer profile data using the handy FormView control. This control includes edit capabilities, so a little work at the beginning will result in a great payoff.

Before you get to this editing page, however, let's take a look at user profiles so you can build your own.

User Profiles in ASP.NET 2.0

The user profile system enables you to define any number of custom data fields that can be stored, along with user login details, in the ASPNETDB database that we're currently using for membership and security information. To tap into this resource, you just declare the fields you want to define for users (along with the data type of those fields) in the web.config file for your application. Behind the scenes, the ASP.NET Framework uses this information to dynamically create classes that you can use to access user details. Functionally, this behavior is exhibited in much the same way that Web Form classes allow you access to controls on a page without ever having to declare them in code-behind files; that is to say, it "just happens" and you can use it.

To declare fields to use in user profiles, you use the <profile> element in the <system.web> section of your web.config file, like so:

```
<profile>
  <properties>
    <add name="param1" type"System.String" />
    <add name="param2" type"System.Int32" />
    <group name="paramGroup1">
      <add name="param3" type"System.String" />
      <add name="param4" type"System.String" />
    </group>
  </properties>
</profile>
```

This information is used to create an object that exposes these properties to the code behind for a Web Form, with the name `Profile`. This object, an instance of a dynamically generated class called `ProfileCommon`, can then be accessed in code behind as follows:

```
Profile.param1 = "New value for param1";
Profile.paramGroup1.param3 = "New value for param3";
```

If a user is logged in, then the preceding code results in these values being stored in the membership database. You can retrieve values from the database in much the same way. And that's pretty much all there is to it. Each user has unique profile values stored in the database, and the preceding code is pretty much all you need to gain access to this information.

Admittedly, we've skimmed over things a little here, for example, data types—you can define whatever data types you want for profile properties as long as they are serializable. Also, in the preceding code, you may note that two properties, `param3` and `param4`, are defined as part of a property group to make things easier. The code to achieve this is so simple that it hardly seemed worth noting.

As with other functionality in the ASP.NET Framework, the preceding behavior is completely customizable. You can, if you want to, create a profile provider to replace this one, adding as much complexity as you need. For the purposes of the BalloonShop application, however, this provides everything you need.

User Profiles in BalloonShop

For the BalloonShop application, you'll use the following profile definition in `web.config`:

```
<profile>
  <properties>
    <add name="CreditCard" type="System.String" />
    <add name="Address1" type="System.String" />
    <add name="Address2" type="System.String" />
    <add name="City" type="System.String" />
    <add name="Region" type="System.String" />
    <add name="PostalCode" type="System.String" />
    <add name="Country" type="System.String" />
```

```
    <add name="ShippingRegion" type="System.String" />
    <add name="DayPhone" type="System.String" />
    <add name="EvePhone" type="System.String" />
    <add name="MobPhone" type="System.String" />
  </properties>
</profile>
```

To keep things simple, all this data is stored in string format. The CreditCard information stored here is an encrypted string that is created using SecurityLib. The ShippingRegion information is actually the ID or a record in the ShippingRegion table, which you'll add as part of the example.

In the next exercise, you'll implement this system, including the custom data-binding scheme. This involves a lot of work and gives us plenty to discuss afterward, but it's well worth the effort!

Exercise: Implementing User Profiles for BalloonShop

1. Add the profile information (shown just before this exercise) to web.config.

2. Add a new table to the **BalloonShop** database called ShippingRegion, with columns as shown in Table 12-1.

Table 12-1. *The ShippingRegion Table*

Column Name	Column Type	Description
ShippingRegionID	int	The ID of the shipping region. Primary key and identity.
ShippingRegion	varchar(100)	The description of the shipping region.

3. Add the values **"Please Select"**, **"US / Canada"**, **"Europe"**, and **"Rest of World"** to the ShippingRegion column in the new table. With auto-numbering of the identity column, "Please Select" should have a ShippingRegionID value of 1—this is important!

4. Add a new class to the **App_Code** directory of the project called **ProfileWrapper**, with code as follows:

```
using System;
using System.Web;
using System.Web.Security;
using SecurityLib;
```

```csharp
/// <summary>
/// A wrapper around profile information, including
/// credit card encryption functionality.
/// </summary>
public class ProfileWrapper
{
  private string address1;
  private string address2;
  private string city;
  private string region;
  private string postalCode;
  private string country;
  private string shippingRegion;
  private string dayPhone;
  private string evePhone;
  private string mobPhone;
  private string email;
  private string creditCard;
  private string creditCardHolder;
  private string creditCardNumber;
  private string creditCardIssueDate;
  private string creditCardIssueNumber;
  private string creditCardExpiryDate;
  private string creditCardType;

  public ProfileWrapper()
  {
    ProfileCommon profile =
      HttpContext.Current.Profile as ProfileCommon;
    address1 = profile.Address1;
    address2 = profile.Address2;
    city = profile.City;
    region = profile.Region;
    postalCode = profile.PostalCode;
    country = profile.Country;
    shippingRegion =
      (profile.ShippingRegion == null
      || profile.ShippingRegion == ""
      ? "1"
      : profile.ShippingRegion);
    dayPhone = profile.DayPhone;
    evePhone = profile.EvePhone;
    mobPhone = profile.MobPhone;
    email = Membership.GetUser(profile.UserName).Email;
```

```
    try
    {
      SecureCard secureCard = new SecureCard(profile.CreditCard);
      creditCard = secureCard.CardNumberX;
      creditCardHolder = secureCard.CardHolder;
      creditCardNumber = secureCard.CardNumber;
      creditCardIssueDate = secureCard.IssueDate;
      creditCardIssueNumber = secureCard.IssueNumber;
      creditCardExpiryDate = secureCard.ExpiryDate;
      creditCardType = secureCard.CardType;
    }
    catch
    {
      creditCard = "Not entered.";
    }
  }

  public void UpdateProfile()
  {
    ProfileCommon profile =
        HttpContext.Current.Profile as ProfileCommon;
    profile.Address1 = address1;
    profile.Address2 = address2;
    profile.City = city;
    profile.Region = region;
    profile.PostalCode = postalCode;
    profile.Country = country;
    profile.ShippingRegion = shippingRegion;
    profile.DayPhone = dayPhone;
    profile.EvePhone = evePhone;
    profile.MobPhone = mobPhone;
    profile.CreditCard = creditCard;
    MembershipUser user = Membership.GetUser(profile.UserName);
    user.Email = email;
    Membership.UpdateUser(user);    try
    {
      SecureCard secureCard = new SecureCard(
          creditCardHolder, creditCardNumber,
          creditCardIssueDate, creditCardExpiryDate,
          creditCardIssueNumber, creditCardType);
      profile.CreditCard = secureCard.EncryptedData;
    }
    catch
    {
      creditCard = "";
    }
  }
}
```

5. For each of the 17 private fields of `ProfileWrapper`, add a corresponding public property. For example, for `address1`, add the following property:

```
public string Address1
{
  get
  {
    return address1;
  }
  set
  {
    address1 = value;
  }
}
```

6. Add a class to **App_Code** called `ProfileDataSource`, with code as follows:

```
using System;
using System.Collections.Generic;

/// <summary>
/// A further wrapper around ProfileWrapper, exposing data
/// in a form usable by ObjectDataSource.
/// </summary>
public class ProfileDataSource
{
  public ProfileDataSource()
  {
  }

  public List<ProfileWrapper> GetData()
  {
    List<ProfileWrapper> data = new List<ProfileWrapper>();
    data.Add(new ProfileWrapper());
    return data;
  }

  public void UpdateData(ProfileWrapper newData)
  {
    newData.UpdateProfile();
  }
}
```

7. Add a new user control to the **UserControls** directory called **CustomerDetailsEdit.ascx**.

8. In the **Design View** for `CustomerDetailsEdit.ascx`, drag an `ObjectDataSource` control onto the page.

9. In `ObjectDataView Tasks,` click `Configure Data Source.`

10. Select `ProfileDataSource` from the drop-down selection, as shown in Figure 12-9.

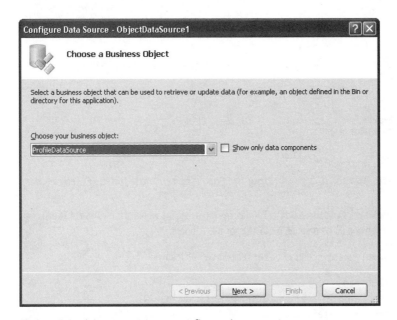

Figure 12-9. *ObjectDataSource configuration, step 1*

11. On the next step of the wizard, select `GetData(), returns List<ProfileWrapper>` for the `SELECT` method and `UpdateDate(ProfileWrapper newData)` for the `UPDATE` method. Leave the `INSERT` and `DELETE` methods blank—users can't add or delete profile information. Click `Finish`.

12. Drag an `SqlDataSource` control onto the page and configure it to use the `BalloonShopConnection` connection string and to get the `ShippingRegionID` and `ShippingRegion` fields from the `ShippingRegion` table. The code for the completed data source control should look as follows in Source View:

```
<asp:SqlDataSource ID="SqlDataSource1" runat="server"
  ConnectionString="<%$ ConnectionStrings:BalloonShopConnection %>"
  SelectCommand="SELECT [ShippingRegionID], [ShippingRegion] FROM
            [ShippingRegion]" />
```

13. In **Design View**, drag a `FormView` control onto `CustomerDetailsEdit.ascx` and choose `ObjectDataSource1` as its data source. The templates are auto-generated from the fields of `ProfileWrapper`, as shown in Figure 12-10.

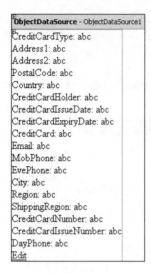

Figure 12-10. *Automatic generation of the FormView template for* `ProfileWrapper`

14. In the **Source View** for `CustomerDetailsEdit.ascx`, delete the whole of the `<InsertItemTemplate>` template, which should be on lines 67 to 128, or thereabouts.

15. Add a `<HeaderTemplate>` and `<FooterTemplate>` as follows:

```
<HeaderTemplate>
  <table border="0" cellpadding="4" cellspacing="0"
    class="UserDetailsTable">
    <tr><td colspan="2" class="UserDetailsTableHead">
      <asp:Label runat="server" ID="TitleLabel" /></td></tr>
</HeaderTemplate>
<FooterTemplate>
  </table>
</FooterTemplate>
```

16. Replace the `<ItemTemplate>` with the following code:

```
<ItemTemplate>
    <tr><td>Address line 1: </td><td width="350px">
      <asp:Label ID="Address1Label" runat="server"
        Text='<%# Bind("Address1") %>' />
    </td></tr>
    <tr><td>Address line 2: </td><td>
      <asp:Label ID="Address2Label" runat="server"
        Text='<%# Bind("Address2") %>' />
    </td></tr>
    <tr><td>City: </td><td>
      <asp:Label ID="CityLabel" runat="server"
        Text='<%# Bind("City") %>' />
    </td></tr>
    <tr><td>Region: </td><td>
```

```
          <asp:Label ID="RegionLabel" runat="server"
            Text='<%# Bind("Region") %>' />
      </td></tr>
      <tr><td>Zip / Postal Code: </td><td>
          <asp:Label ID="PostalCodeLabel" runat="server"
            Text='<%# Bind("PostalCode") %>'>
          </asp:Label>
      </td></tr>
      <tr><td>Country: </td><td>
          <asp:Label ID="CountryLabel" runat="server"
            Text='<%# Bind("Country") %>' />
      </td></tr>
      <tr><td>Shipping Region: </td><td>
          <asp:DropDownList Width="350px" ID="ShippingRegionDropDown"
            runat="server"
            SelectedValue='<%# Bind("ShippingRegion") %>'
            DataSourceID="SqlDataSource1"
            DataTextField="ShippingRegion"
            DataValueField="ShippingRegionID"
            enabled="false">
          </asp:DropDownList>
      </td></tr>
      <tr><td>Daytime Phone no: </td><td>
          <asp:Label ID="DayPhoneLabel" runat="server"
            Text='<%# Bind("DayPhone") %>' />
      </td></tr>
      <tr><td>Evening Phone no: </td><td>
          <asp:Label ID="EvePhoneLabel" runat="server"
            Text='<%# Bind("EvePhone") %>' />
      </td></tr>
      <tr><td>Mobile Phone no: </td><td>
          <asp:Label ID="MobPhoneLabel" runat="server"
            Text='<%# Bind("MobPhone") %>' />
      </td></tr>
      <tr><td>Email: </td><td>
          <asp:Label ID="EmailLabel" runat="server"
            Text='<%# Bind("Email") %>' />
      </td></tr>
      <tr><td>Credit Card: </td><td>
          <asp:Label ID="CreditCardLabel" runat="server"
            Text='<%# Bind("CreditCard") %>' />
      </td></tr>
      <tr><td>
          <asp:Button ID="EditButton" runat="server"
            CausesValidation="False" CommandName="Edit"
            Text="Edit" />
      </td></tr>
</ItemTemplate>
```

17. Replace the `<EditItemTemplate>` with the following code:

```
<EditItemTemplate>
    <tr><td>Address line 1: </td><td width="350px">
      <asp:TextBox Width="340px" ID="Address1TextBox"
        runat="server" Text='<%# Bind("Address1") %>' />
    </td></tr>
    <tr><td>Address line 2: </td><td>
      <asp:TextBox Width="340px" ID="Address2TextBox"
        runat="server" Text='<%# Bind("Address2") %>' />
    </td></tr>
    <tr><td>City: </td><td>
      <asp:TextBox Width="340px" ID="CityTextBox" runat="server"
        Text='<%# Bind("City") %>' />
    </td></tr>
    <tr><td>Region: </td><td>
      <asp:TextBox Width="340px" ID="RegionTextBox"
        runat="server" Text='<%# Bind("Region") %>' />
    </td></tr>
    <tr><td>Zip / Postal Code: </td><td>
      <asp:TextBox Width="340px" ID="PostalCodeTextBox"
        runat="server" Text='<%# Bind("PostalCode") %>' />
    </td></tr>
    <tr><td>Country: </td><td>
      <asp:TextBox Width="340px" ID="CountryTextBox"
        runat="server" Text='<%# Bind("Country") %>' />
    </td></tr>
    <tr><td>Shipping Region: </td><td>
      <asp:DropDownList Width="350px" ID="ShippingRegionDropDown"
        runat="server"
        SelectedValue='<%# Bind("ShippingRegion") %>'
        DataSourceID="SqlDataSource1"
        DataTextField="ShippingRegion"
        DataValueField="ShippingRegionID">
      </asp:DropDownList>
    </td></tr>
    <tr><td>Daytime Phone no: </td><td>
      <asp:TextBox Width="340px" ID="DayPhoneTextBox"
        runat="server" Text='<%# Bind("DayPhone") %>' />
    </td></tr>
    <tr><td>Evening Phone no: </td><td>
      <asp:TextBox Width="340px" ID="EvePhoneTextBox"
        runat="server" Text='<%# Bind("EvePhone") %>' />
    </td></tr>
    <tr><td>Mobile Phone no: </td><td>
      <asp:TextBox Width="340px" ID="MobPhoneTextBox"
        runat="server" Text='<%# Bind("MobPhone") %>' />
    </td></tr>
```

```
    <tr><td>Email: </td><td>
      <asp:TextBox Width="340px" ID="EmailBox" runat="server"
        Text='<%# Bind("Email") %>' />
    </td></tr>
    <tr><td valign="top">Credit Card: </td><td>
      <table cellpadding="0" cellspacing="0" border="0">
        <tr><td width="140px">Cardholder name: </td>
          <td width="200px">
          <asp:TextBox Width="200px" ID="CreditCardHolderLabel"
            runat="server"
            Text='<%# Bind("CreditCardHolder") %>' />
        </td></tr>
        <tr><td>Card type: </td><td>
          <asp:TextBox Width="200px" ID="CreditCardTypeLabel"
            runat="server"
            Text='<%# Bind("CreditCardType") %>' />
        </td></tr>
        <tr><td>Card number: </td><td>
          <asp:TextBox Width="200px" ID="CreditCardNumberLabel"
            runat="server"
            Text='<%# Bind("CreditCardNumber") %>' />
        </td></tr>
        <tr><td>Issue date: </td><td>
          <asp:TextBox Width="200px"
            ID="CreditCardIssueDateLabel" runat="server"
            Text='<%# Bind("CreditCardIssueDate") %>' />
        </td></tr>
        <tr><td>Expiry date: </td><td>
          <asp:TextBox Width="200px"
            ID="CreditCardExpiryDateLabel" runat="server"
            Text='<%# Bind("CreditCardExpiryDate") %>' />
        </td></tr>
        <tr><td>Issue number: </td><td>
          <asp:TextBox Width="200px"
            ID="CreditCardIssueNumberLabel" runat="server"
            Text='<%# Bind("CreditCardIssueNumber") %>' />
        </td></tr>
      </table>
    </td></tr>
    <tr><td>
      <asp:Button ID="UpdateButton" runat="server"
        CausesValidation="True" CommandName="Update"
        Text="Update" /> <asp:Button ID="UpdateCancelButton"
        runat="server" CausesValidation="False"
        CommandName="Cancel" Text="Cancel" />
    </td></tr>
</EditItemTemplate>
```

18. Add the following class definitions to `BalloonShop.css`:

```
.UserDetailsTable
{
    width: 100%;
    background-color: #ccccff;
    font-family: Verdana, Helvetica, sans-serif;
    font-size: 12px;
    border: Solid 2px Navy;
    line-height: 25px;
}
.UserDetailsTableHead
{
    border-bottom: Navy 2px solid;
    background-color: #666699;
    font-family: Verdana, Arial;
    font-weight: bold;
    font-size: 10pt;
    color: #eeeeff;
    padding-left: 3px;
    text-align: center;
}
```

19. Add the following code to `CustomerDetailsEdit.ascx.cs`:

```
public bool Editable
{
  get
  {
    if (ViewState["editable"] != null)
    {
      return (bool)ViewState["editable"];
    }
    else
    {
      return true;
    }
  }
  set
  {
    ViewState["editable"] = value;
  }
}
```

```csharp
public string Title
{
  get
  {
    if (ViewState["title"] != null)
    {
      return ViewState["title"] as string;
    }
    else
    {
      return "Edit User Details";
    }
  }
  set
  {
    ViewState["title"] = value;
  }
}

protected override void OnPreRender(EventArgs e)
{
  // Find and set title text
  Label TitleLabel =
      FormView1.FindControl("TitleLabel") as Label;
  if (TitleLabel != null)
  {
    TitleLabel.Text = Title;
  }

  // Find and set edit button visibility
  Button EditButton =
      FormView1.FindControl("EditButton") as Button;
  if (EditButton != null)
  {
    EditButton.Visible = Editable;
  }
}
```

20. Add a new Web Form to the root of BalloonShop called **CustomerDetails.aspx**, with code as follows:

```
<%@ Page Language="C#" MasterPageFile="~/BalloonShop.master"
  AutoEventWireup="true" CodeFile="CustomerDetails.aspx.cs"
  Inherits="CustomerDetails" Title="BalloonShop : Customer Details" %>
```

```
<%@ Register TagPrefix="uc1" TagName="CustomerDetailsEdit"
  Src="UserControls/CustomerDetailsEdit.ascx" %>
<asp:Content ID="Content1"
  ContentPlaceHolderID="contentPlaceHolder" runat="Server">
  <uc1:customerdetailsedit id="CustomerDetailsEdit1"
    runat="server" />
</asp:Content>
```

21. Modify the `Page_Load` handler in `Customer_Details.aspx.cs` to set the page title:

    ```
    protected void Page_Load(object sender, EventArgs e)
    {
      // Set the title of the page
      this.Title = BalloonShopConfiguration.SiteName +
                   " : Customer Details";
    }
    ```

22. Add the following location security to `web.config`:

    ```
    <!-- Only existing customers can access CustomerDetails.aspx -->
    <location path="CustomerDetails.aspx">
      <system.web>
        <authorization>
          <allow roles="Customers" />
          <deny users="*" />
        </authorization>
      </system.web>
    </location>
    ```

23. In `Register.aspx`, change the `ContinueDestinationPageUrl` property of the `CreateFormWizard` control to `~/CustomerDetails.aspx`.

24. Have a cup of coffee—you've earned it.

25. Fire up a browser and either log in as an existing user and click **Edit Details** or register a new user. Either way, you'll be greeted with the page shown in Figure 12-11.

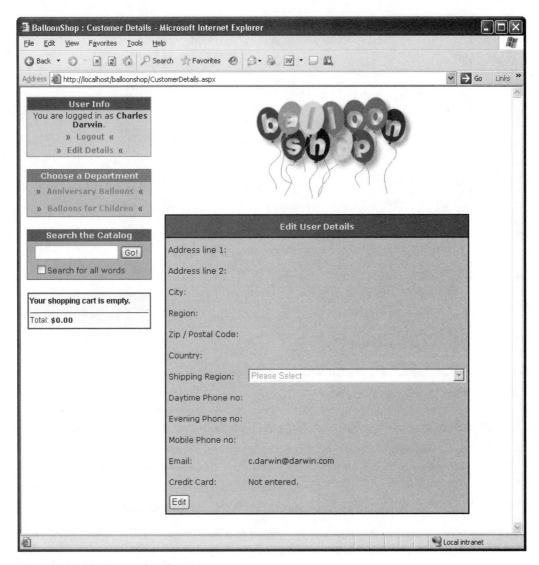

Figure 12-11. *Blank user details page*

26. Click **Edit** and enter some details, as shown in Figure 12-12.

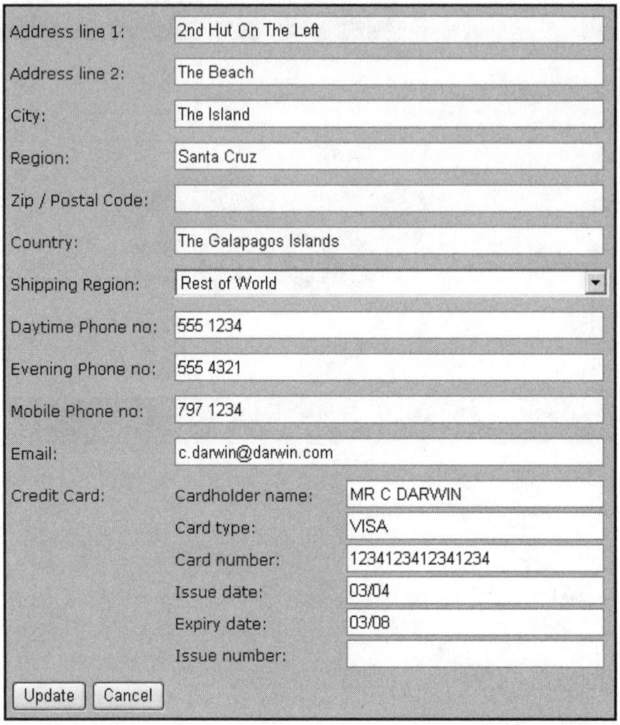

Figure 12-12. *User details page in edit mode*

27. Click **Update** and note how the credit card number is displayed as XXXX-XXXX-XXXX-1234.

28. Log out (you should be redirected to the log in page), and then log back in again as a different user. When you look at the user details for this user, you should see that the details are blank—they are unique to users.

How It Works: Implementing User Profiles for BalloonShop

That was a long exercise! Still, at no point have you seen any particularly complicated code. In fact, most of it was to make the user details edit form look good. Still, there's plenty to analyze, starting with the way that user profile data is exposed to the FormView control via an ObjectDataSource control.

Sadly, there is no direct way to bind user profile data to controls. Many methods are available for doing this (for example, a fellow author and friend, Dave Sussman, created a generic way to do this, see http://blogs. ipona.com/davids/archive/2004/10/29/414.aspx). You could even take the simple option—ignore data binding and build a form yourself, setting Text properties of TextBox or Label controls to appropriate values in the code behind. Because you have encrypted credit card details available, you needed to take a slightly oblique approach to keep the data in the database secure; going with the data-bound approach is also a good test for your ASP.NET development muscles.

To start with, let's look at ProfileWrapper. The code for this class starts with a reference to the SecurityLib library and a bunch of private fields. These fields cover all the fields defined in web.config, along with credit card fields obtained from the SecureCard class in the SecurityLib namespace:

```
using System;
using System.Web;
using System.Web.Security;
using SecurityLib;

/// <summary>
/// A wrapper around profile information, including
/// credit card encryption functionality.
/// </summary>
public class ProfileWrapper
{
  private string address1;
  private string address2;
  private string city;
  private string region;
  private string postalCode;
  private string country;
  private string shippingRegion;
  private string dayPhone;
  private string evePhone;
  private string mobPhone;
  private string email;
  private string creditCard;
  private string creditCardHolder;
  private string creditCardNumber;
  private string creditCardIssueDate;
  private string creditCardIssueNumber;
  private string creditCardExpiryDate;
  private string creditCardType;
```

These fields all have associated public properties, which weren't all listed to save space.

Next, the constructor for the ProfileWrapper class obtains the profile information for the currently logged-in user and populates the preceding fields. Because this class isn't the code behind for a Web Form, you can't use the Page.Profile property to access this information, so instead you used the static HttpContext.Current property to obtain the current context. From this, you get the ProfileCommon instance that you're interested in:

```
public ProfileWrapper()
{
  ProfileCommon profile =
    HttpContext.Current.Profile as ProfileCommon;
```

From this object, you extract all the data you want. Most of this is simply a case of examining properties of the ProfileCommon instance, but in some cases more code is required. For instance, for shippingRegion, we wanted to use a drop-down list rather than a text box (because limited options are available), so we initialized the field accordingly—if profile.ShippingRegion is empty, you instead use the text "1", which matches the ShippingRegionID for "Please Select" in the ShippingRegion table. You could do this for some of the other properties, notably Country, but for simplicity (and brevity) we've kept things simple.

You also extracted the email address of the user by obtaining a `MembershipUser` object via `Membership.GetUser()` and passing the username obtained from the profile as a parameter. You then used the `Email` property of this object to obtain the email address. Strictly speaking, the user's email address isn't part of the user's profile, but it makes sense to expose it here for easy editing.

`creditCard` also needs more work. You needed to decrypt any information stored and use the decrypted data to fill the appropriate fields: `creditCardHolder`, `creditCardNumber`, and so on. Because a decryption failure results in an exception, this decryption is performed in a `try...catch` block.

```
address1 = profile.Address1;
address2 = profile.Address2;
city = profile.City;
region = profile.Region;
postalCode = profile.PostalCode;
country = profile.Country;
shippingRegion =
  (profile.ShippingRegion == null
  || profile.ShippingRegion == ""
  ? "1"
  : profile.ShippingRegion);
dayPhone = profile.DayPhone;
evePhone = profile.EvePhone;
mobPhone = profile.MobPhone;
email = Membership.GetUser(profile.UserName).Email;
try
{
  SecureCard secureCard = new SecureCard(profile.CreditCard);
  creditCard = secureCard.CardNumberX;
  creditCardHolder = secureCard.CardHolder;
  creditCardNumber = secureCard.CardNumber;
  creditCardIssueDate = secureCard.IssueDate;
  creditCardIssueNumber = secureCard.IssueNumber;
  creditCardExpiryDate = secureCard.ExpiryDate;
  creditCardType = secureCard.CardType;
}
catch
{
  creditCard = "Not entered.";
}
}
```

Next the `UpdateProfile` method sets profile data, email data, and credit card details from the data contained in the object instance from which it is called. Again, the code here is simple, with only some minor trickery required to obtain the encrypted form of the credit card data. There's nothing here you haven't seen elsewhere, so there's no need to repeat the code here.

To use object data with the `ObjectDataSource` control, you needed to pass an object supporting `IEnumerable` as the return result of a `SELECT` method. This is because `ObjectDataSource` is designed to work with data lists as well as single data items. `ProfileDataSource` acts as an interface between `ObjectDataSource` and

ProfileWrapper, simply using the IEnumerable that is supporting generic list class List<T> to pass data to ObjectDataSource. The code instantiates an instance of List<ProfileWrapper> and adds a single item, the user's profile data, to this list and then returns it.

```
public List<ProfileWrapper> GetData()
{
  List<ProfileWrapper> data = new List<ProfileWrapper>();
  data.Add(new ProfileWrapper());
  return data;
}
```

Because List<T> actually supports IEnumerable<T>, this is a strongly typed binding, meaning that the UPDATE method is passed an argument of type T when ObjectDataSource calls it. In this case, T is ProfileWrapper, so to update the profile information, you just called the UpdateProfile() method:

```
public void UpdateData(ProfileWrapper newData)
{
  newData.UpdateProfile();
}
```

Next, you used these classes to populate a FormView control via the aforementioned ObjectDataSource control. The templates created needed a bit of modification, because we didn't want to display all the credit card fields on the initial item view. We also wanted to use a drop-down list for the shippingRegion property, and bound that drop-down list to the ShippingRegion table using simple data-binding syntax.

This customization required a lot of code, but most of this was for general display purposes, so there's no real need to go through it in any depth here. Suffice to say that the credit card details get fully displayed for the editing template.

■Note We haven't done it here, but it would be relatively easy to modify this code to enable customers to store multiple credit cards, with one selected as a default to use for purchases. You could, for example, store an array of strings for credit card details, each containing one encrypted card, along with a default card property. Alternatively, you could extend SecureCard to provide a single encrypted string for multiple cards. The only reason this hasn't been done here is to keep things moving—there's no reason to get bogged down in lengthy, uninteresting code at this point. Another feature that's lacking here is the inclusion of validation controls to ensure that required fields are filled in. Again, this is easy to add, but would have filled up another page or so if included here.

You used a user control to store the customer details editing form, CustomerDetailsEdit.ascx. There's a good reason for this—later you'll want to display the same information to customers when they place their orders, giving them a last chance to modify details. To facilitate this reuse, CustomerDetails.ascx.cs includes two public properties, Editable and Title, which can be used to hide the EditButton button and set the title for the FormView control, respectively. This customization happens in the OnPreRender event handler for the control, to cater for the fact that these properties may be set late on in the life cycle of the control, and we still want them to work if this happens. For the Edit Details page, you use the default values for these properties; later you'll supply nondefault values for them.

The page displaying the `CustomerDetailsEdit.ascx` user control (`CustomerDetails.aspx`) needed to have its access limited to users in the `Customers` role, so you added the required security code to `web.config`. Note that the code in `web.config` prevents users in the `Administrators` role from editing profiles. This isn't a problem, however, because administrators don't need to store this information.

Finally, you tested things out by entering some details for a customer and verified that the information added applied only to that customer.

Now that you have this information available, you can move on to the next step—providing a new checkout page.

The Checkout Page

The new checkout page will display an order summary and customer details, which can be reviewed before the customer places an order. This page appears when a customer clicks the Proceed to Checkout button after viewing his shopping cart.

In the next exercise, you'll implement and secure this page.

Exercise: Implementing a new Checkout Page

1. Add a new page to the BalloonShop application called `Checkout.aspx` and modify the code as follows:

```
<%@ Page Language="C#" MasterPageFile="~/BalloonShop.master"
  AutoEventWireup="true" CodeFile="Checkout.aspx.cs"
 Inherits="Checkout" %>

<%@ Register TagPrefix="uc1" TagName="CustomerDetailsEdit"
  Src="UserControls/CustomerDetailsEdit.ascx" %>
<asp:Content ID="Content1"
  ContentPlaceHolderID="contentPlaceHolder" runat="Server">
  <asp:Label ID="titleLabel" runat="server"
    CssClass="ShoppingCartTitle"
    Text="Your Shopping Cart" /> <br />
  <br />
  <asp:GridView ID="grid" runat="server"
    AutoGenerateColumns="False" DataKeyNames="ProductID"
    BorderWidth="1px" Width="100%">
    <Columns>
      <asp:BoundField DataField="Name" HeaderText="Product Name"
        ReadOnly="True" SortExpression="Name" />
      <asp:BoundField DataField="Price" DataFormatString="{0:c}"
        HeaderText="Price" ReadOnly="True"
        SortExpression="Price" />
      <asp:BoundField DataField="Quantity" HeaderText="Quantity"
        ReadOnly="True" SortExpression="Quantity" />
```

```
      <asp:BoundField DataField="Subtotal" DataFormatString="{0:c}"
        HeaderText="Subtotal" ReadOnly="True"
        SortExpression="Subtotal" />
    </Columns>
  </asp:GridView>
  <asp:Label ID="Label2" runat="server" Text="Total amount: "
    CssClass="ProductDescription" />
  <asp:Label ID="totalAmountLabel" runat="server" Text="Label"
    CssClass="ProductPrice" />
  <br />
  <br />
  <uc1:CustomerDetailsEdit ID="CustomerDetailsEdit1" runat="server"
    Editable="false" Title="User Details" />
  <br />
  <asp:Label ID="InfoLabel" runat="server" CssClass="InfoText" />
  <br />
  <br />
  <asp:Button ID="placeOrderButton" runat="server"
    CssClass="ButtonText" Text="Place order"
    OnClick="placeOrderButton_Click" />
</asp:Content>
```

2. Modify **Checkout.aspx.cs** as follows:

```
public partial class Checkout : System.Web.UI.Page
{
  protected void Page_Load(object sender, EventArgs e)
  {
    // Set the title of the page
    this.Title = BalloonShopConfiguration.SiteName +
                 " : Checkout";

    if (!IsPostBack)
      PopulateControls();
  }

  // fill controls with data
  private void PopulateControls()
  {
    // get the items in the shopping cart
    DataTable dt = ShoppingCartAccess.GetItems();
    // populate the list with the shopping cart contents
    grid.DataSource = dt;
    grid.DataBind();
    // setup controls
    titleLabel.Text =
      "These are the products in your shopping cart:";
    grid.Visible = true;
```

```csharp
// display the total amount
decimal amount = ShoppingCartAccess.GetTotalAmount();
totalAmountLabel.Text = String.Format("{0:c}", amount);

// check customer details
bool addressOK = true;
bool cardOK = true;
if (Profile.Address1 + Profile.Address2 == ""
  || Profile.ShippingRegion == ""
  || Profile.ShippingRegion == "Please Select"
  || Profile.Country == "")
{
  addressOK = false;
}
if (Profile.CreditCard == "")
{
  cardOK = false;
}

// report / hide place order button
if (!addressOK)
{
  if (!cardOK)
  {
    InfoLabel.Text =
      "You must provide a valid address and credit card "
      + "before placing your order.";
  }
  else
  {
    InfoLabel.Text =
      "You must provide a valid address before placing your "
      + "order.";
  }
}
else if (!cardOK)
{
  InfoLabel.Text = "You must provide a credit card before "
    + "placing your order.";
}
else
{
  InfoLabel.Text = "Please confirm that the above details are "
    + "correct before proceeding.";
}
placeOrderButton.Visible = addressOK && cardOK;
}
```

```csharp
protected void placeOrderButton_Click(object sender, EventArgs e)
{
    // Store the total amount because the cart
    // is emptied when creating the order
    decimal amount = ShoppingCartAccess.GetTotalAmount();
    // Create the order and store the order ID
    string orderId = ShoppingCartAccess.CreateOrder();
    // Create the PayPal redirect location
    string redirect = "";
    redirect +=
      "https://www.paypal.com/xclick/business=youremail@server.com";
    redirect += "&item_name=BalloonShopOrder " + orderId;
    redirect += "&item_number=" + orderId;
    redirect += "&amount=" + String.Format("{0:c} ", amount);
    redirect += "&return=http://www.YourWebSite.com";
    redirect += "&cancel_return=http://www.YourWebSite.com";
    // Redirect to the payment page
    Response.Redirect(redirect);
}
}
```

3. Add the following class definition to **BalloonShop.css**:

```css
.InfoText
{
    font-family: Verdana, Helvetica, sans-serif;
    font-size: 12px;
}
```

4. Modify **web.config** as follows:

```xml
<!-- Only existing customers can access Checkout.aspx -->
<location path="Checkout.aspx">
  <system.web>
    <authorization>
      <allow roles="Customers" />
      <deny users="*" />
    </authorization>
  </system.web>
</location>
```

5. Modify **ShoppingCart.aspx.cs** as follows:

```csharp
// redirect to the checkout page
protected void checkoutButton_Click(object sender, EventArgs e)
{
    string redirect = "Checkout.aspx";
    // Redirect to the checkout page
    Response.Redirect("Checkout.aspx");
}
```

6. Log in, edit your customer details, and place an order via the shopping cart page. If your details are correct, you should be able to click **Proceed to Checkout**; otherwise, you'll have to add valid customer details before proceeding.

How It Works: Implementing a New Checkout Page

We haven't really done much that is particularly difficult here—most of the work was already done. All we've really done is reorganize existing code to prepare for a new order backend.

The new checkout page, Checkout.aspx, now appears when customers click Proceed to Checkout from the shopping cart view. It displays the current shopping cart using code very similar to—but not identical to—code in ShoppingCart.aspx. The code is different in that editing is no longer possible—quantities and order items are fixed. Checkout.aspx also includes a noneditable version of the CustomerUserDetails.ascx control, customized using the Editable and Title properties you added earlier.

As with ShoppingCart.aspx, you use a code-behind method called PopulateControls() to get and bind to data. The major differences here are that you don't need to check for existing shopping cart items (we know there will be some at this stage), and that you also check for valid address and credit card details before allowing the user to proceed:

```
// check customer details
bool addressOK = true;
bool cardOK = true;
if (Profile.Address1 + Profile.Address2 == ""
  || Profile.ShippingRegion == ""
  || Profile.ShippingRegion == "1"
  || Profile.Country == "")
{
  addressOK = false;
}
if (Profile.CreditCard == "")
{
  cardOK = false;
}
```

This code, which checks the validity of the address and credit card, merits a little extra discussion. First, notice the validation of the address. The address is validated by checking a few of the fields for data (Address1 and Address2 combined *must* contain data for a valid order, and a country and shipping region must be set). This may look overly simple, but it's fine here—if address problems occur further down the line, you can deal with problems as they arise. The shipping region is also interesting because you check for a value of "1", which corresponds to "Please Select" in the database—hence the importance of this record having an ID field value of 1, as noted earlier. As far as credit card details go, you just check that some data is stored, not what that data is. Again, problems here can be dealt with later.

Assuming that the data is okay, the placeOrder button allows users to actually place an order. Notice that the code here is the same code you used in the earlier incarnation of the ShoppingCart.aspx page. In fact, none of the extra details are used. This isn't a problem because you now have everything you need to hook into a proper, fleshed-out order pipeline, as you'll see in subsequent chapters.

A final note—the `web.config` file has again been modified so that users must log in before the checkout page is visible. Using this setting, clicking on Proceed to Checkout takes users straight to the login page if they aren't logged in. This is a nice feature, but really there ought to be more feedback. Some simple text on `Login.aspx` ought to do it:

```
      ...
      </table>
      <span class="InfoText">You must be logged in to place an
        order. If you aren't yet
        registered with the site, click
        <asp:HyperLink runat="server" ID="registerLink"
          NavigateUrl="~/Register.aspx" Text="here"
          ToolTip="Go to the registration page"
          CssClass="UserInfoLink" />. </span>
    </LayoutTemplate>
  </asp:Login>
</asp:Content>
```

Now users will know that they must be registered to place on order and are automatically presented with the tool they need.

Setting Up Secure Connections

Customers can now register on your site, log in, and change details. However, the current system involves sending potentially sensitive information over HTTP. This protocol isn't secure, and the information could be intercepted and stolen. To avoid this, you need to set up the application to work with SSL (Secure Socket Layer) connections using HTTPS (HyperText Transport Protocol [Secure]).

To do this, you have a bit of groundwork to get through first. Unless you've already been using an SSL connection on your web server, you are unlikely to have the correct configuration to do so. This configuration involves obtaining a security certificate for your server and installing it via IIS management.

Security certificates are basically public-private key pairs similar to those discussed earlier in the chapter relating to asymmetric encryption. You can generate these yourself if your domain controller is configured as a certification authority, but this method has its problems. Digital signing of SSL certificates is such that browsers using the certificate will not be able to verify the identity of your certification authority, and may therefore doubt your security. This isn't disastrous, but may affect consumer confidence, because users are presented with a warning message when they attempt to establish a secure connection.

The alternative is to obtain SSL certificates from a known and respected organization that specializes in web security, such as VeriSign. Web browsers such as Internet Explorer have built-in root certificates from organizations such as this and are able to authenticate the digital signature of SSL certificates supplied by them. This means that no warning message will appear and an SSL secured connection will be available with a minimum of fuss.

This section assumes that you take this latter option, although if you want to create your own certificates, that won't affect the end result.

Obtaining an SSL Certificate from VeriSign

Obtaining a certificate from VeriSign is a relatively painless experience, and full instructions are available on the VeriSign web site, (http://www.verisign.com/). You also can get test certificates from VeriSign, which are free to use for a trial period. The basic steps are as follows:

1. Sign up for a trial certificate on the VeriSign web site.

2. Generate a Certificate Signing Request (CSR) via IIS management on your web server. This involves filling out various personal information, including the name of your web site, and so on.

3. Copy the contents of the generated CSR into the VeriSign request system.

4. Shortly afterward, you'll receive a certificate from VeriSign that you copy into IIS management to install the certificate.

There is a little more to it than that, but as noted, detailed instructions are available on the VeriSign web site, and you shouldn't run into any difficulties.

Enforcing SSL Connections

After the certificate is installed, you can access any web pages on your web server using an SSL connection by replacing the http:// part of the URL used to access the page with https:// (assuming that your firewall is set up to allow an SSL connection, which by default uses port 443, if you use a firewall—this doesn't apply to local connections). Obviously, you don't need SSL connections for all areas of the site, and shouldn't enforce it in all places because it can reduce performance. However, you do want to make sure that the checkout, login, and customer detail modification pages are accessible only via SSL. While you're at it, you can also secure the admin pages. This isn't so important at this stage, but later, when you have full order and user admin controls, it doesn't hurt to make things secure here.

There are several ways to achieve this restriction. One way is to configure individual pages via IIS management. Looking at the properties for Login.aspx in IIS management, for example, shows the File Security tab, as shown in Figure 12-13.

■**Note** To access this dialog box, open IIS manager from the Administrative Tools section of Control Panel, navigate through the tree view through IIS/Local Computer/Web Sites/Default Web Site/ BalloonShop, and get the properties for Login.aspx.

From here, you can click the Edit button in the Secure Communications section and tick the Require Secure Channel (SSL) box in the dialog box that appears (don't worry about the other options), as shown in Figure 12-14.

Figure 12-13. *File Security property page*

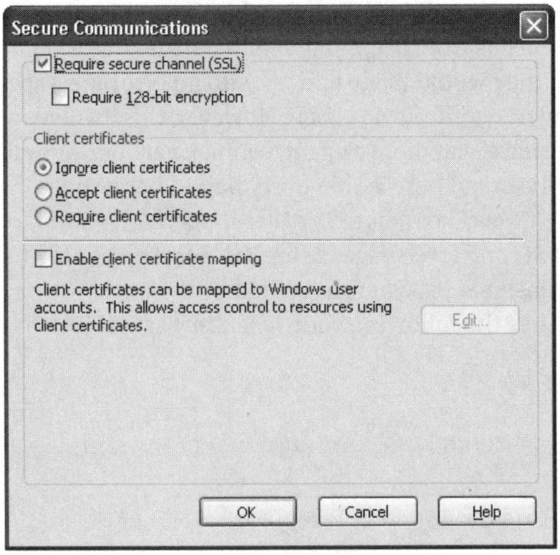

Figure 12-14. *Setting the HTTPS requirement*

After clicking OK, attempts to access the Login.aspx page using HTTP will be rejected. However, this isn't quite the route you want to go down for BalloonShop, because it makes certain things—namely redirections between URLs that start with http:// and URLs that start with https://—slightly difficult to manage. Rather than giving an error message when users attempt to access Login.aspx without SSL, it's better to detect unsecure connections in code and redirect accordingly. This means that users trying to access Login.aspx without SSL are automatically redirected to the same page, but with SSL. Similarly, we want users attempting to use SSL to access a page such as Default.aspx—which doesn't need to be secured—to be redirected to a non-SSL connection to the same page. This results in a seamless experience for users.

We'll look at this in more detail in a moment. First, however, it's worth mentioning an attribute that ASP.NET supplies for use with the <forms> definition in web.config. You can set the attribute requireSSL to true for this element, which will prevent user login cookies from being exchanged over a non-SSL connection. However, this enforces the requirement that, once logged in, users can only be authenticated for pages viewed over SSL. This setting *does not* prevent users from looking at pages such as Default.aspx over a standard HTTP connection. However, user-aware controls (such as UserInfo.ascx in BalloonShop) will not have access to user information unless SSL is used. This attribute is for use only when you are happy to enforce SSL connections site-wide. Because SSL connections introduce a performance hit due to the encryption and decryption required, this isn't recommended for most web sites.

Including Redirections to Enforce Required SSL Connections

One way to enforce SSL connections is to use absolute URLs everywhere a link is used on the site, using for example https://<server>/CustomerDetails.aspx for the Edit Details link in UserInfo.ascx and the http:// protocol for most other links. If you did this in combination with SSL enforcement in IIS, you could prevent users from accessing secured pages quite effectively. If they tried rewriting the URL by hand, they would likely end up with an error message because IIS prevents secured pages from being transmitted via HTTP. However, this involves a lot of work to modify and maintain links, and we have a far more elegant technique at our disposal.

The core concept behind the technique presented here is that every page—bar none—uses a Master Page. This Master Page is either BalloonShop.master or Admin.master. We want to force pages using Admin.master to *always* use SSL, and force pages using BalloonShop.master to *sometimes* use SSL, where the "sometimes" translates as "where specified by the page."

The simplest of these, Admin.master, requires the following code in Admin.master.cs:

```
protected override void OnInit(EventArgs e)
{
  if (!Request.IsSecureConnection)
  {
    Response.Redirect(Request.Url.AbsoluteUri.ToLower().Replace(
      "http://", "https://"), true);
  }
  base.OnInit(e);
}
```

Here you detect whether an SSL connection is in use with Request.IsSecureConnection, and if it isn't, redirect to a page with the same URL as the current page, but starting with https rather than http. You do this at the OnInit stage of the page life cycle; that is, before the page has had a chance to do much processing that would be wasted.

Similarly, in BalloonShop.master.cs, you redirect to an SSL connection if required or to a standard HTTP connection if SSL isn't required. This prevents other, nonsecured pages in the site from being accessed via SSL when not required. To control this redirection, you include a property that pages using BalloonShop.master can set, saying whether they require SSL or not. This property, EnforceSSL, is defined as follows:

```
public bool EnforceSSL
{
  get
  {
    if (ViewState["enforceSSL"] != null)
    {
      return (bool)ViewState["enforceSSL"];
    }
    else
    {
      return false;
    }
  }
  set
  {
    ViewState["enforceSSL"] = value;
  }
}
```

We use view state here to streamline things, but other than that, this is a simple Boolean property.

Now, because this property may be set fairly late in the life cycle of the Master Page, you can't act on it in OnInit. Instead, you check the value of this property in OnPreRender and redirect then (if necessary):

```
protected override void OnPreRender(EventArgs e)
{
  if (EnforceSSL)
  {
    if (!Request.IsSecureConnection)
    {
      Response.Redirect(
        Request.Url.AbsoluteUri.ToLower().Replace(
        "http://", "https://"), true);
    }
  }
  else if (Request.IsSecureConnection)
  {
    Response.Redirect(Request.Url.AbsoluteUri.ToLower().Replace(
      "https://", "http://"), true);
  }
}
```

With this scheme, the user is only aware that something is going on when logging in. At this point the user is redirected from a secure to a nonsecure connection. From that point on, the user is redirected from secure to nonsecure connections transparently—secure when needed, nonsecure when not. Users will, of course, always be able to tell what type of connection they have, because the standard "padlock" symbol is displayed as per usual. The URL will also be there to reassure them.

The code behind required for SSL secured pages is

```
protected override void OnInit(EventArgs e)
{
    (Master as BalloonShop).EnforceSSL = true;
    base.OnInit(e);
}
```

This code needs to be added to Login.aspx.cs, Register.aspx.cs, CustomerDetails. aspx.cs, and Checkout.aspx.cs. Note that the call to base.OnInit(e) is required for proper themes functionality. Without this call, the ASP.NET theme doesn't get applied, and the CSS styles, and so on won't be loaded.

Summary

In this chapter, you've implemented a customer account system that customers can use to store their details for use during order processing. You've looked at many aspects of the customer account system, including encrypting sensitive data, and securing web connections for obtaining it.

You started by creating a set of classes in a new namespace called SecurityLib for hashing and encrypting strings, and a secure credit card representation that makes it easy to exchange credit card details between the encrypted and decrypted format.

After this, you implemented a customer login scheme using a new user role called Customers. This required some, but not many modifications to the existing Forms Authentication scheme, as well as the addition of a registration page. You also added customer details functionality using the ASP.NET Membership controls and the SecurityLib namespace and classes. After all this was implemented, you prepared the way for a new order process with a new checkout page.

Finally, we looked at how to secure data passing over the Internet using secure SSL connections. This involved obtaining and installing a certificate from a known certification authority (VeriSign, for example), restricting access to SSL where appropriate, and modifying the redirection code slightly to use SSL connections.

In the next chapter, we'll look at how to create the framework for the order-processing pipeline, enabling you to automate even more of the supply process.

■ ■ ■

CHAPTER 13

Advanced Customer Orders

The BalloonShop e-commerce application is shaping up nicely. You've added customer account functionality, and you're keeping track of customer addresses and credit card information, which is stored in a secure way. However, you're not currently using this information—you're delegating responsibility for this to PayPal.

In this chapter, you'll make the modifications required for customers to place orders that are associated with their user profile. The main modification here is that the customer associated with an order will be identified by a new piece of information in the Orders table, and much of the rest of the modifications will be made to use this information.

In the next chapter, you'll start to implement a more sophisticated order system, and the code you'll write in this chapter will facilitate this. You'll be adding various new data structures and data access classes to get ready for this. Because of this, you'll be making some modifications that won't seem necessary at this stage, but they'll make your life easier later on.

Also in this chapter, you'll take a look at dealing with another common feature of e-commerce sites: tax and shipping charges. Many options are available for implementing this functionality, but we'll just examine a simple way of doing things and lay the groundwork for your own further development.

Implementing Customer Order Functionality

This section is divided into two parts as follows:

- *Placing customer orders*: In this section, you'll enable customers to place orders.

- *Accessing customer orders*: In this section, you'll enable the order-processing system in later chapters to access customer orders.

Placing Customer Orders

To enable customers to place orders using ASP.NET membership, you need to make several modifications. You'll modify the database and business tier to enable customer orders to be placed and provide new code in the presentation tier to expose this functionality.

Database Modifications

As mentioned previously, the first thing to do is modify the database to make it ready to hold information about customer orders.

The Orders Table

Currently the Orders table doesn't allow for as much information as you'll need to implement customer orders. There are also some modifications that you'll need in later chapters, so you need to add the new columns shown in Table 13-1 to the Orders table.

Table 13-1. *The Orders Table*

Column Name	Column Type	Description
CustomerID	uniqueidentifier	The ID of the customer that placed the order
Status	int	The current status of the order, which you'll use in later chapters to determine what stage of order processing has been reached; default value 0
AuthCode	varchar(50)	The authentication code used to complete the customer credit card transaction
Reference	varchar(50)	The unique reference code of the customer credit card transaction

All except the first of these columns are related to advanced order processing, including credit card transactions, and you'll look at these columns in more detail later. You might also wonder why the CustomerID column is of type uniqueidentifier, which is quite reasonable. The reason is simply because this is how users are identified in the ASP.NET membership system. Effectively, this column provides a link to the aspnet_Users membership table, in the ASPNETDB database.

Note that you won't be using some of the columns that already exist in the Orders table, such as Verified and Completed. This is because this information is now encapsulated in the Status column. You also won't need the old fields relating to customer identification, such as CustomerName, because now this information is stored elsewhere. Don't delete these deprecated columns, however, or you'll lose backward compatibility with code earlier in this book.

■**Note** To enable this database to be used with both the code in this section of the book and the code in the earlier part of this book, it's necessary to make the new columns nullable, because earlier data won't supply values for them.

The CreateCustomerOrder Stored Procedure

Currently, the CreateOrder stored procedure is used to add orders to the database:

```
CREATE PROCEDURE CreateOrder
(@CartID char(36))
AS
/* Insert a new record into Orders */
DECLARE @OrderID int
INSERT INTO Orders DEFAULT VALUES
```

```
/* Save the new Order ID */
SET @OrderID = @@IDENTITY
/* Add the order details to OrderDetail */
INSERT INTO OrderDetail
    (OrderID, ProductID, ProductName, Quantity, UnitCost)
SELECT
    @OrderID, Product.ProductID, Product.Name,
    ShoppingCart.Quantity, Product.Price
FROM Product JOIN ShoppingCart
ON Product.ProductID = ShoppingCart.ProductID
WHERE ShoppingCart.CartID = @CartID
/* Clear the shopping cart */
DELETE FROM ShoppingCart
WHERE CartID = @CartID
/* Return the Order ID */
SELECT @OrderID
```

When an order is created in this new system, more data is added to the database, so you need to use a different (although very similar) stored procedure, CreateCustomerOrder (the differences are shown in bold):

```
CREATE PROCEDURE CreateCustomerOrder
(@CartID char(36),
 @CustomerID uniqueidentifier)
AS
/* Insert a new record into Orders */
DECLARE @OrderID int
INSERT INTO Orders (CustomerID) VALUES (@CustomerID)
/* Save the new Order ID */
SET @OrderID = @@IDENTITY
/* Add the order details to OrderDetail */
INSERT INTO OrderDetail
    (OrderID, ProductID, ProductName, Quantity, UnitCost)
SELECT
    @OrderID, Product.ProductID, Product.Name,
    ShoppingCart.Quantity, Product.Price
FROM Product JOIN ShoppingCart
ON Product.ProductID = ShoppingCart.ProductID
WHERE ShoppingCart.CartID = @CartID
/* Clear the shopping cart */
DELETE FROM ShoppingCart
WHERE CartID = @CartID
/* Return the Order ID */
SELECT @OrderID
```

The new data here is the inclusion of a CustomerID value with the order.

Business Tier Modifications

To use your new stored procedure, you need to modify the ShoppingCartAccess class. Rather than removing the old CreateOrder method, however, add the following method:

```
// Create a new order with customer ID
public static string CreateCommerceLibOrder()
{
  // get a configured DbCommand object
  DbCommand comm = GenericDataAccess.CreateCommand();
  // set the stored procedure name
  comm.CommandText = "CreateCustomerOrder";
  // create parameters
  DbParameter param = comm.CreateParameter();
  param.ParameterName = "@CartID";
  param.Value = shoppingCartId;
  param.DbType = DbType.String;
  param.Size = 36;
  comm.Parameters.Add(param);
  // create a new parameter
  param = comm.CreateParameter();
  param.ParameterName = "@CustomerId";
  param.Value =
     Membership.GetUser(
     HttpContext.Current.User.Identity.Name)
     .ProviderUserKey;
  param.DbType = DbType.Guid;
  param.Size = 16;
  comm.Parameters.Add(param);
  // return the result table
  return GenericDataAccess.ExecuteScalar(comm);
}
```

This new method, CreateCommerceLibOrder, is more or less the same as the old order-placing code, but there is a new parameter to use: @CustomerID. The GUID to use for this customer identification is obtained using the ASP.NET membership classes. You obtain a MembershipUser class using Membership.GetUser by passing the name of the current user obtained from the current context. Next, you use the ProviderUserKey property of the MembershipUser object you receive to obtain the unique GUID that identifies the current user.

Note the naming of this new method, which includes the name CommerceLib. In later chapters, this name helps identify the new code that is associated with the new, advanced order-processing scheme.

Presentation Tier Modifications

You'll use the preceding method in the checkout page you added in the last chapter. You'll do this in the following exercise, as well as add an order confirmation page that users will be redirected to after placing an order.

Exercise: Adding Customer Orders to BalloonShop

1. Modify the **placeOrderButton_Click** method in **Checkout.aspx.cs** as follows:

```csharp
protected void placeOrderButton_Click(object sender,
EventArgs e)
{
  // Store the total amount because the cart
  // is emptied when creating the order
  decimal amount = ShoppingCartAccess.GetTotalAmount();
  // Create the order and store the order ID
  string orderId = ShoppingCartAccess.CreateCommerceLibOrder();
  // Redirect to the confirmation page
  Response.Redirect("OrderPlaced.aspx");
}
```

2. Add a new Web Form to the project called **OrderPlaced.aspx** by using the **BalloonShop.master**
Master Page:

```aspx
<%@ Page Language="C#" MasterPageFile="~/BalloonShop.master"
  AutoEventWireup="true" CodeFile="OrderPlaced.aspx.cs"
  Inherits="OrderPlaced" %>

<asp:Content ID="Content1"
  ContentPlaceHolderID="contentPlaceHolder" runat="Server">
  <span class="InfoText">
    Thank you for your order, please come again!
  </span>
</asp:Content>
```

3. Add the following title-setting code and method override to the code-behind file for this form,
OrderPlaced.aspx.cs:

```csharp
protected override void OnInit(EventArgs e)
{
  (Master as BalloonShop).EnforceSSL = true;
  base.OnInit(e);
} .

protected void Page_Load(object sender, EventArgs e)
{
  // Set the title of the page
  this.Title = BalloonShopConfiguration.SiteName +
               " : Order Placed";
}
```

4. Modify `web.config` as follows:

```
<!-- Only existing customers can access OrderPlaced.aspx -->
<location path="OrderPlaced.aspx">
  <system.web>
    <authorization>
      <allow roles="Customers" />
      <deny users="*" />
    </authorization>
  </system.web>
</location>
```

5. Place an order or two using the new system to check that the code works. You'll need to log on to do this and supply enough details to get past the validation on the checkout page.

How It Works: Adding Customer Orders to BalloonShop

The code added in this exercise is very simple and hardly merits much discussion. Still, you may want to modify the text displayed on `OrderPlaced.aspx` to include additional information that customers might require after placing an order. Also, note that this new page is secured via SSL and the `Customer` role. Customers who aren't logged in won't need to see this page.

After you've implemented more of the new ordering code, you'll be able to provide more information to customers, such as sending them confirmation emails and enabling them to check on order statuses, past and present. For now, however, this is as far as we can take things.

Accessing Customer Orders

After orders have been placed, you'll need to access them. This involves various modifications to the database business tier to provide new data structures and access code. Although essential in the next chapter and beyond, for now, you'll implement a simple (admin only) test form to access customer order data.

Database Modifications

You only need to make one modification here: Add a stored procedure to get access to the new information in the modified `Orders` table. Add the following stored procedure to the BalloonShop database:

```
CREATE PROCEDURE CommerceLibOrderGetInfo
(@OrderID int)
AS
SELECT OrderID,
       DateCreated,
       DateShipped,
       Comments,
       Status,
       CustomerID,
       AuthCode,
```

```
      Reference
FROM Orders
WHERE OrderID = @OrderID
```

This is very similar to the existing `OrderGetInfo` stored procedure, but rewritten to take into account the new columns.

Business Layer Modifications

The current order access code—stored in `App_Code/OrdersAccess.cs`—and the data for an order can be wrapped in a struct called `OrderInfo`. This struct is then used by various methods to manipulate order details.

The `OrderInfo` struct doesn't give you access to the new data stored in the `Orders` table, and it doesn't allow you to access order details or customer and credit card information. In short, you need something a little more advanced.

To achieve this, add a new class called `CommerceLibAccess` to the `App_Code` directory. You'll actually store two other classes in the same file, as per code in previous chapters (excepting the fact that in previous chapters only structs have shared files with a main class). Having a single file makes it easy to group classes that are functionally linked. All the classes in this file will facilitate data access, and you'll start by looking with a class to wrap rows in the `OrderDetail` table. Before doing this, however, add the following namespace references to the `CommerceLibAccess.cs` file:

```
using System.Data.Common;
using System.Text;
using System.Collections.Generic;
using System.Web.Profile;
using SecurityLib;
```

These namespaces provide the class required for us to access and process order and customer information.

The CommerceLibOrderDetailInfo Class

Add the following class to `CommerceLibAccess.cs`:

```
/// <summary>
/// Wraps order detail data
/// </summary>
public class CommerceLibOrderDetailInfo
{
  public int OrderID;
  public int ProductID;
  public string ProductName;
  public int Quantity;
  public double UnitCost;
  public string ItemAsString;
```

```
public double Subtotal
{
  get
  {
    return Quantity * UnitCost;
  }
}

public CommerceLibOrderDetailInfo(DataRow orderDetailRow)
{
  OrderID = Int32.Parse(orderDetailRow["OrderID"].ToString());
  ProductID = Int32.Parse(orderDetailRow["ProductId"].ToString());
  ProductName = orderDetailRow["ProductName"].ToString();
  Quantity = Int32.Parse(orderDetailRow["Quantity"].ToString());
  UnitCost = Double.Parse(orderDetailRow["UnitCost"].ToString());
  // set info property
  Refresh();
}

public void Refresh()
{
  StringBuilder sb = new StringBuilder();
  sb.Append(Quantity.ToString());
  sb.Append(" ");
  sb.Append(ProductName);
  sb.Append(", $");
  sb.Append(UnitCost.ToString());
  sb.Append(" each, total cost $");
  sb.Append(Subtotal.ToString());
  ItemAsString = sb.ToString();
}
}
```

This class wraps a row from the OrderDetail table. Note that we aren't using a struct for this functionality. This is because structs can't have constructors, and to make initialization easier, this class uses a constructor that takes a DataRow object to initialize itself. This constructor simply parses the OrderID, ProductID, ProductName, Quantity, and UnitCost columns and associates them with public fields. We could hide these fields by making them private, and expose them via properties, but for our purposes this access scheme is fine—and is a lot quicker to type in!

The constructor finishes with a call to a publicly accessible Refresh method, which sets a utility field called ItemAsString. This field, as you will see later, makes it easier for us to quickly extract a descriptive piece of text concerning the data contained in a CommerceLib➡ OrderDetailInfo instance.

Subtotal is another piece of information exposed by this class. Like ItemAsString, this is really just for convenience and simply returns the number of items multiplied by the cost of a single item.

The GetOrderDetails Method

The first method to add to the CommerceLibAccess class is one that obtains the OrderDetail rows associated with an order. Add the following method to the class:

```
public static List<CommerceLibOrderDetailInfo>
  GetOrderDetails(string orderId)
{
  // use existing method for DataTable
  DataTable orderDetailsData = OrdersAccess.GetDetails(orderId);
  // create List<>
  List<CommerceLibOrderDetailInfo> orderDetails =
    new List<CommerceLibOrderDetailInfo>(
    orderDetailsData.Rows.Count);
  foreach (DataRow orderDetail in orderDetailsData.Rows)
  {
    orderDetails.Add(
      new CommerceLibOrderDetailInfo(orderDetail));
  }
  return orderDetails;
}
```

There are several things to note here. First, this class returns a generic list of CommerceLibOrderDetailInfo objects. The (in my view, quite fabulous) generic list classes make it easy to perform complex list operations on data without writing any of the code, and they are great timesavers.

We already have a similar method to this one in the OrdersAccess class, so we start by using that method to get a DataTable containing the data we are interested in. Next we take each row in that table, create an instance of the CommerceLibOrderDetailInfo class from it, and add it to the generic list of objects.

The CommerceLibOrderInfo Class

Add the following class to CommerceLibAccess.cs:

```
/// <summary>
/// Wraps order data
/// </summary>
public class CommerceLibOrderInfo
{
  public int OrderID;
  public string DateCreated;
  public string DateShipped;
  public string Comments;
  public int Status;
  public string AuthCode;
  public string Reference;
```

```csharp
    public MembershipUser Customer;
    public ProfileCommon CustomerProfile;
    public SecureCard CreditCard;

    public double TotalCost;
    public string OrderAsString;
    public string CustomerAddressAsString;

    public List<CommerceLibOrderDetailInfo> OrderDetails;

    public CommerceLibOrderInfo(DataRow orderRow)
    {
      OrderID = Int32.Parse(orderRow["OrderID"].ToString());
      DateCreated = orderRow["DateCreated"].ToString();
      DateShipped = orderRow["DateShipped"].ToString();
      Comments = orderRow["Comments"].ToString();
      Status = Int32.Parse(orderRow["Status"].ToString());
      AuthCode = orderRow["AuthCode"].ToString();
      Reference = orderRow["Reference"].ToString();
      Customer = Membership.GetUser(
        new Guid(orderRow["CustomerID"].ToString()));
      CustomerProfile =
        (HttpContext.Current.Profile as ProfileCommon)
          .GetProfile(Customer.UserName);
      CreditCard = new SecureCard(CustomerProfile.CreditCard);
      OrderDetails =
        CommerceLibAccess.GetOrderDetails(
        orderRow["OrderID"].ToString());
      // set info properties
      Refresh();
    }

    public void Refresh()
    {
      // calculate total cost and set data
      StringBuilder sb = new StringBuilder();
      TotalCost = 0.0;
      foreach (CommerceLibOrderDetailInfo item in OrderDetails)
      {
        sb.AppendLine(item.ItemAsString);
        TotalCost += item.Subtotal;
      }
      sb.AppendLine();
      sb.Append("Total order cost: $");
      sb.Append(TotalCost.ToString());
      OrderAsString = sb.ToString();
```

```
    // get customer address string
    sb = new StringBuilder();
    sb.AppendLine(Customer.UserName);
    sb.AppendLine(CustomerProfile.Address1);
    if (CustomerProfile.Address2 != "")
    {
      sb.AppendLine(CustomerProfile.Address2);
    }
    sb.AppendLine(CustomerProfile.City);
    sb.AppendLine(CustomerProfile.Region);
    sb.AppendLine(CustomerProfile.PostalCode);
    sb.AppendLine(CustomerProfile.Country);
    CustomerAddressAsString = sb.ToString();
  }
}
```

This class wraps a row from the Orders table and is a little more complicated than the CommerceLibOrderDetailInfo class. Again, a constructor is used that takes a DataRow object to initialize the class, but this time you need to create user and credit card data using the data extracted.

To obtain this additional information, the code starts by getting an instance of the user references by the order using the GUID stored in CustomerID. The ASP.NET membership system makes this easy—you simply pass the GUID to Membership.GetUser and receive a MembershipUser object. From this object, you can find out the name of the user and pass that to the GetProfile method of the ProfileCommon object currently in use. Strangely, this method isn't a static method, so you need to access the current instance from the current context to do this.

After you've obtained a ProfileCommon instance for the customer, you simply store it in a publicly accessible field, just like the other order information. This will make it easy for you later, because you'll be able to access customer profile information with very simple syntax. From the information stored in the ProfileCommon instance, you also initialize an instance of SecureCard, giving you speedy access to customer credit card details when you need them.

Next, the constructor uses the GetOrderDetails method described previously to obtain the details of the order using the OrderId obtained from the DataRow. Again, this is to enable you to access these order details directly through the CommerceLibOrderInfo class, which is another time-saving operation.

Finally, a Refresh method similar to the one in CommerceLibOrderDetailInfo is used to initialize some utility fields: TotalCost, OrderAsString, and CustomerAddressAsString. You'll use all of these for more speedy access to order details later.

The GetOrder Method

The last thing to add to the CommerceLibAccess class is a method to obtain an order, in the form of a CommerceLibOrderInfo object. To do this, you use the new CommerceLibOrderGetInfo stored procedure. Add the following method to CommerceLibAccess:

```
public static CommerceLibOrderInfo GetOrder(string orderID)
{
  // get a configured DbCommand object
  DbCommand comm = GenericDataAccess.CreateCommand();
  // set the stored procedure name
  comm.CommandText = "CommerceLibOrderGetInfo";
  // create a new parameter
  DbParameter param = comm.CreateParameter();
  param.ParameterName = "@OrderID";
  param.Value = orderID;
  param.DbType = DbType.Int32;
  comm.Parameters.Add(param);
  // obtain the results
  DataTable table = GenericDataAccess.ExecuteSelectCommand(comm);
  DataRow orderRow = table.Rows[0];
  // save the results into an CommerceLibOrderInfo object
  CommerceLibOrderInfo orderInfo =
    new CommerceLibOrderInfo(orderRow);
  return orderInfo;
}
```

Because we've made the data structures nice and simple, there's not really much to shout about here. You get a command in the standard way, using GenericDataAccess.CreateCommand, configure it for your new stored procedure, use it to get a DataTable, and use the first row in the resulting table to initialize a CommerceLibOrderInfo instance. You've already done all the hard work here, in the constructor for CommerceLibOrderInfo.

Presentation Tier Modifications

You haven't added anything to require any data tier modifications yet, but you have implemented a lot of code that is used behind the scenes. To test this code, you'll implement a simple test form that enables administrators to view order information. You're not going to implement massive changes to the order administration code at this stage, because you'll just end up modifying it later after you've finished the new order-processing system.

Exercise: Viewing Customer Orders on a Test Form

1. Add a new Web Form to the BalloonShop application called **OrderTest.aspx** by using the **Admin.master** Master Page:

   ```
   <%@ Page Language="C#" MasterPageFile="~/Admin.master"
     AutoEventWireup="true" CodeFile="OrderTest.aspx.cs"
     Inherits="OrderTest" %>
   ```

```
<asp:Content ID="Content1"
  ContentPlaceHolderID="ContentPlaceHolder1" runat="Server">
 <span class="AdminTitle">
   BalloonShop Customer Order Access Test
 </span>
</asp:Content>
<asp:Content ID="Content2"
  ContentPlaceHolderID="contentPlaceHolder2" runat="Server">
 Order number:
 <asp:TextBox runat="server" ID="orderIDBox" />
 <br />
 <asp:Button runat="server" ID="goButton" Text="Go" />
 <br />
 <br />
 <asp:Label runat="server" ID="resultLabel" />
 <br />
 <br />
 <strong>Customer address:</strong>
 <br />
 <asp:Label runat="server" ID="addressLabel" />
 <br />
 <br />
 <strong>Customer credit card:</strong>
 <br />
 <asp:Label runat="server" ID="creditCardLabel" />
 <br />
 <br />
 <strong>Order details:</strong>
 <br />
 <asp:Label runat="server" ID="orderLabel" />
</asp:Content>
```

2. Switch to **Design View** and double-click on the **Go** button to add an event handler.

3. Modify the code for the event handler as follows:

```
protected void goButton_Click(object sender, EventArgs e)
{
  try
  {
    CommerceLibOrderInfo orderInfo =
      CommerceLibAccess.GetOrder(orderIDBox.Text);
    resultLabel.Text = "Order found.";
```

```
      addressLabel.Text =
        orderInfo.CustomerAddressAsString.Replace(
        "\n", "<br />");
      creditCardLabel.Text = orderInfo.CreditCard.CardNumberX;
      orderLabel.Text =
        orderInfo.OrderAsString.Replace("\n", "<br />");
    }
    catch
    {
      resultLabel.Text =
        "No order found, or order is in old format.";
      addressLabel.Text = "";
      creditCardLabel.Text = "";
      orderLabel.Text = "";
    }
  }
```

4. Modify `web.config` as follows:

```xml
<!-- Only administrators are allowed to access OrderTest.aspx -->
<location path="OrderTest.aspx">
  <system.web>
    <authorization>
      <allow roles="Administrators" />
      <deny users="*" />
    </authorization>
  </system.web>
</location>
```

5. Log into the **BalloonShop Web Application** as an administrator and navigate to the `OrderTest.aspx` page (by typing in the URL, as no page links to this test form).

6. Using the **Database Explorer** in Visual Web Developer Express or any other tool capable of examining data in SQL Server 2005 tables, determine the `OrderId` of an order in the `Orders` table that contains a value for `CustomerID` (that is, an order placed since making the modifications earlier in this chapter). Note that the `Status` field in the database for the order must be 0 or you'll receive an error. It should be 0 already, if you set the default value for the `Status` column to 0 earlier in this chapter.

7. Enter the `OrderID` value in the text box on `OrderTest.aspx` and click **Go**. A typical result is shown in Figure 13-1.

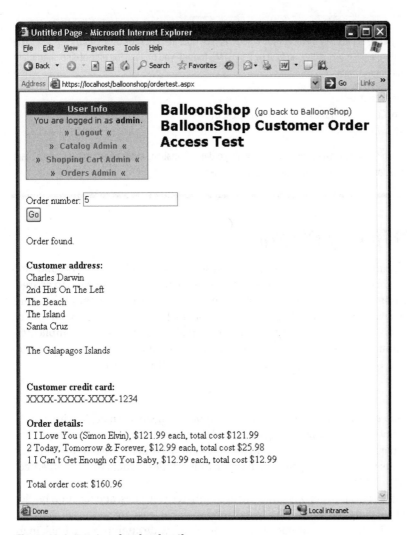

Figure 13-1. *Retrieved order details*

How It Works: Viewing Customer Orders on a Test Form

The simple code in this exercise uses the data tier classes defined earlier to access a customer order. The code is notable for its simplicity. The order information is obtained in a single line of code in the event handler for the Go button:

```
CommerceLibOrderInfo orderInfo =
  CommerceLibAccess.GetOrder(orderIDBox.Text);
```

After an instance of `CommerceLibOrderInfo` has been obtained, the event handler simply populates some `Label` controls on the page using some of the utility members you created earlier. Note that both `CustomerAddressAsString` and `OrderAsString` return a plain text string, so to view it in HTML format, you replace the end-of-line characters with line break elements, for example:

```
addressLabel.Text =
  orderInfo.CustomerAddressAsString.Replace(
  "\n", "<br />");
```

The event handler code also checks for exceptions when obtaining order information, which may occur for nonexistent orders or orders placed before the implementation of customer orders.

Tax and Shipping Charges

One feature that is common to many e-commerce web sites is adding charges for tax and/or shipping. Obviously this isn't always the case—digital download sites have no need to charge for shipping, for example, because no physical shipment is involved. However, the chances are fairly high that you'll want to include additional charges of one kind or another in your orders.

In fact, this can be very simple, although not always. It really depends on how complicated you want to make things. In this chapter, we'll keep things simple and provide basic but extensible functionality for both tax and shipping charges. First, let's discuss the issues.

Tax Issues

The subject of tax and e-commerce web sites has a complicated history. To begin with, you could usually get away with anything. Taxing was poorly enforced, and many sites simply ignored tax completely. This was especially true for international orders, where it was often possible for customers to avoid paying tax much of the time—unless orders were intercepted by customs officers!

Then more people started to become aware of e-commerce web sites, and taxation bodies such as the IRS realized that they were losing a lot of money—or at least not getting all that they could. A flurry of activity ensued as various organizations worldwide attempting to hook in to this revenue stream. A range of solutions was proposed, and some solutions were even implemented with varied complexity and mixed results. Now, things are becoming a little more settled.

The key concept to be aware of when thinking about tax is a **nexus**. A nexus is as "a sufficient presence in the taxing jurisdiction to justify the collection of tax." Effectively, this means that when shipping internationally, you may in most situations not be responsible for what happens unless your company has a significant presence in the destination country. When shipping internally to a country (or within, say, the European Union), you probably will be responsible. The legislation is a little unclear, and we certainly haven't examined the laws for every country in the world, but this general rule tends to hold true.

The other key issues can be summed up by the following:

- Taxation depends on where you are shipping from and where you are shipping to.

- National rules apply.

- The type of product you are selling is important.

Some countries have it easier than others. Within the United Kingdom, for example, you can charge the current VAT rate on all purchases where it applies (some types of product are exempt or charged at a reduced rate) and be relatively happy that you've done all you can. If you want to take things one step further, you can consider an offshore business to ship your goods (Amazon does it, so why shouldn't you?). Other countries, notably the United States, have a much more complex system to deal with. Within the United States, sales tax varies not just from state to state, but often within states as well. In fact, pretty much the only time you'll know exactly what to do is when you are shipping goods to a customer in the same tax area as your business. At other times . . . well, to be perfectly honest, your guess is as good as ours. Many states are aware of the issue, and may well have resolved things by the time you read this, but this is far from certain. Recent estimates (from `http://www.offshore-e-com.com/`) put the loss of revenue from e-commerce trading at between $300 million and $3.8 billion annually; the margin of error here probably informs you that the officials are as confused about all this as we are. Calls have gone out to provide a "taxation calculator" where a source and target ZIP code could be used to obtain a tax rate, but as far as we know, no such service exists yet.

In this book, the taxation scheme you add is as simple as possible. A database table will include information concerning various tax rates that can be applied, and the choice of these will for now depend on the shipping region of the customer. All products are considered to be taxable at the same rate. This does leave a lot to be desired, but at least tax will be calculated and applied. You can replace it with your own system later.

Shipping Issues

Shipping is somewhat simpler to deal with than tax, although again you can make things as complicated as you want. Because sending out orders from a company that trades via an e-commerce frontend is much the same as sending out orders from, say, a mail order company, the practices are very much in place and relatively easy to come to grips with. There may be new ways of doing things at your disposal, but the general principles are well known.

You may well have an existing relationship with a postal service from pre-online trading times, in which case, it's probably easiest to keep things as close to the "old" way of doing things as possible. However, if you're just starting out, or revising the way you do things, you have plenty of options to consider.

The simplest option is not to worry about shipping costs at all, which makes sense if there are no costs, for example, in the case of digital downloads. Alternatively, you could simply include the cost of shipping in the cost of your products. Or you could impose a flat fee regardless of the items ordered or the destination. However, some of these options could involve customers either overpaying or underpaying, which isn't ideal.

The other extreme involved is accounting for the weight and dimensions of all the products ordered and calculating the exact cost yourself. This can be simplified slightly, because some shipping companies (including FedEx, and so on) provide useful APIs to help you. In some cases, you can use a dynamic system to calculate the shipping options available (overnight, three to four days, and so on) based on a number of factors, including package weight and delivery location. The exact methods for doing this, however, can vary a great deal between shipping companies, and we'll leave it to you to implement such a solution if you require it.

In this book, we'll again take a simple line. For each shipping region in the database, you'll provide a number of shipping options for the user to choose from, each of which will have an associated cost. This cost is simply added to the cost of the order. This is the reason why, in Chapter 12, you included a `ShippingRegion` table—its use will soon become apparent.

Implementing Tax and Shipping Charges

As expected, you need to make several modifications to BalloonShop to enable the tax and shipping schemes outlined previously. You have two more database tables to add, Tax and Shipping, as well as modifications to make to the Orders table. You'll need to add new stored procedures and make some modifications to existing ones. Some of the business tier classes need modifications to account for these changes, and the presentation tier must include a method for users to select a shipping method (the taxing scheme is selected automatically). So, without further ado, let's get started.

Database Modifications

In this section, you'll add the new tables and modify the Orders table and stored procedures.

The Tax Table

The Tax table simply provides a number of tax options that are available, each of which has a name and a percentage tax rate. Table 13-2 shows the table structure that you'll need to add.

Table 13-2. *The Tax Table*

Column Name	Column Type	Description
TaxID	int	The ID of the tax option. This column is the primary key and should be configured as an identity so that it will be auto-numbered.
TaxType	varchar(100)	A text description of the tax option.
TaxPercentage	float	The percentage tax rate for this option.

These columns are not nullable. Figure 13-2 shows the data to add to this table.

	TaxID	TaxType	TaxPercentage
	1	Sales Tax at 8.5%	8.5
▶	2	No Tax	0
✳	NULL	NULL	NULL

Figure 13-2. *Data for the Tax table*

The Shipping Table

The Shipping table is also very simple. It provides a number of shipping options, each of which has a name, a cost, and an associated shipping region. Table 13-3 shows the table structure that you'll need to add.

Table 13-3. *The Shipping Table*

Column Name	Column Type	Description
ShippingID	int	The ID of the shipping option. This column is the primary key and identity.
ShippingType	varchar(100)	A text description of the shipping option.
ShippingCost	money	The cost (to the customer) of the shipping option.
ShippingRegionID	int	The ID of the shipping region that this option applies to.

These columns are not nullable. Figure 13-3 shows the data to add to this table.

	ShippingID	ShippingType	ShippingCost	ShippingRegionID
	1	Next Day Delivery ($20)	20.0000	2
	2	3-4 Days ($10)	10.0000	2
	3	7 Days ($5)	5.0000	2
	4	By air (7 days, $25)	25.0000	3
	5	By sea (28 days, $10)	10.0000	3
▶	7	By air (10 days, $35)	35.0000	4
	8	By sea (28 days, $30)	30.0000	4
✱	NULL	NULL	NULL	NULL

Figure 13-3. *Data for the* Shipping *table*

Orders Table Modifications

The modifications to the Orders table are to associate an order with one entry each from the Tax and Shipping tables, as shown in Table 13-4.

Table 13-4. *Orders Table Modifications*

Column Name	Column Type	Description
TaxID	int	The ID of the tax option to use for the order
ShippingID	int	The ID of the shipping option to use for the order

CommerceLibOrderGetInfo Modifications

The existing CommerceLibOrderGetInfo stored procedure now needs to include the tax and shipping data for an order. The new stored procedure is as follows:

```
ALTER PROCEDURE CommerceLibOrderGetInfo
(@OrderID int)
AS
SELECT OrderID,
       DateCreated,
       DateShipped,
       Comments,
       Status,
       CustomerID,
       AuthCode,
       Reference,
       Orders.ShippingID,
       ShippingType,
       ShippingCost,
       Orders.TaxID,
       TaxType,
       TaxPercentage
FROM Orders
LEFT OUTER JOIN Tax ON Tax.TaxID = Orders.TaxID
LEFT OUTER JOIN Shipping ON Shipping.ShippingID = Orders.ShippingID
WHERE OrderID = @OrderID
```

Here there are two joins to the Tax and Shipping tables, both of which are LEFT OUTER joins so that data will be retrieved from the Orders table regardless of a value of TaxID and ShippingID (to enable backward compatibility among other issues).

CreateCustomerOrder Modifications

You also need to modify CreateCustomerOrder so that a tax and a shipping option are added when an order is added. The modifications are as follows:

```
ALTER PROCEDURE CreateCustomerOrder
(@CartID char(36),
 @CustomerID uniqueidentifier,
 @ShippingID int,
 @TaxID int)
AS
/* Insert a new record into Orders */
DECLARE @OrderID int
INSERT INTO Orders (CustomerID, ShippingID, TaxID)
VALUES (@CustomerID, @ShippingID, @TaxID)
/* Save the new Order ID */
SET @OrderID = @@IDENTITY
/* Add the order details to OrderDetail */
INSERT INTO OrderDetail
    (OrderID, ProductID, ProductName, Quantity, UnitCost)
```

```
SELECT
    @OrderID, Product.ProductID, Product.Name,
    ShoppingCart.Quantity, Product.Price
FROM Product JOIN ShoppingCart
ON Product.ProductID = ShoppingCart.ProductID
WHERE ShoppingCart.CartID = @CartID
/* Clear the shopping cart */
DELETE FROM ShoppingCart
WHERE CartID = @CartID
/* Return the Order ID */
SELECT @OrderID
```

The two new parameters to deal with are @ShippingID and @TaxID.

The CommerceLibShippingGetInfo Stored Procedure

You need to add a new stored procedure so that a list of shipping options associated with a shipping region can be obtained. The CommerceLibShippingGetInfo stored procedure achieves this:

```
CREATE PROCEDURE CommerceLibShippingGetInfo
(@ShippingRegionID int)
AS
SELECT ShippingID,
       ShippingType,
       ShippingCost
FROM Shipping
WHERE ShippingRegionID = @ShippingRegionID
```

Business Layer Modifications

To work with the new database tables and stored procedures, you need to make several changes to CommerceLibAccess.cs. You need to add two structs to represent tax and shipping options, TaxInfo and ShippingInfo. You also need to give access to shipping info based on shipping regions and modify CommerceLibOrderInfo to use the tax and shipping structs. You must modify CreateCommerceLibOrder in ShoppingCartAccess to configure tax and shipping for new orders as well.

The TaxInfo and ShippingInfo Structs

These structs use very simple code, which you can add to the top of CommerceLibAccess.cs:

```
/// <summary>
/// Wraps tax data
/// </summary>
public struct TaxInfo
{
  public int TaxID;
  public string TaxType;
  public double TaxPercentage;
}
```

```
/// <summary>
/// Wraps shipping data
/// </summary>
public struct ShippingInfo
{
  public int ShippingID;
  public string ShippingType;
  public double ShippingCost;
  public int ShippingRegionId;
}
```

There's not much to comment on here. The fields in the struct simply match up to the columns in the associated tables.

The GetShippingInfo Method

This method obtains a List<ShippingInfo> object containing shipping information for a shipping region. If it's not there already, this code requires a reference to the System.Collections.Generic namespace in the file. Add this method to the CommerceLibAccess class:

```
public static List<ShippingInfo> GetShippingInfo(
  int shippingRegionId)
{
  // get a configured DbCommand object
  DbCommand comm = GenericDataAccess.CreateCommand();
  // set the stored procedure name
  comm.CommandText = "CommerceLibShippingGetInfo";
  // create a new parameter
  DbParameter param = comm.CreateParameter();
  param.ParameterName = "@ShippingRegionId";
  param.Value = shippingRegionId;
  param.DbType = DbType.Int32;
  comm.Parameters.Add(param);
  // obtain the results
  DataTable table = GenericDataAccess.ExecuteSelectCommand(comm);
  List<ShippingInfo> result = new List<ShippingInfo>();
  foreach (DataRow row in table.Rows)
  {
    ShippingInfo rowData = new ShippingInfo();
    rowData.ShippingID = int.Parse(row["ShippingId"].ToString());
    rowData.ShippingType = row["ShippingType"].ToString();
    rowData.ShippingCost =
      double.Parse(row["ShippingCost"].ToString());
    rowData.ShippingRegionId = shippingRegionId;
    result.Add(rowData);
  }
  return result;
}
```

Here the ID of a shipping region is accepted as a parameter and used to access the CommerceLibShippingGetInfo stored procedure added earlier. The collection is assembled from row data.

CreateCommerceLibOrder Modifications

This method, in ShoppingCartAccess.cs, needs modifying as follows (again, a reference to System.Collections.Generic may be necessary):

```
public static string CreateCommerceLibOrder(int shippingId,
  int taxId)
{
  // get a configured DbCommand object
  DbCommand comm = GenericDataAccess.CreateCommand();
  // set the stored procedure name
  comm.CommandText = "CreateCustomerOrder";
  // create parameters
  DbParameter param = comm.CreateParameter();
  param.ParameterName = "@CartID";
  param.Value = shoppingCartId;
  param.DbType = DbType.String;
  param.Size = 36;
  comm.Parameters.Add(param);
  // create a new parameter
  param = comm.CreateParameter();
  param.ParameterName = "@CustomerId";
  param.Value =
     Membership.GetUser(
     HttpContext.Current.User.Identity.Name)
     .ProviderUserKey;
  param.DbType = DbType.Guid;
  param.Size = 16;
  comm.Parameters.Add(param);
  // create a new parameter
  param = comm.CreateParameter();
  param.ParameterName = "@ShippingId";
  param.Value = shippingId;
  param.DbType = DbType.Int32;
  comm.Parameters.Add(param);
  // create a new parameter
  param = comm.CreateParameter();
  param.ParameterName = "@TaxId";
  param.Value = taxId;
  param.DbType = DbType.Int32;
  comm.Parameters.Add(param);
  // return the result table
  return GenericDataAccess.ExecuteScalar(comm);
}
```

Here two more parameters have been added to match up with the revised stored procedure CreateCustomerOrder.

CommerceLibOrderInfo Modifications

This class requires several modifications. First, you need to add two new fields for tax and shipping info:

```
public class CommerceLibOrderInfo
{
  ...
  public ShippingInfo Shipping;
  public TaxInfo Tax;
```

Next, the constructor needs to be modified to extract this new data from the row returned by the CommerceLibOrderGetInfo stored procedure:

```
public CommerceLibOrderInfo(DataRow orderRow)
{
  ...
  CreditCard = new SecureCard(CustomerProfile.CreditCard);
  OrderDetails =
    CommerceLibAccess.GetOrderDetails(
    orderRow["OrderID"].ToString());
  // Get Shipping Data
  if (orderRow["ShippingID"] != DBNull.Value
    && orderRow["ShippingType"] != DBNull.Value
    && orderRow["ShippingCost"] != DBNull.Value)
  {
    Shipping.ShippingID =
        Int32.Parse(orderRow["ShippingID"].ToString());
    Shipping.ShippingType = orderRow["ShippingType"].ToString();
    Shipping.ShippingCost =
        double.Parse(orderRow["ShippingCost"].ToString());
  }
  else
  {
    Shipping.ShippingID = -1;
  }
  // Get Tax Data
  if (orderRow["TaxID"] != DBNull.Value
    && orderRow["TaxType"] != DBNull.Value
    && orderRow["TaxPercentage"] != DBNull.Value)
```

```
  {
    Tax.TaxID = Int32.Parse(orderRow["TaxID"].ToString());
    Tax.TaxType = orderRow["TaxType"].ToString();
    Tax.TaxPercentage =
      double.Parse(orderRow["TaxPercentage"].ToString());
  }
  else
  {
    Tax.TaxID = -1;
  }
  // set info properties
  Refresh();
}
```

Note here that checks are made for null values for tax and shipping information. If data isn't found for tax information, TaxID will be set to -1. Similarly, no shipping data will result in ShippingID being -1. If all is well, these situations shouldn't occur, but just in case they do (especially if you end up modifying the tax and shipping schemes), this will prevent an error from occurring.

Finally, the Refresh method needs to include tax and shipping costs in its calculation of total cost and in its creation of the OrderAsString field:

```
public void Refresh()
{
  // calculate total cost and set data
  StringBuilder sb = new StringBuilder();
  TotalCost = 0.0;
  foreach (CommerceLibOrderDetailInfo item in OrderDetails)
  {
    sb.AppendLine(item.ItemAsString);
    TotalCost += item.Subtotal;
  }
  // Add shipping cost
  if (Shipping.ShippingID != -1)
  {
    sb.AppendLine("Shipping: " + Shipping.ShippingType);
    TotalCost += Shipping.ShippingCost;
  }
```

```
    // Add tax
    if (Tax.TaxID != -1 && Tax.TaxPercentage != 0.0)
    {
      double taxAmount = Math.Round(TotalCost * Tax.TaxPercentage,
        MidpointRounding.AwayFromZero) / 100.0;
      sb.AppendLine("Tax: " + Tax.TaxType + ", $"
        + taxAmount.ToString());
      TotalCost += taxAmount;
    }
    sb.AppendLine();
    sb.Append("Total order cost: $");
    sb.Append(TotalCost.ToString());
    OrderAsString = sb.ToString();
    ...
  }
```

The calculation of the tax amount involves some mathematical functionality from the System.Math class, but otherwise it's all simple stuff.

Presentation Layer Modifications

Finally we come to the presentation layer. In fact, due to the changes we've made, the only changes to make here are to the checkout page.

Checkout.aspx Modifications

The .aspx page simply needs a means of selecting a shipping type prior to placing an order. This can be achieved using a drop-down list:

```
<asp:Label ID="InfoLabel" runat="server" CssClass="InfoText" />
<br />
<br />
<span class="InfoText">Shipping type:
  <asp:DropDownList ID="shippingSelection" runat="server" /></span>
<br />
<br />
<asp:Button ID="placeOrderButton" runat="server"
  CssClass="ButtonText" Text="Place order"
  OnClick="placeOrderButton_Click" />
</asp:Content>
```

Now you need to populate this list and/or hide it in the code behind.

Checkout.aspx.cs Modifications

The code behind for this page already checks to see whether an order can be placed in PopulateControls, based on whether a valid address and credit card have been entered. You can use this information to set the visibility of the new list control (shippingSelection) and populate the shipping option list accordingly. The code to modify is as follows:

```
private void PopulateControls()
{
  ...
  placeOrderButton.Visible = addressOK && cardOK;
  shippingSelection.Visible = addressOK && cardOK;

  // Populate shipping selection
  if (addressOK && cardOK)
  {
    int shippingRegionId = int.Parse(Profile.ShippingRegion);
    List<ShippingInfo> shippingInfoData =
       CommerceLibAccess.GetShippingInfo(shippingRegionId);
    foreach (ShippingInfo shippingInfo in shippingInfoData)
    {
      shippingSelection.Items.Add(
        new ListItem(shippingInfo.ShippingType,
          shippingInfo.ShippingID.ToString()));
    }
    shippingSelection.SelectedIndex = 0;
  }
}
```

This code uses the CommerceLibAccess.GetShippingInfo method added earlier, and creates ListItem controls dynamically for adding to the drop-down list. Note also that a valid selection in the list is ensured by setting the initially selected item in the drop-down list to the item with an index of 0, that is, the first entry in the list.

Next, you need to modify the placeOrderButton_Click event handler to create an order with tax and shipping option references. For the shipping option, you use the selected item in the drop-down list; for the tax option, you make an arbitrary selection based on the shipping region of the customer and the items you added earlier to the Tax table.

```
protected void placeOrderButton_Click(object sender,
  EventArgs e)
{
  // Store the total amount because the cart
  // is emptied when creating the order
  decimal amount = ShoppingCartAccess.GetTotalAmount();
  // Get shipping ID or default to 0
  int shippingId = 0;
  try
  {
    shippingId = int.Parse(shippingSelection.SelectedValue);
  }
  catch
  {
  }
```

```
  // Get tax ID or default to "No tax"
  string shippingRegion =
    (HttpContext.Current.Profile as ProfileCommon).ShippingRegion;
  int taxId;
  switch (shippingRegion)
  {
    case "2":
      taxId = 1;
      break;
    default:
      taxId = 2;
      break;
  }

  // Create the order and store the order ID
  string orderId =
    ShoppingCartAccess.CreateCommerceLibOrder(shippingId, taxId);
  // Redirect to the conformation page
  Response.Redirect("OrderPlaced.aspx");
}
```

Note that this is one of the most crucial pieces of code in this chapter. Here you'll most likely make any modifications to the tax and shipping systems if you decide to add your own system, because choices are made on this page. The database and business layer changes are far more generic—although that's not to say that modifications wouldn't be necessary.

Exercise: Testing Tax and Shipping Charges

1. Before testing that the new system is working for tax and shipping charges, use the `OrderTest.aspx` page to check that old orders are unaffected. The information retrieved for an old order should be unaffected because the data is unchanged.

2. Place a new order, preferably with a customer in the United States/Canada shipping region (as this is currently the only region where tax is applied). Notice that on the checkout page you must select a shipping option, as shown in Figure 13-4.

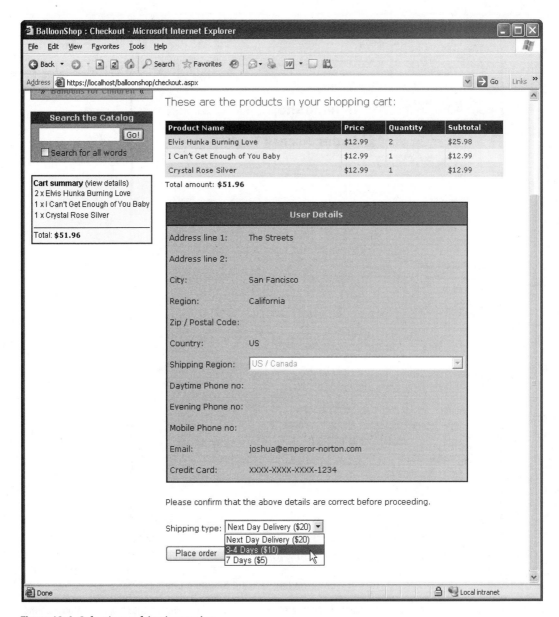

Figure 13-4. *Selecting a shipping region*

3. After placing the order, check the `OrderID` of the order in the database and then retrieve the order using `OrderTest.aspx`. The result is shown in Figure 13-5.

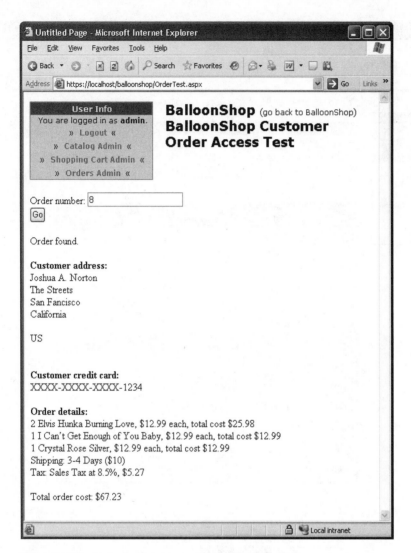

Figure 13-5. *Order including tax and shipping charges*

How It Works: Testing Tax and Shipping Charges

In this chapter leading up to this example, you've pretty much examined how the tax and shipping charges operate, but let's recap.

First, the customer is required to select a shipping region for their address. Without this shipping region being selected, visitors cannot place orders, because they cannot select a shipping option. When a visitor places an order, the shipping region selected is attached to the order in the Orders table. The tax requirement for the order is also attached, although this requires no user input (and is currently selected using a very simple algorithm, although this wouldn't be difficult to change).

Next, when you use the CommerceLibOrderInfo class, the tax and shipping is automatically taken into account in both the total cost and text representation of the order.

Further Development

There are several ways to proceed from here. Perhaps the first might be to add an administration system for tax and shipping options. This hasn't been implemented here partly because it would be trivial given the experience you've had so far in this book, and partly because the techniques laid out here are more of a template for development then a fully developed way of doing things. There are so many options to choose from for both tax and shipping calculations that only the basics are discussed here.

Hooking into online services for tax and shipping cost calculations is an attractive option; for shipping services, this is very much a possibility. In fact, the services offered by shipping companies such as FedEx use a similar way of going about things as the credit card gateway companies we'll look at later in this book. Much of the code you'd have to write to access these services will be very similar to that for credit card processing, although of course you'll have to adapt it to get the specifics right. Sadly, there may be more major changes required, such as adding weights and dimensions to products, but that very much depends on what products you are selling. For items in the BalloonShop catalog, many products are lighter than air, so shipping could be very cheap.

Summary

In this chapter, you've extended the BalloonShop site to enable customers to place orders using all the new data and techniques introduced in Chapter 12. Much of the modification made in this chapter lays the groundwork for the order pipeline to be used in the rest of this book. You've also included a quick way to examine customer orders, although this is by no means a fully fleshed out administration tool—that will come later.

You also implemented a simple system for adding tax and shipping charges to orders. This system is far from being a universal solution, but it works and it's simple. More importantly, the techniques can easily be built on to introduce more complex algorithms and user interaction to select tax and shipping options and price the order accordingly.

From the next chapter onward, you'll be expanding on the customer ordering system even more by starting to develop a professional order pipeline for order processing.

■ ■ ■

CHAPTER 14

Order Pipeline

In this and the next chapter, you'll build your own order-processing pipeline that deals with credit card authorization, stock checking, shipping, sending email notifications, and so on. In fact, we'll leave the credit card processing specifics until Chapter 16, but we'll show you where this process fits in before then.

Order pipeline functionality is an extremely useful capability for an e-commerce site because it allows you to track orders at every stage in the process, and provides auditing information that you can refer to at a later date or if something goes wrong during the order processing. You can do all this without relying on a third party's accounting system, which also can reduce costs. The first section of this chapter discusses what we actually mean by an order pipeline and the specifics that apply to the BalloonShop application.

Such a system can be implemented in various ways, and many people recommend that you use a transactional system such as MTS (Microsoft Transaction Server), or COM+ (Component Object Model+) in more recent operating systems. However, this method adds its own complications and doesn't give you that much that you can't achieve using standard .NET assemblies. Although it's possible to create COM+ components using .NET, the code implementation is more complicated, and debugging code can be tricky. For this reason, we'll stick with the .NET platform here, which has the added advantage that it makes code easier to understand and debug. The bulk of this chapter deals with constructing such a system, which also involves a small modification of the way things currently work and some additions to the database you've been using. However, the code in this chapter isn't much more complicated than the code you've already been using. The real challenges are in the design of the system.

By the end of Chapter 15, you'll be able to follow the progress of customer orders as they pass through various stages of the order pipeline. Although no real credit card processing takes place, you'll end up with a fairly complete system, including a new administration web page that can be used by suppliers to confirm that they have items in stock and to confirm that orders have been shipped. To start with, however, you need a bit more background about what we are actually trying to achieve.

Defining an Order Pipeline

Any commercial transaction, whether in a shop on the street, over the Internet, or anywhere else, has several related tasks that must be carried out before it can be considered complete. For example, you can't simply remove an item of clothing from a fashion boutique without paying for it and say that you have bought it—remuneration is (unfortunately!) an integral part of any purchase. In addition, a transaction can only complete successfully if each of the tasks carried out completes successfully. If a customer's credit card is rejected, for example, then no funds can be taken from it, so a purchase can't be made.

The sequence of tasks carried out as part of a transaction is often thought of in terms of a pipeline. In this analogy, orders start at one end of the pipe and come out of the other end when they are completed. Along the way, they must pass through several pipeline sections, each of which is responsible for a particular task or a related group of tasks. If any pipeline section fails to complete, then the order "gets stuck" and might require outside interaction before it can move further along the pipeline, or it might be canceled completely.

For example, the simple pipeline shown in Figure 14-1 applies to transactions in a street shop.

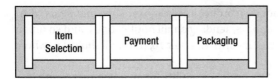

Figure 14-1. *Transactions for a street shop*

Here the last section might be optional, and might involve additional tasks such as gift-wrapping. The payment stage might also take one of several methods of operation, because the customer could pay using cash, credit card, gift certificates, and so on.

As you'll see in the next section, the e-commerce purchasing pipeline becomes longer, but isn't really any more complicated.

Understanding the BalloonShop Order Pipeline

In BalloonShop, the pipeline will look like the one in Figure 14-2.

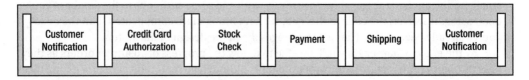

Figure 14-2. *The BalloonShop order pipeline*

The tasks carried out in these pipeline sections are, in order:

- *Customer Notification*: An email is sent notifying the customer that order processing has started and confirming the items to be sent and the address that goods will be sent to.

- *Credit Card Authorization*: The credit card used for purchasing is checked, and the total order amount is set aside (although no payment is taken at this stage).

- *Stock Check*: An email is sent to the supplier with a list of the items that have been ordered. Processing continues when the supplier confirms that the goods are available.

- *Payment*: The credit card transaction is completed using the funds set aside earlier.

- *Shipping*: An email is sent to the supplier confirming that payment for the items ordered has been taken. Processing continues when the supplier confirms that the goods have been shipped.

- *Customer Notification*: An email is sent notifying the customer that the order has been shipped, and thanking them for using the BalloonShop web site.

Note In terms of implementation, as you'll see shortly, there are actually more stages than this, because the stock check and shipping stages consist of two pipeline sections: one for sending the email and one that waits for confirmation.

As orders flow through this pipeline, entries are added to a new database table called Audit. These entries can be examined to see what has happened to an order and are an excellent way of identifying problems if they occur. Each entry in the Orders database also will be flagged with a status, identifying which point in the pipeline it has reached.

To process the pipeline, you'll create classes representing each stage. These classes carry out the required processing and then modify the status of the order in the Orders database to advance the order. You'll also need a coordinating class (or processor), which can be called for any order and will execute the appropriate pipeline stage class. This processor will be called once when the order is placed, and in normal operation, will be called twice more: once for stock confirmation and once for shipping confirmation.

To make life easier, you'll also define a common interface supported by each pipeline stage class to enable the order processor class to access each stage in a standard way. You'll also define several utility functions and expose several common properties in the order processor class, which will be used as and when necessary by the pipeline stages. For example, the ID of the order should be accessible to all pipeline stages, so to save code duplication, you'll put that information in the order processor class.

Now, let's get on to the specifics. You'll build a series of classes that we'll refer to collectively as the CommerceLib classes. These classes could be contained in a separate assembly, but for simplicity, we'll include them in the BalloonShop code. This also simplifies access to customer information because you'll have access to the user profile classes defined by ASP.NET, as used in the last chapter. To differentiate the code from the existing code, however, you'll place all the CommerceLib files in a subdirectory of the App_Code directory and in a CommerceLib namespace. The CommerceLib directory will contain the following classes:

- *OrderProcessor*: The main class for processing orders.

- *OrderProcessorException*: The custom exception class for use in the order processor and pipeline sections.

- *IPipelineSection*: The interface definition for pipeline sections.

- *Customer, OrderDetails, OrderDetail*: The classes used to store data extracted from the database, for ease of access.

- *PSInitialNotification, PSCheckFunds, PSCheckStock, PSStockOK, PSTakePayment, PSShipGoods, PSShipOK, PSFinalNotification*: The pipeline section classes.

The progress of an order through the pipeline as mediated by the order processor relates to the pipeline shown earlier (see Figure 14-3).

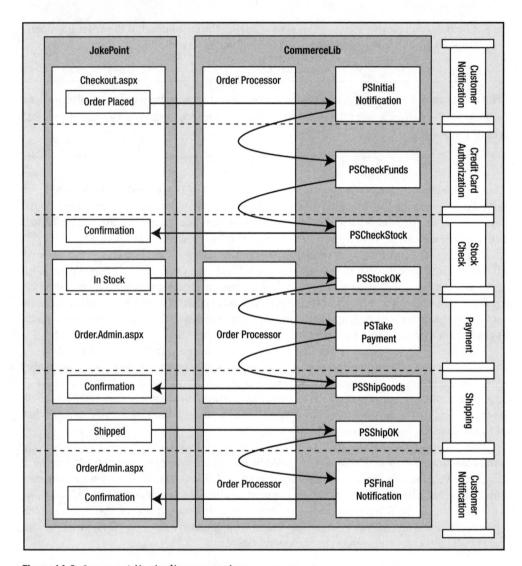

Figure 14-3. *CommerceLib pipeline processing*

The process shown in Figure 14-3 is divided into three sections as follows:

- Customer places order.
- Supplier confirms stock.
- Supplier confirms shipping.

The first stage is as follows:

1. When the customer confirms an order, Checkout.aspx creates the order in the database and calls OrderProcessor to begin order processing.

2. OrderProcessor detects that the order is new and calls PSInitialNotification.

3. PSInitialNotification sends an email to the customer confirming the order and advances the order stage. It also instructs OrderProcessor to continue processing.

4. OrderProcessor detects the new order status and calls PSCheckFunds.

5. PSCheckFunds checks that funds are available on the customer's credit card and stores the details required to complete the transaction if funds are available. If this is successful, then the order stage is advanced and OrderProcessor is told to continue.

6. OrderProcessor detects the new order status and calls PSCheckStock.

7. PSCheckStock sends an email to the supplier with a list of the items ordered, instructs the supplier to confirm via OrderAdmin.aspx, and advances the order status.

8. OrderProcessor terminates.

The second stage is as follows:

1. When the supplier confirms that stock is available, OrderAdmin.aspx calls OrderProcessor to continue order processing.

2. OrderProcessor detects the new order status and calls PSStockOK.

3. PSStockOK advances the order status and tells OrderProcessor to continue.

4. OrderProcessor detects the new order status and calls PSTakePayment.

5. PSTakePayment uses the transaction details stored earlier by PSCheckFunds to complete the transaction, advances the order status, and tells OrderProcessor to continue.

6. OrderProcessor detects the new order status and calls PSShipGoods.

7. PSShipGoods sends an email to the supplier with a confirmation of the items ordered, instructs the supplier to ship these goods to the customer, and advances the order status.

8. OrderProcessor terminates.

The third stage is as follows:

1. When the supplier confirms that the goods have been shipped, OrderAdmin.aspx calls OrderProcessor to continue order processing.

2. OrderProcessor detects the new order status and calls PSShipOK.

3. PSShipOK enters the shipment date in the database, advances the order status, and tells OrderProcessor to continue.

4. OrderProcessor detects the new order status and calls PSFinalNotification.

5. PSFinalNotification sends an email to the customer confirming that the order has been shipped and advances the order stage.

6. OrderProcessor terminates.

If anything goes wrong at any point in the pipeline processing, such as a credit card being declined, an email is sent to an administrator. This administrator then has all the information necessary to check what has happened, get in contact with the customer involved, and cancel or replace the order if necessary.

No point in this process is particularly complicated; it's just that a lot of code is required to put this into action!

Building the Order Pipeline

Building this pipeline involves adding a lot of code, so to simplify things, this process is broken down into stages. First, you'll add the basic framework and include a "dummy" pipeline section to check that things are working. Next, you'll add additional functionality that will be required by the "real" pipeline sections. Then, in the next chapter you'll add these pipeline sections, before integrating credit card functionality in Chapter 16.

The Basic Order Pipeline

To start with, then, let's add the basics.

Database Modifications

There isn't much to change in the database at this point, but you do need to add a new table, Audit, and associated stored procedures.

The Audit Table

During order processing, one of the most important functions of the pipeline is to maintain an up-to-date audit trail. The implementation of this involves adding records to a new database table called Audit. You need to create this table with fields as shown in Table 14-1.

Table 14-1. *The* Audit *Table*

Column Name	Column Type	Description
AuditID	int	Primary key, also set as table identity
OrderID	int	The ID of the order that the audit entry applies to
DateStamp	datetime	The date and time that the audit entry was created, default value GETDATE()
Message	varchar(512)	The text of the audit entry
MessageNumber	int	An identifying number for the audit entry type

Entries will be added by OrderProcessor and by individual pipeline stages to indicate successes and failures. These can then be examined to see what has happened to an order, an important function when it comes to error checking.

The MessageNumber column is interesting because it allows you to associate specific messages with an identifying number. It would be possible to have another database table allowing you to match these message numbers with descriptions, although this isn't really necessary, because the scheme used for numbering (as you'll see later in the chapter) is descriptive. In addition, the Message column already provides human-readable information.

The CreateAudit Stored Procedure

Now that you have the new Audit table, you need a way to add entries. You'll do this with the following stored procedure:

```
CREATE PROCEDURE CreateAudit
(@OrderID int,
 @Message nvarchar(512),
 @MessageNumber int)
AS

INSERT INTO Audit (OrderID, Message, MessageNumber)
VALUES (@OrderID, @Message, @MessageNumber)
```

Business Tier Modifications

There are several new classes to consider here, as well as a new method to add to the CommerceLibAccess class you created earlier. The new classes we'll look at in this section are

- *CommerceLibException*: A standard exception to be used by the order processor.

- *OrderProcessorMailer*: Utility class allowing the order processor to send emails with simple syntax.

- *IPipelineSection*: Standard interface for pipeline sections.

- *OrderProcessor*: Controlling class for order processing.

- *PSDummy*: Test pipeline section.

You'll also need to modify the BalloonShopConfiguration class to include additional order processor configuration properties.

The CreateAudit Method

This method is a wrapper around the CreateAudit stored procedure added earlier and uses standard code. Add the following code to the CommerceLibAccess class:

```
public static void CreateAudit(int orderID, string message,
  int messageNumber)
{
  // get a configured DbCommand object
  DbCommand comm = GenericDataAccess.CreateCommand();
```

```
    // set the stored procedure name
    comm.CommandText = "CreateAudit";
    // create a new parameter
    DbParameter param = comm.CreateParameter();
    param.ParameterName = "@OrderID";
    param.Value = orderID;
    param.DbType = DbType.Int32;
    comm.Parameters.Add(param);
    // create a new parameter
    param = comm.CreateParameter();
    param.ParameterName = "@Message";
    param.Value = message;
    param.DbType = DbType.String;
    param.Size = 512;
    comm.Parameters.Add(param);
    // create a new parameter
    param = comm.CreateParameter();
    param.ParameterName = "@MessageNumber";
    param.Value = messageNumber;
    param.DbType = DbType.Int32;
    comm.Parameters.Add(param);
    // execute the stored procedure
    GenericDataAccess.ExecuteNonQuery(comm);
  }
```

You'll see more details about the `messageNumber` parameter used for auditing later in the chapter, when we analyze the order-processor functionality in an exercise.

The OrderProcessorException Class

This is the first new class that you'll add to the `CommerceLib` library. If you haven't already done so, you need to add a subdirectory called `CommerceLib` to the BalloonShop `App_Code` directory.

Add a new class to this directory called `CommerceLibException` with the following code:

```
namespace CommerceLib
{
  /// <summary>
  /// Standard exception for order processor
  /// </summary>
  public class OrderProcessorException : ApplicationException
  {
    private int sourceStage;

    public OrderProcessorException(string message,
      int exceptionSourceStage) : base(message)
    {
      sourceStage = exceptionSourceStage;
    }
```

```
  public int SourceStage
  {
    get
    {
      return sourceStage;
    }
  }
}
}
```

This code extends the base exception class `ApplicationException`, adding an integer property called `SourceStage`. This property allows you to identify the pipeline section (if any) that is responsible for throwing the exception.

Note that we use `ApplicationException` instead of `Exception` as the base class for this new exception class. This is recommended because the base `Exception` class is the base class for all exceptions; that is, both application and runtime exceptions. `ApplicationException` derives directly from `Exception` and should be used for exceptions thrown from application code. Another class, `SystemException`, which also derives directly from `Exception`, is used by runtime code. This distinction gives you a simple way to see roughly what code is generating exceptions even before examining any exceptions thrown. The Microsoft recommendation is to neither catch nor throw `SystemException` derived classes in your code. In practice, however, we often do, because often `try...catch` blocks have a default `catch` block to catch all exceptions.

BalloonShop Configuration Modifications

The `BalloonShopConfiguration` class already includes a number of configuration properties for the site, or, to be more specific, allows access to properties stored in `web.config`. The `OrderProcessor` class (which you'll add shortly) needs various additional pieces of information in order to function. The new code to add to this class is as follows:

```
public static class BalloonShopConfiguration
{
  ...

  // Returns the email address for customers to contact the site
  public static string CustomerServiceEmail
  {
    get
    {
      return
        ConfigurationManager.AppSettings["CustomerServiceEmail"];
    }
  }

  // The "from" address for auto-generated order processor emails
  public static string OrderProcessorEmail
  {
    get
```

```
    {
      return
        ConfigurationManager.AppSettings["OrderProcessorEmail"];
    }
  }

  // The email address to use to contact the supplier
  public static string SupplierEmail
  {
    get
    {
      return ConfigurationManager.AppSettings["SupplierEmail"];
    }
  }
}
```

The new settings exposed by this class are as follows:

- *CustomerServiceEmail*: The email address that customers can use to send in queries about orders.

- *OrderProcessorEmail*: An email address used as the "from" address for emails sent from the order processor to the administrator.

- *SupplierEmail*: The email address of the product supplier, so that the order processor can send order notifications ready for picking/shipping.

For testing purposes, you can set all of these settings to your email address. Later you will probably want to change some or all of these appropriately.

■**Note** Depending on the size of your enterprise, you may have multiple suppliers, in which case you'll probably want to store supplier information in the BalloonShop database and associate each product or product range with a different supplier. To keep things simple, however, the code in this book assumes that you only have one supplier—which may well use the same email address as the site administrator.

You also need to add the relevant properties to the <appSettings> section of web.config:

```
<appSettings>
  ...
  <add key="CustomerServiceEmail" value="<yourEmail>" />
  <add key="OrderProcessorEmail" value="<yourEmail>" />
  <add key="SupplierEmail" value="<yourEmail>" />
</appSettings>
```

Obviously, you need to replace the values <yourEmail> and <yourEmail> with values appropriate to your system.

The OrderProcessorMailer Class

This class enables code to send emails during order processing. Add a new class to the App_Code/CommerceLib directory with code as follows:

```
namespace CommerceLib
{
  /// <summary>
  /// Mailing utilities for OrderProcessor
  /// </summary>
  public static class OrderProcessorMailer
  {
    public static void MailAdmin(int orderID, string subject,
      string message, int sourceStage)
    {
      // Send mail to administrator
      string to = BalloonShopConfiguration.ErrorLogEmail;
      string from = BalloonShopConfiguration.OrderProcessorEmail;
      string body = "Message: " + message
          + "\nSource: " + sourceStage.ToString()
          + "\nOrder ID: " + orderID.ToString();
      Utilities.SendMail(from, to, subject, body);
    }
  }
}
```

The only method of this class, MailAdmin, uses the Utilities.SendMail method to send an email to the site administrator by using settings from BalloonShopConfiguration. Later, when we need to send mails to customers and suppliers, we'll add more code to this class.

The IPipelineSection Interface

This IPipelineSection interface is implemented by all pipeline section classes, so that OrderProcessor can use them in a standard way. Add the following interface definition in a file called IPipelineSection.cs in the App_Code/CommerceLib directory:

```
namespace CommerceLib
{
  /// <summary>
  /// Standard interface for pipeline sections
  /// </summary>
  public interface IPipelineSection
  {
    void Process(OrderProcessor processor);
  }
}
```

This interface exposes a single method, Process, that OrderProcessor will use to process an order through the pipeline stage in question. This method includes a reference to the calling class, so that pipeline sections will have access to order information and utility methods exposed by the OrderProcessor class.

The OrderProcessor Class

As is probably apparent now, the OrderProcessor class (which is the class responsible for moving an order through the pipeline) is a little more complicated than the classes you've seen so far in this chapter. However, you can start simply and build up additional functionality as needed. To start with, you'll create a version of the OrderProcessor class with the following functionality:

- Dynamically selects a pipeline section supporting IPipelineSection

- Adds basic auditing data

- Gives access to the current order and customer details

- Gives access to administrator mailing

- Mails the administrator in case of error

The code for this class, which you should also add to the App_Code/CommerceLib directory, is as follows:

```
namespace CommerceLib
{
  /// <summary>
  /// Main class, used to obtain order information,
  /// run pipeline sections, audit orders, etc.
  /// </summary>
  public class OrderProcessor
  {
    internal IPipelineSection CurrentPipelineSection;
    internal bool ContinueNow;
    internal CommerceLibOrderInfo Order;

    public OrderProcessor(string orderID)
    {
      // get order
      Order = CommerceLibAccess.GetOrder(orderID);
    }

    public OrderProcessor(CommerceLibOrderInfo orderToProcess)
    {
      // get order
      Order = orderToProcess;
    }

    public void Process()
    {
```

```
      // configure processor
      ContinueNow = true;

      // log start of execution
      CreateAudit("Order Processor started.", 10000);

      // process pipeline section
      try
      {
        while (ContinueNow)
        {
          ContinueNow = false;
          GetCurrentPipelineSection();
          CurrentPipelineSection.Process(this);
        }
      }
      catch (OrderProcessorException ex)
      {
        MailAdmin("Order Processing error occurred.",
          ex.Message, ex.SourceStage);
        CreateAudit("Order Processing error occurred.", 10002);
        throw new OrderProcessorException(
          "Error occurred, order aborted. "
          + "Details mailed to administrator.", 100);
      }
      catch (Exception ex)
      {
        MailAdmin("Order Processing error occurred.", ex.Message,
          100);
        CreateAudit("Order Processing error occurred.", 10002);
        throw new OrderProcessorException(
          "Unknown error, order aborted. "
          + "Details mailed to administrator.", 100);
      }
      finally
      {
        CommerceLibAccess.CreateAudit(Order.OrderID,
          "Order Processor finished.", 10001);
      }
    }

    public void CreateAudit(string message, int messageNumber)
    {
      CommerceLibAccess.CreateAudit(Order.OrderID, message,
        messageNumber);
    }
```

```
    public void MailAdmin(string subject, string message,
      int sourceStage)
    {
      OrderProcessorMailer.MailAdmin(Order.OrderID, subject,
        message, sourceStage);
    }

    private void GetCurrentPipelineSection()
    {
      // select pipeline section to execute based on order status
      // for now just provide a dummy
      CurrentPipelineSection = new PSDummy();
    }
  }
}
```

This class includes two constructors, which are used to initialize the order processor with order information by either using the ID of an order or by simply using a CommerceLibOrderInfo instance. The class also includes its own versions of the CommerceLibAccess.CreateAudit and OrderProcessorMailer.MailAdmin methods, both of which are time savers that enable you to call these methods with the order ID parameter filled in automatically.

We'll walk through the rest of the code here shortly. Suffice to say for now that the only pipeline section used is PSDummy, which you'll add next.

The PSDummy Class

The PSDummy class is a dummy pipeline section that you'll use in your basic pipeline implementation to check that things are working correctly. Add this class to the App_Code/CommerceLib directory:

```
namespace CommerceLib
{
  /// <summary>
  /// Summary description for PSDummy
  /// </summary>
  public class PSDummy : IPipelineSection
  {
    public void Process(OrderProcessor processor)
    {
      processor.CreateAudit("PSDoNothing started.", 99999);
      processor.CreateAudit("Customer: "
        + processor.Order.Customer.UserName, 99999);
      processor.CreateAudit("First item in order: "
        + processor.Order.OrderDetails[0].ItemAsString, 99999);
      processor.MailAdmin("Test.", "Test mail from PSDummy.", 99999);
      processor.CreateAudit("PSDoNothing finished.", 99999);
    }
  }
}
```

The code here uses the AddAudit and MailAdmin methods of OrderProcessor to show that the code has executed correctly. Again, we'll look at this code in more detail shortly.

Presentation Tier Modifications

All you need to do now for the order processor to process an order is to add some very simple code to the checkout page.

Checkout Page Modifications

Modify the code in placeOrderButton_Click in Checkout.aspx.cs as follows:

```
using CommerceLib;

...

  protected void placeOrderButton_Click(object sender, EventArgs e)
  {
    ...
    // Create the order and store the order ID
    string orderId = ShoppingCartAccess.CreateCommerceLibOrder(
      shippingId, taxId);
    // Process order
    OrderProcessor processor = new OrderProcessor(orderId);
    processor.Process();
    // Redirect to the conformation page
    Response.Redirect("OrderPlaced.aspx");
  }
```

Exercise: Basic Order Processing

1. Open the BalloonShop **Web Application** in a browser.

2. Log in as a customer you've previously created, add some products to your cart, and place an order.

3. Check your inbox for new mail. An example of this is shown in Figure 14-4.

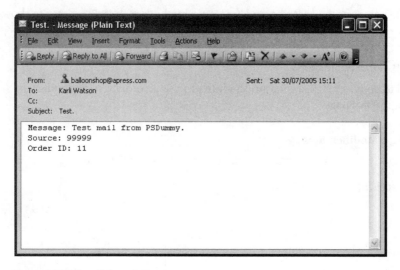

Figure 14-4. *Email from PSDummy*

4. Examine the `Audit` **table** in the database to see the new entries. An example is shown in Figure 14-5 (note that the dates are in `dd/mm/yyyy` format in this figure).

	AuditID	OrderID	DateStamp	Message	MessageNumber
	11	11	30/07/2005 15:11:26	Order Processor started.	10000
	12	11	30/07/2005 15:11:26	PSDoNothing started.	99999
	13	11	30/07/2005 15:11:26	Customer: Charles Darwin	99999
	14	11	30/07/2005 15:11:26	First item in order: 1 Love Rose, $12.99 each, total cost $12.99	99999
	15	11	30/07/2005 15:11:26	PSDoNothing finished.	99999
	16	11	30/07/2005 15:11:26	Order Processor finished.	10001

Figure 14-5. *Audit table entries from PSDummy*

How It Works: Basic Order Processing

The main body of the `OrderProcessor` class is the `Process` method, which is called by the `Checkout.aspx` (and will be called later by the order admin pages) to process an order. The order to be processed is set by the constructor of `OrderProcessor` as noted earlier and is indicated either by an `ID` or a `CommerceLibOrderInfo` object.

The first thing that `Process` does is set `ContinueNow` to true and log the start of its execution in the `Audit` table:

```
public void Process()
{
  // configure processor
  ContinueNow = true;

  // log start of execution
  CreateAudit("Order Processor started.", 10000);
```

■**Note** 10000 is the message number to store for the audit entry—we'll look at these codes in more detail in a little while.

Next we come to the order processing itself. The model used here checks the Boolean ContinueNow field before processing a pipeline section. This allows sections to specify either that processing should continue when they're finished with the current task (by setting ContinueNow to true) or that processing should pause (by setting ContinueNow to false). This is necessary because you need to wait for external input at certain points along the pipeline, such as checking whether stock is available.

The pipeline section to process is selected by the private GetCurrentPipelineSection method, which eventually selects a section based on the status of the order, but currently just has the job of setting the Current➥ PipelineSection field to an instance of PSDummy:

```
private void GetCurrentPipelineSection()
{
  // select pipeline section to execute based on order status
  // for now just provide a dummy
  CurrentPipelineSection = new PSDummy();
}
```

Back to Process, you see this method being called in a try block:

```
// process pipeline section
try
{
  while (ContinueNow)
  {
    ContinueNow = false;
    GetCurrentPipelineSection();
```

Note that ContinueNow is set to false in the while loop—the default behavior is to stop after each pipeline section.

After you have a pipeline section, you need to process it. All sections support the simple IPipelineSection interface, defined as follows:

```
public interface IPipelineSection
{
  void Process(OrderProcessor processor);
}
```

All pipeline sections use a Process method to perform their work, and this method requires an OrderProcessor reference because the pipeline sections need access to the order and customer details exposed by the order processor.

The last part of the while loop (and try block) in OrderProcessor calls this method:

```
      CurrentPipelineSection.Process(this);
    }
  }
```

This calls the `Process` method in `PSDummy`, which we'll come back to shortly.

The last part of the `Process` method in `OrderProcessor` involves catching exceptions, which might be `OrderProcessorException` instances or other exception types. In either case, you send an email to the administrator using the `MailAdmin` method (we'll cover this in a little while), add an audit entry, and throw a new `OrderProcessorException` that can be caught by users of the `OrderProcessor` class:

```
catch (OrderProcessorException ex)
{
  MailAdmin("Order Processing error occurred.",
    ex.Message, ex.SourceStage);
  CreateAudit("Order Processing error occurred.", 10002);
  throw new OrderProcessorException(
    "Error occurred, order aborted. "
    + "Details mailed to administrator.", 100);
}
catch (Exception ex)
{
  MailAdmin("Order Processing error occurred.", ex.Message,
    100);
  CreateAudit("Order Processing error occurred.", 10002);
  throw new OrderProcessorException(
    "Unknown error, order aborted. "
    + "Details mailed to administrator.", 100);
}
```

Regardless of whether processing is successful, you add a final audit entry saying that the processing has completed.

```
finally
{
  CommerceLibAccess.CreateAudit(Order.OrderID,
    "Order Processor finished.", 10001);
}
}
```

At this point, it's worth examining the message number scheme chosen for order-processing audits. In all cases, the audit message number is a five-digit number. The first digit of this number is either 1 if an audit is being added by `OrderProcessor`, or 2 if the audit is added by a pipeline section. The next two digits are used for the pipeline stage that added the audit (which maps directly to the status of the order when the audit was added). The final two digits uniquely identify the message within this scope. For example, so far you've seen the following message numbers:

- *10000*: Order processor started.

- *10001*: Order processor finished.

- *10002*: Order processor error occurred.

Later you'll see a lot of these that start with 2, as you get on to pipeline sections, and include the necessary information for identifying the pipeline section as noted previously. We hope you'll agree that this scheme allows for plenty of flexibility, although you can, of course, use whatever numbers you see fit. As a final note, numbers ending in 00 and 01 are used for starting and finishing messages for both the order processor and pipeline stages, whereas 02 and above are for other messages. There is no real reason for this apart from consistency between the components.

The PSDummy class that is used in this skeleton processor performs some basic functions to check that things are working correctly:

```
public class PSDummy : IPipelineSection
{
  public void Process(OrderProcessor processor)
  {
    processor.CreateAudit("PSDoNothing started.", 99999);
    processor.CreateAudit("Customer: "
      + processor.Order.Customer.UserName, 99999);
    processor.CreateAudit("First item in order: "
      + processor.Order.OrderDetails[0].ItemAsString, 99999);
    processor.MailAdmin("Test.", "Test mail from PSDummy.",
      99999);
    processor.CreateAudit("PSDoNothing finished.", 99999);
  }
}
```

The code here uses the AddAudit and .MailAdmin methods of OrderProcessor to generate something to show that the code has executed correctly. Note that the numbering schemes outlined previously aren't used there, as this isn't a real pipeline section.

That was a lot of code to get through, but it did have the effect of making the client code very simple:

```
// Process order
OrderProcessor processor = new OrderProcessor(orderId);
processor.Process();
```

Short of setting all the configuration details in web.config, there is very little to do because OrderProcessor does a lot of work for you. It's worth noting that the code you have at this point is for the most part a consequence of the design choices made earlier. This is an excellent example of how a strong design can lead straight to powerful and robust code.

Adding More Functionality to OrderProcessor

You need to add a few more bits and pieces to the OrderProcessor class to make it fully functional for use with the pipeline sections that you'll add in the next chapter.

You need to look at

- Updating the status of an order

- Setting and getting credit card authentication details

- Setting the order shipment date

Database Modifications

All the modifications in this section are stored procedures.

The CommerceLibOrderUpdateStatus Stored Procedure

Each pipeline section needs the capability to change the status of an order, advancing it to the next pipeline section. Rather than simply incrementing the status, this functionality is kept flexible, just in case you end up with a more complicated branched pipeline. This requires a new stored procedure, CommerceLibOrderUpdateStatus:

```
CREATE PROCEDURE CommerceLibOrderUpdateStatus
(@OrderID int,
 @Status int)
AS

UPDATE Orders
SET Status = @Status
WHERE OrderID = @OrderID
```

The CommerceLibOrderSetAuthCode Stored Procedure

In Chapter 16, when we deal with credit card usage, you'll need to set data in the AuthCode and Reference fields in the Orders table.

This requires a new stored procedure, CommerceLibOrderSetAuthCode:

```
CREATE PROCEDURE CommerceLibOrderSetAuthCode
(@OrderID int,
 @AuthCode nvarchar(50),
 @Reference nvarchar(50))
AS

UPDATE Orders
SET AuthCode = @AuthCode, Reference = @Reference
WHERE OrderID = @OrderID
```

The CommerceLibOrderSetDateShipped Stored Procedure

When an order is shipped, you should update the shipment date in the database, which can simply be the current date. The new stored procedure to do this, CommerceLibOrder➠ SetDateShipped, is as follows:

```
CREATE PROCEDURE CommerceLibOrderSetDateShipped
(@OrderID int)
AS

UPDATE Orders
SET DateShipped = GetDate()
WHERE OrderID = @OrderID
```

Business Tier Modifications

Next you need to modify CommerceLibAccess to use the new stored procedures. All the methods in this section act in much the same way as some of the other methods of CommerceLibAccess that you've seen already.

The UpdateOrderStatus Method

This method calls the CommerceLibOrderUpdateStatus stored procedure:

```
public static void UpdateOrderStatus(int orderID, int status)
{
  // get a configured DbCommand object
  DbCommand comm = GenericDataAccess.CreateCommand();
  // set the stored procedure name
  comm.CommandText = "CommerceLibOrderUpdateStatus";
  // create a new parameter
  DbParameter param = comm.CreateParameter();
  param.ParameterName = "@OrderID";
  param.Value = orderID;
  param.DbType = DbType.Int32;
  comm.Parameters.Add(param);
  // create a new parameter
  param = comm.CreateParameter();
  param.ParameterName = "@Status";
  param.Value = status;
  param.DbType = DbType.Int32;
  comm.Parameters.Add(param);
  // execute the stored procedure
  GenericDataAccess.ExecuteNonQuery(comm);
}
```

The SetOrderAuthCodeAndReference Method

This method uses the CommerceLibOrderSetAuthCode stored procedure to set the AuthCode and Reference fields in Orders:

```
public static void SetOrderAuthCodeAndReference(int orderID,
  string authCode, string reference)
{
  // get a configured DbCommand object
  DbCommand comm = GenericDataAccess.CreateCommand();
  // set the stored procedure name
  comm.CommandText = "CommerceLibOrderSetAuthCode";
  // create a new parameter
  DbParameter param = comm.CreateParameter();
  param.ParameterName = "@OrderID";
  param.Value = orderID;
  param.DbType = DbType.Int32;
  comm.Parameters.Add(param);
  // create a new parameter
  param = comm.CreateParameter();
  param.ParameterName = "@AuthCode";
  param.Value = authCode;
  param.DbType = DbType.String;
```

```
    param.Size = 50;
    comm.Parameters.Add(param);
    // create a new parameter
    param = comm.CreateParameter();
    param.ParameterName = "@Reference";
    param.Value = reference;
    param.DbType = DbType.String;
    param.Size = 50;
    comm.Parameters.Add(param);
    // execute the stored procedure
    GenericDataAccess.ExecuteNonQuery(comm);
  }
```

The SetOrderDateShipped Method

The last method to add to CommerceLibAccess, SetOrderDateShipped, is as follows:

```
  public static void SetOrderDateShipped(int orderID)
  {
    // get a configured DbCommand object
    DbCommand comm = GenericDataAccess.CreateCommand();
    // set the stored procedure name
    comm.CommandText = "CommerceLibOrderSetDateShipped";
    // create a new parameter
    DbParameter param = comm.CreateParameter();
    param.ParameterName = "@OrderID";
    param.Value = orderID;
    param.DbType = DbType.Int32;
    comm.Parameters.Add(param);
    // execute the stored procedure
    GenericDataAccess.ExecuteNonQuery(comm);
  }
```

CommerceLibOrderInfo Modifications

Finally, for convenience, you can allow the preceding methods to be called via the
CommerceLibOrderInfo class. This enables you to skip the orderID parameter, because
CommerceLibOrderInfo instances know what their IDs are. You can also update local fields while
you make the changes. This requires the following new methods on the CommerceLibOrderInfo
class:

```
  public void UpdateStatus(int status)
  {
    // call static method
    CommerceLibAccess.UpdateOrderStatus(OrderID, status);
    // update field
    Status = status;
  }
```

```
public void SetAuthCodeAndReference(string authCode,
  string reference)
{
  // call static method
  CommerceLibAccess.SetOrderAuthCodeAndReference(OrderID,
    authCode, reference);
  // update fields
  AuthCode = authCode;
  Reference = reference;
}

public void SetDateShipped()
{
  // call static method
  CommerceLibAccess.SetOrderDateShipped(OrderID);
  // update field
  DateShipped = DateTime.Now.ToString();
}
```

Summary

You've started to build the backbone of the application and prepared it for the lion's share of the order pipeline processing functionality, which you'll implement in Chapter 15.

Specifically, we've covered the following:

- The basic framework for your order pipeline

- The database additions for auditing data and storing additional required data in the Orders table

- How to put orders into the pipeline when they are placed in BalloonShop

In the next chapter, you'll go on to implement the order pipeline.

■ ■ ■

CHAPTER 15

Implementing the Pipeline

In the last chapter, you completed the basic functionality of the OrderProcessor component, which is responsible for moving orders through pipeline stages. You've seen a quick demonstration of this using a dummy pipeline section, but you haven't yet implemented the pipeline discussed at the beginning of the last chapter.

In this chapter, you'll add the required pipeline sections so that you can process orders from start to finish, although you won't be adding full credit card transaction functionality until the next chapter.

We'll also look at the web administration of orders by modifying the order admin pages added earlier in the book to take into account the new order-processing system.

Considering the Code for the Pipeline Sections

The OrderProcessor code is complete, except for one important section—the pipeline stage selection. Rather than forcing the processor to use PSDummy, you actually want to select one of the pipeline stages outlined in Chapter 14, depending on the status of the order. Before you do this, let's run through the code for each of the pipeline sections in turn, and some new utility code, which will take you to the point where the order pipeline is complete apart from actual credit card authorization.

Business Tier Modifications

The first thing we'll look at in this section is some modifications to the OrderProcessorMailer class that are required for pipeline sections to send mail to customers and suppliers. After that, we'll move on to the pipeline sections; each section requires a new class in the App_Code/ CommerceLib folder. (Remember that this code is available in the Source Code area of the Apress web site at http://www.apress.com). By the time you get to the next "Exercise" section, you should have eight new classes with the following names (they all start with PS, short for Pipeline Section):

- PSInitialNotification

- PSCheckFunds

- PSCheckStock

- PSStockOK

- PSTakePayment

- PSShipGoods

- PSShipOK

- PSFinalNotification

We'll discuss the classes you are creating as you go.

OrderProcessorMailer Modifications

The OrderProcessorMailer class needs two new methods, MailCustomer and MailSupplier. The new methods to add to OrderProcessorMailer are as follows:

```
public static void MailCustomer(MembershipUser customer,
  string subject, string body)
{
  // Send mail to customer
  string to = customer.Email;
  string from = BalloonShopConfiguration.CustomerServiceEmail;
  Utilities.SendMail(from, to, subject, body);
}

public static void MailSupplier(string subject, string body)
{
  // Send mail to supplier
  string to = BalloonShopConfiguration.SupplierEmail;
  string from = BalloonShopConfiguration.OrderProcessorEmail;
  Utilities.SendMail(from, to, subject, body);
}
```

These methods use properties from BalloonShopConfiguration and the Utilities. SendMail method to send mail to customers and suppliers.

OrderProcessor Modifications

As with MailAdmin, we'll provide some new methods in OrderProcessor for mailing so that pipeline sections don't use OrderProcessorMailer directly. The code for this is simply two new methods as follows:

```
public void MailCustomer(string subject, string message)
{
  OrderProcessorMailer.MailCustomer(Order.Customer, subject,
    message);
}

public void MailSupplier(string subject, string message)
{
  OrderProcessorMailer.MailSupplier(subject, message);
}
```

Doing this is really according to personal taste. It wouldn't really matter if order pipeline sections used OrderProcessorMailer methods, although in the case of MailCustomer it does simplify the syntax slightly.

The PSInitialNotification Class

PSInitialNotification is the first pipeline stage and is responsible for sending an email to the customer confirming that the order has been placed. The code for this class starts off in what will soon become a very familiar fashion (the autogenerated using statements aren't shown here for brevity):

```
using System.Text;

namespace CommerceLib
{
  /// <summary>
  /// 1st pipeline stage - used to send a notification email to
  /// the customer, confirming that the order has been received
  /// </summary>
  public class PSInitialNotification : IPipelineSection
  {
    private OrderProcessor orderProcessor;

    public void Process(OrderProcessor processor)
    {
      // set processor reference
      orderProcessor = processor;
      // audit
      orderProcessor.CreateAudit("PSInitialNotification started.",
        20000);
```

The code contains one additional using statement; the class itself, which implements the IPipelineSection interface; a private field for storing a reference to the order processor; and then the IPipelineSection.Process method implementation. This method starts by storing the reference to OrderProcessor, which all the pipeline sections will do because using the members it exposes (either in the Process method or in other methods) is essential. An audit entry is also added using the numbering scheme introduced earlier (the initial 2 signifies that it's coming from a pipeline section, the next 00 means that it's the first pipeline section, and the final 00 shows that it's the start message for the pipeline section).

The remainder of the Process method sends the email, using the MailCustomer method of OrderProcessor. A private method, GetMailBody(), is used to build a message body, which we'll look at shortly:

```
    try
    {
      // send mail to customer
      orderProcessor.MailCustomer("BalloonShop order received.",
        GetMailBody());
```

After the mail is sent, you add an audit message to change the status of the order and tell the order processor that it's okay to move straight on to the next pipeline section:

```
// audit
orderProcessor.CreateAudit(
  "Notification e-mail sent to customer.", 20002);
// update order status
orderProcessor.Order.UpdateStatus(1);
// continue processing
orderProcessor.ContinueNow = true;
}
```

If an error occurs, an OrderProcessor exception is thrown:

```
catch
{
  // mail sending failure
  throw new OrderProcessorException(
    "Unable to send e-mail to customer.", 0);
}
```

If all goes according to plan, the Process method finishes by adding a final audit entry:

```
// audit
processor.CreateAudit("PSInitialNotification finished.", 20001);
}
```

The GetMailBody method is used to build up an email body to send to the customer using a StringBuilder object for efficiency. The text uses customer and order data, but follows a generally accepted e-commerce email format:

```
private string GetMailBody()
{
  // construct message body
  StringBuilder sb = new StringBuilder();
  sb.Append("Thank you for your order! The products you have "
    + "ordered are as follows:\n\n");
  sb.Append(orderProcessor.Order.OrderAsString);
  sb.Append("\n\nYour order will be shipped to:\n\n");
  sb.Append(orderProcessor.Order.CustomerAddressAsString);
  sb.Append("\n\nOrder reference number:\n\n");
  sb.Append(orderProcessor.Order.OrderID.ToString());
  sb.Append(
    "\n\nYou will receive a confirmation e-mail when this "
    + "order has been dispatched. Thank you for shopping "
    + "at BalloonShop!");
  return sb.ToString();
  }
 }
}
```

When this pipeline stage finishes, processing moves straight on to PSCheckFunds.

The PSCheckFunds Class

The PSCheckFunds pipeline stage is responsible for making sure that the customer has the required funds available on a credit card. For now, you'll provide a dummy implementation of this, and just assume that these funds are available.

The code starts in the same way as PSInitialNotification, although without the reference to the System.Text namespace:

```
namespace CommerceLib
{
  /// <summary>
  /// 2nd pipeline stage - used to check that the customer
  /// has the required funds available for purchase
  /// </summary>
  public class PSCheckFunds : IPipelineSection
  {
    private OrderProcessor orderProcessor;

    public void Process(OrderProcessor processor)
    {
      // set processor reference
      orderProcessor = processor;
      // audit
      orderProcessor.CreateAudit("PSCheckFunds started.", 20100);
```

Even though you aren't actually performing a check, you set the authorization and reference codes for the transaction to make sure that the code in OrderProcessor works properly:

```
      try
      {
        // check customer funds
        // assume they exist for now
        // set order authorization code and reference
        orderProcessor.Order.SetAuthCodeAndReference("AuthCode",
          "Reference");
```

You finish up with some auditing, the code required for continuation, and error checking:

```
        // audit
        orderProcessor.CreateAudit("Funds available for purchase.",
          20102);
        // update order status
        orderProcessor.Order.UpdateStatus(2);
        // continue processing
        orderProcessor.ContinueNow = true;
      }
```

```
    catch
    {
      // fund checking failure
      throw new OrderProcessorException(
        "Error occured while checking funds.", 1);
    }
    // audit
    processor.CreateAudit("PSCheckFunds finished.", 20101);
  }
 }
}
```

When this pipeline stage finishes, processing moves straight on to PSCheckStock.

The PSCheckStock Class

The PSCheckStock pipeline stage sends an email instructing the supplier to check stock availability:

```
using System.Text;

namespace CommerceLib
{
  /// <summary>
  /// 3rd pipeline stage - used to send a notification email to
  /// the supplier, asking whether goods are available
  /// </summary>
  public class PSCheckStock : IPipelineSection
  {
    private OrderProcessor orderProcessor;

    public void Process(OrderProcessor processor)
    {
      // set processor reference
      orderProcessor = processor;
      // audit
      orderProcessor.CreateAudit("PSCheckStock started.", 20200);
```

Mail is sent in a similar way to PSInitialNotification, using a private method to build up the body. This time, however, we use MailSupplier:

```
      try
      {
        // send mail to supplier
        orderProcessor.MailSupplier("BalloonShop stock check.",
          GetMailBody());
```

As before, you finish by auditing and updating the status, although this time you don't tell the order processor to continue straight away:

```
      // audit
      orderProcessor.CreateAudit(
        "Notification e-mail sent to supplier.", 20202);
      // update order status
      orderProcessor.Order.UpdateStatus(3);
    }
    catch
    {
      // mail sending failure
      throw new OrderProcessorException(
        "Unable to send e-mail to supplier.", 2);
    }
    // audit
    processor.CreateAudit("PSCheckStock finished.", 20201);
  }
```

The code for building the message body is simple; it just lists the items in the order and tells the supplier to confirm via the BalloonShop web site (using the order administration page OrdersAdmin.aspx, which you'll modify later):

```
  private string GetMailBody()
  {
    // construct message body
    StringBuilder sb = new StringBuilder();
    sb.Append("The following goods have been ordered:\n\n");
    sb.Append(orderProcessor.Order.OrderAsString);
    sb.Append("\n\nPlease check availability and confirm via ");
    sb.Append("http://balloonshop.apress.com/OrdersAdmin.aspx");
    sb.Append("\n\nOrder reference number:\n\n");
    sb.Append(orderProcessor.Order.OrderID.ToString());
    return sb.ToString();
  }
 }
}
```

Note that the URL used here isn't a real one—you should replace it with a URL of your own. When this pipeline stage finishes, processing pauses. Later, when the supplier confirms that stock is available, processing moves on to PSStockOK.

The PSStockOK Class

The PSStockOK pipeline section doesn't do much at all. It just confirms that the supplier has the product in stock and moves on. Its real purpose is to look for orders that have a status corresponding to this pipeline section and know that they are currently awaiting stock confirmation.

```
namespace CommerceLib
{
  /// <summary>
  /// Summary description for PSStockOK
  /// </summary>
  public class PSStockOK : IPipelineSection
  {
    private OrderProcessor orderProcessor;

    public void Process(OrderProcessor processor)
    {
      // set processor reference
      orderProcessor = processor;
      // audit
      orderProcessor.CreateAudit("PSStockOK started.", 20300);
      // the method is called when the supplier confirms that stock is
      // available, so we don't have to do anything here except audit
      orderProcessor.CreateAudit("Stock confirmed by supplier.",
        20302);
      // update order status
      orderProcessor.Order.UpdateStatus(4);
      // continue processing
      orderProcessor.ContinueNow = true;
      // audit
      processor.CreateAudit("PSStockOK finished.", 20301);
    }
  }
}
```

When this pipeline stage finishes, processing moves straight on to PSTakePayment.

The PSTakePayment Class

The PSTakePayment pipeline section completes the transaction started by PSCheckFunds. As with that section, you only provide a dummy implementation here.

```
namespace CommerceLib
{
  /// <summary>
  /// 5th pipeline stage - takes funds from customer
  /// </summary>
  public class PSTakePayment : IPipelineSection
  {
    private OrderProcessor orderProcessor;
```

```
    public void Process(OrderProcessor processor)
    {
      // set processor reference
      orderProcessor = processor;
      // audit
      orderProcessor.CreateAudit("PSTakePayment started.", 20400);
      try
      {
        // take customer funds
        // assume success for now
        // audit
        orderProcessor.CreateAudit(
          "Funds deducted from customer credit card account.",
          20402);
        // update order status
        orderProcessor.Order.UpdateStatus(5);
        // continue processing
        orderProcessor.ContinueNow = true;
      }
      catch
      {
        // fund checking failure
        throw new OrderProcessorException(
          "Error occured while taking payment.", 4);
      }
      // audit
      processor.CreateAudit("PSTakePayment finished.", 20401);
    }
  }
}
```

When this pipeline stage finishes, processing moves straight on to PSShipGoods.

The PSShipGoods Class

The PSShipGoods pipeline section is remarkably similar to PSCheckStock, because it sends an email to the supplier and stops the pipeline until the supplier has confirmed that stock has shipped. This operation should not be combined with PSCheckStock because after you've checked that the goods are in stock, you need to take payment before shipping the goods.

```
using System.Text;

namespace CommerceLib
{
  /// <summary>
  /// 6th pipeline stage - used to send a notification email to
  /// the supplier, stating that goods can be shipped
  /// </summary>
```

```csharp
public class PSShipGoods : IPipelineSection
{
  private OrderProcessor orderProcessor;

  public void Process(OrderProcessor processor)
  {
    // set processor reference
    orderProcessor = processor;
    // audit
    orderProcessor.CreateAudit("PSShipGoods started.", 20500);
    try
    {
      // send mail to supplier
      orderProcessor.MailSupplier("BalloonShop ship goods.",
        GetMailBody());
      // audit
      orderProcessor.CreateAudit(
        "Ship goods e-mail sent to supplier.", 20502);
      // update order status
      orderProcessor.Order.UpdateStatus(6);
    }
    catch
    {
      // mail sending failure
      throw new OrderProcessorException(
        "Unable to send e-mail to supplier.", 5);
    }
    // audit
    processor.CreateAudit("PSShipGoods finished.", 20501);
  }
```

As before, a private method called GetMailBody is used to build the message body for the
email sent to the supplier:

```csharp
private string GetMailBody()
{
  // construct message body
  StringBuilder sb = new StringBuilder();
  sb.Append(
    "Payment has been received for the following goods:\n\n");
  sb.Append(orderProcessor.Order.OrderAsString);
  sb.Append("\n\nPlease ship to:\n\n");
  sb.Append(orderProcessor.Order.CustomerAddressAsString);
  sb.Append(
    "\n\nWhen goods have been shipped, please confirm via ");
  sb.Append("http://balloonshop.apress.com/OrdersAdmin.aspx");
  sb.Append("\n\nOrder reference number:\n\n");
  sb.Append(orderProcessor.Order.OrderID.ToString());
```

```
      return sb.ToString();
    }
  }
}
```

Again, the URL used here isn't a real one. When this pipeline stage finishes, processing pauses. Later, when the supplier confirms that the order has been shipped, processing moves on to PSShipOK.

The PSShipOK Class

The PSShipOK pipeline section is very similar to PSStockOK, although it has slightly more to do. Because you know that items have shipped, a shipment date value can be added to the Orders table. Technically, this isn't really necessary, because all audit entries are dated. However, this method ensures that all the information is easily accessible in one database table.

```
namespace CommerceLib
{
  /// <summary>
  /// 7th pipeline stage - after confirmation that supplier has
  /// shipped goods
  /// </summary>
  public class PSShipOK : IPipelineSection
  {
    private OrderProcessor orderProcessor;

    public void Process(OrderProcessor processor)
    {
      // set processor reference
      orderProcessor = processor;
      // audit
      orderProcessor.CreateAudit("PSShipOK started.", 20600);
      // set order shipment date
      orderProcessor.Order.SetDateShipped();
      // audit
      orderProcessor.CreateAudit("Order dispatched by supplier.",
        20602);
      // update order status
      orderProcessor.Order.UpdateStatus(7);
      // continue processing
      orderProcessor.ContinueNow = true;
      // audit
      processor.CreateAudit("PSShipOK finished.", 20601);
    }
  }
}
```

When this pipeline stage finishes, processing moves straight on to PSFinalNotification.

The PSFinalNotification Class

The last pipeline section—PSFinalNotification—is very similar to the first, in that it sends email to the customer. This section confirms that the order has shipped:

```
using System.Text;

namespace CommerceLib
{
  /// <summary>
  /// 8th pipeline stage - used to send a notification email to
  /// the customer, confirming that the order has been shipped
  /// </summary>
  public class PSFinalNotification : IPipelineSection
  {
    private OrderProcessor orderProcessor;

    public void Process(OrderProcessor processor)
    {
      // set processor reference
      orderProcessor = processor;
      // audit
      orderProcessor.CreateAudit("PSFinalNotification started.",
        20700);
      try
      {
        // send mail to customer
        orderProcessor.MailCustomer("BalloonShop order dispatched.",
          GetMailBody());
        // audit
        orderProcessor.CreateAudit(
          "Dispatch e-mail sent to customer.", 20702);
        // update order status
        orderProcessor.Order.UpdateStatus(8);
      }
      catch
      {
        // mail sending failure
        throw new OrderProcessorException(
          "Unable to send e-mail to customer.", 7);
      }
      // audit
      processor.CreateAudit("PSFinalNotification finished.", 20701);
    }
```

It uses a familiar-looking GetMailBody method to build the body of the email:

```
    private string GetMailBody()
    {
      // construct message body
      StringBuilder sb = new StringBuilder();
      sb.Append("Your order has now been dispatched! The following "
        + "products have been shipped:\n\n");
      sb.Append(orderProcessor.Order.OrderAsString);
      sb.Append("\n\nYour order has been shipped to:\n\n");
      sb.Append(orderProcessor.Order.CustomerAddressAsString);
      sb.Append("\n\nOrder reference number:\n\n");
      sb.Append(orderProcessor.Order.OrderID.ToString());
      sb.Append("\n\nThank you for shopping at BalloonShop!");
      return sb.ToString();
    }
  }
}
```

When this pipeline section finishes, the order status is changed to 8, which represents a completed order. Further attempts to process the order using OrderProcessor result in an exception being thrown.

The GetCurrentPipelineSection Method

There's one more thing to add to OrderProcessor now that you have the proper pipeline section classes—a full implementation of GetCurrentPipelineSection.

```
    private void GetCurrentPipelineSection()
    {
      // select pipeline section to execute based on order status
      switch (Order.Status)
      {
        case 0:
          CurrentPipelineSection = new PSInitialNotification();
          break;
        case 1:
          CurrentPipelineSection = new PSCheckFunds();
          break;
        case 2:
          CurrentPipelineSection = new PSCheckStock();
          break;
        case 3:
          CurrentPipelineSection = new PSStockOK();
          break;
        case 4:
          CurrentPipelineSection = new PSTakePayment();
          break;
```

```
      case 5:
        CurrentPipelineSection = new PSShipGoods();
        break;
      case 6:
        CurrentPipelineSection = new PSShipOK();
        break;
      case 7:
        CurrentPipelineSection = new PSFinalNotification();
        break;
      case 8:
        throw new OrderProcessorException(
          "Order has already been completed.", 100);
      default:
        throw new OrderProcessorException(
          "Unknown pipeline section requested.", 100);
    }
  }
```

This method simply consists of a large switch statement that selects a pipeline section to execute based on the status of the order being processed.

Presentation Tier Modifications

In a little while, you'll be implementing a new order admin system, allowing suppliers to mark orders as "in stock" or "shipped." Before that, however, you can check that things are working okay by providing a new test page. In fact, you can simply modify the OrderTest.aspx page you used earlier in the book. You'll do this in the following exercise and then we'll analyze the results.

Exercise: Testing the Order Pipeline

1. Modify the code in OrderTest.aspx to add new user interface items as follows:

```
...
<strong>Order details:</strong>
<br />
<asp:Label runat="server" ID="orderLabel" />
<br />
<br />
<strong>Process order:</strong>
<br />
<asp:Button ID="processButton" runat="server" Text="Go"
  Enabled="False" OnClick="processButton_Click" />
<br />
<asp:Label ID="processResultLabel" runat="server" />
</asp:Content>
```

2. Modify the code for **goButton_Click** in **OrderTest.aspx.cs** as follows:

```
using CommerceLib;

...

  protected void goButton_Click(object sender, EventArgs e)
  {
    try
    {
      CommerceLibOrderInfo orderInfo =
        CommerceLibAccess.GetOrder(orderIDBox.Text);
      resultLabel.Text = "Order found.";
      addressLabel.Text =
        orderInfo.CustomerAddressAsString.Replace(
        "\n", "<br />");
      creditCardLabel.Text = orderInfo.CreditCard.CardNumberX;
      orderLabel.Text = orderInfo.OrderAsString.Replace(
        "\n", "<br />");
      processButton.Enabled = true;
      processResultLabel.Text = "";
    }
    catch
    {
      resultLabel.Text =
        "No order found, or order is in old format.";
      addressLabel.Text = "";
      creditCardLabel.Text = "";
      orderLabel.Text = "";
      processButton.Enabled = false;
    }
  }
```

3. Add a new click handler for the **processButton** button in **OrderTest.aspx.cs** as follows:

```
  protected void processButton_Click(object sender, EventArgs e)
  {
    try
    {
      OrderProcessor processor =
        new OrderProcessor(orderIDBox.Text);
      processor.Process();
      CommerceLibOrderInfo orderInfo =
        CommerceLibAccess.GetOrder(orderIDBox.Text);
      processResultLabel.Text = "Order processed, status now: "
        + orderInfo.Status.ToString();
    }
```

```
catch
{
  CommerceLibOrderInfo orderInfo =
    CommerceLibAccess.GetOrder(orderIDBox.Text);
  processResultLabel.Text =
    "Order processing error, status now: "
    + orderInfo.Status.ToString();
}
}
```

4. Save the new files, log in, browse to the **OrderTest.aspx** page, select an existing order by its ID, and then click on the button to process the first phase of the order.

5. Check your (customer account) mail for the customer notification email. An example is shown here:

```
Thank you for your order! The products you have ordered are as
follows:

1 Love Rose, $12.99 each, total cost $12.99
1 Love Cascade Hearts, $12.99 each, total cost $12.99
Shipping: By air (10 days, $35)

Total order cost: $60.98

Your order will be shipped to:

Charles Darwin
2nd Hut On The Left
The Beach
The Island
Santa Cruz

The Galapagos Islands


Order reference number:

11

You will receive a confirmation e-mail when this order has been
dispatched. Thank you for shopping at BalloonShop!
```

6. Check your (administrator) mail for the stock check email (as shown next).

The following goods have been ordered:

1 Love Rose, $12.99 each, total cost $12.99
1 Love Cascade Hearts, $12.99 each, total cost $12.99
Shipping: By air (10 days, $35)

Total order cost: $60.98

Please check availability and confirm via
http://balloonshop.apress.com/OrdersAdmin.aspx

Order reference number:

11

7. Continue processing on the OrderTest.aspx page by clicking the button again, calling
OrderProcessor.Process for the second time.

8. Check your mail for the ship goods email:

Payment has been received for the following goods:

1 Love Rose, $12.99 each, total cost $12.99
1 Love Cascade Hearts, $12.99 each, total cost $12.99
Shipping: By air (10 days, $35)

Total order cost: $60.98

Please ship to:

Charles Darwin
2nd Hut On The Left
The Beach
The Island
Santa Cruz

The Galapagos Islands

When goods have been shipped, please confirm via
http://balloonshop.apress.com/OrdersAdmin.aspx

Order reference number:

11

9. Continue processing on the `OrderTest.aspx` page by clicking the button again, calling
   `OrderProcessor.Process` for the third time.

10. Check your mail for the shipping confirmation email:

Your order has now been dispatched! The following products have
been shipped:

1 Love Rose, $12.99 each, total cost $12.99
1 Love Cascade Hearts, $12.99 each, total cost $12.99
Shipping: By air (10 days, $35)

Total order cost: $60.98

Your order has been shipped to:

Charles Darwin
2nd Hut On The Left
The Beach
The Island
Santa Cruz

The Galapagos Islands

Order reference number:

11

Thank you for shopping at BalloonShop!

11. Examine the new audit entries for the order (see Figure 15-1).

AuditID	OrderID	DateStamp	Message	MessageNumber
25	11	30/07/2005 17:39:46	Order Processor started.	10000
26	11	30/07/2005 17:39:46	PSInitialNotification started.	20000
27	11	30/07/2005 17:39:47	Notification e-mail sent to customer.	20002
28	11	30/07/2005 17:39:47	PSInitialNotification finished.	20001
29	11	30/07/2005 17:39:47	PSCheckFunds started.	20100
30	11	30/07/2005 17:39:47	Funds available for purchase.	20102
31	11	30/07/2005 17:39:47	PSCheckFunds finished.	20101
32	11	30/07/2005 17:39:47	PSCheckStock started.	20200
33	11	30/07/2005 17:39:47	Notification e-mail sent to supplier.	20202
34	11	30/07/2005 17:39:47	PSCheckStock finished.	20201
35	11	30/07/2005 17:39:47	Order Processor finished.	10001
36	11	30/07/2005 17:40:30	Order Processor started.	10000
37	11	30/07/2005 17:40:30	PSStockOK started.	20300
38	11	30/07/2005 17:40:30	Stock confirmed by supplier.	20302
39	11	30/07/2005 17:40:30	PSStockOK finished.	20301
40	11	30/07/2005 17:40:30	PSTakePayment started.	20400
41	11	30/07/2005 17:40:30	Funds deducted from customer credit card account.	20402
42	11	30/07/2005 17:40:30	PSTakePayment finished.	20401
43	11	30/07/2005 17:40:30	PSShipGoods started.	20500
44	11	30/07/2005 17:40:30	Ship goods e-mail sent to supplier.	20502
45	11	30/07/2005 17:40:30	PSShipGoods finished.	20501
46	11	30/07/2005 17:40:30	Order Processor finished.	10001
47	11	30/07/2005 17:40:32	Order Processor started.	10000
48	11	30/07/2005 17:40:32	PSShipOK started.	20600
49	11	30/07/2005 17:40:32	Order dispatched by supplier.	20602
50	11	30/07/2005 17:40:32	PSShipOK finished.	20601
51	11	30/07/2005 17:40:32	PSFinalNotification started.	20700
52	11	30/07/2005 17:40:32	Dispatch e-mail sent to customer.	20702
53	11	30/07/2005 17:40:32	PSFinalNotification finished.	20701
54	11	30/07/2005 17:40:32	Order Processor finished.	10001

Figure 15-1. *Audit entries for completed order*

How It Works: Testing the Order Pipeline

The example code tested your order pipeline by causing a single order to be processed by each pipeline section in turn, and providing the expected results. The modifications to the OrderTest.aspx page and code behind provided a button that simply called the OrderProcessor.Process method on the order being viewed. The other modifications to the code were to enable or disable the processing button depending on whether an order is being viewed.

One interesting point to note is what happens if you continue to try to process an order after it has been completed. The result of clicking the processing button again is shown in Figure 15-2.

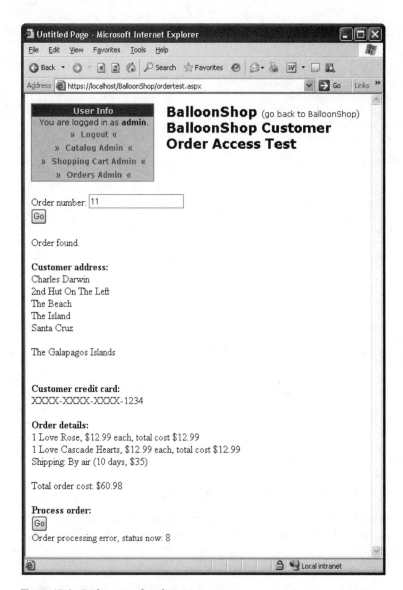

Figure 15-2. *Order completed error*

If you check your mail, you'll see the details:

```
Message: Order has already been completed.
Source: 100
Order ID: 11
```

The error message mailed to the administrator should be enough to get started in detective work, finding out what has happened.

Administering BalloonShop Orders

The current order administration page, implemented in OrdersAdmin.aspx and AdminUserControls\OrderDetailsAdmin.aspx, is no longer applicable to your order system. Now you have new data to handle, new functionality required for suppliers, and an audit trail to display.

This means you need to make several modifications. You'll start, as usual, with the database modifications, which require several new stored procedures. Moving on to the business tier, you'll need to update several methods and add several more to give access to the new stored procedures and allow the presentation tier to obtain and update data. Finally, in the presentation tier, you'll need to update the files responsible for order administration.

Note that your new data structures mean that customer-related information, including the customer name, email address, and postal address, are no longer editable by administrators. It would be possible to do this, but because customers can edit that information themselves, we won't implement it here. In fact, at some point, it might be nice to add a customer administration page, usable by administrators, to check on customer activity and edit customer accounts. We'll leave this task to you because by the end of this book, you'll be familiar with all the necessary techniques.

Database Modifications

As noted, the required additions here are all stored procedures. In addition, they all start with the string CommerceLib to distinguish them from earlier additions. This is especially necessary as many of these stored procedures (and the business tier methods that use them) will replace or upgrade existing functionality.

The CommerceLibOrderGetAuditTrail Stored Procedure

This stored procedure gets the Audit table entries that are associated with a given order:

```
CREATE PROCEDURE CommerceLibOrderGetAuditTrail
(@OrderID int)
AS
SELECT OrderID,
       AuditID,
       DateStamp,
       Message,
       MessageNumber
FROM Audit
WHERE OrderID = @OrderID
```

The CommerceLibOrdersGetByCustomer Stored Procedure

This stored procedure gets the orders that have been made by a specific customer by using the GUID that identifies a customer:

```
CREATE PROCEDURE CommerceLibOrdersGetByCustomer
(@CustomerID uniqueidentifier)
AS
SELECT OrderID,
        DateCreated,
        DateShipped,
        Comments,
        Status,
        CustomerID,
        AuthCode,
        Reference,
        Orders.ShippingID,
        ShippingType,
        ShippingCost,
        Orders.TaxID,
        TaxType,
        TaxPercentage
FROM Orders
LEFT OUTER JOIN Tax ON Tax.TaxID = Orders.TaxID
LEFT OUTER JOIN Shipping ON Shipping.ShippingID = Orders.ShippingID
WHERE CustomerID = @CustomerID
```

The CommerceLibOrdersGetByDate Stored Procedure

This stored procedure mirrors the OrdersGetByDate stored procedure used earlier in the book.
As with that stored procedure, this one gets the orders that were placed between two dates. The
difference here is that different data is returned:

```
CREATE PROCEDURE CommerceLibOrdersGetByDate
(@StartDate smalldatetime,
 @EndDate smalldatetime)
AS

SELECT OrderID,
        DateCreated,
        DateShipped,
        Comments,
        Status,
        CustomerID,
        AuthCode,
        Reference,
        Orders.ShippingID,
        ShippingType,
        ShippingCost,
        Orders.TaxID,
        TaxType,
        TaxPercentage
```

```
FROM Orders
LEFT OUTER JOIN Tax ON Tax.TaxID = Orders.TaxID
LEFT OUTER JOIN Shipping ON Shipping.ShippingID = Orders.ShippingID
WHERE DateCreated BETWEEN @StartDate AND @EndDate
ORDER BY DateCreated DESC
```

The CommerceLibOrdersGetByRecent Stored Procedure

This stored procedure replaces the OrdersGetByRecent stored procedure. It obtains the most recent orders that have been placed, where the number of orders to return is selected by a parameter:

```
CREATE PROCEDURE CommerceLibOrdersGetByRecent
(@Count smallint)
AS

SET ROWCOUNT @Count

SELECT OrderID,
       DateCreated,
       DateShipped,
       Comments,
       Status,
       CustomerID,
       AuthCode,
       Reference,
       Orders.ShippingID,
       ShippingType,
       ShippingCost,
       Orders.TaxID,
       TaxType,
       TaxPercentage
FROM Orders
LEFT OUTER JOIN Tax ON Tax.TaxID = Orders.TaxID
LEFT OUTER JOIN Shipping ON Shipping.ShippingID = Orders.ShippingID
ORDER BY DateCreated DESC

SET ROWCOUNT 0
```

The CommerceLibOrdersGetByStatus Stored Procedure

Again, this stored procedure is a replacement. However, this time the new stored procedure actually replaces two earlier ones: OrdersGetUnverifiedUncanceled and OrdersGetVerified➥ Uncompleted. Because this information is now represented by a single status field, you can provide a single, more versatile stored procedure:

```
CREATE PROCEDURE CommerceLibOrdersGetByStatus
(@Status int)
AS
SELECT OrderID,
       DateCreated,
       DateShipped,
       Comments,
       Status,
       CustomerID,
       AuthCode,
       Reference,
       Orders.ShippingID,
       ShippingType,
       ShippingCost,
       Orders.TaxID,
       TaxType,
       TaxPercentage
FROM Orders
LEFT OUTER JOIN Tax ON Tax.TaxID = Orders.TaxID
LEFT OUTER JOIN Shipping ON Shipping.ShippingID = Orders.ShippingID
WHERE Status = @Status
```

The CommerceLibOrderUpdate Stored Procedure

Finally, this stored procedure replaces the OrderUpdate stored procedure used earlier, making use of your new data:

```
CREATE PROCEDURE CommerceLibOrderUpdate
(@OrderID int,
 @DateCreated smalldatetime,
 @DateShipped smalldatetime = NULL,
 @Status int,
 @Comments varchar(200),
 @AuthCode varchar(50),
 @Reference varchar(50),
 @ShippingID int,
 @TaxID int)
AS
UPDATE Orders
SET DateCreated=@DateCreated,
    DateShipped=@DateShipped,
    Status=@Status,
    Comments=@Comments,
    AuthCode=@AuthCode,
    Reference=@Reference
WHERE OrderID = @OrderID
```

Business Tier Modifications

The modifications in this section apply mainly to the CommerceLibAccess and CommerceLib➥
OrderInfo classes. However, to give easy access to audit trail info, you also need to add a new class, called (surprisingly enough) CommerceLibAuditInfo.

Apart from allowing access to your new data, you have one more thing to add, which you'll do first. You need to provide a human-readable version of order statuses, which you'll use later to display information in the order admin page.

Adding Human-Readable Status Information

You can store order status strings in any number of places. One option is to store them in the database, perhaps in a table called Status. You could then link to the Orders table by matching the existing Orders.Status field to, say, Status.StatusID.

However, it's reasonable to regard status information as static. Although the Orders table is capable of containing any integer for an order status, the CommerceLib code uses order status information in a more formal way. The statuses that exist, in fact, are a consequence of the pipeline structure we've chosen, which is independent of the database. For this reason, you should include status information in your code.

You could store human-readable status strings in web.config, in an external resource file (useful for multilingual sites), or anywhere else you choose. In this chapter, you'll put this information in a static read-only string array in the CommerceLibAccess class, where you can access it from wherever you choose. The indexes of the entries in the array match the status values that are used in your order pipeline. Add the following member to CommerceLibAccess:

```
public static readonly string[] OrderStatuses =
   {"Order placed, notifying customer", // 0
   "Awaiting confirmation of funds",    // 1
   "Notifying supplier–stock check",    // 2
   "Awaiting stock confirmation",       // 3
   "Awaiting credit card payment",      // 4
   "Notifying supplier–shipping",       // 5
   "Awaiting shipment confirmation",    // 6
   "Sending final notification",        // 7
   "Order completed",                   // 8
   "Order cancelled"};                  // 9
```

Note the one new status here—Order cancelled, with a value of 9—for when you want to cancel a customer order.

For the purposes of data binding to the CommerceLibOrderInfo class, you also provide a new public property to expose order statuses as strings. Add the following member to CommerceLibOrderInfo:

```
public string StatusAsString
{
  get
  {
    try
    {
      return CommerceLibAccess.OrderStatuses[Status];
    }
    catch
    {
      return "Status unknown";
    }
  }
}
```

The CommerceLibAuditInfo Class

You'll expose audit trail data via this new class, which is very similar to (although simpler than) the CommerceLibOrderInfo and CommerceLibOrderDetailInfo classes added earlier. As with these classes, you can add CommerceLibAuditInfo to the CommerceLibAccess.cs file:

```
/// <summary>
/// Wraps audit trail data
/// </summary>
public class CommerceLibAuditInfo
{
  #region Private Fields
  private int auditID;
  private int orderID;
  private DateTime dateStamp;
  private string message;
  private int messageNumber;
  #endregion

  #region Public Properties
  public int AuditID
  {
    get
    {
      return auditID;
    }
  }
  public int OrderID
  {
```

```
      get
      {
        return orderID;
      }
    }
    public DateTime DateStamp
    {
      get
      {
        return dateStamp;
      }
    }
    public string Message
    {
      get
      {
        return message;
      }
    }
    public int MessageNumber
    {
      get
      {
        return messageNumber;
      }
    }
    #endregion

    #region Constructor
    public CommerceLibAuditInfo(DataRow auditRow)
    {
      auditID = (int)auditRow["AuditID"];
      orderID = (int)auditRow["OrderID"];
      dateStamp = (DateTime)auditRow["DateStamp"];
      message = auditRow["Message"] as string;
      messageNumber = (int)auditRow["messageNumber"];
    }
    #endregion
}
```

The constructor of this class uses a DataRow object to initialize the class, so next you need a method to get the audit trail for an order.

The GetOrderAuditTrail Method

To get the audit trail for an order, you'll add a new method to CommerceLibAccess called GetOrderAuditTrail, which uses the ID of an order to get audit entries via the

CommerceLibOrderGetAuditTrail stored procedure. Here you can use generic collections by returning audit information in the form of a List<CommerceLibAuditInfo> class.

Add the following method to CommerceLibAccess:

```
public static List<CommerceLibAuditInfo> GetOrderAuditTrail(
  string orderID)
{
  // get a configured DbCommand object
  DbCommand comm = GenericDataAccess.CreateCommand();
  // set the stored procedure name
  comm.CommandText = "CommerceLibOrderGetAuditTrail";
  // create a new parameter
  DbParameter param = comm.CreateParameter();
  param.ParameterName = "@OrderID";
  param.Value = orderID;
  param.DbType = DbType.Int32;
  comm.Parameters.Add(param);
  // obtain the results
  DataTable orderAuditTrailData =
    GenericDataAccess.ExecuteSelectCommand(comm);
  // create List<>
  List<CommerceLibAuditInfo> orderAuditTrail =
    new List<CommerceLibAuditInfo>(
    orderAuditTrailData.Rows.Count);
  foreach (DataRow orderAudit in orderAuditTrailData.Rows)
  {
    orderAuditTrail.Add(new CommerceLibAuditInfo(orderAudit));
  }
  return orderAuditTrail;
}
```

CommerceLibOrderInfo Modifications

To bind to a CommerceLibOrderInfo, you need to do one more thing. Unfortunately, data-bindable objects such as DataGrid don't work with public fields, only properties. This means that every one of the public fields in CommerceLibOrderInfo, for example OrderID, needs to be exposed via a property. For example:

```
public int OrderID;
```

needs to be replaced with

```
private int orderID;
```

```
public int OrderID
{
  get
  {
    return orderID;
  }
  set
  {
    orderID = value;
  }
}
```

Here the private field uses a lowercase first letter to differentiate it from the public property. Yes, this set of changes is very annoying. Unfortunately, we have no alternative. Another thing to change is where tax and shipping info gets set in the constructor. Here you must refer to the private fields for shipping and tax info rather than the properties:

```
// Get Shipping Data
if (orderRow["ShippingID"] != DBNull.Value
  && orderRow["ShippingType"] != DBNull.Value
  && orderRow["ShippingCost"] != DBNull.Value)
{
  shipping.ShippingID =
    Int32.Parse(orderRow["ShippingID"].ToString());
  shipping.ShippingType = orderRow["ShippingType"].ToString();
  shipping.ShippingCost =
    double.Parse(orderRow["ShippingCost"].ToString());
}
else
{
  shipping.ShippingID = -1;
}
// Get Tax Data
if (orderRow["TaxID"] != DBNull.Value
  && orderRow["TaxType"] != DBNull.Value
  && orderRow["TaxPercentage"] != DBNull.Value)
{
  tax.TaxID = Int32.Parse(orderRow["TaxID"].ToString());
  tax.TaxType = orderRow["TaxType"].ToString();
  tax.TaxPercentage =
    double.Parse(orderRow["TaxPercentage"].ToString());
}
else
{
  tax.TaxID = -1;
}
```

CommerceLibOrderDetailInfo Modifications

As with `CommerceLibOrderInfo`, fields need to be upgraded to properties here. For example,

```
public int ProductID;
```

needs to be replaced with

```
private int productID;

public int ProductID
{
  get
  {
    return productID;
  }
  set
  {
    productID = value;
  }
}
```

Exposing an Audit Trail via CommerceLibOrderInfo

The `CommerceLibOrderInfo` class is already versatile, as it exposes customer and order detail information on the fly. You can extend this class even further by allowing access to audit trail information directly. First, you need to add a new private field to `CommerceLibOrderInfo` to hold this data:

```
private List<CommerceLibAuditInfo> auditTrail;
```

Next, you need to give access to this field via a property. Here you can use a "lazy initialization" scheme and only load the audit trail when it's requested. When this happens, you use the new `CommerceLibAccess.GetOrderAuditTrail` method to obtain the audit trail data:

```
public List<CommerceLibAuditInfo> AuditTrail
{
  get
  {
    if (auditTrail == null)
    {
      auditTrail = CommerceLibAccess.GetOrderAuditTrail(
        orderID.ToString());
    }
    return auditTrail;
  }
}
```

The ConvertDataTableToOrders Method

Next you need to add several methods to CommerceLibAccess to let the order admin page obtain lists of CommerceLibOrderInfo objects by using various filters. In all cases, you can return this information in the form of a List<CommerceLibOrderInfo> generic collection. Because the generic GenericDataAccess.ExecuteSelectCommand method you use to get data returns a DataTable, it makes sense to provide a standard way to convert between these list types. Along the way, you can discard invalid or old data (such as existing orders from the code in the first part of this book).

Add the following method to CommerceLibAccess:

```
public static List<CommerceLibOrderInfo>
  ConvertDataTableToOrders(DataTable table)
{
  List<CommerceLibOrderInfo> orders =
    new List<CommerceLibOrderInfo>(table.Rows.Count);
  foreach (DataRow orderRow in table.Rows)
  {
    try
    {
      // try to add order
      orders.Add(new CommerceLibOrderInfo(orderRow));
    }
    catch
    {
      // can't add this order
    }
  }
  return orders;
}
```

The GetOrdersByCustomer Method

This is the first of the new CommerceLibAccess methods that will use the ConvertData➡ TableToOrders method added in the last section. In this case, the method passes the GUID ID of a customer to the CommerceLibOrdersGetByCustomer stored procedure and returns the resultant orders in the form of a List<CommerceLibOrderInfo> collection.

Add the following method to CommerceLibAccess:

```
public static List<CommerceLibOrderInfo> GetOrdersByCustomer(
  string customerID)
{
  // get a configured DbCommand object
  DbCommand comm = GenericDataAccess.CreateCommand();
  // set the stored procedure name
  comm.CommandText = "CommerceLibOrdersGetByCustomer";
  // create a new parameter
  DbParameter param = comm.CreateParameter();
  param.ParameterName = "@CustomerID";
  param.Value = new Guid(customerID);
```

```
      param.DbType = DbType.Guid;
      comm.Parameters.Add(param);
      // obtain the results
      return ConvertDataTableToOrders(
        GenericDataAccess.ExecuteSelectCommand(comm));
    }
```

The GetOrdersByDate Method

Similarly, this method uses the CommerceLibOrdersGetByDate stored procedure to get the orders between two dates.

Add the following method to CommerceLibAccess:

```
public static List<CommerceLibOrderInfo> GetOrdersByDate(
  string startDate, string endDate)
{
  // get a configured DbCommand object
  DbCommand comm = GenericDataAccess.CreateCommand();
  // set the stored procedure name
  comm.CommandText = "CommerceLibOrdersGetByDate";
  // create a new parameter
  DbParameter param = comm.CreateParameter();
  param.ParameterName = "@StartDate";
  param.Value = startDate;
  param.DbType = DbType.Date;
  comm.Parameters.Add(param);
  // create a new parameter
  param = comm.CreateParameter();
  param.ParameterName = "@EndDate";
  param.Value = endDate;
  param.DbType = DbType.Date;
  comm.Parameters.Add(param);
  // obtain the results
  return ConvertDataTableToOrders(
    GenericDataAccess.ExecuteSelectCommand(comm));
}
```

The GetOrdersByRecent Method

This method uses the CommerceLibOrdersGetByRecent stored procedure to get the most recently placed orders. The number of orders to return is determined by the count parameter.

Add the following method to CommerceLibAccess:

```
public static List<CommerceLibOrderInfo> GetOrdersByRecent(
  int count)
{
  // get a configured DbCommand object
  DbCommand comm = GenericDataAccess.CreateCommand();
```

```
    // set the stored procedure name
    comm.CommandText = "CommerceLibOrdersGetByRecent";
    // create a new parameter
    DbParameter param = comm.CreateParameter();
    param.ParameterName = "@Count";
    param.Value = count;
    param.DbType = DbType.Int32;
    comm.Parameters.Add(param);
    // obtain the results
    return ConvertDataTableToOrders(
      GenericDataAccess.ExecuteSelectCommand(comm));
  }
```

The GetOrdersByStatus Method

The last order obtaining stored procedure to use is CommerceLibOrdersGetByStatus.

Add the following method to CommerceLibAccess:

```
  public static List<CommerceLibOrderInfo> GetOrdersByStatus(
    int status)
  {
    // get a configured DbCommand object
    DbCommand comm = GenericDataAccess.CreateCommand();
    // set the stored procedure name
    comm.CommandText = "CommerceLibOrdersGetByStatus";
    // create a new parameter
    DbParameter param = comm.CreateParameter();
    param.ParameterName = "@Status";
    param.Value = status;
    param.DbType = DbType.Int32;
    comm.Parameters.Add(param);
    // obtain the results
    return ConvertDataTableToOrders(
      GenericDataAccess.ExecuteSelectCommand(comm));
  }
```

The UpdateOrder Method

The last business tier addition to make is a method for updating orders. Previously you've achieved this using the OrderAccess.Update method, which used an OrderInfo struct parameter to specify the data to update. Now you have a more "active" representation of order data, namely CommerceLibOrderInfo, so this is no longer a suitable option. Instead, you'll simply have a parameter for each field you want to update.

Add the following method to CommerceLibAccess:

```csharp
public static void UpdateOrder(int orderID,
  string newDateCreated, string newDateShipped,
  int newStatus, string newAuthCode, string newReference,
  string newComments)
{
  // get a configured DbCommand object
  DbCommand comm = GenericDataAccess.CreateCommand();
  // set the stored procedure name
  comm.CommandText = "CommerceLibOrderUpdate";
  // create a new parameter
  DbParameter param = comm.CreateParameter();
  param.ParameterName = "@OrderID";
  param.Value = orderID;
  param.DbType = DbType.Int32;
  comm.Parameters.Add(param);
  // create a new parameter
  param = comm.CreateParameter();
  param.ParameterName = "@DateCreated";
  param.Value = DateTime.Parse(newDateCreated);
  param.DbType = DbType.DateTime;
  comm.Parameters.Add(param);
  // The DateShipped parameter is sent only if data is available
  if (newDateShipped != null)
  {
    param = comm.CreateParameter();
    param.ParameterName = "@DateShipped";
    param.Value = DateTime.Parse(newDateShipped);
    param.DbType = DbType.DateTime;
    comm.Parameters.Add(param);
  }
  // create a new parameter
  param = comm.CreateParameter();
  param.ParameterName = "@Status";
  param.Value = newStatus;
  param.DbType = DbType.Int32;
  comm.Parameters.Add(param);
  // create a new parameter
  param = comm.CreateParameter();
  param.ParameterName = "@AuthCode";
  param.Value = newAuthCode;
  param.DbType = DbType.String;
  comm.Parameters.Add(param);
  // create a new parameter
  param = comm.CreateParameter();
  param.ParameterName = "@Reference";
  param.Value = newReference;
  param.DbType = DbType.String;
```

```
  comm.Parameters.Add(param);
  // create a new parameter
  param = comm.CreateParameter();
  param.ParameterName = "@Comments";
  param.Value = newComments;
  param.DbType = DbType.String;
  comm.Parameters.Add(param);
  // update the order
  GenericDataAccess.ExecuteNonQuery(comm);
}
```

One point to note here concerns the newDateShipped parameter, which is an instance of a string, but might be null. Here you can use the HasValue property to see if a value has been supplied and must also use the Value parameter to pass a value to the SQL parameter, because this expects a plain DateTime value.

Presentation Tier Modifications

As noted earlier, to tie in to the new order information you need to modify both OrdersAdmin.aspx and OrderDetailsAdmin.ascx. The modifications vary between fairly major and quite subtle, because you'll be using roughly the same look and feel.

Modifying the OrdersAdmin.aspx Page

This page could be modified in all manner of ways to achieve the new functionality you want. In some setups, it might be better not to use this page at all, but rather implement this functionality as a Windows Forms application. This may be appropriate, for example, if your suppliers are in-house and on the same network. Alternatively, it might be better to combine this Windows Forms approach with web services.

Whichever method you choose, the basic functionality is the same: Suppliers and administrators should be able to view a list of orders that need attention and edit them or advance them in the pipeline manually. This is simply a case of calling the OrderProcess.Process method as described earlier.

To simplify things in this section, you'll use the same page for both administrators and suppliers. This might not be ideal in all situations, because you might not want to expose all order details and audit information to external suppliers. However, for demonstration purposes, this reduces the amount of code you have to get through. In a more advanced setup, you could provide a new Suppliers role in the existing security setup and restrict the functionality of this page accordingly.

As a starting point, you'll take the existing OrdersAdmin.aspx code and rewrite it to provide the functionality required. In fact, you can simplify the code slightly to achieve this, because you won't need to update order data as completely as you did before.

The first thing to change is the list of filters that can be used to obtain orders. Specifically, you'll add two new ones for obtaining orders by customer or by ID and replace the filters for "unverified, uncanceled" and "verified, uncompleted" orders. The two replacements will be for supplier use—to display orders awaiting stock or shipment.

The most interesting new addition here is the filter for orders by customer. You'll simplify things here by providing a drop-down selection of customer names, which you can obtain (along with IDs) from the ASPNETDB.MDF database. You can set up a connection to this database by dragging an SqlDataSource control (call it CustomerNameDS) onto the existing OrdersAdmin.aspx form and following the wizard steps. The exact process for doing this varies depending on your configuration, but the important thing is to use the following SQL query when requested:

```
SELECT vw_aspnet_Users.UserName, vw_aspnet_Users.UserId
  FROM vw_aspnet_Users
  INNER JOIN aspnet_UsersInRoles
    ON vw_aspnet_Users.UserId = aspnet_UsersInRoles.UserId
  INNER JOIN aspnet_Roles
    ON aspnet_UsersInRoles.RoleId = aspnet_Roles.RoleId
  WHERE (aspnet_Roles.RoleName = 'Customers')
```

You'll likely be prompted to save the connection string along the way, which is a sensible thing to do in case you want to use this database again in the future. You'll end up with code similar to the following:

```
<asp:SqlDataSource ID="CustomerNameDS" runat="server"
  ConnectionString=
  "<%$ ConnectionStrings:BalloonShopAspNetDBConnectionString %>"
  SelectCommand="SELECT vw_aspnet_Users.UserName,
    vw_aspnet_Users.UserId FROM vw_aspnet_Users INNER JOIN
    aspnet_UsersInRoles ON vw_aspnet_Users.UserId =
    aspnet_UsersInRoles.UserId INNER JOIN aspnet_Roles ON
    aspnet_UsersInRoles.RoleId = aspnet_Roles.RoleId WHERE
    (aspnet_Roles.RoleName = 'Customers')" />
```

Next, replace the code in OrdersAdmin.aspx for the existing filters with the following:

```
<span class="AdminPageText">
  Show orders by customer
  <asp:DropDownList ID="userDropDown" runat="server"
    DataSourceID="CustomerNameDS" DataTextField="UserName"
    DataValueField="UserId" />
  <asp:Button ID="byCustomerGo" runat="server"
    CssClass="AdminButtonText" Text="Go"
    OnClick="byCustomerGo_Click" />
  <br />
  Get order by ID
  <asp:TextBox ID="orderIDBox" runat="server" Width="77px" />
  <asp:Button ID="byIDGo" runat="server" CssClass="AdminButtonText"
    Text="Go" OnClick="byIDGo_Click" />
  <br />
  Show the most recent
  <asp:TextBox ID="recentCountTextBox" runat="server" MaxLength="4"
    Width="40px">20</asp:TextBox>
  orders
  <asp:Button ID="byRecentGo" runat="server"
    CssClass="AdminButtonText" Text="Go"
```

```
    OnClick="byRecentGo_Click" />
<br />
Show all orders created between
<asp:TextBox ID="startDateTextBox" runat="server" Width="72px" />
and
<asp:TextBox ID="endDateTextBox" runat="server" Width="72px" />
<asp:Button ID="byDateGo" runat="server"
  CssClass="AdminButtonText" Text="Go"
  OnClick="byDateGo_Click" />
<br />
Show all orders awaiting stock check
<asp:Button ID="awaitingStockGo" runat="server"
  CssClass="AdminButtonText" Text="Go"
  OnClick="awaitingStockGo_Click" />
<br />
Show all orders awaiting shipment
<asp:Button ID="awaitingShippingGo" runat="server"
  CssClass="AdminButtonText" Text="Go"
  OnClick="awaitingShippingGo_Click" />
<br />
...
```

The next line after this code (indicated by the ellipsis) should be the errorLabel label. You can leave this label, and the validation controls that follow, as they are.

Note that the userDropDown control includes the UserId field as its DataValueField. The data for each item is therefore the GUID value that identifies a user, making data retrieval in the code behind very easy, as you'll see shortly.

Next you need to change the columns in the grid control, the GridView that displays order information. You'll leave the styling unchanged, however. The modified set of columns is as follows:

```
<Columns>
  <asp:BoundField DataField="OrderID" HeaderText="Order ID"
    ReadOnly="True" SortExpression="OrderID" />
  <asp:BoundField DataField="DateCreated"
    HeaderText="Date Created" ReadOnly="True"
    SortExpression="DateCreated" />
  <asp:BoundField DataField="DateShipped"
    HeaderText="Date Shipped" ReadOnly="True"
    SortExpression="DateShipped" />
  <asp:BoundField DataField="StatusAsString" HeaderText="Status"
    ReadOnly="True" SortExpression="StatusAsString" />
  <asp:BoundField DataField="CustomerName"
    HeaderText="Customer Name" ReadOnly="True"
    SortExpression="CustomerName" />
  <asp:ButtonField CommandName="Select" Text="Select" />
</Columns>
```

Finally, you need to modify the reference to the `OrderDetailsAdmin.ascx` user control slightly. As you'll see shortly, this user control will now contain a drop-down list control bound to a list of order statuses. To simplify your code, this control requires access to viewstate information, so viewstate needs to be enabled:

```
<uc1:OrderDetailsAdmin id="orderDetailsAdmin" runat="server">
</uc1:OrderDetailsAdmin>
```

Now we can move on to `OrdersAdmin.aspx.cs`. In fact, you can delete all the existing code apart from the `Page_Load` and `grid_SelectedIndexChanged` methods. Next, add the following `using` statement at the top of the file:

```
using System.Collections.Generic;
```

This is required for the generic lists you'll be using. Now you need to supply one method for each Go button. You'll do this in the order they appear in the user interface, starting with the customer filter:

```
// Display orders by customer
protected void byCustomerGo_Click(object sender, EventArgs e)
{
  try
  {
    List<CommerceLibOrderInfo> orders =
      CommerceLibAccess.GetOrdersByCustomer(
      userDropDown.SelectedValue);
    grid.DataSource = orders;
    if (orders.Count == 0)
    {
      errorLabel.Text =
        "<br />Selected customer has made no orders.";
    }
  }
  catch
  {
    errorLabel.Text = "<br />Couldn't get the requested orders!";
  }
  finally
  {
    grid.DataBind();
  }
}
```

Here you get the necessary data with a single line of code. You simply call `CommerceLibAccess.GetOrdersByCustomer`, passing in the selected value from the `userDropDown` control added previously. Now you can see the benefit of storing the GUID that identifies users in the drop-down list control.

After you have a list of orders in the form of a `List<CommerceLibOrderInfo>` collection, you can simply bind that collection to `grid`. The generic collection classes are ideal for this sort of use.

There's also an additional piece of error-checking code here—a check to see if any orders have been returned. If any orders have been returned, you bind the data to the grid as usual (it won't be visible, so this is fine), but report the error via the `errorLabel` control. The `errorLabel` control is also used if an error occurs.

Next we have the filter for a single order. This is necessary for suppliers who, as you may recall, receive an email including the order ID. This means that they can quickly jump to the order that requires their attention. The code is as follows:

```
// Display single order only
protected void byIDGo_Click(object sender, EventArgs e)
{
  try
  {
    // clear order list with empty order list
    List<CommerceLibOrderInfo> orders =
      new List<CommerceLibOrderInfo>();
    grid.DataSource = orders;
    // Save the ID of the selected order in the session
    Session["AdminOrderID"] = orderIDBox.Text;
    // Display the order details admin control
    orderDetailsAdmin.Visible = true;
  }
  catch
  {
    errorLabel.Text = "<br />Couldn't get the requested order!";
  }
  finally
  {
    grid.DataBind();
  }
}
```

Note that a generic list is still used to bind to `grid` here. The only difference is that it will only ever contain a single item.

As a shortcut, the code in this method also stores the retrieved order information automatically. You may recall from earlier chapters that the `OrderDetailsAdmin.ascx` control uses a value stored in session state to bind to an order, so you simply set this value and make the control visible.

If an error occurs, you report it via `errorLabel` in the standard way.

The remainder of the new button click handler methods operate in much the same way. Each one calls one of the new methods of the `CommerceLibAccess` class to obtain a list of orders, and then binds that list to the grid control or displays an error. Next up is the method for obtaining recent orders:

```csharp
// Display the most recent orders
protected void byRecentGo_Click(object sender, EventArgs e)
{
  try
  {
    int recordCount = Int32.Parse(recentCountTextBox.Text);
    List<CommerceLibOrderInfo> orders =
      CommerceLibAccess.GetOrdersByRecent(recordCount);
    grid.DataSource = orders;
    if (orders.Count == 0)
    {
      errorLabel.Text = "<br />No orders to get.";
    }
  }
  catch
  {
    errorLabel.Text = "<br />Couldn't get the requested orders!";
  }
  finally
  {
    grid.DataBind();
  }
}
```

Then we have the method for getting orders between two dates:

```csharp
// Display orders that happened in a specified period of time
protected void byDateGo_Click(object sender, EventArgs e)
{
  try
  {
    string startDate = startDateTextBox.Text;
    string endDate = endDateTextBox.Text;
    List<CommerceLibOrderInfo> orders =
      CommerceLibAccess.GetOrdersByDate(startDate, endDate);
    grid.DataSource = orders;
    if (orders.Count == 0)
    {
      errorLabel.Text =
        "<br />No orders between selected dates.";
    }
  }
  catch
  {
    errorLabel.Text = "<br />Couldn't get the requested orders!";
  }
```

```
    finally
    {
      grid.DataBind();
    }
}
```

And finally, two methods for getting orders that are either awaiting a stock check or shipment, both of which use CommerceLibAccess.GetOrdersByStatus:

```
// Display orders awaiting stock
protected void awaitingStockGo_Click(object sender, EventArgs e)
{
  try
  {
    List<CommerceLibOrderInfo> orders =
      CommerceLibAccess.GetOrdersByStatus(3);
    grid.DataSource = orders;
    if (orders.Count == 0)
    {
      errorLabel.Text = "<br />No orders awaiting stock check.";
    }
  }
  catch
  {
    errorLabel.Text = "<br />Couldn't get the requested orders!";
  }
  finally
  {
    grid.DataBind();
  }
}

// Display orders awaiting shipping
protected void awaitingShippingGo_Click(object sender, EventArgs e)
{
  try
  {
    List<CommerceLibOrderInfo> orders =
      CommerceLibAccess.GetOrdersByStatus(6);
    grid.DataSource = orders;
    if (orders.Count == 0)
    {
      errorLabel.Text = "<br />No orders awaiting shipment.";
    }
  }
```

```
catch
{
  errorLabel.Text = "<br />Couldn't get the requested orders!";
}
finally
{
  grid.DataBind();
}
}
```

The only differences between these two methods are the status code passed and the error messages possible.

The next thing to modify in this file is to tie the new order ID text box to the appropriate button in Page_Load:

```
protected void Page_Load(object sender, EventArgs e)
{
  // Set the title of the page
  this.Title = BalloonShopConfiguration.SiteName +
               " : Orders Admin";
  // associate the check boxes with their buttons
  Utilities.TieButton(this.Page, orderIDBox, byIDGo);
  Utilities.TieButton(this.Page, recentCountTextBox, byRecentGo);
  Utilities.TieButton(this.Page, startDateTextBox, byDateGo);
  Utilities.TieButton(this.Page, endDateTextBox, byDateGo);
}
```

Finally, you need to make a minor modification to the grid_SelectedIndexChanged method. This is because we have reconfigured the OrderDetailsAdmin.ascx control to use viewstate, and because of this, it will remember the state of its Visible property. This control is hidden to start off with, since no data is displayed. When you select an order, this user control must be displayed, so you need to make sure Visible is set to true. The code modification is as follows:

```
// Load the details of the selected order
protected void grid_SelectedIndexChanged(object sender, EventArgs e)
{
  // Save the ID of the selected order in the session
  Session["AdminOrderID"] =
    grid.DataKeys[grid.SelectedIndex].Value.ToString();

  // Display order if it's not already being displayed
  orderDetailsAdmin.Visible = true;
}
```

Modifying the OrderDetailsAdmin.ascx Control

The other control to modify is OrderDetailsAdmin.ascx, which shows the details of an order. Earlier in the book, this control also included the capability to modify order data, but we're removing most of this functionality here, as mentioned earlier. We're also providing the capability for orders to be pushed along the pipeline when they are stuck at the Awaiting Confirmation of Stock and Awaiting Confirmation of Shipment stages. Finally, you'll add a second DataGrid control where audit trail data will be displayed.

The first modifications will be to the OrderDetailsAdmin.ascx, starting with the order information display table. This table needs to be modified as follows:

```
<table class="AdminPageText">
  <tr>
    <td width="130">Total Cost:</td>
    <td><asp:Label ID="totalCostLabel" runat="server"
        CssClass="ProductPrice" /></td>
  </tr>
  <tr>
    <td width="130">Date Created:</td>
    <td><asp:TextBox ID="dateCreatedTextBox" runat="server"
        Width="400px" enabled="false" /></td>
  </tr>
  <tr>
    <td width="130">Date Shipped:</td>
    <td><asp:TextBox ID="dateShippedTextBox" runat="server"
        Width="400px" /></td>
  </tr>
  <tr>
    <td width="130">Status:</td>
    <td><asp:DropDownList ID="statusDropDown" runat="server" /></td>
  </tr>
  <tr>
    <td width="130">Authorization Code:</td>
    <td><asp:TextBox ID="authCodeTextBox" runat="server"
        Width="400px" /></td>
  </tr>
  <tr>
    <td width="130">Reference Number:</td>
    <td><asp:TextBox ID="referenceTextBox" runat="server"
        Width="400px" /></td>
  </tr>
  <tr>
    <td width="130">Comments:</td>
    <td><asp:TextBox ID="commentsTextBox" runat="server"
        Width="400px" /></td>
  </tr>
  <tr>
    <td width="130">Customer Name:</td>
    <td><asp:TextBox ID="customerNameTextBox" runat="server"
        Width="400px" enabled="false" /></td>
  </tr>
```

```
<tr valign="top">
  <td width="130">Shipping Address:</td>
  <td><asp:TextBox ID="shippingAddressTextBox" runat="server"
    Width="400px" Height="200px" TextMode="MultiLine"
    enabled="false" /></td>
</tr>
<tr valign="top">
  <td width="130">Shipping Type:</td>
  <td><asp:TextBox ID="shippingTypeTextBox" runat="server"
    Width="400px" enabled="false" /></td>
</tr>
<tr>
  <td width="130">Customer Email:</td>
  <td><asp:TextBox ID="customerEmailTextBox" runat="server"
    Width="400px" enabled="false" /></td>
</tr>
</table>
```

Apart from the fields removed and the additional fields added, note that the order status is displayed in a DropDownList, and that the customer data fields have their enabled attribute set to false. This is because editing of this data is no longer allowed.

Next, the buttons beneath this table need replacing as follows:

```
<asp:Button ID="editButton" runat="server" CssClass="AdminButtonText"
  Text="Edit" Width="100px" OnClick="editButton_Click" />
<asp:Button ID="updateButton" runat="server"
  CssClass="AdminButtonText" Text="Update" Width="100px"
  OnClick="updateButton_Click" />
<asp:Button ID="cancelButton" runat="server"
  CssClass="AdminButtonText" Text="Cancel" Width="100px"
  OnClick="cancelButton_Click" />
<br />
<asp:Button ID="processOrderButton" runat="server"
  CssClass="AdminButtonText" Text="Process Order"
  Width="310px" OnClick="processOrderButton_Click" />
<br />
<asp:Button ID="cancelOrderButton" runat="server"
  CssClass="AdminButtonText" Text="Cancel Order"
  Width="310px" OnClick="cancelOrderButton_Click" />
```

The buttons for marking the order as verified or completed are replaced with a single button for processing the order. You'll change the text on this button as appropriate, because you can also use it when suppliers are checking stock or shipping orders. The cancel order button has also changed slightly, in keeping with the new scheme.

Finally, you need to add a new DataGrid for the audit trail, using the same style as the DataGrid for order details:

```
<asp:Label ID="Label1" runat="server" CssClass="AdminPageText"
  Text="Order audit trail:" />
```

```
<br />
<asp:GridView ID="auditGrid" runat="server"
  AutoGenerateColumns="False" BackColor="White"
  BorderColor="#E7E7FF" BorderStyle="None" BorderWidth="1px"
  CellPadding="3" GridLines="Horizontal" Width="100%">
  <FooterStyle BackColor="#B5C7DE" ForeColor="#4A3C8C" />
  <RowStyle BackColor="#E7E7FF" ForeColor="#4A3C8C" />
  <Columns>
    <asp:BoundField DataField="AuditID" HeaderText="Audit ID"
      ReadOnly="True" SortExpression="AuditID" />
    <asp:BoundField DataField="DateStamp" HeaderText="Date Stamp"
      ReadOnly="True" SortExpression="DateStamp" />
    <asp:BoundField DataField="MessageNumber"
      HeaderText="Message Number" ReadOnly="True"
      SortExpression="MessageNumber" />
    <asp:BoundField DataField="Message" HeaderText="Message"
      ReadOnly="True" SortExpression="Message" />
  </Columns>
  <PagerStyle BackColor="#E7E7FF" ForeColor="#4A3C8C"
    HorizontalAlign="Right" />
  <SelectedRowStyle BackColor="#738A9C" Font-Bold="True"
    ForeColor="#F7F7F7" />
  <HeaderStyle BackColor="#4A3C8C" Font-Bold="True"
    ForeColor="#F7F7F7" />
  <AlternatingRowStyle BackColor="#F7F7F7" />
</asp:GridView>
```

Next you come to the code behind OrderDetailsAdmins.ascx. The first modifications here are to remove the button handlers you no longer need (markVerifiedButton_Click, markCompletedButton_Click, and markCanceledButton_Click) and add a reference to CommerceLib. Next, you need to populate the list items in the statusDropDown control. You do this in Page_Load, but only when not in postback mode (or if no items yet exist), because otherwise we'd lose the selected item:

```
protected void Page_Load(object sender, EventArgs e)
{
  // populate statuses if necessary
  if (!IsPostBack || statusDropDown.Items.Count == 0)
  {
    for (int index = 0; index <
      CommerceLibAccess.OrderStatuses.Length; index++)
    {
      statusDropDown.Items.Add(
        new ListItem(CommerceLibAccess.OrderStatuses[index],
        index.ToString()));
    }
  }
}
```

This code uses the static string array added to CommerceLibAccess earlier. The next modification is to PopulateControls(), because the data we are populating is different. The new version of this method starts as follows:

```
// populate the form with data
private void PopulateControls()
{
  // obtain order ID from the session
  string orderId = Session["AdminOrderID"].ToString();
  // obtain order info
  CommerceLibOrderInfo orderInfo =
    CommerceLibAccess.GetOrder(orderId);
  // populate labels and text boxes with order info
  orderIdLabel.Text = "Displaying Order #" + orderId;
  totalCostLabel.Text = String.Format("{0:c} ",
    orderInfo.TotalCost);
  dateCreatedTextBox.Text = orderInfo.DateCreated.ToString();
  dateShippedTextBox.Text = orderInfo.DateShipped.ToString();
  statusDropDown.SelectedIndex = orderInfo.Status;
  authCodeTextBox.Text = orderInfo.AuthCode;
  referenceTextBox.Text = orderInfo.Reference;
  commentsTextBox.Text = orderInfo.Comments;
  customerNameTextBox.Text = orderInfo.CustomerName;
  shippingAddressTextBox.Text = orderInfo.CustomerAddressAsString;
  shippingTypeTextBox.Text = orderInfo.Shipping.ShippingType;
  customerEmailTextBox.Text = orderInfo.Customer.Email;
```

This is very similar to the original code, but uses a CommerceLibOrderInfo object to populate the (slightly different) fields. Because you've changed the buttons too, you need to decide which of them to enable and what text to display on the order processing button.

```
  // Decide which one of the buttons should
  // be enabled and which should be disabled
  switch (orderInfo.Status)
  {
    case 8:
    case 9:
      // if the order was canceled or completed...
      processOrderButton.Text = "Process Order";
      processOrderButton.Enabled = false;
      cancelOrderButton.Enabled = false;
      break;
    case 3:
      // if the order is awaiting a stock check...
      processOrderButton.Text = "Confirm Stock for Order";
      processOrderButton.Enabled = true;
      cancelOrderButton.Enabled = true;
      break;
```

```
  case 6:
    // if the order is awaiting shipment...
    processOrderButton.Text = "Confirm Order Shipment";
    processOrderButton.Enabled = true;
    cancelOrderButton.Enabled = true;
    break;
  default:
    // otherwise...
    processOrderButton.Text = "Process Order";
    processOrderButton.Enabled = true;
    cancelOrderButton.Enabled = true;
    break;
}
```

A switch statement is used here to enable or disable buttons according to the current status. The rest of the code in PopulateControls() binds order info and audit trail data and is as follows:

```
  // fill the data grid with order details
  grid.DataSource = orderInfo.OrderDetails;
  grid.DataBind();

  // fill the audit data grid with audit trail
  auditGrid.DataSource = orderInfo.AuditTrail;
  auditGrid.DataBind();
}
```

The SetEditMode method is also slightly different because the controls to enable or disable have changed:

```
// enable or disable edit mode
private void SetEditMode(bool enable)
{
  dateShippedTextBox.Enabled = enable;
  statusDropDown.Enabled = enable;
  authCodeTextBox.Enabled = enable;
  referenceTextBox.Enabled = enable;
  commentsTextBox.Enabled = enable;
  editButton.Enabled = !enable;
  updateButton.Enabled = enable;
  cancelButton.Enabled = enable;
}
```

The code for the Edit and Cancel buttons remains unchanged, but Update needs rewriting to use the new business tier method. The code is as follows:

```
// update order information
protected void updateButton_Click(object sender, EventArgs e)
{
  try
  {
```

```
      // Get new order data
      int orderID = int.Parse(Session["AdminOrderID"].ToString());
      string dateCreated = dateCreatedTextBox.Text;
      string dateShipped = dateShippedTextBox.Text;
      int status = int.Parse(statusDropDown.SelectedValue);
      string authCode = authCodeTextBox.Text;
      string reference = referenceTextBox.Text;
      string comments = commentsTextBox.Text;
      // Update the order
      CommerceLibAccess.UpdateOrder(orderID, dateCreated,
        dateShipped, status, authCode, reference, comments);
    }
    catch
    {
      // In case of an error, we simply ignore it
    }
    // Exit edit mode and populate the form again
    SetEditMode(false);
    PopulateControls();
    Page.DataBind();
  }
```

Again, the code is only slightly different. You extract the data in a similar way, but use several local variables rather than a single `OrderInfo` instance. These variables are passed to `CommerceLibAccess.UpdateOrder` to update the order.

The code for the order-processing button is, thanks to the order processor class, very simple:

```
// continue order processing
protected void processOrderButton_Click(object sender, EventArgs e)
{
  string orderId = Session["AdminOrderID"].ToString();
  OrderProcessor processor = new OrderProcessor(orderId);
  processor.Process();
  PopulateControls();
}
```

You instantiate an `OrderProcessor` instance for the selected order (found from the string in the session state) and call `Process()`. This same call works for suppliers and administrators. Whatever stage the order has reached, this call attempts to push it forward. After order processing (which may involve a lot of work, but should be quick if all goes well), you repopulate the order data to update it.

Finally, you have the code required to cancel an order, which just means setting the status to 9. The code is already in place to do this, and you call it as follows:

```
// cancel order
protected void cancelOrderButton_Click(object sender, EventArgs e)
{
  string orderId = Session["AdminOrderID"].ToString();
  CommerceLibAccess.UpdateOrderStatus(int.Parse(orderId), 9);
  PopulateControls();
}
```

Testing the Order Administration Page

All that remains now is to check that everything is working properly. To do this, use the web interface to place an order and then examine it via the OrdersAdmin.aspx page. You should see that the order is awaiting confirmation of stock, as shown in Figure 15-3.

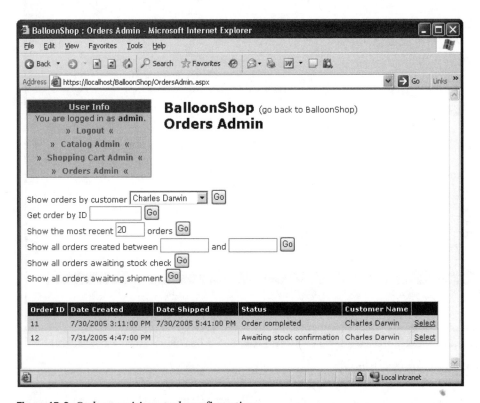

Figure 15-3. *Order awaiting stock confirmation*

Click Select and scroll down until the button for confirming stock appears, as shown in Figure 15-4.

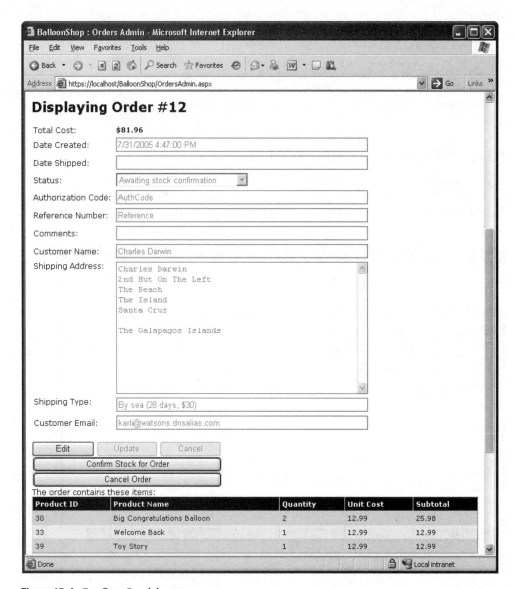

Figure 15-4. *Confirm Stock button*

Click the Confirm Stock for Order button, and the order is processed. Because this happens very quickly, you are soon presented with the next stage, a prompt to confirm shipment. Click the Confirm Order Shipment button and the order is completed.

If you scroll down further, you can see all audit trail messages that have been stored in the database concerning this order, as shown in Figure 15-5.

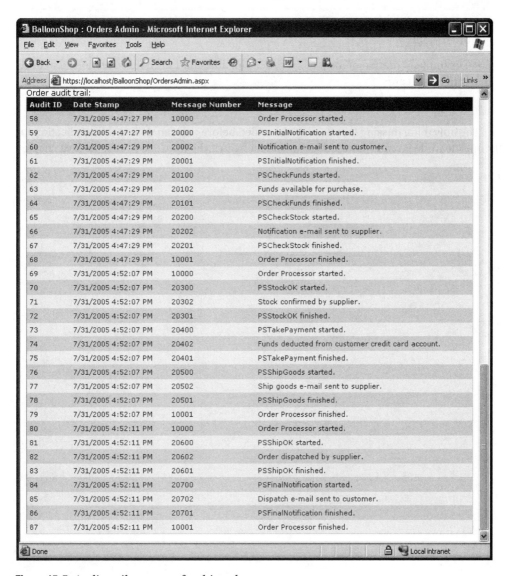

Figure 15-5. *Audit trail messages for this order*

Summary

You've taken giant strides toward completing your e-commerce application in this chapter. Now you have a fully audited, secure backbone for the application.

Specifically, we've covered the following:

- Modifications to the BalloonShop application to enable your own pipeline processing

- The basic framework for the order pipeline

- The database additions for auditing data and storing additional required data in the Orders table

- The implementation of most of the order pipeline, apart from those sections that deal with credit cards

- A simple implementation of an order administration web page

The only thing missing that needs to be added before you can deliver this application to the outside world is credit card processing functionality, which we'll look at in the next chapter.

CHAPTER 16

Credit Card Transactions

The last thing you need to do before launching the e-commerce site is enable credit card processing. In this chapter, we'll look at how you can build this into the pipeline you created in the last chapter.

We'll start by looking at the theory behind credit card transactions, the sort of organizations that help you achieve credit card processing, and the sort of transactions that are possible. Moving on, we'll take two example organizations and discuss the specifics of their transaction APIs (Application Program Interfaces, the means by which you access credit card transaction functionality). After this, you'll build a new set of classes to help you use one of these transaction APIs via some simple test code.

Finally, you'll integrate the API with the BalloonShop e-commerce application and order-processing pipeline.

Learning the Credit Card Transaction Fundamentals

Banks and other financial institutions use secure networks for their transactions, based on the X.25 protocol rather than TCP/IP (Transmission Control Protocol/Internet Protocol, the primary means by which data is transmitted across the Internet). X.25 isn't something you need to know anything about, apart from the fact that it's a different protocol for networking and isn't compatible with TCP/IP. As such, X.25 networks are completely separate from the Internet, and although it's possible to get direct access to them, this is unlikely to be a reasonable option. To do so, you might have to enter into some serious negotiation with the owner of the network you want to use. The owner will want to be 100% sure that you are a reliable customer who is capable of enforcing the necessary safeguards to prevent an attack on the system. The owner of the network won't be handing out these licenses to just anyone, because most people can't afford the security measures required (which include locking your servers in a cage, sending daily backup tapes down a secure chute, having three individuals with separate keys to access these tapes, and so on).

The alternative is to go via a gateway provider. This enables you to perform your side of the credit card transaction protocol over the Internet (using a secure protocol), while relying on your chosen gateway to communicate with X.25 networks. Although there is a cost involved with this (it's a fact of life, unfortunately), at least the provider has reached some deal with financial institutions to keep costs low. This saving is passed on to you (after the gateway takes its share), so it's likely to be much cheaper than having your own X.25 connection. This method is also cheaper than using a third party such as PayPal, because you only need the minimum functionality when you're handling your own order pipeline. You don't need, for example, to use all the order-auditing functionality offered by a company such as PayPal, because in the last chapter, you already built all this functionality.

Working with Credit Card Payment Gateways

Unlike with PayPal, to work with a gateway organization, you first need to open a merchant bank account. This can be done at most banks and will get you a merchant ID that you can use when signing up with the gateway. The next step is to find a suitable gateway. Unfortunately, this can be a lot of hard work, as you'll have to shop around for the best deal!

It isn't hard to find a gateway, but it is hard to find the right one. Literally hundreds of companies are ready to take a cut of your sales. A quick search on the Internet for "credit card gateway" will get you a long list. The web sites of these companies are for the most part pure brochureware—you'll find yourself reading through pages of text about how they are the best and most secure at what they do, only to end up with a form to fill in so that a customer service representative can call you to "discuss your needs." In the long run, you can rest assured that at least you will probably only have to go through the procedure once.

You'll probably find that most of the organizations offering this service offer similar packages, so there may be very little that influences your choice. However, key points to look for include which banks they will do business with (your merchant bank account will have to be at one of these), which currencies they deal in, and, of course, what the costs are.

In this chapter, we'll look at two of the few organizations that are easy to deal with—DataCash and VeriSign PayFlow Pro.

Table 16-1 shows some of the gateway services available.

Table 16-1. *Gateway Services*

United States	Web Address	United Kingdom	Web Address
First Data	http://www.firstdata.com/	WorldPay	http://www.worldpay.com/
Cardservice International	http://www.cardservice.com/	DataCash	http://www.datacash.com/
VeriSign Pay Flow Pro	http://www.verisign.com/	VeriSign Pay Flow Pro	http://www.verisign.com/
ICVerify	http://www.icverify.com/		

DataCash

DataCash is a UK-based credit card gateway organization. Unfortunately, this means that you'll need a UK merchant bank account if you want to use it in your final application, but you don't have to worry about this for now. The reason for using DataCash in this chapter is that you don't have to do very much to get access to a rather useful test account—you don't even need a merchant bank account. All you need is a business email address, as it is DataCash policy that personal addresses can't be used for signing up. As you'll see later in this chapter, you can perform test transactions using so-called "magic" credit card numbers supplied by DataCash, which will accept or decline transactions without performing any actual financial transactions. This is fantastic for development purposes, because you don't want to use your own credit cards for testing!

The important point to bear in mind is that the techniques covered in this chapter apply to every existing credit card gateway. The specifics may change slightly if you switch to a different organization, but you'll have done most of the hard work already.

■**Note** Before you ask, no, we're not sales representatives for DataCash. It's just that we've spent many hours (days?) looking into credit card transactions, and so far we've yet to find a more developer-friendly way of getting started.

PayFlow Pro

PayFlow Pro is a service supplied by the globally recognized Internet company VeriSign. This company has established itself as an excellent resource for Internet security and e-commerce applications, so it comes as no surprise that VeriSign has an entry in the competitive credit card gateway arena.

In fact, the first edition of this book did not cover the PayFlow Pro service. However, because readers have had great success with it, we feel obliged to cover it here.

■**Note** The authors of this book are in no way affiliated with VeriSign.

Understanding Credit Card Transactions

Whichever gateway you use; the basic principles of credit card transactions are the same. First, the sort of transactions you'll be dealing with in an e-commerce web site are known as Card Not Present (CNP) transactions, which means you don't have the credit card in front of you, and you can't check the customer signature. This isn't a problem; after all, you've probably been performing CNP transactions for some time now: online, over the phone, by mail, and so on. It's just something to be aware of should you see the CNP acronym.

Several advanced services are offered by various gateways, including cardholder address verification, security code checking, fraud screening, and so on. Each of these adds an additional layer of complexity to your credit card processing, and we're not going to go into details here. Rather, this chapter provides a starting point from which you can add these services if required. With all these optional extras, the choice will involve how much money is passing through your system and a trade-off between the costs of implementation and the potential costs if something goes wrong that could be prevented if you use these extra services. If you are interested in these services, the customer service representative mentioned previously will be happy to explain things.

You can perform several types of transaction, including the following:

- *Authorization*: Basic type, checks card for funds and deducts them.

- *Preauthorization*: Checks cards for funds and allocates them if available, but doesn't deduct them immediately.

- *Fulfillment*: Completes a preauthorization transaction, deducting the funds already allocated.

- *Refund*: Refunds a completed transaction or simply puts money on a credit card.

Again, the specifics vary, but these are the basic types.

In this chapter, you'll use the pre/fulfill model, in which you don't take payment until just before you instruct your supplier to ship goods. This has been hinted at previously by the structure of the pipeline you created in the last chapter.

Implementing Credit Card Processing

Now that we've covered the basics, we need to look at how to get things working in the BalloonShop application using the DataCash system. First, you need to obtain a test account with DataCash:

1. Go to `http://www.datacash.com/`.

2. Head to the `Apply Now` section of the web site and click `Get a Test Account`.

3. Enter your details and submit.

4. From the email you receive, make a note of your account username and password, as well as the additional information required for accessing the DataCash reporting system.

The next step is normally to download one of DataCash's toolkits for easy integration. However, because DataCash doesn't provide a .NET-compatible implementation, you must use the XML API for performing transactions. Basically, this involves sending XML requests to a certain URL using an SSL connection and deciphering the XML result. This is easy to do in .NET.

■**Note** After we look at DataCash in detail, we'll examine the PayFlow Pro system, although we won't show the code implementation. The code is, however, available in the Source Code area of the Apress web site (`http://www.apress.com`) for this book.

Considering the DataCash XML API

You'll be doing a lot of XML manipulation when communicating with DataCash because you'll need to create XML documents to send to DataCash and extract data from XML responses. In this section, we'll take a quick look at the XML required for the operations you'll be performing and the responses you can expect.

Preauthentication Request

When you send a preauthentication request to DataCash, you need to include the following information:

- DataCash username (known as the DataCash Client)

- DataCash password

- A unique transaction reference number (explained later in this section)

- The amount of money to be debited

- The currency used for the transaction (USD, GBP, and so on)

- The type of the transaction (for preauthentication, the code pre is used)

- The credit card number

- The credit card expiry date

- The credit card issue date (if applicable to the type of credit card being used)

- The credit card issue number (if applicable to the type of credit card being used)

The reference number must be a number between 6 and 12 digits long, which you choose to uniquely identify the transaction with an order. Because you can't use a short number, you can't just use the order ID values you've been using until now for orders. However, you can use this order ID as the starting point for creating a reference number, simply by adding a high number, such as 1,000,000. You can't duplicate the reference number in any future transactions, so you can be sure that after a transaction is completed, it won't execute again, which might otherwise result in charging the customer twice. This does mean, however, that if a credit card is rejected, you might need to create a whole new order for the customer, but that shouldn't be a problem if required.

The XML request is formatted in the following way, with the values detailed previously shown in bold:

```
<?xml version="1.0" encoding="UTF-8"?>
<Request>
  <Authentication>
    <password>DataCash password</password>
    <client>DataCash client</client>
  </Authentication>
  <Transaction>
    <TxnDetails>
      <merchantreference>Unique reference number</merchantreference>
      <amount currency='Currency Type'>Cash amount</amount>
    </TxnDetails>
    <CardTxn>
      <method>pre</method>
```

```
      <Card>
        <pan>Credit card number</pan>
        <expirydate>Credit card expiry date</expirydate>
      </Card>
    </CardTxn>
  </Transaction>
</Request>
```

Response to Preauthentication Request

The response to a preauthentication request includes the following information:

- A status code number indicating what happened; 1 if the transaction was successful, or one of several other codes if something else happens. For a complete list of return codes for a DataCash server, log in to https://testserver.datacash.com/software/download.cgi with your account details and download the relevant document.

- A reason for the status, which is basically a string explaining the status in English. For a status of 1, this string is ACCEPTED.

- An authentication code used to fulfill the transaction.

- A reference code for use by DataCash.

- The time that the transaction was processed.

- The mode of the transaction, which is TEST when using the test account.

- Confirmation of the type of credit card used.

- Confirmation of the country that the credit card was issued in.

- The authorization code used by the bank (for reference only).

The XML for this is formatted as follows:

```
<?xml version="1.0" encoding="utf-8"?>
<Response>
  <status>Status code</status>
  <reason>Reason</reason>
  <merchantreference>Authentication code</merchantreference>
  <datacash_reference>Reference number</datacash_reference>
  <time>Time</time>
  <mode>TEST</mode>
  <CardTxn>
    <card_scheme>Card Type</card_scheme>
    <country>Country</country>
    <issuer>Card issuing bank</issuer>
    <authcode>Bank authorization code</authcode>
  </CardTxn>
</Response>
```

Fulfillment Request

For a fulfillment request, you need to send the following information:

- DataCash username (known as the DataCash Client)

- DataCash password

- The type of the transaction (for fulfillment, you use the code `fulfil`)

- The authentication code received earlier

- The reference number received earlier

Optionally, you can include additional information, such as a confirmation of the amount to be debited from the credit card, although this isn't really necessary.

This is formatted as follows:

```
<?xml version="1.0" encoding="UTF-8"?>
<Request>
  <Authentication>
    <password>DataCash password</password>
    <client>DataCash client</client>
  </Authentication>
  <Transaction>
    <HistoricTxn>
      <reference>Reference Number</reference>
      <authcode>Authentication code</authcode>
      <method>fulfil</method>
    </HistoricTxn>
  </Transaction>
</Request>
```

Fulfillment Response

The response to a fulfillment request includes the following information:

- A status code number indicating what happened; 1 if the transaction was successful, or one of several other codes if something else happens. Again for a complete list of the codes, log in to `https://testserver.datacash.com/software/download.cgi` with your account details and download the relevant document.

- A reason for the status, which is basically a string explaining the status in English. For a status of 1, this string is `FULFILLED OK`.

- Two copies of the reference code for use by DataCash.

- The time that the transaction was processed.

- The mode of the transaction, which is `TEST` when using the test account.

The XML for this is formatted as follows:

```xml
<?xml version="1.0" encoding="utf-8"?>
<Response>
  <status>Status code</status>
  <reason>Reason</reason>
  <merchantreference>Reference Code</merchantreference>
  <datacash_reference>Reference Code</datacash_reference>
  <time>Time</time>
  <mode>TEST</mode>
</Response>
```

Exchanging XML Data

You could build up the XML documents shown previously piece by piece, but the .NET Framework allows you to do things in a much better way. The solution presented here involves XML serialization. It's possible to configure any .NET class so that it can be serialized as an XML document, and that XML documents also can be used to instantiate classes. This involves converting all public fields and properties into XML data and is the basis for the web services functionality in .NET.

The default behavior for this is to create XML documents with elements named the same as the public fields and properties that you are serializing. For example, you might have the following class and member:

```csharp
public class TestClass
{
  public string TestMember;
}
```

This is serialized as follows:

```xml
<?xml version="1.0" encoding="utf-8"?>
<TestClass>
  <TestMember>Value</TestMember>
</TestClass>
```

You can override this behavior using XML serialization attributes. You can force pieces of data to be formatted in elements with custom names, as attributes, as plain text, and so on.

For example, you could force the previous class to serialize as an attribute as follows:

```csharp
public class TestClass
{
  [XmlAttribute("TestAttribute")]
  public string TestMember;
}
```

The [XmlAttribute()] part means that the member that follows should be serialized as an attribute, and the string parameter names the attribute. This class now serializes as follows:

```
<?xml version="1.0" encoding="utf-8"?>
<TestClass TestAttribute="Value" />
```

You can use several of these attributes, and you'll see some of them in the example that follows. This example demonstrates how you can create classes that represent DataCash requests and responses, which are capable of serializing to and deserializing from an XML representation. This makes it easy to send data to DataCash and allows you to use the full power of .NET classes to provide an intelligent way of accessing data.

In the example that follows, you'll create the classes necessary to exchange data with DataCash and try out these classes using some simple client code. Note that several classes are used to build up the XML because the structure involves several nested elements rather than a flat structure.

Exercise: Communicating with DataCash

1. Create a new subdirectory in the **App_Code** directory of BalloonShop, called **DataCashLib**.

2. Add the following classes starting with **AmountClass**:

   ```
   using System.Xml.Serialization;

   namespace DataCashLib
   {
     public class AmountClass
     {
       [XmlAttribute("currency")]
       public string Currency;

       [XmlText()]
       public string Amount;
     }
   }
   ```

3. Add the following class, **AuthenticationClass** (note that all the classes that follow have a using reference to System.Xml.Serialization and are in the DataCashLib namespace, just like the preceding AmountClass, but this extra code isn't shown from now on to save space):

   ```
   public class AuthenticationClass
   {
     [XmlElement("password")]
     public string Password;

     [XmlElement("client")]
     public string Client;
   }
   ```

4. Add the following class, **CardClass**:

```
public class CardClass
{
  [XmlElement("pan")]
  public string CardNumber;

  [XmlElement("expirydate")]
  public string ExpiryDate;

  [XmlElement("startdate")]
  public string StartDate;

  [XmlElement("issuenumber")]
  public string IssueNumber;
}
```

5. Add the following class, **CardTxnRequestClass**:

```
public class CardTxnRequestClass
{
  [XmlElement("method")]
  public string Method;

  [XmlElement("Card")]
  public CardClass Card = new CardClass();
}
```

6. Add the following class, **CardTxnResponseClass**:

```
public class CardTxnResponseClass
{
  [XmlElement("card_scheme")]
  public string CardScheme;

  [XmlElement("country")]
  public string Country;

  [XmlElement("issuer")]
  public string Issuer;

  [XmlElement("authcode")]
  public string AuthCode;
}
```

7. Add the following class, **HistoricTxnClass**:

```
public class HistoricTxnClass
{
  [XmlElement("reference")]
  public string Reference;

  [XmlElement("authcode")]
  public string AuthCode;

  [XmlElement("method")]
  public string Method;

  [XmlElement("tran_code")]
  public string TranCode;

  [XmlElement("duedate")]
  public string DueDate;
}
```

8. Add the following class, **TxnDetailsClass**:

```
public class TxnDetailsClass
{
  [XmlElement("merchantreference")]
  public string MerchantReference;

  [XmlElement("amount")]
  public AmountClass Amount = new AmountClass();
}
```

9. Add the following class, **TransactionClass**:

```
public class TransactionClass
{
  [XmlElement("TxnDetails")]
  public TxnDetailsClass TxnDetails = new TxnDetailsClass();
  private CardTxnRequestClass cardTxn;

  private HistoricTxnClass historicTxn;
```

```csharp
[XmlElement("CardTxn")]
public CardTxnRequestClass CardTxn
{
  get
  {
    if (historicTxn == null)
    {
      if (cardTxn == null)
      {
        cardTxn = new CardTxnRequestClass();
      }
      return cardTxn;
    }
    else
    {
      return null;
    }
  }
  set
  {
    cardTxn = value;
  }
}

[XmlElement("HistoricTxn")]
public HistoricTxnClass HistoricTxn
{
  get
  {
    if (cardTxn == null)
    {
      if (historicTxn == null)
      {
        historicTxn = new HistoricTxnClass();
      }
      return historicTxn;
    }
    else
    {
      return null;
    }
  }
  set
  {
    historicTxn = value;
  }
}
}
```

10. Add the following class, **DataCashRequest** (this class also requires using references to System.Net, System.Text, and System.IO):

```
[XmlRoot("Request")]
public class DataCashRequest
{
  [XmlElement("Authentication")]
  public AuthenticationClass Authentication =
    new AuthenticationClass();

  [XmlElement("Transaction")]
  public TransactionClass Transaction = new TransactionClass();

  public DataCashResponse GetResponse(string url)
  {
    // Configure HTTP Request
    HttpWebRequest httpRequest = WebRequest.Create(url)
      as HttpWebRequest;
    httpRequest.Method = "POST";

    // Prepare correct encoding for XML serialization
    UTF8Encoding encoding = new UTF8Encoding();

    // Use Xml property to obtain serialized XML data
    // Convert into bytes using encoding specified above and
    // get length
    byte[] bodyBytes = encoding.GetBytes(Xml);
    httpRequest.ContentLength = bodyBytes.Length;

    // Get HTTP Request stream for putting XML data into
    Stream httpRequestBodyStream =
      httpRequest.GetRequestStream();

    // Fill stream with serialized XML data
    httpRequestBodyStream.Write(bodyBytes, 0, bodyBytes.Length);
    httpRequestBodyStream.Close();

    // Get HTTP Response
    HttpWebResponse httpResponse = httpRequest.GetResponse()
      as HttpWebResponse;
    StreamReader httpResponseStream =
      new StreamReader(httpResponse.GetResponseStream(),
      System.Text.Encoding.ASCII);

    // Extract XML from response
    string httpResponseBody = httpResponseStream.ReadToEnd();
    httpResponseStream.Close();
```

```
      // Ignore everything that isn't XML by removing headers
      httpResponseBody = httpResponseBody.Substring(
        httpResponseBody.IndexOf("<?xml"));

      // Deserialize XML into DataCashResponse
      XmlSerializer serializer =
        new XmlSerializer(typeof(DataCashResponse));
      StringReader responseReader =
        new StringReader(httpResponseBody);

      // Return DataCashResponse result
      return serializer.Deserialize(responseReader)
        as DataCashResponse;
    }

    [XmlIgnore()]
    public string Xml
    {
      get
      {
        // Prepare XML serializer
        XmlSerializer serializer =
          new XmlSerializer(typeof(DataCashRequest));

        // Serialize into StringBuilder
        StringBuilder sb = new StringBuilder();
        StringWriter sw = new StringWriter(sb);
        serializer.Serialize(sw, this);
        sw.Flush();

        // Replace UTF-16 encoding with UTF-8 encoding
        string xml = sb.ToString();
        xml = xml.Replace("utf-16", "utf-8");
        return xml;
      }
    }
}
```

11. Add the following class, **DataCashResponse** (which needs additional using references to System.Text and System.IO):

```
[XmlRoot("Response")]
public class DataCashResponse
{
  [XmlElement("status")]
  public string Status;
```

```
[XmlElement("reason")]
public string Reason;

[XmlElement("information")]
public string information;

[XmlElement("merchantreference")]
public string MerchantReference;

[XmlElement("datacash_reference")]
public string DatacashReference;

[XmlElement("time")]
public string Time;

[XmlElement("mode")]
public string Mode;

[XmlElement("CardTxn")]
public CardTxnResponseClass CardTxn;

[XmlIgnore()]
public string Xml
{
  get
  {
    // Prepare XML serializer
    XmlSerializer serializer =
      new XmlSerializer(typeof(DataCashResponse));
    // Serialize into StringBuilder
    StringBuilder sb = new StringBuilder();
    StringWriter sw = new StringWriter(sb);
    serializer.Serialize(sw, this);
    sw.Flush();

    // Replace UTF-16 encoding with UTF-8 encoding
    string xml = sb.ToString();
    xml = xml.Replace("utf-16", "utf-8");
    return xml;
  }
}
}
```

12. Now you've finished adding the classes, so add a new Web Form to the root of BalloonShop called
DataCashLibTest.aspx, for testing (use the standard BalloonShop Master Page for now).

13. Add a single multiline `TextBox` control to the page called `OutputBox` and make it big enough to see plenty of text.

14. Add `using` references to `DataCashLib` and `System.Text` to the top of `DataCashLibTest.aspx.cs`.

15. Modify the code in `Program.cs` as follows, replacing the values for `dataCashClient` and `dataCashPassword` with your own values (obtained when you signed up with DataCash). You'll also have to change the Merchant Reference number to be a different value, or else you'll get a duplicate reference response returned to you (this class needs `using` references to `System.IO`, `System.Xml.Serialization`, and `DataCashLib`):

```
static void Main(string[] args)
{
   // Initialize variables
   DataCashRequest request;
   XmlSerializer requestSerializer =
       new XmlSerializer(typeof(DataCashRequest));
   DataCashResponse response;
   XmlSerializer responseSerializer =
       new XmlSerializer(typeof(DataCashResponse));
   StringBuilder xmlBuilder;
   StringWriter xmlWriter;
   string dataCashUrl =
       "https://testserver.datacash.com/Transaction";
   string dataCashClient = "99341800";
   string dataCashPassword = "bbdNsX7p";

   // Construct pre request
   request = new DataCashRequest();
   request.Authentication.Client = dataCashClient;
   request.Authentication.Password = dataCashPassword;
   request.Transaction.TxnDetails.MerchantReference = "9999999";
   request.Transaction.TxnDetails.Amount.Amount = "49.99";
   request.Transaction.TxnDetails.Amount.Currency = "GBP";
   request.Transaction.CardTxn.Method = "pre";
   request.Transaction.CardTxn.Card.CardNumber =
       "4444333322221111";
   request.Transaction.CardTxn.Card.ExpiryDate = "10/07";

   // Display pre request
   Console.WriteLine("Pre Request:");
   xmlBuilder = new StringBuilder();
   xmlWriter = new StringWriter(xmlBuilder);
   requestSerializer.Serialize(xmlWriter, request);
   Console.WriteLine(xmlBuilder.ToString());
   Console.WriteLine();
```

```
    // Get pre response
    response = request.GetResponse(dataCashUrl);

    // Display pre response
    Console.WriteLine("Pre Response:");
    xmlBuilder = new StringBuilder();
    xmlWriter = new StringWriter(xmlBuilder);
    responseSerializer.Serialize(xmlWriter, response);
    Console.WriteLine(xmlBuilder.ToString());
    Console.WriteLine();

    // Construct fulfil request
    request = new DataCashRequest();
    request.Authentication.Client = dataCashClient;
    request.Authentication.Password = dataCashPassword;
    request.Transaction.HistoricTxn.Method = "fulfill";
    request.Transaction.HistoricTxn.AuthCode =
        response.MerchantReference;
    request.Transaction.HistoricTxn.Reference =
        response.DatacashReference;

    // Display fulfil request
    Console.WriteLine("Fulfil Request:");
    xmlBuilder = new StringBuilder();
    xmlWriter = new StringWriter(xmlBuilder);
    requestSerializer.Serialize(xmlWriter, request);
    Console.WriteLine(xmlBuilder.ToString());
    Console.WriteLine();

    // Get fulfil response
    response = request.GetResponse(dataCashUrl);

    // Display fulfil response
    Console.WriteLine("Fulfil Response:");
    xmlBuilder = new StringBuilder();
    xmlWriter = new StringWriter(xmlBuilder);
    responseSerializer.Serialize(xmlWriter, response);
    Console.WriteLine(xmlBuilder.ToString());

    // Await user input to finish
    Console.ReadKey();
}
```

16. Now build and run the solution. The text displayed in the **OutputBox** text box is as follows:

```
Pre Request:
<?xml version="1.0" encoding="utf-16"?>
<Request xmlns:xsi=http://www.w3.org/2001/XMLSchema-instance
  xmlns:xsd="http://www.w3.org/2001/XMLSchema">
  <Authentication>
    <password>bbdNsX7p</password>
    <client>99341800</client>
  </Authentication>
  <Transaction>
    <CardTxn>
      <method>pre</method>
      <Card>
        <pan>4444333322221111</pan>
        <expirydate>10/07</expirydate>
      </Card>
    </CardTxn>
    <TxnDetails>
      <merchantreference>9999999</merchantreference>
      <amount currency="GBP">49.99</amount>
    </TxnDetails>
  </Transaction>
</Request>

Pre Response:
<?xml version="1.0" encoding="utf-16"?>
<Response xmlns:xsi=http://www.w3.org/2001/XMLSchema-instance
  xmlns:xsd="http://www.w3.org/2001/XMLSchema">
  <status>1</status>
  <reason>ACCEPTED</reason>
  <merchantreference>9999999</merchantreference>
  <datacash_reference>4000200041287947</datacash_reference>
  <time>1122838608</time>
  <mode>TEST</mode>
  <CardTxn>
    <card_scheme>VISA</card_scheme>
    <country>United Kingdom</country>
    <authcode>953441</authcode>
  </CardTxn>
</Response>
```

Fulfil Request:

```
<?xml version="1.0" encoding="utf-16"?>
<Request xmlns:xsi=http://www.w3.org/2001/XMLSchema-instance
  xmlns:xsd="http://www.w3.org/2001/XMLSchema">
  <Authentication>
    <password>bbdNsX7p</password>
    <client>99341800</client>
  </Authentication>
  <Transaction>
    <HistoricTxn>
      <reference>4000200041287947</reference>
      <authcode>9999999</authcode>
      <method>fulfill</method>
    </HistoricTxn>
    <TxnDetails>
      <amount />
    </TxnDetails>
  </Transaction>
</Request>
```

Fulfil Response:

```
<?xml version="1.0" encoding="utf-16"?>
<Response xmlns:xsi=http://www.w3.org/2001/XMLSchema-instance
  xmlns:xsd="http://www.w3.org/2001/XMLSchema">
  <status>1</status>
  <reason>FULFILLED OK</reason>
  <merchantreference>4000200041287947</merchantreference>
  <datacash_reference>4000200041287947</datacash_reference>
  <time>1122838608</time>
  <mode>TEST</mode>
</Response>
```

17. Log on to **https://testserver.datacash.com/reporting2** to see the transaction log for your DataCash account (note that this view takes awhile to update, so you might not see the transaction right away). This report is shown in Figure 16-1, with a more detailed view in Figure 16-2.

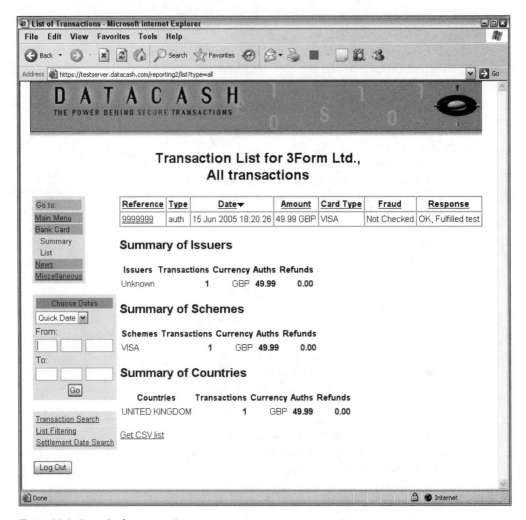

Figure 16-1. *DataCash transaction report*

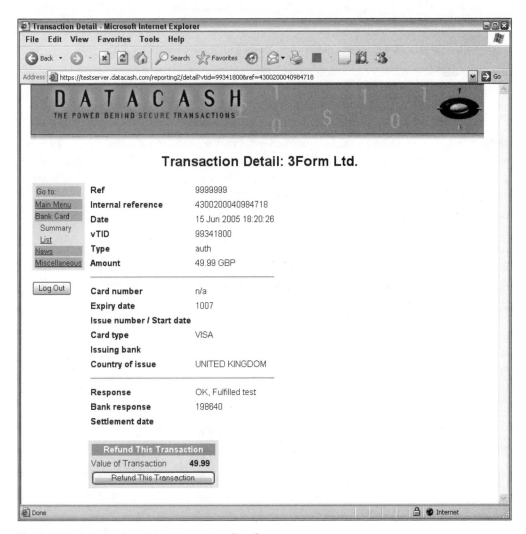

Figure 16-2. *DataCash transaction report details*

How It Works: Communicating with DataCash

You've created code to represent the XML documents that you're exchanging. Two root classes—DataCashRequest and DataCashResponse—encapsulate XML requests and responses. These classes contain instances of the other classes defined, which contain instances of other classes, and so on, relating to the structure of the XML documents described earlier.

Each of the members of these classes has an associated XML serialization attribute, matching the data with the way it will be formatted when the request or response classes are serialized. For example, many of the string members appear as follows:

```
[XmlElement("status")]
public string Status;
```

The Status field will be formatted as follows:

```
<status>Status data</status>
```

The correct capitalization is included while at the same time allowing you to set the status data using standard PascalCasing format.

■**Note** PascalCasing is where variable names start with a capital letter, and each subsequent word in the name also has a capital letter, such as ThisIsAVariable. One alternative scheme is camelCasing, where the first word isn't capitalized, for example thisIsAVariable. The capitalization in the names of these casing schemes serves as a reminder of their usage.

One of the classes used, TransactionClass, is slightly more complicated than the others, because the <Transaction> element contains one of either <CardTxn> or <HistoricTxn>, depending on whether the request is a pre request or a fulfil request. Instead of using fields, this class uses properties that ensure that only one of these two elements is used.

The DataCashRequest class also has a method called GetResponse that sends the request and packages the returned response as a DataCashResponse class. In the code to do this, you start by creating an HttpWebRequest instance for the URL supplied as a parameter:

```
public DataCashResponse GetResponse(string url)
{
  HttpWebRequest httpRequest = WebRequest.Create(url)
    as HttpWebRequest;
```

This request is then defined as a POST request with the appropriate encoding:

```
httpRequest.Method = "POST";
UTF8Encoding encoding = new UTF8Encoding();
```

■**Note** HTTP requests can be sent in a number of formats, the most common being GET and POST. The difference here is that GET requests have just a URL and header information; POST requests have all this plus a message body. Think of an HTTP POST request as if it were an email, with the HTTP response being the email reply. In both cases, header information is like the address and subject of the email, and body information is like the message body of an email.

Next you need to supply the body of the POST request, which is the XML document you want to send. To do this, you get the serialized version of the data contained in the object via the Xml property (which simply serializes the DataCashRequest instance into XML, by using the XML serialization attributes):

```
byte[] bodyBytes = encoding.GetBytes(Xml);
```

You also need to specify the length of the data contained in the HTTP header for the request:

```
httpRequest.ContentLength = bodyBytes.Length;
```

Next you take the XML data and place it into the request via standard stream manipulation code:

```
Stream httpRequestBodyStream =
   httpRequest.GetRequestStream();
httpRequestBodyStream.Write(bodyBytes, 0, bodyBytes.Length);
httpRequestBodyStream.Close();
```

After you have the request class, you can obtain the response, also via stream manipulation:

```
HttpWebResponse httpResponse = httpRequest.GetResponse()
   as HttpWebResponse;
StreamReader httpResponseStream =
   new StreamReader(httpResponse.GetResponseStream(),
      System.Text.Encoding.ASCII);
string httpResponseBody = httpResponseStream.ReadToEnd();
   httpResponseStream.Close();
```

You only need the XML data contained in this stream, so clip off the headers at the beginning of the data returned before deserializing it. You do this using the `String.Substring` method to obtain the section of the string that starts with `"<?xml"`, the location of which is found using the `String.IndexOf` method.

```
httpResponseBody =
   httpResponseBody.Substring(
      httpResponseBody.IndexOf("<?xml"));
XmlSerializer serializer =
   new XmlSerializer(typeof(DataCashResponse));
StringReader responseReader =
   new StringReader(httpResponseBody);
```

Finally, you cast the deserialized object into a `DataCashResponse` object for further manipulation:

```
return serializer.Deserialize(responseReader)
   as DataCashResponse;
}
```

After the transaction has completed, you can check that everything has worked properly via the DataCash reporting web interface.

Integrating DataCash with BalloonShop

Now you have a new set of classes that you can use to perform credit card transactions. However, you need to modify a few things to integrate it with your existing e-commerce application and pipeline.

Business Tier Modifications

In fact, *all* the modifications you'll make to BalloonShop occur at the business tier because we've slipped in the data and presentation tier modifications already. We also have AuthCode and Reference fields ready to use for the database. In the presentation tier, we have the user interface elements in place to check on these values. All you have to do is make the PSCheckFunds and PSTakePayment pipeline sections work.

Modifying the BalloonShopConfiguration Class

Before modifying the pipeline itself, you have to modify the order-processor configuration, because you now have three new pieces of information that CommerceLib requires to operate:

- DataCash Client

- DataCash password

- DataCash URL

You can give access to this information via the BalloonShopConfiguration class as with the other similar information required for order processing. Add the following three properties to BalloonShopConfiguration:

```
// DataCash client code
public static string DataCashClient
{
  get
  {
    return ConfigurationManager.AppSettings["DataCashClient"];
  }
}

// DataCase password
public static string DataCashPassword
{
  get
  {
    return ConfigurationManager.AppSettings["DataCashPassword"];
  }
}

// DataCash server URL
public static string DataCashUrl
{
  get
  {
    return ConfigurationManager.AppSettings["DataCashUrl"];
  }
}
```

This uses information in the web.config file of BalloonShop. Modify web.config as follows, supplying your own client and password data as before:

```
<appSettings>
  ...
  <add key="DataCashClient" value="99110400" />
  <add key="DataCashPassword" value="rUD27uD" />
  <add key="DataCashUrl"
    value="https://testserver.datacash.com/Transaction" />
</appSettings>
```

Modifying the PSCheckFunds Pipeline Section Class

The final changes involve modifying the pipeline section classes that deal with credit card transactions. The infrastructure for storing and retrieving authentication code and reference information has already been included, via the OrderProcessor.SetOrderAuthCodeAndReference method and the AuthCode and Reference properties.

The modifications to PSCheckFunds are as follows:

```
using DataCashLib;

namespace CommerceLib
{
  /// <summary>
  /// 2nd pipeline stage - used to check that the customer
  /// has the required funds available for purchase
  /// </summary>
  public class PSCheckFunds : IPipelineSection
  {
    private OrderProcessor orderProcessor;

    public void Process(OrderProcessor processor)
    {
      // set processor reference
      orderProcessor = processor;
      // audit
      orderProcessor.CreateAudit("PSCheckFunds started.", 20100);
      try
      {
        // check customer funds via DataCash gateway
        // configure DataCash XML request
        DataCashRequest request = new DataCashRequest();
        request.Authentication.Client =
            BalloonShopConfiguration.DataCashClient;
        request.Authentication.Password =
            BalloonShopConfiguration.DataCashPassword;
```

```
request.Transaction.TxnDetails.MerchantReference =
  orderProcessor.Order.OrderID.ToString()
  .PadLeft(6, '0').PadLeft(7, '5');
request.Transaction.TxnDetails.Amount.Amount =
  orderProcessor.Order.TotalCost.ToString();
request.Transaction.TxnDetails.Amount.Currency = "GBP";
request.Transaction.CardTxn.Method = "pre";
request.Transaction.CardTxn.Card.CardNumber =
  orderProcessor.Order.CreditCard.CardNumber;
request.Transaction.CardTxn.Card.ExpiryDate =
  orderProcessor.Order.CreditCard.ExpiryDate;
if (orderProcessor.Order.CreditCard.IssueDate != "")
{
  request.Transaction.CardTxn.Card.StartDate =
    orderProcessor.Order.CreditCard.IssueDate;
}
if (orderProcessor.Order.CreditCard.IssueNumber != "")
{
  request.Transaction.CardTxn.Card.IssueNumber =
    orderProcessor.Order.CreditCard.IssueNumber;
}
// get DataCash response
DataCashResponse response =
  request.GetResponse(
  BalloonShopConfiguration.DataCashUrl);
if (response.Status == "1")
{
  // update order authorization code and reference
  orderProcessor.Order.SetAuthCodeAndReference(
    response.MerchantReference,
    response.DatacashReference);
  // audit
  orderProcessor.CreateAudit(
    "Funds available for purchase.", 20102);
  // update order status
  orderProcessor.Order.UpdateStatus(2);
  // continue processing
  orderProcessor.ContinueNow = true;
}
else
{
  // audit
  orderProcessor.CreateAudit(
    "Funds not available for purchase.", 20103);
  // mail admin
```

```
        orderProcessor.MailAdmin("Credit card declined.",
          "XML data exchanged:\n" + request.Xml + "\n\n"
          + response.Xml, 1);
      }
    }
    catch
    {
      // fund checking failure
      throw new OrderProcessorException(
        "Error occured while checking funds.", 1);
    }
    // audit
    processor.CreateAudit("PSCheckFunds finished.", 20101);
  }
 }
}
```

Modifying the PSTakePayment Pipeline Section Class

The modifications to PSTakePayment are as follows:

```
using DataCashLib;

namespace CommerceLib
{
  /// <summary>
  /// 5th pipeline stage - takes funds from customer
  /// </summary>
  public class PSTakePayment : IPipelineSection
  {
    private OrderProcessor orderProcessor;

    public void Process(OrderProcessor processor)
    {
      // set processor reference
      orderProcessor = processor;
      // audit
      orderProcessor.CreateAudit("PSTakePayment started.", 20400);
      try
      {
        // take customer funds via DataCash gateway
        // configure DataCash XML request
        DataCashRequest request = new DataCashRequest();
        request.Authentication.Client =
          BalloonShopConfiguration.DataCashClient;
```

```
      request.Authentication.Password =
        BalloonShopConfiguration.DataCashPassword;
      request.Transaction.HistoricTxn.Method =
        "fulfill";
      request.Transaction.HistoricTxn.AuthCode =
        orderProcessor.Order.AuthCode;
      request.Transaction.HistoricTxn.Reference =
        orderProcessor.Order.Reference;
      // get DataCash response
      DataCashResponse response =
        request.GetResponse(
        BalloonShopConfiguration.DataCashUrl);
      if (response.Status == "1")
      {
        // audit
        orderProcessor.CreateAudit(
          "Funds deducted from customer credit card account.",
          20402);
        // update order status
        orderProcessor.Order.UpdateStatus(5);
        // continue processing
        orderProcessor.ContinueNow = true;
      }
      else
      {
        // audit
        orderProcessor.CreateAudit(
         "Error taking funds from customer credit card account.",
          20403);
        // mail admin
        orderProcessor.MailAdmin(
          "Credit card fulfillment declined.",
          "XML data exchanged:\n" + request.Xml + "\n\n" +
          response.Xml, 1);
      }
    }
    catch
    {
      // fund checking failure
      throw new OrderProcessorException(
        "Error occured while taking payment.", 4);
    }
    // audit
    processor.CreateAudit("PSTakePayment finished.", 20401);
  }
 }
}
```

Testing the Pipeline

Now that you have all this in place, it's important to test with a few orders. You can do this easily by making sure you create a customer with "magic" credit card details. As mentioned earlier in the chapter, these are numbers that DataCash supplies for testing purposes and can be used to obtain specific responses from DataCash. A sample of these numbers is shown in Table 16-2; a full list is available on the DataCash web site.

Table 16-2. *DataCash Credit Card Test Numbers*

Card Type	Card Number	Return Code	Description	Sample Message
Switch	4936000000000000001	1	Authorized with random auth code.	AUTH CODE ??????
	4936000000000000019	7	Decline the transaction.	DECLINED
	6333000000000005	1	Authorized with random auth code.	AUTH CODE ??????
	6333000000000013	7	Decline the transaction.	DECLINED
	6333000000123450	1	Authorized with random auth code.	AUTH CODE ??????
Visa	4242424242424242	7	Decline the transaction.	DECLINED
	4444333322221111	1	Authorized with random auth code.	AUTH CODE ??????
	4546389010000131	1	Authorized with random auth code.	AUTH CODE ??????

Going Live

Moving from the test account to the live one is now simply a matter of replacing the DataCash information in web.config. After you have set up a merchant bank account, you can use these details to set up a new DataCash account, obtaining new client and password data along the way. You also need to change the URL that you send data to—it needs to be the live server. The URL for this is https://transaction.datacash.com/Transaction. Other than removing the test user accounts from the database, this is all you need to do before exposing your newly completed e-commerce application to customers.

Using the PayFlow Pro API

To use PayFlow Pro, you need to sign up via the web site, which you can access at http://www.verisign.com/products/payflow/pro/. After you register, you can log on to the VeriSign Manager web site and download the API and documentation necessary to use PayFlow Pro.

One advantage that PayFlow Pro has over DataCash is the provision of a .NET API, simplifying communications with the credit card gateway. However, one disadvantage is that the syntax required to use it is a little more convoluted. Instead of sending and receiving XML files, you send and receive strings consisting of name-value pairs, separated by ampersands. Effectively, you use a similar syntax to query strings appended to URLs.

The .NET API comes with instructions for installing the various DLLs necessary to communicate with the PayFlow Pro gateway and includes sample code to test things out. The C# test application starts with the following declarations:

```
using System;
using PayFlowPro;

class PFProdotNETExample
{
  public static void Main()
  {
    PFPro pfpro = new PFPro();
    string Response;

    int pCtlx;
```

These variables are used to send and receive a string that authorizes a credit card transaction. Four more variables must be set to values used when signing up with PayFlow Pro:

```
    string User = "user";
    string Vendor = "vendor";
    string Partner = "partner";
    string Password = "password";
```

You probably won't have to change the following variable definitions in this example unless you use a proxy server. Note that port 443 is used for communications, which is the same as saying, "use https"; that is, it causes an SSL connection to be used.

```
    string HostAddress = "test-payflow.verisign.com";
    int HostPort = 443;
    string ParmList = "&TRXTYPE=S&TENDER=C&ACCT=5105105105105100
      &EXPDATE=1209&AMT=14.42&COMMENT1[3]=123
      &COMMENT2=Good Customer&INVNUM=1234567890
      &STREET=5199 JOHNSON&ZIP=94588";
    int Timeout = 30;
    string ProxyAddress = "";
    int ProxyPort = 0;
    string ProxyLogon = "";
    string ProxyPassword = "";
```

The most important variable here is ParmList (shown with extra spacing here for clarity), which includes most of the parameters required for the transaction, including the credit card details, transaction amount, and transaction type. A transaction type of S (shorthand for Sale) is used, which is an Authorization type transaction in PayFlow Pro. Alternatively, you can use transaction types of A (for Authorization) and D (for Delayed Capture) to perform a pre/fulfil type transaction.

The rest of the parameters required are created from the values set earlier in the code, and the two parameter strings are concatenated:

```
string UserAuth = "USER=" + User + "&VENDOR=" + Vendor +
  "&PARTNER=" + Partner + "&PWD=" + Password;

ParmList = UserAuth + ParmList;
```

Next, after some basic information output, the transaction is carried out. This involves creating a context in which to carry out the transaction, which just means configuring the API with host information, and so on, getting a response to the transaction query, and destroying the context:

```
Console.WriteLine("Running PFProdotNETExample using C#...");
Console.WriteLine("");

pCtlx = pfpro.CreateContext(HostAddress, HostPort, Timeout,
  ProxyAddress, ProxyPort, ProxyLogon, ProxyPassword);

Response = pfpro.SubmitTransaction(pCtlx, ParmList);

pfpro.DestroyContext(pCtlx);

Console.WriteLine(Response);
  }
}
```

The result is along the lines of

```
RESULT=0&PNREF=VXYZ00912465&ERRCODE=00&AUTHCODE=09TEST&AVSADDR=Y&AVSZIP=N&
```

■Note To carry out a successful transaction, you must first configure your account in the VeriSign Manager. Specifically, most test transactions will fail due to no transaction amount ceiling being set and failure of address verification (AVS). If you set a suitably high amount ceiling and disable AVS, you can carry out successful transactions.

You can use the information in the PayFlow Pro documentation to decipher this as follows:

- *RESULT=0*: A value of 0, as shown here, means a successful transaction. Any other number indicates an error.

- *PNREF= VXYZ00912465*: A unique reference number assigned by VeriSign.

- *ERRCODE=00*: Error code.

- *AUTHCODE=09TEST*: Approval code.

- *AVSADDR=Y&AVSZIP=N*: Address verification information.

When using pre/fulfil transactions, you need to use the PNREF value as the ORIGID parameter in the fulfillment stage.

Integrating PayFlow Pro with BalloonShop

As with DataCash, you need to modify things in a few places to use this API. Rather than showing all the code for this, we can just review the steps required:

- Add configuration settings to web.config. For PayFlow Pro, you need to set user, vendor, partner, and password settings for verification, and the host to send data to (test-payflow. verisign.com for testing). Optionally, you could configure other context information here, matching the values shown in the test code in the last section (port, timeout, and proxy information).

- Modify OrderProcessorConfiguration to give access to these configured values.

- Modify PSCheckFunds and PSTakePayment to use this new information to communicate with PayFlow Pro. This involves building a request string, interpreting response strings, and storing authorization codes in the database as with DataCash.

In addition, to use the PayFlow Pro library, you need to add a reference to BalloonShop to use PFProdotNET.dll (the .NET API for PayFlow Pro) and copy the certs directory to the C:\WINDOWS\system32 directory (as described in the sample application documentation).

The downloadable code for this chapter includes a version of BalloonShop modified to use PayFlow Pro and the modifications to BalloonShop required to use this new code.

Summary

In this chapter, you've completed the e-commerce application by integrating BalloonShop with credit card authorization. Short of putting your own products in, hooking it up with your suppliers, getting a merchant bank account, and putting it on the web, you're ready to go. Okay, so that's still a lot of work, but none of it is particularly difficult. We've done the hard work for you.

Specifically, in this chapter, we've looked at the theory behind credit card transactions on the web and looked at one full implementation—DataCash. You created a set of classes that can be used to access DataCash and integrated it with your application. We also looked at PayFlow Pro. The code required to use this credit card gateway is included in the Source Code area for this book on the Apress web site (http://www.apress.com).

■ ■ ■

CHAPTER 17

Integrating Amazon Web Services

In the dynamic world of the Internet, sometimes it isn't enough to just have an important web presence; you also need to interact with functionality provided by third parties to achieve your goals. So far in this book, you already saw how to integrate external functionality to process payments from your customers.

In this chapter, you'll learn new possibilities for integrating functionality from an external source, this time through a web service. A **web service** is a piece of functionality that is exposed through a web interface using standard Internet protocols such as HTTP. The messages exchanged by the client and the server are encoded using an XML-based protocol named SOAP (Simple Object Access Protocol) or by using REST (Representational State Transfer). You'll learn more about these technologies a bit later.

The beauty of using web services is that the client and the server can use any technology, any language, and any platform. As long as they exchange information with a standard protocol such as SOAP over HTTP, there's no problem if the client is a cell phone, and the server is a Java application running on a SUN server, for example.

The possibilities are exciting, and we recommend you purchase a book that specializes in web services to discover more about their world. Have a look at the list of public web services at `http://www.xmethods.net` to get an idea of the kinds of external functionality you can integrate into your application.

In this chapter, you'll learn how to integrate the **Amazon E-Commerce Service** (ECS; web services interface provided by Amazon.com, formerly known as Amazon Web Services—AWS) to sell Amazon.com products through your BalloonShop web site.

You already have an e-commerce web site that sells balloons to its customers. You can go further and make some more money from their passion for balloons by incorporating some other kinds of balloon-related gifts from Amazon.com into your site. For free? Oh no . . . You'll display Amazon.com's product details on your site, but the final checkout will be processed by Amazon.com, and Amazon.com will deliver in your bank account a small commission fee for purchases made from your web site. Sounds like easy money, doesn't it?

In this chapter, you'll learn how to use ECS to add a special department called "**Amazon Balloons**" to your web store, which you can see in Figure 17-1. This will be a "special" department in that it will be handled differently than the others—for example, payment is handled directly by Amazon when the visitor wants to buy a product. This chapter explores just a small subset of ECS's full power, so if you really want to make a fortune out of this service, you should dig deeper to find more substance.

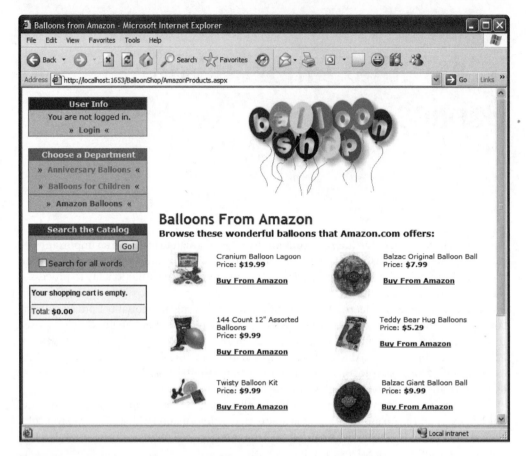

Figure 17-1. *Integrating the "Amazon Balloons" department into BalloonShop*

The rest of this chapter is divided into two parts. In the first part, you'll learn how to access the Amazon E-Commerce Service (ECS); in the second part, you'll implement this functionality in the BalloonShop web site.

■Tip The code in this chapter is independent of the rest of the site, so all you need to get started integrating Amazon functionality is the code from the first four chapters (so you have a working product catalog). Of course, with minor adjustments, you can also adapt this code to your own personal solutions.

Accessing the Amazon E-Commerce Service

Most service providers (including Amazon.com) use SOAP or REST (or both) to expose web services functionality to Internet client programs. You can choose to make a web service request by using either REST or SOAP, and you get the exact same results with both options. In this chapter, you'll learn how to access ECS 4.0 using both REST and SOAP.

REST (Representational State Transfer) uses carefully crafted URLs with specific name-value pairs to call specific methods on the servers. REST is considered to be the easiest way to communicate with the web services that expose this interface. Nonofficial sources say that 85% of ECS clients went the REST way. When using REST, all you have to do to perform an Amazon search is to make a classical HTTP GET request and you'll receive the response in XML format.

SOAP (Simple Object Access Protocol) is an XML-based standard for encoding the information transferred in a web service request or response. SOAP is fostered by a number of organizations, including powerful companies such as Microsoft, IBM, and Sun.

When accessing ECS, you can send the request either through REST or by sending a SOAP message. The web service returns an XML response with the data you requested. You'll learn more about REST and SOAP by playing with ECS.

You need to understand that in this chapter we'll touch just a bit of the functionality provided by the Amazon ECS. A serious discussion on the subject would probably need a separate book, but what you'll see in this chapter is enough to get you on the right track. Also, be aware that in this chapter we integrate functionality from Amazon U.S., but similar web service functionality is provided by the other Amazon branches.

■**Note** You can find a number of links to articles that discuss accessing ECS with REST and SOAP at
http://www.aspnetworld.com/articles/2004032401.aspx.

Creating Your Amazon E-Commerce Service Account

You can reach the official documentation for ECS at http://www.amazon.com/webservices. You can find the latest version of the documentation at http://www.amazon.com/gp/aws/sdk/—bookmark this URL as you'll find it very useful. Before moving on, you need to create your account with the Amazon ECS. To access ECS, you need a *Subscription ID*, which is like a password that identifies your account in the ECS system. If you don't already have one, apply now for a Subscription ID at http://www.amazon.com/gp/aws/registration/registration-form.html/—the Subscription ID is a string of 20 characters, such as 1R4EY7DQYOATN521WQR2.

Getting an Amazon Associate ID

The Subscription ID you created earlier is your key to retrieving data through the Amazon ECS. This data allows you to compose the "Amazon Balloons" department that you saw in Figure 17-1.

What the Subscription ID can't do is give you a commission from the Amazon.com products that you sell through your web site. To get your money, you need to apply to get an **Associate ID**. The Associate ID is used in the Buy From Amazon links you'll display in your special Amazon department, and it's the key that Amazon uses to identify you as the origin of that sale.

The Associate ID can even be used in static web pages that contain links to Amazon.com products, and it doesn't require you to also have an ECS Subscription ID, which has different purposes.

So before moving further, if you want to get any money out of your "Amazon Balloons" department, go get your Associate ID from http://associates.amazon.com/gp/associates/apply/main.html. Otherwise, if at the moment you're just interested in learning about the ECS, feel free to skip this step for now.

Accessing Amazon Web Services Using REST

REST web services are accessed by requesting a properly formed URL. Try the following link in your browser (don't forget to replace the string [Your Subscription ID] with your real Subscription ID that you got earlier):

```
http://webservices.amazon.com/onca/xml?Service=AWSECommerceService
&SubscriptionId=[Your Subscription ID]
&Operation=ItemLookup
&IdType=ASIN
&ItemId=1590594681
```

Your browser will display an XML structure with information about the book you are reading now (see Figure 17-2).

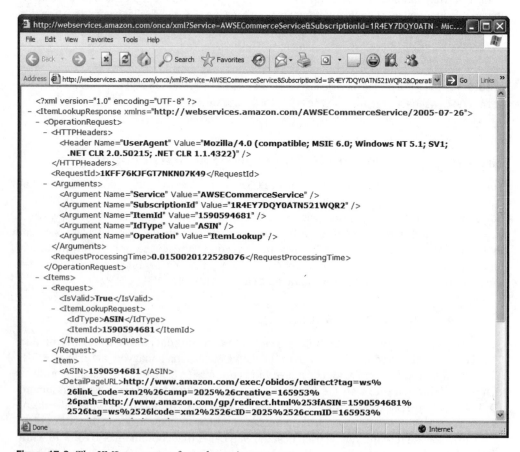

Figure 17-2. *The XML response of a web service request*

■**Caution** Always remember to replace [`Your Subscription ID`] with your own Subscription ID. The figures display the Subscription ID the authors used when writing the book, but obviously, you should use your own.

Pretty cool, huh? You have just seen REST in action. Every product in the Amazon database has a unique identifier called an ASIN (Amazon.com Standard Item Number). For books, the ASIN is the book's ISBN (this book has the ASIN 1590594681).

The web service request you just made tells ECS the following: I have a Subscription ID (`SubscriptionId=[Your Subscription ID]`), and I want to make an item lookup operation (`Operation=ItemLookup`) to learn more about the product with the 1590594681 ASIN (`IdType=ASIN&ItemId=1590594681`).

You didn't get much information about this book in this example—no price or availability information and no links to the cover picture or customer reviews. ECS 4 introduces a finer control of the data you want to receive using response groups (a response group is a set of data about the product).

■**Note** At the time of writing, ECS offers a list of more than 35 possible response groups. In this book, we'll only explain the purpose of the response groups we're using for BalloonShop; for the complete list, visit the official ECS documentation.

So let's ask for some more data by using response groups. At the end of the link you've composed earlier, add the following string to get more specific information about the book: `&ResponseGroup=SalesRank,Request,Small,Images,OfferSummary`. The complete link should look like this now:

```
http://webservices.amazon.com/onca/xml?Service=AWSECommerceService
&SubscriptionId=[Your Subscription ID]
&Operation=ItemLookup
&IdType=ASIN
&ItemId=1590594681
&ResponseGroup=Request,SalesRank,Small,Images,OfferSummary
```

The new XML response from Amazon.com includes more details about the Amazon.com item as shown in Figure 17-3.

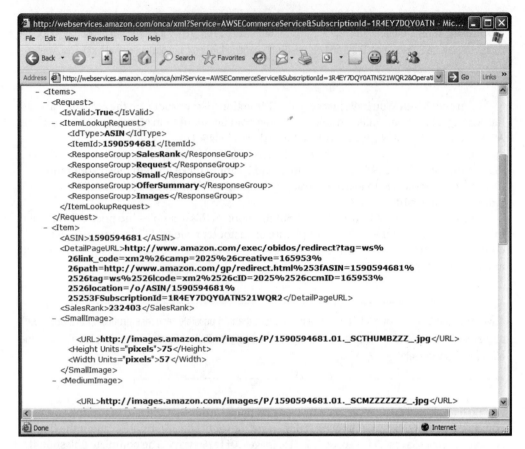

Figure 17-3. *The XML response of a web service request*

We've just mixed five response groups: SalesRank, Request, Small, Images, and OfferSummary. To learn more about the response groups, go to http://www.amazon.com/gp/aws/sdk/, click the HTML link for the latest version of the documentation, click the Response Groups link, expand the API Reference entry, and click Response Groups. Here's the description for the five response groups used in the previous example:

- Request response group is a default response group in every kind of operation, and it returns the list of name-value pairs you used to make the request.

- SalesRank response group returns data about the current Amazon.com sales rank of the product.

- Small response group returns general item data (ASIN, item name, URL, and so on) about items included in the response. This is a default response group for an ItemLookup operation (like we have in this example).

- Images response group gives you the addresses for the three pictures (small, medium, and large) for each item in the response.

- OfferSummary response group returns price information for each item in the response.

To populate the future "Amazon Balloons" department, you'll search the Amazon.com Toys department for the "balloons" keyword. The REST URL looks like this:

```
http://webservices.amazon.com/onca/xml?Service=AWSECommerceService
&SubscriptionId=[Your Subscription ID]
&Operation=ItemSearch
&SearchKeywords=balloons
&SearchIndex=Toys
&ResponseGroup=Request,Medium
```

Accessing Amazon Web Services Using SOAP

Using SOAP, you use a very complex API to access the needed Amazon.com functionality. The following code, which performs the same search operation for balloons that you did earlier with REST, is using the `AWSECommerceService`, `ItemSearch`, `ItemSearchRequest`, and `ItemSearchResponse` objects from the Amazon API to perform the operation:

```
// Create Amazon objects
AWSECommerceService amazonService = new AWSECommerceService();
ItemSearch itemSearch = new ItemSearch();
ItemSearchRequest itemSearchRequest = new ItemSearchRequest();
ItemSearchResponse itemSearchResponse;
// Set up Amazon objects
itemSearch.SubscriptionId = "your Subscription ID";
itemSearchRequest.Keywords = "balloons";
itemSearchRequest.SearchIndex = "Toys";
itemSearchRequest.ResponseGroup = new string[] {"Request", "Medium"};
itemSearch.Request = new AmazonEcs.ItemSearchRequest[1] { itemSearchRequest };
// Perform the search
itemSearchResponse = amazonService.ItemSearch(itemSearch);
```

Analyzing all the possibilities offered by ECS would be the subject of a whole book, but we've done our best to comment the code and make it self-documenting and easy to understand. For detailed information on each of the ECS objects used, consult the ECS documentation.

Integrating the Amazon E-Commerce Service with BalloonShop

The goal is to allow your customers to buy some Amazon.com balloons through your web store. For this, you'll add a special department named "Amazon Balloons," with no categories, to your departments list. When this department is clicked, your products list will be populated with some Amazon.com products, each of them having a `Buy from Amazon` link attached to it instead of the usual `Add to Cart` link.

■**Caution** If you want to add this kind of functionality for your real e-commerce web site, you'll probably want to customize this functionality. Don't forget to read (and comply to) the Amazon E-Commerce Service terms and conditions, before using this service in the real world.

Figure 17-4 shows the new "Amazon Balloons" department you're going to add.

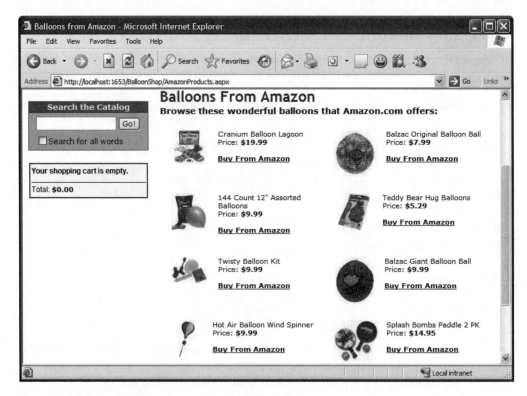

Figure 17-4. *Displaying Amazon products in BalloonShop*

After you have the Subscription ID, and eventually the Associate ID, ready, it's time to decide what Amazon products you want added to your future "Amazon Balloons" department. For the purposes of BalloonShop, we've decided to retrieve the results by doing a search on the "balloons" keyword, on the Toys Amazon store, as shown earlier.

Writing the Amazon Access Code

Follow the steps in the exercise to build the code that accesses Amazon ECS system using both SOAP and REST.

Exercise: Accessing Amazon ECS

1. Let's begin by adding a Web Reference to the Amazon ECS. This is only required if you plan to access ECS through SOAP. Right-click the project entry in **Solution Explorer** and choose **Add Web Reference**.

2. In the dialog box that appears, enter the address of the **ECS Web Service**:

   ```
   http://webservices.amazon.com/AWSECommerceService/AWSECommerceService.wsdl
   ```

3. Click **Go**.

4. Change the **Web Reference name** to something easier to type, such as **AmazonEcs**, and click **Add Reference** (see Figure 17-5). A new folder in your project named App_WebReferences will contain your new reference to the Amazon ECS.

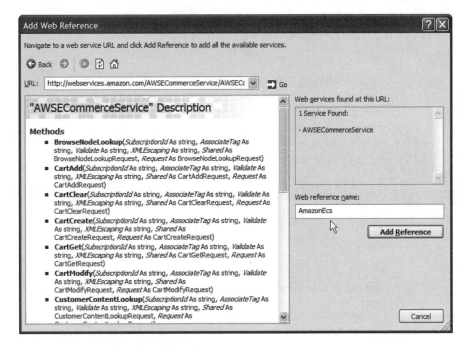

Figure 17-5. *Adding a new Web Reference to your project*

5. Open web.config and add the following configuration parameters:

   ```
   <appSettings>
     <add key="CartPersistDays" value="10" />
     <add key="MailServer" value="localhost" />
     <add key="EnableErrorLogEmail" value="false" />
     <add key="ErrorLogEmail" value="cristian_darie@yahoo.com" />
     <add key="ProductsPerPage" value="6"/>
     <add key="ProductDescriptionLength" value="60"/>
     <add key="SiteName" value="BalloonShop"/>
   ```

```
  <add key="AmazonRestUrl"
 value="http://webservices.amazon.com/onca/xml?Service=AWSECommerceService"/>
  <add key="AmazonSubscriptionID" value="1R4EY7DQY0ATN521WQR2"/>
  <add key="AmazonAssociateID" value="cristiand-20"/>
  <add key="AmazonSearchKeywords" value="balloons"/>
  <add key="AmazonSearchIndex" value="Toys"/>
  <add key="AmazonResponseGroups" value="Request,Medium"/>
  <add key="AmazonEcs.AWSECommerceService"
value="http://soap.amazon.com/onca/soap?Service=AWSECommerceService"/>
</appSettings>
```

6. Add the following properties to the `BalloonShopConfiguration` class to allow for easier retrieval of the data you saved to `web.config`:

```
// Amazon ECS REST URL
public static string AmazonRestUrl
{
    get
    {
        return ConfigurationManager.AppSettings["AmazonRestUrl"];
    }
}


// Subscription ID to access ECS
public static string SubscriptionId
{
    get
    {
        return ConfigurationManager.AppSettings["AmazonSubscriptionID"];
    }
}


// the Amazon.com associate ID
public static string AssociateId
{
    get
    {
        return ConfigurationManager.AppSettings["AmazonAssociateID"];
    }
}


// keywords used to do the Amazon search
public static string SearchKeywords
{
```

```
        get
        {
            return ConfigurationManager.AppSettings["AmazonSearchKeywords"];
        }
    }

    // search location
    public static string SearchIndex
    {
        get
        {
            return ConfigurationManager.AppSettings["AmazonSearchIndex"];
        }
    }

    // the Amazon response groups
    public static string ResponseGroups
    {
        get
        {
            return ConfigurationManager.AppSettings["AmazonResponseGroups"];
        }
    }
```

7. Add a new class named **AmazonAccess** to your **App_Code** folder.

8. Start coding your new class by adding references to the **System.Xml** and **AmazonEcs** namespaces:

```
using System.Xml;
using AmazonEcs;
```

9. Continue by adding the **GetResponseTable** method, which returns a configured DataTable object to be filled with the Amazon search results. This DataTable will ultimately be returned to the presentation tier, which will display the product data to the visitors.

```
public class AmazonAccess
{
  public AmazonAccess()
  {
    //
    // TODO: Add constructor logic here
    //
  }
```

```
// returns a configured DataTable object that can be read by the UI
private static DataTable GetResponseTable()
{
  DataTable dt = new DataTable();
  dt.Columns.Add(new DataColumn("ASIN", Type.GetType("System.String")));
  Columns.Add(new DataColumn("ProductName", Type.GetType("System.String")));
  dt.Columns.Add(new DataColumn("ProductPrice",
Type.GetType("System.String")));
  dt.Columns.Add(new DataColumn("ProductImageUrl", Type.GetType
("System.String")));
  return dt;
}
}
```

10. Add the `GetAmazonDataWithSoap` method, which does pretty much what it says.

```
// perform the Amazon search with SOAP and return results as a DataTable
public static DataTable GetAmazonDataWithSoap()
{
  // Create Amazon objects
  AWSECommerceService amazonService = new AWSECommerceService();
  ItemSearch itemSearch = new ItemSearch();
  ItemSearchRequest itemSearchRequest = new ItemSearchRequest();
  ItemSearchResponse itemSearchResponse;
  // Setup Amazon objects
  itemSearch.SubscriptionId = BalloonShopConfiguration.SubscriptionId;
  itemSearchRequest.Keywords = BalloonShopConfiguration.SearchKeywords;
  itemSearchRequest.SearchIndex = BalloonShopConfiguration.SearchIndex;
  itemSearchRequest.ResponseGroup =
BalloonShopConfiguration.ResponseGroups.Split(',');
  itemSearch.Request = new AmazonEcs.ItemSearchRequest[1]
{ itemSearchRequest };

  // Will store search results
  DataTable responseTable = GetResponseTable();
  // If any problems occur, we prefer to send back empty result set
  // instead of throwing exception
  try
  {
    itemSearchResponse = amazonService.ItemSearch(itemSearch);
    Item[] results = itemSearchResponse.Items[0].Item;
    // Browse the results
    foreach (AmazonEcs.Item item in results)
    {
      // product with incomplete information will be ignored
      try
      {
```

```
        //create a datarow, populate it and add it to the table
        DataRow dataRow = responseTable.NewRow();
        dataRow["ASIN"] = item.ASIN;
        dataRow["ProductName"] = item.ItemAttributes.Title;
        dataRow["ProductImageUrl"] = item.SmallImage.URL;
        dataRow["ProductPrice"] = item.OfferSummary.LowestNewPrice.
FormattedPrice;
        responseTable.Rows.Add(dataRow);
      }
      catch
      {
        // Ignore products with incomplete information
      }
    }
  }
  catch (Exception e)
  {
    // ignore the error
  }
  // return the results
  return responseTable;
}
```

11. Finally, add the `GetAmazonDataWithRest` method:

```
// perform the Amazon search with REST and return results as a DataTable
public static DataTable GetAmazonDataWithRest()
{
  // The response data table
  DataTable responseTable = GetResponseTable();
  // Compose the Amazon REST request URL
  string amazonRequest = string.Format("{0}&SubscriptionId=
{1}&Operation=ItemSearch&Keywords={2}&SearchIndex={3}&ResponseGroup={4}",
      BalloonShopConfiguration.AmazonRestUrl,
      BalloonShopConfiguration.SubscriptionId,
      BalloonShopConfiguration.SearchKeywords,
      BalloonShopConfiguration.SearchIndex,
      BalloonShopConfiguration.ResponseGroups);
  // If any problems occur, we prefer to send back empty result set
  // instead of throwing exception
  try
  {
    // Load the Amazon response
    XmlDocument responseXmlDoc = new XmlDocument();
    responseXmlDoc.Load(amazonRequest);
    // Prepare XML document for searching
    XmlNamespaceManager xnm = new XmlNamespaceManager
```

```
        (responseXmlDoc.NameTable);
            xnm.AddNamespace("amz", "http://webservices.amazon.com/
        AWSECommerceService/2005-07-26");
            // Get the list of Item nodes
            XmlNodeList itemNodes = responseXmlDoc.SelectNodes("/amz:Item
        SearchResponse/amz:Items/amz:Item", xnm);
            // Copy node data to the DataTable
            foreach (XmlNode itemNode in itemNodes)
            {
              try
              {
                // Create a new datarow and populate it with data
                DataRow dataRow = responseTable.NewRow();
                dataRow["ASIN"] = itemNode["ASIN"].InnerText;
                dataRow["ProductName"] =
    itemNode["ItemAttributes"]["Title"].InnerText;
                dataRow["ProductImageUrl"] = itemNode["SmallImage"]["URL"].InnerText;
                dataRow["ProductPrice"] = itemNode["OfferSummary"]
        ["LowestNewPrice"]["FormattedPrice"].InnerText;
                // Add the row to the results table
                responseTable.Rows.Add(dataRow);
              }
              catch
              {
                // Ignore products with incomplete information
              }
            }
          }
          catch
          {
            // Ignore all possible errors
          }
          return responseTable;
        }
```

How It Works: Working with Amazon ECS

The important points you need to understand from this exercise follow:

- The search parameter commands were saved to web.config, so you can do various changes to the behavior of the "Amazon Balloons" pages without modifying any C# code.

- To enable accessing ECS, you added a Web Reference to its WDSL file. Visual Studio was kind enough to do the rest for you, giving you direct access to the classes exposed by Amazon. To make your life even easier, you wrote a reference to the AmazonEcs namespace at the beginning of your file.

- The heart of the AmazonAccess class is composed of the two GetAmazon... methods, which offer identical functionality to the presentation tier, but using different access technologies: one uses SOAP; the other uses REST.

To understand these two methods, we suggest starting with the REST one. After composing the REST URL, the request is submitted to Amazon, and the results are saved to an XML document (which will look something like what you saw in Figure 17-1 and Figure 17-2).

```
// Load the Amazon response
XmlDocument responseXmlDoc = new XmlDocument();
responseXmlDoc.Load(amazonRequest);
```

The logic that follows is extremely simple. On the retrieved XML document we make an Xpath query to filter the `Item` nodes, because these contain the data we're interested in. By analyzing the response hierarchy, you will know what nodes to ask for to get your data. We also catch and ignore the eventual exceptions that can happen in case one of the nodes we're trying to query doesn't exist.

Although the logic is simple enough, its implementation details can look a bit confusing if you're not used to parsing and working with XML documents. We strongly recommend that you grab some additional documentation on that topic, as its importance to everyday development projects has increased dramatically in the past few years.

`GetAmazonDataWithSoap` does the exact same actions, but this time by using the Amazon ECS API and the classes provided by it, instead of manually parsing an XML response file.

Implementing the Presentation Tier

Let's have another look at what we want to achieve in Figure 17-1 and Figure 17-4.

Exercise: Displaying Amazon.com Products in BalloonShop

1. Open `DepartmentsList.ascx` in **Source View** and add the `FooterStyle` element, like this:

```
<FooterTemplate>
   &raquo;
    <a href="AmazonProducts.aspx"
class='<%# Request.AppRelativeCurrentExecutionFilePath ==
"~/AmazonProducts.aspx" ? "DepartmentSelected" : "DepartmentUnselected" %>' >
      Amazon Balloons
    </a>
   &laquo;
</FooterTemplate>
<FooterStyle CssClass="DepartmentListContent" />
</asp:DataList>
```

2. Add a new **Web User Control** to your `UserControls` folder, named `AmazonProductsList.ascx`.

3. While `AmazonProductsList.ascx` is in **Source View**, add this bit of code to it:

```
<%@ Control Language="C#" AutoEventWireup="true" CodeFile=
"AmazonProductsList.ascx.cs"
  Inherits="AmazonProductsList" %>
<asp:DataList ID="list" runat="server" RepeatColumns="2"
```

```
      EnableViewState="False">
       <ItemTemplate>
         <table height="100" cellpadding="0" align="left">
           <tr>
             <td valign="top" align="center" width="110">
               <img src='<%# Eval("ProductImageUrl") %>' border="0" />
             </td>
             <td valign="top" width="250">
               <span class="ProductDescription">
                 <%# Eval("ProductName") %>
                 <br />
                 Price: </span><span class="ProductPrice">
                 <%# Eval("ProductPrice") %>
                 <br /><br />
                 <a target="_blank" href="http://www.amazon.com/exec/obidos/ASIN/
<%# Eval("ASIN") %>/ref=nosim/<%# BalloonShopConfiguration.AssociateId %>">
                   Buy From Amazon
                 </a>
               </span>
             </td>
           </tr>
         </table>
       </ItemTemplate>
     </asp:DataList>
```

4. Switch to the code-behind file, and complete the **Page_Load** method with the following code:

```
protected void Page_Load(object sender, EventArgs e)
{
  if (!IsPostBack)
  {
    // fill the DataList with Amazon products. Calling any of
    // GetAmazonDataWithRest or GetAmazonDataWithSoap should return
    // the same results
    list.DataSource = AmazonAccess.GetAmazonDataWithRest();
    list.DataBind();
  }
}
```

5. Add a new Web Form to your solution named **AmazonProducts.aspx** based on the
   BalloonShop.master Master Page.

6. Open `AmazonProducts.aspx` in **Source View** and modify it like this:

```
<%@ Page Language="C#" MasterPageFile="~/BalloonShop.master"
AutoEventWireup="true" CodeFile="AmazonProducts.aspx.cs" Inherits=
"AmazonProducts" Title="Balloonshop : Balloons from Amazon" %>
<asp:Content ID="Content1" ContentPlaceHolderID="contentPlaceHolder"
 Runat="Server">
  <span class="CatalogTitle">Balloons From Amazon</span>
  <br />
  <span class="CatalogDescription">Browse these wonderful balloons
 that Amazon.com offers: </span>
  <br />
</asp:Content>
```

7. Switch `AmazonProducts.aspx` to **Design View** and drag the `AmazonProductsList.ascx` control from solution explorer to the bottom of the page, as shown in Figure 17-6.

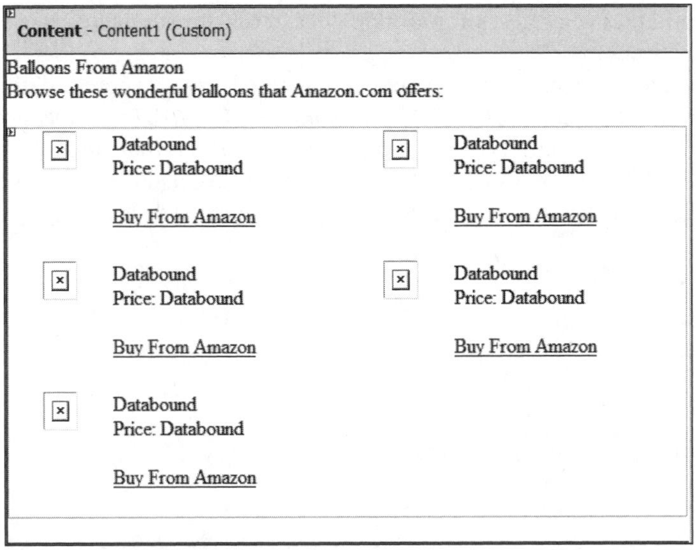

Figure 17-6. *Designing the Amazon page*

How It Works: Displaying Amazon.com Products in BalloonShop

In this exercise, you simply updated BalloonShop to display Amazon.com products by employing the techniques you studied in the first part of the chapter. The new functionality isn't especially complex, but the possibilities are exciting. When the `Buy from Amazon` links are clicked, Amazon.com associates that customer and what she purchases to your Associate ID (which is mentioned in the links).

The code-behind file `AmazonProductsList.ascx.cs` calls `AmazonAccess.GetAmazonDataWithRest()` to get the data to populate the list of products. This data is read to build the Amazon links to the retrieved products:

```
<a target="_blank" href="http://www.amazon.com/exec/obidos/ASIN/
<%# Eval("ASIN") %>/ref=nosim/<%# BalloonShopConfiguration.AssociateId %>">
```

However, you must know that Amazon offers many ways in which you can allow your visitors to buy their products. If you log in to the Associates page, you'll see a number of link types you can build and integrate into your web site.

Perhaps the most interesting and powerful is the possibility to create and manage Amazon shopping carts from your C# code, by using the Amazon API. If you're really into integrating Amazon.com into your web site, you should study the ECS documentation carefully and make the most of it.

Summary

In this chapter, you learned how to access Amazon Web Services using REST and SOAP. You can use the same techniques when accessing any kind of external functionality exposed through these protocols.

Congratulations, you have just finished your journey into learning about building e-commerce web sites with *Beginning ASP.NET 2.0 E-Commerce in C# 2005: From Novice to Professional*! You have the knowledge to build your own customized solutions that are even more interesting and powerful than what we showed you in this book. We really hope you enjoyed reading this book, and we wish you good luck with your own personal development projects!

Installing the Software

The good news is that all the software required to follow this book and build the BalloonShop Web Application is freely downloadable from the Internet. This appendix covers the installation process for the following required programs:

- Visual Web Developer 2005 Express Edition

- SQL Server 2005 Express Edition

- SQL Server Express Manager

- IIS 5.x

What Do These Programs Do?

Although the question sounds a bit funny, it's actually good to have a quick overview of the products you're about to install.

Visual Web Developer 2005 is the lightweight Visual Studio product that allows you to build ASP.NET 2.0 applications. This is the toy you'll use all the way in this book to build your BalloonShop web site. The installation process automatically installs the .NET Framework 2.0, in case you don't already have it on your system.

In the process of installing Visual Web Developer 2005, you'll be given the option to install SQL Server 2005 Express Edition along with it, and we suggest you do so. You need SQL Server 2005 Express Edition anyway, and the interaction with Visual Web Developer 2005 sometimes works better if they're installed together.

SQL Server 2005 will be used as your database engine. The first thing to say about SQL Server 2005 Express Edition is that it's free, but it's entirely compatible with the commercial versions of SQL Server 2005. This means that as well as providing the perfect system for you to learn and experiment with, a complete Web Application can initially be produced and distributed without incurring any costs for the database server. If the system expands at a later date, it can be ported to the commercial distribution of SQL Server with next to no effort.

All the features that Express Edition supports are also supported by the other versions of SQL Server, but the converse is not true. However, none of this extra functionality is required for this book.

Some of the limitations of SQL Server Express are that it supports only one CPU (but it can be installed on any server), it can use maximum 1GB addressable RAM, the maximum database size is limited to 4GB, and the many enterprise features are (obviously) not present. Visit `http://www.microsoft.com/sql/2005/productinfo/sql2005features.asp` to find the feature comparison list for the various versions of SQL Server 2005.

Installing Visual Web Developer 2005 Express Edition and SQL Server 2005 Express Edition

The following steps describe the process to install and activate Visual Web Developer 2005 Express Edition and SQL Server 2005 Express Edition.

▪**Note** The installation steps were tested with the beta 2 versions of Visual Web Developer 2005 Express Edition and SQL Server 2005 Express Edition.

---

1. Go to `http://lab.msdn.microsoft.com/express/`, find the **Visual Web Developer 2005 Express Edition** box, and click **Learn More Now**. Click **Download Now**. You'll download a file named `vwdsetup.exe`.

2. After download completes, execute `vwdsetup.exe`. You'll be taken through a number of setup screens. The important one is where you're asked to choose optional products that you might want to install. Check to install **SQL Server 2005 Express Edition**. You might also want to install Microsoft MSDN Express Library 2005 Beta 2, which contains the product documentation.

   You'll eventually get to the Download screen, where the setup program downloads other necessary components from the Microsoft site. After the download completes, the process continues by installing the downloaded components.

3. After installation is complete, you're informed that you must complete a registration process to get your free activation key in a maximum of 30 days. Follow the activation procedure to get the activation key, which will be something like `NGBQ2KCKL31KXX`.

4. Execute Visual Web Developer product by choosing **Start ➤ All Programs ➤ Visual Web Developer 2005 Express Edition**. The product will look something like Figure A-1.

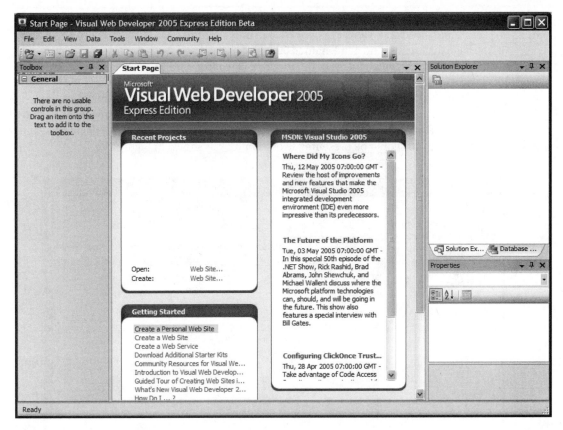

Figure A-1. *The Start Page in Visual Web Developer 2005*

5. If you already have a registration key, go to **Help ➤ Activate Product**. In the page that opens, enter the activation key and then click **Activate Now**.

Installing SQL Server 2005 Express Manager

SQL Server 2005 Express Manager is a very useful tool that allows you to access and manipulate your databases and execute SQL queries on them. This tool is not necessary, but it certainly is useful, and it's free, so we highly recommend you install it.

■Note You need the SQL Express Manager to easily execute the SQL Scripts provided in the Source Code area for this book on the Apress web site (http://www.apress.com).

The installation procedure is very simple. First, go to http://lab.msdn.microsoft.com/express/, find the **Visual Web Developer 2005 Express Edition** box, and click **Learn More Now**. In the page that opens, find a link named Download SQL Server 2005 Express Manager, which will get you to the download page of the product. Download and install it.

After the product is installed, you'll find it by choosing **Start ➤ All Programs ➤ Microsoft SQL Server 2005 ➤ SQL Server Express Manager**. When executing the program, first you'll need to add login credentials to the database. If you installed the product using default data, the Server Instance will be (local)\SqlExpress. Leave **Windows Authentication** checked and click **Connect**. You should be presented with a window as shown in Figure A-2.

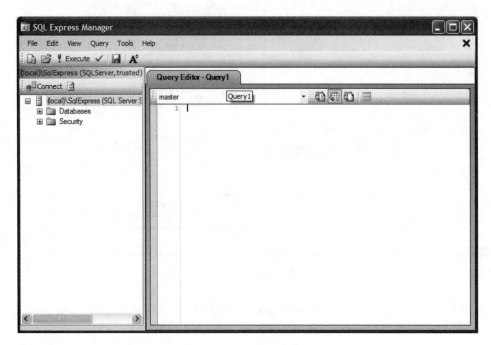

Figure A-2. *SQL Express Manager*

Installing the IIS 5.x Web Server

Previous versions of Visual Studio required you to have IIS on the local machine to build and run Web Applications. This was inconvenient for users whose operating system didn't support IIS, such as Windows XP Home Edition.

Visual Web Developer 2005 Express Edition, on the other hand, contains a built-in web server (Cassini), so you don't need IIS any more. The code in this book has been tested with both Cassini and IIS, so you can safely use either, but if you have a choice, we suggest you work with IIS. It offers better performance and guarantees that your site looks on the development machine the same as it will look on the production machines (which will run IIS, obviously).

The following pages are for users who prefer using IIS and don't already have it installed on their machines. We'll look at the installation process for IIS on Windows 2000 Professional and Windows XP Professional together because they don't differ significantly. The main difference is that Windows 2000 installs IIS 5.0, whereas Windows XP installs IIS 5.1. The options for installing are exactly the same; the only thing that might differ is the look of the dialog boxes.

Because your computer might be already running IIS 5.*x*, we'll describe a process for checking whether this is the case as part of the installation process. You should also note that to install anything (not just ASP.NET, but literally anything) on Windows 2000/XP, you need to be logged in as a user with administrative rights.

Installing IIS 5.x on a Web Server Machine

To install IIS 5.x, follow these steps:

1. Go to the **Control Panel** and select the **Add or Remove Programs** icon. The dialog box shown in Figure A-3 appears, displaying a list of your currently installed programs.

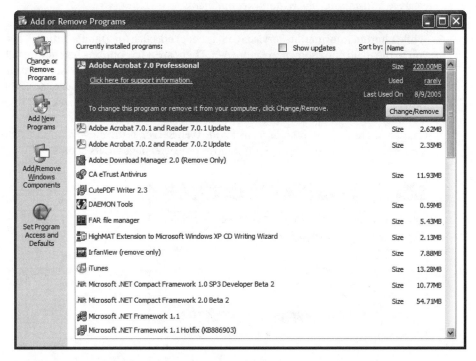

Figure A-3. *The Add or Remove Programs window*

2. Select the **Add/Remove Windows Components** icon on the left side of the dialog box to get to the screen that allows you to install new Windows components (see Figure A-4). Make sure the **Internet Information Services (IIS)** check box is checked.

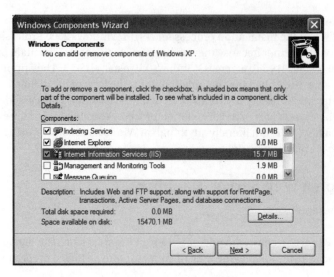

Figure A-4. *Installing new Windows components*

3. While Internet Information Services (IIS) is checked, click the **Details** button. This takes you to the dialog box shown in Figure A-5. There are a few options here for installing various optional bits of functionality. Make sure the **FrontPage 2000 Server Extensions** entry is checked. The **Internet Information Services Snap-In** is also very desirable, as you'll see in the book, so make sure this is checked, too. You need to check **SMTP Service** if you'll want to send administrative emails through your own server, as shown in Chapter 3. The last component, **World Wide Web Server**, is the most important, because it's the server that allows your computer to serve web pages to its clients.

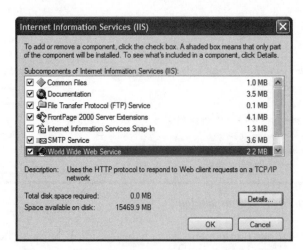

Figure A-5. *IIS dialog box*

4. For the purpose of this installation, make sure all the check boxes in this dialog box are checked. Then, click **OK** to return to the previous dialog box.

IIS starts up automatically as soon as your installation is complete, and thereafter whenever you boot up Windows.

IIS installs most of its bits and pieces under the (Windows root)\system32\inetsrv directory. However, more interesting to you at the moment is the \Inetpub\wwwroot directory, which is also created at this time. This directory is the default root web directory, and contains subdirectories that will provide the home for the web page files that you create. When loading http://localhost/ in Internet Explorer, the application in \Inetpub\wwwroot is loaded by default. In Chapter 2, you learn how to create the BalloonShop virtual directory under the root virtual directory (so it's accessible through http://localhost/BalloonShop), and make it point to a custom physical folder (not a subfolder of \Inetpub\wwwroot).

Working with IIS

Having installed IIS web server software onto your machine, you'll need some means of administering its contents and settings. In this section, you'll meet the user interface provided for IIS 5.*x*.

Whenever you need to administer IIS, you can simply call up the Internet Information Services administration applet (see Figure A-6) by choosing Control Panel ➤ Administrative Tools.

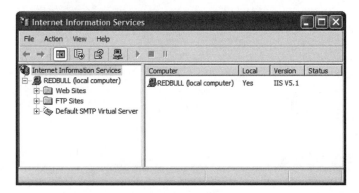

Figure A-6. *The IIS Administration tool*

Having opened the IIS applet, you can perform all your web-management tasks from this window. For example, you can stop or start the web server or the SMTP server. You will need to start the SMTP server to be able to send emails from this machine. The properties of the web site are accessible via the Default Web Site node.

To test that your IIS installation actually works, you can try loading the web address of your computer in a web browser such as Internet Explorer. You can access the default address through http://127.0.0.1/ (127.0.0.1 is the IP of the local computer), or alternatively through http://localhost/ (localhost is an alias for the 127.0.0.1 address), or http://*computer_name*/. You can view or change your computer's name through the Control Panel ➤ System applet (there you'll find a tab named Computer Name or Network Identification).

In the book, in any examples that require you to specify a web server name, the server name will be shown as localhost, implicitly assuming that your web server and browser are being run on the same machine. If they reside on different machines, you simply need to substitute the computer name of the appropriate web server machine.

■■■

Project Management Considerations

It feels great to finish building a complete e-commerce store, doesn't it? For the purposes of this book, we dealt with many design issues on a chapter-by-chapter basis, while also presenting the theory concepts. However, in real-world projects, many times you'll need to do the whole design work from the start. This appendix discusses how to manage building complete solutions in a professional manner.

Maybe it seems easier to just start coding without any upfront design, and with some luck, you might even create something that works the second day; however, when it comes to large projects, you'll face a lot of problems in the long term by doing that.

A project's life cycle includes more than simply coding away and building something ready to run—it should not be done hastily. For example, for almost any real-world software project, a critical part of its success is the database design, even if it's only a small part of the project's cycle. This makes perfect sense if you think that e-commerce sites, web portals, search engines, and customer interfaces for service providers (banking, IT, insurance, and so on) are all basically interfaces to a backend database.

Of course, the way you display the data and the reports you present to the visitor also play an important role in the success of the software. However, you can think of the database as the foundation of a house; if you did something wrong there, no matter how nice or trendy the house looks, it will still be torn down by the first wind.

Developing Software Solutions

The technical design of a software solution is only a part of a software project's life cycle. To give you an idea of the steps involved in managing a complete software solution, imagine a real-world example, such as building an ERP (Enterprise Resource Planning) application for a clothing factory.

First of all, you need to know exactly what the client needs from the software, so you talk to the client about the goals of implementing such software in its network. This is the stage of gathering system requirements and software requirements for the application you need to build.

After the project manager fully understands the customer's requirements and discusses a budget allocation and a timeline for the project, a team of analysts works with the customer's commercial office to get information about the tasks performed in the factory, the work schedule, and the manufacturing equipment they have. Your analysts must be in touch with the region's economic regime, the employer's legal obligations, the import/export conditions, and so on—facts that are clarified with the commercial, economic, and personnel departments of the company. The analysts build the database and describe the reports and the operations that the software must do.

After adjustments (if necessary) by the customer, the analytical part ends by adding a written annex to the contract with all these features agreed on by the customer and a timeline. After this, any modification in the database structure, the reports, or software functionality will be charged extra.

Next, the design team creates a user-friendly, attractive interface that can be presented to the customer and changed to fit the customer's artistic taste. After this phase is completed, the coding part begins. This shouldn't take a long time because the programmers know exactly what they need to do. When they finish coding, the software is installed on a test platform at the customer site, and the customer team simulates using the software for a definite period of time. During the testing period, the eventual programming and design bugs are revealed and fixed by the programmers. At the end of this phase, the customer should have a software application that runs by the agreed specifications and deploys on the production machines. That's the end of the project; the final payments are made, and every modification the customer asks for in the future is billed.

That was a short version of a story about commercial software. Of course, the theory doesn't apply the same for all software projects. In the case of smaller projects, such as many e-commerce sites, several, if not all, the tasks can be performed by a single person.

Considering the Theory Behind Project Management

Many theories exist about how to manage the software development life cycle (SDLC). No model is deemed the best, because choosing a SDLC model depends on the particularities of your project. We'll take a look at the most popular project-management theories in the following pages.

The Waterfall (or Traditional) Method

The Waterfall method, also known as the traditional method, is the father of all methodologies. It consists of breaking the software project into six or seven phases that must be processed in sequential order to deliver the final product. The input of each phase consists of the output of the preceding one (see Figure B-1).

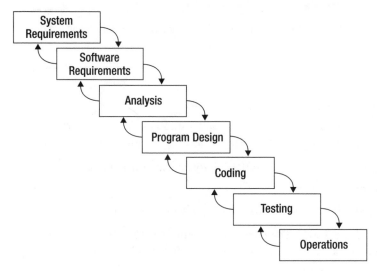

Figure B-1. *The Waterfall model*

Establishing the requirements is the first phase and can be divided in two as shown in Figure B-1. First, you must establish the system requirements of the project; at the end of this phase, you have a paper describing all the hardware needed for implementing, testing, and deploying the application. You also need the software platforms your application will be developed and tested on. The first two phases must include an opportunity study at the beginning and a feasibility study at the end. Basically, the first question is "Do we really need this from the business point of view?" After you establish the requirements, the feasibility study provides a high-level cost and benefit analysis so that a ROI (return of investment) can be estimated.

In the Analysis phase, the analysts work with the customer to fully understand the customer needs. They have to spend time with the customer's staff to define the software functionalities, transcribing them in a professional analysis for the software engineers.

In the Program Design phase, the design team reads the specifications of the analysis and develops some prototypes that the customer must agree on. Usually, that is throwaway code.

In the Coding phase, programmers effectively code the application. This happens after the customer agrees on the software design delivered by the Program Design phase.

If a testing platform is provided, the programmers install the application there and test all the functionalities of the software. All the bugs discovered are corrected, and at the end of the testing phase, the software must be ready to go in production. If a testing platform is not provided, the programmers have to simulate or conduct the testing on the actual platform the software will run on; however, at the end of the testing phase, the programmers must install a fresh copy of the bug-free software they created.

Everything is completed after deployment at the beginning of the Operations phase.

▪**Note** Every phase has a feedback to the precedent phase where new ideas can be added and errors are corrected.

Advantages of the Waterfall Theory

The main advantages of the Waterfall method are its simplicity and the fact that everything is documented and agreed upon with the customer. This leads to some important benefits:

- Because everything is planned from the start, it's easy for the project manager to correctly estimate project costs and timelines.

- The rigorous initial planning makes the project goals clear.

- All requirements are analyzed and validated by the customer, so the customer can estimate the benefits incurred by the software application before it's actually implemented.

Disadvantages of the Waterfall Theory

The disadvantages of the Waterfall model are

- The customer is not able to see the product until it's completely finished. At that stage, it can be very expensive to make any changes to the project.

- It has little flexibility for scope changes during the project's development.

- The architecture limitations are often not discovered until late in the development cycle.

- Because testing happens at the end of the coding phase, unexpected problems with the code might force developers to find quick fixes at the expense of the planned architecture.

- The Waterfall method doesn't work on projects whose requirements can't be rigorously planned from the start.

The Spiral Method

As a development of the Waterfall method, the Spiral method is more suitable for large, expensive, and complicated projects. Barry Boehm first described it in 1988 as an iterative waterfall in which every iteration provides increased software capability (see Figure B-2, which represents the diagram created by Barry Boehm).

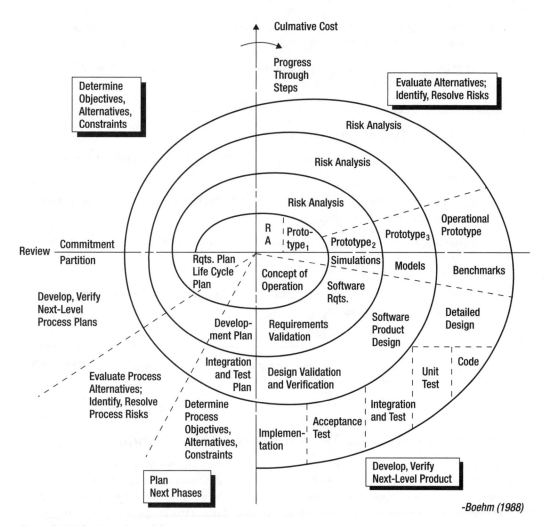

Figure B-2. *The Spiral model*

It consists of a spiral divided into four quadrants. Each quadrant represents a management process: Identify, Design, Construct, and Evaluate. The system goes through four cycles of these four processes:

- *Proof-of-concept cycle*: Define the business goals, capture the requirements, develop a conceptual design, construct a "proof-of-concept," establish test plans, and conduct a risk analysis. Share results with user.

- *First-build cycle*: Derive system requirements, develop logic design, construct first build, and evaluate results. Share results with user.

- *Second-build cycle*: Derive subsystem requirements, produce physical design, construct second build, and evaluate results. Share results with user.

- *Final-build cycle*: Derive unit requirements, produce final design, construct final build, and test all levels. Seek user acceptance.

The main advantages of the Spiral method proposed by Boehm are

- The entire application is built while working with the client.

- Any gaps in the Requirement phase of the Waterfall method are identified as work progresses.

- The spiral representation conveys very clearly the cyclical nature of the project and the progression through its lifespan.

However, the Spiral method has some disadvantages of its own:

- Requires serious discipline on the part of the client.

- Executive control can be difficult because in most projects the client is not responsible for the schedule and budget.

Note The Spiral method is more suitable for software in which the entire problem is well defined from the start, such as modeling and simulating software.

The Rapid Application Development (RAD) Method

RAD is another common project-management method that is, in essence, "try before you buy." Whereas in the Waterfall and even Spiral methods, the client was working with a lot of documentation, in the RAD approach, the client works with the software as it's being developed. The belief is that the client can produce better feedback when working with a live system as opposed to working strictly with documentation. When using RAD as a project-management method, customer rejection is significantly less when going into production.

The RAD method consists of the following phases:

- Business modeling

- Data modeling

- Process modeling

- Application generation

- Testing and turnover

The RAD approach allows rapid generation and change of user interface features. The client works with the software just like in the production environment.

The main disadvantage of RAD is that the client will always want more enhancements to the software—not always important ones—and the developer must try to satisfy the client's needs. This can result in an unending cycle of requirements, going away from the main purpose of the project.

Extreme Programming (XP) Methodology

Extreme Programming (XP) is a very controversial method not only because it's the newest, but also because it eliminates a lot of phases from the traditional Waterfall method. XP is simple and based on communication, feedback, and courage.

The professional analysts are replaced with the client, who is very active in the process. The client writes a document named "User Stories," which is a simple description of the desired functionality of the software. The programmers read the document and give an estimated timeframe of every functionality implementation. After receiving the time estimates, the customer chooses a group of functionalities to be developed first. This is called an **iteration**.

The developers use a **test-driven** design in the implementation phase, meaning that a testing method for the desired functionality is conceived before the code is actually written. Usually, every piece of code is written by a programmer under the supervision of another programmer who tests the functionality of the code.

After the code for the entire iteration is complete, it's then given an acceptance test with the customer, who approves (or disapproves) the iteration. The programmer keeps developing or improving code for that iteration until it passes the acceptance test.

The software is deployed in a number of **releases**, composed of one or more iterations; the software gets to the final release when all iterations that contain all the functionalities described in the User Stories document pass the acceptance test.

Picking a Method

More project management methods exist than the ones described so far. Because no single method is best, a good project manager must know in theory a little about all of them to choose the best one for the current project. Choosing the wrong tactic for a project might lead to failure, so the project manager must carefully consider all options before choosing how to deal with a particular project. A strategy like this will never work: "Okay, we have to build an e-commerce site. Let's do XP with this one, and maybe we'll Spiral the next one!"

In many cases, it's best to use a mix of methods to suit your project. For example, if the client doesn't know for sure what it wants, you can use bits of XP and collaborate closely with the client during the development based on a User Stories document, add a few steps from the Waterfall method, and do some RAD on the way.

Anyway, it's very important to keep some of these procedures in mind for your next projects, because the way you manage your projects can save you time, money, and stress.

Understanding the E-Commerce Project Cycle

For most e-commerce projects, your best bet will be something with a Waterfall flavor, but with a bit of changes here or there.

If you have some knowledge about management and a good artistic spirit for web design, after you read this book, the e-commerce project can be a "one man show." First of all, you need to organize the tasks so that they take place in a logical, sequential order.

Understanding the customer needs should not be difficult. The customer wants an e-store where a range of products can be advertised and bought. You need to know the type of products the customer wants on the site and a little about future strategy (today the customer is only selling balloons, but in the future the customer might want to sell candies). This is very important because the database and the whole architecture must be designed from the start to support future changes. You might also want to find out how the shipping department is organized to optimize the handling and shipping process.

Most of the customers require artistic and functional design, so, in most cases, the next phase is **creating a web prototype**. Whether you do it yourself or hire a web designer, the prototype should be only a web site template—only HTML code with something like "Product Name Here" instead of an actual product—without the need of any databases. Depending on the artistic taste of the customer, you might have to build several prototypes until you agree on a design. Alternatively, you can create a more complex prototype that has some basic functionality and even a simple database behind the scenes. The prototype will help you get a feel about how the final application will work and can help you get some initial feedback from the future users. With ASP.NET 2.0, you can very easily write simple throwaway interfaces using the new data-bound controls and data-binding techniques. After you've passed the prototypes phase, it's time to start implementing the real application.

Designing the database is, as we said, a critical phase of the project. The logical database design is developed from the requirements-gathering phase, and is agreed on with the customer. The logical design of a database describes what data you need to store and the relationships between different entities of data (such as the relationship between products and departments), but doesn't include strict implementation details, such as the associate table used to physically implement Many-to-Many relationships. If you're an advanced database designer, you'll create an optimal physical database structure yourself.

A number of tools—such as Microsoft Visio—enable you to design the database visually. These tools have very powerful features for designing relational database structures, and even generate the SQL code to turn them into real databases. Regardless of the database engine you're using, design your tables in a visual way (even with a pen and paper) rather than writing SQL queries.

If you don't have resources to buy such an expensive program (yeah, the really professional ones can be very expensive), you can use Visual Web Developer, which is free and comes packed with some useful diagramming features.

Next, you **implement the data tier objects**. This is the place you start playing with your database because you need to implement the data access logic that will support the other tiers in your application. In the process, you'll probably want to populate the database with some fictive examples to have a base for testing your queries. Before writing the queries as data tier objects, test them using a visual interface to the database engine that allows executing and debugging SQL queries. This will make your life easier when debugging the SQL code, because as all SQL developers know, the code doesn't always work as you expect it to the first time.

After the data tier is in place, you can continue by **building the middle tier** of your application. In the middle tier, you implement the error-handling, data-manipulation strategies and the business logic for your project. In this book, you learned some good techniques, but you might want to choose other ones for your particular project.

Building the user interface (the ASP.NET Web Forms, Web User Controls, and Master Pages) should be the next step. You already have a prototype that is usable only for design, because at the stage you created the prototypes, you didn't have a functional foundation. Usually, interface prototypes in software projects are throwaway code, but the ASP.NET forms and controls generate the actual look of your web site (with the design the customer agreed on).

A final testing phase is very important at the end of the project. The database will be populated with real records, and a simulation is made to test the efficiency of the ordering process. Every process should be tested before going into production, so you must give your customer enough time to test every functionality of the site, to make some test orders, and to evaluate the shipping process. During this stage, any programming errors should be revealed for you to correct.

After the code is ready and tested on your local machine, the next step is to **find/provide a hosting solution**. Perhaps the best strategy is to host the project at a specialized provider, and if the site proves to be successful, the customer can invest in its own hosting solution.

Maintaining Relationships with Your Customers

In the ideal project, you include all the possible clauses in a contract; after you deliver the site and finish the project, you never want to hear from the customer again, except for developing new functionalities or changing the design, in which case, you charge the customer extra.

The most unwanted thing would be for the customer to ask you to make changes without paying for them, and that's possible if you are not careful with the contract and with the tools you provide the customer for administration.

For example, many e-commerce sites have poor catalog admin pages, which are nightmares for the programmers. Avoiding such a nightmare can be possible by providing proper tools and interfaces for the customer and, most importantly, describing how they work (eventually a user's manual). Many programmers don't take this detail seriously and prefer to bring the site up with an incomplete or hard-to-use catalog admin page, not knowing what's coming.

If the database is complicated, you must describe all the fields in a manual and how they must be completed; if an error occurs when the customer tries to submit a form to a database, you have to make the error page as eloquent as possible. Also, try to work with the persons who will use the tools you provide in the design stage and take a couple of hours to instruct them personally on how to use the tools. This will save you a lot of explanations over the phone or even going to the customer's office without being paid.

Index

forums.apress.com